Democracy in America

from the
library of
Desiree
Garcia

RUSSIAN AMERICA
Pop. 50.000.

NORTH PACIFIC OCEAN

STATISTICAL MAP
OF
THE CONTINENT
OF
NORTH AMERICA.
1855.

Explanation of the Signs.
F. Epoch of the foundation of a State.
Pop. Present Population.

Remarks.
Surface of the Territory of the United States,
2.016.410 Square Miles.
Average height of the Alleghany Mountains,
3000 to 6000 Feet.
Number of Whites and Blacks in the States in which
Slavery is abolished, Whites 8.685.434. Blacks 170.620.
Number of Whites and Blacks in the Slave States,
Whites 3.960.814. Blacks 2.209.112.

R.Martin & G. Lithog. 26, Long Acre.

A French version of this map
appeared in the 1835 first edition.

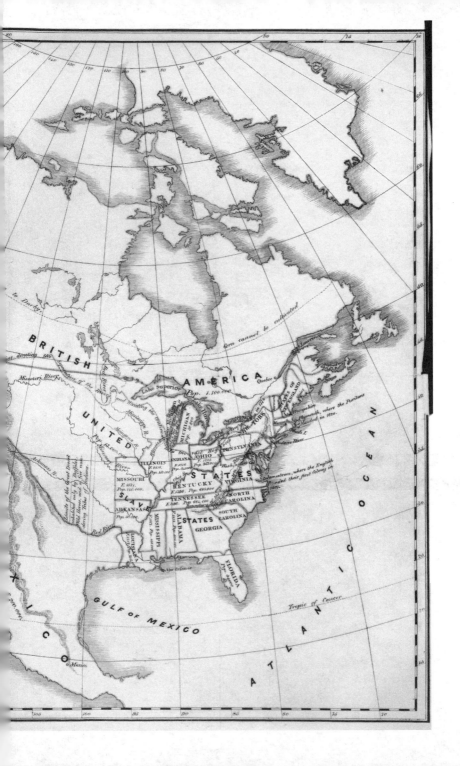

Alexis de Tocqueville

Democracy in America

The Arthur Goldhammer Translation

VOLUME I

EDITED AND WITH AN INTRODUCTION BY

Olivier Zunz

LIBRARY OF AMERICA PAPERBACK CLASSICS

FIRST LIBRARY OF AMERICA PAPERBACK CLASSIC EDITION
February 2012

Manufactured in the United States of America

OLIVIER ZUNZ
WROTE THE CHRONOLOGY AND
OLIVIER ZUNZ AND ARTHUR GOLDHAMMER
WROTE THE NOTES FOR THIS VOLUME

Contents

INTRODUCTION

by Olivier Zunz

Alexis de Tocqueville intuited at a young age that American democracy could become a model for the modern world.[1] So, when political circumstances early in his career prompted him to travel to the United States, he was naturally eager to see it for himself.

Tocqueville had ample personal reasons for his interest in democracy. His family, of the oldest and most influential nobility, had suffered immensely in the French Revolution. Tocqueville's great grandfather, the reformist minister Malesherbes, had unsuccessfully defended Louis XVI before the revolutionary tribunal. He paid for his political courage with his own life, but not before he was forced to witness the death of his daughter and granddaughter at the guillotine. Tocqueville's parents narrowly escaped death. They remained marginalized during the Napoleonic Empire, which they considered illegitimate, but regained some prominence with the restoration of a Bourbon monarch in 1814. Alexis was then nine years old.

In July 1830, Tocqueville was working as apprentice magistrate at the Versailles courthouse when a popular upheaval abolished the Bourbon dynasty for the final time. Compared to the sustained violence of the Terror, the July Revolution was mild. But the events briefly forced Tocqueville's parents into hiding, and it seemed as though dangerous times were returning.

Although Tocqueville felt the Bourbons had mismanaged the country and deserved their fate, he only halfheartedly supported the new constitutional monarchy under Louis-Philippe. For Tocqueville, the political turmoil underscored the dilemma of democratic reform in France. It once again had been necessary to shed blood to secure liberty, and Tocqueville saw no end to the vicious cycle of revolution, reform, and despotism. Passed over for promotion and left with limited prospects, he was ready to try something radically different.

As he would explain in *Democracy in America*, he left France to observe the one country that had "witnessed the effects of

the democratic revolution" but "without having had the revolution itself"—at least not in the sense of a social revolution.
The War for Independence merely threw off the British yoke
but did not fundamentally alter the social order, as the French
revolution did in France. Twenty-five years old and ambitious,
he hoped the experience would serve as a springboard for
something bigger than an uncertain legal career.

His good friend Gustave de Beaumont, a colleague at the
courthouse, joined him in this venture. Using their political
connections, the pair secured an official but unpaid mission to
report on American penitentiaries, part of an effort to reform
the French prison system. Sailing from Le Havre on April 2,
1831, they spent the voyage practicing their English, studying
American history and geography, and treatises in political
economy, and plotting their itinerary.

In their nine months in America, Tocqueville and Beaumont
traveled from New York to the Great Lakes, from Quebec and
New England down the East Coast, into the interior and down
the Mississippi to New Orleans, before crossing the South more
rapidly and returning to New York by way of Washington, D.C.
(see the Chronology in this volume). Recalled by the French
government before they completed their planned circuit, they
departed for France on February 20, 1832. Neither would ever
return to the United States.

Following the pair's return to France, Beaumont wrote most
of the promised prison report (*On the Penitentiary System in
the United States and its Application in France*). He also produced *Marie, or, Slavery in the United States*, a documentary
novel condemning race relations in America, which Tocqueville
announced as a work of "true insights and deep truths." As for
Tocqueville, he labored for eight years on a two-volume treatise, *Democracy in America*, publishing the first installment in
1835 and the second in 1840. Brilliantly framing modern history as a continuous struggle between liberty and equality,
Democracy became the enduring legacy of this voyage.

APPROACHING THE TASK OF INVESTIGATION

Tocqueville claimed that no amount of reading could have
prepared him for the spectacle of a democracy at work. I am

"tempted to burn my books," he wrote. Tocqueville was careful not to let any author intrude too obviously on his own thinking. He explained that he needed to reinvent concepts and examine facts totally on his own, or he would lose "absolutely all real talent."[2] French literary critic Sainte Beuve was perhaps especially perceptive, but also too severe, when he remarked that Tocqueville had "begun to think before learning anything," with the result "that his thinking was sometimes empty."[3] That Tocqueville was rarely explicit about the source of some of his ideas has intrigued and sometimes frustrated close readers detecting likely borrowings from Benjamin Constant, Madame de Staël, Pierre-Paul Royer-Collard, and others. But although he rarely acknowledged them, Tocqueville did have intellectual guides.

One source that shaped his preconceptions about America was Chateaubriand's novels, which he read from an early age. The great romantic writer was a member of Tocqueville's extended family. He was the brother-in-law of Tocqueville's guillotined aunt, saw the young Alexis grow up, and developed affection for him. Chateaubriand went to America in exile during the French Revolution and memorably portrayed its awe-inspiring landscapes as well as the beautiful Indian woman Atala, who converted to the Catholic faith. Tocqueville took direct inspiration from Chateaubriand in his description of the Michigan forest in *Two Weeks in the Wilderness*, a text published posthumously, but he emancipated himself from the romantic master in *Democracy*, where he adhered to a classical style of composition better suited to his analytical skills.

Tocqueville also found early inspiration in the writings of Blaise Pascal, who helped him search his own anxious personality. We cannot say at what age Tocqueville began reading Pascal, though it is likely that his beloved Jansenist tutor, Abbé Lesueur, steered him towards the *Pensées*. From reflecting on Pascal's writings he developed acute psychological insight into the restlessness that he found to be characteristic of a young democratic society. His debt to Pascal is especially apparent in his treatment of this theme in his notebooks as well as in the second volume of *Democracy*.

As a teenager, Tocqueville read Rousseau and Voltaire in his father's library, two men his great-grandfather had protected from censorship while director of the book trade under Louis XV. The experience cost him his religious faith, a loss that caused him a great deal of unease. Tocqueville maintained an especially conflicted relationship with Rousseau in the writing of *Democracy*. Like many in his generation, he greatly admired Rousseau's modern appreciation of the individual but resisted the idea of a "common me" or a "general will," which he and others blamed for so much bloodshed during the French Revolution. Tocqueville mentioned Rousseau by name once in his draft manuscript, but struck it out before the final version.[4]

One book Tocqueville did acknowledge as a direct source of inspiration was Montesquieu's *The Spirit of the Laws*. In his foreword, Montesquieu had argued he needed "new terms" to express "new ideas." Tocqueville in turn promoted not just new words but a whole "new political science" for understanding a world "totally new." Tocqueville borrowed from Montesquieu the concept of national character, the idea of studying mores as a prologue to understanding political regimes, and the dialectic between virtue and interest.

Although Tocqueville did not mention François Guizot in *Democracy*, he owed a great deal to the teaching of this master historian. He had already finished law school and was working at the tribunal when he and Beaumont attended Guizot's "truly extraordinary" lectures at the Sorbonne in 1829. From America, while groping for an analytical framework for his observations, Tocqueville asked his friend and colleague Ernest de Chabrol to go to his apartment in Versailles, find the lectures, and send them on to a New York address.[5] Guizot, even more than Montesquieu, gave Tocqueville the concept of a "social state"—a unique combination of circumstances, laws, customs, and ideas that shapes political institutions and gives them direction. Later in his political career, Tocqueville would come to resent Guizot as the strongman of the July monarchy who stood for the status quo. But when Tocqueville traveled across America, he turned to Guizot's writings for critical guidance.

TALKING TO AMERICANS

While Tocqueville approached his investigation of American democracy with an urgency prompted by the July Revolution and with key concepts of state and society that shaped his thinking, he learned enormously from the Americans he and Beaumont met and interviewed. The two had secured some letters of recommendation to distinguished Americans, but these turned out to be unnecessary as locals everywhere welcomed two French commissioners so eager to be instructed about the United States.[6] As Tocqueville wrote to his mother shortly after arriving in New York, "You have no idea how much help and benefit we will have received here from people eager to assist us in our mission. Americans of every class seem to vie with one another to see who can be most useful and agreeable to us."[7] Americans, for their part, found Tocqueville and Beaumont to be a relief from a seemingly unending stream of travel writers (mostly British) who had only contempt for American manners.

In interviews with roughly two hundred informants, Tocqueville proved to be an astute interlocutor, allowing people to talk about what they knew best without ever losing track of his larger purpose of understanding democracy. He transcribed "invaluable information" in notebooks, and he instructed family members, and such friends as his cousin Louis de Kergorlay, classmate Eugène Stöffels, and colleague Ernest de Chabrol, to keep his letters, as did Beaumont. With this paper trail, we can follow the two travelers everywhere they went, read a report of every conversation they had, and compare their observations. Tocqueville transcribed verbatim large sections of his notebooks and letters in volume I of *Democracy in America*, and this helped connect conclusions to the incidents and observations that elicited them.

Of all the places he visited, Tocqueville felt most at home in New England. This was not something he had expected, but it became readily apparent that the Boston gentry and the young French aristocrat shared a similar anxiety. How could power, they asked, devolve from educated people like themselves to uneducated adventurers who had no experience of government?

Tocqueville's hosts were all well-bred members of the New England elite, heirs of the Federalist political tradition that had been delivered a coup de grâce by General Jackson's election in 1828. First on the list was defeated former president John Quincy Adams, with whom Tocqueville dined at the home of diplomat Alexander Hill Everett, formerly the American minister to Spain. Tocqueville became close to Everett's brother, Edward, a prolific writer, Unitarian minister, and future Secretary of State, who remained a correspondent for life. He renewed his acquaintance with Jared Sparks, whom he had met in Paris: another Unitarian minister, proprietor and editor of the *North American Review*, and Harvard's first professor of history.[8] Sparks turned out to be Tocqueville's most valuable informant. He helped lead him to two of the major ideas of volume I. The first posited the New England town as the cradle of American democracy, an idea Sparks explored in a long personal memorandum to Tocqueville. The second, that majority rule posed a possible threat to democracy, became one of *Democracy's* signature insights. Tocqueville felt a sense of kinship with the New Englanders who would later form the Whig party to give formal expression to their misgivings. As he continued his travels, he questioned the universal white male suffrage that could send a man such as Davy Crockett to Congress: "It is striking to discover how low," under conditions of equality, "the people's choice may go, and how far astray."[9]

Tocqueville saw in American lawyers a kind of natural aristocracy of knowledge whose conservative instincts would help balance democracy's excesses. As a lawyer himself, Tocqueville might have been on familiar ground with American colleagues, but actually he had to struggle mightily to wrap his mind around the vast body of American case law—far removed from the Roman legal tradition in which he had trained. Tocqueville had critical conversations with attorney John C. Spencer—a New York State legislator and future treasury secretary, and the man who would arrange for the first American edition of *Democracy* in 1838—about the judiciary, bicameralism, freedom of speech and the press, and the relationship between church and state. He also met with the young Salmon Chase, whom Abraham Lincoln later made chief justice. He came away from his discussions with these figures impressed by the special power American judges held in deciding whether a law was constitutional. This meant courts could single-handedly void the work of both executive and legislative branches. He also saw the jury as an unparalleled school of democracy.

Tocqueville searched out men of prominence and responsibility to talk to wherever he went. On the Michigan frontier, it was Father Gabriel Richard from Detroit, a pioneer elected to the House of Representatives even though he was a Catholic priest; in Philadelphia, it was Robert Vaux, a Quaker and leading prison reformer; on the steamboat going down the Mississippi, it was Sam Houston who instructed him on both President Jackson and the Indians. But Tocqueville and Beaumont also met ordinary Americans as well as those who lived on the margins of society, and these encounters influenced and deepened their understanding of America. On the frontier of settlement, they shared the pioneers' log cabins. In the Great Lakes, they communicated as best they could with Indians who knew some French. For their prison investigation, they interviewed not only the great penitentiary reformers but the prisoners themselves. Tocqueville sat down with the men held in solitary confinement in the Cherry Hill penitentiary in Philadelphia. From Sing Sing, Tocqueville wrote to his cousin Le Peletier d'Aunay, who had been instrumental in getting the two friends the prison assignment, that "save for sleeping in a cell and being whipped with a rope, we are leading almost the same lives as the inmates."[10]

Before returning to France, the two friends stayed in Washington, D.C., where Edward Livingston, Jackson's Secretary of State, arranged for them to visit the President and attend sessions of Congress, while providing many documents they brought back to France. Tocqueville was extremely grateful to Livingston for this assistance. He was the only informant that Tocqueville thanked by name in the first volume of *Democracy*, though it was published as Livingston, now minister to France, broke off relations with the French government at the height of the indemnity crisis over sums owed for the seizure of American ships during the Napoleonic blockade of the continent.

Upon returning to Paris in 1832, Tocqueville, exhausted and unsure of how to direct his life, slipped into a bout of depression. But he steeled his resolve, literally locked himself up in an attic room in his parents' home, and got to work on his book. He read the American Founding Fathers and the debates over the Constitution (he had read only parts of *The Federalist* during the trip), and the law books of New York Chancellor James Kent and Supreme Court Justice Joseph Story. He came out only occasionally to seek advice from friends and family.

THE 1835 VOLUME

What did Tocqueville ultimately conclude from his interviews, reading notes, observations, and the intense writing effort? How did the new political science turn out?

Tocqueville set out to convince his French readers that democracy could work well and perpetuate itself without fear of being corrupted by despotism—whether the latter originated with an individual or the crowd. It was a "providential fact" that democracy could promote liberty. America proved it, pure and simple.

Tocqueville was especially keen on showing that Americans had practiced a form of what Isaiah Berlin would later call "positive" liberty from the very first settlement in New England.[11] Tocqueville found John Winthrop's definition of liberty, as he read it in Cotton Mather's writings, congenial, and he adapted it to his purpose. Liberty was not an "enemy of all authority" but "a civil and moral" quality that made it possible for individuals, singly or in groups, to realize their potential. With liberty empowering individuals, equality could spread.

In America, Tocqueville came to think of equality in a new light. He used the words equality and democracy interchangeably. Equality among Americans resulted not from a loss of autonomy and power, as happened to the French nobility under the absolute monarchy, but instead from the exercise of liberty. New England Puritans, Tocqueville explained, practiced self-government from day one (he had little to say about those he called the "gold seekers" of Virginia). This exercise of liberty generated an immense and beneficial burst of energy. Jared Sparks gave Tocqueville the critical historical sequence: In America, "the local community was organized before the county, the county before the state, and the state before the Union." The larger units never replaced the smaller ones. Thus multiple centers of authority coexisted, and this protected against tyranny.

Tocqueville impressed on his readers the importance of this "point of departure" for the subsequent constitutional history of the country. In elaborating a federal constitution, the founding fathers were careful to divide "the powers of sovereignty into two distinct groups." They gave the central government great authority but at the same time protected the parts from the whole. They combined them advantageously, and by dividing sovereignty, sustained and fostered liberty.

This was a tough sell to a French political audience committed to administrative centralization inherited from kings and revolutionaries alike, and strengthened under Napoleonic rule, but Tocqueville kept pressing the point. He wanted to see both central and local initiatives. He even added as an appendix to the 12th edition (1848) a disquisition on federalism in Switzerland to show that the Swiss failure to properly balance central and local powers crippled government. Tocqueville also kept pushing for legislative bicameralism at home in France. While on the Constitutional Committee of the French Second Republic in 1848, Tocqueville was still corresponding with John Spencer on the need for a diversity of voices in government.[12]

American readers deeply appreciated that a foreigner could understand so well their "compound republic." They were taken by surprise, however, when Tocqueville added to what they knew about themselves, focusing on the associations that were such an important part of American life. Tocqueville witnessed a benevolent empire of bible, tract, and missionary societies, Sunday schools, educational associations, and local charities in the Jacksonian era. Americans had not yet fully absorbed its consequences, and it is a sign of Tocqueville's genius that he was able to do this for them. James Madison had thought "different interests and parties" were useful safeguards against abuses of power.[13] But George Washington had denounced political "combinations and Associations, under whatever plausible character" as a threat to effective government.[14] Tocqueville changed the terms of the debate by seeing in associations a key mechanism for promoting liberty.

Tocqueville explained that Americans knew how to employ

voluntary associations as a means to initiate change. He described the process very concretely: "Suppose a person conceives of an idea for a project that has a direct bearing on the welfare of society. It would never occur to him to call upon the authorities for assistance. Instead, he will publicize his plan, offer to carry it out, enlist other individuals to pool their forces with his own, and struggle with all his might to overcome every obstacle. No doubt his efforts will often prove less successful than if the state had acted in his stead. In the long run, however, the overall result of all these individual enterprises will far outstrip anything the government could do." The free circulation of ideas in the press only further facilitated the creative process.

Tocqueville could have added that Protestant sectarianism only reinforced the associational impulse. Religious disestablishment that encouraged the creation of new churches was proceeding under his eyes, and Sparks alerted him to it. Old denominations fractured and new ones emerged. Tocqueville, who was concerned primarily with problems of dogma in his discussion of American Protestantism, did not focus his discussion of religion on the voluntarism he was otherwise analyzing; still, he rightly insisted that American churches, in contrast to the French Catholic church, which had sided with monarchs, had also been a pillar of liberty.

Thus emerged a picture of American democracy with multiple centers of power, and enduring habits of liberty and self-government. Nonetheless, Tocqueville conceded, there was a price to pay for democracy. "Democracy does not give the people the most skillful government," he pointed out, "but what it does even the most skillful government is powerless to achieve: it spreads throughout society a restless activity, a superabundant strength, an energy that never exists without it, and which, if circumstances are even slightly favorable, can accomplish miracles. These are its true advantages."

This was the very positive image of American democracy that Tocqueville meant to convey. At the same time, Tocqueville was conscious of the objections he would inevitably hear from French readers, and he was by temperament inclined to articulate and to a certain extent endorse these opposing viewpoints. He therefore also underscored the many challenges to American democracy from within. No matter how much fragmentation guaranteed liberty, Tocqueville argued, the spread of equality still threatened to corrupt it.

What Tocqueville feared most from equality was a deadening uniformity of thought, which he believed he detected in America. He depicted Americans as victims of a crippling conformity of opinion, justified only in part by the great instability of conditions, yet aggravated by an extreme case of national pride that made self-criticism unlikely. He complained that one could not even criticize the weather in America.

Sparks had told him that the dogma of the country was that the majority was always right. Tocqueville called this dogma the "tyranny of the majority" and saw manifestations of it almost everywhere. This opinion, of course, did not fare well with Tocqueville's American readers. Spencer, in his notes to the American edition of *Democracy in America*, put the best face he could on it by explaining that Tocqueville was criticizing, not Americans in general, but only the Jacksonians and the "tyranny of party." The Jacksonians, for their part, flatly rejected Tocqueville's views. Thomas Hart Benton, senator from Missouri, criticized Tocqueville for relying on the "book learning" of the "enlightened classes." For him, what Tocqueville described as the "tyranny of the majority" was better understood as "the intelligence of the masses."[15]

Tocqueville's insistence on this point was not just the result of his observations in America. It was also a reaction to the tactics of the French left, and it was meant as a rebuttal to them. In denouncing the tyranny of the majority, Tocqueville pursued his debate with Rousseau. He unmistakably targeted Rousseau when he wrote, "There are those who have made so bold as to insist that a people, insofar as it deals with matters of interest to itself alone, cannot overstep the bounds of justice and reason entirely, hence that there is no reason to be afraid of bestowing all power on the majority that represents that people. But to speak thus is to speak the language of a slave." To counter Rousseau, Tocqueville relied on Madison's reflections on the positive role of factions. Even though both Sparks and Everett were engaged in extensive dialogue with Madison at the time of Tocqueville's visit, they did not appreciate his comparative treatment. Sparks complained that Tocqueville

xxii   INTRODUCTION

had made too much of his remarks, while Everett argued that Tocqueville had misrepresented both Madison and Jefferson.[16] But again, Tocqueville had intentionally mixed his political and analytical goals, hidden his sources, and blurred the terms of comparison.

Tocqueville reserved his most direct challenge to American democracy for the last chapter on the "three races," where he condemned the forced displacement of the Indians and the harsh realities of life for blacks—slave or free. He was very wise in devoting a totally separate chapter to race and stating bluntly that the topic required a distinct treatment, for there was no way he could think of the lives of nonwhites on American soil as democratic. Treating race relations independently was thus an effective way of challenging Americans to extend democracy beyond the white race.

Tocqueville was not immediately sympathetic to the plight of the Indians. He had had a hard time overcoming a prejudice derived from his first sight of intoxicated Native Americans begging in upstate New York. This was quite a shock to someone who had taken for granted a romantic vision of proud and independent savages from the novels of Chateaubriand and James Fenimore Cooper. But he was still able to catch a glimpse of his ideal character in the wilderness. He severely condemned Jackson's policy of removal and the subsequent Trail of Tears, an early manifestation of which he witnessed while traveling down the Mississippi. But he was resigned to the fate of the Indians, whose social state was so much at odds with that of the advancing civilization of the whites.

As an abolitionist, yet one who favored some compensatory compromise with slave owners, Tocqueville reasoned that slavery was as poisonous a system for the masters as for the slaves. This conviction led him to introduce in this first volume a discussion of the concept of "self-interest" that would occupy so much of volume 2. He argued that it was in the "self-interest of the master" to abolish slavery and realize as soon as possible the advantages of free labor.

Tocqueville was a universalist, who while recognizing the civilizing mission of advanced societies, never accepted the superiority of one race over another and remained a committed abolitionist. But he was far more indulgent with Americans than his travel companion Beaumont, who felt that racism was the "seeds of death" of American democracy.[17] Unfortunately, the two travelers had not seen enough of the American South to anchor their respective viewpoints in direct observation. Tocqueville accepted Beaumont's distinct views, and their friendship never wavered. But their different assessment of the future of American democracy most likely prevented them from writing together the book they had once envisioned as a joint work.

Finally, after two and a half years of self-imposed isolation, Tocqueville gave the book to the publisher Gosselin for printing. In a last bout of anxiety, he wrote to his cousin Camille d'Orglandes, "It would be best for me if no one read the book, and I have not yet lost hope that this happiness will be mine."[18] But the reading public decided otherwise. The book's enduring success has been closely tied to both the expanding reach of democracy and the influence of the United States. It has to this day helped not only Americans but citizens of others nations understand what it means to live in a democratic society.

Thanks to my friends Charlie Feigenoff, Arthur Goldhammer, Christopher Loomis, and Max Rudin for important suggestions when writing this introduction.

[1]Before Tocqueville turned twenty, Tocqueville to Camille d'Orglandes, November 29, 1834, in Olivier Zunz, ed., *Alexis de Tocqueville and Gustave de Beaumont in America: Their Friendship and Their Travels*, trans. Arthur Goldhammer (Charlottesville: University of Virginia Press, 2010) [hereafter *Tocqueville/Beaumont*], 563.

[2]Tocqueville to Prosper Duvergier de Hauranne, September 1, 1856, in Olivier Zunz and Alan Kahan, eds., *The Tocqueville Reader: A Life in Letters and Politics* (Oxford: Blackwell, 2002) [hereafter *Tocqueville Reader*], 273–74.

[3]Sainte Beuve, Moniteur Universel, December 31, 1860, republished in *Causeries du Lundi* (Paris: Garnier Frères, 1862), XV: 105n1.

[4]*Democracy in America*, ed. Eduardo Nolla, trans. James T. Schleifer (Indianapolis: Liberty Fund, 2010), I: 58.

[5]Tocqueville to Ernest de Chabrol, May, 18, 1831, in *Tocqueville/Beaumont*, 23.

[6]George Wilson Pierson, *Tocqueville in America* (1938; Baltimore: Johns Hopkins University Press, 1996), 36.

[7]Tocqueville to his mother, May 14, 1831, in *Tocqueville/Beaumont*, 9.

[8]André Jardin, *Tocqueville: A Biography*, trans. Lydia Davis with Robert Hemenway (Baltimore: Johns Hopkins University Press), 150.

[9]Notebook E, *Tocqueville/Beaumont*, 351.

[10]Tocqueville to Félix Le Peletier d'Aunay, June 7, 1831, in *Tocqueville/Beaumont*, 443.

[11]Isaiah Berlin, *Two Concepts of Liberty: An Inaugural Lecture Delivered Before the University of Oxford on 31 October 1958* (Oxford: Clarendon Press, 1958).

[12]John C. Spencer to Alexis de Tocqueville, June 10, 1848, in *Tocqueville on America after 1840: Letters and Other Writings* ed. Aurelian Craiutu and Jeremy Jennings (Cambridge: Cambridge University Press, 2009), 93–96.

[13]Publius, "The Federalist X," November 22, 1787, in *The Debate on the Constitution, Part One* (New York: The Library of America, 1993), 410.

[14]George Washington, "Farewell Address," September 19, 1796, in *George Washington: Writings* (New York: The Library of America, 1997), 968.

[15]Olivier Zunz, "Tocqueville and the Americans: *Democracy in America* as Read in Nineteenth-Century-America," in *The Cambridge Companion to Tocqueville* ed. Cheryl B. Welch (Cambridge: Cambridge University Press, 2006) [hereafter "Tocqueville and the Americans"], 368–69.

[16]"Tocqueville and the Americans," 368.

[17]Gustave de Beaumont, *Ireland: Social, Political, and Religious*, ed. and trans. W.C. Taylor (1839; Cambridge, MA, Harvard University Press, 2006), 376.

[18]Tocqueville to Camille d'Organdes, November 29, 1834, in *Tocqueville/Beaumont*, 563.

DEMOCRACY IN AMERICA
VOLUME I

INTRODUCTION

AMONG the new things that attracted my attention during my stay in the United States, none struck me more forcefully than the equality of conditions. I readily discovered what a prodigious influence this basic fact exerts on the workings of society. It imparts a certain direction to the public spirit and a certain shape to laws, establishes new maxims for governing, and fosters distinctive habits in the governed.

I quickly recognized that the influence of this same fact extends well beyond political mores and laws and that it holds no less sway over civil society than over government. It creates opinions, engenders feelings, suggests customs, and modifies everything that it does not produce.

As I pursued my study of American society, I therefore came increasingly to see the equality of conditions as the original fact from which each particular fact seemed to derive. It stood constantly before me as the focal point toward which all my observations converged.

Then I began to think again about our own hemisphere, and it seemed to me that I could make out there something quite similar to what I saw in the new world. I saw an equality of conditions which, although it had yet to reach the extreme of development it had attained in the United States, nevertheless resembled it more closely every day. And the same democracy that ruled the societies of America seemed to be advancing rapidly toward power in Europe.

In that moment I conceived the book that you are about to read.

A great democratic revolution is taking place among us. Everyone sees it, but not everyone judges it in the same way. There are those who regard it as something new and, believing it to be an accident, still hope to arrest it, while others deem it irresistible because in their view it is the oldest, most continuous, most permanent fact known to history.

Let us cast our minds back to France as she was seven hundred years ago. A small number of families owned the land and ruled its inhabitants. The right to command was part of a man's inheritance, handed down from generation to generation. Men

3

could act on one another only by means of force. All power stemmed from a single source: ownership of land.

At this point, however, the clergy established and quickly extended its political power. Its ranks were open to all, to the poor as well as the rich, the commoner as well as the lord. Equality began to insinuate itself into government through the Church, and a man who might have vegetated in eternal slavery as a serf could, as a priest, take his place among nobles and often sit above kings.

With the passage of time society became more civilized and more stable, and relations among men became more numerous and more complex. The need for civil laws was urgently felt. People began to specialize in the study of law. They emerged from the obscure precincts of the tribunals and the dusty recesses of judicial registries and went to sit at the prince's court alongside feudal barons clad in ermine and mail.

Kings ruined themselves in great enterprises. Nobles spent themselves in private wars. Commoners enriched themselves in commerce. Money began to exert an influence over affairs of state. Trade was a new source of wealth, which led to power, and financiers became a power in politics that was an object of scorn as well as flattery.

Little by little enlightenment spread. The taste for literature and the arts revived. Mind became an ingredient of success. Science was a means of government and intelligence a social force. Men of letters took up affairs of state.

As new avenues to power opened up, however, the value of birth declined. In the eleventh century nobility was an inestimable prize. In the thirteenth century it could be bought. The first ennoblement took place in 1270, and equality was at last introduced into government by way of aristocracy itself.

Over the past seven hundred years, the nobility at times chose to counter royal authority or deny power to its rivals by giving political power to the people.

Even more frequently the king invited the inferior classes of the state to participate in government in order to humble the aristocracy.

In France kings proved themselves to be the most energetic and constant of levelers. When they were ambitious and strong, they sought to raise the people to the level of the nobles, and when they were moderate and weak, they allowed the people to take their place above the king. Some kings served democracy through their talents, others through their vices. Louis XI and Louis XIV tried hard to equalize everyone below the throne, and Louis XV descended with all his court into the dust.

Once citizens began to hold land by other than feudal tenure, and transferable wealth, being conspicuous, created new wellsprings of power and influence, no discovery in the arts, no improvement in commerce or industry, failed to create a comparable number of new elements of equality among men. From that moment on, every newly discovered process, every newly conceived need, every new desire that craved to be satisfied, marked further steps toward universal leveling. The taste for luxury, the love of war, the sway of fashion, indeed, all the passions of the human heart from the most superficial to the most profound, seemed to conspire to impoverish the rich and enrich the poor.

Once works of the intelligence became sources of power and wealth, people were obliged to look upon every scientific advance, every new discovery and idea, as a germ of power placed within the people's grasp. Poetry, eloquence, memory, the graces of the spirit, the fires of the imagination, profundity of thought — all these gifts, which heaven distributes at random, benefited democracy, and even if they happened to be in the possession of democracy's adversaries, they still served its cause by setting in relief the natural greatness of man. Democracy's conquests therefore spread with those of civilization and enlightenment, and literature was an arsenal open to all from which the weak and the poor daily drew arms.

If we run through the pages of our history, we find scarcely a single great event of the past seven hundred years that did not redound to equality's benefit.

The Crusades and the wars with England decimated the nobles and divided their estates. Municipal institutions introduced democratic liberty into the heart of the feudal monarchy. With the invention of firearms peasant and noble became equals on the field of battle. The printing press was a resource on which the intelligence of both could draw equally. The post brought enlightenment to the pauper's doorstep as well as to the palace gate. Protestantism held that all men are equally equipped to find their way to heaven. America, on being discovered, opened a thousand new paths to fortune and brought wealth and power to obscure adventurers.

If, starting in the eleventh century, we examine the state of French society at fifty-year intervals, we see a twofold revolution taking place. The noble has moved steadily down the social ladder, and the commoner has moved steadily up. One is descending, the other rising. Every fifty years they move closer together; soon they will touch.

None of these changes is peculiar to France. Wherever we look in the Christian world, we see the same ongoing revolution.

Everywhere a diversity of historical incident has redounded to democracy's benefit. Everyone played a part: those who strove to ensure democracy's success as well as those who never dreamt of serving it; those who fought for it as well as those who declared themselves its enemies. Driven pell-mell down a single path, all worked toward a single goal, some in spite of themselves, others unwittingly — blind instruments in the hands of God.

The gradual development of the equality of conditions is therefore a providential fact. It has the essential characteristics of one: it is universal, durable, and daily proves itself to be beyond the reach of man's powers. Not a single event, not a single individual, fails to contribute to its development.

Is it wise to believe that a social movement that originated so far in the past can be halted by the efforts of a single generation? Does anyone think that democracy, having destroyed feudalism and vanquished kings, will be daunted by the bourgeois and the rich? Will it stop now that it has become so strong and its adversaries so weak?

Where are we headed, then? No one can say, because we have no basis for comparison. Already today conditions among Christians are more equal than they have ever been at any previous time anywhere in the world. Thus the magnitude of what has been done already prevents us from anticipating what can still be done.

This entire book was written in the grip of a kind of religious terror occasioned in the soul of the author by the sight of this irresistible revolution, which for centuries now has sur-mounted every obstacle and continues to advance amid the ruins it has created.

We can discover indubitable signs of God's will even if God Himself remains silent. We have only to examine the habitual course of nature and the constant tendency of events. Though the Creator does not raise His voice, still I am certain that the curves along which the stars move through space are traced by His finger.

If, after a lengthy period of observation and sincere medi-tation, people were to become convinced that the gradual and progressive development of equality was at once their past and their future, the process would immediately take on a sacred character, as if it were an expression of the sovereign master's will. To wish to arrest democracy would then seem tanta-mount to a struggle against God himself, and nations would have no choice but to accommodate to the social state im-posed on them by Providence.

The Christian peoples today present an alarming spectacle. The change that has them in its grip is already so powerful that it cannot be stopped yet not so rapid that there is no hope of altering its direction. Their fate is still in their hands, but not for much longer.

To educate democracy — if possible to revive its beliefs; to purify its mores; to regulate its impulses; to substitute, little by little, knowledge of affairs for inexperience and under-standing of true interests for blind instinct; to adapt govern-ment to its time and place; to alter it to fit circumstances and individuals — this is the primary duty imposed on the leaders of society today.

A world that is totally new demands a new political science.

To this need, however, we have given little thought. Im-mersed in a rapidly flowing stream, we stubbornly fix our eyes on the few pieces of debris still visible on the shore, while the current carries us away and propels us backward into the abyss.

There is no European nation in which the great social revolution that I have just described has proceeded more rap-idly than in France, but its progress here has always been haphazard.

Heads of state have never thought to prepare for this revolution in advance. It has come in spite of them, or without their knowledge. The nation's most powerful, intelligent, and morally responsible classes have never tried to take hold of the movement in order to guide it. Democracy has therefore been abandoned to its savage instincts. It has grown up like those children deprived of parental care who raise themselves in the streets of our cities and who know nothing of society but its vices and miseries. Almost before anyone was aware of its existence, it seized power unexpectedly. From then on each man has abjectly catered to the least of its desires. Once, it was worshiped as the very image of force. Later, after its strength had been sapped by its own excesses, legislators imprudently sought to destroy it rather than educate and discipline it. Instead of teaching it to govern, they thought only of expelling it from government.

Consequently, the democratic revolution has altered the material basis of society without bringing about the concomitant changes in laws, ideas, habits, and mores necessary to make it useful. Thus we have democracy minus that which ought to attenuate its vices and bring its natural advantages to the fore. We already see the evils it entails but know nothing as yet of the good it may bring.

When monarchy, supported by aristocracy, peaceably governed the nations of Europe, society for all its miseries nevertheless enjoyed several kinds of happiness that are difficult to appreciate or even imagine today.

The power of a few subjects raised insurmountable barriers against the tyranny of the prince; and kings, sensing the almost divine character that cloaked their authority in the eyes of the multitude, drew from the very respect they inspired the will not to abuse their power.

Nobles, despite the vast distance that separated them from the people, took a benevolent and tranquil interest in their fate, much as the shepherd concerns himself with the fate of his flock. Without regarding the poor as equals, they watched over the destiny of those whose welfare had been entrusted to them by Providence.

The people, never having imagined a social condition other than their own and never expecting to become the equals of their leaders, accepted what benefits came their way and did not challenge their leaders' rights. They loved their superiors when they were clement and just and submitted to their rigors without hardship or ignominy as if bowing to inevitable woes imposed by the hand of God. Usage and custom set limits to tyranny, moreover, and established a kind of law in the very teeth of might.

Because the noble had no idea that anyone might wish to deprive him of privileges that he believed to be legitimate, and because the serf looked upon his inferiority as a consequence of nature's immutable order, it is easy to imagine how a sort of reciprocal good will might have been established between two classes so differently favored by fate. In this society one saw inequality and misery, but souls were not degraded.

Men do not become depraved through the exercise of power or the habit of obedience but rather by wielding a power that they consider to be illegitimate or by obeying a power that they regard as usurped and oppressive.

On one side were wealth, force, and leisure, accompanied by the indulgence of luxury, the refinement of taste, the pleasures of the mind, and the cultivation of the arts; on the other, labor, coarseness, and ignorance.

But within this ignorant and coarse multitude one also found energetic passions, generous sentiments, deep beliefs, and uncultivated virtues.

Thus organized, the body social could lay claim to stability, power, and above all glory.

But then distinctions of rank began to blur; the barriers that had separated man from man began to fall. Estates were divided, power was shared, enlightenment spread, intellectual capacities grew more equal. The social state became democratic, and in the end democracy peacefully established its dominion over institutions and mores.

Under such conditions, I can conceive of a society in which all people would think of themselves as the authors of the law, which they would consequently love and readily obey; and in which the authority of the government would be respected as necessary rather than divinely ordained, so that a person's love for the head of state would be not a passion but a reasoned and tranquil sentiment. Because each individual would possess certain rights he could be sure of retaining, a manly confidence would develop between classes, a reciprocal condescension as devoid of pride as of servility.

The people, instructed as to their true interests, would recognize that in order to enjoy the benefits of society one has to accept its burdens. Citizens joined together in free association might then replace the individual power of nobles, and the state would be protected against tyranny and license.

To be sure, a democratic state constituted in this way would not stand still, but changes in the body of society would be orderly and progressive. Such a society would be less brilliant than an aristocracy but also less plagued by misery. Pleasures would be less extreme, prosperity more general. Knowledge would be less exalted but ignorance more rare. Feelings would be less passionate and habits milder. There would be more vices and fewer crimes.

In the absence of enthusiasm and ardent belief, citizens could nevertheless be summoned to make great sacrifices by appealing to their reason and experience. All men being equally weak, each would feel equally in need of his fellow man's support and, knowing that cooperation was the condition of that support, would readily see that his private interest was subsumed in the general interest.

The nation taken as a whole would be less brilliant, less glorious, and perhaps less powerful, but the majority of citizens would be better off. People would prefer peace to war, not out of despair of living better but out of appreciation of living well.

In such an order there might be some things that were neither good nor useful, but society would at least have appropriated as much of the good and useful as possible. In renouncing forever such social benefits as aristocracy might have been able to provide, society would have absorbed all the good that democracy had to offer.

But we — what have we done? In rejecting the social state of our ancestors and casting aside their institutions, ideas, and mores, what have we put in their place?

The prestige of royal power has evaporated, but the majesty of the law has failed to take its place. People nowadays despise authority yet still fear it, and fear extracts from them more than they previously gave out of respect and love.

It strikes me that we have destroyed those individuals who once had the wherewithal to battle tyranny on their own. Privileges once vested in families, corporations, and individuals are now bequeathed to the government alone. The sometimes oppressive but often protective power of a small number of citizens has given way to the weakness of all.

The breakup of fortunes has diminished the distance that once separated the poor from the rich. In coming together, however, they seem to have discovered new reasons to hate one another. Gripped by terror or envy, each rejects the other's claims to power. Neither has any idea of rights. Force is for both today's only means of persuasion and tomorrow's only guarantee.

The poor man for the most part clings to his forebears' prejudices without their faith and to their ignorance without their virtues. He accepts the doctrine of interest as the guide for his actions without understanding the science of that doctrine, and his selfishness is as unenlightened now as his selfless devotion was before.

Society is tranquil not because it is conscious of its strength and well-being but, on the contrary, because it believes itself to be weak and infirm. It fears that the slightest effort might do it in. Everyone senses that something is wrong, but no one has the courage or energy necessary to set it right. People feel desire, regret, sorrow, and joy, but nothing visible or lasting comes of it, much as the passion of an old man culminates in impotence and nothing more.

Thus we have abandoned what was good in our former state without acquiring what useful things our present state might have to offer. Having destroyed an aristocratic society, we seem ready to go on living complacently amid the rubble forever.

What is happening in the intellectual world is no less deplorable.

French democracy, hindered in its forward progress or left to cope unaided with its own unruly passions, toppled anything that stood in its way, shaking what it did not destroy. Rather than gradually taking control of society so as to rule in peace, it marches on through the chaos and tumult of battle. In the heat of struggle, people have been driven beyond the natural limits of their own opinions by the opinions and excesses of their adversaries, to the point where they have lost sight of their objectives and begun to speak in ways that have little to do with their true feelings and secret instincts.

This is the source of the peculiar confusion we have been forced to witness.

I search my memory in vain and find nothing to excite greater sorrow and pity than what is taking place before our very eyes. The natural bonds that join opinion to taste and action to belief seem lately to have been broken. The harmony that has been observed throughout history between man's feelings and his ideas has apparently been destroyed, and the laws of moral analogy have seemingly been abolished.

Among us one still encounters zealous Christians who love to draw spiritual nourishment from the verities of the other life. They will no doubt thrill to the cause of human liberty, the source of all moral greatness. Christianity, which made all men equal in the sight of God, will not shrink from seeing all citizens as equal in the eyes of the law. But through a strange concatenation of events, religion has for the time being become enmeshed with the powers that democracy is bent on destroying. Often it spurns the equality it loves and curses freedom as an enemy instead of taking it by the hand and sanctifying its efforts.

Alongside these religious men I see others who look not to heaven but to earth. Champions of freedom, which they see as the source not only of the noblest virtues but above all of the greatest goods, they sincerely wish to establish its power and secure its benefits for mankind. In my view they should hasten to invoke the aid of religion, for they must know that without morality freedom cannot reign and without faith there is no basis for morality. Yet they have seen religion in the ranks of their adversaries, and for them that is enough: some attack it, and the rest dare not hasten to its defense.

In centuries past some base and venal souls spoke out in favor of slavery, while others of independent mind and generous heart fought a hopeless battle to preserve human freedom. Nowadays, however, it is common to meet men of noble and proud mien whose opinions directly contradict their tastes, men who vaunt a servile and base condition they have never known themselves. By contrast, others speak of freedom as if they could feel what is sacred and grand in it, and vociferously demand for humanity rights they have always failed to recognize.

I see virtuous, peaceful men whose untainted morals, tranquil habits, comfortable circumstances, and enlightened thinking mark them out as natural leaders. Sincere and ardent patriots, they would make great sacrifices for their country. Yet civilization often finds them among its adversaries. They cannot distinguish its abuses from its benefits, and in their minds the idea of evil is inextricably linked to the idea of the new.

Alongside them I see other men who, in the name of progress, seek to reduce man to a material being. They look for what is useful without concern for what is just; they seek science removed from faith and prosperity apart from virtue. Having styled themselves champions of modern civilization, they have arrogantly placed themselves at its head, usurping a position abandoned by others which they are quite unworthy of occupying themselves.

Where, then, do things stand?

Religious men do battle against liberty, and friends of liberty attack religion. Noble and generous spirits extol slavery, while base and servile souls advocate independence. Honest and enlightened citizens oppose all progress, while men with neither patriotism nor morals style themselves apostles of civilization and enlightenment!

Has every other century been like this one? Has man always confronted, as he does today, a world in which nothing makes sense? In which virtue is without genius and genius without honor? In which the love of order is indistinguishable from the lust of tyrants? In which the sacred cult of liberty is confounded with contempt for the law? In which conscience casts but an ambiguous light on the actions of men? In which nothing any longer seems forbidden or allowed, honest or shameful, true or false?

Am I to believe that the Creator made man only to allow him to flounder endlessly in a sea of intellectual misery? I do not think so. For the societies of Europe God envisions a future calmer and more certain than the present. Though I cannot penetrate His designs, I will not for that reason cease to believe in them. I would rather doubt my reason than His justice.

There is one country in the world in which the great social revolution of which I speak seems almost to have attained its natural limits. It has been effected there with simplicity and ease. Or, to put it another way, one might say that this country has witnessed the effects of the democratic revolution that we are now undergoing without having had the revolution itself.

The immigrants who settled in America at the beginning of the seventeenth century somehow separated the democratic principle from all the other principles with which it had to contend in the old societies of Europe and transplanted it alone to the shores of the new world. There it could mature under conditions of liberty and, because it advanced in harmony with mores, develop peacefully within the law.

There is no doubt in my mind that sooner or later we will come, as the Americans have come, to an almost complete equality of conditions. I do not conclude from this that we will one day be compelled to draw the same political consequences as the Americans from our similar social state. I am not at all convinced that they have hit upon the only form of government that a democracy may adopt. If, however, the same root cause has given rise to new laws and customs in both countries, then that is reason enough for us to take an immense interest in finding out what effects that cause has produced in each.

I did not study America, then, simply to satisfy my curiosity, though that would have been a legitimate thing to do. I was looking for lessons from which we might profit. Anyone who thinks that I set out to write a panegyric is sorely mistaken, as will be clear to anyone who reads this book. Nor was my goal to advocate any form of government in general, for I am among those who believe that absolute goodness is almost never to be found in laws. I do not even presume to judge whether the social revolution, whose progress seems to me irresistible, has been advantageous or harmful to mankind. I have taken the revolution to be a *fait accompli*, or nearly so, and looked for the nation in which it has unfolded in the fullest, most peaceful way so as to identify its natural consequences and if possible discover ways of making it beneficial to man. I confess that in America I saw more than America. I sought there an image of democracy itself — its inclinations, character, prejudices, and passions. I wanted to become familiar with democracy, if only to find out what we had to hope from it, or to fear.

In the first part of this work, I have therefore attempted to show what shape democracy, left in America to its inclinations and all but abandoned to its natural instincts, imparted to the laws, what influence it had on the course of government, and in general what force it exerted on affairs of state. I wanted to know what benefits it produced, and what ills. I tried to find out what precautions the Americans took to keep it under control, and what others they omitted. And I undertook to point out what factors allowed democracy to govern society.

I had originally intended to write a second part in which I would have described the influence of equality of conditions and democratic government on civil society in America: on habits, ideas, and mores. But my ardor to fulfill this design has begun to wane. My work will have been rendered almost superfluous even before it is begun, for soon another author will set the principal traits of the American character before the reader. By concealing the gravity of his portrait beneath a light veil, he will adorn truth with greater charm than I am capable of.[1]

I do not know whether I have succeeded in communicating what I saw in America, but it was my sincere wish to do so: of that I am sure. So far as I know I never gave in to the temptation to tailor facts to ideas rather than adapt ideas to facts.

---

[1]At the time I published the first edition of this work, M. Gustave de Beaumont, my traveling companion in America, was still working on his book, entitled *Marie, or Slavery in the United States*, which has since appeared. M. de Beaumont's principal aim was to set in relief and call attention to the situation of Negroes in Anglo-American society. His work will shed a vivid new light on the question of slavery, a question vital for the united republics. Unless I am mistaken, M. de Beaumont's book will not only arouse the keen interest of those who look to it as a source of emotions and descriptions but should also win a more solid and durable success among readers who more than anything else desire true insights and deep truths.

Whenever it was possible to make a point with the aid of written documents, I was careful to consult either the original text or the most authentic and reputable sources.[2] I have indicated those sources in footnotes, so that anyone may verify them. When it came to opinions, political practices, or remarks on manners, I sought out the best-informed people. On important and controversial matters, I did not rely on one informant alone but based my opinion on all the testimony taken together.

For this the reader will have to take my word. In many instances I might have supported my opinion by citing the names of authorities either familiar to everyone or worthy of being so. A stranger sitting at fireside with his host will often hear important truths that might be withheld from a friend. With the stranger it is a relief to break an enforced silence, and the stranger's indiscretion need not be feared because his stay will be short. When information was confided to me, I wrote it down immediately, but these notes will never leave my files. I would rather hinder my work's chance of success than add my name to the list of travelers who repay the generous hospitality of their hosts with embarrassment and chagrin.

I am well aware that, despite the care I have taken in writing this book, nothing would be easier than to criticize it, should anyone wish to do so.

Anyone who cares to examine the book closely will find, I think, one dominant thought running through its various parts. But I have been obliged to look at a wide range of subjects, and anyone who wishes to set a single, isolated fact against the body of facts collected here, or a particular idea against the whole body of ideas, will find it easy to do so. I therefore ask only that the reader do me the favor of reading

---

[2]Legislative and administrative documents were made available to me with a kindness whose memory will always elicit my gratitude. Among the American officials who assisted my research, I will mention especially Mr. Edward Livingston, the Secretary of State (now minister plenipotentiary in Paris). During my visit to Congress, Mr. Livingston was kind enough to provide me with most of the documents I possess dealing with the federal government. Mr. Livingston is one of those rare men whom one likes from having read their writings, whom one admires and honors before meeting them, and to whom one is happy to owe a debt of gratitude.

my work in the same spirit in which I wrote it, and of judging the book on the basis of the general impression that it leaves, just as I made up my mind on the basis not of a single fact but of the preponderance of facts.

Bear in mind, too, that the author who wishes to make himself intelligible is obliged to explore all the theoretical consequences of his ideas, often pushing them to the limit of the false and impractical. In action it is sometimes necessary to brush the rules of logic aside, but in reasoned argument this is never the case. It is almost as difficult to be inconsistent in language as it is to be consistent in action.

To conclude, I will point out myself what many readers are likely to regard as the major defect of my book. It is not precisely tailored to anyone's point of view. In writing it, I had no intention of serving or opposing any party. I did not try to look at things differently from the parties, but I did try to see further. They busy themselves with tomorrow only, while I aimed to think about the future.

PART I

Chapter 1

THE OUTWARD CONFIGURATION
OF NORTH AMERICA

North America divided into two vast regions, one sloping toward the North Pole, the other toward the equator. — Mississippi valley. — Traces found there of the revolutions of the globe. — The Atlantic Coast, on which the English colonies were founded. — Differences in the appearance of South America and North America at the time of their discovery. — Forests of North America. — Prairies. — Roving tribes of natives. — Their appearance, mores, and languages. — Traces of an unknown people.

NORTH AMERICA, in its outward configuration, exhibits certain general features that strike the eye at first glance. Land and water, mountains and valleys, seem to have been separated with methodical care. Despite the profuse variety of landscape and scenery, a simple majesty of design stands out.

The continent is divided into two vast regions of roughly equal size.

One is bounded on the north by the North Pole and on the east and west by the two great oceans. It stretches southward to form a triangle, whose irregular sides touch at last below the great lakes of Canada.

The second starts where the first leaves off, spanning the remainder of the continent.

The first region slopes gently toward the pole, the second toward the equator.

The land comprised by the first region declines so imperceptibly to the north that one might almost describe it as a plateau. Within this vast land mass one finds neither high mountains nor deep valleys.

Streams snake their way through it almost at random. Rivers intertwine, mingle, separate, and meet again. They spread into vast marshes, losing themselves in the watery labyrinth they create, and only after countless detours find their way at last to the polar seas. The great lakes that bound this first region are not contained, as are most lakes in the Old World, by hills or rocks. Their flat banks rise only a few feet above the water's surface. Hence each lake is like a vast bowl filled to the brim. The slightest change in the structure of the globe would send waves from these lakes racing off toward either the North Pole or the tropical sea.

The second region is more uneven in elevation and better suited to permanent human habitation. Two long mountain ranges divide it along its length: one of these, known as the Alleghenies, follows the shores of the Atlantic Ocean; the other runs parallel to the South Seas.

Between these two mountain ranges lies a territory of 228,343 square leagues.[1] Its area is therefore roughly six times the size of France.[2]

Yet this vast territory comprises but a single valley, which descends at one end from the rounded summits of the Alleghenies and rises at the other to the peaks of the Rocky Mountains without encountering any obstacles in between.

At the bottom of this valley flows an immense river. Water flowing down from the mountains feeds this river from every direction.

The French used to call it the Saint-Louis in memory of their far-off fatherland, and the Indians, in their grandiloquent tongue, have named it the Father of Waters, or Mississippi.

The source of the Mississippi lies in the area of overlap between the two great regions I mentioned earlier, not far from the highest point of the plateau that divides them.

Nearby rises another river,[3] which discharges its waters into the polar seas. The Mississippi itself seems at first to hesitate as to its proper course: it turns back on itself several times, and only after tarrying awhile amid lakes and marshes does it finally make up its mind and slowly wend its way southward.

Flowing tranquilly at times through the bed of clay that nature has dug for it, at other times swollen by storms, the Mississippi waters more than a thousand leagues along its course.[4]

---

[1] 1,341,649 square miles. See *Darby's View of the United States*, p. 469. I have reduced these miles to leagues of 2,000 *toises*.

[2] France is 35,181 square leagues.

[3] The Red River.

[4] 2,500 miles, 1,032 leagues. See *Description des États-Unis*, by Warden, vol. 1, p. 186.

Six hundred leagues[5] north of its mouth, the river has already attained a mean depth of fifteen feet, and ships of 300 tons can navigate nearly 200 leagues upstream. Fifty-seven major navigable rivers feed its flow. Its tributaries include a river of 1,300 leagues,[6] another of 900 leagues,[7] another of 600,[8] another of 500,[9] and four of 200,[10] to say nothing of countless small streams whose waters, flowing into it from every direction, are absorbed into its current.

The valley watered by the Mississippi seems to have been created for it alone. There, like a god, the river dispenses good and evil at will. Nature has seen to it that the fertility of its bottomland is inexhaustible. The farther one ventures from its banks, the sparser the vegetation becomes and the poorer the soil; everything withers or dies. Nowhere have the great convulsions of the globe left more obvious traces than in the Mississippi valley. The whole aspect of the region attests to the effects of water. Both barrenness and fertility are consequences of its power. The tides of the primeval ocean piled up thick layers of vegetable matter in the valley's bottom, and with the passage of time these deposits were leveled out. The river's right bank is lined with vast plains as flat as if a farmer had smoothed them with a roller. Toward the mountains, however, the terrain becomes increasingly uneven and barren. The soil seems pierced in a thousand places by primitive rocks, which stand out like the bones of a skeleton from which time has stripped away muscle and flesh. The surface of the earth is covered with pulverized granite and irregularly shaped stones, among which a few plants manage to force their way: it is as though the debris of some vast edifice lay scattered about a fertile field. When the stones and powder are analyzed, their composition is easily seen to be the same as that of the arid, jagged peaks of the Rockies. Having flushed the soil

---

[5]1,364 miles, 563 leagues. See *ibid.*, vol. 1, p. 169.

[6]The Missouri. See *ibid.*, vol. 1, p. 132 (1,278 leagues).

[7]The Arkansas. See *ibid.*, vol. 1, p. 188 (877 leagues).

[8]The Red River. See *ibid.*, vol. 1, p. 190 (598 leagues).

[9]The Ohio. See *ibid.*, vol. 1, p. 192 (490 leagues).

[10]The Illinois, Saint Pierre, Saint Francis, and Moingona. For the measurements of these rivers, I have used the statute mile and the *lieue de poste* of 2,000 *toises*.

down into the valley, the water no doubt carried off even some of the rocks, hurling them onto nearby slopes and grinding them together until finally the base of the mountain range was strewn with debris snatched from its summits.*

All in all, the Mississippi valley is the most magnificent place God ever prepared for men to dwell in, yet it is still but a vast wilderness.

East of the Alleghenies, from the base of the mountains to the Atlantic Ocean, lies a long strip of rock and sand that appears to have been left behind by the receding ocean. Although this strip averages only forty-eight leagues in width,[11] it is three hundred ninety leagues in length.[12] In this part of the American continent the soil yields to the farmer's labors only grudgingly. The vegetation is meager and unvarying.

It was on this inhospitable coast that the efforts of human industry were first concentrated. On this arid tongue of land the English colonies that would one day become the United States of America were born and matured. And there the center of power remains today, while in the hinterland the true elements of the great people to whom the future of the continent no doubt belongs are being assembled almost in secret.

When Europeans first landed on the shores of the West Indies and, later, on the coast of South America, they thought they had been transported into the fabled realms celebrated by the poets. The sea sparkled with the fires of the tropics. Its extraordinarily limpid waters revealed to sailors for the first time the depth of the abyss.[13] Here and there small perfumed isles seemed to float like baskets of flowers on the calm surface of the sea. Wherever the eye turned, these enchanted places seemed to have been made to meet man's needs or else calculated to suit his pleasures. Most of the trees were laden

---

*See Note I, page 477.

[11]100 miles.

[12]900 miles.

[13]The sea around the West Indies is so clear, according to Malte-Brun, vol. 5, p. 726, that one can make out coral and fish at a depth of sixty fathoms. Ships seem to float in the air. A sort of vertigo grips the traveler, who looks through the crystalline fluid at submarine gardens where shells and golden fish shine among tufts of sea wrack and tangles of seaweed.

with nutritious fruits, and the ones least useful to man charmed him with the brilliance and variety of their colors. In a forest of fragrant citrus, wild figs, round-leafed myrtle, acacia, and oleander, all laced with flowering vines, a multitude of birds unknown in Europe spread wings iridescent with purple and azure, and joined their voices to the chorus of a nature teeming with vitality and life.*

Death lay concealed beneath this brilliant cloak, but no one saw it at the time. In the very air of these climates, moreover, there prevailed I know not what enervating influence, which bound man to the present and made him careless of the future.

North America presented a different aspect: there, everything was grave, serious, solemn. It seemed to have been created to become the domain of the intelligence, and the other to become the abode of the senses.

A storm-tossed, fog-shrouded ocean washed its beaches. Granite boulders and sandy inlets lined its perimeter. The forests that blanketed its shores were dark and melancholy, and hardly anything grew in them other than pine, larch, live oak, wild olive, and laurel.

Breaching this outer rampart led to the thick shade of the central forest, where the largest of the trees found in either hemisphere grew side by side. Sycamore, catalpa, sugar maple, and Virginia poplar twined their branches with those of oak, beech, and linden.

As in forests under man's dominion, death here worked its ceaseless ravages, but no one took it upon himself to remove the debris it left behind. Dead wood therefore piled up faster than it could decay to make way for new growth. Yet even in the midst of all this debris, the work of reproduction continued without letup. Climbing vines and other plants crept among fallen trees and worked their way into decaying remains; they lifted and broke the shriveled bark that still clung to the dead wood, thereby clearing the way for young shoots. Thus death in a way served life. Each looked the other in the face, seemingly keen to mingle and confound their works.

Within these forests a profound obscurity reigned. A thousand streams, their courses not yet guided by human industry,

*See Note II, page 477.

ensured that the air was always moist. Barely anything could be seen beyond a few flowers, some wild fruits, an occasional bird.

Only the fall of a tree toppled by old age, the hiss of a waterfall, the bellowing of buffalo, and the whistle of the wind troubled the silence of nature.

To the east of the great river, the woods gave way in places to boundless prairies. Had nature, in her infinite variety, deprived these fertile fields of the seed of trees, or had the forests that once covered them been destroyed by the hand of man? Neither tradition nor scientific research has yet provided an answer.

This immense wilderness was not entirely devoid of human presence, however. For centuries a few tribes had roved the dark forests and prairie pastures. From the mouth of the Saint Lawrence to the delta of the Mississippi, from the Atlantic to the Pacific, these savages resembled one another in certain ways attesting to a common origin. But they differed from all other known races.[14] They were neither white like Europeans nor yellow like most Asians nor black like Negroes. Their skin was of reddish complexion, their hair long and shiny, their lips thin, and their cheekbones quite pronounced. The languages spoken by the savage tribes of America differed in their vocabulary but obeyed the same grammatical rules, and those rules differed in several respects from the ones previously known to govern the formation of human tongues.

The idiom of the Americans seemed the product of new combinations. It bespoke an effort of intelligence on the part of its inventors of which the Indians of today scarcely seem capable.[*]

[14]Certain resemblances have subsequently been discovered between the physical appearance, language, and habits of the Indians of North America and those of the Tungus, Manchus, Mongols, Tartars, and other nomadic tribes of Asia. These tribes live close to the Bering Strait, which has given rise to the hypothesis that at some point in the distant past they migrated to the deserted continent of America. But science has yet to clarify this point. On this question, see Malte-Brun, vol. 5; the works of M. von Humboldt; Fischer, *Conjectures sur l'origine des Américains*; Adair, *History of the American Indians*.

[*]See Note III, page 478.

The social state of these people also differed in several respects from anything to be seen in the Old World. They seemed to have multiplied freely in their wilderness, without contact with more civilized races. They therefore exhibited none of those dubious and incoherent notions of good and evil, no sign of that profound corruption that generally accompanies the ignorance and crude manners of once-civilized nations that have reverted to barbarism. The Indian owed nothing except to himself: his virtues, his vices, and his prejudices were his own. He had grown up in the savage independence of his nature.

If the common people of civilized countries are coarse, it is not only because they are ignorant and poor but also because, in that condition, they find themselves in daily contact with enlightened and wealthy men.

The daily contrast between their own misfortune and weakness and the prosperity and power of a few of their fellow human beings stirs anger in their hearts at the same time as fear. Their sense of inferiority and dependence vexes and humiliates them. This internal state of the soul is reflected in their mores as well as their language. They are at once insolent and base.

The truth of this is easily proved by observation. The people are coarser in aristocratic countries than anywhere else, and coarser in opulent cities than in the countryside.

Wherever men of such great wealth and power are found, the weak and poor are all but overwhelmed by their baseness. Seeing no way to restore equality, they despair utterly for themselves and allow themselves to sink below the threshold of human dignity.

This unfortunate effect of contrasting conditions is not a factor in the life of the savage. The Indians, though all ignorant and poor, are also all equal and free.

When the first Europeans arrived, the natives of North America still had no notion of the value of wealth and seemed indifferent to the well-being that civilized men could acquire with their riches. Yet there was nothing coarse about them. Their actions were governed by a habitual reserve and a kind of aristocratic politeness.

Mild and hospitable in peace yet merciless in war beyond all previously known limits of human ferocity, the Indian would brave starvation to assist the stranger who knocked on the door of his hut at night, yet he would also tear his prisoner's still-quivering limbs from his body with his own hands. Not even in the most famous ancient republics do we find examples of stouter courage, prouder spirit, or more uncompromising love of independence than lay hidden in those days in the wild forests of the New World.[15] Europeans made little impression when they landed on the shores of North America. Their presence occasioned neither envy nor fear. What hold could they have over men such as these? The Indian knew how to live without needs, suffer without complaint, and die with a song on his lips.[16] Like all other members of the great human family, these savages also believed in the existence of a better world and worshiped God, the creator of the universe, under a variety of names. Their notions concerning the great intellectual truths were in general simple and philosophical.[*]

However primitive the people whose character we have just described may appear, there can be no doubt that another, more civilized people, more advanced in all things, lived previously in the same regions.

An obscure tradition common to most of the Indian tribes of the Atlantic coast informs us that those same tribes once lived west of the Mississippi. Along the banks of the Ohio and throughout the central valley, mounds built by human hands are even now a daily discovery. If one digs to the center of

[15] President Jefferson (*Notes sur la Virginie*, p. 148) reports that when the Iroquois were attacked by superior forces, the old men, who scorned to fly, or to survive the capture of their town, braved death, like the old Romans in the sack of Rome by the Gauls. Later (p. 150), he says that "there never was an instance known of an Indian begging his life when in the power of his enemies: on the contrary, that he courts death by every possible insult and provocation."

[16] See Lepage-Dupratz, *Histoire de la Louisiane*; Charlevoix, *Histoire de la Nouvelle-France*; letters of R. Hecwelder, *Transactions of the American Philosophical Society*, vol. 1; Jefferson, *Notes sur la Virginie*, pp. 135–190. Especially great weight should be attached to what Jefferson says in view of the personal merit of the writer, his special position, and the positive and exact century in which he wrote.

[*] See Note IV, page 479.

these mounds, it is said that they rarely fail to yield up human bones, strange instruments, weapons, and various kinds of utensils made of metal, or suggestive of customs, with which today's tribes are unfamiliar.

The Indians of our day are unable to supply any information about the history of this unknown people. Nor did those who were alive three hundred years ago, when America was discovered, tell us anything from which we can even so much as piece together a hypothesis. Traditions — those perishable yet perpetually reborn monuments of the primitive world — shed no light on the subject. Yet thousands of our fellow human beings lived here. Of this there can be no doubt. When did they arrive? Where did they come from? What became of them? What was their history? When and how did they perish? No one knows.

How strange it is that there are peoples who have vanished from this earth so completely that the very memory of their name has been effaced! Their languages are lost, their glory has evaporated like a sound that dies without an echo. Yet I do not know if any people has ever vanished without leaving at least a tomb as a token of its passing. Thus, of all man's works, the most durable is still that which best recalls his wretchedness and nothingness!

Although the vast country just described was inhabited by numerous tribes of native peoples, one can justly say that at the time of its discovery it was still no more than a wilderness. The Indians occupied it but did not possess it. It is through agriculture that man takes possession of the soil, and the first inhabitants of North America lived by hunting. Their implacable prejudices, their unbridled passions, their vices, and, perhaps most of all, their savage virtues marked them out for inevitable destruction. The ruin of these tribes began the day that Europeans landed on their shores. It has continued ever since and is even now being carried through to completion. Providence placed these people among the riches of the New World but made their enjoyment brief. They were there, in a sense, only *in anticipation*. These coasts, so well suited to trade and industry, these rivers so deep, this inexhaustible Mississippi valley, this whole continent, in fact, seemed but an empty cradle awaiting the birth of a great nation.

Here civilized men would attempt to build society on new foundations. Applying for the first time theories either previously unknown or deemed inapplicable, they would stage for the world a spectacle for which nothing in the history of the past had prepared it.

Chapter 2

ON THE POINT OF DEPARTURE AND ITS IMPORTANCE FOR THE FUTURE OF THE ANGLO-AMERICANS

Usefulness of knowing a people's point of departure in order to understand its social state and laws. — America is the only country in which it has been possible to perceive clearly the point of departure of a great people. — In what respects all the people who came to English America were similar. — In what respects they differed. — Remark applicable to all the Europeans who settled on the shores of the New World. — Colonization of Virginia. — Colonization of New England. — Original character of the early inhabitants of New England. — Their arrival. — Their first laws. — Social contract. — Penal code borrowed from the Law of Moses. — Religious ardor. — Republican spirit. — Intimate union of spirit of religion and spirit of liberty.

A MAN is born. His first years pass unnoticed in the pleasures and travails of childhood. He grows up. Manhood begins. At last the doors of the world open to receive him. He enters into contact with his fellow man. People begin to study him, and think they can perceive the seeds that will develop into the vices and virtues of maturity.

This, if I am not mistaken, is a great error.

Go back in time. Examine the babe when still in its mother's arms. See the external world reflected for the first time in the still-dark mirror of his intelligence. Contemplate the first models to make an impression on him. Listen to the words that first awaken his dormant powers of thought. Take note, finally, of the first battles he is obliged to fight. Only then will you understand where the prejudices, habits, and passions that will dominate his life come from. In a manner of speaking, the whole man already lies swaddled in his cradle.

Something analogous happens with nations. Every people bears the mark of its origins. The circumstances that surround its birth and aid its development also influence the subsequent course of its existence.

If we could trace societies back to their elements and examine the earliest records of their history, I have no doubt that we would discover the first cause of their prejudices, habits, and dominant passions, indeed, of every aspect of what has been called the national character. We would discover explanations for customs that today seem at odds with prevailing mores; for laws that seem to clash with accepted principles; and for the inconsistent opinions that one occasionally encounters in a society — opinions reminiscent of the fragments of broken chain that one sometimes finds dangling from the vaults of an old building, no longer supporting anything. This might explain the destiny of certain peoples, who seem propelled by an unknown force toward an end undivined even by themselves. Until now, however, the facts needed for such a study have been lacking. Nations developed an analytic spirit only as they grew old, and before it occurred to them to reflect on their beginnings, time had already shrouded the moment of their inception in fog, and ignorance and pride had surrounded it with fables behind which the truth lay hidden.

America is the only country in which it has been possible to witness the natural and tranquil course of a society's development and to pinpoint the influence of a state's point of departure on its future.

By the time the peoples of Europe landed on the shores of the New World, the traits of their national characters were already fully formed. Each of them had a distinct physiognomy. Having already achieved that degree of civilization which inclines men to study themselves, they left us a faithful portrait of their opinions, mores, and laws. We know the men of the fifteenth century almost as well as we know ourselves. America therefore exposes to the light of day what the ignorance and barbarity of the earliest times conceal.

Close enough to the time when the societies of America were founded to be acquainted in detail with their elements, yet far enough away to form a judgment of what those seeds have produced, we seem destined to see further into human events than our predecessors did. Providence has placed within our reach a torch our fathers lacked, a torch that allows us, when examining the destiny of nations, to make out first causes that the obscurity of the past hid from our forebears.

If, after attentively studying the history of America, one carefully examines its political and social state, one becomes firmly convinced of the following truth: that there is not a single opinion, habit, or law, I might almost say not a single event, which the point of departure cannot readily explain. Hence anyone who reads this book will find in the present chapter the germ of what follows and the key to virtually the entire work.

The immigrants who came at various times to occupy the territory of what is now the American Union differed from one another in many respects. Their goals were not the same, and they governed themselves according to a variety of principles.

Nevertheless, those men shared certain traits in common, and all found themselves in a similar situation.

The bond of language is perhaps the strongest and most durable that exists among men. All the immigrants spoke the same language; all were children of the same people. Born in a country riven by centuries of partisan strife, in which one faction after another had been obliged to seek the protection of the law, their political education had been conducted in this harsh school, and they shared more notions of rights and more principles of true liberty than most other European peoples. By the time of the earliest immigrations, local government, that prolific seed of free institutions, was already deeply ingrained in English habits, and the dogma of popular sovereignty thereby implanted itself at the very heart of the Tudor monarchy.

At that time the Christian world was agitated by religious controversy. With a kind of frenzy, England had plunged headlong into the fray. A people whose character had always been grave and deliberate now became austere and argumentative. Education improved greatly in the course of these intellectual struggles; the cultivation of the intellect achieved a new depth. At a time when religion was on everyone's lips, morals grew purer. All of these general national features were reflected to one degree or another in the physiognomies of those sons of England who arrived on the opposite shore of the Atlantic in search of a new future.

A further remark, to which I shall have occasion to return later, applies not only to the English but also to the French, the Spanish, and all the other Europeans who settled one after another on the shores of the New World. All the new European colonies invariably contained at least the germ, if not the mature form, of a complete democracy. There were two reasons for this: it is fair to say that, on the whole when emigrants left the mother country, they had no notion of any kind of superiority of some over others. It was scarcely the happy and powerful who chose exile, and poverty, together with misfortune, is the best guarantee we know of equality among men. On occasion, however, a great lord might flee to America in the wake of a political or religious quarrel. Although laws establishing a hierarchy of ranks were adopted there, it soon became clear that American soil was implacably hostile to landed aristocracy. People realized that if this refractory soil was to be cultivated, it would take nothing less than the constant and self-interested effort of those who owned the land. When the ground was tilled, its fruits proved insufficient to enrich both a master and a farmer. It was therefore natural for the land to be divided into small holdings, each just large enough to be farmed by its owner without assistance. But aristocracy is rooted in the soil; it is attached to, and dependent on, land. It is not just privilege that establishes an aristocracy and not just birth that constitutes it; it is property in land, passed on from generation to generation. A nation may engender both vast wealth and grinding poverty, but if that wealth is not territorial, one finds only rich or poor among its people, not aristocrats in the true sense of the word.

Hence there was a marked family resemblance among the various English colonies at their inception. From the first, all seemed destined to encourage the growth of liberty: not the aristocratic liberty of the mother country but bourgeois and democratic liberty, of which history as yet offered no fully developed model.

Such was the general complexion of things, but we must also pay careful attention to any number of distinct variations.

Within the great Anglo American family we find two main branches, which have thus far matured without altogether losing their identity, one in the south, the other in the north.

Virginia was home to the first English colony. Immigrants arrived there in 1607. Europe at that time was still singularly preoccupied by the idea that gold and silver mines constitute the wealth of nations: a disastrous idea that did more to impoverish the European nations that embraced it, and destroyed more men in America, than war and iniquitous laws combined. It was therefore gold-seekers who were sent to Virginia,[1] men without resources or discipline whose restless, turbulent spirit caused trouble for the colony in its early days[2] and rendered its progress uncertain. Then came working men and farmers, a more moral and tranquil breed but not much above the lower classes of England in any respect.[3] No noble thought or immaterial contrivance presided over the foundation of these new settlements. No sooner was the colony created than slavery was introduced.[4] This capital fact was to exert an immense influence on the character, laws, and entire future of the South.

Slavery, as I will explain later, dishonors labor. It introduces idleness into society and, with it, ignorance and pride, poverty and luxury. It saps the powers of the mind and lulls human activity to sleep. The influence of slavery, combined with the English character, explains the mores and social state of the South.

In the North, the English background was the same, but the foreground was painted in very different shades. I beg the reader's indulgence while I fill in a few details.

[1]The charter granted by the English crown in 1609 stipulated that the colonists were to pay the crown one-fifth of what their mines yielded in gold and silver. See Marshall, *Vie de Washington*, vol. 1, pp. 18–66.

[2]According to Stith (*History of Virginia*), many of the new colonists were young people from troubled families whose parents had shipped them off to thwart some ignominious fate; the rest were former servants, bankrupt swindlers, debauchees, and other people of the sort, more likely to pillage and destroy than to consolidate the new settlement. Seditious leaders found it easy to enlist support for all sorts of extravagant adventures. On the history of Virginia, see Smith, *History of Virginia from the First Settlements to the Year 1624*; William Stith, *History of Virginia*; and Beverley, *History of Virginia from the Earliest Period*, translated into French in 1807.

[3]It was only later that a certain number of wealthy English landowners settled in the colony.

[4]Slavery was introduced in 1620 by a Dutch vessel that landed twenty Negroes on the banks of the James River. See Chalmer.

It was in the English colonies of the North, better known as the New England states,[5] that the two or three principal ideas which today form the basis of the social theory of the United States were first combined.

The principles of New England spread initially to nearby states. Little by little they made their way to the farthest reaches of the confederation until ultimately they had, if I may put it this way, *penetrated* throughout. Their influence extended beyond New England's borders, to the entire American continent. The civilization of New England was like a bonfire on a hilltop, which, having spread its warmth to its immediate vicinity, tinges even the distant horizon with its glow.

The founding of New England presented a novel spectacle: everything about it was singular and original.

The first inhabitants of most other colonies were men with neither education nor means, men driven from the land of their birth by poverty or misconduct; or else they were greedy speculators and industrial entrepreneurs. Some colonies could not claim even that much about their origins: Santo Domingo was founded by pirates, and even now the courts of England are making it their mission to populate Australia.

The immigrants who settled on the shores of New England all belonged to the well-to-do classes of the mother country. From the first, what was striking about their gathering on American soil was that here was a society with neither great lords nor commoners, indeed, one might almost say with neither rich nor poor. These people possessed a proportionately greater quantity of enlightenment than any European nation today. All, virtually without exception, had received a reasonably advanced education, and any number were renowned in Europe for their talents and learning. Other colonies had been founded by adventurers without families. The people who immigrated to New England brought with them admirable elements of order and morality. They went into the wilderness with their wives and children. But what distinguished them most of all from other colonizers was the very

---

[5]The New England states are those situated east of the Hudson. Today there are six: Connecticut, Rhode Island, Massachusetts, Vermont, New Hampshire, and Maine.

purpose of their enterprise. It was by no means necessity that forced them to leave their native land. They left behind enviable social positions and secure incomes. They did not travel to the New World in the hope of improving their situation or enhancing their wealth. They tore themselves away from the pleasures of home in obedience to a purely intellectual need. They braved the inevitable miseries of exile because they wished to ensure the victory of *an idea*.

These immigrants, or, as they so aptly styled themselves, "pilgrims," belonged to that English sect whose austere principles had earned it the name "Puritan." Puritanism was not just a religious doctrine. In several respects it coincided with the most absolute democratic and republican theories. It was this aspect of Puritanism that had aroused its most dangerous adversaries against it. Persecuted by the government of the mother country and offended by the routine ways of a society at odds with the rigorous principles by which they lived, the Puritans sought a land so barbarous and so neglected that they might still be allowed to live there as they wished and pray to God in liberty.

A few quotations will throw more light on the spirit of these pious adventurers than anything I might say.

Nathaniel Morton, the historian of New England's early years, broaches his subject thus:[6]

I have always thought that it was a sacred duty for us, whose fathers received so many and such memorable tokens of divine goodness in the establishment of this colony, to perpetuate the memory of it in writing. What we have seen, and what has been recounted to us by our fathers, we must make known to our children, so that the generations to come may learn to praise the Lord; so that the progeny of Abraham his servant, and the sons of Jacob his chosen, may always keep the memory of the miraculous works of God (Psalms CV:5–6). They must know how the Lord brought his vine into the desert; how he planted it and cast out the pagans; how he prepared a place for it, rooted it deeply, and then allowed it to spread and cover the land far and wide (Psalms LXXX:13–15); and not only that, but also how he guided his people toward his holy tabernacle, and established it on the mountain of his inheritance (Exodus XV:13). These facts should

---

[6] *New England's Memorial*, p. 14, Boston, 1826. See also Hutchinson, *History*, vol. II, p. 440.

be known, so that God may derive from them the honor that is due Him, and so that some rays of His glory may fall upon the venerable names of the saints that served him as instruments.

No reader of this opening passage can fail to be moved in spite of himself by its solemn religious feeling. It breathes the air of antiquity and is redolent of a kind of biblical fragrance. The writer's conviction elevates his style. One begins to see with his eyes, not a small band of adventurers gone to seek their fortune across the sea but the seed of a great people set down in a promised land by the hand of God.

The author goes on to describe the departure of the first emigrants:[7]

So they left this city (Delft-Haleft), which had been for them a resting place. Meanwhile they were calm; they knew that they were pilgrims and strangers here below. They were not attached to the things of the earth but lifted their eyes to heaven, their cherished fatherland, where God had prepared for them his holy city. They finally reached the port where the vessel awaited them. A great many friends who could not depart with them had nevertheless wished to follow them that far. The night passed without sleep; it was spent in effusions of friendship, pious discourse, and expressions full of true Christian tenderness. The next day they went on board; their friends wanted to accompany them still. It was then that deep sighs were heard, and tears were seen to flow from all eyes, and even strangers were moved by the sound of long farewells and ardent prayers. When the departure signal was given, they fell to their knees, and their pastor, lifting eyes filled with tears up to heaven, commended them to the mercy of the Lord. At last they took leave of one another and uttered that farewell which, for many of them, was to be the last.

The emigrants, counting women and children as well as men, numbered about one hundred and fifty. Their purpose was to found a colony on the banks of the Hudson. But having roamed the ocean for quite some time, they were finally forced to land on the arid coast of New England, on the spot where the city of Plymouth now stands. The rock upon which the Pilgrims first set foot can still be seen.[8]

[7] *New England's Memorial*, p. 22.
[8] This rock has become an object of veneration in the United States. I have seen fragments of it preserved in any number of cities of the Union. Does this not clearly prove that man's power and grandeur lie entirely within his

"But before continuing," says the historian whom I have already cited,[9] "consider for a moment the present condition of these poor people, and admire the goodness of God, who saved them."

They had now crossed the vast ocean, they were coming to the end of their voyage, but they saw no friends to receive them, no dwelling to offer them shelter. It was the middle of winter, and those who know our climate know how harsh the winters are and what furious gales ravage our coasts. In this season, it is difficult to travel to known places, hence more difficult still to settle on new shores. Around them there was nothing to be seen but a hideous and desolate wilderness, full of wild animals and wild men, whose ferocity and number they could not gauge. The ground was frozen. The land was covered with forests and brush, all of barbarous aspect. Behind them they saw only the immense ocean that separated them from the civilized world. What little peace and hope was to be found could only be glimpsed by turning their eyes upward.

It must not be imagined that the piety of the Puritans was purely speculative, or that it took no notice of worldly affairs. Puritanism, as I have said, was almost as much a political theory as it was a religious doctrine. No sooner had the immigrants landed on the inhospitable shores described above by Nathaniel Morton than they set about organizing a society. They immediately adopted a covenant, which read:[10]

"We, whose names follow, who, for the glory of God, the development of the Christian faith, and the honor of our fatherland have undertaken to establish the first colony on these remote shores, we agree in the present document, by mutual and solemn consent, and before God, to form ourselves into a body of political society, for the purpose of governing ourselves and working toward the accomplishment

---

soul? A rock is touched momentarily by the feet of a few wretched individuals, and that rock becomes famous. It draws the attention of a great people. Pieces of it are venerated, and its dust is distributed far and wide. What has become of the doorstep of many a palace? Does anyone care?

[9]*New England's Memorial*, p. 35.

[10]The immigrants who founded the state of Rhode Island in 1638, those who settled in New Haven in 1637, the first inhabitants of Connecticut in 1639, and the founders of Providence in 1640 also began by drafting a social contract, which was submitted to everyone concerned for their approval.

of these designs; and in virtue of this contract, we agree to promulgate laws, acts, and ordinances, and to institute as needed officials to whom we promise submission and obedience."

This took place in 1620. From then on, emigration continued without letup. The religious and political passions that tore the British Empire apart throughout the reign of Charles I drove additional hordes of sectarians onto the coast of America every year. In England, the breeding ground of Puritanism remained among the middle classes. It was from those classes that most of the emigrants sprang. The population of New England increased rapidly, and while people in the mother country continued to be classified despotically according to the hierarchy of rank, the colony increasingly exhibited the new spectacle of a society homogeneous in all its parts. Democracy such as antiquity had never dared to dream of leapt full-grown and fully armed from the middle of the old feudal society.

Content to be rid of the seeds of fresh unrest and future revolutions, the English government was undismayed by the flood of emigrants. Indeed, it did what it could to encourage them and seemed little concerned by the fate of those who sought, on American soil, asylum from the harshness of its laws. It was as though it looked upon New England as a region best left to the imagination of dreamers and abandoned to innovators to experiment with at will.

The English colonies always enjoyed greater internal freedom and political independence than did the colonies of other peoples: this was one of the chief causes of their prosperity. But nowhere was this principle of liberty more comprehensively applied than in the states of New England.

At the time, it was generally agreed that the lands of the New World belonged to the European nation that was first to discover them.

Almost the entire coast of North America thus became an English possession toward the end of the sixteenth century. The British government employed a variety of means to populate these new dominions. In some cases, the king made a portion of the New World subject to a governor of his choosing, who was charged with administering the country in the king's name and under his direct orders.[11] This was the colonial system adopted by the rest of Europe. In other cases, he awarded ownership of certain regions to an individual or company.[12] All civil and political powers were then concentrated in the hands of one or more individuals, who sold the land and governed its inhabitants under crown supervision and control. Finally, under a third system, the king granted a group of immigrants the right to form a political society under the patronage of the mother country and to govern themselves in any respect not contrary to its laws.

This mode of colonization, so propitious to liberty, was put into practice only in New England.[13]

In 1628, Charles I granted a charter of this kind to the founders of the Massachusetts colony.[14]

In general, however, charters were granted to the colonies of New England only long after their existence had become an accomplished fact. Plymouth, Providence, New Haven, and the states of Connecticut and Rhode Island[15] were founded without the cooperation and in a sense without the knowledge of the mother country. Although the new inhabitants did not deny the supremacy of the metropolis, neither did they look to it as the source of all power: they constituted themselves, and it was only thirty or forty years later, under

[11]This was the case with New York.

[12]Maryland, the Carolinas, Pennsylvania, and New Jersey were included in this group. See *Pitkin's History*, vol. 1, pp. 11–31.

[13]See, in the work entitled *Historical Collection of State Papers and Other Authentic Documents Intended as Materials for an History of the United States of America* by Ebenezer Hazard, printed in Philadelphia in 1792, innumerable documents precious for their content and authenticity concerning the early days of the colonies, including the various charters granted to them by the Crown of England, as well as the first acts of their governments.

See also the analysis of these various charters by Mr. Justice Story of the Supreme Court of the United States in the introduction to his *Commentary on the Constitution of the United States*.

From all these documents it emerges that the principles of representative government and the external forms of political freedom were introduced into all the colonies almost from their inception. These principles were more fully elaborated in the north than in the south, but they existed everywhere.

[14]See *Pitkin's History*, p. 35, vol. 1. See *The History of the Colony of Massachusetts* by Hutchinson, vol. 1, p. 9.

[15]*Ibid.*, pp. 42–47.

Charles II, that a royal charter was issued to legalize their existence.

Thus it is often difficult, in examining New England's earliest historical and legislative records, to perceive the bond between the immigrants and the land of their ancestors. We find them regularly exercising sovereign powers: they appoint magistrates, make peace and war, establish rules of order, and adopt laws as if answerable to God alone.[16]

Nothing is more curious and at the same time more instructive than the legislation of this period. Here above all lies the key to the great social enigma with which the United States confronts the world today.

As a characteristic example of that legislation, we may choose the code of laws adopted in 1650 by the small state of Connecticut.[17]

Connecticut's lawmakers first took up the question of penal laws.[18] In drafting those laws, they hit on the strange idea of drawing upon sacred texts:

"Whosoever shall worship any deity other than the Lord God," they began, "shall be put to death."

This was followed by ten or twelve similar provisions taken literally from Deuteronomy, Exodus, and Leviticus.

Blasphemy, witchcraft, adultery,[19] and rape were punishable by death. A son who failed to honor his father and mother was subject to the same penalty. Thus the laws of a rude and

[16]When the residents of Massachusetts established courts of law and adopted rules of civil and criminal procedure, they departed from English custom: in 1650 the king's name still did not appear at the head of judicial warrants. See Hutchinson, vol. 1, p. 452.

[17]*Code of 1650*, p. 28 (Hartford, 1830).

[18]See also, in Hutchinson's *History*, vol. 1, pp. 435–456, the analysis of the Penal Code adopted in 1648 by the Massachusetts Bay Colony. This code was based on principles similar to those on which the Connecticut code was based.

[19]Adultery was also punishable by death in Massachusetts, and Hutchinson, vol. 1, p. 441, says that several people were in fact executed for this crime. In this connection, he mentions a curious anecdote that dates back to 1663. A married women had amorous relations with a young man. After being left a widow, she married him. Several years passed. People at last came to suspect that the couple had been intimate prior to their marriage, and criminal charges were brought. They were imprisoned and just barely escaped being put to death.

half-civilized people were carried over into a society of enlightened spirit and gentle mores. Never was the death penalty more frequently prescribed by statute or more seldom enforced.

The men who framed these penal codes were primarily concerned with maintaining the moral order and sound mores of their society. They therefore repeatedly intruded upon the realm of conscience, and virtually no sin was exempt from the scrutiny of the courts. The reader has seen how harshly these laws punished adultery and rape. Even social intercourse between unmarried individuals was subject to severe censure. Judges were permitted to impose one of three penalties: a fine, a whipping, or a wedding.[20] To judge by the records of the old courts of New Haven, moreover, prosecutions for such crimes were not infrequent. On May 1, 1660, for example, a young woman was fined and reprimanded after being accused of making indiscreet remarks and allowing herself to be kissed.[21] The Code of 1650 abounded with preventive measures. Sloth and drunkenness were severely punished.[22] Innkeepers were not permitted to serve more than a specified quantity of wine to each consumer. Fines and floggings were meted out for mere lies if likely to cause harm.[23] Elsewhere, legislators totally oblivious of the great principles of religious freedom that they had claimed for themselves in Europe imposed fines intended to frighten people into attending religious services[24] and often went so far as to mandate severe punishment[25] or

[20]*Code of 1650*, p. 48.
It appears that in some cases judges imposed all three penalties, as can be seen in a verdict of 1643 (p. 114, *New Haven Antiquities*, which indicates that one Margaret Bedford, convicted of having engaged in reprehensible acts, was to be punished by whipping and then obliged to marry Nicholas Jemmings, her accomplice).

[21]*New Haven Antiquities*, p. 104. See also Hutchinson's *History*, vol. 1, p. 436, for several equally extraordinary verdicts.

[22]*Ibid.*, 1650, pp. 50, 57.

[23]*Ibid.*, p. 64.

[24]*Ibid.*, p. 44.

[25]This was not peculiar to Connecticut. See, for example, the Massachusetts law of September 13, 1644, banishing Anabaptists: *Historical Collection of State Papers*, vol. 1, p. 538. See also the law published on October 14, 1656, against the Quakers: "Whereas there is a pernicious sect, commonly called Quakers, lately arisen . . ." Subsequent provisions of this law stipulate large

even death for Christians who wished to worship God in some way other than their own.[26] In their ardor to regulate, legislators sometimes stooped to consider matters unworthy of their august function. For instance, the previously mentioned code included a law prohibiting the use of tobacco.[27] However, we must not lose sight of the fact that these bizarre and even tyrannical laws were not imposed from above but freely approved by the votes of all affected by them, or that their mores were even more austere and puritanical than their laws. In 1649, an association was formed in Boston for the solemn purpose of stamping out the worldly luxury of long hair.[28*]

Surely such lapses constitute a stain upon the human spirit. They attest to the inferiority of our nature, which, by virtue of our incapacity to maintain a firm grasp on truth and justice, is generally reduced to a choice between extremes.

Alongside these penal laws, so profoundly marked by narrow sectarian thinking as well as by religious passions warmed by persecution and still fermenting in the souls of men, there was also a body of political laws, in some ways closely linked to the former, and yet which, though drafted some two hundred years ago, still seems far in advance of the spirit of liberty of our own age.

The general principles upon which modern constitutions are based — principles that most Europeans barely comprehended in the seventeenth century and whose triumph in Great Britain was still incomplete — were all recognized and incorporated into the laws of New England: involvement of the people in public affairs, free voting on taxes, accountability of government officials, individual liberty, and trial by

---

fines to be imposed on the captain of any vessel bringing Quakers into the region. Any Quaker found in the colony was subject to flogging and imprisonment in a workhouse. Any who continued to defend their views were subject first to fine, then imprisonment, and finally banishment. Same collection, vol. 1, p. 630.

[26]Under the penal code of Massachusetts, any Catholic priest who set foot in the colony after being expelled was subject to the death penalty.

[27]*Code of 1650*, p. 96.

[28]*New England's Memorial*, p. 316.

*See Note V, page 481.

jury — all of these were adopted without debate and put into practice.

There, these fundamental principles were applied and elaborated to a degree that no European nation has yet dared to attempt.

In Connecticut, the electorate from the beginning comprised the totality of all citizens, and the reason for this is simple:[29] in that nascent community there prevailed an almost perfect equality of wealth and a still greater equality of intellect.[30]

In Connecticut at that time, all officials of the executive branch of government were elected, including the governor of the state.[31]

Citizens above the age of sixteen were required to bear arms. They formed a national militia, which chose its own officers and was required to maintain itself in a constant state of readiness to defend the country.[32]

In the laws of Connecticut and the other New England states we witness the inception and development of that local independence which is still today the wellspring and lifeblood of liberty in America.

In most European nations, political existence began in the upper reaches of society and was communicated, gradually and always incompletely, to other parts of the social body.

In America, by contrast, the local community was organized before the county, the county before the state, and the state before the Union.

In New England local governments were fully constituted and had achieved their mature form by 1650. Each individual locality became a focal point of passions and interests, duties and rights. A real and active, wholly democratic and republican political life flourished within each community. The colonies still acknowledged the supremacy of the metropolis.

---

[29]Constitution of 1638, p. 17.

[30]In 1641, the General Assembly of Rhode Island unanimously declared that the government of the state was a democracy and that power was vested in the body of free men, who alone had the right to make the laws and see to it that they were carried out. *Code of 1650*, p. 70.

[31]*Pitkin's History*, p. 47.

[32]Constitution of 1638, p. 12.

Monarchy was the law of the state, but already the republic was alive in local government.

Local governments appointed all of their own magistrates. They assessed property and apportioned and levied taxes.[33] New England's towns did not adopt a representative form of government. As in Athens, matters affecting everyone's interests were discussed in public places and in general assemblies of citizens.

When one studies closely the laws adopted in the early years of the American republics, one is struck by the lawmakers' knowledge of government as well as by their advanced theories.

It is clear that they had a loftier and more comprehensive idea of society's duties toward its members than did their European counterparts, and that they imposed on society obligations from which it was elsewhere exempt. In New England provision was made from the first for the care of the poor.[34] Strenuous efforts were made to maintain the roads, and officials were appointed to monitor their condition.[35] Town governments kept open records of deliberations at public meetings as well as of deaths, marriages, and births of their citizens.[36] Clerks were designated to maintain these records.[37] Officials were assigned to administer intestate property, others to establish the boundaries of inherited land, and still others whose principal function was to preserve the public tranquillity.[38]

Legislation concerned itself with a thousand details in order to anticipate and satisfy a host of social needs which even now are only dimly perceived in France.

But, from the beginning, the originality of American civilization was most clearly apparent in the provisions made for public education.

"Whereas," says the law, "Satan, the enemy of the human race, finds his most powerful weapons in the ignorance of men, and it is important that the enlightenment brought here

---

[33]*Code of 1650*, p. 80.
[34]*Ibid.*, p. 78.
[35]*Ibid.*, p. 49.
[36]See Hutchinson's *History*, vol. 1, p. 455.
[37]*Code of 1650*, p. 86
[38]*Ibid.*, p. 40

by our forefathers not remain buried in their graves; and whereas the education of children is one of the primary interests of the state, with the assistance of the Lord."[39] Subsequent clauses of the law established schools in every town and required citizens to pay taxes to support them or else face significant fines. In the most populous districts, high schools were established in the same way. Municipal magistrates were made responsible for seeing that parents sent their children to school. They were authorized to impose fines on any parent who refused to do so. If resistance continued, society, putting itself in the place of the family, might seize the child and deprive its father of natural rights so egregiously abused.[40] The reader will no doubt have been struck by the preamble to these statutes: in America, it was religion that showed the way to enlightenment; it was respect for divine law that showed man the way to freedom.

If, having made this rapid survey of American society as it was in 1650, we examine now the state of Europe, and, more particularly, continental Europe, at the same time, we are in for a rude shock: everywhere on the continent absolute monarchy stood in triumph upon the debris of the oligarchic and feudal liberty of the Middle Ages. Never, perhaps, was the idea of rights more completely neglected than in the midst of this brilliant and literary Europe. Never were people less involved in political life or less concerned with notions of true liberty. Yet even then the very principles ignored or despised by the nations of Europe were being proclaimed in the wilderness of the New World and held out as the future symbol of a great people. The boldest theories ever conceived by the mind of man were put into practice in a society in appearance quite humble, and with which perhaps no statesman of the day deigned to concern himself. Left to its own devices, the human imagination improvised an unprecedented body of laws. From the bosom of this obscure democracy, which had yet to produce a single general or philosopher or great writer, a man could step forth to address a free people and give, to the acclamation of all, this beautiful definition of liberty:

[39]*Ibid.*, p. 90.
[40]*Ibid.*, p. 83.

Make no mistake about what we ought to understand by our independence. There is in fact a corrupt sort of liberty, the use of which is common to animals and men, and which consists in doing whatever they like. This liberty is the enemy of all authority; it is impatient of all rules. With it, we become inferior to ourselves. It is the enemy of truth and peace, and God believed it his duty to rise against it! But there is a civil and moral liberty that finds its strength in union, and which it is the mission of power itself to protect: this is the liberty to do what is just and good without fear. This sacred liberty we must defend in all circumstances and if necessary risk our life for it.[41]

I have already said enough to put the character of Anglo-American civilization in its true light. It is the result (and this point of departure should be constantly kept in mind) of two quite distinct elements, which elsewhere have often been at war but in America have somehow been incorporated into one another and marvelously combined. I allude to the *spirit of religion* and the *spirit of liberty*.

The founders of New England were at once ardent sectarians and impassioned innovators. Strictly bound by certain religious beliefs, they were free from all political prejudice.

Accordingly, two distinct though not contradictory tendencies are apparent everywhere, in mores as well as laws.

Some men are willing to sacrifice friends, family, and country for the sake of a religious opinion. We may assume that if they are willing to pay so high a price for an intellectual prize, they must be totally absorbed by its pursuit. Yet we find these same men seeking, with almost equal ardor, material wealth and moral gratifications, heaven in the other world and prosperity and freedom in this.

In their hands, political principles, laws, and human institutions seem to be malleable things, capable of being shaped and combined at will.

The walls that imprisoned the society into which they were born fall before them. Old opinions, which ruled the world for centuries, vanish. Limitless opportunities, fields without

[41]*Mather's Magnalia Christi Americana*, vol. 2, p. 13. The speech is that of Winthrop, who was accused of having acted arbitrarily as a judge. After he made the speech from which I have taken this excerpt, however, he was acquitted amidst applause, and he was still reelected as governor of the state. See Marshall, vol. 1, p. 166.

horizon, open up before them. The human spirit hastens to explore these and sets out in every conceivable direction. When it reaches the limits of the political world, however, it stops of its own accord. In trepidation it forgoes the use of its most redoubtable faculties. It forswears doubt. It renounces the need to innovate. It refrains from even lifting the veil of the sanctuary. It bows respectfully before truths it accepts without argument.

Thus, in the moral world, everything is arranged, coordinated, anticipated, and decided in advance. In the political world, everything is agitated, contested, and uncertain. On the one hand, passive albeit voluntary obedience; on the other, independence, contempt for experience, and jealousy of all authority.

Far from clashing, these two tendencies, in appearance so contradictory, advance in harmony and seem to support each other.

Religion looks upon civil liberty as a noble exercise of man's faculties, and on the world of politics as a realm intended by the Creator for the application of man's intelligence. Free and powerful in its own sphere and satisfied with the place ascribed to it, religion knows that its empire is more secure when it reigns through its own intrinsic strength and dominates the hearts of men without assistance.

Liberty looks upon religion as its comrade in battle and victory, as the cradle of its infancy and divine source of its rights. It regards religion as the safeguard of mores, and mores as the guarantee of law and surety for its own duration.*

REASONS FOR CERTAIN PECULIAR FEATURES OF THE LAWS AND CUSTOMS OF THE ANGLO-AMERICANS

Some relics of aristocratic institutions amid the most complete democracy. — Why? — Need to distinguish carefully between that which is Puritan in origin and that which is English.

The reader must not draw unduly general or absolute conclusions from what has just been said. The social condition,

*See Note VI, page 484.

religion, and mores of the first immigrants no doubt exerted an immense influence on the destiny of their adopted land. Nevertheless, it was not within their power to found a society whose point of departure lay exclusively within themselves. No one can free himself entirely from the past. Intentionally or not, they combined ideas and customs of their own with others that they took from their education and from the national traditions of their homeland.

If we wish to make an informed judgment about the Anglo-Americans as they are today, we must therefore take care to distinguish between that which is Puritan in origin and that which is English.

In the United States one encounters laws and customs that contrast with everything around them. These laws appear to have been drafted in a spirit contrary to the dominant spirit of American legislation; these mores seem to conflict with the state of society in general. If the English colonies had been founded in a century of darkness, or if their origins were already lost in the night of time, the problem would be insoluble.

I will cite but a single example to illustrate what I mean.

Only two means of action are provided for under American civil and criminal law: *imprisonment* and *bail*. In any legal proceeding, the first step is to obtain bail from the defendant, or, if he declines, to incarcerate him. Only afterward is the validity of the title or the gravity of the charge discussed.

Such legislation is obviously directed against the poor and favors only the rich.

The poor man cannot always make bail, even in a civil case, and if he is compelled to await justice in prison, enforced idleness will soon reduce him to misery.

By contrast, the rich man can always avoid imprisonment in a civil case. Worse yet, if he has committed a crime, he can easily avoid punishment by vanishing after making bail. Thus all the penalties of the law are for him reduced to fines.[42] What legislation could be more aristocratic than this?

---

[42]There are no doubt some crimes for which bail is not allowed, but their number is quite small.

In America, however, it is the poor who make the law, and usually they reserve society's greatest benefits for themselves. The explanation of this paradox must be sought in England: the laws I speak of are English.[43] The Americans have not changed them, even though they run counter to the general tenor of American legislation and to the preponderance of American ideas.

Apart from customs, the thing that a nation is least likely to change is its civil legislation. The only people truly conversant with the civil code are specialists in the law, that is, those who have a direct interest in maintaining it as it is, good or bad, for the simple reason that they are familiar with it. Most people have only a vague knowledge of the law. They perceive its effects only in particular cases, have difficulty in discerning its general implications, and obey it without thinking.

I have mentioned one example, but I might have called attention to any number of others.

American society, if I may put it this way, is like a painting that is democratic on the surface but from time to time allows the old aristocratic colors to peep through.

[43]See Blackstone and Delolme, book 1, chap. 10.

Chapter 3

SOCIAL STATE OF THE ANGLO-AMERICANS

T HE social state is ordinarily the result of a fact, sometimes of laws, usually of these two causes taken together. Once it exists, however, it can itself be considered the primary cause of most of the laws, customs, and ideas that govern the conduct of nations. What it does not produce, it modifies.

If one would know a people's legislation and mores, one must therefore begin by studying its social state.

WHAT IS MOST STRIKING ABOUT THE SOCIAL STATE OF THE ANGLO-AMERICANS IS THAT IT IS ESSENTIALLY DEMOCRATIC

First immigrants to New England. — Equal among themselves. — Aristocratic laws introduced in the South. Epoch of the Revolution. — Change in the laws of inheritance. — Effects produced by this change. — Equality pushed to its ultimate limits in the new states of the West. — Equality of intellect.

Many important remarks could be made about the social state of the Anglo-Americans, but one stands out above all the rest.

The social state of the Americans is eminently democratic. It has had this character since the birth of the colonies; it has it even more today.

I said in the previous chapter that a very high degree of equality prevailed among the immigrants who settled on the coast of New England. The very seed of aristocracy was never sown in this part of the Union. Only intellectual influences could be established there. People became accustomed to venerating certain names as emblems of enlightenment and virtue. The voices of a few citizens obtained a kind of power over them that might reasonably have been called aristocratic had it been possible always to pass it on from father to son.

Such was the case east of the Hudson. Southwest of that river and all the way to Florida, things were different.

Great English landowners settled in most of the states southwest of the Hudson. Aristocratic principles were imported along with English laws of inheritance. Earlier I stated the reasons why it proved impossible to establish a powerful aristocracy in America. Although those reasons also obtained southwest of the Hudson, their influence there was less potent than it was east of that river. In the South, a single man could, with the help of slaves, cultivate a vast expanse of land. Hence in this part of the continent it was possible to find wealthy landowners. But their influence was not precisely aristocratic as that term is understood in Europe, because they possessed no privileges and because the use of slaves to cultivate the land left them without tenants and consequently without patronage. Still, the great landowners south of the Hudson constituted a superior class, with ideas and tastes of its own and generally concentrating political activity within its own ranks. It was a sort of aristocracy that differed little from the mass of the population, whose passions and interests it readily embraced, arousing neither love nor hatred. In short, it was feeble and not particularly robust. In the South it was this class that took command of the insurrection. To it the American Revolution is indebted for its greatest men.

In that time the whole of society was shaken. The people, in whose name one had fought, became a force to be reckoned with, and conceived the desire to act on their own. Democratic instincts were awakened. Smashing the yoke of the metropolis had fostered a taste for independence of every kind. Little by little, the influence of individuals ceased to make itself felt. Custom and law began to march in step toward a common goal.

But it was the law of inheritance that drove equality to take the last step.

I am astonished that ancient and modern writers on public matters have not ascribed greater influence over human affairs to the laws governing inheritance.[1] Such laws belong, of course, to the civil order, but they should be placed first

---

[1] By "inheritance laws" I mean all laws whose principal purpose is to regulate the disposition of property after the death of its owner.

The law of entail is one such law. To be sure, one of its consequences is also to prevent the owner from disposing of his property before his death. But

among political institutions because of their incredible influence on a people's social state, of which the political laws are merely the expression. Furthermore, inheritance laws act on society in a sure and uniform way; in a sense, they lay hold of each generation before it is born. Through them, man is armed with an almost divine power over the future of his fellow men. Once the legislator has regulated inheritance among citizens, he can rest for centuries. Once his work has been set in motion, he can remove his hands from his creation. The machine acts under its own power and seems almost to steer itself toward a goal designated in advance. If constructed in a certain way, it collects, concentrates, and aggregates property and, before long, power as well around a single head. It causes aristocracy to spring, as it were, from the soil. If guided by other principles and launched on a different path, its effect is still more rapid; it divides, partitions, and disseminates wealth and power. In that case the rapidity of its progress is sometimes frightening; abandoning hope of halting its progress, people at least try to place difficulties and obstacles in its path. They would counteract its effects by contrary efforts, but in vain. The machinery of the law crushes or shatters anything in its way, it rises up from the earth only to hammer down again and again until nothing remains but a shifting, impalpable dust, on which democracy rests.

When the law of inheritance permits, and *a fortiori* when it orders, a father's property to be divided equally among his children, its effects are of two kinds. It is important to distinguish carefully between them, even though both tend toward the same end.

By virtue of the law of inheritance, the death of any owner of property entails a revolution in ownership. Not only do goods change masters, they also change nature, so to speak. They are broken up into ever smaller portions.

This is the direct and, as it were, material effect of the law. In countries whose laws provide for equal partition, property,

---

it imposes the obligation to preserve property for one purpose only, that it may be transmitted intact to its heir. The principal purpose of the law of entail is therefore to regulate the disposition of property after its owner's death. The rest is merely a matter of the means employed to achieve that end.

and especially landed wealth, necessarily has a permanent tendency to shrink. If the law were left to its own devices, however, the effects of such legislation would become apparent only over the long run. For to the extent that families consist of no more than two children (and the family average in a country populated like France is said to be just three), the children, sharing the wealth of their father and mother, will not be poorer than each parent individually.

But the law of equal partition does not exert its influence solely on the fate of property. It also works upon the very soul of the owner, whose passions are enlisted in its behalf. It is the indirect effects of the law that rapidly destroy great fortunes and especially great estates.

Among peoples whose law of inheritance is based upon primogeniture, landed estates ordinarily pass undivided from generation to generation. As a result, the family spirit in a sense becomes materialized in the earth. The family represents the land; the land represents the family. The land perpetuates the family's name, its origins, its glory, its power, and its virtues. It is an imperishable witness to the past and a precious guarantee of continued existence.

When the law of inheritance requires equal partition, it destroys the intimate bond that once existed between family spirit and preservation of the land. The land ceases to represent the family, because within the space of a generation or two it cannot avoid being divided and must therefore shrink until ultimately it disappears entirely. The sons of a great landowner, if few in number or favored by fortune, may nurse hopes of rivaling the wealth of the author of their days, but not of owning the same property. The composition of their fortunes must necessarily be different from his.

Now, the moment you deprive landowners of any great interest they may have in preserving the land, whether of sentiment, memories, pride, or ambition, you may rest assured that sooner or later they will sell. They have a great pecuniary interest in doing so, since movable capital yields more interest than other forms of capital and lends itself more readily to gratifying the passions of the moment.

Once divided, great landed estates can never be put back together, for the small holder derives proportionately greater income from his field than the great landowner does from his.[2] The former will therefore demand a far higher price for his land than did the latter. Thus the economic calculations that led the rich man to sell his vast properties will, for even stronger reasons, prevent him from buying small holdings in order to reconstitute a large one.

What is called family spirit is often based on an egotistical illusion. A person may seek to perpetuate and, as it were, immortalize himself in his posterity. When family spirit attains its limits, individual selfishness reasserts its penchants. Because the family is now present in mind only as a vague, indefinite, uncertain thing, the individual focuses his attention on present comforts. He thinks only of establishing the next generation, and nothing more.

Hence he does not seek to perpetuate his family, or at any rate seeks to perpetuate it by means other than landed property.

Thus the law of inheritance not only makes it difficult for families to keep their estates intact, it deprives them of the desire even to attempt to do so and leads them in a way to cooperate with the law in their own ruin.

The law of equal partition proceeds along two paths: by acting on things, it acts on men, and by acting on men, it strikes at things.

In these two ways it succeeds in attacking landed property at its root, soon causing families and fortunes to disappear.[3]

---

[2] I do not mean that the small holder is a better farmer, but he farms with greater ardor and care and makes up with toil for what he lacks in skill.

[3] Because land is the most substantial form of property, one occasionally encounters wealthy men who are prepared to make great sacrifices in order to acquire it and who will readily sacrifice a considerable portion of their income to pay for its upkeep. But they are accidents. The love of real estate is common nowadays only among the poor. The small holder, who is less enlightened, less imaginative, and less passionate than the great landowner, is generally preoccupied solely by the desire to augment his holdings, and inheritances, marriages, and the hazards of commerce often provide him, little by little, with the means to do so.

Thus, along with the tendency that impels men to divide the land, there exists another, which leads them to aggregate it. This tendency, which suffices to prevent the division of property *ad infinitum*, is not powerful enough to create great landed fortunes, much less to confine such fortunes within the same families.

Surely it is not for us, Frenchmen of the nineteenth century and daily witnesses to the political and social changes to which the law of inheritance has given rise, to cast doubt on its power. Every day we watch as, again and again, it cuts swaths across our land, knocking down the walls of our homes and destroying the enclosures around our fields. But if the law of inheritance has already done a great deal among us, much remains to be achieved. Here, memories, opinions, and habits constitute powerful obstacles in its path.

In the United States its work of destruction is almost complete. There one can study its chief results.

English laws governing the transmission of property were abolished in nearly all the states at the time of the Revolution.

The law of entail was amended so as to place only an imperceptible restriction on the free circulation of property.*

The first generation passed away. The division of the land began. The pace of change increased as time went by. Today, barely sixty years later, the face of society is already unrecognizable. The families of the great landowners have nearly all been absorbed into the common mass. In the state of New York, where there were many such families, just two have managed to remain afloat above the chasm that awaits. The sons of once opulent citizens are today merchants, lawyers, and doctors. Most have fallen into the uttermost depths of obscurity. The last vestiges of hereditary rank and distinction have been destroyed. Everywhere the law of inheritance has fixed its level.

Not that there are no wealthy people in the United States, just as there are everywhere. Indeed, I know of no other country where the love of money occupies as great a place in the hearts of men or where people are more deeply contemptuous of the theory of permanent equality of wealth. But wealth circulates there with incredible rapidity, and experience teaches that it is rare for two successive generations to garner its favors.

This picture, which to some may seem overdrawn, still gives only an incomplete idea of what is happening in the new states of the West and Southwest.

*See Note VII, page 492.

At the end of the last century, bold adventurers began to make their way into the valleys of the Mississippi. This was almost a new discovery of America. Before long, the majority of new immigrants were headed for that region. Hitherto unknown societies sprang up in the wilderness overnight. States that had been nameless only a few years before took their place in the American Union. In the West it was possible to observe democracy pushed to its ultimate limit. In these states, in a sense improvised by fortune, people lived on land to which they had come only a short while before. They barely knew one another, and none knew the history of his nearest neighbor. In this part of the American continent, the population therefore escaped the influence not only of great names and great wealth but also of that natural aristocracy which derives from enlightenment and virtue. Here, no one exercised the respectable power that men grant to the memory of a life wholly devoted to doing good in the public eye. The new states of the West were already inhabited, but no society yet existed there.

In America, however, it is not only fortunes that are equal; equality extends to some degree to intelligence itself.

I do not think that there is any other country in the world where, as a proportion of the population, the ignorant are so few and the learned still fewer.

Primary education is within the reach of everyone; higher education is within the reach of virtually no one.

This is not hard to understand. In a sense, it is the necessary result of what I have set forth above.

Almost all Americans are comfortably well-off. Hence they can easily acquire the rudiments of human knowledge.

In America, few people are wealthy. Almost all Americans therefore need to practice a profession. Now, every profession requires a period of apprenticeship. Americans can therefore afford to devote only the first few years of life to the general cultivation of the intelligence. At fifteen they embark on a career. Thus their education usually ends at the time of life when ours begins. If it continues beyond that period, its aim becomes exclusively specialized and lucrative. One studies a science as one takes up a craft, and one takes from it only those applications whose present utility is recognized.

In America, most of the rich started out poor. Almost all men of leisure were occupied in youth. Hence in the time of life when a person might have a taste for study, he has no time for it, and when he has acquired time to devote to it, he no longer has the taste.

Hence there is no class in America in which the penchant for intellectual pleasures is passed on along with hereditary wealth and leisure, and which holds works of the intelligence in high esteem.

Thus the will to devote oneself to such works is lacking, and so is the ability.

A certain middling level of human understanding has been established in America. Minds of every sort have approached this standard, some by raising themselves up, others by lowering themselves.

One therefore finds a vast multitude of individuals who share virtually the same number of notions in matters of religion, history, science, political economy, law, and government.

Intellectual inequality comes directly from God, and man can do nothing to prevent it.

Yet even if intelligence remains, as God willed, unequally distributed, the resources at its disposal are, as we have just seen, equal.

Today, therefore, the aristocratic element in America, weak from the outset, has been if not destroyed then at least weakened to the point where it is difficult to ascribe to it any influence whatsoever in the course of affairs.

By contrast, time, events, and laws have made the democratic element not only preponderant but, in a manner of speaking, unrivaled. No familial or corporate influence can be discerned. Indeed, it is often impossible to detect any individual influence that is in any way durable.

America's social state therefore exhibits the most curious phenomenon. Men there can be seen to be more equal in fortune and intelligence — more equally strong, in other words — than they are in any other country, or were at any other time in recorded history.

POLITICAL CONSEQUENCES OF THE SOCIAL
STATE OF THE ANGLO-AMERICANS

The political consequences of such a social state are easy to deduce.

It is impossible to imagine that equality will not ultimately enter into the world of politics as it enters into everything else. It is impossible to conceive of men as eternally unequal in one respect but equal in all others. Eventually, therefore, they will be equal in everything.

Now, I know of only two ways to achieve the reign of equality in the world of politics: rights must be given either to each citizen or to none.

For nations that have achieved the same social state as the Anglo-Americans, it is therefore quite difficult to perceive a middle term between the sovereignty of all and the absolute power of a single individual.

One must not dissimulate the fact that the social state I have just described lends itself almost as readily to one of these two consequences as to the other.

There is in fact a manly and legitimate passion for equality that spurs all men to wish to be strong and esteemed. This passion tends to elevate the lesser to the rank of the greater. But one also finds in the human heart a depraved taste for equality, which impels the weak to want to bring the strong down to their level, and which reduces men to preferring equality in servitude to inequality in freedom. Not that peoples whose social state is democratic naturally despise liberty; on the contrary, they have an instinctive taste for it. But liberty is not the principal and constant object of their desire. What they love with a love that is eternal is equality. They lunge toward liberty with an abrupt impulse or sudden effort and, if they fail to achieve their goal, resign themselves to their defeat. But nothing could satisfy them without equality, and, rather than lose it, they would perish.

Furthermore, when citizens are all almost equal, it becomes difficult for them to defend their independence against the aggressions of power. As none of them is strong enough to fight alone with advantage, the only guarantee of liberty is for everyone to combine forces. But such a combination is not always in evidence.

A people may therefore derive two great political consequences from the same social state. Those consequences differ prodigiously, but both arise from the same fact.

As the first people to face the redoubtable alternative I have just described, the Anglo-Americans were fortunate enough to escape from absolute power. Their circumstances, background, enlightenment, and, most of all, mores enabled them to establish and maintain the sovereignty of the people.

Chapter 4

ON THE PRINCIPLE OF POPULAR SOVEREIGNTY IN AMERICA

It dominates all of American society. — Application of this principle by the Americans before their Revolution. — Its development as a result of the Revolution. — Gradual and ineluctable lowering of the property qualification.

ANY discussion of the political laws of the United States has to begin with the dogma of popular sovereignty.

The principle of the sovereignty of the people, which to some extent always underlies nearly all human institutions, is ordinarily wrapped in obscurity. People obey it without recognizing it; if light should chance briefly to fall on it, they are quick to relegate it to the darkness of the sanctuary.

The national will is one of those phrases that intriguers in all times and despots in all ages have most abundantly abused. Some have seen the expression of that will in the purchased suffrage of a few hirelings of power; others in the votes of an interested or fearful minority. Indeed, some have even divined it fully articulated in the people's silence and have believed that from the *fact* of obedience arises the *right* for them to command.

In America, the principle of popular sovereignty is not, as in certain nations, hidden or sterile; it is recognized by mores, proclaimed by laws. It expands with freedom's expansion and meets no obstacle on the way to its ultimate ends.

If there is any country in the world where one may hope to assess the true value of the dogma of popular sovereignty, to study its application to the affairs of society and judge its benefits and dangers, that country is surely America.

I said earlier that, from the beginning, the principle of the sovereignty of the people was the fundamental principle of most of the English colonies in America.

It was nevertheless far from dominating the government of society then as it does now.

Two obstacles, one external, the other internal, slowed its inroads.

It could not manifest itself openly in law, because the colonies were still constrained to obey the metropolis. It was therefore reduced to taking refuge in provincial assemblies and above all in town governments. There it spread in secret.

American society at that time was not yet prepared to embrace all its consequences. As I explained in the previous chapter, enlightenment in New England and wealth south of the Hudson long exerted a kind of aristocratic influence, which tended to concentrate society's powers in the hands of a few. It was still by no means the case that all public officials were elected and all citizens were voters. Everywhere, the right to vote was still limited in certain ways and subject to a property qualification. The bar was set quite low in the North, substantially higher in the South.

Then came the American Revolution. The dogma of popular sovereignty emerged from the towns and took possession of the government. All classes enlisted in its cause. People fought and triumphed in its name. It became the law of laws.

A change almost equally rapid took place within society. The law of inheritance completed its task of breaking down local influences.

By the time this effect of the law and the Revolution began to be apparent to all, victory had already declared itself irrevocably in favor of democracy. Power was, in point of fact, in democracy's hands. To struggle against it was no longer even allowed. The upper classes therefore submitted without a murmur or a fight to an evil that was now inevitable. What happened to them was what usually happens to powers that fall: individual members of these classes succumbed to self-interest. Since they could no longer wrest power from the hands of the people, and since none of them detested the multitude enough to take pleasure in defying it, their only thought was to win its good will at any price. Those whose interests were most threatened by democratic laws therefore vied with one another to vote for them. Consequently, the upper classes did not arouse popular passions against themselves, but they did hasten the triumph of the new order. Thus, strange to say, the democratic spirit proved most irresistible in states where aristocracy had been most deeply rooted.

The state of Maryland, which had been founded by great lords, was the first to proclaim universal suffrage[1] and introduced the most democratic forms throughout its government.

Once a people begins to tamper with the property qualification, it is easy to foresee that sooner or later it will eliminate it entirely. Of the rules that govern societies, this is one of the most invariable. The more broadly voting rights are extended, the more one feels the need to extend them still further, for with each new concession, the forces of democracy increase, and its demands grow with its newfound power. The ambition of those who remain below the qualification level is spurred in proportion to the number who stand above it. At last the exception becomes the rule; concessions follow one upon the other, and there is no stopping until universal suffrage is achieved.

In our own day, the principle of popular sovereignty has been elaborated in practice in every conceivable way. It has disentangled itself from the many fictions with which it has elsewhere carefully been wreathed. It adapts its form to the necessities of each particular case. Sometimes the people as a body make the laws as in Athens; at other times deputies created by universal suffrage represent them and act in their name, under their almost immediate surveillance.

There are countries in which a power in some sense external to the social body acts on it and forces it to march in a certain direction.

There are other countries in which force is divided, being placed at once inside society and outside it. Nothing of the kind exists in the United States. There, society acts by itself and on itself. No power exists but within its bosom. Virtually no one is to be found who dares to conceive, much less to express, the idea of seeking power from another source. The people participate in the drafting of the laws through the choice of legislators and in their enforcement through the election of agents of the executive power. So feeble and limited is the share of government left to the administration, and so

---

[1] Amendments made to the Constitution of Maryland in 1801 and 1809.

much does the latter reflect its popular origins and obey the power from which it emanates, that it is fair to say that the people govern themselves. The people reign over the American political world as God reigns over the universe. They are the cause and end of all things; everything proceeds from them, and to them everything returns.*

*See Note VIII, page 494.

Chapter 5

NECESSITY OF STUDYING WHAT HAPPENS IN PARTICULAR STATES BEFORE SPEAKING OF THE GOVERNMENT OF THE UNION

IN THE following chapter I propose to examine the American form of government, which is based on the principle of popular sovereignty. What means of action does it possess? What advantages does it offer? What impediments and dangers does it face?

A first difficulty arises: the United States has a complex constitution. One finds there two distinct, interlocking societies, the one embedded, as it were, in the other. One also finds two completely separate and almost independent governments: one, customary and not precisely defined, which responds to society's daily needs; the other, exceptional and circumscribed, which deals exclusively with certain general interests. In short, there are twenty-four small, sovereign nations, which together form the great body of the Union.

To examine the Union before studying the states is to start down a route strewn with obstacles. The federal government was the last form of government to emerge in the United States. It was merely a modification of the republic, a summary of political principles already disseminated throughout the society and subsisting independently of it. As I have just noted, moreover, the federal government is only an exception; the government of the states is the common rule. Any writer who tries to describe this picture as a whole before examining its details will inevitably lapse into obscurity and repetition.

The great political principles that govern American society today originated and developed in the *states*; of this there can be no doubt. Hence one must know the states if one would possess the key to the rest.

The states that make up the American Union today resemble one another in the outward aspect of their institutions. Political and administrative action is concentrated in three vital centers, which might be compared to the various nerve centers that contribute to the movement of the human body.

At the lowest level is the *town*; above it, the *county*; and finally the *state*.

ON THE SYSTEM OF LOCAL GOVERNMENT IN AMERICA

Why the author begins his examination of political institutions with local government. — Local government is found among all peoples. — Difficulty of establishing and preserving local independence. — Its importance. — Why the author has chosen the organization of local government in New England as the principal object of his examination.

It is no accident that I examine local government first.

The locality (*commune*) is the only association that is so much a part of nature that wherever men come together, towns spontaneously arise.

Communal society therefore exists among all peoples, regardless of their customs or laws. It is man who creates kingdoms and republics; the community seems to stem directly from the hands of God. But if communities have existed since there were men, local independence is a rare and fragile thing. A nation can always establish great political assemblies, because among its people are always to be found a certain number for whom education to some extent makes up for lack of practical experience. A village is composed of coarse elements that often resist the shaping hand of the legislator. As nations become more enlightened, the difficulty of establishing local independence increases rather than decreases. A very civilized society finds it relatively difficult to tolerate experiments with local independence. It rebels at the sight of numerous errors and despairs of success before the final result of the experiment is achieved.

Of all the forms of liberty, that of local government, which is so difficult to establish, is also the most vulnerable to the encroachments of power. Left to themselves, local institutions are scarcely capable of combating a strong and enterprising government. If they are to defend themselves successfully, they must be fully mature and fully integrated into national ideas and habits. Unless local independence has become a part of a nation's mores, it is easily destroyed, and it can become a part of a nation's mores only after it has been embodied for a considerable length of time in law.

In a manner of speaking, therefore, local independence is beyond the reach of human effort. It is seldom created but in a sense springs up of its own accord. It develops almost in secret in the depths of semi-barbarous society. Under the continuing influence of laws and mores, circumstances, and, above all, time, it establishes itself on a firm foundation. It is fair to say that not a single nation on the continent of Europe has achieved it.

Yet it is at the local level that the strength of a free people lies. Local institutions are to liberty what elementary schools are to knowledge; they bring it within reach of the people, allow them to savor its peaceful use, and accustom them to rely on it. Without local institutions, a nation may give itself a free government, but it will not have a free spirit. Fleeting passions, momentary interests, or chance circumstances may give it the outward forms of independence, but despotism repressed within the body of society will eventually resurface.

To help the reader understand the general principles on which the political organization of towns and counties in the United States is based, I felt it would be useful to take a particular state as a model, examine in detail what took place there, and only then cast a rapid glance at the rest of the country.

I chose one of the states of New England.

Towns and counties are not organized in the same way in all parts of the Union. Yet it is easy to see that virtually identical principles governed the organization of both throughout.

Now, it seemed to me that those principles were more fully developed in New England, where their consequences were more far-reaching than anywhere else. In New England the principles in question stood out, as it were, with greater relief, and a foreigner could therefore observe them more easily.

The local institutions of New England constitute a complete and orderly whole. They are old. They owe their strength not only to law but even more to custom. And they exert a prodigious influence on the entire society.

For all of these reasons they are worthy of our attention.

THE LIMITS OF THE TOWN

The New England town is midway between the *canton* and the *commune* of France. The population generally ranges between two and three thousand.[1] Hence it is not so large that the interests of all the inhabitants are not more or less the same, yet populous enough to be sure of finding among its citizens the qualities necessary for good administration.

TOWN POWERS IN NEW ENGLAND

The people, origin of all powers in the town as elsewhere. — They deal with the most important matters themselves. — No municipal council. — Most authority in the town concentrated in the hands of selectmen. — How the selectmen act. — Town meeting. — List of town officials. — Obligatory and paid offices.

In the town as elsewhere the people are the source of all social power, but nowhere do they exercise their power more directly. The people in America are a master who must be pleased to the ultimate extent possible.

In New England, when general affairs of the state are at issue, the majority acts through representatives. This was inevitable. In the town, however, where legislative and governmental action is closer to the governed, the representative system is not accepted practice. There is no municipal council. The voters, after electing town officials, sit as a body and supervise all activities of those officials except those that simply involve execution of the laws of the state.[2]

Such a state of affairs is so contrary to our ideas and so at odds with our habits that it will be necessary to cite several examples to make my meaning clear.

[1] The number of towns in the state of Massachusetts in 1830 was 305. The number of inhabitants was 610,014, which yields a figure of approximately 2,000 people per town on the average.

[2] The same rules are not applicable to large cities, which generally have a mayor and city council divided into two branches, but this is an exception that has to be authorized by law. See the law of February 22, 1822, which sets forth the powers of the city of Boston. *Laws of Massachusetts*, vol. 2, p. 588. This applies to large cities. It is also common for smaller cities to be subject to special forms of government. In 1832, 104 localities were administered this way in the state of New York (*Williams' Register*).

As we shall see in a moment, town offices are extremely numerous and their responsibilities minutely divided. Yet most administrative powers are concentrated in the hands of a small number of annually elected officials known as *selectmen*.[3]

The general laws of the state impose certain obligations on the selectmen. They need no authorization from their constituents to fulfill these obligations and are held personally accountable if they fail to do so. Under state law, for example, they are responsible for drawing up town voting lists. If they do not, they are guilty of a crime. In all matters left to the town, however, the selectmen carry out the will of the people, just as in France the mayor is the executor of decisions of the municipal council. Usually the selectmen act on their own private responsibility, and in practice they remain bound by principles previously laid down by the majority. If, however, they should wish to alter the established order in any way or initiate a new enterprise, they must look to the source of their power. Suppose the question of building a school arises. The selectmen will invite all the voters to convene on a certain day at a designated place. There, they will explain why there is a need and indicate what resources are available to satisfy it, how much money will have to be spent, and where the school should be located. The town meeting, consulted on all these issues, will approve the plan in principle, choose the site, vote the tax, and entrust the execution of its wishes to the selectmen.

Only the selectmen are permitted to convene a town meeting, but they can be compelled to do so. If ten property owners conceive of a project and wish to obtain the consent of the town, they may ask that a town meeting be convened. The selectmen are obliged to do as they are bidden, and when the meeting is held, their only privilege is to preside.[4]

These political mores and social customs will no doubt seem quite alien to Frenchmen. It is not my intention at this

[3]Small towns elect three, large ones nine. See *The Town Officer*, p. 186. See also the principal laws of Massachusetts regarding selectmen: Law of February 20, 1786, vol. 1, p. 219; February 24, 1796, vol. 1, p. 488; March 7, 1801, vol. 2, p. 45; June 16, 1795, vol. 1, p. 475; March 12, 1808, vol. 2, p. 186; February 28, 1787, vol. 1, p. 302; June 22, 1797, vol. 1, p. 539.

[4]See *Laws of Massachusetts*, vol. 1, p. 150; law of March 25, 1786.

point to judge them or to explain the hidden causes that bring them into being and breathe life into them. I merely note their existence.

The selectmen are elected every year in the month of April or May. At the same time the town meeting also chooses a host of other municipal officials[5] to take charge of certain important administrative details. Tax assessors are responsible for setting taxes, while tax collectors are responsible for collecting them. An officer known as a constable is responsible for maintaining order, supervising public places, and enforcing laws. The town clerk keeps minutes of all meetings and compiles vital statistics. The treasurer safeguards the town's funds. In addition to these officials, the overseer of the poor has the duty — and it is a very difficult one — of implementing legislation concerning the indigent; the school committee is in charge of public education; and surveyors of highways are responsible for all details concerning roads, both major and minor. This completes the list of principal town officials, but the division of functions does not end here. Other town officials[6] include parish commissioners, who are supposed to regulate expenditures for religion, and inspectors of various kinds, some of whom are responsible for directing the efforts of citizens when a fire breaks out; others with overseeing the harvest; still others with finding interim solutions to problems stemming from the enclosure of land; and, finally, officials whose job it is to oversee the measurement of wood and to inspect weights and measures.

There are, in all, nineteen principal offices in the town. Every resident is obliged to serve in these various offices or face a fine, but, in addition, most of these positions are paid, so that poor citizens can devote time to them without hardship. Under the American system, however, officials are not paid a fixed salary. Generally speaking, each official act has a price, and officials are paid in proportion to what they do.

---

[5]*Ibid.*
[6]All these officials actually exist in practice.
For details about the duties of all these town officials, see the book entitled *Town Officer* (Worcester, 1827) by Isaac Goodwin and the collection of the general laws of Massachusetts in 3 vols. (Boston, 1823).

TOWN LIFE

Each individual is the best judge of what concerns himself alone. — Corollary of the principle of popular sovereignty. — Application of these doctrines in American towns. — The New England town, sovereign in all that pertains to itself alone, subject in everything else. — The town's obligations to the state. — In France, the government lends its agents to the commune. *— In America, the town lends its agents to the government.*

I remarked earlier that the principle of popular sovereignty looms over each and every aspect of the Anglo-American political system. Every page of this book will reveal new applications of this doctrine.

In nations where the dogma of popular sovereignty reigns, each individual constitutes an equal share of the sovereign and participates equally in the government of the state.

Thus each individual is supposed to be as enlightened, as virtuous, and as strong as every other individual.

Why, then, does the individual obey society, and what are the natural limits of his obedience?

He obeys society, not because he is inferior to those who rule it, or less capable of governing himself than anyone else, but because union with his fellow men seems useful to him, and because he knows that such union cannot exist without a regulatory power.

In everything to do with the duties of citizens to one another, he has therefore become subject. In everything that regards himself alone, he remains master. He is free and owes an account of his actions only to God. Whence this maxim: the individual is the best as well as the only judge of his own interest, and society has the right to direct his actions only when it feels injured by his activities or when it requires his cooperation.

This doctrine is universally accepted in the United States. Elsewhere I shall examine what general influence it exerts even over life's most routine activities, but for the time being the subject is towns.

The town, taken as a whole and in relation to the central government, is merely an individual like any other, to which the theory I just mentioned applies.

In the United States, therefore, local liberty is a consequence of the dogma of popular sovereignty itself. To one degree or another, all the American republics have recognized the independence of the town, but circumstances in New England were particularly favorable to its development.

In this part of the Union, political life first developed in the towns. One might almost say that, in the beginning, each town was an independent nation. When the kings of England later insisted on their share of sovereignty, they seized only the central power. They left the towns as they had found them. From then on, the towns of New England were subject, but in the beginning they were not, or at least not to any great extent. Thus their powers were not granted to them. On the contrary, it would appear that it was the towns that relinquished a portion of their independence to the state. This distinction is important, and the reader should take care to bear it in mind.

Broadly speaking, towns are subject to the state only where what I shall call a *social* interest is involved, that is, an interest they share with others.

In everything that pertains to themselves alone, towns remain independent bodies. I do not believe that there is a single resident of New England who would grant the state government the right to intervene in matters of exclusively local interest.

One therefore finds New England towns buying and selling property, attacking others and defending themselves in court, and increasing or decreasing their budgets, while no administrative authority would even think of standing in their way.[7]

Yet there are certain social duties that the towns are bound to satisfy. If, for instance, the state needs money, the town is not free to grant or withhold its cooperation.[8] If the state wishes to build a road, the town cannot bar access to its territory. If the state issues a regulation regarding public order, the town is bound to enforce it. If the state wishes to impose uniform standards on education throughout its territory, towns

[7]See *Laws of Massachusetts*, law of March 23, 1786, vol. 1, p. 250.
[8]*Ibid.*, law of February 20, 1786, vol. 1, p. 217.

are bound to build schools as required by law.[9] When we come to discuss the administration of the United States, we shall see how and by whom towns can be required to obey in various cases. Here I mean only to establish the existence of the obligation. This obligation is strict, but the state government, in laying it down, is merely stating a principle. When it comes to execution of the law, the town generally reclaims its full individual rights. For example, taxes are indeed voted by the legislature, but the town apportions and collects them. The existence of a school may be obligatory, but it is the town that builds it, pays for it, and runs it.

In France, local taxes are collected by the state's tax collector. In America, state taxes are collected by the town's tax collector.

In France, in other words, the central government lends its agents to the *commune*. In America, the town lends its officials to the government. This fact alone suffices to make clear the degree to which the two societies differ.

ON THE TOWN SPIRIT IN NEW ENGLAND

Why the New England town wins the affections of the people who live in it. — Difficulty of creating community spirit in Europe. — Communal rights and duties help forge community spirit in America. — In the United States the "homeland" has a more distinctive physiognomy than in other countries. — How community spirit manifests itself in New England. — Its happy effects.

In America, not only do community institutions exist; so does a community spirit that sustains them and breathes life into them.

The New England town combines two advantages in which people take a keen interest wherever they are found, namely, independence and power. To be sure, the town's actions are strictly circumscribed, but within limits its movements are free. This independence alone would bestow real importance on the town, even if its population and size did not.

[9]See, in the same collection, the laws of June 25, 1789 and March 8, 1827, vol. 1, p. 367, and vol. 3, p. 179.

It must be granted that men generally bestow their affections where there is strength. Love of country will not endure for long in a conquered nation. The New Englander is attached to his town not so much because he is born there as because he sees the town as a free and powerful corporation of which he is a part and which it is worth his trouble to seek to direct.

In Europe, it is common for people in government to regret the absence of community spirit, because everyone agrees that it is an important element of order and public tranquillity. Yet they do not know how to foster such a spirit. Their fear is that to allow towns to be strong and independent would be to divide social power and lay the state open to anarchy. Deprive a town of strength and independence, however, and its inhabitants cease to be citizens; they are reduced to mere subjects of an administration.

Note, too, another important fact: the New England town is constituted in such a way as to elicit the warmest of affections, while nothing in its vicinity holds much appeal for the more ambitious passions of the human heart.

County officials are not elected, and their authority is limited. The state itself is of only secondary importance; it leads an obscure and tranquil existence. Few men are willing to travel far from the place where the majority of their interests lie and disturb their settled lives to win the right to administer its affairs.

The federal government confers power and glory on its leaders, but it is given to very few men to shape its destiny. The presidency is a high office seldom achieved by anyone not well advanced in age. When a person accedes to other high federal offices, it is in a sense by luck and comes only after celebrity has been achieved in some other career. Ambition cannot settle on such offices as its one and only goal. It is in the town, amidst the ordinary relationships of life, that the desire for esteem, the needs stemming from real interests, and the thirst for power and notoriety come to be concentrated; these passions, which so often roil society, change in character when they find a vent close to home, in the bosom, as it were, of the family.

Much artful care has been taken in American towns to — if I may put it this way — *disperse* power in order to interest as many people as possible in public affairs. It is not just that the voters are summoned from time to time to perform acts of government. There are also a great many officcs, and a host of different officials, each of whom represents, within a limited sphere, the powerful corporation in whose name they all act. How many men thereby exploit the power of the town for their own benefit and take an interest in public affairs for reasons of their own!

The American system, even as it shares municipal power among a large number of citizens, does not hesitate to multiply the number of civic duties. In the United States people rightly believe that love of country is a form of religion to which people become attached through practicing it.

As a result, people are constantly made aware of the life of the community. They participate in that life daily by fulfilling some duty or exercising some right. This political existence impresses upon society a constant but at the same time peaceful motion that stirs it without disturbing it.

Americans are devoted to their communities for the same reason that highlanders love their mountains. An American thinks of his homeland as a place with marked, characteristic features; it has a more distinctive physiognomy than people elsewhere ascribe to their country.

In general, the towns of New England lead a happy existence. Their government is to their taste as well as of their choice. Amid the profound peace and material prosperity that prevail in America, stormy episodes in municipal life are rare. Management of town interests is easy. The people have long since completed their political education, or perhaps it would be more accurate to say that they arrived already educated on the land they now occupy. In New England, divisions by rank do not exist, not even as a memory. Hence no portion of the town is tempted to oppress any other portion, and injustices, which affect only isolated individuals, are lost in the general contentment. Though the government is not without defects — indeed, it is easy to point them out — they do not strike the eye, because the government really does emanate from the governed, and as long as it continues to struggle its way forward, it will be protected by a sort of paternal pride. In any case, the people have nothing else to compare it with. England formerly ruled the colonies, but the people always governed local affairs. The sovereignty of the people in the town is therefore not just an ancient state but a primordial one.

The New Englander is attached to his town because it is strong and independent; he takes an interest in it because he helps direct its affairs; he loves it because it gives him no reason to complain about his lot in life. He invests his ambition and his future in the town and participates in all aspects of community life. In the limited sphere that is within his reach, he tries his hand at governing society. He becomes accustomed to the forms without which liberty advances only by way of revolution, becomes imbued with their spirit, develops a taste for order, comprehends the harmony of powers, and, finally, acquires clear and practical ideas about the nature of his duties and the extent of his rights.

ON THE COUNTY IN NEW ENGLAND

The New England county, analogue of the French arrondissement. *— Created for purely administrative reasons. — Has no representation. — Is administered by unelected officials.*

The American county is analogous in many ways to the *arrondissement* of France. Its limits, like those of the *arrondissement*, were drawn arbitrarily. It forms a body whose various parts have no necessary relation among themselves, and no one feels bound to it by affection, memory, or communal existence. It was created for purely administrative reasons.

The town was too small to confine the administration of justice within its limits. The county therefore became the primary judicial center. Every county has a court of justice,[10] a sheriff to carry out the orders of the courts, and a prison that is supposed to hold criminals.

Some needs are felt almost equally by all the towns in the county. It was natural to establish a central authority to deal with them. In Massachusetts, that authority was placed in the

[10]See the law of February 14, 1821, *Laws of Massachusetts*, vol. 1, p. 551.

hands of a number of officials appointed by the governor of the state on the advice[11] of his council.[12]

County administrators have only limited and exceptional powers, which pertain exclusively to a very small number of cases spelled out in advance. The state and town suffice to deal with routine matters. County administrators draw up the county budget, but the legislature must approve it.[13] No assembly represents the county directly or indirectly.

Therefore, to be frank, the county has no political existence.

In most American constitutions one can discern a tendency on the part of lawmakers to divide executive power while concentrating legislative power. The vitality of the New England town stems from the town itself, and the source of that vitality has been left untouched. By contrast, to breathe life into the county would have required artificial means, and the usefulness of doing so was not apparent. All the towns together are represented by a single institution, the state, the center of all national powers. Towns can act and the state can act, but beyond that it is fair to say that the only forces are individual.

ON ADMINISTRATION
IN NEW ENGLAND

In America the administration is invisible. — Why? — Europeans believe that they establish a foundation for liberty when they deprive the social power of some of its rights; Americans, when they divide the exercise of that power. — Almost all administration in the proper sense of the term is confined within the town and divided among town officials. — No trace of an administrative hierarchy is visible either in the town or above it. — Why this is so. — How it comes to pass nevertheless that the state is administered in a uniform manner. — Who is charged with requiring town and county administrations to obey the law? — On the introduction of judicial power into the administration. — Consequence of extending the principle of election to all officials. — On the justice of the peace in New England. — Appointed by whom? — Administers the county. — Sees to the administration of the towns. — Court of Sessions. — Manner in

---

[11] See the law of February 20, 1819, *Laws of Massachusetts*, vol. 2, p. 494.
[12] The Governor's Council is an elective body.
[13] See the law of November 2, 1791, *Laws of Massachusetts*, vol. 1, p. 61.

which it acts. — Who brings cases before it? — The right of inspection and complaint dispersed along with other administrative functions. — Informers encouraged by the sharing of fines.

What most strikes the European who travels through the United States is the absence of what we would call government or administration. In America you find written laws; you see them enforced daily. Things seem to be in motion all around you, yet the force that drives them is not apparent. The hand that guides the social machinery constantly evades detection.

Yet just as all peoples, in order to express their thoughts, must have recourse to certain grammatical forms intrinsic to human language, so, too, must all societies, in order to exist, subject themselves to a certain measure of authority, or else lapse into anarchy. That authority may be distributed in a variety of ways, but it must always exist somewhere.

There are two ways of diminishing the force of authority in a nation.

The first is to weaken power at the source by depriving society of the right or faculty to defend itself in certain cases. To weaken authority in this way is generally what Europeans call establishing a basis for liberty.

There is a second way of diminishing the action of authority: this consists not in depriving society of certain of its rights or in paralyzing its efforts but in dividing the use of its forces among several hands, increasing the number of officials while attributing to each one whatever power he needs to discharge his assigned responsibilities. There exist peoples among whom such a division of social powers can still lead to anarchy; in itself, however, it is not anarchic. Authority divided in this way becomes less irresistible and less dangerous, to be sure, but it is not destroyed.

The revolution in the United States was the result of a mature, reflective preference for liberty and not a vague, indefinite instinct for independence. It did not depend on the passions of disorder. On the contrary, it demonstrated love of order and legality as it went forward.

In the United States, therefore, it was never claimed that man in a free country has the right to do whatever he pleases.

Indeed, the range of social obligations imposed on him was wider than in other countries. The idea was not to attack the power of society at its source and to challenge its rights; instead, people confined themselves to dividing the exercise of that power. In so doing, they wanted to ensure that authority would be great and the official small, so that society would continue to be well regulated and remain free.

There is no other country in the world where the law speaks so absolute a language as in America or where the right to apply it is divided among so many hands.

There is nothing centralized or hierarchical in the constitution of administrative power in the United States. That is why it goes unnoticed. Administrative power exists, but its representatives are not easy to find.

We saw earlier that the towns of New England were not placed under any supervisory authority. They therefore assume responsibility for tending to their own special interests.

Usually, moreover, town officials are charged either with assisting in the execution of the general laws of the state or with executing those laws themselves.[14]

Apart from general laws, the state sometimes issues general regulations regarding public order, but ordinarily it is the towns and town officials who, conjointly with justices of the peace and in accordance with local needs, regulate the details of social existence and issue orders dealing with matters of public health, law and order, and the morality of citizens.[15]

---

[14]See *Town Officer*, especially under the headings "selectmen," "assessors," "collectors," "schools," "surveyors of highways," and so on. To take just one example among a thousand, the state bans travel without a reason on Sundays. Town officials known as "tithing men" are specifically designated to help in the enforcement of this law.

See the law of March 8, 1792, *Laws of Massachusetts*, vol. 1, p. 410.

The selectmen draw up voting lists for the election of the governor and convey the results of the voting to the secretary of state. Law of February 24, 1796, *ibid.*, vol. 1, p. 488.

[15]Example: the selectmen authorize the construction of sewers and designate places where slaughterhouses may be built and where certain types of business that are noxious to their neighbors may be conducted.

See the law of June 7, 1785, vol. 1, p. 193.

Finally, it is municipal officials who, on their own initiative and without need of outside prompting, meet the unforeseen needs that often arise in societies.[16]

From the foregoing it follows that, in Massachusetts, administrative power is limited almost entirely to the local level;[17] but there it is divided among many hands.

In the French *commune* there is really only one administrative official: the mayor.

We have seen that in the New England town there are some nineteen town officials.

These nineteen officials are generally independent of one another. The law carefully circumscribes their responsibilities. Within the limits laid down by the law, each official has the full powers necessary to perform the duties of his office and is not subordinate to any local authority.

If we look above the local level, we find scarcely any trace of administrative hierarchy. County officials will sometimes modify a decision taken by a town or town official,[18] but in general we can say that county administrators do not have the right to control the conduct of town administrators.[19] They are in command only in matters pertaining to the county.

In a very small number of cases designated in advance, town and county officials are bound to communicate the results of

---

[16]Example: the selectmen oversee public health in case of contagious disease and take necessary measures in conjunction with justices of the peace. Law of June 22, 1797, vol. 1, p. 539.

[17]I say *almost* because various aspects of town life are dealt with either by justices of the peace acting alone or by all the justices gathered as a body in the county seat. Example: the justices of the peace grant licenses. See the law of February 28, 1787, vol. 1, p. 297.

[18]Example: licenses are awarded only to applicants submitting a certificate of good behavior issued by the selectmen. If the selectmen refuse to issue this certificate, the individual can complain to the justices of the peace gathered together in a Court of Sessions, and they may grant the license. See the law of March 12, 1808, vol. 2, p. 186. Towns have the right to issue by-laws and to enforce them by imposing fixed fines, but the by-laws must be approved by the Court of Sessions. See the law of March 23, 1786, vol. 1, p. 254.

[19]In Massachusetts, county administrators are often called upon to evaluate the actions of town administrators. As we shall see later, however, they examine those actions as a judicial power, not an administrative authority.

their actions to officials of the central government.[20] But the central government is not represented by a man charged with issuing general regulations regarding public welfare or injunctions concerning enforcement of the laws; or with communicating regularly with town and county administrators, inspecting their behavior, directing their activities, and punishing their faults.

Hence there is no central hub toward which the spokes of administrative power converge.

When everything is on virtually the same plane, how is it possible to conduct the business of society? How can counties and their administrators and towns and their administrators be made to obey?

In the states of New England, the extent of legislative power is greater than it is in France. The legislator insinuates himself, as it were, into the very heart of the administration. The law descends to minute details. It prescribes principles and at the same time means of applying those principles. It thereby subjects secondary bodies and their administrators to a multitude of strict and rigorously defined obligations.

It follows that, if all secondary bodies and officials abide by the law, the society will function in a uniform manner throughout. It remains to be seen, however, how the secondary bodies and their officials can be obliged to abide by the law.

It can be stated as a general rule that society has at its disposal only two means of obliging officials to obey the law:

It can entrust one of them with the discretionary power to direct the others and remove them in case of disobedience;

Or it can charge the courts with imposing judicial penalties on violators.

One is not always free to choose one or the other of these methods, however.

The right to direct the work of an official assumes the right to remove him from office if he fails to follow orders or to promote him if he is zealous in the discharge of his duties. Elected officials cannot be removed or promoted, however.

---

[20]Example: town school committees are required to make an annual report to the secretary of state on the condition of the schools. See the law of March 10, 1827, vol. 3, p. 183.

Elective offices are by their very nature irrevocable until the mandate of the voters expires. In fact, when all public offices are filled by election, elected officials have nothing to expect or fear from anyone but the voters. Hence no true official hierarchy can exist, since the right to issue orders and the right to deal effectively with disobedience cannot be vested in the same person, and there is no way to combine the power to command with the power to reward and punish.

Peoples who allow elections to play a part in the auxiliary machinery of government are therefore compelled to rely heavily on judicial sanctions as a tool of administration.

This is not evident at first glance. Those who govern regard it as a first concession to make offices elective and as a second concession to make elected officials subject to judicial writ. They are equally afraid of both innovations, and since they are more urgently pressed to grant the former than they are to grant the latter, they permit the official to be elected but leave him independent of the judge. Yet one of these two measures is the only counterweight that can be set against the other. Mark this well: an elective power that is not subject to a judicial power sooner or later escapes all control or is destroyed. The courts are the only possible intermediary between the central power and elected administrative bodies. Only the courts can force elected officials to obey without violating the rights of voters.

The extension of judicial power into the world of politics must therefore be correlated with the extension of elective power. If the two things do not go together, the state will ultimately lapse into anarchy or servitude.

In all ages it has been observed that judicial habits prepare men rather poorly for the exercise of administrative power.

From their English forefathers the Americans borrowed the idea for an institution that has no counterpart on the continent of Europe, namely, the justices of the peace.

The justice of the peace stands midway between the man of the world and the official, the administrator and the judge. The justice of the peace is an enlightened citizen, though not necessarily well-versed in the law. Thus he is charged only with overseeing the general order of society, something that requires more common sense and uprightness of character than it does learning. When the justice of the peace becomes involved in matters of administration, he brings to the table a certain preference for formal procedures and openness, which makes him an instrument highly inimical to despotism. Yet he does not show himself to be a slave to the kind of legal superstitions that render magistrates so little capable of governing.

The Americans appropriated the institution of justices of the peace while eliminating the aristocratic character that attached to this institution in the mother country.

The governor of Massachusetts[21] appoints a certain number of justices of the peace in each county for a term of seven years.[22]

In addition, he designates three justices of the peace in each county to form what is called the *Court of Sessions*.

Individually, the justices of the peace take part in public administration. Sometimes they are charged with administrative functions jointly with elected officials.[23] Sometimes they sit as a court before which officials bring summary charges against citizens who refuse to obey, or citizens complain of offenses by officials. But it is in the Court of Sessions that justices of the peace exercise their most important administrative functions.

The Court of Sessions meets twice a year in the county seat. In Massachusetts, it is this court that is responsible for ensuring that most[24] public officials obey the law.[25]

[21]We shall see later what the governor is. For now I should say that the governor represents the executive power of the entire state.

[22]See the Constitution of Massachusetts, chap. II, section I, paragraph 9; chap. 3, paragraph 3.

[23]One example among many: a foreigner comes to a town from a country ravaged by a contagious disease. He falls ill. With the advice of the selectmen, two justices of the peace can order the county sheriff to transport the man elsewhere and watch over him. Law of June 22, 1797, vol. I, p. 540.

In general, justices of the peace intervene in all important administrative actions, to which they impart a semi-judicial character.

[24]I say *most* because certain administrative offenses are in fact transferred to the ordinary courts. Example: when a town refuses to provide the funds necessary for its schools or to appoint a school committee, it is sentenced to pay a very substantial fine. This fine is imposed by a court known as the Supreme Judicial Court or by the Court of Common Pleas. See the law of March 10, 1827, vol. 3, p. 190. The same is true when a town fails to provide munitions of war. Law of February 21, 1822, vol. 2, p. 570.

[25]The justices of the peace, acting in their individual capacity, take part in the government of towns and counties. The most important actions taken by the towns generally require the consent of a justice of the peace.

I stated earlier that the county was merely an administrative entity.[26] It is the Court of Sessions itself that deals with the small number of interests that affect several towns at the same time or all the towns of the county at once and therefore cannot be assigned to any one of them in particular.

As far as the county is concerned, the duties of the Court of Sessions are therefore purely administrative, and if it often introduces judicial forms into its procedures, it does so only as a way of clarifying the issue[27] and giving a certain guarantee to those under its jurisdiction. When the administration of the towns has to be dealt with, however, it almost always acts a judicial body and only rarely as an administrative body.

The first difficulty that arises is to compel the town, an almost independent power, to obey the general laws of the state.

We saw earlier that towns must every year appoint a certain number of officials known as assessors to apportion the tax. A town tries to avoid the obligation to pay taxes by failing to appoint assessors. The Court of Sessions condemns it to pay a substantial fine.[28] The fine is levied on all the residents of the town collectively. The county sheriff, an officer of the court, enforces its orders. By such means power in the United States seems keen to hide itself from scrutiny. There, administrative orders are almost always veiled as judicial writs. Such orders are only more powerful as a result, because they then have behind them the almost irresistible force that men grant to legal forms.

Such a course of action is easy to follow and simple to understand. What is required of the town is generally clear and

---

[26]The list of county matters with which the Court of Sessions concerns itself is as follows:

1. Building of prisons and courts of justice.
2. The proposed county budget (which must be approved by a vote of the state legislature).
3. The apportionment of taxes thus voted on.
4. The award of certain licenses.
5. The construction and maintenance of county roads.

[27]For example, when a road is under consideration, the Court of Sessions resolves most practical questions with the aid of a jury.

[28]See the law of February 20, 1786, vol. 1, p. 217.

well-defined. It involves a simple action, not a complicated one, a principle, not a detailed application.[29] The difficulty begins, however, when the obedience required is not that of the town but of the town's officials.

Ultimately, all the reprehensible actions that a public official may commit can be classified in one of the following categories:

He can do what the law commands him to do but without ardor or zeal.

He can fail to do what the law commands him to do.

Or, finally, he can do what the law forbids him to do.

Only in the latter two cases can the courts punish the official's conduct. Absent a positive and appreciable act, there is no basis for judicial action.

Thus, if the selectmen fail to respect the formal requirements of the law in the case of a town election, they can be fined.[30]

But when the public official does his duty in an unintelligent way, or when he obeys the prescriptions of law without ardor or zeal, he is wholly beyond the reach of any judicial body.

Even when the Court of Sessions assumes its administrative prerogatives, it is powerless in such cases to force the official to fulfill his obligations entirely. Only the fear of dismissal can prevent such quasi-offenses, and the Court of Sessions is not the source of power in the towns; it cannot dismiss officials that it does not appoint.

In order to ascertain the existence of negligence or lack of zeal, moreover, the subordinate official would have to be subjected to constant scrutiny. The Court of Sessions sits only

[29]There is an indirect way of making the town obey. Towns are obliged by law to maintain their roads in good condition. If they neglect to approve the funds required for such maintenance, the town official in charge of roads is authorized to raise the necessary money by fiat. Since he is personally responsible to individual citizens for the state of the roads and can be sued by them in the Court of Sessions, one can be certain that he will use the extraordinary powers granted to him by the law against the town. Thus by threatening the official, the Court of Sessions compels the town to obey. See the law of March 5, 1787, vol. 1, p. 305.

[30]*Laws of Massachusetts*, vol. 2, p. 45.

twice a year, however; it makes no investigation; it judges only such reprehensible acts as are brought before it.

Only the arbitrary power to remove public officials from office can guarantee the sort of enlightened and active obedience that no judicial sanction can impose.

In France we seek this final guarantee through *administrative hierarchy*; in America it is sought through *election*.

To sum up in a few words what I have just set forth:

If a New England public official commits a *crime* in the exercise of his functions, the ordinary courts are *always* called upon to administer justice.

If he commits an *administrative error*, a purely administrative court is responsible for punishing him, and when the matter is grave or urgent, the judge does what the official should have done.[31]

Finally, if the official is guilty of one of those elusive offenses that human justice can neither define nor assess, he appears annually before a tribunal from which there is no appeal and which can strip him of power in an instant; his power ends with his mandate.

There are certainly great advantages to this system, but it meets with practical difficulties that need to be pointed out.

I have already noted that the administrative tribunal known as the Court of Sessions has no right to oversee the work of town officials; it can act, in legal terms, only when suit is filed. This is the difficult point in the system.

The people of New England never assigned a public prosecutor to the Court of Sessions,[32] and we need to appreciate why it would have been difficult for them to do so. Had they simply assigned a prosecutor to each county seat and not provided him with agents in the towns, why should that prosecutor have been any better informed about what was going

---

[31]Example: if a town obstinately refuses to appoint assessors, the court of sessions will appoint them, and the officials thus chosen are invested with the same powers as the elected officials. See the previously cited law of February 20, 1787.

[32]I say no prosecutor is assigned *to the court of sessions*. There is an official who fills certain of the duties of a public prosecutor assigned to the common courts.

on in the county than the members of the Court of Sessions themselves? Had they provided him with agents in each town, they would have centralized in his hands the most redoubtable of powers, that of judicial administration. Laws, moreover, are the children of habit, and nothing of the kind existed in English law.

Therefore the Americans severed the right to supervise from the right to file charges of malfeasance, just as they divided all other administrative functions.

Under the terms of the law, the members of the grand jury are supposed to apprise the tribunal under whose auspices they act of offenses of all kinds that may be committed in their county.[33] There are certain major administrative offenses that the regular prosecutor is responsible for prosecuting.[34] More often, the fiscal officer is responsible for punishing delinquents and collecting fines. Thus the town treasurer is charged with prosecuting most administrative offenses committed within his area of responsibility.

American legislation appeals above all to particular interest.[35] In studying the laws of the United States, one encounters this great principle again and again.

American legislators display relatively little confidence in human honesty, but they always assume that man is intelligent. Hence they usually rely on personal interest for the execution of the laws.

When an individual suffers immediate and palpable harm as a result of an administrative offense, it is indeed plausible to assume that personal interest is enough to ensure that suit will be filed.

It is easy to foresee, however, that if it is a question of a legal prescription that, while useful to society, is not currently felt to be useful by any individual, each person will hesitate to

[33]Grand jurors are obliged, for example, to alert the courts to roads in poor condition. *Laws of Massachusetts*, vol. 1, p. 308.

[34]If, for example, the county treasurer fails to submit his books. *Laws of Massachusetts*, vol. 1, p. 406.

[35]One example among a thousand: if a private individual damages his carriage or injures himself on a poorly maintained road, he has the right to file suit in the court of sessions against the town or county responsible for maintaining the road. *Laws of Massachusetts*, vol. 1, p. 309.

come forward as the accuser. In this way, by a sort of tacit agreement, laws might well fall into disuse.

Thus, forced by their system to adopt an extreme remedy, the Americans are obliged to motivate potential plaintiffs by authorizing them in certain cases to share in the proceeds of any fines.[36]

This is a dangerous procedure, which ensures the execution of the laws by degrading the morality of the people.

Above the county officials, there is no administrative power as such but only a governmental power.

GENERAL IDEAS ABOUT ADMINISTRATION IN THE UNITED STATES

How the states of the union differ among themselves in their system of administration. — Community life less active and less comprehensive as one travels southward. — The power of the official then becomes greater, that of the voter, smaller. — Administration passes from the town to the county. — States of New York, Ohio, Pennsylvania. — Administrative principles applicable to the entire Union. — Election of public officials or impossibility of removing them from office. — Absence of hierarchy. — Introduction of judicial procedures into administration.

I stated earlier that after examining the constitution of town and county in New England in detail, I would cast a general glance at the rest of the Union.

---

[36]In case of invasion or insurrection, if town officials neglect to provide the militia with necessary items and munitions, the town may be required to pay a fine of 200 to 500 dollars (1,000 to 2,500 francs).

In such a case, it is easy to imagine that there may be no one with the motive or desire to assume the role of accuser. The law therefore adds that the fine is "to be sued for and recovered by any person, who may prosecute for the same, . . . one moiety to the prosecutor." See the law of March 6, 1810, vol. 2, p. 236.

Similar measures are found quite frequently in the laws of Massachusetts.

Sometimes it is not the private citizen whom the law incites in this way to pursue public officials; it is rather the official whom it encourages to punish disobedience by private citizens. For example: a citizen refuses to perform his assigned share of work on a highway. The surveyor of highways must file suit, and if a judgment is secured, half of the fine goes to the official. See the previously cited laws, vol. 1, p. 308.

Towns exist in every state, and there is life in every town, but nowhere else do we find towns identical to those of New England.

As one proceeds southward, the vitality of the town seems to diminish. Towns have fewer officials, rights, and duties. The people do not exert as direct an influence on affairs. Town meetings are less frequent and deal with a narrower range of issues. Hence the power of elected officials is greater, and that of the voters smaller; the community spirit is less aroused and less powerful.[37]

One begins to notice these differences in the state of New York. They are already quite palpable in Pennsylvania but become less striking as one proceeds toward the Northwest. Most of the immigrants who founded the states of the Northwest came from New England, and they took the administrative habits of the mother country with them to their adopted homeland. An Ohio town has much in common with a Massachusetts town.

In Massachusetts, as we have seen, the mainspring of public administration is located in the town. The town is the focal point of people's interests and affections. This is no longer the case, however, as one moves into states where enlightenment is less universally shared and where, in consequence, the town provides fewer guarantees of wisdom and performs fewer basic administrative functions. As one moves away from New England, therefore, communal life shifts in a sense to the county. The county becomes the great administrative center and constitutes the intermediate power between the government and ordinary citizens.

[37]For details, see *The Revised Statutes of the State of New York*, at part I, chap. II, entitled: "Of the Powers, Duties and Privileges of Towns," vol. I, pp. 336–364.

In the compendium entitled *Digest of the Laws of Pennsylvania*, see the words Assessors, Collectors, Constables, Overseers of the Poor, Supervisor of Highways. And in the compendium entitled *Acts of a General Nature of the State of Ohio*, see the law of February 25, 1834, pertaining to towns, p. 412. See also specific clauses dealing with various town officials such as Township's Clerk, Trustees, Overseers of the Poor, Fence Viewers, Appraisers of Property, Township's Treasurer, Constables, Supervisors of Highways.

I said earlier that in Massachusetts, county affairs are directed by the Court of Sessions. The Court of Sessions consists of a certain number of magistrates appointed by the governor and his council. The county has no representation, and its budget is voted by the state legislature.

By contrast, in the great state of New York and in the states of Ohio and Pennsylvania, the residents of each county elect a certain number of representatives; these representatives then meet to form the county's representative assembly.[38]

Within certain limits, the assembly has the power to levy taxes on the county's inhabitants. In this respect it constitutes a genuine legislature. The assembly also administers the county and in several cases directs the administration of the towns and limits their powers to a far greater degree than in Massachusetts.

These are the main differences apparent in the constitution of towns and counties in the various confederated states. If I wished to go into detail about means of execution, I would have many other dissimilarities to report. But my aim is not to give a course on American administrative law.

I have said enough, I think, to make clear the general principles on which administration is based in the United States. Those principles are applied in a variety of ways. Their consequences are more or less numerous, depending on the place, but fundamentally they are the same everywhere. The laws vary; their aspect changes; but the spirit that animates them is identical.

Towns and counties are not constituted in the same way everywhere. Yet we can say that the organization of towns and counties in the United States is everywhere based on the same idea, namely, that each is the best judge of what pertains only to itself and best equipped to provide for its own particular

[38]See *Revised Statutes of the State of New York*, part I, chap. 11, vol. 1, p. 340; chap. 12, p. 366. *Acts of the State of Ohio*. Law of February 25, 1824, relative to the county commissioners, p. 263.

See *Digest of the Laws of Pennsylvania*, at the words "Count-Rates" and "Levies," p. 170.

In the state of New York, each town elects a deputy, and this deputy participates in the administration of both the county and the town.

needs. Towns and counties are therefore responsible for looking after their own special interests. The state governs and
does not administer. One meets with exceptions to this principle but not with a contrary principle.

The first consequence of this doctrine was to have all the
administrators of towns and counties chosen by the residents
themselves, or at least to have those officials chosen exclusively
from among their number.

Because administrators were everywhere elected, or at least
impossible to remove from office, it proved impossible to introduce hierarchical rules. Hence there are almost as many independent officials as there are offices. Administrative power
has been scattered among a multitude of hands.

Because there was no administrative hierarchy anywhere,
and because administrators were elected and could not be removed until their mandate was complete, it became necessary
to allow the courts to intervene to one degree or another in
matters of administration. This led to a system of fines, by
means of which secondary bodies and their representatives are
compelled to obey the law. This system is found throughout
the Union.

Finally, the power to punish administrative offenses and,
where necessary, to take administrative action, was not granted
to the same judges in all the states.

In creating the institution of justices of the peace, the
Anglo-Americans drew on a common source; it is found in
all the states. But they did not always use that source in the
same way.

Everywhere justices of the peace contribute to the administration of the towns and counties,[39] whether by administering themselves or by punishing certain administrative offenses.
In most states, however, the most serious of these offenses are
referred to the common courts.

Election of administrative officials or impossibility of removing them from office, absence of administrative hierarchy,

---

[39] There are even states in the South in which county court magistrates are
responsible for all the details of administration. See *The Statutes of the State of
Tennessee* at arts. "Judiciary," "Taxes," etc.

introduction of judicial procedures into the secondary government of society — these are the principal characteristics of American administration from Maine to Florida.

There are a few states in which we glimpse the first signs of administrative centralization. The state of New York has proceeded furthest down this road.

In the state of New York, officials of the central government exercise a kind of supervisory control over the behavior of secondary bodies in certain cases.[40] In certain other cases they form a kind of appellate tribunal.[41] In the state of New York, judicial sanctions are less widely used as a means of administration than is the case elsewhere. The power to

[40]Example: the direction of public education is centralized in the hands of the government. The legislature appoints the regents of the university, with the governor and lieutenant-governor of the state as *ex officio* members (*Revised Statutes*, vol. 1, p. 456). The regents of the university visit schools and academies every year and issue an annual report to the legislature. Their oversight is no mere formality, for the following reasons. Schools must have a charter in order to become corporations entitled to buy, sell, and own property. This charter is granted by the legislature only on the advice of the regents. Every year, the state distributes to secondary schools and academies the interest from a special fund set up to encourage study. The regents decide how this money is to be distributed. See chap. 15, "Public Education," *Revised Statutes*, vol. 1, p. 455.

Each year, the commissioners of public schools are required to send a report on the situation to the superintendent of the republic. *Id.*, p. 588.

A similar report must be made to him annually on the number and condition of the poor. *Id.*, p. 631.

[41]If a person feels injured by the actions of school commissioners (who are town officials), he may appeal to the superintendent of primary schools, whose decision is final. *Revised Statutes*, vol. 1, p. 487.

In the laws of the state of New York one occasionally finds measures similar to those cited here as examples. In general, however, these attempts at centralization have not gone very far and have yielded little. High state officials are granted the power to supervise and direct lower-level officials but not to reward or punish them. Almost never is the same individual responsible both for issuing orders and punishing disobedience. He therefore has the right to command but not the ability to enforce obedience.

In 1830, the superintendent of schools complained in his annual report to the legislature that a number of school commissioners had failed, despite his warnings, to submit their accounts as required. "If this omission is repeated," he added, "I shall be forced, pursuant to law, to prosecute them in the competent courts."

prosecute administrative offenses is also entrusted to fewer people.[42]

There are slight indications of a similar tendency in a few other states.[43] In general, however, what is most striking about public administration in the United States is its extraordinarily decentralized character.

ON THE STATE

I have discussed towns and administration; I turn now to the state and government.

Here I can proceed quickly without fear of being misunderstood. What I have to say is set forth in published constitutions that anyone can obtain easily.[44] These constitutions are themselves based on a simple and rational theory.

Most of the forms that they set forth have been adopted by all constitutional peoples, so that they have become familiar to us.

My exposition here can therefore be short. Later I will try to judge what I am about to describe.

LEGISLATIVE POWER OF THE STATE

Division of the legislative body into two houses. — Senate. — House of Representatives. — Different prerogatives of the two bodies.

The legislative power of the state is entrusted to two assemblies, the first of which is generally called the "senate."

The senate is usually a legislative body, but sometimes it becomes an administrative and judicial body.

It takes part in administration in several ways under different constitutions.[45] But by concurring in the choice of officials it regularly ventures into the sphere of executive power.

[42]Example: the office of the district attorney in each county is responsible for collecting all fines of more than $50 unless that power is expressly assigned by law to another official. *Revised Statutes*, part I, chap. 10, vol. 1, p. 383.

[43]There are a number of signs of administrative centralization in Massachusetts. Example: town school committees are required to submit annual reports to the secretary of state. *Laws of Massachusetts*, vol. 1, p. 367.

[44]See the text of the Constitution of New York.

[45]In Massachusetts, the Senate has no administrative function.

It shares in judicial power by pronouncing judgment on certain political offenses and also by ruling on certain civil cases.[46] Its members are always few in number.

The other branch of the legislature, which is usually called the house of representatives, plays no role in administrative power and shares in judicial power only when it brings charges against public officials before the senate.

The same conditions of eligibility apply to members of both houses almost everywhere. Both are elected in the same way by the same citizens.

The only difference between them stems from the fact that the term of a senator is generally longer than that of a representative. A representative rarely remains in office for more than a year; a senator ordinarily sits for two or three years.

By granting senators the privilege of remaining in office for several years and stipulating that only a fraction of the senate be replaced at each election, the law strives to ensure that the legislature contains a core of men well-versed in public affairs and capable of exerting a useful influence on newcomers.

When Americans divided the legislative body into two branches, their goal was therefore not to establish one hereditary assembly and another elective assembly; nor did they seek to make one branch an aristocratic body and the other a representative of democracy. Neither was their purpose to make the former a bulwark of power while leaving the latter to deal with the interests and passions of the people.

To divide legislative power, thus to slow the movement of political assemblies, and to create an appellate tribunal for revision of the laws — such are the only advantages that result from the present constitution of the two houses in the United States.

Time and experience have shown Americans that, even reduced to these two advantages, the division of legislative powers is still a necessity of the first order. Alone among the united republics, Pennsylvania initially attempted to establish a single assembly. Franklin himself, carried away by the logical consequences of the dogma of popular sovereignty, concurred in this measure. But the legislators were soon forced

---

[46]As in the state of New York.

to change the law and constitute two houses. This marked the final consecration of the division of legislative power. Hence the need for several bodies to share the work of legislation may now be taken as a demonstrated truth. This theory — all but unknown to the republics of antiquity; introduced into the world, like most great truths, almost by chance; and neglected by any number of modern nations — has today become an axiom of political science.

ON THE EXECUTIVE POWER OF THE STATE

What the governor is in an American state. — What position he occupies vis-à-vis the legislature. — What his rights and duties are. — His dependence on the people.

The executive power of the state has the governor as its representative.

I have not chosen the word "representative" at random. The governor does indeed represent the executive power, but he exercises only some of its rights.

The supreme magistrate, called the governor, is set alongside the legislature as a moderator and advisor. He is armed with a suspensive veto, which allows him to halt or at least slow the movement of the legislature if he so chooses. He expounds the needs of the state before the legislature and suggests what he considers to be useful means of meeting those needs. He is the natural executor of the wishes of the legislature in all enterprises involving the state as a whole.[47] When the legislature is not in session, he must take any measures necessary to protect the state from violent shocks and unforeseen dangers.

The governor holds all the military power of the state in his hands. He is the commander of the militia and the head of the armed forces.

When the people flout the power they have by common consent granted to the law, the governor assumes command

---

[47]In practice, it is not always the governor who carries out plans conceived by the legislature. When the legislature approves a project in principle, it often appoints special agents to oversee its execution.

of the physical might of the state, breaks the resistance, and restores the customary order.

Otherwise, the governor plays no role in the administration of towns and counties, or at any rate only a very indirect role through the nomination of justices of the peace, whom he cannot then remove.[48]

The governor is an elected official. Indeed, his term of office is usually limited to one or two years, so that he is always strictly dependent on the majority that created him.

ON THE POLITICAL EFFECTS OF ADMINISTRATIVE DECENTRALIZATION IN THE UNITED STATES

Distinction to be made between governmental centralization and administrative centralization. — In the United States, no administrative centralization but very great governmental centralization. — Some unfortunate consequences of the extreme administrative decentralization found in the United States. — Administrative advantages of this arrangement. — The force that administers society, less regulated, less enlightened, less educated, much greater than in Europe. — Political advantages of this arrangement. — In the United States the influence of the nation is felt everywhere. — Support of the governed for the government. — Provincial institutions more necessary to the extent that the social state becomes more democratic. — Why.

"Centralization" is a word that is constantly repeated of late but whose meaning no one seeks to clarify.

There are, however, two very different kinds of centralization, and it is important to be clear about the difference.

Certain interests, such as the enactment of general laws and relations with foreigners, are common to all parts of the nation.

Other interests are special to certain parts of the nation: local projects, for instance.

To concentrate the power to direct the former in one place or one pair of hands is to establish what I shall call governmental centralization.

---

[48]In several states justices of the peace are not appointed by the governor.

To concentrate the power to direct the latter in the same way is to establish what I shall name administrative centralization.

In some respects the distinction between the two kinds of centralization becomes blurred. But if we consider the totality of matters falling specifically within the purview of each, we can easily distinguish them.

Clearly, governmental centralization gathers immense force when coupled with administrative centralization. It thereby accustoms people to ignore their own wills completely and constantly and to obey, not a single order on a single occasion, but always and in every way. It not only subdues them by force but also ensnares them through their habits. It isolates them and then plucks them one by one from the common mass.

These two types of centralization support each other and share a mutual attraction, but I cannot believe that they are inseparable.

Under Louis XIV, France witnessed the greatest conceivable centralization of its government, because the same man both made the general laws and had the power to interpret them, represented France abroad, and acted in her name. *"L'État, c'est moi,"* he said; and he was right.

Yet under Louis XIV there was far less administrative centralization than there is today.

Today we see one power, England, which has achieved a very high degree of governmental centralization. There the state seems to act as one person. It can arouse immense masses at will, muster its full might, and bring it to bear wherever it wishes.

England, which has achieved such great things over the past fifty years, has no administrative centralization.

For my part, I cannot conceive that a nation can endure, much less prosper, without a high degree of governmental centralization.

But I think that administrative centralization serves only to sap the strength of nations that are subjected to it, because it steadily weakens their civic spirit. To be sure, administrative centralization can gather all of a nation's available forces at a specific time and place, but it impedes the reproduction of those forces. It ensures the nation's victory on the day of battle but over the long run diminishes its might. It can therefore contribute admirably to the passing grandeur of one man but not to the enduring prosperity of an entire people.

Mark this well: when people say that a state cannot act because it is not centralized, they are almost always talking about governmental centralization, though they do not know it. It is often said that the German Empire was never able to take full advantage of its strengths. Granted. But why? Because the national force there was never centralized; because the state was never able to make people obey its general laws; because the separate parts of that great body always had the right or option to withhold their cooperation from the repositories of common authority in the very matters that touched the interests of all citizens; in other words, because there was no governmental centralization. The same remark is applicable to the Middle Ages: all the miseries of feudal society stemmed from the fact that the power not just to administer but to govern was divided among a thousand hands and fragmented in a thousand ways. The absence of all governmental centralization at that time prevented the nations of Europe from advancing energetically toward any goal.

We have seen that administrative centralization does not exist in the United States. Almost no trace of hierarchy is to be found there. Decentralization has been carried to a degree that I believe no European nation could tolerate without profound uneasiness, and which even in America has unfortunate effects. Yet in the United States there is a high degree of governmental centralization. It would be easy to prove that state power there is more concentrated than it was in any of Europe's old monarchies. Not only is there but a single body that makes the laws in every state; not only is there but a single power that can create political life around it; but, in general, Americans have avoided convoking numerous district and county assemblies lest those assemblies be tempted to exceed their administrative prerogatives and impede the action of the government. In America no state legislature has to contend with any power capable of resisting it. Nothing can stand in its way: not privilege or local immunity or personal influence or even the authority of reason, for the legislature represents the majority, which claims to be the sole organ of reason. Hence there is nothing to limit its action but its own will. Alongside it, and under its control, stands the representative of executive power, who with the backing of physical force must compel malcontents to obey.

The weakness of the system is not apparent until one examines certain governmental actions in detail.

The American republics maintain no permanent armed force to curb minorities, but to date no minority has ever been reduced to waging war, and the need for an army has yet to be felt. The state usually relies on town or county officials in its dealings with citizens. In New England, for example, the town assessor apportions the tax; the town tax collector collects it; the town treasurer transmits the proceeds to the public treasury; and any claims that arise are submitted to the common courts. Such a method of collecting taxes is slow and cumbersome. It would constantly hobble any government with great pecuniary needs. In general, it is desirable that a government have, in all matters essential to its existence, officials of its own, chosen by it and serving at its pleasure, and also that it should possess the means to act quickly. But given the way the central power is organized in America, it will always be easy to introduce more energetic and effective means of action as needed.

Therefore, despite what is often repeated, the republics of the New World will not perish because there is no centralization in the United States. One can maintain that American governments, far from being insufficiently centralized, are all too centralized, as I shall prove later on. Every day their legislatures swallow up a little more of the debris of governmental power. They tend to accumulate these remnants in themselves, just as the Convention did. When social power is centralized in this way, it constantly changes hands, because it is subordinate to the power of the people. Because it can do whatever it pleases, it often lacks wisdom and foresight. That is the danger it faces. The threat of death that hangs over it is thus due to its strength, not to its weakness.

Administrative decentralization in America produces a variety of effects.

As we have seen, the Americans isolated administration from government almost entirely. In so doing they seem to me to have trespassed the limits of sound reason, because order, even in secondary matters, is still a national interest.[49]

Since the state has no administrative officials of its own assigned to fixed locations throughout its territory and to whom it can issue a common set of guidelines, it rarely attempts to establish general rules of order. Yet the need for such rules is sorely felt. A European frequently notes their absence. The apparent disorder that prevails on the surface persuades him at first sight that there is complete anarchy in the society. Only when he looks into things more deeply does he disabuse himself.

Certain ventures are of interest to the state as a whole yet cannot be carried out because there is no administration at the state level to direct them. Abandoned to the care of towns and counties, left to elected and temporary agents, they yield no result or produce nothing lasting.

Partisans of centralization in Europe contend that governmental power administers localities better than they could administer themselves. That may be true when the central power is enlightened and the localities are unenlightened, when it is active and they are inert, when it is in the habit of acting and they are in the habit of obeying. One can even appreciate that the more centralization increases, the more pronounced these two tendencies become, so that the capability of one side and the incapability of the other stand out.

I deny that this is so, however, when, as in America, the people are enlightened, alert to their own interests, and accustomed to thinking about them.

Indeed, in that case, I am convinced that the collective strength of citizens will always be a more powerful force than governmental authority for producing social well-being.

[49]Even when the authority that represents the state does not itself engage in administration, it should not, in my view, relinquish the right to oversee administration at the local level. Suppose, for example, that there were in each county an agent of the government responsible for referring to the courts offenses committed in the towns and county. Would not order then be respected more uniformly without compromising the independence of localities? Yet nothing of the kind exists in America. Above the county courts there is nothing, and in a sense it is a matter of chance whether the administrative offenses that those courts ought to punish are brought to their attention.

I grant that it is difficult to say precisely how a slumbering people can be awakened and endowed with the passions and enlightenment it lacks. I am not unaware that it is an arduous enterprise to persuade people that they ought to be concerned with their own affairs. In many cases it would be less difficult to interest them in the details of court etiquette than in the repair of their town hall.

But I also think that when the central administration claims that it can dispense entirely with the free participation of those whose interests are primarily at stake, then it is either deceiving itself or trying to deceive you.

No central power, no matter how enlightened or intelligent one imagines it to be, can by itself embrace all the details of the life of a great people. It cannot, because such a labor is beyond human strength. If it tries to build and operate such a complex machine on its own, it will either content itself with something far short of its goal or exhaust itself in futile efforts.

To be sure, centralization can easily impose a certain uniformity on men's external actions, and in the end one comes to desire that uniformity for itself, independent of the things to which it is applied, just as religious fanatics will worship a statue and forget the deity it represents. Centralization easily succeeds in imposing an appearance of regularity on everyday affairs; in cleverly regulating the details of social organization; in suppressing minor disorders and petty crimes; in maintaining a social status quo that is, strictly speaking, neither decadence nor progress; and in maintaining the social body in a state of administrative somnolence that administrators are in the habit of describing as proper order and public tranquillity.[50] In short, it excels at preventing, not at doing. When it is a matter of stirring a society to its depths or of spurring it forward at a rapid pace, centralization's strength deserts it. If even the slightest cooperation is required of individuals, the

[50]China seems to me the most perfect symbol of the kind of social well-being that a highly centralized administration can offer to peoples who submit to it. Travelers tell us that the Chinese have tranquillity without prosperity, industry without progress, stability without force, and material order without public morality. Their society always gets on fairly well but never very well. I imagine that when China is opened to Europeans, they will find the finest model of administrative centralization that exists in the universe.

vast machine turns out to be astonishingly feeble. It is suddenly reduced to impotence.

Centralization may then, in despair, call upon citizens for help. But it speaks to them in these terms: "You shall do what I want, just as much as I want, and in precisely the way I want. You shall assume responsibility for the details without aspiring to direct the whole. You shall work in the dark, and later you will judge my work by its results." One cannot enlist the cooperation of human beings on such terms. The human will requires freedom in its manner and responsibility in its actions. Man is so made that he would rather stand still than forgo his independence in order to move toward a goal he knows nothing about.

I will not deny that in the United States one often regrets the absence of the uniform rules that seem to regulate our lives at every turn.

On occasion, one encounters striking examples there of indifference and social neglect. Now and then, serious blemishes come to light, blemishes that seem completely at odds with the surrounding civilization.

Useful enterprises that require constant care and rigorous exactitude for success often end up being abandoned, because in America as elsewhere the people proceed by momentary efforts and sudden impulses.

Europeans, accustomed to having officials constantly at hand and meddling in almost everything, find the various cogs of the town's administrative machinery difficult to get used to. In general, it is fair to say that the small details of social organization that make life pleasant and convenient are neglected in America, but the guarantees essential to man in society exist there as much as they do anywhere. Among the Americans, the force that administers the state is less well regulated, less enlightened, less intelligent, but a hundred times greater than in Europe. There is no other country in the world in which people ultimately do more to ensure the well-being of society. I know of no other nation that has managed to build schools as numerous or as effective, or temples better suited to the religious needs of the people, or that does a better job of maintaining local roads. One should not look to the United States, therefore, for uniform or lasting vision, minute attention to detail, or perfection of administrative procedure.[51] What one finds there is an image of strength, a little untamed, to be sure, but full of vigor; and of life, not without mishap, to be sure, but also dynamic and energetic.

If pressed, moreover, I am even willing to concede that a remote and alien central authority might provide the villages and counties of the United States with an administration more efficient than that achieved by officials chosen from their midst. If required, I am willing to grant that America would be more secure, and that wiser and more judicious use would be made of its social resources, if the administration of the whole country were concentrated in one person's hands. Yet I would still prefer the system of decentralization to its opposite because of the *political* advantages that the Americans derive from it.

What good does it do me, after all, if an ever-watchful authority keeps an eye out to ensure that my pleasures will be tranquil and races ahead of me to ward off all danger, sparing me the need even to think about such things, if that authority, even as it removes the smallest thorns from my path, is also absolute master of my liberty and my life; if it monopo-

[51]A talented writer, whose comparison of the finances of the United States with those of France has proved that intelligence cannot always substitute for knowledge of the facts, rightly reproaches Americans for the kind of confusion that can often be found in their town budgets. After citing the budget of a French *département* as a model, he adds: "Thanks to centralization, the admirable creation of a great man, municipal budgets throughout the kingdom are just as orderly or methodical in the humblest of villages as in the greatest of cities." This is a result that I admire, to be sure, yet I find most French *communes* mired, despite their impeccable bookkeeping, in profound ignorance as to their true interests and in a state of apathy so invincible that the society seems to vegetate rather than thrive. Meanwhile, in the same American towns whose budgets are so unmethodical and so utterly lacking in uniformity, I find an enlightened, active, enterprising population; there I contemplate a society that is always at work. This is a stunning sight, for to my way of thinking the principal goal of a good government is to foster the well-being of the people, not to establish a certain order in the midst of their misery. I wonder, therefore, if it might not be possible to ascribe the prosperity of the American town and the disorderly state of its finances to the same cause, and, likewise, the distress of the French *commune* and the perfection of its budget. In any case, I am suspicious of a good that I find mingled with so many ills and find it easy to console myself for an ill that is compensated by so many goods.

lizes vitality and existence to such a degree that when it languishes, everything around it must also languish; when it sleeps, everything must also sleep; and when it dies, everything must also perish?

There are some nations in Europe whose inhabitants think of themselves in a sense as colonists, indifferent to the fate of the place they live in. The greatest changes occur in their country without their cooperation. They are not even aware of precisely what has taken place. They suspect it; they have heard of the event by chance. More than that, they are unconcerned with the fortunes of their village, the safety of their streets, the fate of their church and its vestry. They think that such things have nothing to do with them, that they belong to a powerful stranger called "the government." They enjoy these goods as tenants, without a sense of ownership, and never give a thought to how they might be improved. They are so divorced from their own interests that even when their own security and that of their children is finally compromised, they do not seek to avert the danger themselves but cross their arms and wait for the nation as a whole to come to their aid. Yet as utterly as they sacrifice their own free will, they are no fonder of obedience than anyone else. They submit, it is true, to the whims of a clerk, but no sooner is force removed than they are glad to defy the law as a defeated enemy. Thus one finds them ever wavering between servitude and license.

When a nation has reached this point, it must either change its laws and mores or perish, for the well of public virtue has run dry: in such a place one no longer finds citizens but only subjects.

Such nations, I contend, are ripe for conquest. If they do not vanish from the world's stage, it is because they are surrounded by nations like themselves or worse. Within their breast lurks an ineffable patriotic instinct and I know not what unthinking pride in the name they bear, what vague souvenir of past glory, which, though not connected with anything in particular, is enough to arouse conservative impulses when needed.

It would be a mistake to take reassurance from the fact that people have at times made prodigious efforts to defend countries in which they lived, so to speak, as foreigners. Look carefully at these cases and you will see that religion was almost always the prime mover.

For them, the permanence, glory, and prosperity of the nation had become sacred dogmas, and in defending their homeland they were also defending that holy city of which they were citizens.

The Turkish populations never took any part in directing the affairs of society, yet they accomplished great things as long as they saw the sultans' conquests as triumphs for the religion of Mohammed. Today, the religion is vanishing, and only the despotism remains: the result is collapse.

When Montesquieu attributed a peculiar force to despotism, he did it an honor that in my opinion it does not deserve. By itself, despotism cannot maintain anything for any length of time. When one looks at the matter closely, it becomes clear that what caused absolutist governments to prosper for so long was not fear but religion.

Look where you will, you will never find genuine power among men without the free consent of their wills. There is no power in the world other than patriotism or religion capable of making all citizens march steadily as one toward a single goal.

It is not within the power of the law to revive dying beliefs, but it is within the power of the law to instill in people an interest in the fate of their country. It is within the power of the law to awaken and guide the vague patriotic instinct that dwells permanently in the heart of man and, by linking that instinct to everyday thoughts, passions, and habits, to turn it into a conscious and durable emotion. Let it not be said that it is too late to try: nations do not grow old in the same way as men. Each new generation born among them is fresh material for the lawmaker to mold.

What I admire most in America is not the *administrative* effects of decentralization but the *political* effects. In the United States, patriotic sentiment is pervasive. Whether at the village level or at the level of the Union as a whole, the public interest is a matter of concern. People care about their country's interests as though they were their own. They glory in the nation's glory. In its successes they see their own work and are exalted by it. They rejoice in the general prosperity, from which they profit. They feel for their homeland a feeling analogous to what a man feels for his family, so that a kind of egoism also contributes to their interest in the state.

In the public official the European often sees nothing but force; the American sees right. Thus one can say that in America man never obeys man; he obeys justice, or the law.

Accordingly, his opinion of himself may be inflated, but it is almost always salutary. He trusts fearlessly in his own powers, which he believes to be equal to any situation. Suppose a person conceives of an idea for a project that has a direct bearing on the welfare of society. It would never occur to him to call upon the authorities for assistance. Instead, he will publicize his plan, offer to carry it out, enlist other individuals to pool their forces with his own, and struggle with all his might to overcome every obstacle. No doubt his efforts will often prove less successful than if the state had acted in his stead. In the long run, however, the overall result of all these individual enterprises will far outstrip anything the government could do.

Administrative authority arouses neither jealousy nor hatred because it is close to the people upon whom it is exercised. Since its means of actions are limited, no one feels that he can rely on it exclusively.

Therefore, when a public official acts within the limits of his prerogatives, he is not left to his own resources as in Europe. No one believes that the duties of individuals cease once the representative of the public has acted. On the contrary, everyone offers him guidance, support, and backing.

When the action of individual forces is coupled with that of social forces, it is often possible to accomplish things that would be beyond the reach of the most concentrated and energetic administration.*

I could cite many facts in support of what I am saying, but I would rather look at just one, and choose that which I know best.

*See Note IX, page 495.

In America, the means available to the authorities for discovering crimes and prosecuting criminals are few.

There is no administrative branch of the police; passports are unknown. The police who investigate criminal offenses cannot be compared with our *police judiciaire*. District attorneys have small staffs of investigators, and they are not always permitted to initiate investigations. Questioning of the accused is rapid and oral. Yet I doubt that in any other country crime so seldom goes unpunished.

The reason for this is that everyone believes he has an interest in providing evidence of crime and in apprehending criminals.

During my stay in the United States, I saw the inhabitants of one county in which a major crime had been committed spontaneously organize committees to apprehend the guilty party and turn him over to the courts.

In Europe, the criminal is an unfortunate who is fighting to save his head from agents of the government. The people are merely onlookers in this contest. In America, he is an enemy of the human race and has all humanity against him.

I believe that provincial institutions are useful to all peoples, but nowhere is the need for such institutions more real, in my view, than among peoples whose social state is democratic.

In an aristocracy, one is always sure of maintaining a certain order within liberty.

Because those who govern have a great deal to lose, order is for them a major interest.

It is also fair to say that in an aristocracy, the people are protected against the excesses of despotism, because organized forces prepared to resist the despot are always at hand.

A democracy without provincial institutions possesses no guarantee against such evils.

How can a multitude be made to bear the burden of liberty in great matters when it has not learned to make use of it in small ones?

How can tyranny be resisted in a country where individuals are weak and no common interest binds them together?

Those who fear license, like those who dread absolute power, should therefore desire the gradual development of provincial liberties.

I am convinced, moreover, that no nation is more likely to succumb to the yoke of administrative centralization than one whose social state is democratic.

Several causes contribute to this result, including, among others, the following:

The constant tendency in democratic nations is to concentrate all governmental might in the hands of the one power that directly represents the people, because beyond the people one sees only equal individuals merged indistinctly into a common mass.

Now, when all the prerogatives of government are already vested in a single power, it is difficult for that power to refrain from entering into the details of administration, and over the long run there will be no shortage of opportunities to do so. We have witnessed this ourselves.

The French Revolution exhibited two contradictory tendencies that we must take care not to confuse, one favorable to liberty, the other favorable to despotism.

In the old monarchy, the king alone made law. Below the sovereign power stood the half-shattered remnants of provincial institutions. Those institutions were incoherent, poorly organized, and often absurd. In the hands of the aristocracy they had served at times as instruments of oppression.

The Revolution declared its opposition to both royalty and provincial institutions. Its hatred was directed at everything that preceded it, both absolute power and that which had been able to moderate the rigors thereof. It was at once republican and centralizing.

This dual nature of the French Revolution is a fact that the friends of absolute power have been careful to seize upon. When you see them defending administrative centralization, do you think they labor on behalf of despotism? Not at all: they are defending one of the great conquests of the Revolution.* In this way, it is possible both to remain popular and to oppose the rights of the people, to be a secret servant of tyranny and an avowed lover of liberty.

I have visited the two nations in which the system of provincial liberties has been developed to the highest degree,

*See Note X, page 495.

and I have listened to the voices of the two parties that divide those nations.

In America, I found men who secretly aspired to destroy their country's democratic institutions. In England, I found other men who loudly attacked aristocracy. I did not meet a single person who did not look upon provincial liberty as a great good.

In both countries, I heard the ills of the state imputed to an infinite variety of causes, but never to local liberties.

I heard citizens attribute their nation's greatness or prosperity to a multitude of reasons, but to a man they emphasized provincial liberties first and foremost.

Am I to believe that men so fundamentally divided that they do not agree about religious doctrine or political theory find themselves in agreement about only one thing, something they are better equipped than anyone else to judge because they see it in operation every day with their own eyes, and yet they are mistaken?

Only peoples among whom provincial institutions are entirely or almost entirely non-existent deny their usefulness. In other words, the only people who speak ill of such institutions are those who know nothing about them.

Chapter 6

ON JUDICIAL POWER IN THE UNITED STATES AND ITS EFFECT ON POLITICAL SOCIETY

The Anglo-Americans have preserved all the characteristics of the judicial power that distinguish it in other nations. — They have, however, made it a major political power. — How. — In what respects the judicial system of the Anglo-Americans differs from all others. — Why American judges have the right to declare laws unconstitutional. — How American judges use that right. — Precautions taken by lawmakers to prevent abuse of that right.

I FELT obliged to devote a separate chapter to the judicial power. So great is its political importance that, had I mentioned it only in passing, it seemed to me that I might diminish it in the reader's eye.

There have been confederations elsewhere than in America. Republics have arisen in places other than on the shores of the New World. A number of European states have adopted the representative system. But I do not think that, to date, any other nation in the world has constituted judicial power in the same way as the Americans.

What is most difficult for a foreigner to understand in the United States is the organization of the judiciary. There is virtually no political event in which he does not hear the authority of the judge invoked, and from this he naturally concludes that in the United States the judge ranks among the preeminent political powers. When he subsequently examines the constitution of the courts, their prerogatives and customary procedures strike him at first sight as entirely judicial. In his eyes, the magistrate seems to intervene in public affairs only by chance; but the same chance recurs daily.

When the Parlement of Paris made remonstrances and refused to register an edict, or when it summoned a prevaricating functionary to appear at its bar, the political influence of judicial power was plain to see. But nothing of the kind is visible in the United States.

The Americans have preserved all the characteristics customarily associated with the judicial power. They have scrupulously circumscribed its action within the usual ambit.

The first characteristic of judicial power among all peoples
is to serve as an arbiter. In order for the courts to have grounds
to act, there has to be a dispute. In order for there to be a
judge, there has to be a trial. As long as a law does not give
rise to a dispute, the judicial power has no reason to concern
itself with that law. The law exists, but the judicial power takes
no notice of it. When a judge attacks a law pertinent to a case
that lies before him, he expands his prerogatives but does not
step outside his proper sphere, because in a sense he must
judge the law in order to judge the case. If, however, he were
to pronounce on the law irrespective of any case that lay
before him, he would step outside his sphere altogether and
encroach upon that of the legislative power.

The second characteristic of judicial power is that it pronounces on particular cases and not on general principles. If
a judge, in deciding a particular question, destroys a general
principle because it is clear that any consequence deriving
from that principle will be struck down in the same way, he
does not exceed his natural purview. But if he attacks the general principle directly and demolishes it without having a
particular case in mind, he exceeds the limits that by general
agreement of all peoples circumscribe his authority. He becomes something more important and perhaps more useful
than a magistrate, but he ceases to represent the judicial
power.

The third characteristic of judicial power is that it can act
only when called upon, or, to use the language of the law,
when it is *seised* of a case. This characteristic is not as widely
encountered as the other two. Nevertheless, I believe that, despite the exceptions, it may be considered essential. By its
nature, the judicial power takes no action on its own. If it is
to be roused, it must be set in motion. A crime is brought to
its attention, and it punishes the guilty party. It is called upon
to redress an injustice, and it rectifies the wrong. A text is submitted to it, and it interprets that text. But it does not prosecute criminals, seek out injustice, or examine facts on its own.
The judicial power would in a sense do violence to its passive

nature if it were to take the initiative and set itself up as censor of the laws.

The Americans have preserved these three distinctive characteristics of judicial power. An American judge can render a decision only when there is litigation. He concerns himself only with particular cases. And in order to act, he must always wait until the matter has been laid before him.

The American judge is therefore exactly like the magistrates of other nations. Yet he is vested with immense political power.

Where does this power come from? The American judge moves within the same ambit and relies upon the same means as other judges. Why does he possess a power that they do not?

The source of that power lies in one fact: Americans have granted judges the right to base their decisions on the *Constitution* rather than on *laws*. In other words, they have allowed judges not to apply laws they deem to be unconstitutional.

I know that a similar right has sometimes been claimed by the courts of other countries, but it has never been granted to them. In America it is recognized by all powers. Not a single party or even a single person contests it.

The explanation for this must lie in the very principle of American constitutions.

In France, the Constitution is, or is supposed to be, an immutable work. No power can change anything in it: that is the accepted theory.*

In England, Parliament is acknowledged to have the right to modify the Constitution. In England, therefore, the Constitution can change constantly; or, rather, it does not exist. Parliament, besides being a legislative body, is also a constituent one.†

In America, political theories are simpler and more rational.

An American constitution is not supposed to be immutable, as in France. It cannot be modified by the ordinary powers of society, as in England. It is a thing apart: since it represents the will of all the people, it is binding on legislators as well as

*See Note XI, page 496.
†See Note XII, page 497.

on ordinary citizens, but it can be changed by the will of the people in accordance with an established process under certain specific conditions.

Thus, in America, the Constitution may vary, but as long as it exists, it is the source of all power. Ultimate force rests solely in it.

It is easy to see how these differences must influence the position and rights of the judicial body in the three countries I have mentioned.

If courts in France could disobey laws on the grounds that they found them unconstitutional, constituent power would really be in their hands, since they alone would have the right to interpret a constitution whose terms no one else could change. They would therefore set themselves in the place of the nation and dominate society, insofar at least as the inherent weakness of the judicial power allowed.

I know that by denying judges the right to declare laws unconstitutional, we indirectly give the legislative body the power to change the Constitution, because no legal barrier now stands in its way. Yet it is still better to grant the power to change the people's Constitution to men who imperfectly represent the will of the people rather than to men who represent only themselves.

It would be even more unreasonable to give English judges the right to resist the will of the legislative body, since Parliament, which makes the law, also makes the Constitution, and one cannot in any case call a law unconstitutional when it emanates from the three powers.

But neither of these arguments is applicable to America.

In the United States, the Constitution rules legislators as it rules ordinary citizens. It is therefore the primary law, and cannot be modified by a law. Hence it is just for courts to obey the Constitution in preference to all the laws. This flows from the very essence of the judicial power: to choose among the provisions of law those that bind him most narrowly is in a sense the magistrate's natural right.

In France, the Constitution is also the first of laws, and judges have an equal right to take it as the basis of their decisions. But they cannot exercise that right without trampling on a right still more sacred than their own: that of the society in whose name they act. Here, ordinary reason must give way to the reason of state.

In America, where the nation can always oblige magistrates to obey by amending its Constitution, no such danger is to be feared. On this point politics and logic are therefore in agreement, and both the people and the judge retain their privileges.

In the courts of the United States, if a law is invoked that the judge deems to be contrary to the Constitution, he may therefore refuse to apply it. This is the only power peculiar to the American magistrate, but from it flows great political influence.

Very few laws are of a nature to escape judicial scrutiny for long, for there are very few laws that are not adverse to some person's interest and that litigants cannot or should not invoke before the courts.

Now, the moment a judge refuses to apply a law in a case, it loses part of its moral force. People injured by it are put on notice that there exists a way to avoid the obligation to obey it: cases multiply, and the law subsides into impotence. At that point one of two things happens: either the people change the Constitution, or the legislature repeals the law.

Americans have thus entrusted their courts with immense political power. But by obliging them to attack laws only by judicial means, they have greatly diminished the dangers of that power.

Had the judge been allowed to attack laws in a theoretical and general fashion, had he been permitted to seize the initiative and censure the legislator, his entry onto the stage of politics would have been impressive indeed. As the champion or adversary of one party, he would have invited all the passions that divide the country to join the fray. But when a judge strikes down a law in some obscure debate and with some particular application in mind, he partially conceals the importance of his attack from the public eye. His decision is designed only to strike at some individual interest; if the law is injured, it is only by chance.

Furthermore, the law thus censured is not nullified; its moral force is diminished, but its material effect remains. Only gradually does it succumb to the repeated blows of jurisprudence.

It is easy to see, moreover, that by leaving it up to private interest to instigate censure of the laws, and by tying the case brought against the law intimately to the case brought against an individual, one ensures that legislation will not be subject to frivolous attack. Under this system, the law is no longer exposed to daily aggression by the parties. In pointing out the faults of the legislator, one fills a real need: one starts with a positive, palpable fact, since it must serve as the basis of a trial.

I am not sure whether these procedures of the American courts, in addition to being more conducive to public order, are not also more conducive to liberty.

If judges had to attack legislators head on, there would be times when they would be afraid to do so and other times when partisan spirit would compel them to risk it repeatedly. Hence the laws would be attacked when the power from which they emanate was weak, and people would submit to them without a murmur when it was strong. In other words, the laws would often be attacked when it was most useful to respect them, and they would be respected when it became easy to oppress in their name.

The American judge is lured onto political terrain in spite of himself, however. He judges the law only because he has to judge a case, and he cannot avoid judging the case. The political question that he must resolve is bound up with the interests of the litigants, and he cannot refuse to decide the case without denying justice to the parties. In fulfilling the strict duties imposed on the magistrate by profession, he acts as a citizen. It is true that judicial censure exercised in this way by the courts cannot cover all the laws, because there are some that can never give rise to the sort of clearly formulated contest that we call a trial. And when such a contest is possible, it is conceivable that no one will be found to bring the case before the courts.

Americans have often felt this inconvenience, but they have left the remedy incomplete lest they invest it in every case with a dangerous efficacy.

Confined within proper limits, the power granted to American courts to pronounce on the unconstitutionality of laws still constitutes one of the most powerful barriers ever erected against the tyranny of political assemblies.

OTHER POWERS GRANTED TO
AMERICAN JUDGES

In the United States, all citizens have the right to accuse public officials before the ordinary courts. — How they use that right. — Article 75 of the French Constitution of Year VIII. — The Americans and the English cannot understand the sense of this article.

It hardly needs mentioning that among a free people, like the Americans, every citizen has the right to bring charges against public officials to the attention of ordinary judges, and every judge has the right to pronounce sentence on public officials, for it is only natural that this should be the case.

To allow the courts to punish agents of the executive power when they violate the law is not to grant them any special privilege. To forbid them to do so is rather to take away one of their natural rights.

The fact that officials in the United States are responsible before the courts did not seem to me to weaken the springs of government.

On the contrary, it seemed to me that the Americans, by acting in this way, increased the respect that is due to those who govern, since they are far more careful to avoid criticism.

Nor did I see many political cases being brought in the United States, and this I find easy to explain. A trial of any kind is always a difficult and costly undertaking. It is easy to accuse a public figure in the newspapers, but grave reasons must exist before anyone will decide to file charges against him in court. In order to prosecute an official under the law, just cause for complaint has to exist, and officials are unlikely to provide such a cause if they are afraid of being prosecuted.

This does not depend on the republican form that the Americans have adopted, because the same experience can be had every day in England.

These two peoples did not believe that they had secured their independence by allowing the principal agents of government to be impeached. They thought that freedom could be guaranteed far better by enabling the least of citizens to bring suit routinely in small matters than by relying on grand proceedings that are either never invoked or initiated only when it is too late.

In the Middle Ages, when criminals were very difficult to apprehend, judges often inflicted dreadful tortures on those unfortunate enough to fall into their hands. This did nothing to diminish the number of the guilty. Since then, people have learned that by making justice both more certain and more mild, they also make it more effective.

The Americans and the English think that arbitrariness and tyranny ought to be treated like theft: prosecution should be facilitated and punishment alleviated.

In Year VIII of the French Republic, there appeared a constitution whose article 75 was conceived in these terms: "Agents of the government, other than ministers, cannot be prosecuted for acts relating to their functions except by decision of the Council of State; in that case, the prosecution takes place before the ordinary courts."

The Constitution of Year VIII passed away, but not this article, which lingered after it. It is still invoked every day in opposition to citizens' just demands.

I have often tried to make the sense of this article 75 clear to Americans and Englishmen, and I have always had a hard time of it.

What first struck them was that the Council of State in France is a high court that sits at the center of the kingdom. There was a sort of tyranny in obliging all litigants to appear before it in preliminary hearings.

But when I tried to make them understand that the Council of State was not a judicial body in the ordinary sense of the word but an administrative body whose members are subordinate to the king, so that the king, after issuing to one of his servants, known as a prefect, a sovereign order to commit an iniquitous act could then issue to another of his servants, known as a councilor of state, a sovereign order not to punish the offender; and when I pointed out to them that the citizen injured by the prince's order was reduced to asking the prince himself for permission to seek justice; they refused to believe in such enormities and accused me of either falsehood or ignorance.

Under the old monarchy it was common for Parlement to order the arrest of public officials guilty of some offense. In some cases, royal authority intervened and ordered the case dismissed. Despotism thereby openly showed its face, and to obey was merely to submit to force.

We have thus given up much of the ground that our fathers had won; for under the banner of justice and in the name of the law we permit things to be done that could only be imposed on them by violence.

Chapter 7

ON POLITICAL JUDGMENT
IN THE UNITED STATES

What the author means by political judgment. — How political judgment is understood in France, England, and the United States. — In America the political judge is concerned only with public officials. — He orders removal from office rather than imposing punishment. — Political judgment, an ordinary means of government. — Political judgment as understood in the United States is, in spite or perhaps because of its mildness, a very powerful weapon in the hands of the majority.

B Y political judgment I mean the decision pronounced by a political body temporarily vested with the right to judge.

In absolute governments, extraordinary judicial procedures are pointless: because the prince, in whose name the accused is prosecuted, is master of the courts as of everything else, he need seek no warrant for his action beyond the conception of his might that exists in his subjects' minds. The only thing he might conceivably have to fear is that even the outward appearance of justice might fail to be maintained, and that those seeking to strengthen his authority might thereby bring it into disrepute.

But in most free countries, where the majority's influence on the courts cannot be compared with that of an absolute prince, judicial power has at times been placed temporarily in the hands of society's representatives. To confound the powers temporarily in this way seemed preferable to violating the necessary principle of unity of government. England, France, and the United States have made political judgment a part of their laws, and it is interesting to see the different uses they make of it.

In England the House of Lords and in France the Chambre des Pairs sit as the nation's high criminal court.[1] Neither house tries all political offenses, but both are competent to do so.

---

[1] In England, moreover, the House of Lords sits as the final court of appeals in certain civil cases. See Blackstone, book III, chap. 4.

The right to accuse is vested in another political body. In this respect there is only one difference between the two countries: in England, the members of the House of Commons can accuse anyone they please before the House of Lords, whereas in France deputies can impeach only ministers of the king.

Furthermore, the upper chamber in both countries may apply to offenders any law in the penal code.

In the United States, as in Europe, the right to accuse is vested in one of the two branches of the legislature, while the right to judge is vested in the other. The House of Representatives denounces the offender; the Senate punishes him.

Only the *representatives* can lay the matter before the Senate, however, and they may bring charges only against *public officials*. Thus the jurisdiction of the Senate is more limited than that of the Court of Peers in France, while the representatives have a broader right to impeach.

But the greatest difference between America and Europe is this: in Europe, political tribunals can apply all the provisions of the penal code; in America, once they have stripped the offender of his public functions and declared him unworthy to hold further public office, their powers are exhausted, and the task of the ordinary courts begins.

Suppose that the President of the United States has committed a crime of high treason.

The House of Representatives impeaches him, and the senators remove him from office. He then appears before a jury, which alone can deprive him of life and liberty.

We can now see our subject in a vivid light.

When Europeans made political judgment a part of their law, they aimed to strike at great criminals regardless of their birth, rank, or power in the state. In order to accomplish this, they temporarily invested a great political body with all the prerogatives of the courts.

The legislator was thereby transformed into a magistrate. He was able to establish the existence of a crime and try and punish the criminal. In granting the legislator the rights of a judge, the law imposed on him all the obligations thereof and required him to respect all legal formalities.

When a political tribunal in France or England hears a case against a public official and pronounces sentence on him, it *ipso facto* deprives him of office and may also declare him un-worthy to occupy any future office, but here the removal from office and banishment from politics are consequences of the judgment rather than its content.

In Europe, political judgment is therefore more a judicial act than an administrative measure.

The opposite is true in the United States, where it is easy to see that political judgment is more an administrative meas-ure than a judicial act.

It is true that the judgment of the Senate is judicial in form. In rendering it, the senators are obliged to respect procedural formalities and customs. It is also judicial as to its grounds for legal action; in general, the Senate is obliged to base its de-cision on a violation of common law. But its objective is administrative.

If the principal aim of American lawmakers had really been to arm a political body with great judicial power, they would not have limited the purview of that body to public officials, because the most dangerous enemies of the state may not hold office. This is especially true in republics, where power stems primarily from the favor of political parties, and a man is often all the more formidable because he exercises no legal power of any kind.

If American lawmakers had wanted to invest society itself with the power to ward off great crimes as judges do, by sowing fear of punishment, they would have allowed politi-cal tribunals to avail themselves of all the resources of the penal code; instead they equipped those tribunals with a less than adequate weapon, one ill-suited to dealing with the most dangerous of criminals. For what does banishment from pol-itics signify to a person bent on overthrowing the law itself?

The primary purpose of political judgment in the United States is therefore to withdraw power from a person who has made poor use of it and to prevent power from being granted to that same citizen in the future. This is clearly an administrative act that has been cloaked in the solemnity of a judgment.

In this matter the Americans have therefore created some-thing mixed. They have applied the guarantees inherent in political judgment to the question of administrative removal from office, and they have deprived political judgment of its severest sanctions.

Once this principle has been established, everything else follows. It becomes clear why American constitutions make civilian officials subject to the jurisdiction of the Senate yet exempt military officers, whose crimes are nevertheless more to be feared. In the civilian order, American officials cannot be dismissed in the ordinary sense of the term: some enjoy tenure of office, while others derive their powers from a mandate that cannot be abrogated. So, in order to deprive them of power, they must be brought to judgment. But military officers serve at the pleasure of the chief of state, who is himself a civilian official. If a blow is struck at the chief of state, it strikes them as well.[2]

If we now compare the European to the American system with an eye to the actual or potential effects of each, the differences we find are no less marked.

In France and England, political judgment is seen as an exceptional weapon that society should use only to save itself in moments of great peril.

There is no denying that political judgment as it is understood in Europe violates the conservative principle of the division of powers and poses a constant threat to life and liberty.

Political judgment in the United States violates the principle of the division of powers only indirectly; it does not threaten citizens in their very existence; it does not hover, as in Europe, over everyone's head, since it is aimed only at those who, in accepting public office, agree in advance to the rigors thereof.

It is less fearsome as well as less effective.

Consequently, the lawmakers of the United States saw it not as an extreme remedy for society's great ills but as an ordinary means of government.

In this respect, it may have more real influence on society in America than in Europe. Indeed, one should be careful not to be misled by the apparent mildness of American legislation regarding political judgments. Note, first of all, that in the

---

[2]An officer cannot be deprived of his rank but he can be relieved of his command.

United States the tribunal that pronounces such judgments is composed of the same elements and subject to the same influences as the body charged with making accusations, which lends almost irresistible force to the vindictive passions of the parties. Although political judges in the United States cannot pronounce sentences as severe as those pronounced by political judges in Europe, there is in consequence a smaller chance that they will render an acquittal. The sentence is less terrible and more certain.

When Europeans established political tribunals, their primary purpose was to *punish* the guilty, whereas the primary purpose of the Americans was to *deprive them of power*. Political judgment in the United States is in some ways a preventive measure. Hence judges there must not be bound by the very precise definitions of criminal law.

There is nothing more frightening than the vagueness of American laws defining political crimes as such: "The President . . . shall be removed from office on impeachment for, and conviction of, treason, bribery or other high crimes and misdemeanors" (says Article 1, Section 4, of the Constitution of the United States). Most state constitutions are even more obscure.

"The Senate shall be a court with full authority to hear and determine all impeachments made by the House of Representatives against any officer or officers of the Commonwealth for misconduct and maladministration in their offices," says the Constitution of Massachusetts.[3] "All officers offending against the state either by maladministration, corruption, neglect of duty, or any other high crime or misdemeanor, shall be impeachable by the House of Delegates," says the Constitution of Virginia. There are constitutions that specify no crime so as to place no limit on the responsibility of public officials.[4]

But what makes American laws on this matter so fearsome stems, I daresay, from their very mildness.

We have seen that in Europe, the removal of an official from office and his banishment from politics were among the con-

---

[3]Chapter 1, Section 2, Subsection 8.
[4]See the Constitutions of Illinois, Maine, Connecticut, and Georgia.

sequences of his punishment while in America they were the punishment itself. This yields the following result: in Europe, political tribunals possess awesome powers, which in some cases they do not know how to use; and for fear of punishing too much they may not punish at all. In America, however, no one shrinks from imposing a punishment that does not cause humanity to moan: to condemn a political enemy to death in order to deprive him of power is in everyone's eyes a horrible crime of murder; to declare one's adversary unworthy of wielding that same power, and to deprive him of it without depriving him of life and liberty, may seem the fair outcome of a struggle.

Though easy to pronounce, such a judgment is nevertheless the height of misfortune for those to whom it is ordinarily applied. Great criminals may well brave its futile rigors; ordinary men will see it as a doom that ruins their position, stains their honor, and condemns them to a shameful idleness worse than death.

Political judgment exerts all the more influence on the direction of society in the United States because it seems less terrifying. It does not act directly on the governed but makes those who govern entirely subject to the will of the majority. It does not give the legislature a power so immense that it can be exercised only in time of crisis. It allows it to assume a moderate and regular authority that can be used day in and day out. Although it is a less powerful weapon, it is also more convenient to use and easier to abuse.

By preventing political tribunals from pronouncing judicial sentences, the Americans therefore seem to me to have avoided the most dreadful consequences of legislative tyranny rather than the tyranny itself. All things considered, I am not sure that political judgment as it is understood in the United States is not the most formidable weapon ever placed in the hands of the majority.

I think that it will be easy to recognize when the American Republics begin to degenerate: it will suffice to see whether the number of political judgments increases.[*]

---

[*]See Note XIII, page 498.

Chapter 8

ON THE FEDERAL CONSTITUTION

So FAR I have looked upon each state as forming a complete whole, and I have shown the various mechanisms that the people of each state set in motion and the way in which they did so. But all these states, which I have treated as independent, are in certain cases obliged to obey a superior authority, that of the Union. The time has come to examine the portion of sovereignty that was conceded to the Union and to cast a rapid glance at the federal constitution.[1]

HISTORY OF THE FEDERAL CONSTITUTION

Origin of the first Union. — Its weakness. — Congress appeals to the constituent power. — Interval of two years between that moment and the promulgation of the new Constitution.

As I said earlier, the thirteen colonies that simultaneously threw off the English yoke at the end of the last century shared the same religion, the same language, the same mores, and almost the same laws; they fought a common enemy; they should therefore have had powerful reasons to unite closely with one another and consolidate as a single nation.

But each of them, having always enjoyed a separate existence and a government close to home, had developed its own interests and distinctive customs and was reluctant to enter into a solid and total union that would have submerged the individual importance of each in the common importance of all. Hence two conflicting tendencies arose: one that drove the Anglo-Americans to unite and another that impelled them to divide.

As long as war with the mother country continued, necessity ensured that the principle of union would prevail. And while the laws that constituted that union were defective, the common bond survived in spite of them.[2]

[1] See the text of the federal constitution.

[2] See the articles of the first confederation, formed in 1778. This federal constitution was not adopted by all the states until 1781.

See also the analysis of this constitution in *The Federalist* from no. 15

As soon as peace was concluded, however, the flaws in that legislation became glaringly apparent: the state seemed suddenly to dissolve. Each colony, having become an independent republic, laid claim to full sovereignty. The federal government, condemned to weakness by its own constitution and no longer sustained by a sense of public danger, saw its flag insulted by the great nations of Europe, even as it failed to muster resources sufficient to stand up to the Indian nations or to pay the interest on debts contracted during the War for Independence. On the point of perishing, it officially declared itself impotent and appealed to the constituent power.[3]

If ever America achieved, however briefly, that high pinnacle of glory that it forever occupies in the proud imagination of its inhabitants, it was in that supreme moment, when the national government in a sense abdicated its authority.

That a people should fight hard to achieve its independence is a spectacle by no means uncommon; one finds it repeated in century after century. The efforts of the Americans to free themselves from the yoke of the English have been greatly exaggerated, moreover. Separated from its enemies by 1,300 leagues of ocean and aided by a powerful ally, the United States owed its victory far more to its situation than to the valor of its armies or the patriotism of its citizens. Who would be so brazen as to compare America's war to the wars of the French Revolution, or the efforts of the Americans to ours, when France, attacked by the whole of Europe, without money, without credit, and without allies, hurled a twentieth of her population at the enemy, with one hand snuffing out the fire that devoured her entrails and with the other brandishing the torch in every direction? What is new in the history of societies, however, is the sight of a great nation, warned by its lawmakers that the wheels of government are grinding to a halt, calmly and fearlessly turning its gaze upon itself, sounding the depths of its ills, refraining from action for two whole years while patiently seeking a remedy, and

---

through no. 22, and Mr. Story in his *Commentaries on the Constitution of the United States*, pp. 85–115.

[3]Congress made this declaration on February 21, 1787.

when at last that remedy is found, submitting to it voluntarily without costing humanity a single tear or drop of blood.

When the inadequacy of the first federal constitution became apparent, the effervescence of political passions stirred by the revolution had somewhat subsided, and all the great men it had brought to prominence were still alive. America was thus twice blessed. The assembly responsible for drafting the second Constitution had relatively few members[4] but included the finest minds and noblest characters the New World had ever seen. George Washington presided.

After lengthy and mature deliberation, this national commission at last submitted to the people for adoption the body of organic laws that still governs the Union today. All the states ratified it, one after another.[5] The new federal government commenced its functions in 1789, after a two-year interregnum. Thus the American Revolution ended just as ours began.

SUMMARY OF THE FEDERAL CONSTITUTION

Division of powers between federal and state sovereignty. — State government is the rule and federal government the exception.

The first question the Americans faced was that of dividing sovereignty in such a way that the various states of the Union would continue to govern themselves in all matters pertaining solely to their internal prosperity yet without causing the nation as a whole, represented by the Union, to cease to exist as a body or to fail to meet its general needs. The question was complex, and difficult to resolve.

It was impossible to specify fully and precisely in advance the share of power that was to be granted to each of the two governments between which sovereignty was to be divided. Who can foresee the life of a nation in all its detail?

---

[4]It was composed of 55 members. Washington, Madison, Hamilton, and the two Morrises were included.

[5]It was not the legislators who ratified the Constitution. The people chose representatives specifically for this sole purpose. The new Constitution was discussed in depth in each of these assemblies.

The duties and rights of the federal government were simple and fairly easy to define, because the Union had been formed to respond to a small number of important general needs. By contrast, the duties and rights of state governments were manifold and complex, because the states were involved in every detail of social life.

Hence the prerogatives of the federal government were carefully defined, and it was stipulated that any prerogative not comprised within that definition was to be retained by the states. Thus state governments remained the rule; the federal government was the exception.[6]

But since it was foreseen that in practice questions might arise as to the precise limits of this exceptional government, and that it would be dangerous to leave the resolution of such questions to the ordinary courts instituted in the various states by the states themselves, a high federal court was created,[7] a unique tribunal, one of whose prerogatives was to maintain the division of powers between the two rival governments as established by the Constitution.[8]

---

[6]See amendments to the federal Constitution. *Federalist*, no. 32. Story, p. 711. Kent's *Commentaries*, vol. 1, p. 364.

Note, moreover, that whenever the Constitution does not reserve to Congress the *exclusive* right to deal with certain matters, the states may do so until it pleases Congress to act. For example, Congress has the right to pass a general law regarding bankruptcy. It does not do so. Each state may then adopt a law of its own. What is more, this point was not established until after the matter had been debated in the courts. It is merely a matter of jurisprudence.

[7]The action of this court is indirect, as we shall see later on.

[8]*Federalist* no. 41 explains the division of sovereignty between the Union and the individual states as follows: "The powers delegated by the proposed Constitution to the federal government are few and defined. Those which are to remain in the state governments are numerous and indefinite. The former will be exercised principally on external objects, as war, peace, negotiation, and foreign commerce. . . . The powers reserved to the several States will extend to all the objects which, in the ordinary course of affairs, concern the lives, liberties, and properties of the people and the internal order, improvement, and prosperity of the State."

I shall often have occasion to quote *The Federalist* in this work. When the proposed legislation that has since become the Constitution of the United States was still before the people awaiting ratification, three men, already celebrated and since to become more so — John Jay, Hamilton, and Madison — joined forces in order to point out to the nation the advantages of the plan being submitted to it. To that end, they published in the form of a newsletter

PREROGATIVES OF THE FEDERAL GOVERNMENT

Power granted to the federal government to make peace and war and establish general taxes. — Internal political matters within its purview. — The government of the Union more centralized in some respects than was the royal government under the old French monarchy.

Nations, when dealing with one another, are no more than individuals. It is above all to gain advantage in dealing with foreigners that a nation needs a single government.

The Union was therefore granted the exclusive right to make peace and war, to negotiate commercial treaties, to raise armies, and to equip fleets.[9]

The need for a national government to direct the internal affairs of society is less imperiously felt.

Still, there are certain general interests that only a general authority can usefully provide for.

The right to regulate all things pertaining to the value of money was left to the Union. The Union was also made responsible for the postal service. It was given the right to open the great avenues of communication that were to unite the various parts of the country.[10]

Broadly speaking, each state government was considered to be free to act within its own sphere. Yet a state government might abuse that independence and, by acting imprudently, compromise the security of the Union as a whole. In these rare cases, spelled out in advance, the federal government was to be allowed to intervene in the internal affairs of the states.[11]

---

a series of articles, which together form a complete treatise. They called this newsletter *The Federalist*, and that title has carried over to the publication in book form.

The Federalist is a beautiful book, and although it is specifically concerned with America, statesmen of all countries ought to be familiar with it.

[9]See Constitution, sec. 8; *Federalist*, nos. 41 and 42; Kent's *Commentaries*, vol. I, pp. 207 ff.; Story, pp. 358–382 and 409–416.

[10]There are several other rights of this kind, such as the right to establish a general law of bankruptcy and the right to grant patents. One has a fairly clear sense of what made it necessary for the entire Union to intervene in such matters.

[11]Even in these cases its intervention is indirect. The Union intervenes through its courts, as we shall see later on.

Thus, even though each of the confederated republics was recognized as having the power to change its laws, none was permitted to pass retroactive laws or to establish a body of nobles.[12]

Finally, since the federal government had to be able to meet its assigned obligations, it was granted the unlimited right to levy taxes.[13]

If we take into account the division of powers established by the federal Constitution, as well as the portion of sovereignty that the individual states reserved to themselves as opposed to the share of power taken by the Union, it is easy to see that the framers of the federal Constitution had formed very clear and very accurate ideas about what I earlier called governmental centralization.

The United States is not only a republic but also a confederation. Yet national authority there is in some respects more centralized than it used to be in several of Europe's absolute monarchies. I shall mention just two examples of this.

France used to have thirteen sovereign courts, which ordinarily enjoyed the right to interpret the law with no possibility of appeal. It also had certain provinces known as *pays d'États*, which could refuse to cooperate when the sovereign authority charged with representing the nation ordered that a tax be levied.

The Union has but a single tribunal to interpret the law, just as it has a single legislature to make it. A tax voted by the representatives of the nation is an obligation placed upon each and every citizen. In these two essential respects, the Union is therefore more centralized than the French monarchy once was. Yet the Union is a mere assemblage of confederated republics.

In Spain, certain provinces had the power to set up their own customs systems, a power that by its very essence is linked to national sovereignty.

In America, only Congress has the right to regulate interstate commerce. The government of the confederation is therefore more centralized in this respect than that of the Spanish realm.

---

[12]Federal Constitution, art. 1, sec. 10.

[13]Constitution, secs. 8, 9, and 10; *Federalist*, nos. 30–36 inclusive, 41, 42, 43, and 44; Kent's *Commentaries*, vol. 1, pp. 207 and 381; Story, pp. 329, 514.

Of course, since royal governments in France and Spain were always in a position to carry out, by force if need be, measures that they had no right to carry out under the kingdom's constitution, the ultimate result was the same. Here, however, I am speaking theoretically.

FEDERAL POWERS

Once the sphere of action of the federal government had been clearly delineated, the next problem was to set that government's wheels in motion.

LEGISLATIVE POWERS

Division of the legislative body into two branches. — Differences in the composition of the two houses. — The principle of state independence triumphs in the composition of the Senate. — The dogma of national sovereignty in the composition of the House of Representatives. — Singular effects resulting from the fact that constitutions are logical only when peoples are young.

In many respects, the organization of the powers of the Union followed the plan laid down in advance by the various state constitutions.

The federal legislative body of the Union consisted of a Senate and a House of Representatives.

In a spirit of conciliation, different rules were applied to the composition of each of these assemblies.

Earlier I pointed out that when the federal constitution was being drafted, two opposing sets of interests were in contention. From those two sets of interests came two distinct bodies of opinion.

One group of people wanted the Union to be a league of independent states, a sort of congress, in which representatives of separate nations would come together to discuss certain matters of common interest.

Another group wanted to consolidate all inhabitants of the former colonies into a single nation and to give them a government capable of acting, within a limited sphere to be sure, as that nation's sole and unique representative. The practical consequences of these two theories were very different.

For instance, if there was to be a league rather than a national government, it was up to the majority of states to make the law and not the majority of inhabitants of the Union. Each state, whether large or small, would then remain an independent power and join the union on a footing of perfect equality with every other state.

If, on the other hand, the inhabitants of the United States were seen as constituting a single nation, it was natural that the law should be made solely by a majority of the citizens of the Union.

Obviously the small states could not agree to this doctrine without completely ceasing to exist where matters of federal sovereignty were concerned. Instead of being coequal powers, the small states would then have been reduced to an insignificant fraction of a large population. The first system would have awarded them unreasonable power; the second would have reduced them to insignificance.

What happened in this situation was what almost always happens when interests and logic clash: the rules of logic were bent. The framers adopted a middle path that peremptorily reconciled two theoretically irreconcilable systems.

The principle of state independence triumphed in the composition of the Senate, the dogma of national sovereignty in the composition of the House of Representatives.

Each state would send two senators to Congress along with a number of representatives proportional to its population.[14]

[14]Every ten years, Congress recalculates the number of congressmen that each state is to send to the House of Representatives. The total number was 69 in 1789; in 1833 it was 240. (*American Almanac*, 1834, p. 194.)

The Constitution stated that there should be no more than one representative for every 30,000 people, but no minimum was specified. Congress has not felt it necessary to increase the number of representatives in proportion to the population. Under the terms of the first law on the subject, of April 14, 1792 (see Story, *Laws of the United States*, vol. 1, p. 235), it was decided that there should be one representative for every 33,000 inhabitants. The most recent law, passed in 1832, set the figure at one representative for every 48,000 inhabitants. The population represented consists of all free men plus three-fifths of the number of slaves.

As a result of this arrangement, the state of New York today has forty representatives in Congress and only two senators; the state of Delaware has two senators and only one representative. In the Senate, Delaware is therefore the equal of New York, while New York has forty times as much influence as Delaware in the House of Representatives. Thus a minority of the nation, dominating the Senate, can completely paralyze the will of the majority, represented by the other house; this is contrary to the spirit of constitutional government.

All this shows how rare and difficult it is to make the law logical and rational in all its parts.

In any nation, diverse interests always emerge in the long run, and various rights are consecrated by the passage of time. When the time comes to establish a general constitution, those interests and rights become natural obstacles to pursuing any political principle to its logical end. Only at the inception of a society is it possible to frame its laws in a fully logical fashion. If a nation enjoys such an advantage, do not be too hasty to conclude that it is wise; think instead that it is young.

When the federal constitution was drafted, the Anglo-Americans had just two interests, and these were diametrically opposed: each state had an interest in preserving its individuality, while the people as a whole had an interest in forming a union. A compromise had to be reached.

It must be granted, however, that this part of the Constitution has yet to produce the ills that one might have feared.

All the states are young. One is much like another. Their mores, ideas, and needs are homogeneous. Though some are larger than others, differences of size alone have not given rise to strongly opposing interests. Thus, in the Senate, the smaller states have never joined forces to thwart the designs of the larger ones. In any case, the legal expression of the will of an entire people is so irresistible that, when the majority speaks through the House of Representatives, the Senate finds itself very weak by comparison.

Bear in mind, moreover, that it was not within the power of American lawmakers to create a single, unified nation out of the people to whom they wished to give laws. The aim of the federal constitution was not to eliminate the states but

simply to circumscribe their existence. Because these subsidiary bodies were to be left with real power (which could
not be taken away from them), the use of force to bend them
to the will of the majority was renounced in advance. That
being the case, there was nothing extraordinary about trying
to ensure that the powers of the individual states would mesh
smoothly with the machinery of the federal government. To
do so was merely to acknowledge an existing fact: that of a
recognized power that had to be accommodated rather than
coerced.

ANOTHER DIFFERENCE BETWEEN
THE SENATE AND THE HOUSE
OF REPRESENTATIVES

*The Senate named by provincial legislators. — The representatives,
by the people. — Election of the former in two stages. — A single
stage for the latter. — Duration of the mandate for each. —
Prerogatives.*

The Senate differs from the other house not only by
virtue of the principle of representation itself but also with
respect to its mode of election, term of office, and range of
prerogatives.

The House of Representatives is named by the people; the
Senate, by the legislators of each state.

One is the product of direct election, the other of election
in two stages.

A representative's term of office is just two years; that of a
senator, six years.

The House of Representatives has only legislative functions.
It shares judicial power only when it impeaches public officials. The Senate cooperates in the shaping of the laws. It
judges political offenses that are placed before it by the House
of Representatives. It is also the nation's high executive council. Treaties concluded by the president must be ratified by the
Senate. His appointments do not become final unless approved by the same body.[15]

---

[15]See *Federalist*, nos. 52–66. Story, pp. 199–314. Constitution, secs. 2 and 3.

ON THE EXECUTIVE POWER[16]

Dependence of the president. — Elective and responsible. — Free within his sphere; the Senate oversees but does not direct him. — The president's salary is fixed when he takes office. — Suspensive veto.

American lawmakers faced a difficult task: they wished to create an executive power dependent on the majority yet with enough power of its own to act freely within its sphere.

In order to maintain the republican form of government, it was essential that the representative of the executive power be subject to the national will.

The president is an elected official. His honor, property, liberty, and life stand as constant guarantees to the people that he will make good use of his power. In exercising that power, moreover, he is not entirely independent: the Senate oversees him in relations with foreign powers as well as in the distribution of appointments, so that he can neither corrupt nor be corrupted.

The Union's lawgivers recognized that the executive power could not properly or usefully perform its task unless they could make it stronger and more stable than it was in the individual states.

The president, they therefore decided, was to be elected for four years and could be re-elected. His future assured, he could muster the courage and resources necessary to work for the public good.

They made the president the sole and unique representative of the executive power of the Union. They even refrained from subjecting his decisions to the approval of a council: councils are dangerous because they not only weaken the government but diminish the responsibility of those who govern. The Senate has the power to nullify certain presidential actions, but it cannot force him to act or share executive power with him.

Legislative action on the executive can be direct. We have just seen that care was taken in America to ensure that this would not be the case there. Legislative action can also be indirect.

Congress, by depriving public officials of their salaries, can strip away a portion of their independence. There is reason to

---

[16]*Federalist*, nos. 67–77. Constitution, art. 2. Story, pp. 315, 515–780. Kent's *Commentaries*, p. 255.

fear that a body that is mistress of the law may gradually whittle away the share of power that the Constitution sought to reserve to others.

This dependence of the executive power is one of the defects inherent in republican constitutions. The Americans were unable to eliminate the temptation for legislative assemblies to seize the reins of government, but they were able to make it less irresistible.

The president's salary is fixed when he takes office for as long as he remains in power. In addition, the president is armed with a suspensive veto, which enables him to halt the passage of laws that might undermine the independence granted to him under the Constitution. Still, the battle between the president and Congress is inevitably unequal, since the latter, by persevering in its designs, is in a position to overcome any and all resistance to its wishes. Nevertheless, the veto forces it to revisit its decisions. Congress must reconsider the vetoed bill, which does not carry unless it receives a two-thirds majority. Furthermore, the veto is in a way an appeal to the people. For the executive, which but for this guarantee might have been subject to secret pressures, it is an opportunity to plead its case and make its reasons known. But if the legislature persists in its designs, can it not vanquish all resistance? To that I respond that there is in every constitution, regardless of its nature, a point at which the legislator is obliged to place his faith in the good sense and virtue of his fellow citizens. That point is nearer to hand and more obvious in a republic, more remote and carefully hidden in a monarchy, but it always exists somewhere. In no country can the law foresee every eventuality, nor should institutions take the place of reason and mores.

HOW THE POSITION OF THE PRESIDENT OF THE UNITED STATES DIFFERS FROM THAT OF A CONSTITUTIONAL KING IN FRANCE

Executive power in the United States limited and exceptional, like the sovereignty in whose name it acts. — Executive power in France, like sovereignty, extends to everything. — The king is among the authors of the law. — The president is only the executor of the law. — Other differences stemming from the different duration of the two powers. — The president is checked in the exercise of executive power. — The king is free. — Despite these differences, France resembles a republic more than the Union resembles a monarchy. — Comparison of the number of officials who serve under the executive in the two countries.

Executive power plays so great a role in the destiny of nations that I want to dwell for a moment on the place it occupies among the Americans.

In order to get a clear and precise idea of the position of the president of the United States, it is useful to compare it to the position of the king in one of Europe's constitutional monarchies.

In this comparison I shall pay little heed to the outward signs of power. These are more likely to deceive the observer than to guide him.

When a monarchy is gradually transformed into a republic, the executive power retains titles, honors, respect, and even wealth long after it has lost the reality of power. The English, after cutting off the head of one of their kings and driving another from the throne, still kneel before the successors of those deposed monarchs.

On the other hand, when a republic falls under the yoke of one man, power will continue to affect simple, unpretentious, and modest manners, as if the ruler did not already loom above all others. When the emperors reigned as despots over the lives and fortunes of their fellow citizens, they were still addressed as "Caesar" and continued to dine with friends on familiar terms.

We must therefore delve beneath the surface.

Sovereignty in the United States is divided between the Union and the states, whereas in France it is unified and concentrated. From this comes the first and greatest difference that I see between the president of the United States and the king of France.

In the United States, executive power is limited and exceptional, as is the sovereignty in whose name it acts; in France, it extends, just as sovereignty does, to everything.

The Americans have a federal government; we have a national government.

Therein lies a first cause of inferiority, inherent in the very nature of things. But it is not the only one. Second in importance is the fact that sovereignty can be defined, strictly speaking, as the right to make laws.

The king of France really constitutes a part of the sovereign power, since laws do not exist if he refuses to sanction them. He is also the executor of those laws.

The president, too, is the executor of the law, but he does not really participate in making it, because even if he withholds his consent, he cannot prevent a law from existing. Hence he is not a part of the sovereign power; he is simply its agent.

In France, the king is not only a part of the sovereign power, he also participates in the formation of the legislature, which is the other part. He does this by appointing the members of one chamber and by terminating the mandate of the other whenever he pleases. The president of the United States plays no role in determining the composition of the legislative body, and he cannot dissolve it.

The king shares the right to propose new laws with the two chambers of the legislature.

The president has no comparable right to initiate legislation.

The king is represented in the chambers of the legislature by agents who set forth his views, support his opinions, and enforce respect for his maxims of government.

The president does not have free access to Congress. His ministers are also barred. His only means of bringing his influence and opinions to bear on that great body are indirect.

The king of France is thus on an equal footing with the legislature, which cannot act without him, just as he cannot act without it.

The president stands beside the legislature as an inferior and dependent power.

In the exercise of executive power as such, wherein the position of the president seems closest to that of the king of France, he is still inferior for a number of very important reasons.

First, the king has this advantage over the president, that his power is of longer duration, and duration is one of the primary sources of strength. People neither love nor fear anything that is not likely to exist for long.

The president of the United States is an elected official whose term of office is four years. The king of France is a hereditary leader.

In exercising executive power, the president of the United States is subject to constant and jealous scrutiny. He prepares treaties but does not make them. He may nominate but cannot appoint federal officials.[17]

The king of France is absolute master in the sphere of executive power.

The president of the United States is responsible for his actions. French law says that the person of the king of France is inviolable.

Above both, however, stands a guiding power: that of public opinion. This power is less defined in France than in the United States, and less recognized, less explicitly formulated in law, but it does in fact exist. In America it asserts itself through elections and decrees; in France, through revolutions. France and the United States therefore have this in common despite the differences between their constitutions, that public opinion is in effect the dominant power. The fundamental source of the law, by nature essentially republican, is therefore in fact the same in both countries, although public opinion may be interpreted rather more freely in one than in the other, and the consequences drawn from it may often differ. Therefore I believe that France, with its king, more closely resembles a republic than the Union, with its president, resembles a monarchy.

In everything I have said until now, I was careful to mention only major differences. Had I chosen to go into detail, the contrast would have been even more striking. But I have too much to say to be anything but brief.

As I have noted, the power of the president of the United States is exercised only within the sphere of limited sovereignty, whereas that of the king of France acts within the circle of full sovereignty.

I could have shown that in France, the governmental power of the king even transcends its natural limits, as extensive as

[17]The Constitution was ambiguous about whether the president is required to accept the advice of the Senate about removing federal officials from office as well as about appointing them. *Federalist 77* seemed to establish the affirmative, but in 1789 Congress quite rightly decided that, since the president was responsible, he could not be forced to rely on agents who did not have his confidence. See Kent's *Commentaries*, vol. I, p. 289.

they are, to involve itself in a thousand ways in the administration of individual interests.

To this source of influence I would add that which results from the large number of public officials, nearly all of whom owe their appointments to the executive power. In France this number has exceeded all known limits: it now stands at 138,000.[18] Each of those 138,000 appointments ought to be seen as a source of strength. The president's power to appoint public officials is not absolute, and the number of such appointments scarcely exceeds 12,000.[19]

ACCIDENTAL CAUSES THAT MAY INCREASE THE INFLUENCE OF THE EXECUTIVE POWER

External security of the Union. — Expectant politics. — Army of 6,000 soldiers. — Only a few ships. — The president enjoys great prerogatives that he has no occasion to use. — With respect to those prerogatives which he does have occasion to use, he is weak.

If executive power is weaker in America than in France, the cause lies perhaps more with circumstances than with laws.

It is chiefly in the realm of foreign relations that the executive power of a nation finds occasion to demonstrate its skill and strength.

If the existence of the Union were under constant threat, if its great interests were daily intertwined with those of other powerful nations, the executive power would take on increased importance in the public eye, because people would expect more of it, and it would do more.

To be sure, the president of the United States is the head of the army, but that army consists of six thousand soldiers. He commands the fleet, but the fleet has only a few vessels. He directs the Union's dealings with foreign nations, but the

---

[18]Every year the state pays these officials a sum amounting to 200,000,000 francs.

[19]A compendium known as the *National Calendar* is published every year in the United States; it contains the names of all federal officials. The figure given here is based on the *National Calendar* for 1833.

It follows from what I have said that the king of France has at his disposal eleven times as many offices as the president of the United States, even though the population of France is only one and a half times that of the Union.

United States has no neighbors. Separated from the rest of the world by the Atlantic Ocean and still too weak to seek to rule the sea, it has no enemies, and only rarely do its interests intersect with those of other nations of the globe.

What this shows is that government practice should not be judged in light of theory.

The president of the United States possesses prerogatives that are almost royal in magnitude, which he has no occasion to use, and the powers that he has been able to use until now have been very circumscribed: the law allows him to be strong, but circumstances keep him weak.

By contrast, it is circumstances even more than laws that have made royal authority in France a more powerful force.

In France, the executive power must constantly contend with immense obstacles and muster immense resources to overcome them. Its magnitude is enhanced by the grandeur of its undertakings and the importance of the events whose course it influences, yet without modification to its constitution.

Even if the laws had made it initially as weak and as circumscribed as that of the Union, its influence would soon have become much greater.

WHY THE PRESIDENT OF THE UNITED STATES DOES NOT NEED A MAJORITY IN BOTH HOUSES IN ORDER TO LEAD THE GOVERNMENT

In Europe it is an accepted axiom that a constitutional king cannot govern when the opinion of the legislative chambers does not coincide with his own.

As we have seen, several presidents of the United States have lost the support of the majority of Congress without being obliged to leave office and without any great harm to society as a result.

I have heard this fact cited as proof of the independence and strength of the executive power in America. A few moments' reflection will suffice, however, to see it rather as proof of the executive's lack of power.

A king in Europe needs the support of the legislature to fulfill his constitutional task, which is immense. A constitutional king in Europe is not only the executor of the law: he is so completely entrusted with its execution that even if the law were against him, he could paralyze its power. He needs the houses of the legislature to make the law; they need him to execute it. Neither of the two powers can live without the other. The machinery of government grinds to a halt the moment there is discord between them.

In America, the president cannot prevent laws from being passed. He cannot shirk the obligation to carry them out. His zealous and sincere cooperation is no doubt useful to the operation of the government, but it is not necessary. In all essential respects his actions are directly or indirectly subject to scrutiny by the legislature. In those areas where he is entirely independent of the legislature, he can do almost nothing. Thus it is his weakness rather than his strength that allows him to carry on in opposition to the legislative power.

In Europe, there must be agreement between the king and the houses of the legislature because conflict between them can be serious. In America, agreement is not obligatory because conflict is impossible.

ON THE ELECTION OF
THE PRESIDENT

The danger of the electoral system increases in proportion to the extent of the executive power's prerogatives. — Americans can adopt this system because they can do without a strong executive power. — How circumstances favored the establishment of the electoral system. — Why the election of the president does not alter the principles of government. — Influence of the election of the president on the fate of lower-level officials.

Experience and historians have amply taught us the dangers inherent in choosing the chief executive of a great nation through the system of election.

I shall therefore discuss those dangers only as they pertain to America.

The magnitude of the danger posed by the electoral system depends on the role and importance of the executive power in the state, the mode of election, and the circumstances in which the nation finds itself at the time of the election.

The use of the electoral system to choose the head of state has been criticized, not without reason, because it is such an incitement to personal ambition, and so inflames the passion for power, that men have often been known to resort to force when they failed to achieve their ends by legal means.

It is clear that the more prerogatives the executive has, the greater the allure. And the greater the incitement to the ambition of the candidates, the greater the support they are able to enlist from countless men of lesser ambition, who hope for a share of power when their candidate triumphs.

The dangers of the electoral system therefore increase in direct proportion to the influence that the executive power exerts on affairs of state.

Poland's revolutions ought to be attributed not just to the electoral system in general but also to the fact that the official elected was the head of a great monarchy.

Before we can discuss the value of the electoral system in itself, a prior question must therefore be answered: namely, whether the geographical position, laws, habits, mores, and opinions of the nation into which that system is to be introduced permit the establishment of an executive power that is weak and dependent. For in my opinion it is a contradiction to want the representative of the state to be both armed with vast power and elected. I know only one way of transforming a hereditary monarchy into an elective power: its sphere of action must first be limited, and its prerogatives gradually reduced, and little by little the people must become accustomed to living without its assistance. Yet European republicans pay scant attention to these requirements. Since many of them hate tyranny only because they must endure its rigors, the extent of executive power does not trouble them. They attack only its origin without perceiving the close bond between the two things.

No one has yet been willing to risk life and honor to become president of the United States, because the power of a president is merely temporary, limited, and dependent. Fortune must hold out an immense prize if it is to entice men upon a desperate adventure. No candidate has thus far been able to arouse ardent sympathies and dangerous popular passions. The reason for this is simple: even if a man becomes the head of the government, he cannot reward his friends with much in the way of power, wealth, or glory, and his influence within the state is too feeble for any faction to feel that its success or ruin depends on his elevation to power.

Hereditary monarchies have one great advantage: because the private interest of one family is intimately intertwined with the interests of the state, those interests are not left untended even for a moment. I do not know if monarchies manage affairs of state better than they are managed elsewhere, but at least there is always someone watching over them to the best of his abilities, whether for good or ill.

In elective states, by contrast, the machinery of government is in a sense left to function on its own for a considerable period of time prior to an election. Laws can no doubt be designed to ensure that elections are swift and their effects instantaneous, so that the seat of executive power is virtually never vacant. Despite the best efforts of the lawmakers, however, a void exists in people's minds.

As the election approaches, the chief executive thinks of nothing but the battle to come. He has no future; he cannot embark on any new venture and is at best halfhearted in pursuing things that he might have to leave for others to complete. "I am now so near the moment of retiring," President Jefferson wrote on January 21, 1809 (six weeks before the election), "that I take no part in affairs beyond the expression of an opinion. I think it fair that my successor should now originate those measures of which he will be charged with the execution and responsibility."

The nation, for its part, is focused on only one thing. Its sole concern is to watch over the impending labor of childbirth.

The greater the role that the executive power plays in directing the affairs of government, the greater and more necessary its habitual functions, the more dangerous such a state of affairs becomes. In a nation that has become used to being governed by the executive, and still more in a nation that has become accustomed to being administered by it, elections are invariably sources of profound disruption.

In the United States, the executive power can slacken its efforts with impunity, because those efforts are feeble and circumscribed.

When the head of government is elected, the stability of the state's domestic and foreign policy almost always suffers as a result. Therein lies one of the principal flaws of the system.

But the degree to which this flaw manifests itself depends on the share of power accorded to the elected official. In Rome, the principles of government did not vary even though new consuls were chosen every year, because the Senate was the ruling power, and the Senate was a hereditary body. In most of the monarchies of Europe, if the king were elected, the face of the kingdom would change with each new choice.

In America, the president exerts a fairly substantial influence on affairs of state, but he does not control their direction. The preponderance of power lies in the national representation as a whole. Not just the president but the people en masse must change if the fundamental principles of policy are to change. Thus in America, the fact that the chief executive is elected does little palpable harm to the stability of government.

Still, lack of stability is so intrinsic a flaw of the electoral system that its effects are quite apparent within the president's sphere of action, however limited it might be.

The Americans rightly judged that in order for the chief executive to carry out his mission and bear full responsibility for his actions, he ought to be left as free as possible to choose his own agents and to dismiss them at will. Congress keeps an eye on what the president does rather than dictate what he ought to do. As a result, the fate of all federal employees hangs in the balance with each new election.

In Europe's constitutional monarchies, people complain that the destiny of obscure administrative officials often depends on the fate of ministers. It is far worse in states where the head of government is elected. The reason for this is simple: in constitutional monarchies, ministers are rapidly replaced, but the principal representative of the executive power never changes; hence the spirit of innovation is confined within certain limits. What changes in the administrative system is therefore more a matter of detail than of principle.

One cannot suddenly substitute one administrative system for another without provoking a revolution of sorts. In America, such a revolution takes place every four years at the behest of the law.

As for the hardship that such legislation imposes on individuals, it must be granted that the unpredictability inherent in the lot of American officials does not produce the evils that one might expect. In the United States, it is so easy for a man to create an independent life for himself that an official who loses his post may find his circumstances more difficult but will never find it impossible to earn a living.

I said at the beginning of this chapter that the dangers of electing the chief executive were greater or smaller depending on the circumstances in which the nation found itself at the time of the election.

Try as one might to diminish the role of the executive power, its influence will remain great in one area regardless of the role assigned to it by law, namely, in the area of foreign policy. A negotiation can scarcely be undertaken and carried through to fruition except by one man.

The more precarious and perilous the position in which a nation finds itself, the greater the need for continuity and stability in the direction of foreign affairs, and the greater the danger of electing the head of state.

The policy of the Americans toward the rest of the world is simple. One might almost say that no one needs them, nor do they need anyone. Their independence is never threatened.

The role of the executive power in America is therefore limited as much by circumstances as by laws. The president can change his views frequently without damaging the state or causing it to perish.

No matter what prerogatives are vested in the executive, the time immediately before and during an election must always be considered a period of national crisis.

The more difficult the country's domestic situation and the greater the perils it has to face abroad, the more dangerous that time of crisis is. Very few European nations would be able to choose a new leader without fear of laying themselves open to conquest or anarchy.

In America, society is so constituted that it can sustain itself without assistance. Foreign dangers are never pressing. The election of a president is a cause of agitation, not ruin.

MODE OF ELECTION

Shrewdness of American lawmakers in choosing the mode of election. — Creation of a special electoral body. — Separate vote of special electors. — In what circumstances the House of Representatives is called upon to choose the president. — What has happened in the twelve elections that have taken place since the Constitution has been in effect.

Apart from the dangers inherent in the principle of election, many other dangers stem from electoral procedures and can be avoided if lawmakers are careful.

When a people in arms gathers in some public place to choose its leader, it exposes itself not only to the dangers of the electoral system as such but also to those of civil war inherent in such a procedure.

When Polish laws made the choice of king subject to the veto of one man, they invited the murder of that man, or laid down a prescription for anarchy.

The more one studies the institutions of the United States and the more closely one examines the country's social and political situation, the more marvelous the harmony between fortune and human effort seems. America was a new nation, yet the people who lived there had long been accustomed to the exercise of liberty elsewhere. These were two great causes of domestic order. What is more, America had no reason to fear conquest. Taking advantage of these favorable circumstances, American lawmakers found it easy to make the executive power weak and dependent. And having made it so, they took no risk in making it elective as well.

All that remained for them to do after that was to choose the least dangerous of the various systems of election. The rules they established in this regard admirably complemented the guarantees already furnished by the country's physical and political constitution.

The problem was to find a mode of election that would allow the people to express their authentic will without unduly arousing their passions, yet keep them in suspense as briefly as possible. It was accepted from the outset that a *simple* majority would decide the issue. But it was still hard to know how that majority could be determined without the delays that everyone wanted above all to avoid.

In a large country, a man seldom receives a majority of the votes on the first ballot. In a republic of confederated states, where local influences are much more powerful and highly developed, the difficulty is compounded.

In order to overcome this second hurdle, America's lawmakers proposed to delegate the nation's electoral powers to a representative body.

This mode of election made a majority more likely, for the smaller the number of electors, the easier it is for them to come to an agreement. The system also offered greater guarantees that the choice would be a good one.

But should the right to elect the president be entrusted to the legislative body itself — the usual representative of the nation — or to an electoral college whose sole purpose would be to choose the president?

The Americans chose the latter course. They believed that the men chosen to make the nation's ordinary laws only partially represented the wishes of the people in regard to the election of its principal official. Because those men were elected for more than one year, the will they represented might already have changed. It was felt that if the legislature were charged with electing the chief executive, its members would become the target of corrupting maneuvers and pawns of intrigue long before the election, whereas special electors, like jurors, would remain unknown to the populace until the day they were called upon to act, and would come forward only long enough to make their decision known.

It was therefore stipulated that each state should choose a certain number of electors,[20] who would in turn elect the president. Moreover, because the framers were aware that the bodies charged with choosing heads of government in countries that hold elections inevitably became focal points of

[20]Equal to the number of members they sent to Congress. The number of electors in the election of 1833 was 288 (*The National Calendar*).

passion and intrigue and sometimes usurped powers not assigned to them, and because their activities, and the concomitant uncertainties, were in some cases so prolonged as to
imperil the state, it was further stipulated that all the electors
would vote on a fixed date but would not meet in a single
location.[21]

This two-stage election procedure made a majority probable but not certain, because the electors might differ among
themselves just as much as the people who chose them.

In that eventuality, three courses of action were available:
one could choose new electors, consult those already chosen
a second time, or, lastly, defer the choice to a new authority.

The first two methods, apart from their uncertainty, also introduced delays and perpetuated a state of agitation that was
invariably dangerous.

The third was therefore chosen, and it was agreed that the
votes of the electors would be transmitted under seal to the
president of the Senate, who, on the date fixed, would proceed to count those votes in the presence of both houses. If
none of the candidates obtained a majority, the representatives would proceed immediately to elect the president. But
care was taken to limit this right. The representatives were required to elect one of the three candidates who had received
the most votes.[22]

Clearly, then, it is only in rare circumstances, difficult to
predict in advance, that the nation's ordinary representatives
are entrusted with the election of the president, and even then
they may not choose anyone other than a citizen already designated by a substantial minority of the special electors. This

[21]The electors for each state do meet, but they transmit the record of their
individual votes and not just of the resulting majority to the seat of the central government.

[22]In this situation, the election is decided by a majority of the states, not
of the ballots cast in the election, so that New York has no greater influence
in the deliberations than Rhode Island. Thus, one first consults the citizens
of the Union as if they constituted but a single people; only if they cannot
agree does one revive the division of the Union into states and accord to each
state a separate and independent vote.

Here is yet another of the bizarre features of the federal constitution, which
can only be explained as the result of a clash of conflicting interests.

is a happy formula, which strikes a balance between the respect owed to the will of the people and the state's interest in a quick decision and guarantees of order. The decision to allow the House of Representatives to settle the issue in case of a split did not resolve all the problems, however, for if the majority in the House remained in doubt, the Constitution had no remedy to offer. Yet by designating mandatory candidates, limiting their number to three, and entrusting the decision to a few enlightened men, it smoothed away all the obstacles[23] within its power. The others were inherent in the elective system itself.

In the forty-four years since the federal constitution came into existence, the United States has elected its president twelve times.

Ten of those elections were decided instantly by the simultaneous vote of special electors at various locations throughout the country.

To date, the House of Representatives has only twice availed itself of the exceptional power vested in it in case of a split. The first time was in 1801, when Mr. Jefferson was elected, and the second in 1825, when Mr. Quincy Adams was chosen.

CRISIS OF THE ELECTION

A presidential election can be seen as a moment of national crisis.
— Why. — Passions of the people. — Preoccupation of the president.
— Calm that follows the agitation of the election.

Thus far I have discussed how the circumstances in which the United States found itself favored the adoption of the elective system and pointed out what precautions the lawmakers took to reduce the dangers inherent in that system. Americans are used to holding elections of all sorts. Experience has taught them what degree of agitation can result and when it should be stopped. Because the country is so vast and its population so dispersed, clashes between its various parties are less likely than they are elsewhere, and also less perilous. The political

---

[23]In 1801, however, Jefferson was not elected until the thirty-sixth ballot.

circumstances under which elections have thus far been carried out have presented no real danger.

All this notwithstanding, a presidential election in the United States may be looked upon as a time of national crisis.

To be sure, the president's influence over the country's affairs is weak and indirect, but it encompasses the entire nation. The choice of the president is of only moderate concern to each citizen, but it does concern them all. No matter how minor an interest may be, it takes on great importance when it becomes general.

Compared to a European monarch, the president has relatively few means of enlisting partisans. Still, the number of posts he controls is sufficient to ensure that several thousand voters have a direct or indirect interest in his cause.

Furthermore, political parties in the United States, like political parties everywhere, feel a need to rally around an individual in order to communicate more effectively with the masses. Thus they generally use the name of the presidential candidate as a symbol: they make him the personification of their theories. Hence the parties have a great interest in winning presidential elections, not so much in order to secure the president's aid in achieving the triumph of their doctrines as to demonstrate by electing him that those doctrines enjoy the support of the majority.

Long before the appointed date arrives, the election becomes everyone's major, not to say sole, preoccupation. The ardor of the various factions intensifies, and whatever artificial passions the imagination can create in a happy and tranquil country make their presence felt.

The president, for his part, is consumed by the need to defend his record. He no longer governs in the interest of the state but rather in the interest of his reelection. He prostrates himself before the majority, and often, rather than resist its passions as his duty requires, he courts favor by catering to its whims.

As the election draws near, intrigues intensify, and agitation increases and spreads. The citizens divide into several camps, each behind its candidate. A fever grips the entire nation. The election becomes the daily grist of the public papers, the sub-

ject of private conversations, the aim of all activity, the object
of all thought, the sole interest of the moment.

Immediately after fortune renders its verdict, of course, this
ardor dissipates, calm is restored, and the river, having briefly
overflowed its banks, returns peacefully to its bed. But is it
not astonishing that such a storm could have arisen?

ON THE REELECTION OF
THE PRESIDENT

*When the chief executive can be reelected, the state itself becomes in-
volved in intrigue and corruption. — The desire to be reelected dominates all the thinking of the president of the United States. —
Drawbacks of reelection unique to America. — Democracy's natural flaw is the gradual subjugation of all powers to the slightest desire
of the majority. — Reelection of the president encourages this flaw.*

Were the men who gave the United States its laws right or
wrong to permit the reelection of the president?

To prevent the reelection of the chief executive at first seems
contrary to reason. One knows the extent to which the talent
and character of a single individual can influence the destiny
of an entire nation, especially in difficult situations and
times of crisis. Laws prohibiting citizens from reelecting their
supreme official would deprive them of the best means of
saving the state or ensuring its prosperity. They would also
have the bizarre effect of excluding a man from government
just when he had proved that he was capable of governing
well.

These are no doubt powerful arguments, but can we not
put forward still more powerful arguments against them?

Intrigue and corruption are natural vices of elective governments. When the head of state can be reelected, however,
those vices spread without limit and compromise the country's
very existence. If a mere candidate chooses to engage in intrigue, his maneuvers are necessarily confined within a limited
sphere. By contrast, when the head of state himself enters
the running, he enlists the power of the government in his
own behalf.

In the former case, intrigue and corruption are the work of one man with limited resources. In the latter, it is the state itself, with its immense resources, that becomes involved.

An ordinary citizen who employs corrupt means to achieve power can do only indirect damage to public prosperity. But if the representative of the executive power joins the fray, the government becomes a secondary interest for him; his primary interest is to secure his election. Negotiations, like laws, cease to be anything to him other than campaign tactics. Government posts become rewards for services rendered not to the nation but to its leader. Even if the action of the government is not always contrary to the national interest, it no longer serves that interest. Every action is tailored solely to the purposes of the leader.

It is impossible to observe the ordinary course of affairs in the United States without noticing that the desire to be re-elected dominates the thoughts of the president; that the whole policy of his administration is directed toward this end, his every action bent to this purpose; and that, particularly when the crisis looms, his own individual interest supplants the general interest in his mind.

The principle of reelection therefore makes the corrupting influence of elective government more extensive and more dangerous. It tends to degrade the nation's political morality and to substitute shrewdness for patriotism.

In America, it strikes even more directly at the very sources of the nation's existence.

Every government harbors within itself a natural flaw that seems inextricably intertwined with the very principle of its existence; the genius of the legislator consists in clearly perceiving that flaw. A state can triumph over a multitude of bad laws, and the harm they do is often exaggerated. But any law whose effect is to foster the spread of this deadly germ is ultimately fatal, though its harmful consequences may not be immediately apparent.

In absolute monarchies the seed of destruction lies in the boundless and unreasonable extension of royal power. Any measure that removes the constitutional counterweight to that power is therefore radically wrong, even if its effects go unnoticed for a long time.

Similarly, in countries where democracy governs, and in which everything revolves around the people, laws that accelerate or increase the influence of the people strike directly at the government's existence.

The greatest merit of the men who gave America its laws is that they clearly recognized this truth and had the courage to put it into practice.

They saw that there must be authorities outside the people, not completely independent of them yet endowed with a fairly substantial degree of liberty within their own sphere of responsibility. Though obliged to accept the permanent guidance of the majority, these authorities would nevertheless have the capacity to counter its caprices and reject its dangerous demands.

To that end, the lawgivers concentrated all the executive power of the nation in the hands of one person. They granted extensive prerogatives to the president and armed him with the veto so that he might resist the encroachments of the legislature.

By introducing the principle of reelection, however, they partly negated their efforts. They conferred great power on the president and stripped him of the will to make use of it.

Had the president been ineligible for reelection, he would not have been independent of the people, for he would still have been accountable to them. But he would not have needed their favor so much as to be obliged always to bend to their will in all matters.

Because the president of the United States is eligible for reelection (especially now that political morality has grown lax and men of great character are vanishing from the scene), he is but a docile instrument in the hands of the majority. What it loves, he loves, and what it hates, he hates. He caters to its wishes, anticipates its grievances, and bows to its every whim. Instead of guiding the majority, as the framers of the law intended, he follows in its wake.

Thus, in order to avoid depriving the state of one man's talents, they rendered those talents almost useless. And in order to secure a resource for extraordinary times, they exposed the country to daily dangers.

ON THE FEDERAL COURTS[24]

Political importance of judicial power in the United States. — Difficulty of treating this subject. — Utility of justice in confederations. — What courts were available to the Union? — Need for federal courts. — Organization of federal justice. — The Supreme Court. — How it differs from all the courts of justice we know.

I have examined the legislative power and the executive power of the Union. It remains for me to consider the judicial power.

Here I must be frank about my fears.

Judicial institutions exert a great influence over the destiny of the Anglo-Americans. They occupy a very important place among political institutions properly so called. In this respect they are particularly worthy of our attention.

But how can I make the political action of American courts clear without going into detail about their constitution and procedures? And how can I delve in detail into such an intrinsically arid subject without repelling the reader? How can I remain clear without ceasing to be brief?

I do not flatter myself that I have avoided these various perils. Men of the world will find me tedious; lawyers will think me superficial. But this is a drawback inherent in the subject in general as well as in the more specialized material with which I am about to deal.

The greatest difficulty lay not in knowing how to constitute the federal government but in determining how people could be made to obey its laws.

Governments in general have only two ways of overcoming the resistance of the people they govern: the physical force they find in themselves and the moral force they derive from decisions of the courts.

A government that has no choice but to resort to war to

---

[24]See chapter 6, entitled "On Judicial Power in the United States." This chapter sets forth the general principles to which Americans adhere in judicial matters. See also the federal constitution, art. 3.

See also *Federalist* 78–83 and Thomas Sergeant, *Constitutional Law, being a View of the Practice and Jurisdiction of the Courts of the United States*.

See also Story, pp. 134–162, 489–511, 581, 668. See the fundamental law of September 14, 1789, in the compendium by Story entitled *Laws of the United States*, vol. 1, p. 53.

enforce its laws stands on the brink of ruin. One of two things is likely happen. If weak and moderate, it will employ force only as an ultimate remedy and wink at countless instances in which the law is partially flouted. Little by little the state will thereby lapse into anarchy.

If bold and powerful, it will resort to violence constantly and soon degenerate into pure military despotism. To the governed, action and inaction are equally catastrophic.

The paramount aim of justice is to substitute the idea of right for the idea of violence, to place intermediaries between the government and the use of physical force.

The presumptive power that people are generally willing to grant to interventions of the courts is surprising. So great is that power that it attaches to judicial forms even when drained of all substance; it gives body to the mere shadow of justice.

The moral force vested in the courts makes the recourse to physical force infinitely more rare than it would otherwise be, for in most cases moral force takes its place. And if, in the end, physical force is necessary, it is backed by moral force and therefore twice as powerful.

A federal government needs the support of justice even more than other types of government because it is by nature weaker, and resistance to it can be organized more easily.[25] If constrained always to use violence as its first resort, such a government would be inadequate to its task.

Hence the Union, in order to compel citizens to obey, and to repel attacks upon its laws, had particular need of courts.

But what courts should it rely upon? Each state already had its own judicial power. Should the state courts be used? Or was it necessary to create a federal judiciary? It is easy to demonstrate that the Union could not adapt the state court systems for its own use.

For the security and liberty of all citizens, the judicial power should surely be separate from all other powers. But it is no less essential to the very existence of the nation that the various

---

[25]Federal laws have the greatest need of courts and yet do the least to establish them. This is because most federations have been formed by independent states, which had no real intention of obeying the central government: even as they granted it the right to command, they were careful to reserve for themselves the faculty to disobey.

powers of the state should all stem from the same source, be subject to the same principles, and respect the same limits: in short, that they should be *harmonious* and *homogeneous*. It would never occur to anyone, I presume, that crimes committed in France should be judged in foreign courts in order to be more certain of the judges' impartiality.

Vis-à-vis the federal government, the Americans are a single people, but a people among whom political bodies have been allowed to remain that are dependent on the national government in some respects, independent in others. Those bodies have their own specific origins, their own doctrines, and their own special ways of doing things. To entrust the execution of the laws of the Union to the courts instituted by those political bodies was to deliver the nation to foreign judges.

Vis-à-vis the Union, moreover, each state is not only a foreign power but a constant adversary, because any sovereignty lost by the Union inevitably enhances that of the states.

To have made the courts of the several states responsible for enforcing the laws of the Union would therefore have been to deliver the nation into the hands of judges who were not only foreign but also partial.

Furthermore, it was not just the character of the state courts that rendered them incapable of serving a national purpose; it was above all their number.

At the time the federal constitution was drafted, there were already thirteen courts in the United States whose decisions could not be appealed. Today there are twenty-four. How can a state survive when its fundamental laws can be interpreted and applied in twenty-four different ways at once! Such a system is as contrary to reason as it is to the lessons of experience.

America's lawmakers therefore agreed to create a federal judiciary to enforce the laws of the Union and decide certain questions of general interest whose nature was carefully spelled out in advance.

All judicial power in the Union was concentrated in a single court, the Supreme Court of the United States. But in order to expedite the handling of cases, lower courts were also established. In less important cases their decisions were final, while in more important ones they sat as courts of the first instance. Members of the Supreme Court were not elected by the people or the legislature; the president of the United States was required to choose them with the advice of the Senate.

In order to make these judges independent of the other powers, it was decided that they should be appointed for life and that their salaries, once fixed, should not be subject to the control of the legislature.[26]

It was fairly easy to proclaim the establishment of a federal judiciary in principle, but when it came time to fix its prerogatives, a host of difficulties arose.

DEFINING THE JURISDICTION OF THE FEDERAL COURTS

Difficulty of defining the jurisdiction of the diverse courts in confederations. — The courts of the Union are granted the right to determine their own jurisdiction. — Why this rule threatened the portion of sovereignty that the individual states reserved to themselves. — The sovereignty of those states limited by the laws and the interpretation of the laws. — Danger to the individual states is therefore more apparent than real.

The first difficulty to arise was the following: since the constitution of the United States set up two distinct and opposing sovereignties, each represented in the realm of justice by

---

[26]The Union was divided into districts. Each district was assigned a resident federal judge. The court over which that judge presided was known as the district court.

In addition, each justice of the Supreme Court was required to tour a certain portion of the republic annually and to hear certain more important cases on the spot. The court over which this magistrate presided was designated the circuit court.

Finally, the most serious cases were to be brought, either directly or on appeal, to the Supreme Court, where all the circuit judges assembled for a formal session once each year.

The jury system was introduced in the federal courts in the same way as in the state courts, and for similar cases.

Clearly, there is virtually no analogy between the Supreme Court of the United States and our Cour de Cassation. The Supreme Court can hear cases in the first instance, whereas the Cour de Cassation hears cases only on first or second appeal. To be sure, the Supreme Court, like the Cour de Cassation, is a single court charged with establishing a uniform jurisprudence. But the Supreme Court judges facts as well as law and *itself* pronounces judgment

a different system of courts, frequent clashes were impossible to avoid no matter how carefully one established their respective jurisdictions. In such a situation, who should have the right to define competence?

When a people forms but a single polity, if a question of competence arises between two courts, it is generally brought before a third court, which acts as arbiter.

This is easily done, because in such nations questions of judicial competence have no bearing on questions of national sovereignty.

But in case of jurisdictional dispute between a high state court and a high federal court, it was impossible to establish a court that would have been superior to both and yet neither a federal court nor a state court.

Hence it was necessary to grant one of the two courts the right to judge cases to which it was a party, and to accept or refuse jurisdiction when a dispute arose. This privilege could not be granted to the courts of the several states. To do so would have been to destroy the sovereignty of the Union in practice after having established it in law, because interpretation of the Constitution would soon have restored to each state the portion of independence that the terms of the Constitution had taken away.

The federal courts were created in order to deny the courts of each state the right to decide questions of national interest in their own way. It was hoped that this would result in a uniform body of jurisprudence for interpreting the laws of the Union. That goal would not have been achieved if the state courts, while abstaining from judgment in federal cases, had been allowed to render judgment whenever they claimed that a case was not federal.

The right to decide all questions of jurisdiction was therefore vested in the Supreme Court of the United States.[27]

---

without sending cases back down to another court — two things which the Cour de Cassation cannot do.

See the fundamental law of September 24, 1789, in Story, *Laws of the United States*, vol. 1, p. 53.

[27]Furthermore, in order to diminish the frequency of jurisdictional disputes, it was decided that in a very large number of federal cases, the state courts would render a decision concurrently with the federal courts, but in

No more dangerous blow was dealt to the sovereignty of the states. That sovereignty was now restricted not only by the laws but also by the interpretation of the laws; by a known limit and another that was unknown; by a fixed rule and an arbitrary rule. To be sure, the Constitution had imposed precise limits on federal sovereignty. But whenever that sovereignty finds itself in competition with the sovereignty of the states, a federal court must decide the issue.

Yet the dangers with which this way of proceeding seemed to threaten the sovereignty of the states were not in fact as great as they appeared to be.

We shall see later on that in America, real force resides more in state governments than in the federal government. Federal judges are aware of the relative weakness of the power in whose name they act, and they are more likely to forgo a right of jurisdiction in cases where the law grants them one than they are to claim such a right illegally.

JURISDICTION IN VARIOUS CASES

Federal jurisdiction governed by the nature of the case and the parties to the case. — Cases involving ambassadors, — the Union, — a particular state. — Judged by whom. — Cases arising out of the laws of the Union. — Why judged by the federal courts. — Cases involving nonperformance of contracts tried in federal courts. — Consequence of this.

After establishing the means by which the competence of the federal courts would be determined, the framers of the Union decided what cases should fall under federal jurisdiction.

They agreed that certain parties could be judged only by the federal courts, regardless of the nature of the case.

They also established that certain cases could be decided only by those same courts, regardless of the quality of the parties.

---

such cases the condemned party would be entitled to appeal the judgment to the Supreme Court of the United States. The Supreme Court of Virginia challenged the right of the Supreme Court of the United States to appellate jurisdiction over its judgments, but it did not prevail. See *Kent's Commentaries*, vol. 1, pp. 300, 370 ff. See *Story's Comm.*, p. 646, and the fundamental law of 1789; *Laws of the United States*, vol. 1, p. 53.

Thus the parties to a case and the nature of the case became the criteria by which the competence of the federal courts was determined.

Ambassadors represent nations friendly to the Union. Anything affecting the interests of an ambassador must to some extent affect the interests of the Union as a whole. When an ambassador is party to a case, that case has a bearing on the well-being of the nation. Under the circumstances it is natural that a federal court should render judgment.

The Union itself can be a party to a case. In such a situation, it would be contrary to reason as well as to the common custom of nations to seek the judgment of a court representing another sovereign power. It is for the federal courts alone to decide.

When two individuals from two different states are parties to a lawsuit, there are reasons to object to the case's being heard by a court in either state. It is safer to choose a tribunal that will not arouse the suspicions of either party, and quite naturally it is the federal courts that come to mind.

When the two parties to a suit are not isolated individuals but states, this consideration of equity is reinforced by a political consideration of the utmost importance, for in such a case the nature of the parties lends national significance to the proceedings. Any litigation between states, however slight, has implications for the peace of the Union as a whole.[28]

Jurisdiction was in many instances to be determined by the nature of the case itself. For instance, all questions of maritime law were to be decided by the federal courts.[29]

The reason for this is easily stated: nearly all such questions hinge on the interpretation of international law. In this re-

[28]The Constitution also stipulates that any litigation between a state and a citizen or citizens of another state falls within the jurisdiction of the federal courts. Soon the question arose as to whether the Constitution meant to include all such litigation no matter which party was the plaintiff. The Supreme Court said yes, but this decision alarmed the states, which feared that they could be forced to appear against their wishes in federal court on any grounds whatsoever. The Constitution was therefore amended so that the judicial power of the Union does not extend to cases *brought* against a state by a citizen of another state.

See *Story's Commentaries*, p. 624.

[29]Example: all acts of piracy.

spect, they bear on the interests of the Union as a whole in its relations with foreigners. Since, moreover, the sea does not belong to one judicial district any more than to another, only a national court can claim jurisdiction over cases of maritime origin.

The Constitution assigns all cases whose nature requires them to be heard in federal court to a single category.

The rule that it lays down in this regard is simple, but it encompasses a vast system of ideas and a multitude of facts.

The federal courts, the Constitution declares, shall judge all cases *arising under the laws of the United States.*

Two examples will make the thinking of the framers on this point perfectly clear.

The Constitution forbids states to make laws regarding the circulation of currency. Suppose that, in spite of this prohibition, a state passes such a law. Because this law is contrary to the Constitution, the parties affected by it refuse to obey. They must make their case in a federal court, because the ground of their action is found in the laws of the United States.

Suppose now that Congress establishes an import duty. Difficulties arise as to its collection. Again, the matter must be brought before the federal courts, because what is at issue is the interpretation of a law of the United States.

This rule is in perfect accord with the fundamental principles of the Constitution.

To be sure, the Union as constituted in 1789 had only limited sovereignty, but the intention was that within its sphere it should mold a single, unified people.[30] Within its sphere, it was sovereign. Once that principle had been laid down and acknowledged, everything else followed easily, because once one accepts that the United States, within the limits laid down by the Constitution, comprises a single people, then that people must be granted the rights that belong to all peoples.

Now, since the dawn of society, it has been generally agreed that every people has the right to have all questions concerning

---

[30] Some restrictions were of course placed on this principle with the introduction of individual states as independent powers in the Senate and the decision to have the states vote separately in the House of Representatives in presidential elections, but these are exceptions. The contrary principle prevails.

the execution of its own laws judged by its own courts. Someone may object that the Union is in the unusual position of comprising one people only with respect to certain purposes; for all other purposes it does not exist. What follows from this? Precisely this: that at least in regard to all laws pertaining to those purposes, the Union enjoys all the rights that would be granted to a fully sovereign entity. The real point of the objection is to know what those purposes are. Once that has been decided (and we saw earlier, in our discussion of jurisdiction, how this was done), there really is no issue, for once it has been established that a case is federal, that is, that it falls under the sovereign powers reserved to the Union by the Constitution, then it naturally follows that judgment should be rendered solely by a federal court.

If, therefore, someone wants to attack the laws of the United States or to invoke them in his own defense, he is obliged to turn to the federal courts.

Accordingly, the jurisdiction of the federal courts expands and contracts with the sovereignty of the Union itself.

We saw earlier that the principal aim of the lawmakers of 1789 was to divide the powers of sovereignty into two distinct groups. Into one group they placed those powers pertaining to the general interests of the Union, while into the other they placed those powers pertaining to the special interests of certain of its parts.

Their principal concern was to arm the federal government with sufficient powers to defend itself within its proper sphere against encroachments by the individual states.

As for the latter, the general principle adopted was to leave them free in their own sphere. There, the central government cannot dictate what they ought to do or even monitor their behavior.

In the chapter on the division of powers I indicated that this latter principle was not always respected. There are certain laws that an individual state cannot make, even though those laws might appear to pertain solely to its own interests.

When a state of the Union promulgates such a law, citizens injured by its enforcement can appeal to the federal courts.

Thus, the jurisdiction of the federal courts extends not only to all cases arising under the laws of the Union but also to all cases stemming from laws that individual states may adopt that are contrary to the Constitution.

The states are prohibited from promulgating retroactive laws in criminal matters. A man sentenced on the basis of such a law may appeal to the federal courts.

The Constitution also prohibits states from making laws "impairing the obligations of contracts."[31]

Any individual who believes that a state law infringes on a contractual right can refuse to obey that law and appeal to the federal courts.[32]

More than any other provision of the Constitution, this one seems to me to pose a threat to the sovereignty of the states.

The rights granted to the federal government for what are obviously national purposes are well defined and easy to understand. The rights granted to it indirectly by the aforementioned article are not so readily comprehensible, and their limits not clearly delineated. Indeed, there are a multitude of political laws that affect the existence of contracts and

---

[31]It is perfectly clear, says Mr. Story, p. 503, that any law that extends, restricts or alters the stipulated intentions of the parties to a contract alters or "impairs" that contract. The same author goes on to define what federal jurisprudence means by a contract. The definition is quite broad. A concession made by a state to an individual and accepted by that individual is a contract and cannot be revoked by a subsequent law. A charter granted by a state to a company is a contract and is a law as binding on the state as it is on the concessionaire. Hence the article of the Constitution that we are discussing here protects many but not all *acquired rights*. I may be the perfectly legitimate owner of a piece of property without having obtained ownership by means of a contract. My ownership is an acquired right, and that right is not guaranteed by the federal constitution.

[32]Mr. Story cites a remarkable example of this on p. 508. Dartmouth College in New Hampshire was founded on the basis of a charter granted to certain individuals before the American Revolution. By virtue of this charter, the administrators of the college formed what is called in American parlance a "corporation." The New Hampshire legislature felt obliged to alter the terms of the original charter and transferred all rights, privileges, and franchises resulting therefrom to a new group of administrators. The old administrators resisted and appealed to the federal courts, which found in their favor. Since the original charter had been an authentic contract between the state and the concessionaires, the new law could not alter its provisions without violating rights acquired by virtue of a contract, thereby violating Article 1, section 10, of the United States Constitution.

might thereby provide the central government with a pretext for encroaching upon the powers of the states.

PROCEDURE OF THE FEDERAL COURTS

Natural weakness of the judiciary in confederations. — Efforts that lawmakers ought to make to ensure that, insofar as possible, only isolated individuals and not states will appear before federal courts. — How the Americans achieved this. — Direct action of federal courts on ordinary individuals. — Indirect attack on states that violate the laws of the Union. — Decisions of the federal courts do not destroy state law but weaken it.

I have discussed the powers of the federal courts. It is just as important to see how those powers are exercised.

In countries where sovereignty is undivided, the irresistible force of the judiciary derives from the fact that the courts represent the entire nation in conflict with the single individual against whom the court issues its judgment. The idea of right is associated with the idea of might, which supports it.

In countries where sovereignty is divided, however, this is not always the case. The judiciary in such countries often has to contend not with an isolated individual but with a fraction of the nation. Its moral force and physical might are thereby diminished.

In federal states, therefore, the position of the courts is weakened and that of the justiciable parties strengthened.

Those who make laws for confederations must constantly strive to make a place for the courts analogous to that which they occupy in nations where sovereignty is undivided. In other words, they must seek constantly to ensure that the federal courts represent the nation and that the justiciable parties represent particular interests.

Any government, regardless of its nature, needs to act upon the people it governs, in order to force them to give the government its due. It needs to act against them in order to defend itself from their attacks.

As for direct action by the government on the governed in order to force them to obey the laws, the Constitution of the United States (in its master stroke) arranged things so that the federal courts, acting in the name of those laws, would have to deal only with individuals. In fact, since it was stipulated that the confederation comprised a single, unique people within the limits set forth by the Constitution, it followed that the government created by that Constitution and acting within its limits was invested with all the powers of a national government, the chief of which is the ability to transmit its injunctions directly to ordinary citizens, without intermediaries. So, for example, when the Union ordered the levying of a tax, it was not obliged to turn to the states to collect that tax but could rather demand a fair share from each American citizen. Consequently, the federal courts charged with enforcing this law of the Union were obliged to condemn not recalcitrant states but individual taxpayers. Like the courts in other countries, the federal courts had to contend only with individuals.

Note that here the Union chose its own adversary, and it chose a weak one. It was only natural that that adversary would fall.

But when the Union, rather than attack, is forced to defend itself, the difficulty increases. The Constitution grants the states the power to make laws. Those laws may violate the Union's rights. Inevitably in such a case the federal government finds itself locked in struggle with the sovereign power that made the law. At that point its only option is to choose which of the available courses of action is the least dangerous. That course is laid down in advance by the general principles that I set forth previously.[33]

One might think that in the case I just postulated, the Union would be allowed to take the state to a federal court, which would declare the offending law null and void. This would have been a logical course to follow. But then the federal court would have found itself in direct conflict with a state, which was what the framers wanted as much as possible to avoid.

The Americans believed that it was almost impossible to enforce a new law without injuring some particular interest.

The authors of the federal constitution relied on that particular interest to attack the legislative measure about which

---

[33]See the chapter entitled "On the Judicial Power in America."

the Union might have cause to complain. They offered it a safe harbor.

Suppose that a state sells land to a company. A year later, a new law disposes of the same land in a different way, thereby violating the clause in the Constitution that prohibits altering rights acquired by contract. When the person who has purchased the land under the terms of the new law attempts to take possession, the owner whose title derives from the previous law files suit in federal court and has the new purchaser's title declared null and void.[34] Thus, in reality, the federal courts are at grips with the sovereignty of the state, but they attack it only indirectly and on a matter of detail. They thereby strike at the consequences of the law, but not at its source. They do not destroy it, but rather weaken it.

We come now to one last hypothetical situation.

Each state forms a corporation, which enjoys a separate legal existence and its own civil rights. It can consequently bring suit and have suits brought against it in the courts. For example, a state can file suit against another state.

In that event, it is not a question of the Union attacking a state law but rather of judging a case to which a state is a party. Such a case is just like any other; only the quality of the parties is different. Here, the danger indicated at the beginning of this chapter still exists, but now there is no way to avoid it. It is inherent in the very nature of a federal constitution, the result of which is always to create within the nation entities powerful enough that it is difficult for the courts to take action against them.

ELEVATED RANK OF THE SUPREME COURT AMONG THE GREAT POWERS OF THE STATE

No people has created a more powerful judiciary than the Americans. — Extent of the judiciary's prerogatives. — Its political influence. — The peace of the Union, and indeed its very existence, depend on the wisdom of the seven federal judges.

When, after examining the organization of the Supreme Court in detail, one comes to consider all the prerogatives

---

[34]See *Kent's Commentaries*, vol. i, p. 387.

with which it was endowed, it soon becomes clear that no other people has ever constituted a mightier judicial power.

The Supreme Court stands above any known tribunal both by the *nature* of its powers and by the *categories* of parties subject to its jurisdiction.

In all the civilized nations of Europe, governments have always been extremely reluctant to allow ordinary courts to decide questions bearing on governmental interests. Naturally this reluctance is greatest when the government is most absolute. By contrast, as liberty increases, the prerogatives of the courts steadily grow. Yet no European nation has yet reached the conclusion that every judicial question, no matter where it originates, can be left to common-law judges.

The Americans have put this theory into practice. The Supreme Court of the United States is the nation's sole and unique tribunal.

It is charged with the interpretation of laws and treaties; questions relative to maritime commerce and, more generally, all questions pertaining to international law fall within its exclusive competence. It is even fair to say that its prerogatives are almost entirely political, although its constitution is entirely judicial. Its sole purpose is to enforce the laws of the Union, and the Union regulates only relations between the government and the governed and between the nation and foreigners. Relations of citizens with one another are almost all governed by the sovereignty of the states.

There is a second and still greater reason for the importance of this court. In the courts of European nations only individuals may appear as parties, but the Supreme Court of the United States compels sovereigns to appear at its bar. When the Clerk of the Court mounts the steps of the tribunal to announce "the State of New York versus the State of Ohio," one senses that these are not the chambers of any ordinary court of justice. And to think that one of the attorneys in the case represents a million people and the other two million is to be astonished by the responsibility borne by the seven judges whose decision will soon bring either joy or despair to so many of their fellow citizens.

The peace, prosperity, and very existence of the Union rest constantly in the hands of the seven federal judges. Without them, the Constitution would be a dead letter. It is to them that the executive power appeals to resist the encroachments of the legislature; that the legislature appeals to defend itself against the assaults of the executive; that the Union appeals to gain the obedience of the states; that the states appeal to rebuff the exaggerated claims of the Union; that public interest appeals against private interest; and that the spirit of conservation appeals against democratic instability. Their power is immense, but it is a power of opinion. They are all-powerful so long as the people consent to obey the law, but when the people scoff at the law, they can do nothing. Now, the power of opinion is the most difficult kind of power to use, because it is impossible to say exactly where its limits lie. It is often as dangerous to underestimate it as to overestimate it.

Federal judges must therefore be more than just good citizens, educated and upright men, for these are qualities necessary in any magistrate; they must also be statesmen. They must know how to discern the spirit of their time, to confront obstacles that can be overcome, and to steer out of the current when the flood threatens to sweep them away along with the sovereignty of the Union and the obedience due its laws.

The president may fail yet the state not suffer, because the president's duties are limited. Congress may err yet the Union not perish, because standing above Congress is the electorate, which can change the spirit of Congress by changing its members.

Should imprudent or corrupt men ever fill the Supreme Court, however, the confederation would have to fear anarchy or civil war.

Make no mistake, moreover: the fundamental source of danger lies not in the constitution of the Supreme Court but in the very nature of federal governments. Nowhere is a strongly constituted judiciary more essential than in a confederated nation, as we have seen, because nowhere are the individual entities capable of braving the will of society stronger or better equipped to resist the use of physical force by the government.

Now, the more necessary it is that a power be strong, the more imperative it is that it be granted breadth and independence. The broader and more independent a power is, the more dangerous its abuse becomes. Hence the root of the evil is not in the constitution of this power but in the constitution of the state itself, which makes the existence of such a power necessary.

IN WHAT RESPECTS THE FEDERAL CONSTITUTION IS SUPERIOR TO THE CONSTITUTIONS OF THE STATES

How the Constitution of the Union may be compared with the constitutions of particular states. — Credit for the superiority of the Union's Constitution is due in particular to the wisdom of federal lawmakers. — The legislature of the Union is less dependent on the people than are the legislatures of the states. — The executive power is freer in its sphere. — The judicial power is less subject to the will of the majority. — Practical consequences of this. — Federal lawmakers diminished the dangers inherent in the government of democracy; state lawmakers increased those dangers.

The federal constitution differs essentially from the constitutions of the states in the goal that it sets for itself, but it is very similar in the means of attaining that goal. The object of government is different, but the forms of government are the same. With these specific points in mind, it is useful to compare the two types of constitution.

I think that the federal constitution is superior to all the state constitutions. There are several reasons for this.

The present Constitution of the Union was conceived after the constitutions of most of the states. It was therefore possible to take advantage of the experience acquired.

That this was only a subsidiary cause, however, becomes clear when one recollects that since the establishment of the federal constitution, eleven new states have been added to the American confederation, and these states almost always exacerbated rather than attenuated the flaws in the constitutions of their predecessors.

The most important reason for the superiority of the federal constitution has to do with the character of the lawmakers themselves.

At the time the Constitution was being drafted, the ruin of the confederation seemed imminent. It is fair to say that it was obvious to everyone. In that extremity, the people chose not the men they liked best, perhaps, but those they esteemed most.

I have already pointed out that the men who framed the laws of the Union were almost all remarkable for their enlightenment and still more remarkable for their patriotism.

They all grew up in the midst of a social crisis, during which the spirit of liberty was locked in constant struggle with a strong and dominating authority. When that struggle ended, and while the mob, its passions aroused, continued as usual to contend with dangers that had long since ceased to exist, they stopped and took a calmer, more penetrating look at their country. They saw that a definitive revolution had been accomplished, and that the perils that menaced the people could henceforth arise only from abuses of liberty. What they thought, they had the courage to say, because for that very liberty they felt in the bottom of their hearts a sincere and ardent love. They dared to propose limiting it because they were sure they had no wish to destroy it.[35]

Most state constitutions provide for only a one-year term in the House of Representatives and a two-year term in the Senate. Members of the legislature are thus forever bound in the narrowest possible way by their constituents' every whim.

The Union's framers believed that this extreme dependency of the legislature on the voters denatured the principal effects of the representative system by vesting in the people not only the source of all power but also the government.

[35]In this period the celebrated Alexander Hamilton, who was among the most influential drafters of the Constitution, was not afraid to publish the following in *Federalist* no. 71:

"There are some who would be inclined to regard the servile pliancy of the Executive to a prevailing current, either in the community or in the legislature, as its best recommendation. But such men entertain very crude notions, as well, of the purpose for which government was instituted, as of the true means by which the public happiness may be promoted.

"The republican principle demands that the deliberate sense of the community should govern the conduct of those to whom they entrust the management of their affairs; but it does not require an unqualified complaisance to every sudden breeze of passion, or to every transient impulse which the people may receive from the arts of men who flatter their prejudices to betray their interests.

"It is a just observation, that the people commonly *intend* the PUBLIC GOOD. This often applies to their very errors. But their good sense would

They lengthened the representative's term of office in order to allow him greater latitude to exercise his own judgment.

Like the various state constitutions, the federal constitution divided the legislature into two branches.

In the states, however, the two parts of the legislature were composed of the same elements and elected in the same way. As a result, the passions and wishes of the majority manifested themselves just as easily, and found an organ and an instrument just as rapidly, in one house as in the other. This made the drafting of laws a violent and precipitous process.

The federal constitution made both houses of the legislature dependent on the votes of the people, but it established different rules of eligibility and a different mode of election for each, so that if one of the two branches of the legislature did not represent different interests from the other, as is the case in some nations, it did at least represent a superior wisdom.

In order to become a senator, a man had to have reached a mature age, and the responsibility of electing senators was bestowed on select assemblies composed of a relatively small number of people.

Democracies are by their very nature inclined to concentrate all social force in the hands of the legislature. Since the legislative power is the one that emanates most directly from the people, it is also the one that shares most fully in the people's omnipotence.

---

despise the adulator who should pretend that they always *reason right* about the *means* of promoting it. They know from experience that they sometimes err; and the wonder is that they so seldom err as they do, beset, as they continually are, by the wiles of parasites and sycophants, by the snares of the ambitious, the avaricious, the desperate, by the artifices of men who possess their confidence more than they deserve it, and of those who seek to possess rather than to deserve it.

"When occasions present themselves, in which the interests of the people are at variance with their inclinations, it is the duty of the persons whom they have appointed to be the guardians of those interests, to withstand the temporary delusion, in order to give them time and opportunity for more cool and sedate reflection. Instances might be cited in which a conduct of this kind has saved the people from very fatal consequences of their own mistakes, and has procured lasting monuments of their gratitude to the men who had courage and magnanimity enough to serve them at the peril of their displeasure."

One therefore finds in the legislature a habitual tendency to gather all authority unto itself.

This concentration of powers not only hinders the proper conduct of government but also gives rise to despotism of the majority.

State lawmakers frequently gave in to these democratic instincts; those of the Union always courageously resisted them.

In the states, executive power was entrusted to an official who seemed to be placed on a par with the legislature but who in reality was but a blind and passive instrument of its will. On what source of power could he draw? The length of his term of office? In general he was elected for only one year. His prerogatives? He had none to speak of. The legislature could reduce him to impotence by choosing to enforce its laws through special commissions made up of legislators themselves. If it wished, it could even deny the governor his salary, thus effectively removing him from office.

The federal constitution concentrated all the rights of the executive power, as well as all the responsibilities, in a single man. It gave the president four years of existence; it assured him of receiving his salary throughout his term of office; it gave him powers of patronage and armed him with a veto. In short, after carefully circumscribing the limits of executive power, it sought to make the executive strong and free within its proper sphere.

Of all the powers, the judicial power is the one that remained most independent of the legislative under the constitutions of the states.

Yet in all the states, the legislature reserved the right to fix the compensation of judges, which inevitably leaves those judges subject to its immediate influence.

In some states, judges are appointed for only a limited period of time, which again deprives them of much of their power and freedom.

In other states, legislative and judicial powers are thoroughly confounded. In New York, for example, the senate sits as the state's high court in certain cases.

By contrast, the federal constitution took care to separate the judicial power from all the others. It also made judges in-

dependent by declaring that their salaries should not be tampered with and that they should remain on the bench for life.
The practical consequences of these differences are easy to see. It is obvious to any attentive observer that the business of the Union is infinitely better conducted than that of any of the states.

The federal government is more just and moderate in its conduct than the government of any of the states. There is more wisdom in its views, more foresight and shrewdness in its planning, and more skill, continuity, and firmness in the execution of its designs.

This chapter can be summed up in a few words.

Two principal dangers threaten the existence of democracies:

The complete subjugation of the legislative power to the will of the electorate.

The concentration in the legislative power of all the other powers of government.

The men who framed the constitutions of the states encouraged the growth of these dangers. Those who framed the constitution of the Union did what they could to make them less formidable.

WHAT DISTINGUISHES THE FEDERAL CONSTITUTION OF THE UNITED STATES OF AMERICA FROM ALL OTHER FEDERAL CONSTITUTIONS

The American confederation seems to resemble all other confederations. — Yet its effects are different. — What accounts for this? — How this confederation differs from all others. — The American government is not a federal government but an incomplete national government.

The United States of America is not the first or only example of a confederation. Even if we leave Antiquity out of the discussion, we find several examples in modern Europe: Switzerland, the Germanic Empire, and the Republic of the Netherlands either once were or still are confederations.

When one studies the constitutions of these various countries, one is surprised to discover that the powers they grant to the federal government are virtually the same as those granted by the American Constitution to the government of the United States. Like the American Constitution, these European constitutions give the central power the right to make peace and war, to raise men and money, to provide for general needs, and to regulate the common interests of the nation.

Yet the federal government in each of these countries almost always remained feeble and powerless, whereas that of the Union deals with affairs vigorously and easily.

What is more, the first American Union did not survive because its government was too weak, yet that government, weak as it was, was granted powers as extensive as those enjoyed by the federal government today. Indeed, it is fair to say that in some respects its privileges were even greater.

The present Constitution therefore embodies certain new principles, which, though not striking at first glance, have exerted a profound influence.

This Constitution, which at first sight seems indistinguishable from the federal constitutions that preceded it, is in fact based on an entirely new theory, a theory that must be counted as one of the great discoveries of contemporary political science.

In all confederations prior to the American confederation of 1789, the peoples that allied for a common purpose agreed to obey the injunctions of a federal government, but they retained the right to promulgate the laws of the union themselves and oversee their enforcement.

The American states that united in 1789 agreed that the federal government should be allowed not only to dictate laws to them but also to enforce its own laws.

The right is the same in both cases; only the exercise of that right is different. But the effects of that one difference are immense.

In all the confederations that preceded the American Union as we know it today, the federal government was obliged to rely on the separate governments included in the confederation in order to meet its own needs. If a prescribed measure displeased one of those governments, it could always circumvent the requirement to obey. If strong, it could resort to arms; if weak, it could tolerate resistance to the laws of the union that it had accepted as its own, invoke its very weakness as a pretext, and rely on the force of inertia to have its way.

Thus, inevitably, one of two things came to pass: either the most powerful of the united peoples seized the powers of the federal authority and dominated the others in its name;[36] or the federal government was abandoned to its own forces, anarchy established itself among the confederates, and the union lost the power to act.[37]

In America, the subjects of the Union are not states but ordinary citizens. When the Union wants to levy a tax, it addresses itself not to the government of Massachusetts but to each of the state's inhabitants. Previous federal governments confronted peoples; the Union confronts individuals. Its strength is not borrowed but drawn from within. It has its own administrators, its own courts, its own law enforcement officers, and its own army.

To be sure, the patriotic spirit, collective passions, and provincial prejudices of each state still tend to diminish significantly the scope of the federal power thus constituted and to create centers of resistance to its wishes. Because the sovereignty of the federal government is limited, it cannot be as powerful as a government with full sovereignty. But that is an evil inherent in any federal system.

In America, each state has far fewer opportunities and temptations to resist. And if the thought of resistance does arise, it cannot be acted upon without openly violating the laws of the Union, disrupting the normal course of justice, and raising the banner of revolt. In other words, the state must immediately adopt an extreme position, and that is a step that men are extremely reluctant to take.

In previous confederations, rights accorded to the union were sources of conflict rather than power, because they

[36]This is what happened to the Greeks under Philip when it fell to him to carry out a decree of the Amphictyons. It also happened in the Republic of the Netherlands, which was always ruled by one province, Holland. The same thing is happening now in the Germanic states. Austria and Prussia have set themselves up as agents of the Diet and dominate the whole confederation in its name.

[37]This has always been the case in the Swiss Confederation. Switzerland would have ceased to exist centuries ago were it not for jealousies among its neighbors.

encouraged the union to increase its demands without giving it additional means to enforce its will. Hence the actual weakness of federal governments almost always increased in direct proportion to their nominal powers.

This is not the case in the American Union. Like most ordinary governments, the federal government can do whatever it has been given the right to do.

The human mind invents things more readily than words. That is why so many improper terms and inadequate expressions are in use.

Several nations form a permanent league and establish a supreme authority. This authority does not act directly on ordinary citizens, as a national government might do, but it does act on each of the confederated peoples taken as a body.

Such a government, so different from all others, is called federal.

Subsequently, a new form of society is found in which several peoples actually merge to form a single people, united with respect to certain common interests while remaining in all other respects separate, mere confederates.

Here the central government acts directly on the people it governs, administering them and judging them as national governments do, but it does so only within a limited sphere. Clearly this is not a federal government; it is an incomplete national government. This was how people discovered a new form of government, one that was neither precisely national nor precisely federal. To date, that is as far as anyone has gone: the new word that ought to express this new thing does not yet exist.

Because other unions failed to achieve this new form of confederation, they faced civil war, subjugation, or stagnation. The nations that constituted those unions were all either insufficiently enlightened to see the remedy for their ills or insufficiently courageous to use it.

The first American Union suffered from the same flaws.

In America, however, the confederated states had long been parts of a single empire before achieving independence. Therefore they had not acquired the habit of fully governing themselves, and national prejudices had not been able to strike deep roots. More enlightened than the rest of the world, they were equally enlightened among themselves. The passions that ordinarily lead nations to oppose the extension of federal power they felt only feebly. And those passions were combated by the greatest citizens. Even as Americans experienced the malady, they steadfastly contemplated the remedy. They corrected their laws and saved the country.

ON THE ADVANTAGES OF THE FEDERAL SYSTEM IN GENERAL, AND ITS SPECIAL UTILITY FOR AMERICA

Happiness and liberty enjoyed by small nations. — Power of great nations. — Great empires encourage the development of civilization. — That force is often the first element of prosperity for a nation. — The purpose of the federal system is to combine the advantages of a small territory with those of a large one. — Advantages that the United States derives from this system. — The law bends to the needs of the people, the people do not bend to the necessities of the law. — Activity, progress, taste for and use of freedom by the American people. — The public spirit of the Union is but the epitome *of provincial patriotism. — Things and ideas circulate freely throughout the United States. — The Union is free and happy like a small nation and respected like a large one.*

In small nations, society's eye penetrates everywhere. The improving spirit delves into even the minutest details: because the nation's ambition is much tempered by its weakness, its efforts and resources are almost entirely turned inward and are not likely to be dissipated in the vain cloud of glory. Since each person's capabilities are generally limited, so are his desires. Moderate fortunes make conditions almost equal. Mores seem simple and tranquil. Thus, all things considered, and allowing for varying degrees of morality and enlightenment, one ordinarily finds greater prosperity, meets more people, and encounters a more tranquil existence in small nations than in large ones.

When tyranny establishes itself in a small nation, it is more disruptive than in a large one, because its scope is more limited, and it therefore affects everything within its reach. Deprived of any great purpose, it occupies itself with a multitude of small ones. It is both violent and petty. From the political world, which is, properly speaking, its domain, it moves into private life. After actions, it aspires to regiment tastes; after the state, it seeks to govern families. But such tyranny is rare. In fact, liberty is the natural condition of small societies. Government in such countries offers too little enticement to ambition, and the resources of private individuals are too limited, to readily permit the concentration of sovereign power in one person's hands. If this does occur, it is not difficult for the governed to unite and, by making common cause, to overthrow tyranny along with the tyrant.

Small nations have therefore always been the cradle of political liberty. As it happens, most of them have lost that liberty as they grew, which shows that it was a product of the smallness of the nation's size rather than of the character of its people.

The history of the world offers no example of a large nation that remained a republic for long,[38] and this fact has led people to assert that such a thing is impracticable. For my own part, I think that it is highly imprudent for man, who each day fails to grasp what is real and present and who is constantly surprised by the unexpected in the things he knows best, to try to prescribe the limits of the possible and judge the future. What one can say with certainty is that the existence of a large republic will always be far more vulnerable than that of a small one.

All the passions fatal to republics increase with the extent of the territory, while the virtues that sustain them do not increase at the same rate.

The ambition of individuals increases with the power of the state; the strength of parties, with the importance of the goal they set for themselves; but the love of country that must counter these destructive passions is no greater in a vast republic than in a tiny one. Indeed, it would be easy to prove that love of country is less developed and less powerful in a large republic than in a small one. Great wealth and profound misery, big cities, depraved morals, individual selfishness, and complication of interests are among the perils that almost

[38] Here I am speaking not of a confederation of small republics but of a large, consolidated republic.

always exist in large states. Several of these things pose no threat to the existence of monarchies, and some may even contribute to their longevity. In monarchies, moreover, the government has forces of its own. It uses the people and does not depend on them. The greater the people, the more powerful the prince. But a republican government has only the support of the majority with which to counter these dangers. That element of strength is proportionately no greater in a vast republic than in a small one. Thus, while the means of attack constantly increase in number and power, the force of resistance remains the same. One can even say that that force decreases, because the more the population grows, and the more diversified minds and interests become, the more difficult it is to form a cohesive majority.

It has been observed, moreover, that the intensity of human passions is increased not only by the loftiness of the goal toward which those passions are directed but also by the multitude of individuals who experience them simultaneously. There is not a man alive who has not experienced the intensification of emotion that comes of sharing one's feelings with a crowd as opposed to experiencing those same feelings alone. In a large republic, political passions become irresistible, not only because the stakes are immense but also because millions of people experience them in the same way at the same time.

One may therefore venture this general conclusion, that nothing is more inimical to human welfare and freedom than great empires.

Nevertheless, large states have distinct advantages that must be recognized.

Not only is the desire for power among the common people in such states more ardent than it is elsewhere, but in certain souls the love of glory is also more highly developed, for such souls find in the applause of a great people an object worthy of their effort and apt to raise them as it were above themselves. In large states, stimuli to thought operate more rapidly and more powerfully, and ideas circulate more freely. Great cities are in essence vast intellectual centers wherein the multifarious emanations of the human spirit may shine and combine: this fact explains why enlightenment and civilization in general progress more rapidly in large nations than in small ones. In addition, major discoveries often require a greater concentration of national resources than the government of a small nation can manage. In a great nation, the government has more general ideas and can free itself more completely from the routine of precedent and the self-interest of localities. Its designs are more ingenious, and its manner bolder.

Domestic prosperity is more comprehensive and widespread in small nations so long as they remain at peace, but war is more harmful to them than it is to large countries. In the latter, remoteness from the border sometimes allows the better part of the population to remain safe from danger for centuries on end. For such a country, war is more a cause of discomfort than of ruin.

In this connection as in so many others, moreover, one consideration dominates all others: that of necessity.

If all nations were small and none were large, humanity would surely be freer and happier. But one cannot prevent the existence of great nations.

This introduces into the world a new element of national prosperity, namely, force. What does it matter if a nation presents an image of prosperity and freedom if it is constantly vulnerable to pillage and conquest? What good does it do a nation to excel in manufacturing and commerce if another country rules the seas and imposes its laws on markets everywhere? Small nations are often miserable not because they are small but because they are weak; large ones prosper not because they are large but because they are strong. For all nations, therefore, force is often a precondition of prosperity and even of existence. Barring unusual circumstances, therefore, small nations always end up annexed to great ones, either coerced by violence or of their own volition. I know of no condition more deplorable than that of a nation that cannot defend itself or supply its own needs.

The federal system was created in order to combine the various advantages of largeness with those of smallness.

A glance at the United States of America is enough to reveal the many benefits that it derives from having adopted such a system.

In large, centralized nations, lawmakers are obliged to give the laws a uniform character that does not comport with the diversity of places and customs. Lacking knowledge of particular cases, they can proceed only on the basis of general rules. Men are therefore obliged to bend to the necessities of legislation, because legislation is incapable of accommodating the needs and customs of men. This is a great source of trouble and woe.

Confederations do not suffer from this drawback: Congress governs the main activities of social life, but all the details are left to legislation by the states.

It is impossible to imagine the degree to which this division of sovereignty contributes to the well-being of the states. Each state of the Union is a small society in which, because there is no need to be concerned with either self-defense or outward expansion, public power and individual energy are entirely directed toward internal improvement. The central government of each state, being close to the people it governs, is daily informed of any needs that may arise. Every year, new plans are put forward, debated in town meetings and before the state legislature, and reported in the press, thereby arousing the interest of all citizens and enlisting their zealous support. The need for improvement constantly stirs but does not trouble the American republics. Ambition for power is supplanted by love of prosperity, a more common passion but also a less dangerous one. In America it is widely believed that the continued existence of republican forms in the New World depends on the continued existence of the federal system. Much of the misery that afflicts the new states of South America is attributed to the fact that people there tried to establish large republics rather than divide sovereignty.

There can be no doubt that in the United States the taste for, and experience of, republican government began in the towns and provincial assemblies. In a small state like Connecticut, for example, where a great political issue might be the construction of a canal or highway, where the state has no army to pay and no war to support and is incapable of bringing its leaders much in the way of either wealth or glory, one can imagine nothing more natural or more appropriate to the nature of things than a republic. Now, this same republican spirit, these same mores and habits of a free people, having arisen and flourished in the various states, later found it easy to establish themselves throughout the land. The public spirit of the Union itself was in a sense simply a concentrated form of provincial patriotism. Each citizen of the United States took the interest aroused by his little republic and carried it over into love of the common fatherland. In defending the Union, the citizen defended the growing prosperity of his own province, along with his right to govern its affairs and his prospects for winning approval of improvements likely to make him a wealthier man: things that in the ordinary course of events are more likely to sway the hearts of men than are the general interests of the country and the glory of the nation.

If, moreover, the spirit and mores of the American people made them more apt than others to bring prosperity to a great republic, the federal system made their task far less difficult. The confederation of all the American states does not suffer from the drawbacks that usually arise when large numbers of people live together. The union is a republic that is large in size, but it may be likened to a small republic because of the relatively small number of issues with which its government is concerned. Its actions are important, but they are rare. Since the sovereignty of the Union is hobbled and incomplete, the exercise of that sovereignty poses no danger to liberty. Nor does it arouse the immoderate desire for power and notoriety that are so fatal to large republics. Since things do not necessarily converge toward a common center, one does not find vast metropolises or immense riches or great misery or sudden revolution. Political passions, instead of spreading like wildfire and engulfing the entire country in an instant, are countered by the individual interests and passions of each state.

Within the Union, however, things and ideas circulate freely, as in a single nation. Nothing impedes the burgeoning spirit of enterprise. The government attracts talented and enlightened people. And within the borders of the Union there reigns a profound peace, as within a country governed by a unified regime. Beyond its borders, the United States ranks as one of the most powerful nations on earth. To foreign commerce it offers more than eight hundred leagues of coastline, and since it holds in its hands the keys to an entire continent, it can command respect for its flag throughout the seven seas.

The Union is free and happy like a small nation, glorious and strong like a large one.

WHY THE FEDERAL SYSTEM IS NOT WITHIN THE REACH OF ALL PEOPLES, AND WHY THE ANGLO-AMERICANS WERE ABLE TO ADOPT IT

In any federal system, there are inherent flaws that lawmakers cannot combat. — Complexity of any federal system. — Citizens are required to make daily use of their intelligence. — Practical knowledge of the Americans as to the business of government. — Relative weakness of the government of the Union, another inherent flaw of the federal system. — The Americans diminished the seriousness of that flaw but were unable to eliminate it. — The sovereignty of individual states appears to be weaker but is in fact stronger than that of the Union. — Why. — In confederated nations there must exist natural causes of union independent of the laws. — What those causes are among the Anglo-Americans. — Maine and Georgia, though separated by four hundred leagues, are more naturally united than Normandy and Brittany. — War is the principal stumbling block to successful confederation. — The example of the United States proves this. — The Union need not fear any great wars. — Why. — Dangers that the nations of Europe would face if they were to adopt the American federal system.

If, after much effort, lawmakers are able to exert an indirect influence on the destiny of a nation, they are celebrated for their genius. But often it is a country's geographical situation, about which they can do nothing; or a social state that developed without their concurrence; or mores and ideas of whose origins they know nothing; or a point of departure of which they are ignorant that acts on society with irresistible force, against which lawmakers struggle in vain and which ultimately carries them along with it.

The legislator is like a navigator on the high seas. He can steer the vessel on which he sails, but he cannot alter its construction, raise the wind, or stop the ocean from swelling beneath his feet.

I have shown what advantages the Americans derive from the federal system. I have yet to explain what allowed them to adopt that system, whose benefits it is not given to all peoples to enjoy.

One finds in the federal system accidental flaws stemming from the laws; these can be corrected by lawmakers. One also encounters other flaws, which, because they are inherent in the system, cannot be eliminated by nations that adopt it. Hence those nations must find in themselves the strength necessary to cope with the natural imperfections of their government.

Among the flaws inherent in any federal system, the most visible is the complexity of the system's operation. The federal system necessarily brings two sovereign powers together. Lawmakers can make the activities of these two powers as simple and as equal as possible and limit each to a clearly defined sphere of action, but they cannot reduce the two to one or prevent clashes on certain issues.

No matter what one does, therefore, the federal system rests on a complicated theory, the application of which requires citizens to rely daily on the light of reason.

Generally speaking, only simple conceptions can grip the mind of a nation. An idea that is clear and precise even though false will always have greater power in the world than an idea that is true but complex. That is why political parties, which are like small nations within a large one, are always quick to adopt a symbol or name or principle that may only imperfectly represent the goal they set for themselves or the means they employ yet without which they could neither engage in action nor survive. Governments that are based on a single idea or easily identified sentiment may not be the best, but they are surely the strongest and most durable.

By contrast, when one looks at the Constitution of the United States, the most perfect of all known federal constitutions, it is frightening to discover the range of diverse knowledge and discernment that it assumes in the people it is supposed to govern. The government of the Union rests almost entirely on legal fictions. The Union is an ideal nation that exists only in the mind, as it were, and whose extent and limits can be discovered only through an effort of intelligence.

Even if the general theory is well understood, difficulties of application remain: they are innumerable, for the sovereignty of the Union is so enmeshed with that of the states that it is impossible at first glance to see where the boundaries lie. Everything is conventional and artificial in such a government, which is suitable only for a people long accustomed to managing its own affairs, among whom political science has filtered down to the lowest ranks of society. Nothing makes me admire the common sense and practical intelligence of the Americans more than the way in which they avoid the countless difficulties arising from their federal constitution. Seldom have I met an ordinary American who could not distinguish with surprising ease between obligations stemming from laws passed by Congress and obligations originating in the laws of his state, and who, having distinguished matters falling within the general prerogatives of the Union from those that the local legislature is supposed to deal with, could not indicate the point where the competence of the federal courts begins and where that of state courts leaves off.

The Constitution of the United States resembles those beautiful creations of human industry that bring abundant glory and wealth to their inventors yet in other hands remain sterile.

One sees this today in Mexico.

The inhabitants of Mexico, wishing to establish a federal system, took the federal constitution of their neighbors the Anglo-Americans as their model and copied it almost entirely.[39] In borrowing the letter of the law, however, they were unable to borrow as well the spirit that animated it. Again and again we therefore find them ensnaring themselves in the machinery of their divided government. With sovereignty no longer circumscribed by the constitution, the states trespass upon that of the union and the union upon that of the states. Even today Mexico is still lurching from anarchy to military despotism and back again.

The second and most fatal of the flaws inherent in the federal system, in my view, is the relative weakness of the government of the union.

The principle on which all confederations are based is the fragmentation of sovereignty. Lawmakers can make this fragmentation less apparent and even conceal it for a time, but

[39]See the Mexican Constitution of 1824.

they cannot eliminate it entirely. Yet a fragmented sovereignty will always be weaker than one that is complete.

In our discussion of the Constitution of the United States, we saw how artfully the Americans managed to circumscribe the power of the Union within the narrow ambit of a federal government yet at the same time give it the appearance and, to a certain extent, the power of a national government.

By proceeding in this way, the Union's lawmakers diminished the danger inherent in the nature of confederations but were unable to eliminate it entirely.

It is said that the American government does not address itself to the states: it transmits its injunctions directly to its citizens and obliges them individually to bend to the common will.

But if federal law were to collide violently with the interests and prejudices of a state, would there not be reason to fear that each citizen of that state would find it in his interest to wed the cause of the man who refused to obey? Because the authority of the Union would harm all citizens of the state in the same way at the same time, any attempt by the federal government to divide in order to conquer them would fail. They would instinctively feel obliged to unite in their own defense, and the portion of sovereignty left to the state would provide a natural rallying point. Fiction would then give way to reality, and one might well see a clash between an organized regional power and the central authority.

I would say much the same thing about federal justice. If a court of the Union were to violate an important state law in a specific case, the real if not apparent conflict would be between the injured state, represented by a citizen, and the Union, represented by its courts.[40]

---

[40]Example: the Constitution gives the Union the right to sell unoccupied land for its own benefit. Suppose that Ohio were to claim the same right for unoccupied land within its borders on the grounds that the Constitution meant to include only territory not yet subject to the jurisdiction of any state, and consequently that it wished to sell the same land. To be sure, the legal issue before the courts would arise between purchasers holding a title to the land issued by the Union and purchasers holding a title issued by the state, not between the Union and Ohio. But if the Court of the United States found that the federal buyer held good title to the land while the Ohio courts upheld the title of his competitor, what would become of the legal fiction then?

One would have to be quite inexperienced in the ways of the world to imagine that if ways of satisfying human passions are allowed to exist, legal fictions can somehow prevent people from discovering and using them.

Thus, while American lawmakers reduced the probability of a clash between the two sovereign powers, they did not eliminate all sources of conflict.

It is possible to go even further and say that they were not able to ensure that, in case of conflict, federal power would prevail.

They gave the Union money and soldiers, but the states retained the love and favor of the people.

The sovereignty of the Union is an abstraction whose external referents are few in number. The sovereignty of the states is readily apparent to all the senses; it is easily understood, and its actions are at every moment plain to see. The sovereignty of the Union is new, whereas the sovereignty of the states was born with the nation itself.

The sovereignty of the Union is the work of art. The sovereignty of the states is natural; it exists by itself, without effort, like a father's authority in a family.

People feel the sovereignty of the Union only as it impinges on a few great interests. It represents a vast, remote fatherland, a vague and indefinite sentiment. The sovereignty of the states in a sense envelops each citizen and affects every detail of his daily life. It is responsible for safeguarding his property, his liberty, and his life. Its influence on his well-being or misery is never-ending. The sovereignty of the states is sustained by memories, habits, local prejudices, regional and familial self-interest — in short, by all the things that make the patriotic instinct such a powerful force in the heart of man. How can one doubt its advantages?

Since lawmakers cannot prevent dangerous clashes between the two sovereignties that the federal system brings together, their efforts to dissuade confederated peoples from waging war must be combined with specific measures to lead them toward peace.

From this it follows that the federal pact cannot long endure unless the peoples to whom it applies satisfy a certain number of prerequisites for union, prerequisites which, if met, ease the business of living together and facilitate the task of government.

If the federal system is to succeed, not only good laws but also favorable circumstances are required.

In the past, nations that entered into confederations with other nations have always shared certain common interests, which served in a sense as the intellectual basis of their association.

Apart from material interests, however, man also has ideas and feelings. If a confederation is to endure for long, a homogeneity of civilization is no less necessary than a homogeneity of needs among its member nations. The civilization of the canton of Vaud is to the civilization of the canton of Uri as the nineteenth century is to the fifteenth: hence Switzerland has never really had a federal government. Only on the map do its various cantons constitute a union, as would become apparent if a central authority ever attempted to apply a uniform set of laws throughout its territory.

One fact about the United States admirably facilitates the existence of the federal government. Not only do the various states share almost the same interests, origin, and language, but they are also civilized to the same degree, so that it is usually easy for them to come to agreement. I doubt that there is any nation in Europe, however small, whose various parts are not less homogeneous than the people of America, who occupy a territory at least half the size of Europe.

The distance from Maine to Georgia is roughly four hundred leagues, but the difference between the civilization of Maine and that of Georgia is less than that between the civilization of Normandy and that of Brittany. It is therefore only natural that Maine and Georgia, though situated at opposite ends of a vast empire, should find more genuine opportunities to form a confederation than do Normandy and Brittany, which are separated by only a narrow stream.

In addition to the opportunities for confederation that American lawmakers found in the mores and habits of the people, the country's geographical situation afforded additional opportunities to which primary credit for the adoption and persistence of the federal system must be ascribed.

The most important of all the actions that bring the existence of a people to the world's attention is war. In war, a people acts as a single individual toward foreign peoples: it fights for its very existence.

As long as the issue is simply one of preserving the peace within a country's borders and promoting its prosperity, skill in government, reason among the governed, and a certain natural attachment that men almost always feel toward their fatherland can easily suffice. But in order for a nation to wage war on a grand scale, its citizens must be prepared to make numerous and painful sacrifices. Anyone who believes that large numbers of people are capable of accepting such social obligations voluntarily has but little knowledge of humankind.

So it is that all nations that have had to wage great wars have been forced, almost against their will, to increase the powers of government. Those that failed to do so were conquered. A long war almost always brings a nation face-to-face with an unhappy alternative: defeat will lead to destruction, while triumph will end in despotism.

In general, therefore, it is in war that the weakness of a government reveals itself most visibly and dangerously, and I have shown that the inherent flaw of federal governments is to be very weak.

In the federal system, not only is there no administrative centralization or anything that resembles it, but governmental centralization itself is at best incomplete, and this is always a great cause of weakness when a nation must defend itself against other nations in which governmental centralization is complete.

In the federal constitution of the United States, which grants the central government more real powers than any other federal constitution, this evil is still keenly felt.

A single example will allow the reader to judge for himself.

The Constitution gives Congress the right to call the various state militias to active duty when it becomes necessary to put down an insurrection or repel an invasion. Another article states that the president of the United States then becomes the commander-in-chief of the militia.

During the War of 1812, the president ordered the militias of the north to deploy on the country's borders. Connecticut and Massachusetts, whose interests suffered as a result of the war, refused to dispatch their contingents.

The Constitution, they claimed, authorizes the federal government to use the militias in case of *insurrection* or *invasion*, but neither had yet occurred. They further claimed that the same Constitution that gave the Union the right to call up the militia reserved to the states the right to appoint its officers. Hence in their view it followed that, even in war, no official of the Union had the right to command the state militias except the president in person, whereas in this war they were being asked to serve in an army commanded by someone else.

These absurd and destructive doctrines were approved not only by the governors and legislatures of these two states but also by the state courts, and the federal government was forced to look elsewhere for the troops it needed.[41]

What, then, is to prevent the American Union, protected though it is by the relative perfection of its laws, from falling apart in the midst of a great war? The answer is that it has no great wars to fear.

Situated in the center of a vast continent with limitless room for the expansion of human endeavor, the Union is almost as isolated from the rest of the world as if it were surrounded by water on all sides.

Only a million people live in Canada, and they are divided into two hostile nations. The rigors of the climate limit the extent of its territory and close its ports six months out of the year.

Between Canada and the Gulf of Mexico one finds a few half-destroyed savage tribes that cannot stand up to six thousand soldiers.

[41]*Kent's Commentaries*, vol. 1, p. 244. Note that I have taken this example from a period subsequent to the establishment of the present Constitution. Had I wished to go back as far as the time of the first confederation, I could have cited far more conclusive instances. At that time a genuine enthusiasm reigned in the nation, and the Revolution was represented by an eminently popular man, yet Congress, strictly speaking, had absolutely no resources at its disposal. It was constantly short of men and money. Its best laid plans came to naught, and the Union, always on the point of perishing, was saved far more by the weakness of its enemies than by its own strength.

At one point in the south, the Union comes into contact with the empire of Mexico. Some day great wars will probably come from that quarter. For many years to come, however, Mexico's relatively backward state of civilization, corrupt mores, and miserable condition will prevent her from assuming an eminent place among the nations of the world. As for the powers of Europe, distance makes them less formidable than they might otherwise be.*

The great good fortune of the United States is therefore not to have hit upon a federal constitution that enables it to endure a great war but rather to be so situated that it need not fear such a war.

No one can be more appreciative of the advantages of the federal system than I. I see it as one of the most potent arrangements there is for making men prosperous and free. I envy the lot of the nations that have been permitted to adopt it. Yet I refuse to believe that a confederated nation can hold out for long against an equally powerful nation whose government is centralized.

Any nation confronting the great military monarchies of Europe that chose to fragment its sovereignty would, in my view, thereby abdicate its power and perhaps its name and very existence.

How admirable is the position of the New World, where man still has no enemies other than himself! To be happy and free he has only to wish it.

*See Note XIV, page 499.

PART II

Thus far I have examined institutions, reviewed published laws, and depicted the political society of the United States as it is presently constituted.

Yet standing above all the institutions and outside all the forms of political society is a sovereign power, that of the people, which can abolish or change these things as it pleases.

It remains for me to examine the ways in which that power, which dominates the laws, proceeds; and to explain what its instincts and passions are; what secret forces propel, impede, or guide it on its irresistible course; what effects flow from its omnipotence; and what future lies in store for it.

Chapter 1

WHY IT IS STRICTLY ACCURATE TO SAY THAT IN THE UNITED STATES IT IS THE PEOPLE WHO GOVERN

In America, the people choose those who make the law and those who carry it out. They constitute the juries that punish infractions of that law. Institutions are democratic not only in principle but in all their ramifications. For example, the people choose their representatives *directly*, and in general they do so *every year*, the better to ensure their subservience. Hence it is really the people who rule, and even though the form of government is representative, it is clear that there can be no durable obstacles capable of preventing the opinions, prejudices, interests, and even passions of the people from making their influence felt on the daily direction of society.

In the United States, as in every country where the people rule, it is the majority that governs in the people's name.

That majority consists mainly of peaceful citizens who, whether by taste or interest, sincerely desire what is good for the country. Around them political parties constantly contend for their adherence and support.

Chapter 2

PARTIES IN THE UNITED STATES

Important distinction to be made among parties. — Parties that treat one another like rival nations. — Parties properly so-called. — Difference between great and minor parties. — When they come into being. — Their various characteristics. — America has had great parties. — It no longer does. — Federalists. — Republicans. — Defeat of the Federalists. — Difficulty of creating parties in the United States. — What people try in order to do so. — Aristocratic or democratic characteristics found in all parties. — General Jackson's battle with the bank.

I MUST begin by making an important distinction among parties.

Some countries are so vast that even though the various populations that live in them are united under a single sovereignty, they have contradictory interests, which give rise to permanent tensions. Under such circumstances, these diverse populations constitute not parties in the strict sense but rather distinct nations. If civil war should break out, the conflict will be one between rival peoples rather than factions.

But when citizens differ about matters that interest all portions of the country equally, such as the general principles of government, then what may truly be called parties come into being.

Parties are an evil inherent in free governments, but their character and instincts are not always the same.

There are times when nations feel tormented by such great evils that a total change of political constitution begins to seem feasible. And there are times when the malaise strikes even deeper, and the social state itself is compromised. In such times great revolutions occur, and great parties arise.

Between these centuries of disorder and woe, there are other times when societies take their rest, and the human race seems to pause for breath. In fact, such interludes are more apparent than real. Time no more stops for nations than it does for individuals. Both advance daily toward a future of which they know nothing. If they seem to stand still, it is because their progress eludes us. To a runner, a person who is merely walking may seem to be standing still.

In any case, the changes affecting the political constitutions and social states of nations may at times be so slow and difficult to perceive that it becomes plausible to believe that an end has been achieved. The human spirit, convinced that the ground on which it stands is solid, sets itself a certain horizon and does not look beyond it.

Such times are ripe for intrigue and minor parties.

The political parties that I call great are those that dedicate themselves more to principles than to their consequences; to generalities and not particulars; to ideas and not to men. Such parties generally have nobler features, more generous passions, more genuine convictions, and a franker, bolder manner than others. Private interest, which always plays the greatest role in political passions, is here more skillfully hidden beneath the veil of public interest. At times it even succeeds in concealing itself from those whom it animates and impels to act.

By contrast, minor parties are generally without political faith. Because they do not feel ennobled and sustained by any great purpose, their character bears the stamp of self-interest, which clearly manifests itself in every action they undertake. They always become hotly passionate for coldly calculated reasons; their language is violent, but their course is timid and uncertain. Their tactics are squalid, as is the goal they set for themselves. Hence when a period of calm succeeds a violent revolution, great men seem suddenly to vanish, and souls turn inward.

Great parties stand society on its head; minor parties agitate it. Great parties tear society apart; minor parties corrupt it. The former may at times save society at the cost of disrupting it, while the latter invariably provoke agitation without profit.

America has had great parties in the past, but today they no longer exist. This change has contributed greatly to its happiness but not to its morality.

When the War of Independence ended and the time came to lay the foundation of a new government, the nation found itself divided into two camps. The views of both camps were as old as the world, and in one form or another one finds them under various names in all free societies. One camp wished to restrain the power of the people, the other to extend it without limit.

In America, the struggle between these two camps never took the violent form that has often distinguished it in other countries. Both parties were in agreement about the most essential points. Neither had to destroy an ancient order or overturn an entire society in order to prevail. Hence the lives and livelihoods of thousands of individuals did not depend on the triumph of one set of principles rather than another. But those principles did affect immaterial interests of the utmost importance, such as the love of equality and independence. This was enough to arouse violent passions.

The party that wanted to limit the power of the people sought above all to apply its doctrines to the Constitution of the Union, which earned it the name *federal*.

The other party, which posed as the only party to love liberty, claimed the title *republican*.

America is the land of democracy. The Federalists were therefore always in the minority, but their ranks included nearly all the great men to come out of the War of Independence, and their moral power was considerable. Circumstances favored them, moreover. The collapse of the first confederation had made people afraid that the country might lapse into anarchy, and the Federalists took advantage of this temporary state of affairs. For ten or twelve years, they controlled the business of government and were able to put some of their principles into practice. Not all of them, however, because with each passing day the opposition became more violent, so much so that no one dared to stand against it.

In 1801, the Republicans finally took control of the government. Thomas Jefferson was elected president. He brought his party the benefit of his famous name, great talents, and immense popularity.

The Federalists had always relied on artificial means and temporary resources to maintain themselves in power. Had it not been for the virtues and talents of their leaders and the fortune of circumstance, they would never have come to office at all. When the Republicans' turn finally came, it was as if the opposition party was engulfed by a sudden flood. The vast majority of the people voted against it, and Federalists found themselves in so small a minority that they lost faith in themselves. From that moment on, the Republican, or Democratic, party marched from conquest to conquest and eventually took complete control of society.

Feeling defeated, devoid of resources, and isolated in the nation's midst, the Federalists divided. Some joined the victors, while others furled their banner and changed their name. By now they have long since ceased to exist as a party.

The Federalist accession to power was in my view one of the most fortunate events attending the birth of the great American Union. The Federalists fought against the irresistible penchant of their century and their country. Their theories, whether sound or flawed, suffered from being inapplicable in their entirety to the society they wished to govern; what came to pass under Jefferson would therefore have come to pass sooner or later in any case. But at least their government left the new republic time to establish itself and later enabled it to survive the rapid evolution of doctrines the Federalists themselves had opposed. Indeed, many of their principles ultimately became part of their adversaries' creed. And the federal Constitution, which still exists today, is a lasting monument to their patriotism and wisdom.

So it is, then, that one sees no great political parties in the United States today. There are any number of parties that pose a threat to the future of the Union, but none that seem to be attacking the present form of the government or the general course of society. The parties that threaten the Union are based not on principles but on material interests. In the various provinces of such a vast empire, those interests constitute not so much parties as rival nations. In the recent past, for example, the North supported a system of restrictions on commerce, and the South took up arms in favor of freedom of trade, solely because the North is a manufacturing region and the South an agricultural one and the restrictions profit one at the expense of the other.

Though lacking great parties, the United States is teeming with minor ones, and public opinion is endlessly divided over insignificant issues. The effort expended on creating political parties — not an easy thing to do nowadays — can scarcely be imagined. Religious hatred does not exist in the United States, because religion is universally respected and no sect is dominant. Class hatred does not exist, because the people are everything, and no one yet dares to oppose them. Finally, there is no public misery to exploit, because the material condition of the country is so favorable to industry that it suffices to leave man to his own devices to enable him to achieve wonders. Yet ambition inevitably leads to the creation of parties, because it is difficult to throw a man out of power simply because one wants to take his place. All the skill of the politician therefore goes into organizing parties. In the United States, a politician first tries to identify his own interests and find out what similar interests might be joined with his. He then casts about to discover whether there might not by chance exist some doctrine or principle around which this new association might be organized, so that it may present itself to the world and gain ready acceptance. This might be compared to the royal imprimatur that our forefathers used to print on the first page of their works and incorporate into the book even though it was not part of its contents.

That done, the new force can be introduced into the world of politics.

To a foreigner, nearly all the domestic quarrels of the Americans seem at first glance either incomprehensible or puerile, and one is hard put to decide whether one ought to pity a people that takes such wretched trifles seriously or envy it the good fortune that permits it to do so.

But when one begins to study closely the secret instincts that govern factions in America, it is easy to see that most of them can be more or less accurately described as belonging to one of the two great parties that have always existed in free societies. The more deeply one enters into the intimate thoughts of these two parties, the clearer it becomes that one wants to limit the use of public power and the other to extend it.

I am not saying that the overt or covert aim of parties in America is always to see to it that either aristocracy or democracy prevails. I do say that in every political party aristocratic or democratic passions play a central role, and while these may not be visible to the casual observer, they do constitute the party's heart and soul.

I shall cite a recent example: the president launches an attack on the Bank of the United States. The country is aroused, and people take sides. In general, the enlightened classes take the side of the bank, while the people favor the president. Do you suppose that the people are capable of explaining the grounds for their opinion on such a difficult question, whose fine points even experienced men find daunting? Not at all. But the bank is an important institution that enjoys an independent existence. The people, who can demolish or exalt whatever power they choose, can do nothing about it, and this astonishes them. In a society where everything is in flux, this immovable object is offensive to their eyes, and they want to see if they can oblige it to change along with everything else.

VESTIGES OF THE ARISTOCRATIC PARTY IN THE UNITED STATES

Hidden opposition of the rich to democracy. — They withdraw into private life. — In the privacy of their homes they reveal their taste for exclusive pleasures and luxury. — Their simplicity outside the home. — Their affected condescension toward the people.

When the balance of power among the parties is upset in a nation where opinion is divided, one party may emerge with an irresistible preponderance over the others. It smashes every obstacle, crushes its adversaries, and exploits the whole of society for its own benefit. The losers, despairing of success, withdraw into hiding or lapse into silence. Stillness and silence reign everywhere. The entire nation seems united in a single thought. The victorious party then steps forward and says, "I have restored peace to the country, and I deserve thanks."

But under this apparent unanimity lurk deep divisions and a genuine opposition.

This is what happened in America: when the democratic party gained the upper hand, it took exclusive control of affairs. Since then, it has persistently molded mores and laws to its desires.

Today it is fair to say that the wealthy classes in the United States are almost entirely out of politics, and that wealth, far from being a privilege there, is a real cause of disfavor and an obstacle to attaining power.

The rich would therefore rather give up the fight than engage in often unequal battle with the poorest of their fellow citizens. Unable to assume a position in public life comparable to that which they occupy in private life, they abandon the former and concentrate on the latter. Within the state they form a society apart, with its own distinctive tastes and pleasures.

The rich resign themselves to this state of affairs as to an incurable ill. They take great care not to give so much as a hint that it wounds them. In public one hears them extol the blessings of republican government and the advantages of democratic institutions. For after hating one's enemies, what is more natural than flattering them?

Do you see this opulent citizen? Does he not resemble a Jew of the Middle Ages, afraid lest anyone suspect his riches? His dress is simple, his demeanor modest. Within the four walls of his home, luxury is adored. Into this sanctuary he allows only a few select guests, whom he insolently calls his equals. There is not a nobleman anywhere in Europe who is more exclusive in his pleasures than this man or more jealous of the least advantages conferred by a privileged position. Yet this same man leaves home to go work in a dusty hole in the business district downtown, where anyone is free to call on him. On the way there he passes his shoemaker, and the two men stop and begin to converse. What can they be saying to each other? These two citizens are discussing affairs of state, and they will not part without shaking hands.

But beneath this conventional enthusiasm, beyond this obsequious politeness toward the dominant power, it is easy to see that the rich feel a deep disgust with their country's democratic institutions. The people are a power they fear and despise. If democratic misrule someday leads to a political crisis, or if monarchy were ever to appear as a practical possibility in the United States, the truth of what I am saying will soon become apparent.

Political parties in pursuit of success can avail themselves of two primary weapons: *newspapers* and *associations*.

Chapter 3

ON FREEDOM OF THE PRESS IN THE UNITED STATES

Difficulty of restricting the freedom of the press. — Particular reasons that certain nations have for cherishing this freedom. — Freedom of the press is a necessary consequence of popular sovereignty as it is understood in America. — Violence of language in the periodical press in the United States. — The periodical press has its own instincts, as the example of the United States proves. — Opinion of the Americans concerning judicial punishment of offenses by the press. — Why the press is less powerful in the United States than in France.

FREEDOM of the press makes its power felt by influencing opinions of all kinds, not just political opinions. It affects mores as well as laws. In another part of this work, I shall attempt to determine the degree to which freedom of the press has influenced civil society in the United States. I shall try to determine the direction it has imparted to ideas and the habits of mind and feeling it has imposed on Americans. For now, however, I wish to examine the freedom of the press only as it affects the world of politics.

I confess that I do not feel toward the freedom of the press that complete and instantaneous love that one grants to things that by their very nature are supremely good. I love it out of consideration for the evils that it prevents far more than for the good that it does.

If someone were to show me a tenable intermediate position between complete independence of thought and total servitude, I might adopt it, but can such a position be found? Suppose you wish to curb the license of the press and restore order: how do you proceed? You begin by subjecting writers to trial by jury. But the jurors acquit, and what was only the opinion of an isolated individual becomes the opinion of the country. You have therefore done too much and yet not enough; you have no choice but to continue. You haul authors before permanent magistrates. But the judges are obliged to hear the case before pronouncing sentence. What a person might have been afraid to say in a book, he may proclaim with impunity in his plea. What he might have said obscurely in his text is then repeated in a thousand others. Expression is the external form of thought, its body, one might say, but it is not thought itself. Your courts may place the body under arrest, but the soul eludes them and subtly slips through their fingers. You have therefore done too much and yet not enough; you have no choice but to continue. Next, you abandon the writers to censors. Fine! The goal is near. But is the political platform not still free? You have therefore accomplished nothing; nay, you have made things worse. Might you perchance be treating thought as a material power of the sort that increases as the number of its agents increases? Will you count writers as you count soldiers in an army? The power of thought is not like a physical power: indeed, it is often the case that the smaller the number of people who express a thought, the more powerful it is. A forceful speaker who stirs a silent assembly with his speech exercises more power than the confused utterances of a thousand orators. And if a person can speak freely in even one public place, it is as if he had spoken publicly in every village. Hence you must suppress the freedom to speak as well as to write. Now at last you have reached your destination: everyone is silent. But what destination is it that you have reached? You began with an abuse of freedom and ended under a despot's heel.

You have gone from extreme independence to extreme servitude without finding in the vast distance separating the two a single place to rest.

There are peoples who, quite apart from the general reasons I have just stated, have specific reasons to cherish the freedom of the press.

In some nations that claim to be free, any agent of the government may violate the law with impunity, yet the country's constitution grants the oppressed no right to complain of this abuse of power before the courts. In such a country, the independence of the press can no longer be regarded as one among many guarantees of the citizens' freedom and security; it is the only guarantee.

Therefore, if the men who govern such a country were to

propose depriving the press of its independence, the people might respond with one voice: "Allow us to prosecute your crimes before ordinary judges, and perhaps then we will agree not to invoke the court of public opinion."

In a country where the dogma of popular sovereignty ostensibly reigns, censorship is not merely dangerous but monstrously absurd.

If each individual is granted the right to govern society, one has to presume that he also possesses the ability to choose among the various opinions that agitate his contemporaries and to appreciate the various facts that may guide his judgment.

Popular sovereignty and freedom of the press are therefore entirely consistent. By contrast, censorship and universal suffrage are contradictory and cannot coexist for long in the political institutions of any nation. Among the twelve million people who live in the United States, *not a single one* has yet proposed restricting the freedom of the press.

The first newspaper I laid eyes on upon arriving in America contained the following article, which I translate faithfully:

Throughout this whole business, the language of Jackson (the President) has been that of a heartless despot whose sole concern is to cling to power. Ambition is his crime, and it will be his punishment. Intrigue is his vocation, and intrigue will thwart his designs and cost him his power. He governs by corruption, and his criminal manipulations will end in embarrassment and shame. In the political arena he has shown himself to be a shameless and unrestrained gambler. He has been successful thus far, but the hour of reckoning is near. Soon he will be obliged to give back what he has won, cast aside his loaded dice, and retire from the scene to a place where he can curse his folly to his heart's content, for repentance is a virtue he knows nothing of. (*Vincennes Gazette*)

Many people in France assume that the violence of the press is due to the unstable state of our society, to our political passions, and to the general malaise that these things occasion. Hence they are always waiting for a time when, tranquillity having been restored to society, calm will likewise return to the press. For my part, I am perfectly willing to attribute the press's exorbitant influence on us to the causes set forth above, but I do not think those causes have much effect on its language. The periodical press seems to me to have instincts and passions of its own, independent of the circumstances in which it operates. What is happening in America is in my view proof of this assertion.

Of all the countries in the world today, America is perhaps the one that harbors the fewest seeds of revolution. Yet the American press has the same destructive tastes as the press in France, and the same violence, though without comparable grounds for anger. In America as in France, the press constitutes an extraordinary power, so peculiarly compounded of goods and evils that without it liberty cannot survive and with it order can scarcely be maintained.

What needs to be said is that the press has much less power in the United States than in France. Yet nothing is rarer in the United States than a prosecution of the press. The reason for this is simple: the Americans, having accepted the dogma of popular sovereignty, have been sincere in their application of it. It never occurred to them to mold an eternal constitution out of elements that change from day to day. Hence it is no crime to attack an existing law so long as one has no intention of evading that law by violent means.

The Americans believe, moreover, that the courts are powerless to moderate the press and that, because human language is too supple for judicial analysis, these kinds of offenses have a way of vanishing when the arm of the law reaches out to grasp them. In order to influence the press effectively, in their view, one would have to find a tribunal that was not only devoted to the existing order but also capable of placing itself above the surrounding swirl of public opinion; a court that would render its judgments without publicity, issue its decisions without legal grounds, and punish intentions even more than words. Anyone with the power to create and maintain such a tribunal would waste his time attacking the freedom of the press, for he would be the absolute master of society itself and in a position to rid himself of writers along with their writing. When it comes to the press, therefore, there really is no middle ground between servitude and license. In order to reap the priceless goods that derive from the freedom of the press, one must learn to accept the inevitable evils that it breeds. To seek the former without the latter is to succumb to the sort of illusion that sick nations indulge when, tired of fighting and exhausted by their exertions, they seek ways to oblige hostile opinions and contrary principles to coexist within the same territory.

There are many reasons why newspapers in America lack power. The primary ones are as follows.

The freedom to write, like any other freedom, is more redoubtable when new. A people that has never heard affairs of state discussed will believe the first orator to capture its ear. Among the Anglo-Americans, this freedom is as old as the colonies themselves. Furthermore, the press, skilled as it is at inflaming human passions, cannot create them out of whole cloth. In America, political life is active, varied, and even agitated, but it is rarely roiled by deep passions. Such passions seldom arise unless material interests are compromised, and in the United States material interests prosper. To appreciate the difference between the Anglo-Americans and us in this regard, I have only to glance at their newspapers and ours. In France, commercial advertising occupies only a very limited space, and even news articles are relatively few in number. The vital part of a newspaper is the section that features political debates. In America, three-quarters of the bulky newspaper that is set before you is filled with advertising, and the rest is mostly filled with political news and unremarkable anecdotes. Only occasionally does one find in some forgotten corner of the paper an impassioned debate of the sort that constitutes the French reader's daily fodder.

The effective force of any power is increased as control is centralized. This is a general law of nature confirmed by observation and appreciated with the surest of instincts by the least of despots.

In France, the press combines two distinct types of centralization.

Almost all its power is concentrated in one place and, in a sense, in the same hands, for the number of its organs is very small.

A press constituted in this way in the midst of a skeptical nation will enjoy almost limitless power. It is an enemy with which a government may enter into a truce for a more or less lengthy period of time but with which it has difficulty living in a permanent state of opposition.

Neither of these two types of centralization exists in America.

The United States has no capital. Enlightenment, like power, is disseminated throughout this vast country. Hence the beams of human intelligence do not all emanate from a common center but crisscross in every direction. Nowhere have the Americans established any central direction over their thinking, any more than they have established any central direction over affairs of state.

This is in part a consequence of local circumstances beyond the control of human beings. But it is also a result of the law, in the following respects:

In the United States, there is no licensing of printers and newspapers need no official stamp or registration. Finally, journalists are not required to put up bonds of surety.

As a result, it is simple and easy to establish a newspaper. A small number of subscribers is enough to cover the journalist's costs. Hence the number of periodicals and semi-periodicals in the United States beggars belief. The most enlightened Americans attribute the press's lack of power to this incredible dispersion of its forces. It is an axiom of political science in the United States that the only way to neutralize the influence of the newspapers is to multiply their number. I cannot imagine why such an obvious truth has yet to become a commonplace in France. It is easy for me to understand why those who wish to make revolutions with the aid of the press seek to endow it with but a few powerful organs. But I can conceive of absolutely no reason why the official proponents of the established order and the natural champions of existing laws think they can diminish the influence of the press by concentrating it. To me it seems that the governments of Europe treat the press as knights used to treat their adversaries: having found out for themselves that centralization is a powerful weapon, they want to make sure that their enemy wields the same weapon, no doubt in order to reap greater glory for themselves by resisting that enemy's onslaughts.

There is hardly a town in the United States without a newspaper. With such a large number of combatants in the field, it is easy to see that discipline and unity of action are impossible to achieve. Thus each paper flies its own standard. To be sure, all of the Union's political papers are either for or against the administration. But they attack and defend it in a thousand different ways. Therefore newspapers in the United States cannot create currents of opinion so powerful that not even the most formidable of dams can withstand them. Other effects of this dispersion of the press's strength are no less worthy of note. Because it is easy to start a newspaper, anybody can do it. On the other hand, the competition is such that newspapers cannot expect to earn very large profits, which discourages people with great business acumen from embarking on this kind of venture. Even if newspapers were a source of wealth, moreover, their sheer number would ensure that there would not be enough talented writers to run them. In the United States, therefore, the position of the journalist is not a very high one; his education is rudimentary at best, and his ideas are often expressed in a vulgar way. In every domain, however, the majority lays down the law; it establishes certain styles to which everyone must conform. Taken together, these common habits define a spirit: there is a spirit of the courthouse just as there is a spirit of the royal court. The spirit of the journalist in France is to discuss great state interests in violent but lofty and often eloquent terms. If this is not always the case, it is because there are exceptions to every rule. In America, the spirit of the journalist is to appeal crudely, directly, and artlessly to the passions of the people he is addressing, forsaking principles in order to portray individuals, pursue them into their private lives, and lay bare their weaknesses and vices.

Such abuse of thought can only be deplored. Later I shall have occasion to look into the influence that newspapers exercise on the taste and morality of the American people, but for now, to reiterate, I am concerned only with the world of politics. One cannot conceal the fact that the license of the press, through its political effects, helps indirectly to preserve public tranquillity. As a result, men of whom their countrymen already hold a high opinion do not dare write in the newspapers and thereby forfeit the most redoubtable weapon they possess for stirring up popular passions in their favor.[1] Even more important, the personal views expressed by journalists carry, as it were, no weight with their readers. What readers look for in a newspaper is knowledge of the facts, and it is only by altering or distorting the facts that the journalist can gain some influence for his views.

Even with such limited resources, the press wields enormous power in America. It carries the currents of political life into every section of this vast country. Ever vigilant, it regularly lays bare the secret springs of politics and obliges public men to appear before the court of public opinion. It is the press that rallies interests around certain doctrines and formulates the creeds of the political parties. It is through the press that the parties speak to one another without meeting face-to-face and understand one another without direct contact. When numerous organs of the press take a common line, their influence over the long run becomes almost irresistible, and public opinion, battered incessantly on one side only, ultimately gives in to their bludgeoning.

In the United States, each individual newspaper has little power, but the power of the periodical press in general is second only to that of the people.[*]

Opinions that become established under the influence of the free press in the United States are often more tenacious than those formed elsewhere under the influence of censorship.

In the United States, democracy brings a steady flow of new men into positions of leadership. The government is therefore not much concerned with continuity and order in its measures. But the general principles of government there are more stable than in many other countries, and the principal opinions that dominate society have proved more durable. When

---

[1]They write in the newspapers only in rare cases, when they wish to address the people and speak in their own name, as, for example, when slanderous allegations have been made about them and they want to put the true facts on the record.

[*]See Note XV, page 500.

an idea, whether just or unreasonable, takes possession of the American mind, nothing is more difficult than to get rid of it.

The same thing has been observed in England, the European country which for a century now has exhibited the greatest freedom of thought and the most invincible prejudices.

I attribute this effect to the same cause that might seem at first glance to prevent it from happening, namely, freedom of the press. Nations that enjoy this freedom cling to their opinions as much out of pride as out of conviction. They love them because they seem right and also because they are of their own choosing, and they cling to them not only as to something that is true but also as to something that is their own.

There are several other reasons as well.

A great man once said that *ignorance lies at both ends of knowledge*. It might have been truer to say that deep convictions are found only at the two ends, and that in the middle lies doubt. Indeed, one can distinguish among three distinct and often successive states of human intelligence.

Man firmly believes a thing because he accepts it without looking deeply into it. He begins to doubt when objections are raised. In many cases he succeeds in laying all his doubts to rest and begins to believe again. Then he no longer clings to a truth plucked at random from the darkness but stares truth in the face and marches directly toward its light.[2]

When freedom of the press finds men in the first of these two states, it does not immediately alter their habit of believing firmly but uncritically; it merely changes the object of their uncritical beliefs from one day to the next. From one end of the intellectual horizon to the other, man therefore continues to see only one point at a time, but that point changes constantly. This is when sudden revolutions occur. Woe unto those generations that abruptly introduce freedom of the press for the first time!

Soon, however, nearly the whole range of new ideas is explored. With experience comes doubt and universal mistrust.

---

[2] I am not sure, however, that reflective, self-assured convictions of this kind ever exalt man to the same degree of ardor and devotion that dogmatic beliefs inspire.

We can be sure that the majority of men will remain in one of these two states: they will either believe without knowing why, or not know precisely what they ought to believe.

As for the other type of conviction — the reflective, self-assured conviction that grows out of knowledge and emerges from the agitation of doubt itself — it will never be granted to more than a very small number of men to achieve it as a reward for their efforts.

It has been observed that in centuries of religious fervor men sometimes changed faiths, while in centuries of doubt each man clung stubbornly to his own beliefs. The same thing happens in politics under freedom of the press. Since all social theories are criticized and combated one after another, anyone who once adheres to one of them holds on to it not so much because he is sure that it is good as because he is not sure that anything else is better.

In such centuries, people are not so ready to die for their opinions, but they do not change them, and one finds both fewer martyrs and fewer apostates.

An additional and still more powerful reason is this: when opinions are in doubt, people end up relying on instinct and material interest to guide them, for these are far plainer to see, easier to grasp, and by nature more permanent than opinions.

It is very difficult to decide whether democracy governs better, or aristocracy. But it is clear that democracy hinders some people and aristocracy oppresses others.

That you are rich and I am poor is a self-evident truth that needs no discussion.

Chapter 4

ON POLITICAL ASSOCIATION IN THE UNITED STATES

Daily use of the right of association by the Anglo-Americans. — Three types of political association. — How the Americans apply the representative system to associations. — Dangers resulting from this for the state. — Important tariff convention of 1831. — Legislative character of this convention. — Why the unlimited exercise of the right of association is not as dangerous in the United States as elsewhere. — Why it may be regarded as necessary there. — Usefulness of associations in democratic nations.

No country in the world has made better use of association than the United States, and nowhere has that powerful instrument been applied to a wider range of purposes.

Apart from those permanent associations established by law and known as towns, cities, and counties, a host of others would never have existed or flourished but for the initiative of individuals.

Americans are taught from birth that they must overcome life's woes and impediments on their own. Social authority makes them mistrustful and anxious, and they rely upon its power only when they cannot do without it. This first becomes apparent in the schools, where children play by their own rules and punish infractions they define themselves. One encounters the same spirit in all aspects of social life. An obstruction blocks a public road, interrupting the flow of traffic. The neighbors immediately set up a deliberative body. Out of this improvised assembly comes an executive power that will remedy the ill before it occurs to anyone to appeal to an authority prior to that of the interested parties. Should pleasure be the object, people will join together to organize the celebration and enhance its splendor. Finally, they will unite to resist purely abstract enemies: collectively they combat intemperance. In the United States, people associate for purposes pertaining to public security, commerce and industry, morality and religion. There is nothing the human will despairs of achieving through the free action of the collective power of individuals.

Later I shall have occasion to speak of the effects of association in civil life. For now I must confine myself to the world of politics.

Since the right of association is taken for granted, citizens are free to use it in a variety of ways.

An association consists solely in the decision of a certain number of individuals to adhere publicly to certain doctrines, and to commit themselves to seek the triumph of those doctrines in a certain way. The right to associate is therefore almost identical with the freedom to write, yet associations already possess greater power than the press. When an opinion is represented by an association, it has to be expressed in a clearer, more precise form than would otherwise be the case. It calls upon supporters to stand up and be counted and enlists them in the cause. They learn about one another, and their ardor increases with their number. The association links the efforts of divergent minds and vigorously propels them toward a single goal, which it unambiguously designates.

The second stage in the exercise of the right of association is the ability to assemble. When a political association is permitted to establish centers of action at important places around the country, its activity increases and the extent of its influence grows. Men can see one another, pool their resources, and exchange views with a forcefulness and warmth that the written word can never achieve.

In the political realm, moreover, there is a final stage in the exercise of the right of association: people who share a common view can join together in electoral bodies and choose delegates to represent them in a central assembly. This is, properly speaking, the representative system applied to a party.

In the first case, in other words, men who share the same view establish a purely intellectual bond. In the second case, they meet in small assemblies that represent only a fraction of the party. Finally, in the third case, they form something like a separate nation within the nation, a government within the government. Their delegates, like the delegates of the majority, represent the full collective strength of their constituents, and, like delegates of a majority, they appear as national representatives with all the moral force that that confers. Unlike the majority, of course, these delegates do not have the right to make law, but they do have the power to attack existing laws and propose new ones that ought to exist.

Imagine a people not entirely habituated to the use of freedom, or one among whom deep political passions are brewing. Suppose, further, that alongside the majority that makes the laws there is a minority that concerns itself solely with *preambles* and stops short of *enactments*. I cannot help thinking that public order is exposed to great dangers.

It is, to be sure, a long way from proving that a law is in itself better than another law to proving that it ought to take the place of that other law. Although that great distance may still be obvious to enlightened men, it is already beyond the imagination of the multitude. A time may come, moreover, when the nation is almost equally divided between two parties, each of which claims to represent the majority. If, alongside the ruling power, another power of almost equal moral authority gains a foothold, is there any reason to believe that it will limit itself to talk without action for very long?

Will it always be deterred by the metaphysical consideration that the purpose of an association is to guide rather than coerce opinion and give advice about the law rather than make it?

The more I consider the chief effects of the independence of the press, the more convinced I am that, among the moderns, independence of the press is the most important, indeed the essential, ingredient of liberty. A people that wants to remain free therefore has the right to insist that the independence of the press be respected at all costs. But the freedom to write should not be confused with *unlimited* freedom to associate in political matters, which is not exactly the same thing. The latter is both less necessary and more dangerous than the former. A nation can set limits to the freedom to associate without ceasing to be its own master. There are times when it should do so in order to continue being its own master.

In America, the freedom to associate for political purposes is unlimited.

One example will make the degree to which it is tolerated clearer than anything I might add.

The reader will recall the furor that erupted in America over the question of the tariff, or freedom of trade. The tariff aroused not only public opinion but also very powerful material interests either for or against it. The North cited the tariff as part of the reason for its prosperity, while the South blamed it for nearly all its woes. It is no exaggeration to say that for many years the tariff was the only issue to stir up really disruptive political passions in the United States.

In 1831, when the dispute was at its most venomous, an obscure citizen of Massachusetts took it upon himself to propose, through the newspapers, that opponents of the tariff send deputies to Philadelphia to discuss ways of restoring freedom of trade. Through the power of the press, this proposal was conveyed throughout the country, from Maine to New Orleans, within a matter of days. The enemies of the tariff ardently supported it. They held meetings everywhere and chose deputies. Most were well-known figures, and a few were famous. South Carolina, which has since then taken up arms in the same cause, sent sixty-three delegates. On October 1, 1831, this assembly, which as is customary in America chose to call itself a convention, gathered in Philadelphia. It attracted more than two hundred delegates. Its debates were public and from the first were quite legislative in character. The delegates discussed the extent of congressional powers, theories of free trade, and, finally, the various provisions of the tariff. After ten days, the delegates dispersed, but not before drafting a petition to the American people. This petition contended that: 1) Congress had no power to make a tariff and that the existing tariff was unconstitutional; 2) it was not in the interest of any people, and, in particular, of the American people, that trade should be anything other than free.

Granted, the unlimited freedom to associate in the political realm has thus far not produced the catastrophic results in the United States that one might expect elsewhere. The right of association is an English import, and it has always existed in America. Its use is by now habitual and customary.

In our own time, freedom of association has become a necessary guarantee against the tyranny of the majority. Once a political party becomes dominant in the United States, all public power passes into its hands. Its partisan friends fill all offices and control all organized forces. Since the most distinguished men of the opposing party cannot penetrate the barrier that stands between them and power, they need to establish themselves outside the government. The minority needs to bring all its moral force to bear on the material power that oppresses it. Thus one danger is set against another more redoubtable still.

The omnipotence of the majority in my view poses so great a peril to the American republics that the use of dangerous means to limit it seems to me still to be a good thing.

At this point I shall venture to express a thought that may remind the reader of what I said earlier about local liberties: nowhere are associations more necessary to prevent either the despotism of the parties or the arbitrariness of the prince than in countries whose social state is democratic. In aristocratic nations, secondary bodies constitute natural associations that halt abuses of power. In countries where such associations do not exist, unless private individuals can artificially and temporarily create something that resembles them, I see no impediment to any form of tyranny, and a great people can be oppressed with impunity by a handful of factious individuals or a single man.

The convocation of a great political convention (and there are conventions of many kinds) may be a necessary step, but it is always, even in America, a grave occurrence, and one that friends of that country cannot but look upon with fear.

This can be seen clearly in the convention of 1831, when the distinguished men who served as delegates devoted all their efforts to moderating the convention's rhetoric and limiting its objectives. It is likely that the convention nevertheless exerted a profound influence on the thinking of malcontents and laid the groundwork for the open rebellion against the commercial laws of the Union that broke out in 1832.

One should not shut one's eyes to the fact that unlimited freedom of association in the political realm is, of all forms of liberty, the last that a people can tolerate. If it does not plunge them into anarchy, it often brings them close to it. Yet in one respect this very dangerous freedom does offer guarantees. In

countries where associations are free, secret societies are unknown. In America, people join factions, but they do not
become conspirators.

On the different ways in which the right of association is understood in Europe and the United States, and the different use that is made of it.

The freedom most natural to man, after the freedom to act
alone, is the freedom to combine his efforts with those of his
fellow man and to act in common. The right of association
therefore seems to me by its very nature almost as inalienable
as the freedom of the individual. The legislator cannot wish
to destroy it without attacking society itself. Yet if there are
peoples among whom the freedom to unite is purely beneficial and a source of prosperity, there are others who pervert
it through abuse, transforming an element of life into a cause
of destruction. Thus it seems to me that a comparison of the
various forms of association in countries where that freedom
is understood and in countries where it degenerates into license would be useful to both governments and parties.

Most Europeans still look upon associations as a weapon of
war, to be organized in haste and immediately tried out on
some field of battle.

People do indeed associate for the purpose of discussion,
but the thought of impending action weighs on everyone's
mind. An association is an army. Discussion offers an opportunity to count heads and stir spirits, after which it is time to
march out and meet the enemy. The members of an association may regard legal resources as a useful means of action but
never as the only path to success.

In the United States, the right of association is understood
differently. In America, citizens of the minority associate primarily to ascertain their numerical strength and thereby
weaken the moral ascendancy of the majority. The second purpose of association is to promote competition among ideas in
order to discover which arguments are most likely to make an
impression on the majority, for the minority always hopes to
attract enough additional support to become the majority and
as such to wield power.

Political associations in the United States are therefore peaceful as to their purposes and legal as to the means they employ, and when they claim to want to win only by legal means, they are generally telling the truth. The obvious differences between us and the Americans in this respect are explained by several things.

In Europe, there exist parties so different from the majority that they can never hope to gain its support, yet they believe themselves strong enough to take it on in battle. When a party of this kind forms an association, its aim is not to convince but to combat. In America, men whose opinions place them at a considerable distance from the majority can do nothing to thwart its power; everyone else hopes to win its support.

The right of association is therefore dangerous only to the degree that it is impossible for a great party to become the majority. In a country like the United States, where only shades of difference separate one opinion from another, the right of association may remain virtually unlimited.

If we are still inclined to look upon freedom of association as nothing more than the right to make war on the government, it is because we lack experience in the exercise of freedom. With consciousness of strength comes violence as the first idea to occur to a party or individual. The idea of persuasion comes only later; it is born of experience.

The English, though deeply divided, rarely abuse the right of association because they have longer experience of its use.

What is more, we ourselves have such a passion for war that there is no undertaking, no matter how senseless or how disruptive to the state, in which we do not think it glorious to die arms in hand.

But of all the causes that help to moderate the violence of political association in the United States, the most powerful, perhaps, is universal suffrage. In countries where universal suffrage is allowed, the majority is never in doubt, because no party can reasonably portray itself as the representative of those who did not vote. Associations therefore know that they do not represent the majority, and everyone else knows it too. The very existence of associations proves this, for if they did represent the majority, they would change the law themselves rather than petition for its reform.

[handwritten margin notes: "against extreme of demo"; "exercise demo universal would political particip dimer"; "Paradox"]

The moral force of the government that these associations attack is thereby greatly enhanced, while their own moral force is greatly diminished.

In Europe, there is virtually no association that does not claim to represent, or believe that it does represent, the will of the majority. This claim or belief adds prodigiously to the association's strength and serves marvelously to justify its actions, for what is more excusable than violence in the cause of righteousness oppressed?

Thus in the immense complexity of human laws it is sometimes the case that extreme freedom corrects the abuses of freedom and extreme democracy guards against the dangers of democracy.

In Europe, associations see themselves in a sense as the legislative and executive council of a nation that cannot speak for itself. With this idea in mind, they take action and issue orders. In America, where in everyone's eyes associations represent only a minority within the nation, they talk and circulate petitions.

The means employed by associations in Europe accord with the goal they set for themselves.

Since their principal goal is to act and not to talk, to fight and not to persuade, they are naturally inclined to organize themselves in ways that eschew civil norms and to adopt military habits and principles. Hence they centralize control of their forces as much as they can and place the power of all in the hands of a very few.

The members of such associations respond to orders as soldiers in the field. They profess the dogma of passive obedience, or perhaps it would be better to say that upon enlisting they offer up all they possess of judgment and free will in a moment of sacrifice. Within such organizations a tyranny often prevails that is more unbearable still than the tyranny exerted over society by the government they attack.

This greatly diminishes their moral force. They thereby forfeit the sacred character that attaches to the struggle of the oppressed against their oppressors. For how can a person willing to bow down to certain of his fellow men, to surrender his will and even his mind to them, claim that he wants to be free?

American associations also establish their own governments, but those governments are, if I may put it this way, civilian governments. Individual independence has its place in them: as in the society at large, everyone marches simultaneously toward the same goal, but there is no requirement that everyone follow exactly the same path. No one sacrifices his will or his reason. Instead, everyone lends his will and his reason to the common enterprise in order to ensure its success.

Chapter 5

ON THE GOVERNMENT OF DEMOCRACY IN AMERICA

I AM well aware that I tread now on live coals. Every word in this chapter will inevitably offend one or another of the parties that divide my country. I shall nevertheless conceal nothing of what I think.

In Europe we find it difficult to judge the true character and permanent instincts of democracy because in Europe two opposing principles are locked in struggle, and we do not know precisely how much is to be attributed to the principles themselves and how much to the passions arising from the battle between them.

Things are different in America. There, the people rule unimpeded. They need fear no danger nor avenge any insult.

In America, democracy is left to its own propensities. Its manner is natural and its movement free. This is where it must be judged. And to whom should such a study be interesting and profitable if not to us, who are swept along each day by an irresistible force and blindly advance, perhaps toward despotism, perhaps toward a republic, but certainly toward a democratic social state?

ON UNIVERSAL SUFFRAGE

I said earlier that every state of the union adopted universal suffrage. One sees it at work in communities occupying very different places on the social scale. I had the opportunity to observe its effects in various places and among races of men made virtual strangers to one another by language, religion, and mores: in Louisiana as well as New England, in Georgia as well as Canada. I noted that in America universal suffrage was a long way from yielding all the benefits or causing all the ills that people expect from it in Europe, and that its effects were generally different from what Europeans assume.

CONCERNING THE PEOPLE'S CHOICES AND THE INSTINCTIVE PREFERENCES OF AMERICAN DEMOCRACY

In the United States the most outstanding men are rarely called upon to direct public affairs. — Reasons for this. — The envy that the lower classes of France feel toward the upper classes is not a French sentiment but a democratic one. — Why distinguished Americans often avoid political careers.

Many people in Europe believe but do not say, or say but do not believe, that one of the great advantages of universal suffrage is that it brings men worthy of public trust into positions of leadership. The people, it is argued, may not know how to govern themselves, but they always sincerely want what is good for the state, and their instinct is unlikely to overlook men animated by the same desire and eminently capable of wielding power.

For my part, I must say that what I saw in America gives me no reason to believe that this is the case. On arriving in the United States, I was surprised to discover how common talent was among the governed and how rare in government. There is no escaping the fact that in the United States today the most outstanding men are seldom called to public office, and one is forced to acknowledge that this situation arose as democracy developed beyond all former bounds. It is clear that over the past half century the race of American statesmen has singularly shrunk in stature.

Several causes of this phenomenon may be adduced.

Whatever one does, there are limits to the degree to which the people can be enlightened. Try as one might to make knowledge more accessible, improve teaching methods, and reduce the cost of acquiring learning, there is no way for people to educate themselves and develop their intelligence unless they can devote time to the effort.

How easy or hard it is for people to live without working therefore sets a necessary limit to their intellectual progress. In some countries that limit is a long way from being reached; in others it is not so far off. But in order for there to be no limit, the people would need to be freed of worries about their material needs, in which case they would no longer be the people. Hence it is as difficult to conceive of a society in which everyone is highly enlightened as of a state in which every citizen is wealthy; the two difficulties are related. I am perfectly willing to concede that most citizens very sincerely want what is good for their country. Taking this one step further, I would go so far as to add that in general the lower classes of society seem to me less likely than the upper classes to adulterate this desire with considerations of personal interest. What the lower classes invariably lack to one degree or another, however, is the art of judging the means to the end they sincerely wish to achieve. What a lengthy period of study and variety of ideas are necessary to form an exact idea of the character of a single man! The greatest geniuses fail at this, yet the multitude is supposed to succeed! The people never have enough time or resources to devote to the effort. They must always judge hastily and seize on whatever is most visible. That is why charlatans of every stripe are so clever at pleasing them, while more often than not their true friends fail.

What democracy lacks, moreover, is not always the capacity to choose men of merit but the desire and taste to do so.

We must not blind ourselves to the fact that democratic institutions develop the sentiment of envy in the human heart to a very high degree. This is not so much because such institutions give everyone the means to equal everyone else as because those means continually prove unavailing to those who employ them. Democratic institutions awaken and flatter the passion for equality without ever being able to satisfy it to the full. No sooner does full equality seem within the people's reach than it flies from their grasp, and its flight, as Pascal said, is eternal. The people passionately seek a good that is all the more precious because it is close enough to be familiar yet far enough away that it cannot be savored. The chance of success spurs them on; the uncertainty of success vexes them. They struggle, they tire, they grow bitter. Anything that is beyond them in any quarter then seems an obstacle to their desires, and no form of superiority is so legitimate that the sight of it is not wearisome to their eyes.

Many people imagine that it is only in France that the lower classes harbor the secret instinct to do whatever they can to keep control of affairs out of the hands of the upper classes. This is not true: the instinct I have in mind is not French but democratic. Political circumstances may have been such as to color its character with a peculiar bitterness, but they did not bring it into being.

In the United States, the people do not feel hatred toward the upper classes of society, but they feel little benevolence toward them and are careful to keep them out of power. They do not fear great talents but have little taste for them. In general, one finds that anything that rises up without the support of the people has a hard time winning their favor.

While the natural instincts of democracy lead the people to banish distinguished men from power, an instinct no less powerful leads distinguished men to shun careers in politics, in which it is so very difficult to remain entirely true to oneself or to advance without self-abasement. Chancellor Kent expresses this thought in the most naïve way possible. After lavishing praise on that portion of the Constitution that grants the executive the power to nominate judges, that celebrated writer added this: "The fittest men would probably have too much reservedness of manners and severity of morals to secure an election resting on universal suffrage." (Kent's *Commentaries*, vol. 1, p. 272.) That was printed in America in 1830, and no one contradicted it.

I am satisfied that anyone who looks upon universal suffrage as a guarantee of good choices is operating under a total illusion. Universal suffrage has other advantages, but not that one.

FACTORS THAT MAY PARTIALLY CORRECT THESE INSTINCTS OF DEMOCRACY

Contrary effects of great dangers on nations and individuals. — Why America saw so many outstanding men in leading government posts fifty years ago. — Influence of enlightenment and mores on the people's choices. — Example of New England. — The states of the Southwest. — How certain laws influence the people's choices. — Two-stage election. — Its effects on the composition of the Senate.

When great perils threaten the state, the people fortunately often choose the citizens best qualified to save it.

It has been observed that a man facing urgent danger rarely remains as he was: he will either rise well above his habitual level or sink well below it. The same thing happens to peoples. Extreme peril does not always impel a nation to rise to meet it; it is sometimes fatal. It can arouse passions without offering guidance and cloud a nation's intelligence rather than enlighten it. The Jews went on slaughtering one another amid the smoking ruins of the Temple. In nations as well as individuals, however, it is more common to see the very imminence of danger act as midwife to extraordinary virtues. At such times great characters stand out as a monument hidden by the dark of night will stand out in the illumination of a blaze. Genius no longer shuns the light, and the people, struck by the perils they face, forget for a time their envious passions. Under such circumstances it is not rare to see famous names emerge from the ballot box. I said earlier that today's American statesmen seem vastly inferior to those who guided affairs fifty years ago. This is due not only to laws but also to circumstances. When America was fighting for the most just of causes, that of one people throwing off the yoke of another, and the goal was to win a place in the world for a new nation, the loftiness of the aim ennobled the soul of everyone involved. In the general excitement, superior men made haste to present themselves to the people, and the people, enfolding those men in their arms, chose them as their leaders. But such moments are rare, and judgment must be based on the ordinary course of events.

If fleeting events can at times counter the passions of democracy, enlightenment and above all mores exert a no less powerful but more durable influence on its proclivities. This is quite apparent in the United States.

In New England, where education and liberty are the daughters of morality and religion, and where society, already old and long-established, has been able to develop its own maxims and habits, the people have become accustomed to respecting intellectual and moral superiority, and to submitting to it without discomfort, even as they have done away with all the forms of superiority that wealth and birth ever created among men. Thus one finds democracy making better choices in New England than anywhere else.

By contrast, as one proceeds southward into states where the social bond is less venerable and less powerful, where education is less widespread, and where the principles of morality, religion, and liberty have been blended in a less congenial way, one finds that talent and virtue in government become increasingly rare.

When at last one reaches the new states of the Southwest, where society, organized only yesterday, is still but a swarm of adventurers and speculators, one is dismayed to learn the identity of the men to whom public authority has been entrusted, and one asks oneself what force it is that allows the state to grow and society to prosper there independent of legislation and its stewards.

Some laws, though democratic in nature, are nevertheless still capable of partially correcting democracy's dangerous instincts.

When you enter the chamber of the House of Representatives in Washington, you are struck by the vulgar appearance of that august assembly. Often the eye searches in vain for a famous man. Nearly all the members are obscure individuals whose names call no image to mind. Most are local lawyers or businessmen or even members of the lowest classes of society. In a country where education is almost universal, it is said that not all of the people's representatives are capable of writing correctly.

A short distance away is the chamber of the Senate, whose narrow confines contain a substantial proportion of America's famous men. Scarcely a man is to be seen there who has not distinguished himself by some recent achievement. Among the senators are eloquent attorneys, distinguished generals, clever magistrates, and well-known statesmen. Every word uttered in this assembly would do honor to Europe's greatest parliamentary debates.

What accounts for this bizarre contrast? Why is the elite of the nation in this chamber rather than the other? Why is the first assembly made up of so many vulgar elements, when the second seems to enjoy a monopoly of talent and enlightenment? Yet both emanate from the people; both are the product of universal suffrage, and America has yet to hear a single voice protest that the Senate is hostile to the people's interests. What, then, accounts for such an enormous difference? I see only one thing capable of explaining it: the election that chooses the members of the House of Representatives is direct; that which determines the composition of the Senate involves two stages. All the citizens of each state vote for the state legislature, whereupon, under the terms of the federal Constitution, that legislature is transformed into an electoral body, which in turn chooses the members of the Senate. The senators therefore reflect, albeit indirectly, the outcome of universal suffrage, for the legislature that chooses the senators is not an aristocratic or privileged body that derives its electoral right from its very nature. It is in essence subordinate to the totality of the state's citizens, who elect its members, generally every year, and who can always guide its choices by filling it with new members. But the popular will, in passing through this select body, is somehow refined by the process and emerges cloaked in nobler and more beautiful robes. The men elected in this way are therefore always precisely representative of the ruling majority, but they represent only the lofty thoughts at large in the nation, the generous instincts that animate it, and not the petty passions that often agitate it or the vices that dishonor it.

It is easy to foresee a time in the future when the American republics will be forced to multiply two-stage elections in their electoral system or else come to grief on democracy's shoals.

I am quite prepared to admit that I see two-stage elections as the only way to bring experience of political liberty within reach of all classes of the people. Those who hope to use this as the exclusive weapon of one party and those who fear it are to my mind equally mistaken.

THE INFLUENCE OF AMERICAN DEMOCRACY ON ELECTION LAWS

Infrequent elections leave the state vulnerable to major crises. — Frequent elections keep it in a state of feverish agitation. — The Americans chose the second of these two evils. — Mutability of the law. — Opinion of Hamilton, Madison, and Jefferson on this subject.

When intervals between elections are long, the state risks being overthrown at every election.

With each new election the parties make a prodigious effort to seize an opportunity that offers itself so rarely. The woes of losing candidates being all but incurable, there is every reason to fear that ambition will be driven to desperate lengths. If, on the other hand, battle is soon to be joined again on equal terms, losers will bide their time.

When one election follows rapidly on the heels of another, their frequency keeps society in feverish activity and public affairs in a state of constant volatility.

Choose one course and there is a chance that the state will suffer from malaise; choose the other and there is a chance of revolution. The first system is prejudicial to good government; the second threatens the government's very existence.

The Americans chose to brave the first evil rather than the second. In this choice they were guided far more by instinct than by reason, because democracy stimulates the taste for variety to the point of passion. The result of this is a singular mutability in legislation.

Many Americans regard the instability of their laws as a necessary consequence of a system whose general effects are useful. Yet I do not think that there is anyone in the United States who would deny that such instability exists or who does not look upon it as a great evil.

Hamilton, after demonstrating the usefulness of a power capable of preventing or at any rate delaying the promulgation of bad laws, adds: "It may perhaps be said that the power of preventing bad laws includes that of preventing good ones; and may be used to the one purpose as well as to the other. But this objection will have little weight with those who can properly estimate the mischiefs of that inconstancy and mutability in the laws which *forms the greatest blemish in the character and genius of our governments*" (*Federalist* 73).

"The facility and excess of law-making seem to be the diseases to which our governments are most liable," says Madison (*Federalist* 62).

Jefferson himself, the greatest democrat yet to emerge from the bosom of American democracy, pointed to the same dangers:

"The instability of our laws is really an immense evil. I think it would be well to provide in our constitutions that there shall always be a twelve-month between the ingrossing a bill and passing it; that it should then be offered to its passage without changing a word; and that if circumstances should be thought to require a speedier passage, it should take two-thirds of both Houses instead of a bare majority."[1]

ON PUBLIC OFFICIALS UNDER THE CONTROL OF AMERICAN DEMOCRACY

Simplicity of American officials. — Absence of uniforms. — All officials are paid. — Political consequences of this fact. — In America there are no public careers. — What results from this.

Public officials in the United States blend in with the multitude of citizens. They have neither palaces nor guards nor formal uniforms. The simple manners of government officials reflect not just a peculiarly American cast of mind but fundamental principles of American society.

In the eyes of democracy, government is not a good but a necessary evil. Some power must be accorded to government officials, for what use would they be without it? But the external appearance of power is not indispensable to the business of government; it offends the public eye to no good purpose.

Public officials themselves are well aware that they have been granted the right to wield power over others only on condition that in regard to manners they descend to the same level as everyone else.

I can imagine no one more straightforward in his actions, more accessible to all the world, more attentive to requests, or more civil in his answers than a public man in the United States.

I like this natural style in the government of democracy; in the inner strength that attaches more to the office than to the official, more to the man than to outward signs of power, I see something virile, which I admire.

As for the possible influence of uniforms, I think that people greatly exaggerate the importance these are likely to have in a century such as ours. I have not noticed that Amer-

[1]Letter to Madison, December 20, 1787, translation by M. Conseil.

ican public officials in the performance of their official duties are treated with less consideration or respect because they are obliged to stand solely on their own merits.

I strongly doubt, moreover, that special dress induces public men to respect themselves if they are not naturally inclined to do so, because I cannot believe that they respect their clothing more than their person.

When I see magistrates in France treating the parties before them rudely or derisively, shrugging their shoulders at the strategy of the defense, or smiling indulgently as an indictment is read, I wish that someone would strip off their robes to see whether dressing as ordinary citizens dress might remind these judges of the natural dignity of the human race.

No public official in the United States wears a uniform, but all receive salaries.

This, even more than the other things discussed thus far, follows naturally from democratic principles. A democracy can surround its magistrates with pomp and cover them with silk and gold without striking directly at the principle of its existence. Such privileges are temporary; they are inherent in the office, not the man. But to establish unpaid offices is to create a class of wealthy and independent officials, to form the core of an aristocracy. Even if the people retain the right to choose, the exercise of that right is then necessarily limited.

When a democratic republic stops paying salaries to its officials, I think it is fair to conclude that it is on the way to transforming itself into a monarchy. And when a monarchy begins to compensate offices that previously went unremunerated, it is a sure sign that the state is on its way to becoming either despotic or republican.

Hence in my view the replacement of unpaid offices by paid ones is in itself a genuine revolution.

I regard the total absence of unpaid offices in America as one of the most visible signs of democracy's absolute sway there. Services rendered to the public, regardless of their nature, are compensated. Hence everyone has not only the right to render such services but also the opportunity to do so.

In democratic states, any citizen may seek public employment, yet not everyone is tempted to run for office. The choice of the voters is often limited not by the prerequisites of candidacy but by the number and capabilities of the candidates.

In nations where the principle of election informs every aspect of public life, there is no such thing as a public career in the strict sense. Men come to office only by chance, as it were, and there is no assurance that they will remain. This is especially true when elections are held annually. In periods of calm, therefore, public offices offer little enticement to ambition. In the United States, the men willing to brave the vicissitudes of politics are those of modest desire. Men of great talent and towering passions generally avoid power in order to pursue wealth. And often a man will assume responsibility for the state only if he feels he has little gift for managing his own affairs.

It is to these causes as much as to poor choices by the voters that one must attribute the large number of very ordinary men in public office. I do not know if the people of the United States would vote for superior men if they ran for office, but there can be no doubt that such men do not run.

ON THE ARBITRARY POWER OF MAGISTRATES[2] UNDER THE RULE OF AMERICAN DEMOCRACY

Why the arbitrariness of magistrates is greater under absolute monarchies and in democratic republics than in temperate monarchies. — Arbitrariness of magistrates in New England.

There are two types of government in which a good deal of arbitrariness enters into the actions of magistrates: the absolute government of a single individual and the government of democracy.

In each case, almost analogous causes yield identical effects.

In despotic states, no man's fate is secure — that of the public official no more than that of the ordinary private citizen. Since the sovereign always controls the lives and fortunes and sometimes the honor of the men he employs, he is convinced that he has nothing to fear from them and allows them

---

[2] I here use the word *magistrates* in its most extended sense to refer to all who are charged with the execution of the laws.

considerable freedom of action because he feels sure they will never use it against him.

In despotic states, the sovereign is so enamored of his power that he is afraid of being constrained by his own rules. He likes his underlings to work in a more or less haphazard way so as to be sure of never encountering a tendency opposed to his desires.

In democracies, the majority is free each year to strip away power from those to whom it has been entrusted; hence it, too, need have no fear that such power will be used against it. Since the majority always has the sovereign right to communicate its will to the people it has chosen to govern, it would rather leave them to their own devices than bind them with inflexible rules, which, by limiting their power, would in a sense limit its power.

Indeed, upon looking closely into the matter, one finds that the arbitrariness of magistrates under democratic rule is even greater than in despotic states.

In such states, the sovereign can instantly punish any faults that he perceives, but he cannot presume to perceive all the faults that he ought to punish. By contrast, in democracies, the sovereign is not only all-powerful but also ubiquitous. Thus the American official is far freer within the scope of his legal powers than is any official in Europe. Often he is simply shown the desired end, and the means are left to his discretion.

In New England, for example, it is up to the selectmen of each town to draw up a jury list. The only rule is that jurors must be chosen from among citizens with the right to vote and must be men of good reputation.[3]

In France, we would think it a threat to life and liberty to entrust so formidable a right to any official, no matter who he might be.

In New England, the same magistrates are allowed to post the names of drunkards in taverns and fine anyone who serves them wine.[4]

[3]See the law of February 27, 1813. *General Collection of the Laws of Massachusetts*, vol. 2, p. 331. I should add that jury members are subsequently chosen by lot from the jury lists.

[4]Law of February 28, 1787. See *General Collection of the Laws of Massachusetts*, vol. 1, p. 302.

Such censorial power would revolt subjects of the most absolute of monarchies, but in New England citizens submit to it without complaint.

Nowhere has the law left more room for arbitrariness than in democratic republics, because there seems to be no need to be afraid of it. Indeed, it is fair to say that magistrates in democratic republics become freer as voting rights are extended down the social scale and terms of office made briefer.

That is why it is so difficult to transform a democratic republic into a monarchical state. In such a state, magistrates, though no longer elected, usually retain the powers and habits of elected officials. This leads to despotism.

Only in temperate monarchies does the law, in addition to circumscribing the actions of public officials, also take care to guide them at every step. The reason for this is easily stated.

In temperate monarchies, power is divided between the people and the prince. It is in the interest of both that the position of the magistrate be stable.

The prince is unwilling to place the fate of officials in the hands of the people lest those officials betray his authority. The people, for their part, are afraid that if magistrates are absolutely dependent on the will of the prince, they will serve only to oppress liberty. Hence it is arranged that magistrates should, in a sense, be subordinate to no one.

The same considerations that lead the prince and the people to grant officials their independence also lead them to seek guarantees against abuses of that independence, so that it will not be used against the authority of the former or the liberty of the latter. Accordingly, both agree that a line of conduct needs to be laid down in advance for officials to follow, and

---

Here is the text:

"The Selectmen in each town shall cause to be posted in the houses and shops of all taverners, innholders, and retailers within such towns a list of the names of all persons reputed common drunkards, common tipplers, or common gamesters, misspending their time and estate in such houses. And every keeper of such house or shop, after notice given him, that shall be convicted before one or more justices of the Peace, of entertaining or suffering any of the persons in such list, to drink or tipple, or game, in his or her house, or any of the dependencies thereof, or of selling them spiritous liquor, shall forfeit and pay the sum of thirty shillings."

both have a common interest in imposing rules that officials cannot evade.

ADMINISTRATIVE INSTABILITY
IN THE UNITED STATES

In America, the record of society's actions is often scantier than that of a family's actions. — Newspapers, the only historical record. — How extreme administrative instability is inimical to the art of government.

In America, men remain in power for but an instant before fading back into a population which itself changes from day to day, so that the record of society's actions there is often scantier than that of an ordinary family's actions. Public administration is in a sense oral and traditional. Little is written down, and what is written is scattered by the slightest wind, like the leaves of the Sibyl, and vanishes forever.

The only historical record in the United States is the newspapers. If an issue is missing, the chain of time is broken, and the present severed from the past. I have no doubt that fifty years from now it will be more difficult to obtain authentic documents about the details of social life in America today than about the administration of France in the Middle Ages. And if the United States were to be surprised by a barbarian invasion, it would be necessary to consult the history of other nations to learn anything about the people who lived there.

Administrative instability began as a habit, but now I would almost say that people have developed a taste for it. No one bothers about how things were done in the past. No one seeks to adopt a method. No archives are assembled. No one collects documents even when it would be easy to do so. If a person chances to have documents in his possession, he is likely to be careless with them. I have among my papers original documents given to me by public officials in response to some of my questions. In America, society seems to live from day to day, like an army in the field. Yet surely the art of administration is a science, and any science, in order to progress, needs to accumulate discoveries generation after generation. A man, in the short space of his lifetime, notices some fact; another man conceives of some idea; still another invents a method or discovers a formula. Humanity gathers up these various fruits of individual experience and molds the sciences. It is very difficult for American administrators to learn from one another. Hence they bring to the conduct of society such enlightenment as they find current within it rather than knowledge of their own. Democracy, carried to its ultimate extreme, is therefore inimical to progress in the art of government. In this respect, it is better suited to a people whose administrative education is already complete than to one that is still a novice in affairs of state.

Indeed, the foregoing remark is not limited to administrative science. Democratic government, though based on a very simple and very natural idea, always has a very civilized and thoroughly educated society as its prerequisite.[5] At first glance one might think that it is as old as the world, but on closer examination it is easy to see that it can only have arrived last.

ON PUBLIC EXPENDITURES UNDER AMERICAN DEMOCRACY

The citizens of all societies are divided into a certain number of classes. — What instincts guide each of these classes in the management of state finances. — Why public expenditures inevitably tend to increase when the people govern. — Why there is less to fear from the extravagances of democracy in America. — The use of public funds under democratic rule.

Is the government of democracy economical? First we must know what we intend to compare it to.

The question would be easy to answer if we wished to establish a parallel between a democratic republic and an absolute monarchy. We would find that public expenditures in the former are considerably higher than in the latter. But this is true of all free states, in contrast to states that are not free. There can be no doubt that despotism ruins men more by preventing them from producing than by depriving them of the fruits of production. It dries up the source of riches but often respects acquired wealth. Liberty, by contrast, begets far more

---

[5]Needless to say, I am here speaking of democratic government as it applies to a people and not a small tribe.

wealth than it destroys, and in nations familiar with it, the people's resources always increase faster than taxes.

What concerns me now is to compare one free people with another and to determine what influence democracy has on state finances.

Societies, like organisms, are formed in accordance with certain inviolable rules. They are made up of certain elements, which we find wherever and whenever societies exist.

If one is prepared to idealize, it is always easy to divide a people into three classes.

One class consists of the wealthy. Another includes people who, though not wealthy, are nevertheless well-off in every respect. Into the third class we place those who own little or no property and who must live primarily on work that members of the other two classes provide.

The number of individuals in each class will vary depending on the state of society, but you cannot do away with these three classes altogether.

Obviously, each class will approach the handling of the state's finances with its own peculiar instincts.

Suppose that the first class alone makes the laws. It will likely show little concern for economizing on public expenditures because a tax imposed on a large fortune will subtract only from what is superfluous and cause little pain.

By contrast, suppose that the middle classes alone make the law. One can count on them not to levy harsh taxes, because nothing is as disastrous as a heavy tax on a small fortune.

Of all free governments, in my view, the government of the middle classes will inevitably be, I do not say the most enlightened, much less the most generous, but the most economical.

Suppose now that the lowest of the three classes is exclusively responsible for making the law. I think it highly likely that public expenditures will increase rather than decrease, for two reasons:

Since most voters will then own no taxable property, it will seem that all money spent in the interest of society can only profit them and never harm them; and those who do have some little property will easily find ways to apportion the tax so that it falls solely on the rich and profits only the poor, things that the rich would hardly do if they were in charge of the government.

Hence any country in which sole responsibility for making the laws was borne by the poor[6] could not hope for much economy in public expenditures. These would always be high, either because the people who voted to impose taxes would be immune from paying them or because taxes would be apportioned in such a way as to exempt them. Only under a democratic government, in other words, can those who vote to impose taxes escape the obligation to pay them.

It is idle to object that if the people had a proper understanding of their own interest, they would spare the fortunes of the rich because they must soon feel the effects of any financial difficulties they create. Is it not also in the interest of kings to make their subjects happy and of nobles to know when to open their ranks? If long-run interests had always trumped the passions and needs of the moment, there would never have been tyrannical sovereigns or exclusive aristocracies.

Again, someone may stop me by saying, "Who ever imagined entrusting the poor with sole responsibility for making the law?" Who? Those who established universal suffrage. Is it the majority or the minority that makes the law? The majority, of course. And if I prove that the poor always constitute the majority, can I not add that in countries where the poor are called to the polls, they alone make the law?

It is clear that to date the majority of people of all nations have always owned either no property or so little property that they could not live comfortably without working. Universal suffrage therefore truly hands the government of society to the poor.

The unfortunate consequences of giving the people power over state finances are easy to see when we look at certain democratic republics of Antiquity, whose public treasuries were drained to aid indigent citizens or to provide games and spectacles for the people.

Of course the representative system was all but unknown in

---

[6]Clearly the word *poor* is used here and throughout this chapter in a relative and not an absolute sense. The poor of America may often seem rich compared with those of Europe. Nevertheless, it is reasonable to call them poor by contrast with their wealthier fellow citizens.

Antiquity. Nowadays it is more difficult for popular passions to make themselves felt in public forums. In the long run, however, one can be sure that representatives will always reflect the spirit of the people who elect them and see to it that their predilections as well as their interests prevail.

Furthermore, the extravagance of democracy is less to be feared as the people begin to own property, because then, on the one hand, the people have less need of the money of the rich and, on the other hand, they find it more difficult not to tax themselves. In this respect, universal suffrage would be less dangerous in France than in England, where nearly all taxable property is concentrated in a few hands. America, where the vast majority of citizens own property, finds itself in a situation more favorable than that of France.

There are still other factors that tend to increase the amount of public expenditure in democracies.

When aristocracy governs, the men who conduct the state's affairs are exempt from all need by virtue of their position in society. They are content with their lot, and what they want from society is above all power and glory. Standing as they do above the obscure mass of citizens, they do not always perceive clearly how their own grandeur depends on the general well-being. They do not look on the suffering of the poor without pity, but they cannot feel the poor man's suffering as their own. Provided that the people seem resigned to their fate, aristocrats therefore count themselves satisfied and expect nothing more from government. Aristocracy seeks to maintain things as they are rather than to improve them.

By contrast, when public power is in the hands of the people, the sovereign, knowing its own suffering, seeks general improvement.

The improving spirit bends itself to a thousand different purposes. It delves into a myriad of details and, in particular, undertakes to make improvements that cannot be had for free, for the goal is to improve the lot of the poor man, who cannot help himself.

In democratic societies, moreover, there exists an urge to do something even when the goal is not precise, a sort of permanent fever that turns to innovation of every kind. And innovations are almost always costly.

In monarchies and aristocracies, ambitious men flatter the sovereign's natural thirst for renown and power and thus frequently encourage him to expend large sums.

In democracies, where the sovereign is needy, there is little likelihood of obtaining his benevolence without ameliorating his condition, which can seldom be done without money.

Furthermore, when the people begin to reflect upon their lot, they become aware of a host of needs they had not felt previously that cannot be satisfied without recourse to the resources of the state. That is why public expenditures generally seem to increase with civilization, and why taxes rise as enlightenment spreads.

Finally, there is one additional reason why democratic government is often more expensive than other forms of government. Democracy sometimes seeks to economize on its expenditures but fails to do so because it lacks the art of thrift.

Because the views of democracy change frequently, and the agents of democracy more frequently still, its undertakings are sometimes poorly managed or left unfinished. In the first case, the state spends sums disproportionate to the grandeur of the purpose for which they are intended; in the second case, nothing comes of what it spends.

ON THE INSTINCTS OF AMERICAN DEMOCRACY IN SETTING THE SALARY OF PUBLIC OFFICIALS

In democracies, the people who authorize high salaries have no opportunity to profit from them. — Tendency of American democracy to increase the compensation of lower-level officials and to decrease that of higher-level officials. — Why this is so. — Comparison of salaries of public officials in the United States and France.

There is a powerful reason why democracies generally try to economize on the salaries paid to public officials.

In democracies, high salaries are authorized by a very large number of people, few of whom will ever have the opportunity to receive such generous compensation.

In aristocracies, on the other hand, the people who authorize high salaries almost always entertain vague hopes of profiting from them. They are creating capital for themselves, or at the very least resources for their children.

It must be granted, however, that democracy's extreme parsimony is reserved for its highest-ranking officials.

In America, officials of lower rank are better paid than they are elsewhere, but officials of high rank are far less well paid. These contrary effects stem from a common cause: in both cases it is the people who set the salaries of public officials. The people always think of their own needs, and this comparison enlightens them. Since they live quite comfortably themselves, it seems natural to them that their servants should share their comfort.[7] But when it comes to setting the salaries of high state officials, this rule fails, and decisions cease to be anything but haphazard.

The poor man has no clear idea what needs the upper classes of society might feel. A sum that might seem modest to a wealthy man seems prodigious to a poor one, who makes do with what is necessary. He feels that a state governor who is paid more than two thousand écus a year ought to feel happy and count himself an object of envy.[8]

So, if you try to make him understand that the representative of a great nation must present himself to foreigners with a certain splendor, he will understand you at first. But then he will think of his simple home and of the modest fruits of his arduous labor and dream of all that he might do himself with the very salary that you deem insufficient, and he will be shocked, not to say terrified, at the idea of so much wealth.

Furthermore, the low-level official is on almost the same level as the people, while the high official stands above them. Hence the former can still excite their interest, but the latter begins to arouse their envy.

[7]There is another reason why lower-ranking officials in the United States live so comfortably, one that has nothing to do with the instincts of democracy in general. Private careers of all kinds are highly remunerative. The state would find no one to fill these lower public offices if it were not willing to pay its officials well. It therefore finds itself in the same position as a business, which, despite its wish to economize, is obliged to bear the substantial costs of competition.

[8]The state of Ohio, with a population of one million, pays its governor a salary of only $1,200, or 6,504 francs.

This is quite apparent in the United States, where salaries seem almost to decrease as an official's power increases.[9]

Under the rule of aristocracy, by contrast, some high officials receive quite substantial emoluments, while lesser officials often have barely enough to live on. The reasons for this are obviously analogous to those given above.

If democracy cannot imagine the pleasures of the rich, or is envious of them, aristocracy for its part cannot understand the miseries of the poor, or, rather, is ignorant of them. The poor, properly speaking, are not like the rich; they belong to a different species. Aristocracy therefore shows little concern for the lot of its hirelings. It raises their wages only when the price falls so low that they refuse to serve.

Because democracy tends to be parsimonious with its chief officials, it has been credited with a powerful penchant for thrift that it does not actually possess.

[9]To illustrate the truth of this assertion, it suffices to examine the salaries of some agents of the federal government. I also list the salaries of comparable French officials to give the reader a basis for comparison.

UNITED STATES

Ministry of Finances (*Treasury Department*)

Bailiff (messenger)	3,734 fr.
Lowest paid clerk	5,420
Highest paid clerk	8,672
Secretary general (*chief clerk*)	10,840
Minister (*secretary of state*)	32,520
Head of the government (president)	135,000

FRANCE

Ministry of Finances

Bailiff of the minister	1,500 fr.
Lowest paid clerk	1,000–1,800
Highest paid clerk	3,200–3,600
Secretary general	20,000
Minister	80,000
Head of the government (king)	12,000,000

Perhaps I was wrong to take France as a basis of comparison. In France, where democratic instincts are daily exerting more and more influence over the government, we already see a strong tendency for the chambers to raise the lowest salaries and, even more, to lower the highest ones. For instance, the Minister of Finance, who is paid 80,000 fr. in 1834, used to be paid 160,000 under the Empire; the Directors General of Finance, who are now paid 20,000, then got 50,000.

To be sure, democracy gives those who govern it barely enough to live decently, but it spends enormous sums to meet people's needs and facilitate their pleasures.[10] This is a better use of the revenue from taxes, but it is not thrift. In general, democracy gives little to government officials and much to the people governed. The opposite is true in aristocracies, where the state's money chiefly benefits the class in charge of affairs.

DIFFICULTY OF DISCERNING THE FACTORS THAT ENCOURAGE ECONOMY IN THE AMERICAN GOVERNMENT

Anyone who examines the facts in search of the real influence of laws on the fate of mankind is liable to make great mistakes, because nothing is so difficult to appreciate as a fact.

One nation is by nature frivolous and enthusiastic; another is deliberate and calculating. This may be due in each case to its physical constitution or to some remote cause of which I am unaware.

Some nations love spectacles, noise, and joyful celebration and do not regret seeing millions go up in smoke. Others value only solitary pleasures and seem ashamed to appear content.

In some countries, great value is attached to the beauty of buildings. In others, no value is ascribed to art, and anything that fails to generate revenue is scorned. Finally, there are countries where people love renown, and others where money takes precedence over everything else.

Quite apart from the laws, all these factors exert a very powerful influence on the conduct of state finances.

If Americans have never spent the people's money on public celebrations, it is not only because they vote to approve taxes but because they do not like to celebrate.

[10] See *inter alia* the amounts allocated by American budgets for support of the indigent and free education.

In 1831, the state of New York spent 1,290,000 francs to support the indigent. And the sum set aside for public education was estimated to be at least 5,420,000 francs. (*Williams' New York Annual Register*, 1832, pp. 205 and 243.)

The state of New York had a population of only 1,900,000 in 1830, which is not even twice the population of the Département du Nord.

If they reject ornament in architecture and prize only its material and concrete benefits, it is not only because they constitute a democratic nation but also because they are a commercial people.

The habits of private life carry over into public life, and one has to distinguish carefully between those economies that depend on American institutions and those that depend on American habits and mores.

CAN PUBLIC EXPENDITURES IN THE UNITED STATES BE COMPARED WITH PUBLIC EXPENDITURES IN FRANCE?

National wealth and taxation are two points to consider in evaluating the extent of public expenditures. — The wealth of France and magnitude of her public expenditures are not precisely known. — Why one cannot hope to know the wealth of the Union and the magnitude of its public expenditures. — Research undertaken by the author to learn the amount of taxes in Pennsylvania. — General signs by which the magnitude of a nation's public expenditures can be estimated. — Results of this investigation for the Union.

Great efforts have been made in recent years to compare public expenditures in the United States with public expenditures in France. Nothing has come of all this work, and a few words will suffice, I believe, to show why this was inevitable.

In order to gauge the magnitude of a nation's public expenditures, two things are essential. One must determine, first, the wealth of the nation and, second, the portion of that wealth devoted to state expenses. Anyone who seeks to determine the level of taxation without evaluating the resources that are supposed to sustain it is wasting his effort, for what is interesting to know is not the level of expenditure itself but the ratio of expenditure to revenue.

A tax that a wealthy man can easily pay will reduce a poor man to misery.

The wealth of nations is a composite of several elements: real property is one, and movable property another.

It is difficult to ascertain the extent of cultivable land that a nation possesses and to determine its natural or acquired value. It is even more difficult to estimate the amount of movable property at a nation's disposal. The variety and quantity of the latter make analysis all but impossible.

Accordingly, we find that the nations of Europe that have been civilized the longest, the very ones in which administration is centralized, have thus far failed to establish an exact accounting of their wealth.

In America, no one has even thought of attempting such a thing. And what hope would there be of success in such a new country, where society has yet to achieve a settled and definitive form, and where the national government does not have at its beck and call an army of officials whose efforts it can simultaneously command and control; and where, finally, the art of statistics is not cultivated, because there is no one with the ability to collect the documents or the time to peruse them?

Thus the basic elements needed for our calculations are unavailable. We have no idea of the comparative fortunes of France and the United States. The wealth of the former is not yet known, and the means of establishing that of the latter do not exist.

For the moment, however, I am quite prepared to do without this necessary term of comparison. Instead of attempting to determine the ratio of tax to revenue, I shall limit myself to attempting to ascertain the tax.

As the reader will soon see, however, I did not make my task any easier by thus limiting the scope of my research.

I have no doubt that the central administration of France, with all the officials in its employ, is quite capable of determining the exact amount of direct and indirect taxes that weigh upon the citizens of France. But the French government has yet to complete this task, which is beyond the capability of any individual, or, if it has completed it, it has yet to make the results public. We know what the state's costs are. The total amount of departmental expenditures is known. We do not know what goes on in the *communes*. Hence at this moment no one can state the exact amount of France's public expenditures.

Turning now to America, I see difficulties still more numerous and insurmountable. The Union publishes an exact accounting of its expenditures; I can obtain the budgets of each of the twenty-four states. But who will tell me how much citizens spend on the administration of their counties and towns?[11]

Federal authority cannot be stretched to compel state governments to enlighten us on this point. And even if all the state governments wanted to help us, I doubt that they would be in a position to satisfy our curiosity. Apart from the inherent difficulty of the undertaking, the political organization of the country would work against them. Officials of the towns and counties are not appointed by state administrators and do not report to them. Hence there is reason to believe that if the state wanted to obtain the information we require, it would encounter a major obstacle in the negligence of the lower-level officials on whom it would be obliged to rely.[12]

[11]The Americans, it will be clear, have four types of budgets: the Union has one of its own, as does each state, county, and town. During my stay in America, I conducted extensive research to determine the amount of public expenditures in the towns and counties of the principal states of the Union. It was easy for me to obtain the budgets of the largest towns but impossible for the smaller ones. Hence I have no idea exactly how much towns spend. As for the expenditures of the counties, I have in my possession certain documents, which, though incomplete, may be worthy of the reader's curiosity. I am grateful to Mr. Richards, the former mayor of Philadelphia, for the budgets of thirteen Pennsylvania counties in the year 1830: these include the counties of Lebanon, Centre, Franklin, Lafayette, Montgomery, Luzerne, Dauphin, Butler, Allegheny, Columbia, Northumberland, Northampton, and Philadelphia. In 1830, the population of these counties was 495,207. A glance at a map of Pennsylvania will reveal that these thirteen counties are scattered in every direction and subject to all the general factors influencing the state of the country, so that there is no reason to believe that they do not offer an accurate picture of the financial state of the counties of Pennsylvania. Now, in 1830, these thirteen counties spent 1,800,221 francs, or 3 fr. 64 per inhabitant. I have calculated that in that same year each inhabitant contributed 12 fr. 70 to the federal Union and 3 fr. 80 to the state of Pennsylvania. In other words, each inhabitant contributed the sum of 20 fr. 14 cent. to society to defray all public expenses (except those of the towns). Obviously this result is incomplete in two respects: it applies to only one year and to only a portion of public expenditures. But it has the merit of being accurate.

[12]Those who have tried to compare public expenditures in the United States and France have clearly recognized the impossibility of comparing total expenditures, so they have devoted their attention instead to isolated portions of the budgets of both countries. It is easy to see that this second procedure is as defective as the first.

To what shall I compare, say, our national budget? To the budget of the Union? But the Union is concerned with far fewer matters than our central

In any case, there is no point in asking what Americans might do in this regard, since there can be no doubt that to date they have done nothing.

Today, therefore, there is no one in either America or Europe who can tell us how much each citizen of the Union pays annually to underwrite society's expenditures.[13]

Let us conclude that it is as difficult to compare the social expenditures of the Americans fruitfully with ours as it is to compare the wealth of the Union with that of France. I add that it would even be dangerous to attempt such a thing. When statistics are not based on rigorously accurate calculations, they mislead rather than guide. The mind is easily taken in by the false air of exactitude that even aberrant statistics

---

government, and its expenditures must of course be far lower. Shall I compare our departmental budgets with the budgets of individual states of the Union? No, because in general the states deal with matters that are far more important and far more numerous than our departmental administrations, hence their expenditures are naturally much higher. As for the county budgets, there is nothing in our system of finances that resembles them. Shall we include items from these budgets in state budgets or town budgets? Towns in both countries spend money, but not always in comparable ways. American towns assume responsibility for various matters that are left to the departments or the national government in France. Furthermore, how should town expenditures be defined in America? Town organizations vary from state to state. Shall we take as the norm what is done in New England or in Georgia, in Pennsylvania or in Illinois?

It is easy to see a kind of similarity between certain budgets of the two countries, but since the items included always differ to one degree or another, it is impossible to make a serious comparison.

[13]Even if one succeeded in finding out the precise amount that each French or American citizen pays into the public treasury, one would still have only part of the truth.

Governments demand not only money from taxpayers but also personal services having a certain monetary equivalent. The state raises an army. The entire nation bears the cost of the soldier's pay, but the soldier must give of his own time, whose value depends on the use he could make of it if he were free. The same can be said of service in the militia. A man who belongs to the militia devotes a portion of his precious time to the security of the public and really gives the state what he fails to earn. I could cite many other examples in addition to these. The governments of France and America collect taxes of this kind. These taxes are borne by the citizens. But who can give a precise estimate of the amounts in both countries?

Nor is this the final difficulty that one encounters if one attempts to compare the Union's public expenditures to our own. The state in France imposes

retain and calmly accepts errors that it sees as cloaked in mathematical truth.

Let us therefore abandon figures and seek our proofs elsewhere.

Does a country give the appearance of material prosperity? After paying the state, does the poor man retain resources and the rich man more than what he needs? Does each seem satisfied with his lot and seek each day to improve it further, so that, just as industry does not want for capital, capital in turn does not want for industry? In lieu of concrete documents, these are the signs by which one can tell whether the public expenditures borne by a people are proportionate to its wealth.

An observer who relied on such testimony would no doubt find that the American in the United States gives the state a much smaller part of his income than the Frenchman.

But how could anyone think it would be otherwise?

A part of the French debt is the result of two invasions; the Union has nothing to fear in this regard. Our position requires us to keep a large number of men in arms at all times. The Union's isolation allows it to have only 6,000 soldiers. We maintain nearly 300 vessels. The Americans have only 52.[14] How could the inhabitant of the Union pay the state as much as the inhabitant of France?

There is simply no parallel between the finances of countries in such different situations.

In order to judge whether American democracy is truly

---

certain obligations on itself that the state in America does not, and vice versa. The French government pays the clergy; the American government leaves this responsibility to the faithful. In America, the state cares for the poor; in France it leaves them to the charity of the public. We pay all our officials a fixed salary; the Americans allow officials to collect certain fees. Compulsory labor is required only on certain highways in France but on nearly all roads in the United States. Our roads are open to travelers, who can travel on them for free. In the United States toll roads abound. All these differences in the way in which taxpayers contribute toward the expenses of society make comparison of the two countries difficult, for there are certain expenditures that citizens would not make or would not support to the same degree if the state did not take it upon itself to act in their name.

[14]See the detailed budgets of the Ministry of the Navy for France, and for America, the *National Calendar* of 1833, p. 228.

thrifty, we must therefore look at what goes on in the Union rather than compare the Union to France.

When I look at each of the various republics that constitute the confederation, I find that their governments often lack perseverance in their designs and fail to maintain constant supervision of the men they employ. From this I naturally draw the conclusion that they must often spend the taxpayers' money to no purpose or allocate more of it to their projects than is necessary.

I see that these governments, faithful to their popular origins, make prodigious efforts to satisfy the needs of society's lower classes, to open up the avenues of power to them, and to sow prosperity and enlightenment among them. These governments care for the poor, distribute millions every year to the schools, pay for all services, and generously remunerate even their lowliest agents. If this manner of governing strikes me as useful and reasonable, I am nevertheless forced to admit that it is also spendthrift.

I see the poor man in control of public affairs and directing the expenditure of national resources, and I cannot believe that, profiting as he does from the expenditures of the state, he does not often engage the state to make additional expenditures.

Therefore, without recourse to incomplete figures or shaky comparisons, I conclude that democratic government in America is not, as is sometimes claimed, cheap government. I do not hesitate to predict, moreover, that if great difficulties should ever befall the people of the United States, taxes there will rise to a level just as high as one finds in most of Europe's aristocracies and monarchies.

ON CORRUPTION AND VICES IN THE PEOPLE WHO GOVERN DEMOCRACY AND THEIR EFFECTS ON PUBLIC MORALITY

In aristocracies, rulers sometimes seek to corrupt. — In democracies they are often corrupt themselves. — In the former, their vices corrode the morality of the people directly. — In the latter, they exert an indirect influence that is even more to be feared.

Aristocracy and democracy reproach each other for facilitating corruption. A distinction has to be made.

In aristocratic governments, the men who influence affairs are wealthy and desire only power. In democracies, statesmen are poor and have their fortunes to make.

Hence in aristocratic states the men in government are not very susceptible to corruption and have only a very limited desire for money, whereas the opposite is true in democratic nations.

But because the men who aspire to lead the government in aristocracies are very wealthy, and because the number of people who can help them achieve their goal is often limited, the government is in a sense up for auction. In democracies, by contrast, the men who compete for power are almost never rich, and the number who participate in giving it to them is very large. In democracies there are perhaps no fewer men for sale, but buyers are scarce, and too many people would have to be bought at once to achieve the desired goal.

Among the men who have held power in France over the past forty years, any number have been accused of having made their fortunes at the expense of the state and its allies. This reproach was rarely leveled at public men under the old monarchy. In France, however, the buying of votes is virtually unheard of, whereas in England the practice is notorious and public.

I have never heard of anyone in the United States using his wealth to win over constituencies, but I have frequently heard the integrity of public officials questioned. Still more often have I heard the success of those same officials attributed to base intrigue or criminal manipulation.

Thus if the men who govern aristocracies sometimes seek to corrupt, the leaders of democracies prove corrupt themselves. In aristocracies one attacks the morality of the people directly; in democracies one influences the public conscience in an indirect way that is even more to be feared.

Because the men who head democratic states are almost always suspected of dishonorable conduct, in a way they lend the support of the government to the crimes of which they are accused. Thus they set dangerous examples for struggling virtue and serve as glorious precedents for hidden vice.

There is no point in objecting that dishonest passions are to be found in men of every rank; that often they ascend by birthright to the throne itself; and thus that contemptible men are to be found at the head of aristocratic nations as well as in democracies.

This response does not satisfy me. In the corruption of those who come to power by chance, there stands revealed something coarse and vulgar that makes such corruption contagious to the multitude, whereas in the depravity of great lords there reigns a certain aristocratic refinement, an air of grandeur that commonly makes it incommunicable.

The people can never fathom the obscure labyrinth of the courtly spirit. It is always difficult for them to discern the baseness that lies beneath elegant manners, refined taste, and graceful language. But robbing the public treasury or selling state favors for cash — any wretch can understand such things and aspire to do no less if he gets the chance.

What is to be feared, moreover, is not so much the sight of immorality in the great as that of immorality leading to greatness. In a democracy, ordinary citizens see a man step forth from their ranks and within a few years achieve wealth and power. This spectacle fills them with astonishment and envy. They try to understand how a man who only yesterday was their equal today enjoys the right to rule over them. To attribute his rise to talent and virtue is inconvenient, because it requires them to admit to themselves that they are less virtuous and clever than he. They therefore ascribe primary responsibility to some number of his vices, and often they are right to do so. This results in I know not what odious mingling of the ideas of baseness and power, unworthiness and success, utility and dishonor.

EFFORTS OF WHICH DEMOCRACY IS CAPABLE

The Union has fought for its existence only once. — Enthusiasm at the beginning of the war. — Chilling at the end. — Difficulty of instituting conscription or impressment of seamen in America. — Why democratic nations are less capable of great sustained efforts than other nations.

I warn the reader that I am speaking here of a government that follows the true wishes of the people and not of a government that limits itself solely to issuing orders in the people's name.

There is nothing so irresistible as a tyrannical power that issues orders in the people's name. This is so because in addition to being cloaked in the moral authority stemming from the will of the greatest number, it also acts with the decisiveness, promptness, and tenacity of a single man.

It is rather difficult to say what degree of effort a democratic government is capable of in a time of national crisis.

A great democratic republic has yet to be seen. It would be an insult to republics generally to apply that term to the oligarchy that reigned over France in 1793. The United States is the first example of its kind.

Now, in the half century since the Union was formed, its existence was placed in jeopardy only once, during the War for Independence. The beginning of that great war witnessed extraordinary flashes of enthusiasm to serve the fatherland.[15] As the struggle wore on, however, individual selfishness returned. Money stopped flowing into the public treasury. Men no longer volunteered to serve in the army. The people still wanted independence, but they recoiled from what had to be done to obtain it. "Tax laws have in vain been multiplied — new methods to enforce the collection have in vain been tried," says Hamilton in *Federalist* 12. "The public expectation has been uniformly disappointed, and the treasuries of the states have remained empty. The popular system of administration inherent in the nature of popular government, coinciding with the real scarcity of money, incident to a languid and mutilated state of trade, has hitherto defeated every experiment for extensive collections, and has at length taught the different legislatures the folly of attempting them."

Since that time, the United States has not had to support a single serious war.

In order to judge what sacrifices democracies are capable of imposing on themselves, we must therefore wait until the

---

[15]One of the most striking, in my view, was the decision of Americans to give up drinking tea for a time. Anyone aware of the fact that people generally cling to their habits more tenaciously than to their lives will no doubt be astonished that an entire nation was willing to make such a great and obscure sacrifice.

American nation is obliged to place half of its income in the hands of its government, as England is, or to send a twentieth of its population into battle, as France did.

In America, conscription is unknown. Men are induced to enlist for money. Compulsory recruitment is so contrary to the ideas and so foreign to the habits of the people of the United States that I doubt whether anyone would ever dare introduce it into law. What is called conscription in France is surely the heaviest of our taxes, but without conscription how could we sustain a major continental war?

The Americans have not adopted the English practice of impressing seamen. They have nothing like our French system of *inscription maritime*. The Navy, like the merchant marine, recruits by means of voluntary enlistment.

It is not easy, however, to imagine how a nation can sustain a major war at sea without recourse to one of the methods just mentioned. Although the Union has already fought and won glory on the seas, it has never had a large number of ships, and equipping what few vessels it had has always been very costly.

I have heard American statesmen concede that the Union will find it difficult to maintain its rank on the high seas unless it resorts to impressment or *inscription maritime*. The problem, however, is to compel the people, who govern, to submit to such measures.

There is no denying the fact that free peoples generally respond to danger with far more energy than peoples that are not free, but I am inclined to believe that this is true primarily of free peoples among whom the aristocratic element is dominant. Democracy seems to me far better suited to rule a peaceful society, or, if need be, to make a sudden and vigorous effort, than to brave the great storms that beset the political existence of nations over a long period of time. The reason for this is simple: men will expose themselves to danger and privation out of enthusiasm, but they will continue to expose themselves over a long period of time only as a result of reflection. In what is called instinctive courage there is more calculation than people think, and although passions alone generally account for the initial efforts, it is the desired result that sustains those efforts. One risks part of what one holds dear in order to save the rest.

Now, what democracy often lacks is this clear perception of the future, based on enlightenment and experience. The people feel far more than they reason, and if present ills are great, it is to be feared that they will forget the greater ills that may await them in case of defeat.

There is still another cause that is likely to make the efforts of a democratic government less durable than those of an aristocracy.

Not only do the people see less clearly than the upper classes what they may hope or fear from the future, but they also suffer the ills of the present in a very different way. The nobleman, in risking his life, will find glory as often as peril. In handing over the bulk of his income to the state, he temporarily deprives himself of some of wealth's pleasures. But for the poor man, death is without prestige, and a tax that is a mere annoyance to the rich will often strike at the very roots of his existence.

The relative weakness of democratic republics in times of crisis is perhaps the greatest obstacle in the way of establishing such republics in Europe. In order for a democratic republic to survive easily in a European nation, all the other nations of Europe would have to establish democratic republics at the same time.

I believe that democratic government must in the long run increase the real strength of society. But at a given time and in a given place it cannot assemble as formidable a force as an aristocratic government or an absolute monarchy. If a democratic country were to remain under a republican government for a century, there is reason to believe that by the end of that time it would be wealthier, more populous, and more prosperous than the despotic states on its borders, but during that century it would often have run the risk of being conquered by them.

ON AMERICAN DEMOCRACY'S POWER
OVER ITSELF

The American people are slow to accept, and sometimes reject, measures beneficial to their well-being. — The American faculty for committing errors that can be corrected.

Democracy's difficulty in vanquishing the passions and silencing the needs of the moment for the sake of the future can be observed in the most trivial matters in the United States.

The people, surrounded by flatterers, find it most difficult to overcome their own inclinations. Whenever anyone tries to persuade them to deprive themselves of something or to inconvenience themselves in some way, even for a purpose to which their reason assents, they almost always begin by refusing. Americans have been justly praised for their obedience to the law. One should add that in America the laws are made by the people and for the people. In the United States, therefore, the law favors the very people who, everywhere else, would have the greatest interest in violating it. Hence we may assume that an irksome law whose utility was not evident to the majority would either not carry or not be obeyed.

In the United States, there are no laws regarding fraudulent bankruptcies. Is this perhaps because there are no bankruptcies? No, on the contrary, it is because there are a good many. In the mind of the majority, the fear of being prosecuted as a bankrupt outweighs the fear of being ruined by the bankruptcy of others. Thus the public conscience has developed a sort of guilty tolerance for an offense that everyone individually condemns.

In the new states of the Southwest, citizens almost always take the law into their own hands, and murders are commonplace. This is because manners in the wilderness are too rough, and enlightenment too rare, for anyone to see the point of putting teeth into the law: the people there prefer duels to trials.

Someone in Philadelphia once told me that nearly all crimes in America stemmed from the abuse of strong liquor, which the lower classes could drink at will because of its very low price. "Why," I asked, "do you not impose a tax on spirits?"

To which my informant replied, "Our lawmakers have often thought about it, but it would be difficult to do. They are afraid of provoking a rebellion. And in any case, any representative who voted for such a law would certainly not be reelected." "So," I replied, "in your country drinkers are in the majority, and temperance is unpopular."

When one points such things out to people in government, their only response is, "Let time do its work. When people begin to feel the ill, it will enlighten them and make them aware of their needs." This is often true: if democracy is more likely than a king or body of nobles to make a mistake, it is also more likely to correct that mistake once enlightenment arrives, because within democracy there are generally no interests contrary to that of the majority and hostile to reason. But democracy can discover truth only through experience, and many nations will perish before they have had an opportunity to learn from their mistakes.

Hence the great privilege of the Americans is not only to be more enlightened than other peoples but also to enjoy the faculty of committing errors that can be corrected.

In order to profit readily from past experience, moreover, democracy must already have achieved a certain degree of civilization and enlightenment.

There are nations whose early education was so flawed, and whose character exhibits such a strange mixture of passions, ignorance, and erroneous notions about all things, that they are incapable of discovering the causes of their own misery. Such nations succumb to ills of whose nature they remain ignorant.

I have traveled through vast regions once inhabited by powerful Indian nations that no longer exist. I have lived among what is left of tribes that are obliged every day to look on as their numbers diminish and their savage glories vanish. I have heard these Indians themselves predict the ultimate destiny reserved for their race. Any European can see what has to be done to save these unfortunate peoples from inevitable destruction. Yet they themselves do not see it. They feel the ills that are heaped upon them year after year, and to a man they will reject the remedy and die. One would have to use force to compel them to live.

For the past quarter of a century, people have been astonished to see the new nations of South America repeatedly convulsed by revolution, and they keep waiting for those countries to return to what they call their *natural state*. But who can say that, for the Spaniards of South America, revolution is not today the most natural state? In that part of the world, society is struggling at the bottom of an abyss from which it cannot escape by its own efforts.

The people who live in that beautiful half of the hemisphere seem stubbornly determined to eviscerate one another. Nothing can deter them. Exhaustion brings brief respite, but respite soon leads to renewed furies. When I contemplate their condition, alternating between misery and crime, I am tempted to think that for them despotism would be a godsend.

In my mind, however, "despotism" and "godsend" are two words that may never coexist in the same sentence.

HOW AMERICAN DEMOCRACY CONDUCTS FOREIGN AFFAIRS

Direction imposed on the foreign policy of the United States by Washington and Jefferson. — Almost all the natural defects of democracy influence the direction of foreign affairs, while its virtues are not much in evidence.

We have seen that the federal constitution placed the permanent direction of the nation's foreign interests in the hands of the president and the Senate,[16] a choice that to a certain extent removes the general policy of the Union from the direct and daily influence of the people. Hence one cannot say without qualification that democracy is in charge of America's foreign affairs.

Two men set a direction for American foreign policy that is still being followed today: one was Washington, the other Jefferson.

---

[16]"The president," says the Constitution, art. 2, sec. 2, no. 2, "shall have power, by and with the advice and consent of the Senate, to make treaties." The reader should not lose sight of the fact that senators are elected for six years and that they are chosen by the legislators of each state, hence that they are the product of a two-stage election process.

Washington, in the admirable letter to his fellow citizens that served as his political testament, had this to say:

The great rule of conduct for us in regard to foreign nations is in extending our commercial relations to have with them as little political connection as possible. So far as we have already formed engagements, let them be fulfilled, with perfect good faith. Here let us stop.

Europe has a set of primary interests, which to us have none, or a very remote relation. Hence she must be engaged in frequent controversies, the causes of which are essentially foreign to our concerns. Hence therefore it must be unwise in us to implicate ourselves, by artificial ties, in the ordinary vicissitudes of her politics, or the ordinary combinations and collisions of her friendships, or enmities.

Our detached and distant situation invites and enables us to pursue a different course. If we remain one people, under an efficient government, the period is not far off when we may defy material injury from external annoyance; when we may take such an attitude as will cause the neutrality we may at any time resolve upon to be scrupulously respected; when belligerent nations, under the impossibility of making acquisitions upon us, will not lightly hazard the giving us provocation; when we may choose peace or war, as our interest, guided by justice, shall counsel.

Why forgo the advantages of so peculiar a situation? Why quit our own to stand upon foreign ground? Why, by interweaving our destiny with that of any part of Europe, entangle our peace and prosperity in the toils of European ambition, rivalship, interest, humor or caprice?

'Tis our true policy to steer clear of permanent alliances with any portion of the foreign world. So far, I mean, as we are now at liberty to do it, for let me not be understood as capable of patronizing infidelity to existing arrangements (I hold the maxim no less applicable to public than to private affairs, that honesty is always the best policy). I repeat it therefore, let those engagements be observed in their genuine sense. But in my opinion, it is unnecessary and would be unwise to extend them.

Taking care always to keep ourselves, by suitable establishments, on a respectably defensive posture, we may safely trust to temporary alliances for extraordinary emergencies.

Previously, Washington gave expression to the following admirable and true idea: "The nation which indulges towards another an habitual hatred, or an habitual fondness, is in some degree a slave. It is a slave to its animosity or to its affection . . ."

Washington's political conduct was always guided by these maxims. He managed to keep his country at peace when the rest of the world was at war, and he established the fundamental doctrine that the true interest of Americans was never to take sides in Europe's internal quarrels.

Jefferson went further still and introduced this other maxim into the policy of the Union: "Americans should never solicit privileges from foreign nations so as never to be obliged to grant any themselves."

These two principles, whose palpable truth put them within reach of the multitude, greatly simplified the foreign policy of the United States.

Since the Union does not involve itself in European affairs, it has in a manner of speaking no foreign interests to debate, for it is still without powerful neighbors in America. Placed beyond the passions of the Old World as much by its location as by its will, it has no more need to protect itself from those passions than to espouse them. As for those of the New World, the future hides them still.

The Union is free of prior commitments. It can therefore profit from the experience of the old nations of Europe without being obliged, as they are, to make the best of the past and accommodate it to the present. It is not forced as they are to accept a vast heritage bequeathed by previous generations, a melange of glory and of misery, of national friendships and national hatreds. The foreign policy of the United States is eminently one of wait-and-see: it is far more a matter of abstaining than of doing.

It is therefore quite difficult at present to predict what skills American democracy will develop in the conduct of foreign affairs. In this respect, both its adversaries and its friends must reserve judgment.

For my part, I have no compunction about stating my opinion that when it comes to managing the foreign interests of society, democratic governments seem to me decidedly inferior to others. In democracies, experience, mores, and education almost always lead to the development of that practical, everyday wisdom and understanding of life's commonplace events that we call common sense. Common sense is sufficient for dealing with routine matters, and in a nation whose people are educated, democratic liberty applied to domestic affairs yields goods sufficient to outweigh the evils that democratic government is likely to introduce. But this is not always the case when it comes to relations between nations.

Foreign policy requires virtually none of the distinctive virtues of democracy but does demand the development of nearly all that it lacks. Democracy fosters growth of the state's domestic resources; it promotes prosperity and develops the public spirit; it strengthens respect for the law in the various classes of society. Yet all these things have only an indirect influence on a nation's position relative to other nations. By contrast, democracy finds it difficult to coordinate the details of a great enterprise or to settle on a plan and stick to it stubbornly in spite of obstacles. It has little capacity to devise measures in secret and patiently await their results. Qualities such as these are more likely to be found in a man or an aristocracy. Yet it is precisely these qualities that ensure that over the long run a nation, as indivisible entity, will dominate.

If, by way of contrast, we consider the natural defects of aristocracy, we find that they have almost no effect on the conduct of foreign affairs. The chief vice of which aristocracy stands accused is that it works only for itself and not for the masses. In foreign policy, it is very rare for the aristocracy to have interests distinct from those of the people.

Democracy's tendency to follow sentiment rather than reason in politics and to abandon a mature design in order to satisfy a momentary passion was quite apparent in America when the French Revolution broke out. The most elementary calculation should have been enough, then as now, to convince Americans that it would not be in their interest to take sides in the bloody conflict that was about to engulf Europe but that could do no damage to the United States.

Nevertheless, the sympathy of the American people for France declared itself with such violence that it took nothing less than Washington's inflexible character and immense popularity to prevent a declaration of war against England. And even then, that great man's efforts to throw austere reason into the balance against the generous but ill-considered passions of his fellow citizens nearly cost him the only reward he ever reserved for himself, namely, the love of his country. The majority spoke out against his policy then, but now the entire country approves.[17]

If the Constitution and public favor had not given Washington control over foreign policy, there can be no doubt that the nation would have done then precisely what it now condemns.

Nearly all the nations that have acted powerfully on the world, that have conceived, pursued, and carried out grand designs, from the Romans to the English, were led by an aristocracy. And why should this come as a surprise?

Nothing in the world is so fixed in its views as an aristocracy. The masses can be seduced by their ignorance or their passions. A king, caught off guard, can be induced to vacillate in his designs, and in any case no king is immortal. But an aristocratic body is too numerous to be ensnared yet not numerous enough to yield readily to the intoxication of mindless passion. An aristocratic body is a man of resolve and enlightenment who never dies.

---

[17]See the fifth volume of Marshall's *Life of Washington*: "In a government constituted like that of the United States," he says on p. 314, "the first magistrate cannot, whatever his firmness may be, long hold a dike against the torrent of popular opinion; and the one that prevailed then seemed to lead to war." In fact, in Congress it was apparent at the time that Washington often had the majority of the House against him. In the country at large, the language used against him was of an extremely violent nature: a speaker at one political meeting did not hesitate to compare him to the traitor Arnold (p. 265): "Those who held to the party of the opposition," Marshall writes (p. 335), "claimed that the partisans of the administration composed an aristocratic faction that had submitted to England and that, wanting to establish a monarchy, was consequently the enemy of France; a faction whose members constituted a sort of nobility that had the stock of the Bank as securities and that so feared every measure that could influence its funds that it was insensitive to the affronts that the honor and the interest of the nation commanded it equally to repel."

Chapter 6

WHAT ARE THE REAL ADVANTAGES TO AMERICAN SOCIETY OF DEMOCRATIC GOVERNMENT?

B EFORE beginning this chapter, I feel the need to remind the reader of something I have already mentioned more than once.

The political constitution of the United States is in my view one form that democracy can give to its government. But I do not believe that American institutions are the only or best ones that a democratic people may adopt.

Hence in examining the benefits that Americans derive from democratic government, I am far from arguing or thinking that such advantages can be obtained only by means of identical laws.

ON THE GENERAL TENDENCY OF THE LAWS UNDER AMERICAN DEMOCRACY AND THE INSTINCTS OF THE PEOPLE WHO APPLY THEM

Democracy's flaws are immediately apparent. — Its advantages become clear only in the long run. — American democracy is often clumsy, but the general tendency of its laws is beneficial. — Public officials under American democracy have no permanent interests that differ from those of the majority. — The consequences of this.

The flaws and weaknesses of democratic government are easy to see. They can be demonstrated by obvious facts, while the salutary influence of democratic government is exerted in an imperceptible, not to say occult, manner. Its defects are striking at first glance, but its virtues reveal themselves only over the long run.

The laws of American democracy are often defective or incomplete. Some of them violate established rights or sanction dangerous ones. Even if all the laws were good, the frequency of new legislation would still be a great evil. All this is apparent at a glance.

How is it, then, that the American republics survive and prosper?

In considering laws, one must distinguish carefully between the goals they seek and the way in which they move toward them, and, furthermore, between what is absolutely good in the laws and what is only relatively good.

Suppose that the aim of the lawmaker is to promote the interests of the few at the expense of the many. Suppose, further, that he contrives a law in such a way as to obtain the desired result in the least possible time with the least possible effort. In that case, the law will be well designed, but its purpose will be bad. It will be dangerous to the very extent that it is effective.

The laws of democracy generally tend toward the good of the many, for they emanate from the majority of all citizens, who may be mistaken but cannot be in conflict of interest with themselves.

By contrast, the laws of aristocracy tend to monopolize wealth and power in the hands of a few, because an aristocracy by its very nature constitutes a minority.

One can therefore say in general that the aim of legislation in a democracy is more useful to humanity than that of legislation in an aristocracy.

But there its advantages end.

Aristocracies are infinitely more clever at the science of legislation than democracies can ever be. An aristocracy, because it is self-possessed, is not subject to fleeting enthusiasms. It has long-range designs, which it can mature until a favorable opportunity arises. Aristocracy proceeds intelligently. It has the knack of bringing the collective force of all its laws to bear on a specific point at a specific moment in time.

This is not true of democracy: its laws are almost always defective or ill-timed.

Democracy's resources are therefore more imperfect than those of aristocracy: democracy often works against itself without intending to. But its goals are more utilitarian.

Imagine a society organized by nature or by its constitution in such a way as to withstand the fleeting effects of bad legislation and hold on until the *general tendency* of the law is realized, and you will understand why democratic government, for all its faults, is still the form of government most likely to achieve prosperity.

This is precisely what is happening in the United States. I will repeat here what I have already stated elsewhere: the great privilege of the Americans is the ability to make errors that can be corrected.

I shall say something analogous about public officials.

It is easy to see that American democracy is often mistaken in the choice of men whom it entrusts with power, but not so easy to say why the state prospers in their hands.

Note first that if government officials in a democratic state are less honest or less capable, the people they govern are more enlightened and more alert.

In a democracy, the people, being perpetually concerned with their own affairs and jealous of their rights, refuse to allow their representatives to deviate from a certain general line dictated by their interests.

Note, moreover, that if the democratic official makes poorer use of power than others, he generally holds power for a shorter time.

But there is also another reason more general than this one, as well as more satisfying.

It is no doubt important for the welfare of a nation that the men who govern it should be men of virtue and talent; but what is perhaps even more important is that these government officials should not have interests contrary to those of the masses they govern, for in that case, their virtues might become almost useless, and their talents disastrous.

I say that it is important for government officials not to have interests contrary to or different from the masses they govern; I do not say that it is important for them to have interests similar to those of *all* the people they govern, for I am not sure that such a situation has ever existed.

No one has yet discovered a political structure that promotes the development and prosperity of all classes of society equally. The classes remain as something like distinct nations within the larger nation, and experience has shown that it is almost as dangerous to entrust to one class the fate of all the others as to make one people the arbiter of another's destiny.

When the rich alone govern, the interests of the poor are always imperiled; and when the poor make the law, the interests of the rich are seriously at risk. What, then, is the advantage of democracy? The real advantage of democracy is not, as some say, to promote the prosperity of all but merely to foster the well-being of the greater number.

The officials charged with managing public affairs in the United States are often inferior in talent and morality to the men whom aristocracy would bring to power, but their interests overlap or are identical with those of a majority of their fellow citizens. Although such men may often betray their trust and commit grave errors, they will never systematically adopt a line hostile to the majority and are incapable of turning the government into a dangerous instrument for their own exclusive ends.

Under democracy, moreover, poor administration by one official is an isolated phenomenon whose effects do not outlive his brief term of office. Corruption and incompetence do not become common interests with the power to create permanent bonds among men.

A corrupt or incompetent official will not join forces with another official solely because he, too, is corrupt and incompetent, and two such men will never work in concert to foster corruption and incompetence in their children and their children's children. On the contrary, the ambition and intrigues of one official will help to unmask those of others. In democracies, official vices are for the most part purely personal.

Under aristocratic government, however, men in public life will share a common class interest, which may at times coincide with the interest of the majority but often will not. This common interest creates a durable bond. It encourages officials to work together to achieve a result that is not necessarily the happiness of the greater number. And not only does this similarity of purpose create bonds among government officials, it also unites those officials to a substantial proportion of the governed, for many citizens not employed by the government are nevertheless members of the aristocracy.

The aristocratic official therefore receives steady support from within society as well as from within government.

The common objective that leads officials in aristocracies to wed the interests of some of their contemporaries also encourages them to identify with, and in a sense subordinate their own interest to, that of future generations. They work with an eye to the future as well as to the present. Thus, the passions of the governed, of the aristocratic official himself, and I am tempted to say of his posterity conspire to lead him in the same direction.

Should we count it as surprising if he does not resist? In aristocracies it is therefore common to find even those not corrupted by the class spirit caught up by it and led unwittingly to accommodate society to their own use and prepare it for their progeny.

I do not know if there has ever been another aristocracy as liberal as that of England, or one that has consistently provided the government of the country with men as worthy and enlightened.

Nevertheless, it is easy to see that in English law the poor man's welfare has often been sacrificed to that of the rich man, and the rights of the many to the privileges of a few. England today therefore exhibits every conceivable extreme of fortune, and the wretchedness that one finds there almost rivals her power and glory.

In the United States, where public officials have no class interest to vindicate, the general and constant process of government is beneficial, though government officials are often inept and sometimes contemptible.

Underlying democratic institutions there is thus a hidden tendency that often leads men to contribute, despite their faults and errors, to the general prosperity, while in aristocratic institutions there is at times a secret proclivity that encourages them, for all their talents and virtues, to contribute to the miseries of mankind. Public men in aristocratic governments may do harm without intending to, while in democracies they may do good without recognizing it.

PUBLIC SPIRIT IN THE UNITED STATES

Instinctive love of country. — Considered patriotism. — Their different characters. — Why nations should strive with all their might to achieve the latter when the former disappears. — Efforts by the Americans to do so. — Individual interest intimately related to national interest.

There exists a love of country that stems primarily from the immediate, disinterested, and indefinable sentiment that ties a man's heart to the place where he was born. This instinctive love is intimately connected to a liking for ancient customs, respect for elders, and memory of the past. Those who feel it cherish their country as a man might love his ancestral home. They love the tranquillity they enjoy and value the peaceful habits they acquired there. Attached to the memories that the place evokes, they find it pleasant to live there even in obedience. It is not uncommon for such love of country to be further exalted by religious zeal, in which case it can work miracles. It is itself a kind of religion: it does not reason, it believes, it feels, it acts. Some nations in a way personify the fatherland and glimpse its image in the prince. They transfer to his person some of the sentiments that constitute patriotism. They boast of his triumphs and take pride in his power. There was a time under the old monarchy when Frenchmen felt a kind of joy at surrendering utterly to the arbitrary rule of their monarch and were proud to proclaim that "we live under the world's most powerful king."

Like all unreflective passions, such love of country inspires great but transitory efforts rather than persistent ones. It is apt to save the state in time of crisis only to allow it to wither in time of peace.

When a people is still simple in its mores and firm in its belief, and society rests tranquilly on an ancient order whose legitimacy is not contested, such instinctive love of country can flourish.

Another, more rational form of patriotism also exists: it is less generous, less ardent perhaps, but more fruitful and durable. This second form of patriotism is born of enlightenment. It develops with the aid of laws, grows with the exercise of rights, and eventually comes to be bound up in a way with personal interest. People understand how their country's well-being influences their own. They know that the law allows them to contribute to that well-being, and they take an interest in their country's prosperity, initially as something useful to them but later as their own handiwork.

In the life of a nation, however, there may come a time when ancient customs are transformed, mores decay, faiths are shaken, memories lose their prestige, but enlightenment has yet to complete its work and political rights remain insecure or limited. At such times the only light in which men can see their country is a feeble and dubious one. Patriotic feeling no longer attaches to the soil, which to the people who live on it has become mere inanimate earth; or to ancestral customs, which they have learned to see as confining; or to religion, of which they are skeptical; or to the laws, which they do not make; or to the lawmaker, whom they fear and despise. Hence they cannot see their country anywhere, in either its proper guise or any other, and they withdraw into narrow, unenlightened selfishness. They have escaped prejudice but not yet embraced the empire of reason. Lacking both the instinctive patriotism of monarchy and the considered patriotism of a republic, they find themselves stuck somewhere between the two, surrounded by confusion and misery.

What to do in such a situation? Retreat. But nations no more revert to the sentiments of their youth than do men to the innocent desires of childhood. Though they may long to feel such feelings again, nothing can revive them. So there is no choice but to proceed forthrightly and with all deliberate speed to make the case that the interests of individuals and of the nation are inextricably intertwined, because disinterested love of country has vanished forever.

Far be it from me to suggest that in order to achieve this end, full political rights must immediately be granted to all men. Nevertheless, the most powerful way of persuading men that they have a stake in their country's fate, and perhaps the only way still available to us, is to see to it that they participate in its government. The civic spirit today seems to me intimately intertwined with the exercise of political rights, and I think that from now on the number of citizens in Europe will rise and fall in proportion to the extension of such rights.

How is it that in the United States, whose residents, leaving customs and memories behind, came only recently to the land they now inhabit, where they met as strangers for the first time and where, to put it bluntly, it is scarcely possible for a patriotic instinct to exist — how is it that everyone in the United States takes an interest in the affairs of his town, county, and state as though they were his own? The answer is that, within his own sphere, each person takes an active part in the government of society.

In the United States, the common man has understood how the general prosperity affects his own happiness — a very simple idea, yet one of which the people in most countries have only a very limited grasp. What is more, he has become accustomed to looking upon that prosperity as his own handiwork. He therefore identifies the public fortune with his own, and he works for the good of the state not only out of duty or pride but, I would almost venture to say, out of greed.

There is no need to study American institutions and history to understand the truth of what has just been said; American mores will instruct you sufficiently. Because the American takes part in everything that is done in his country, he believes that he has an interest in defending everything about it that is criticized, for it is not only his country that is attacked but himself. Thus one finds his national pride resorting to every artifice and stooping to every puerile expression of individual vanity.

Nothing inhibits ordinary social intercourse more than the irritable patriotism of the American. A foreigner may be prepared to praise a great deal in the United States, but some things he would like to criticize, and this the American absolutely refuses to allow.

America is therefore a land of liberty where, in order not to offend anyone, a foreigner must not speak freely about individuals or the state, the people or the government, public or private enterprises, indeed about anything he finds there, except perhaps the climate and soil. In fact, one encounters

Americans prepared to defend even the latter two things as though they had had a hand in making them.

In these times we must make up our minds and dare to choose between the patriotism of all and the government of a few, for we cannot have both the social strength and vitality that come from the former and the guarantees of tranquillity that the latter occasionally provides.

ON THE IDEA OF RIGHTS IN
THE UNITED STATES

There can be no great nation without an idea of rights. — By what means can the people be given an idea of rights? — Respect for rights in the United States. — Where it comes from.

Next to the general idea of virtue, I know of no idea more beautiful than that of rights, and, indeed, it would be more accurate to say that the two ideas are indistinguishable. The idea of rights is none other than the idea of virtue introduced into the world of politics.

Men have used the idea of rights to define license and tyranny. Guided by its light, they learned to be independent without arrogance and obedient without baseness. The man who submits to violence bows down and makes himself abject, but the man who obeys orders issued by someone to whom he has granted the right to command shows himself to be nobler in a way than the commander himself. Without virtue there is no such thing as a great man; without rights there is no such thing as a great nation, and, one might almost say, no such thing as society, for what is a group of rational and intelligent beings held together solely by force?

I ask myself how in these times the idea of rights can be inculcated in the minds of men and made palpable, as it were, to their senses. I see only one way of doing it, namely, to allow everyone to exercise certain rights in peace. One sees this clearly in children, who are men in all but strength and experience. When a child begins to move among the objects of the external world, instinct impels him to turn everything he touches to his own use. He has no idea of the property, or even of the existence, of others. But as he is taught the value of things and learns that what he has can be taken away from him, he becomes more circumspect and ultimately comes to respect in others what he wants them to respect in him.

What happens to the child with his playthings happens later to the man with everything he owns. Why, in a quintessentially democratic country like America, does one hear no complaints about property in general such as those that often resound through Europe? Needless to say, it is because there are no proletarians in America. Since everyone has property of his own to defend, everyone recognizes property rights as a matter of principle.

The same is true in the world of politics. In America, the common man has an exalted idea of political rights because he has such rights. He does not attack the rights of others because he does not want them to violate his own. And while in Europe the man of the people will often refuse to bend even to sovereign authority, the American submits without a murmur to the least of his officials.

Evidence of this can be seen in even the smallest details of a nation's existence. In France, few pleasures are reserved exclusively for the upper classes of society. The poor man is admitted almost everywhere the rich man goes: thus we find the poor behaving decently and showing proper respect for whatever helps to procure pleasures in which they share. In England, where enjoyment is the privilege and power the monopoly of the wealthy, one hears complaints that when the poor by stealth somehow gain admission to places set aside for the rich man's pleasures, they like to do indiscriminate damage. But why is this surprising, since everything has been done to ensure that they should have nothing to lose?

Democratic government causes the idea of political rights to filter down to the humblest of citizens, much as the division of property brings the idea of property rights in general within everyone's reach. This, in my view, is one of its greatest merits.

Not that teaching everyone to make use of political rights is an easy thing to do: that is not my point. All I mean to say is that, when it can be done, the effect is great.

And I would add that, if ever there were a century in which an attempt to do so ought to be made, it is this one.

Do you not see that religions are on the wane and that the divine notion of rights is disappearing? Does it not strike you that mores are crumbling and that, along with them, the moral notion of rights is fading away?

Is it not obvious to you that belief is everywhere giving way to reasoning and sentiment to calculation? If, in the midst of this universal upheaval, you do not succeed in linking the idea of rights to the personal interest that stands out as the only fixed point in the human heart, what means of governing the world will be left to you other than fear?

Therefore, when I am told that the laws are weak and the people turbulent; that passions run high, and virtue is powerless; and that in such a situation one must not think of extending democratic rights; I respond that in my view these are the very reasons why one must consider extending them; and quite frankly I think that governments have an even greater interest in doing so than society has, because governments perish, whereas society cannot die, Yet I do not wish to make too much of the American example.

In America, the people were granted political rights at a time when it was difficult to make poor use of them, because citizens were few and their mores simple. As they grew, they did not increase democracy's powers but rather extended its purview.

There can be no doubt that the moment when political rights are granted to a people previously deprived of them is a moment of crisis — a crisis that is often necessary but always dangerous.

A child may kill when he does not understand the value of life. He may take the property of others before he realizes that others can take what is his. Upon being granted political rights, the common man stands in relation to those rights as the child stands to all of nature, and to him in that moment one may apply the celebrated adage, *Homo puer robustus.*

The truth of this is apparent even in America. States whose citizens have enjoyed their rights the longest are states whose citizens are still best equipped to make use of them.

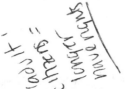

That nothing is more prodigal of wonders than the art of being free is a truth that cannot be repeated too often. But nothing is harder than the apprenticeship of liberty. This is not true of despotism. Despotism often presents itself as the remedy for all ills suffered in the past. It is the upholder of justice, the champion of the oppressed, and the founder of order. Nations are lulled to sleep by the temporary prosperity to which it gives rise, and when they awake, they are miserable. Liberty, in contrast, is usually born in stormy times. It struggles to establish itself amid civil discord, and its benefits can be appreciated only when it is old.

ON RESPECT FOR THE LAW IN THE UNITED STATES

Respect of Americans for the law. — Paternal love they feel for it. — Personal interest that everyone takes in enhancing the power of the law.

It is not always feasible to involve all the people directly or indirectly in the making of the law, but there is no denying the fact that when it is practicable to do so, the law thereby acquires great authority. Legislation that originates with the people may often want for goodness and wisdom, but what it lacks in those respects is compensated by a singular increase in its power.

In the expression of the wills of an entire people there is a prodigious force. When such a force declares itself openly, the very imagination of potential opponents is in some ways daunted.

Parties are well aware of this truth.

They therefore vie for the majority wherever they can. If they fail to obtain it from the voters, they will say that it lies with those who abstained from voting, and if it still eludes them, they will say that it belongs to those who are denied the right to vote.

In the United States, apart from slaves, servants, and paupers whose upkeep is paid for by the towns, there is no one who is excluded from voting and who does not, as a voter, contribute indirectly to the law. Anyone who wishes to attack the laws is therefore reduced to doing one of two things: he must either change the nation's opinion or trample upon its will.

There is also a second reason, more direct and more powerful than the first: in the United States each individual has in a sense a personal interest in seeing to it that everyone obeys the law. For a person who is not in the majority today may find himself in it tomorrow, and the respect that he professes for the will of the legislature now he may later have occasion to demand for himself. No matter how irksome a law may be, the resident of the United States therefore submits to it without protest, not simply because it is the work of the majority but also because he had a hand in making it himself. He looks upon it as a contract to which he is a party.

In the United States, therefore, one does not find large numbers of perpetually agitated people who see the law as their natural enemy and whose view of it is inevitably clouded by fear and suspicion. On the contrary, it is impossible to miss the fact that all classes place great confidence in their country's laws, for which they feel a kind of paternal affection.

I am wrong to say "all classes." Because the European hierarchy of power is stood on its head in America, the rich find themselves in a position analogous to that of the poor in Europe; it is often they who distrust the law. As I have said elsewhere, the real advantage of democratic government is not, as some would claim, to guarantee the interests of all but simply to protect the interests of the greatest number. In the United States, where the poor man governs, the rich must always be afraid that he will abuse his power at their expense.

Such a cast of mind among the rich may lead to muffled discontent, but no violent disruption of society ensues because the same thing that prevents the wealthy from trusting the legislator also prevents them from defying his commandments. They do not make the law because they are rich, and they dare not break the law because of their wealth. In civilized nations, as a general rule, it is only those who have nothing to lose who revolt. Hence, while the laws of democracy are not always respectable, they are almost always respected, because those who would ordinarily violate the law cannot fail to obey laws that they have made and from which they profit, and citizens who might have an interest in breaking the law are inclined by character and position to submit to the will of the law-maker, whatever it happens to be. Furthermore, Americans obey the law not only because it is their own handiwork but also because they can change it if by chance it does them harm. They submit to an injurious law, first because it is an injury they have done to themselves, and second because they know their suffering will be brief.

THE PERVASIVENESS OF POLITICAL ACTIVITY IN THE UNITED STATES AND THE INFLUENCE IT EXERTS ON SOCIETY

The prevalence of political activity in the United States is more difficult to comprehend than the liberty and equality one finds there. — The constant political fervor in the legislatures is merely an episode or extension of this universal fervor. — The difficulty that Americans have with minding their own business. — Political agitation spills over into civil society. — The industriousness of the Americans is partly due to this. — Indirect benefits to society of democratic government.

On traveling from a country that is free to another that is not, one is struck by the extraordinary contrast between the two: in the former bustle and activity are everywhere, whereas in the latter everything seems calm and still. In the one, improvement and progress are on everyone's mind, whereas in the other it almost seems that society, having acquired everything it needs, aspires only to enjoy what it already has. Nevertheless, the country whose happiness is bought at the price of so much agitation is generally richer and more prosperous than the one that appears so satisfied with its lot. And contemplating both, it is hard to understand how it is possible for so many new needs to arise in the former every day, while the latter seems conscious of so few.

Although this remark applies to free countries that have retained the form of monarchies as well as to those ruled by aristocracy, it is more pertinent still to democratic republics. In a democratic republic, it is not just one segment of the population that seeks to improve the state of society; the people as a whole assume the responsibility. The goal is not to serve the needs and convenience of one class but of all classes simultaneously.

The immense liberty that Americans enjoy is not beyond our powers of conception, nor is it difficult to imagine the extreme equality that exists among them. What cannot be understood until it has been seen, however, is the prevalence of political activity in the United States.

To set foot on American soil is to find oneself in tumultuous surroundings. A confused clamor proceeds from every quarter. A thousand voices assail the ear simultaneously, each giving expression to some social need. Everywhere things are in an uproar: the people of one neighborhood have come together to decide whether they should build a church; in another they are busy choosing a representative; elsewhere delegates from the county rush to the city to offer their views on certain local improvements. In yet another village, farmers abandon their fields to discuss plans for a highway or school. Citizens meet for the sole purpose of announcing that they disapprove of the policies of the government, while others hail the men now in office as the fathers of their country. Still others, being of the opinion that drunkenness is the principal cause of the state's woes, solemnly pledge to set an example of temperance.[1]

The great political fervor that keeps American legislatures in a state of constant agitation is the only part of this vast movement that can be seen from abroad, but it is merely an episode in something much larger, and in a way an extension of it: something that begins in the lowest ranks of the populace and from there spreads through all classes of citizens one after another. No one can work harder at being happy than Americans do.

[1]Temperance societies are associations whose members pledge to abstain from drinking strong liquor. At the time I visited the United States, temperance societies already comprised more than 270,000 members, and their effect had been to decrease the annual consumption of spirits by 500,000 gallons in the state of Pennsylvania alone.

It is difficult to say what place political concerns occupy in the lives of Americans. For them, to take an interest in and talk about the government of society is life's most important activity and, in a way, its only pleasure. This is evident in their most basic routines: even women often attend public meetings and find relaxation from the cares of the household in listening to political speeches. For them, political rallies to some extent take the place of shows. Americans do not converse; they argue. They do not talk; they lecture. They always speak to you as though addressing a meeting, and if for some reason they warm to the topic, they will say "Gentlemen" even when addressing a single person.

The inhabitants of some countries accept the political rights granted them by law only with a kind of repugnance. It seems as though they value their time too much to spend it on the interests of the community, and they would rather confine themselves within the narrow limits of self-interest, precisely defined by four ditches lined with hedges.

If, by contrast, an American were reduced to minding only his own business, half of his life would be stolen from him. He would feel as though an immense void had hollowed out his days, and he would become incredibly unhappy.[2]

I am convinced that if despotism ever takes hold in America, it will find conquering the habits to which liberty has given rise even more difficult than subduing the love of liberty itself.

The ceaseless agitation that democratic government introduces into politics then spreads to civil society. I am not sure that in the end this is not the greatest benefit of democratic government, so that I praise it far more for what it causes to be done than for what it does.

There is no denying that the people often manage public affairs very badly. But they could not take part in public affairs at all without broadening their ideas and abandoning set ways of thinking. When a man of the people is called to government, his self-esteem increases. Because he now has power,

[2] The same thing was observed in Rome under the first Caesars.

Montesquieu remarks somewhere that nothing could equal the despair of certain Romans who suddenly returned to the calm of private life after the excitement of a political career.

some very enlightened minds are ready to advise him. People look to him constantly for support and, by trying to deceive him in a thousand ways, manage only to enlighten him. In politics, he takes part in enterprises that he has not himself conceived but that foster in him a taste for enterprise in general. Every day people point out to him new ways of improving common property, and this fosters in him a desire to improve his own property. He may not be happier or more virtuous than his predecessors, but he is more enlightened and more active. I have no doubt that democratic institutions, combined with the physical nature of the country, are responsible for the prodigious development of industry that one sees in the United States — not as the direct cause, as so many people say, but rather as the indirect cause. It is not that the laws are responsible for this development, but rather that the people, in making the laws, learn how to make it happen.

When the enemies of democracy argue that one person alone can do what he sets out to do better than the government of all, it seems to me that they are right. A government run by one man can be more consistent in its efforts than a multitude, assuming equal intelligence on both sides. One man can be more persevering and form a better idea of the whole while achieving greater mastery of detail and more discerning judgment of people. Those who deny these things have never seen a democratic republic or base their judgment on only a small number of examples. Even when local circumstances and the dispositions of the people allow democracy to survive, it lacks the sharp eye that is developed by administrative regularity and methodical order in government; that much is true. Under democratic liberty, projects are not executed with the perfection that intelligent despotism can achieve. Democracy will often abandon its projects before harvesting their fruits, or it will embark on dangerous adventures. In the long run, however, it achieves more than despotism. It does each thing less well, but it does more things. Under its rule, it is not so much what the public administration does that is great, but, above all, what people do without it, and independent of it. Democracy does not give the people the most skillful government, but what it does even the most skillful government is powerless to achieve: it *energy none much*

spreads throughout society a restless activity, a superabundant strength, an energy that never exists without it, and which, if circumstances are even slightly favorable, can accomplish miracles. These are its true advantages.

In this century, when the fate of the Christian world seems to hang in the balance, some are quick to attack democracy as a hostile power, while it is still growing; others already worship it as a new god emerged from the void. But both groups have at best an imperfect knowledge of the object of their hatred or desire. They clash in darkness and strike blows haphazardly at best.

What do you want from society and government? Clarity on this point is essential.

Do you wish to impart a certain loftiness to the human mind, a generous way of looking at the things of this world? Do you want to inspire in men a kind of contempt for material goods? Do you hope to foster or develop profound convictions and lay the groundwork for deep devotion?

Is your goal to refine mores, elevate manners, and promote brilliance in the arts? Do you want poetry, renown, and glory?

Do you seek to organize a people so as to act powerfully on all other peoples? Would you have them embark on enterprises so great that, no matter what comes of their efforts, they will leave a deep imprint on history?

If, in your view, these are the main objectives that men in society ought to set for themselves, do not choose democratic government, for it offers no guarantee that you will reach your goal. *demo offers no goal*

But if it seems useful to you to turn man's intellectual and moral efforts to the necessities of material life and use them to improve his well-being; if reason strikes you as more profitable to man than genius; if your purpose is to create not heroic virtues but tranquil habits; if you would rather see vice than crime and are prepared to accept fewer great deeds in exchange for fewer atrocities; if, instead of a brilliant society as a stage for your actions, you are willing to settle for a prosperous one; and if, finally, the principal purpose of a government is not, in your view, to make the nation as a whole as glorious or powerful as can be but to achieve for each individual the greatest possible well-being while avoiding misery

want [?] il habit everyone, lessen pwr.

as much as possible; then equalize conditions and constitute a democratic government.

But if the time for choice is past and a force superior to man is already, without consulting your wishes, propelling you toward one of these two forms of government, try at least to get out of it all the good that it can do; and knowing its good instincts as well as its wicked inclinations, strive to limit the effect of the latter and promote the former.

if in a rough situation, take out good of it & prepare the

Chapter 7

ON THE OMNIPOTENCE OF THE MAJORITY IN THE UNITED STATES AND ITS EFFECTS

Natural strength of the majority in democracies. — Most of the American constitutions have artificially increased this natural strength. — How. — Binding mandates. — Moral sway of the majority. — Opinion of its infallibility. — Respect for its rights. — What increases it in the United States.

IT IS of the very essence of democratic government that the majority has absolute sway, for in a democracy nothing resists the majority.

Most American constitutions also attempt to increase this natural strength of the majority by artificial means.[1]

Of all political powers, the legislature is the one that obeys the majority most willingly. Americans wanted members of the legislature to be elected *directly* by the people, and for a *very short* term, so as to oblige representatives to conform not only to the general views but also to the daily passions of their constituents.

They recruited members of both houses from the same classes and elected them in the same way, so that shifts in the legislative body are almost as rapid and no less irresistible than in a single assembly.

Having constituted the legislature in this way, they concentrated nearly all of government in its hands.

Even as the law strengthened the powers that were naturally strong, it steadily weakened those that were naturally weak. It accorded neither stability nor independence to the representatives of the executive power and, by subjecting them

---

[1]When we examined the federal Constitution, we saw that the framers of the Union worked against this tendency. As a result of their efforts, the federal government is more independent in its sphere than the state governments are in theirs. But the federal government is concerned with little other than foreign affairs; American society is really ruled by the state governments.

entirely to the whims of the legislature, deprived them of what little influence the nature of democratic government would have allowed them to exert.

In a number of states, the law made the judicial power subject to election by the majority, and in all it made the existence of the judicial power partially dependent on the legislative by allowing representatives to set the salaries of judges year by year.

Custom has accomplished even more than law.

A custom that will ultimately undercut the guarantees of representative government is increasingly common in America. It is not at all unusual for voters to chart a course of action for their elected representatives and to impose on them certain binding obligations. The result is as if the majority itself undertook to deliberate in the public square, albeit without the tumult.

A number of specific circumstances tend, moreover, to make the power of the majority in America not just predominant but irresistible.

The moral ascendancy of the majority rests in part on the idea that there is more enlightenment and wisdom in an assembly of many than in the mind of one, or that the number of legislators matters more than the manner of their selection. It is the theory of equality applied to intelligence. This doctrine strikes at the last refuge of man's pride. Hence the minority is reluctant to accept it and takes time to get used to it. Thus the power of the majority, like all powers — and perhaps more than others — needs to endure if it is to appear legitimate. On first establishing itself, it gains obedience through coercion. Only after people have lived for a long time under its laws do they begin to respect it.

The idea that the enlightenment of the majority gives it the right to govern society came to the United States with its first settlers. This idea, which alone would suffice to create a free people, has by now been incorporated into the nation's mores, and its influence extends to the least significant of life's daily routines.

The French, under the old monarchy, held fast to the idea that the king could never fail. When he did do wrong, they blamed his advisors. This made it wonderfully easy to obey.

One could murmur against the law without ceasing to love and respect the man who made it. Americans take the same view of the majority.

The moral ascendancy of the majority also rests on the principle that the interests of the many ought to be preferred to those of the few. Now, it is easy to see that respect for the right of the greater number increases or decreases depending on the state of the parties. When a nation is torn by several great and irreconcilable interests, the privilege of the majority is often ignored, because it becomes too painful to submit to it.

If there were a class of citizens in America whom lawmakers were endeavoring to strip of advantages possessed for centuries and to reduce from a lofty position to the status of the multitude, it is likely that the minority would not readily submit to the resulting laws.

But because the United States was settled by equals, no natural and permanent conflict among their interests yet exists.

Social states do exist in which members of the minority cannot hope to win over the majority, because in order to do so they would have to abandon the very cause for which they are fighting against it. For example, an aristocracy cannot become a majority while clinging to its exclusive privileges, but it cannot let go of those privileges without ceasing to be an aristocracy.

In the United States, political questions of such an absolute and general kind cannot arise, and all parties are prepared to recognize the rights of the majority, because all hope some day to exercise those rights.

Hence the majority in the United States enjoys immense actual power together with a power of opinion that is almost as great. And once it has made up its mind about a question, there is nothing that can stop it or even slow it long enough to hear the cries of those whom it crushes in passing.

The consequences of this state of affairs are dire and spell danger for the future.

HOW THE OMNIPOTENCE OF THE MAJORITY IN AMERICA INCREASES THE LEGISLATIVE AND ADMINISTRATIVE INSTABILITY THAT IS NATURAL IN DEMOCRACIES

How the Americans increase the natural legislative instability of democracy by changing legislators every year and arming them with almost unlimited power. — The same effect on administration. — In America the impetus toward social improvement is far greater than in Europe but not as steady.

I spoke earlier about the natural flaws of democratic government, every one of which increases as the power of the majority increases.

To begin with the most obvious of all:

Legislative instability is an evil inherent in democratic government, because it is in the nature of democracies to bring new men to power. But the severity of this evil depends on the power and means of action accorded to the legislator.

In America, sovereign power is vested in the authority that makes the laws. It can quickly and irrevocably indulge its every desire, and each year it is supplied with new representatives. In other words, the arrangement chosen was precisely that which encourages democratic instability in every way possible and allows matters of the utmost importance to be decided by the changing will of the people.

Thus, of all the countries in the world today, America is the one in which the duration of laws is the shortest. Nearly all American constitutions have been amended within the past thirty years. Hence no American state has left the basic principle of its laws untouched for that length of time.

As for the laws themselves, a glance at the various state archives is enough to convince oneself that legislative action in America never slows down. The problem is not that American democracy is by nature more unstable than any other democracy, but rather that it has been given the means to indulge its natural penchant toward instability in the shaping of its laws.[2]

---

[2]The legislative enactments of the state of Massachusetts alone from 1780 to the present already fill three stout volumes. Note, moreover, that the collection to which I refer was revised in 1823, and many laws that had become

The omnipotence of the majority and the rapid and absolute way in which its wishes are carried out in the United States not only make the law unstable but exert a similar influence on the execution of the law and the actions of the public administration.

Since the majority is the only power that it is important to please, its projects enlist ardent support, but the moment its attention turns elsewhere, all efforts cease; whereas in the free states of Europe in which the administrative power enjoys an independent existence and a secure position, the will of the legislator continues to be carried out even when he concerns himself with other matters.

In America, certain improvements elicit far more enthusiasm and energy than they do in other countries.

In Europe, the social force employed in these efforts is infinitely less great, but more continuous.

Several years ago, some pious individuals undertook to improve the state of the prisons. Their voices moved the public, and the rehabilitation of criminals became a popular cause.

New prisons were then built. For the first time, the idea of reforming criminals as well as punishing them gained influence inside prison walls. But this praiseworthy revolution, which the public had so enthusiastically joined and which acquired irresistible force thanks to the simultaneous efforts of so many citizens, could not be accomplished overnight.

Alongside the new penitentiaries, whose development was hastened by the wishes of the majority, the old prisons continued to exist and to house large numbers of inmates. The old prisons seemed to become more insalubrious and corrupting while the new ones instituted additional reforms and improved health conditions even more. Both effects are easy to understand: the majority, preoccupied with the idea of founding new prisons, had forgotten the ones that already existed. Because everyone averted their eyes from matters that no longer held the master's attention, oversight ceased. The

outdated or irrelevant were eliminated. Yet the state of Massachusetts, whose population is no greater than one of our *départements*, is reputed to be the most stable state in the entire Union, as well as the most persevering and sagacious in its undertakings.

salutary bonds of discipline first slackened, then broke. And in the end one found standing cheek by jowl not only prisons that may be taken as durable monuments to the sweetness and light of our time but dungeons reminiscent of the barbarity of the Middle Ages.

TYRANNY OF THE MAJORITY

How the principle of popular sovereignty should be understood. — Impossibility of conceiving a mixed government. — Sovereign power must exist somewhere. — Precautions that should be taken to moderate its action. — Such precautions were not taken in the United States. — What results from this.

I regard as impious and detestable the maxim that in matters of government the majority of a people has the right to do absolutely anything, yet I place the origin of all powers in the will of the majority. Am I in contradiction with myself?

There exists one general law that was made or at any rate adopted not only by a majority of this or that people but by a majority of all people. That law is justice.

Justice therefore sets a limit to the right of each people. A nation is like a jury charged with representing universal society and applying the justice which is its law. Should the jury, which represents society, have more power than the society whose laws it applies?

Therefore, when I refuse to obey an unjust law, I do not deny the majority's right to command; I am simply appealing from the sovereignty of the people to the sovereignty of the human race.

There are those who have made so bold as to insist that a people, insofar as it deals with matters of interest to itself alone, cannot overstep the bounds of justice and reason entirely, hence that there is no reason to be afraid of bestowing all power on the majority that represents that people. But to speak thus is to speak the language of a slave.

For what is a majority taken collectively if not an individual with opinions and, more often than not, interests contrary to those of another individual known as the minority? Now, if you are willing to concede that a man to whom omnipotence has been granted can abuse it to the detriment of his adversaries, why will you not concede that the same may be true of a majority? Do men, in banding together, change character? Do they become more patient of obstacles as they gain in strength?[3] I, for one, do not believe it. And if I refuse to grant to any one of my fellow men the power to do whatever he likes, I will never grant that same power to some number of my fellow men.

In saying this, I do not mean to say that I think liberty can be preserved by establishing a government based on a mix of principles chosen in such a way that one truly opposes another.

What is called mixed government has always seemed to me a chimera. In fact, there is no such thing as mixed government (in the sense in which that term is used), because in the end one discovers that in every society there is one principle of action that dominates all the others.

Eighteenth-century England, which has been singled out as an example of this type of government, was essentially an aristocratic state, though it did contain important elements of democracy, because laws and mores there were such that the aristocracy would always predominate in the long run and direct public affairs as it saw fit.

The error came from the fact that observers of the constant conflict between the interests of the high nobility and those of the people thought only of the struggle and paid no attention to the result, which is what mattered. When a society really reaches the point of having a mixed government, which is to say a government equally divided between contrary principles, either revolution erupts or society dissolves.

I therefore think that a place must always be provided for one social power superior to all others, but I believe that liberty is imperiled if that power meets with no obstacle capable of slowing its advance and giving it time to moderate itself.

---

[3] No one would want to argue that a people cannot abuse its strength in regard to another people. But parties are like small nations within the larger one and relate to one another as foreigners.

If one admits that a nation can be tyrannical toward another nation, how can one deny that a party can be tyrannical toward another party?

Omnipotence in itself seems to me a bad and dangerous thing. Its exercise appears to me beyond the strength of any man, whoever he may be. As I see it, only God can be all-powerful without danger, because his wisdom and justice are always equal to his power. Thus there is no authority on earth so inherently worthy of respect, or invested with a right so sacred, that I would want to let it act without oversight or rule without impediment. Therefore, when I see the right and wherewithal to do all accorded to any power whatsoever, whether it be called people or king, democracy or aristocracy, and whether it be exercised in a monarchy or a republic, I say, therein lies the seed of tyranny, and I seek to live elsewhere, under different laws.

My chief complaint against democratic government as it has been organized in the United States is not that it is weak, as many in Europe maintain, but rather that its strength is irresistible. What I find most repugnant in America is not the extreme liberty that prevails there but the virtual absence of any guarantee against tyranny.

When a man or party suffers from an injustice in the United States, to whom can he turn? To public opinion? It constitutes the majority. To the legislature? It represents the majority and obeys it blindly. To the executive? It is elected by the majority and serves as its passive instrument. To public force? Public force is nothing but the majority in arms. To the jury? The jury is the majority invested with the right to pronounce judgment. In some states, judges themselves are elected by the majority. However iniquitous or unreasonable the measure that strikes you may be, you must therefore submit to it.[4]

---

[4] During the War of 1812, a striking example of the excesses to which the despotism of the majority may lead occurred in Baltimore. At that time the war was very popular there. One newspaper, which was strongly opposed, incurred the wrath of the city's inhabitants. A crowd assembled, smashed the presses, and attacked the homes of journalists. An attempt was made to call in the militia, but the troops failed to answer the call. To save the lives of the unfortunate victims of the public's fury, it was decided that they should be taken to prison like criminals; but this precaution proved vain: during the night another crowd gathered; because officials had been unsuccessful in summoning the militia, the prison was stormed; one of the journalists was killed,

Suppose, on the contrary, a legislative body constituted in such a way as to represent the majority without being necessarily the slave of its passions; an executive power with a force of its own; and a judicial power independent of the two others. You would still have a democratic government, but almost no danger of tyranny would remain.

I am not saying that recourse to tyranny is frequent in America today, only that no guarantee against it can be found, and that the reasons for the mildness of government must be sought in circumstances and mores rather than in the laws.

EFFECTS OF THE OMNIPOTENCE OF THE MAJORITY ON THE ARBITRARINESS OF AMERICAN PUBLIC OFFICIALS

Liberty of American officials within the sphere marked out for them by law. — Their power.

It is important to mark well the distinction between arbitrariness and tyranny. Tyranny can use the law itself as an instrument, in which case it is not arbitrary. Arbitrariness can be used in the interest of the governed, in which case it is not tyrannical.

---

and the others were left for dead. The perpetrators were tried but acquitted by a jury.

One day I asked a Pennsylvanian to "explain to me, please, how in a state founded by Quakers and renowned for its tolerance, freed Negroes are not allowed to exercise the rights of citizens. They pay taxes. Is it not right that they should vote?" — "Do not insult us," he replied, "by thinking that our legislators would commit an act of such gross injustice and intolerance." — "So, Blacks have the right to vote in your state?" — "Certainly." — "Then why is it that in the electoral college this morning I did not see a single one?" — "That is not the fault of the law," the American told me. "Negroes have the right to go to the polls, but they voluntarily abstain." — "How extraordinarily modest of them!" — "Oh! It isn't that they refuse to vote, but they are afraid of being mistreated if they do. The law here has no teeth if the majority refuses to support it. But the majority harbors strong prejudices against the Negroes, and our officials do not feel strong enough to guarantee the rights that the legislature has bestowed on them." — "What! Do you mean to say that the majority, which enjoys the privilege of making the law, also insists on the privilege of disobeying it?"

Tyranny ordinarily makes use of arbitrary power but if need be can do without it.

In the United States, the omnipotence of the majority not only encourages legal despotism in the legislator but at the same time favors arbitrariness in the magistrate. The majority, having absolute sway over both the making and execution of the law as well as control of both government agents and the people they govern, looks upon public officials as its passive agents and is willing to leave it to them to serve its designs. Hence it does not concern itself in advance with the details of their duties and scarcely troubles itself to define their rights. It treats them as a master might treat his servants if they were never out of his sight and he could thus correct their behavior whenever necessary.

In general, the law leaves American officials much freer than ours within the sphere marked out for them. At times the majority even allows them to act outside that sphere. Backed by the opinion of the many and strengthened by their support, officials will then dare to do things that astonish even a European accustomed to the sight of arbitrary rule. Within the bosom of liberty habits are thus formed that may one day do it great harm.

ON THE POWER THAT THE MAJORITY IN AMERICA EXERCISES OVER THOUGHT

In the United States, once the majority has made up its mind about an issue, debate ceases. — Why. — Moral power that the majority exercises over thought. — Democratic republics transform despotism into something immaterial.

It is when one comes to examine the way in which thought is exercised in the United States that one perceives quite clearly the degree to which the power of the majority exceeds all the powers we are acquainted with in Europe. Thought is an invisible, almost intangible power that makes a mockery of tyranny in all its forms. The most absolute sovereigns in Europe today are powerless to prevent certain thoughts hostile to their authority from silently circulating through their states and even within their courts. The same cannot be said of America: as long as the majority remains in doubt, people talk, but as soon as it makes up its mind once and for all, everyone falls silent, and friends and enemies alike seemingly hitch themselves to its chariot. The reason for this is simple: no monarch is so absolute that he can gather in his hands all the forces of society and overcome all resistance, as a majority can do if vested with the right to make and execute the laws.

A king's only power is material, moreover: it affects actions but has no way of influencing wills. In the majority, however, is vested a force that is moral as well as material, which shapes wills as much as actions and inhibits not only deeds but also the desire to do them.

I know of no country where there is in general less independence of mind and true freedom of discussion than in America.

There is no religious or political theory that cannot be preached freely in the constitutional states of Europe or that cannot spread from one to another, for there is no country in Europe so subject to a single power that a person who wishes to speak the truth there cannot find support capable of protecting him from the consequences of his independence. If he is unfortunate enough to live under an absolute government, he will often find the people on his side; if he lives in a free country, he can if necessary seek the protection of royal authority. The aristocratic segment of society will support him in democratic countries and the democratic segment in others. But in a democracy organized as in the United States, there is only one power, one source of strength and success, and nothing outside it.

In America, the majority erects a formidable barrier around thought. Within the limits thus laid down, the writer is free, but woe unto him who dares to venture beyond those limits. Not that he need fear an auto-da-fé, but he must face all sorts of unpleasantness and daily persecution. He has no chance of a political career, for he has offended the only power capable of opening the way to one. He is denied everything, including glory. Before publishing his opinions, he thought he had supporters, but having revealed himself to all, he finds that his support seems to have vanished, because his critics voice their opinions loudly, while those who think as he does but who lack his courage hold their tongues and take their distance. In the end, he gives in, he bends under the burden of such unremitting effort and retreats into silence, as if he felt remorse for having spoken the truth.

Chains and executioners: such were the crude instruments on which tyranny once relied. But civilization has today brought improvement to everything, even to despotism, which seemed to have nothing left to learn.

Princes made violence a physical thing, but today's democratic republics have made it as intellectual as the human will it seeks to coerce. Under the absolute government of one man, despotism tried to reach the soul by striking crudely at the body; and the soul, eluding such blows, rose gloriously above it. Tyranny in democratic republics does not proceed in the same way, however. It ignores the body and goes straight for the soul. The master no longer says: You will think as I do or die. He says: You are free not to think as I do. You may keep your life, your property, and everything else. But from this day forth you shall be as a stranger among us. You will retain your civic privileges, but they will be of no use to you. For if you seek the votes of your fellow citizens, they will withhold them, and if you seek only their esteem, they will feign to refuse even that. You will remain among men, but you will forfeit your rights to humanity. When you approach your fellow creatures, they will shun you as one who is impure. And even those who believe in your innocence will abandon you, lest they, too, be shunned in turn. Go in peace, I will not take your life, but the life I leave you with is worse than death.

Absolute monarchies brought dishonor to despotism. Let us be wary lest democratic republics rehabilitate it and make it less odious and degrading in the eyes of the many by making it more onerous for a few.

In the proudest nations of the Old World, writers published works intended to paint a faithful portrait of contemporary vices and follies. La Bruyère was living in the palace of Louis XIV when he wrote his chapter on the high nobility, and Molière criticized the Court in plays that were performed before courtiers. But the power that rules the United States does not like to be mocked in this way. The slightest reproach offends it; the least sting of truth drives it wild. Everything must be praised, from its stylistic flourishes to its most stalwart virtues. No writer, no matter how renowned, can avoid this obligation to sing the praises of his fellow citizens. Thus the majority lives in perpetual self-adoration, and there are certain truths that only foreigners or experience can bring to American ears.

If America still has no great writers, we need seek no further for the reason: literary genius cannot exist without freedom of spirit, and freedom of spirit does not exist in America.

The Inquisition was never able to prevent the circulation in Spain of books contrary to the religion of the majority. In the United States the majority has such sway that it can do better: it has banished even the thought of publishing such books. One meets unbelievers in America, but unbelief has, as it were, no organ.

Some governments seek to safeguard mores by condemning the authors of licentious books. In the United States, no one is condemned for such works, but no one is tempted to write them — not because all the citizens are pure, but because the majority are sober in their ways.

In this instance power is no doubt used to good effect, so my point has to do only with the nature of that power in itself. The irresistible power of the majority is a constant fact, whereas its good use is only an accident.

EFFECTS OF THE TYRANNY OF THE MAJORITY ON THE NATIONAL CHARACTER OF THE AMERICANS; ON THE COURTLY SPIRIT IN THE UNITED STATES

The effects of the tyranny of the majority have thus far affected the mores of society more than the behavior. — They impede the development of great characters. — Democratic republics organized as the United States is organized bring the courtly spirit within reach of the majority. — Evidence of this spirit in the United States. — Why there is more patriotism among the people than among those who govern in their name.

The influence of the foregoing on political society has thus far been feeble, but the unfortunate consequences for the national character of Americans are already apparent. The steadily increasing effect of the despotism of the majority is, I believe, the chief reason for the small number of remarkable men in American politics today.

When the American Revolution declared itself, remarkable men came forward in droves. In those days, public opinion gave direction to their wills but did not tyrannize them. The famous men of the day freely took part in the intellectual movement of their time yet possessed a grandeur all their own. Their brilliance, rather than being borrowed from the nation, spilled over onto it.

In absolute governments, the high nobles who surround the throne flatter the passions of the master and voluntarily bend to his whims. But the masses of the nation are not inclined toward servitude; often they submit out of weakness, habit, or ignorance, and occasionally out of love for royalty or the king. It is not unknown for a people to take pleasure and pride of a sort in sacrificing their will to that of the prince, thereby marking a kind of independence of soul in the very act of obedience. In such nations degradation is far less common than misery. There is a great difference, moreover, between doing what one does not approve of and pretending to approve of what one does: one is the attitude of a man who is weak, the other a habit that only a lackey would acquire.

In free countries, where to one degree or another each individual is expected to offer an opinion about affairs of state; in democratic republics, where public life is forever intertwined with private life and where the sovereign can be approached in many different ways and one has only to raise one's voice in order to be heard; one finds many more people trying to speculate about the weaknesses and take advantage of the passions of the sovereign than is the case in absolute monarchies. Not that men are by nature worse in such countries than they are elsewhere, but the temptation is greater, and more people are exposed to it at any one time. The result is a far more general debasement of the soul.

Democratic republics bring the courtly spirit within reach of the many and expose all classes to it simultaneously. This is one of the chief reproaches that one can lay at their door.

This is especially true in democratic states organized as the

American republics are, where the ascendancy of the majority is so absolute and so irresistible that one has in a way to renounce one's rights as a citizen, not to say one's quality as a man, if one wishes to deviate from the path it has laid down.

Among the droves of men with political ambitions in the United States, I found very few with that virile candor, that manly independence of thought, that often distinguished Americans in earlier times and that is invariably the preeminent trait of great characters wherever it exists. At first sight one might suppose that all American minds were formed on the same model, so likely are they to follow exactly the same paths. To be sure, a foreigner does sometimes meet Americans who avoid the usual slogans. They will occasionally deplore defects in the law, or democracy's capriciousness and want of enlightenment. Often they will go so far as to note flaws that taint the national character and indicate ways in which these might be corrected. Yet no one but you listens to them, and you, to whom they confide these secret thoughts, are only a foreigner, who will soon depart. On you they are more than willing to bestow truths for which you have no use, while in public they speak a different language.

If these lines are ever read in America, I am sure of two things: first, that all of my readers, to a man, will speak out to condemn me, and second, that in the depths of their conscience many of them will absolve me of any wrong.

I have heard Americans speak of their homeland. I have met with true patriotism among the people; I have often searched for it in vain among their leaders. This fact is easily understood by analogy: despotism corrupts the person who submits to it far more than the person who imposes it. In absolute monarchies, the king often has great virtues, but the courtiers are always vile.

To be sure, courtiers in America do not say "Sire" and "Your Majesty," a great and capital difference. But they do speak constantly of their master's natural enlightenment. They do not offer prizes for the best answer to the question, "Which of the prince's virtues is most worthy of admiration?" for they are certain that he has all the virtues without having acquired them, indeed without wanting to acquire them. They do not bestow their wives and daughters on him in the hope that he will deign to elevate them to the rank of mistress. But in sacrificing their opinions to him, they prostitute themselves.

Moralists and philosophers in America are not obliged to shroud their opinions in veils of allegory, but before venturing a nettlesome truth they say, "We know that the people to whom we speak are too far above human weaknesses ever to lose control of themselves. We would not speak thus were we not addressing men whose virtues and intelligence so far outshine all others as to render them alone worthy to remain free."

Could Louis XIV's sycophants have been any more adept at flattering their master?

My own view is that baseness will adhere to force and flattery to power in every government, regardless of its nature. And I know only one way of preventing men from debasing themselves: by not granting anyone omnipotence and, with it, the sovereign power to defile.

THE GREATEST DANGER TO THE AMERICAN REPUBLICS COMES FROM THE OMNIPOTENCE OF THE MAJORITY

Democratic republics are more likely to perish through misuse of power than through lack of it. — The governments of the American republics are more centralized and energetic than those of the monarchies of Europe. — The danger that results from this. — Opinion of Madison and Jefferson on this subject.

Governments usually perish through either impotence or tyranny. In the first case, power slips from their grasp; in the second, it is wrested from them.

Many people, when they see democratic states lapse into anarchy, assume that the government in such states must be naturally weak and impotent. The truth is that once war has been ignited among the parties, government ceases to exert any influence over society. But I do not believe that it is in the nature of a democratic power to lack for strength and resources. On the contrary, I think that what causes such a power to perish is almost always abuse of its forces and misuse of its resources. Anarchy is almost always a consequence of tyranny or incompetence rather than impotence.

Stability must not be confused with strength, or grandeur with duration. In democratic republics, the power that guides[5] society is not stable, for it often changes hands, and goals. But wherever it turns its attention, its force is almost irresistible. The governments of the American republics seem to me just as centralized and more energetic than those of Europe's absolute monarchies. I therefore do not think that they will perish from weakness.[6]

If America ever loses its liberty, the fault will surely lie with the omnipotence of the majority, which may drive minorities to despair and force them to resort to physical force. This may lead to anarchy, but to an anarchy that will come as a consequence of despotism.

President James Madison expressed the same thought (see *Federalist* 51).

"It is of great importance in a republic," he says, "not only to guard the society against the oppression of its rulers, but to guard one part of the society against the injustice of the other part. . . . Justice is the end of government. It is the end of civil society. It ever has been and ever will be pursued until it be obtained or until liberty be lost in the pursuit. In a society under the forms of which the stronger faction can readily unite and oppress the weaker, anarchy may as truly be said to reign as in the state of nature, where the weaker individual is not secured against the violence of the stronger; and as, in the latter state, even the stronger individuals are prompted, by the uncertainty of their condition, to submit to a government which may protect the weak as well as themselves; so, in the former state, will the more powerful factions or parties be gradually induced, by a like motive, to wish for a government which will protect all parties, the weaker as well as the more powerful. It can be little doubted that if the State of Rhode Island was separated from the confederacy and left to itself, the insecurity of rights under the popular form of government within such narrow limits would be displayed by

---

[5] Power can be centralized in an assembly; then it is strong but not stable. It can be centralized in a man: then it is less strong but more stable.

[6] I trust that there is no need to point out to the reader that here, as in the rest of this chapter, I am speaking not of the federal government but of the government of each of the states, which the majority rules despotically.

such reiterated oppressions of factious majorities that some power altogether independent of the people would soon be called for by the voice of the very factions whose misrule had proved the necessity of it."

Jefferson also said: "The executive in our governments is not the sole, it is scarcely the principal object of my jealousy. The tyranny of the legislatures is the most formidable dread at present, and will be for long years. That of the executive will come in its turn, but it will be at a remote period."[7]

I would rather cite Jefferson on this matter than anyone else, because I consider him to be the most powerful apostle that democracy has ever had.

[7]Letter from Jefferson to Madison, March 15, 1789.

Chapter 8

ON THAT WHICH TEMPERS THE TYRANNY OF THE MAJORITY IN THE UNITED STATES

ABSENCE OF ADMINISTRATIVE CENTRALIZATION

The majority of the nation does not think of itself as governing without assistance. — It is obliged to rely on town and county officials to carry out its sovereign wishes.

I distinguished earlier between two types of centralization; one I called governmental, and the other administrative.

Only the first exists in America; the second is virtually unknown.

If the ruling power in America possessed both these means of government and enjoyed not only the right to issue orders of all kinds but also the capability and habit of carrying out those orders; if it not only laid down general principles of government but also concerned itself with the details of applying those principles; and if it dealt not only with the country's major interests but also descended to the limit of individual interests, then liberty would soon be banished from the New World.

But if the majority in the United States often has the tastes and instincts of a despot, the most advanced instruments of tyranny are still lacking.

In none of the American republics has the central government ever been concerned with more than a small number of issues — those important enough to attract its attention. It has never sought to regulate social matters of lesser moment, nor is there any indication that it even aspired to do so. The majority, as it became more and more absolute, never expanded the prerogatives of the central power. It merely made that power omnipotent in its own sphere. Thus despotism may be very oppressive in one respect, but it cannot be oppressive in all.

The majority of the nation — no matter how caught up by its passions, no matter how ardently committed to its goals — cannot ensure that all citizens everywhere will comply with its desires in the same way at the same time. Once the central government representing the majority has issued its sovereign commands, it must rely for the execution of those commands on agents who in many cases do not report to it, and whose actions it cannot constantly oversee. Municipal bodies and county administrations are thus like hidden reefs that turn back or divide the tide of popular will. Were the law oppressive, liberty would still find safe haven in the manner of its execution. The majority cannot concern itself with the details — I daresay the childish whims — of administrative tyranny. It cannot even imagine that it might, for it lacks full consciousness of its power. It is aware only of its natural strengths and has no idea of the extent to which the art of administration can further them.

This point is worth a moment's reflection. I say this without fear of contradiction: if a democratic republic like the one in the United States were ever to be established in a country where autocratic rule had already introduced administrative centralization, and where both custom and law had absorbed its influence, that country would come to know a despotism more intolerable than any that has ever existed in Europe's absolute monarchies. To discover anything comparable one would have to look to Asia.

ON THE LEGAL SPIRIT IN THE UNITED STATES, AND HOW IT SERVES AS A COUNTERWEIGHT TO DEMOCRACY

Usefulness of investigating the natural instincts of the legal spirit. — Lawyers called to play an important role in a society struggling to be born. — How the nature of legal work gives an aristocratic turn to legal thinking. — Incidental factors that may check this tendency. — Ease with which the aristocracy makes common cause with lawyers. — How despots can make advantageous use of lawyers. — Lawyers are the only aristocratic element whose nature is such as to combine readily with the natural elements of democracy. — Specific factors that tend to give an aristocratic turn to the English and American legal mind. — The American aristocracy is at the bar and on the bench. — Influence of lawyers on American society. — How the legal spirit affects the legislature and the administration and in the end gives the people themselves some of the instincts of the magistrate.

Upon visiting Americans and studying their laws, one finds that the authority they have bestowed on lawyers, and the influence they have allowed lawyers to exert in government, today constitute the most powerful barriers against the excesses of democracy. This effect seems to me to have a general cause, about which it is useful to inquire, because it may recur elsewhere.

Lawyers have had a hand in all the political changes that have taken place in Europe over the past five hundred years. Sometimes they served as instruments of political power, and sometimes political power became their instrument. In the Middle Ages, lawyers worked wonders in extending the dominion of kings. Since then, they have worked prodigiously to limit royal power. In England they threw in their lot with the aristocracy; in France they became its most dangerous enemies. Do lawyers thus yield to sudden and momentary impulses, or do they respond to circumstances in ways more or less dictated by their natural instincts, which continually reassert themselves? I should like to clarify this point, for it may be that lawyers are called to play a leading role in the political society that is even now struggling to be born.

Men who make a special study of the law take from their work certain habits of order, a taste for forms, and a sort of instinctive love of regular sequence in ideas that naturally foster in them a strong opposition to the revolutionary spirit and the unthinking passions of democracy.

The special knowledge that lawyers acquire through the study of law assures them of a distinctive rank in society. They constitute a kind of privileged class among the intelligent. The practice of their profession brings daily reminders of their superiority. They are masters of a body of knowledge that, while necessary, is not widely understood. They serve as arbiters among citizens, and the habit of guiding the blind passions of

litigants toward a desired goal inspires in them a certain contempt for the judgment of the multitude. What is more, they
naturally constitute a *corporation* — not in the sense that they
agree with one another and act in concert, but in the sense
that common studies and like methods link their intellects,
just as common interest may unify their wills.

One therefore finds, hidden in the depths of lawyers' souls,
some of the tastes and habits of aristocracy. The legal profession shares aristocracy's instinctive preference for order and
natural love of formalities, as well as its deep distaste for
the actions of the multitude and secret contempt for popular
government.

I do not mean to say that these natural penchants of lawyers
are strong enough to be irresistible. What rules lawyers as it
rules other men is private interest, and above all the interest
of the moment.

Imagine a society in which men of law cannot assume a rank
in the world of politics analogous to the one they occupy in
private life. One can be certain that in a society organized
in this way, lawyers will be very active agents of revolution.
But one must inquire whether the impetus to destroy or
change is the result of a permanent disposition of the legal
mind or an accident. It is true that lawyers played a singularly
important role in overthrowing the French monarchy in 1789.
But it remains to be seen whether they acted as they did because they had studied law or because they had no share in
making it.

Five hundred years ago, the English aristocracy claimed to
lead the people and speak in their name; today it supports the
throne and defends royal authority. Yet the aristocracy has instincts and penchants of its own.

One must be careful, too, not to take isolated members of
a body for the body itself.

In any free government, no matter what its form, lawyers
will always be found in the front ranks of all parties. The same
remark also applies to the aristocracy. Nearly every democratic
movement that has agitated the world has been directed by
nobles.

No elite corps can satisfy all the ambitions that exist within
it. Talent and passion are always in more abundant supply

than opportunities for their employment, and many who cannot achieve greatness as quickly as they would like by availing themselves of the privileges of the corps will seek to do so by attacking those privileges instead.

Hence I do not claim that there will ever be a time when *all* lawyers will be friends of order and enemies of change, nor do I claim that most lawyers *always* are.

I do say that in a society in which no one contests the right of lawyers to occupy the high position that is naturally their due, their spirit will be eminently conservative and anti-democratic.

When aristocracy closes its ranks to lawyers, it makes enemies of them — enemies all the more dangerous in that, though inferior to the aristocracy in wealth and power, they are independent of it by virtue of their work and feel equal to it by virtue of their enlightenment.

But whenever nobles have allowed lawyers to share some of their privileges, the two classes have found it quite easy to make common cause and have discovered that they belong, as it were, to the same family.

I am also inclined to believe that kings will always find it easy to turn lawyers into most useful instruments of royal authority.

There is infinitely more natural affinity between men of law and executive power than between men of law and the people, though lawyers often have to topple executive power. By the same token, there is more natural affinity between nobles and the king than between nobles and the people, although the upper classes of society have often joined with the other classes to combat royal power.

What lawyers love above all is a life of order, and the greatest guarantee of order is authority. One must not forget, moreover, that while lawyers may prize liberty, they generally place a far higher value on legality. They are less afraid of tyranny than of arbitrariness, and so long as the legislator himself sees to it that men are deprived of their independence, the lawyer is more or less content.

I therefore believe that a prince who seeks to ward off the threat of democracy by tearing down judicial power and diminishing the political influence of lawyers in his state is making a great mistake. He lets go of the substance of authority to seize the shadow.

I have no doubt that he would do better to bring lawyers into government. Were he to entrust them with despotism in its violent form, he might well reclaim it graced with the features of justice and law.

Democratic government encourages lawyers to assume political power. When the rich man, the noble, and the prince are excluded from government, lawyers step into the breach almost as if it were their right, for they are the only enlightened, able men not counted among the people whom the people may choose.

If lawyers are naturally drawn by their tastes to the aristocracy and the prince, they are naturally drawn to the people by their interests.

Thus lawyers favor democratic government without sharing its inclinations or imitating its weaknesses — two reasons why they enjoy power through it and over it.

The people in a democracy do not distrust the legal profession, because they know that it is in the interest of lawyers to serve their cause. They can listen to legal counsel without becoming angry, because they do not suspect lawyers of ulterior motives. In fact, lawyers do not seek to overthrow the government that democracy has chosen for itself, but they do endeavor constantly to divert it from its intrinsic course by means that are alien to its nature. The lawyer belongs to the people by interest and birth and to the aristocracy by habit and taste. He is in a sense the natural liaison between the two, the link that joins one to the other.

The legal profession is the only aristocratic element that can mix readily with the natural elements of democracy to form useful and durable compounds. I am not unaware of the defects inherent in the legal spirit. Unless it is added to the democratic spirit, however, I doubt that democracy can govern society for long, and I do not believe that any republic can survive today unless the influence of lawyers on its affairs increases as the power of the people grows.

The aristocratic character that I detect in the legal spirit is far more pronounced in the United States and England than in other countries. This has to do not only with the way in which English and American lawyers study the law but also with the nature of legislation itself and the position of the interpreter of law in the two countries.

The English and Americans have retained the law of precedents. In other words, they continue to base their legal opinions and judicial decisions on the opinions and decisions of their forebears.

Therefore, an English or American lawyer almost always combines a taste and respect for what is old with a liking for what is regular and legal.

This influences the legal spirit in yet another way, and consequently the course of society as well.

The English or American lawyer investigates what was done, the French lawyer what was most likely intended. One wants decisions; the other, reasons.

When one listens to an English or American lawyer, it is surprising to note how often he cites the opinions of others and how little he speaks of his own, whereas the contrary is true in France.

No case is too small for a French lawyer to plead without introducing a whole system of ideas of his own, and he will delve deep into constitutional principles just so that it may please the court to move the boundary of a contested inheritance by a few yards in a certain direction.

The willingness of the English or American lawyer to forswear his own interpretation in favor of that of his forebears — indeed, the need to subject his thinking to a kind of servitude — must make the legal mind more timid in its habits and more static in its inclinations in England and America than in France.

Our written laws are often difficult to understand, but anyone can read them. By contrast, there is nothing more obscure to the uninitiated, nothing less within their grasp, than a body of law based on precedent. The need for lawyers in England and the United States, together with the exalted idea that attaches to their enlightened way of thinking, increasingly sets them apart from the people and in the end places them in a class all their own. The French lawyer is merely a man of learning, but the English or American man of law in some ways resembles an Egyptian priest. Like the priest, he is the sole interpreter of an occult body of knowledge.

The position that men of law occupy in England and America has no less great an influence on their habits and opinions. The English aristocracy, always keen to attract to its side elements of society bearing some natural resemblance to itself, has shown lawyers great consideration and offered them a substantial share of power. Within English society, lawyers do not occupy the first rank, but they are content with the rank they hold. They form something like a cadet branch of the English aristocracy and love and respect the senior branch even if they do not share all its privileges. English lawyers therefore combine the aristocratic interests of their profession with the aristocratic ideas and tastes of the circles in which they move.

Thus it is in England especially that one sees in most vivid relief the type of lawyer I am attempting to portray: the English lawyer esteems the law not so much because it is good as because it is old. And if he finds himself obliged to amend some provision of the law in order to adapt it to the changes that time wreaks on society, he will resort to the most incredible subtleties in order to persuade himself that in adding something to the work of his forebears, he is merely developing their ideas and completing their labors. There is no hope of wringing from him an admission of innovation: he would rather court absurdity than confess to so great a crime. This type of legal mind, which seems indifferent to the spirit and attentive only to the letter of the law and which would sooner relinquish reason and humanity than venture beyond its limits, was born in England.

English law is like an ancient tree onto which lawyers have repeatedly grafted the most exotic shoots, hoping that, though their fruits might differ, at least their foliage would blend with that of the venerable trunk.

In America, there are no noblemen or men of letters, and the people distrust the wealthy. Lawyers therefore constitute the superior political class and the most intellectual segment of society. Thus they can only lose by innovating: this adds a conservative interest to their natural preference for order.

If I were asked where I see the aristocracy in America, I would answer without hesitation that I do not find it among the rich, who share no common bond. The American aristocracy congregates in the courtroom: at the bar or on the bench.

The more one reflects on what goes on in the United States, the more convinced one becomes that the legal profession is the most powerful, if not the only, counterweight to democracy.

In the United States it is easy to see the degree to which not only the qualities but also even the flaws of the legal mind suit it to the task of neutralizing the vices inherent in popular government.

When the American people allow themselves to become intoxicated by passion or to be carried away by their own ideas, lawyers apply an almost imperceptible brake that slows them down and brings them to a halt. The democratic instincts of the people are secretly opposed by the aristocratic inclinations of the lawyers; the people's love of novelty, by the lawyers' superstitious respect for what is old; the immensity of the people's designs, by the narrowness of the lawyers' views; the people's contempt for rules, by the lawyers' love of formalities; and the people's ardor, by the lawyers' habitually dilatory ways.

The courts are the most visible of the organs that lawyers use to influence democracy.

The judge is a lawyer who, quite apart from the predilection for order and rules that he takes from his legal studies, finds further reason to love stability in the fact that he cannot be removed from office. His legal knowledge had already assured him of a high place among his fellow men. His political power completes the task of assigning him a rank apart and gives him the instincts of the privileged classes.

Armed with the right to declare laws unconstitutional, the American magistrate continually intervenes in political affairs.[1] He cannot compel the people to make laws, but he can at least insist that they not break faith with the laws they have made and remain consistent with themselves.

I am not unaware of the hidden tendency in the United States that leads the people to curtail the power of the judiciary.

[1]See what I say about judicial power in Part I.

Under the provisions of most state constitutions, the government may, at the request of both chambers of the legislature, remove judges from the bench. Some constitutions provide for *election* of members of the courts and require them to submit to frequent reelection. I venture to predict that these innovations will sooner or later lead to disastrous results, and that some day it will become clear that to reduce the independence of magistrates in this way is to attack not only the judicial power but the democratic republic itself.

Do not suppose, moreover, that in the United States the legal spirit is confined to the courthouse. Its influence is far more extensive.

Lawyers, who constitute the only enlightened class not distrusted by the people, are naturally called upon to fill most public offices. The legislatures are full of them, and they head many administrative departments. They therefore exercise considerable influence on both the making and execution of the law. Yet they are obliged to yield to the current of public opinion that sweeps them along. Nevertheless, it is easy to find indications of what they would do if they were free. For all the innovations that Americans have brought to their political laws, they have made only minor changes in their civil laws, and even then only with great difficulty, though any number of those laws are strongly out of keeping with their social state. The reason for this is that when it comes to civil law, the majority has no choice but to rely on lawyers, and American lawyers, when free to choose, will not innovate.

It is an odd experience for a Frenchman to hear Americans complain about the static thinking of lawyers and their prejudice in favor of what is established.

The influence of the legal spirit extends well beyond the specific limits set forth above.

There is virtually no political question in the United States that does not sooner or later resolve itself into a judicial question. Hence the parties in their daily polemics find themselves obliged to borrow the ideas and language of the courts. Since most public men either were or are lawyers, it is only natural for them to bring their professional habits and ways of thinking to their dealing with the public's business. Jury duty makes people of all classes familiar with legal ways. In a sense, the language of the judiciary becomes the vulgar tongue. Thus the legal spirit, born in law schools and courtrooms, gradually spreads beyond their walls. It infiltrates all of society, as it were, filtering down to the lowest ranks, with the result that in the end all the people acquire some of the habits and tastes of the magistrate.

Lawyers in the United States constitute a power that arouses little fear, that is barely perceived, that flies no banner of its own, that supplely bends to the exigencies of the times and surrenders without resistance to every movement of the social body. Yet it envelops the whole of society, worms its way into each of the constituent classes, works on the society in secret, influences it constantly without its knowledge, and in the end shapes it to its own desires.

ON THE JURY IN THE UNITED STATES CONSIDERED AS A POLITICAL INSTITUTION

The jury, as one mode of popular sovereignty, must be seen in relation to the laws establishing that sovereignty. — Composition of juries in the United States. — Effects of trial by jury on the national character. — Education of the people through jury service. — How trial by jury tends to establish the influence of magistrates and spread the legal spirit.

My subject having led naturally to the matter of justice in the United States, I must turn now to the question of the jury before moving on.

The jury is both a judicial institution and a political institution, and it is important to distinguish between the two.

If the question were one of determining how much juries, particularly juries in civil cases, contribute to the fair administration of justice, I concede that their utility might be contested.

The jury system developed in a society that was not very advanced, in which the courts had little to deal with beyond simple questions of fact, and it is no easy matter to adapt it to the needs of a highly civilized people whose social relations have become strikingly complex and taken on a scholarly, intellectual character.[2]

For now my primary focus is the political aspect of the jury: to proceed in any other way would take me away from my subject, so I will say just a few words about the jury as a judicial instrument. When the English adopted the jury system, they were still a semi-barbarous people. Since that time, they have become one of the most enlightened nations on the planet, and their devotion to the jury system seems to have kept pace with their enlightenment. They have ventured forth from their native soil and spread throughout the world: some established colonies; others, independent states. The main body of the nation kept its king. Some of the emigrants founded powerful republics. But praise for the jury system has been uniform wherever Englishmen are found.[3] Wherever they went, they established that system or hastened to restore it. A judicial institution that wins the approbation of a great people over so many centuries, that has been ardently embraced by societies in all phases of civilization, in all climates,

---

[2] It would be both profitable and interesting to consider the jury as a judicial institution, to measure its effects in the United States, and to investigate how Americans have benefited from it. This question alone provides matter enough for an entire book, and a book that would be of great interest in France. It would be interesting to inquire, for instance, how much of the American jury system could be transplanted to France, and by what stages it could be introduced. The American state that could shed the most light on this subject is probably Louisiana. The population of Louisiana is a mixture of French and English. Both French law and English law are present as well, and the two bodies of law are gradually merging. The most useful books to consult are probably the two-volume *Digest of the Laws of Louisiana*, and perhaps more useful still, a manual of civil procedure in both French and English entitled *Traité sur les règles des actions civiles*, published in 1830 in New Orleans by Buisson. This work has a special advantage in that it offers the French reader a reliable and authentic explanation of English legal terms. In all countries the language of the law is something like a separate dialect, and nowhere more so than among the English.

[3] English and American lawyers are unanimous on this point. Mr. Story, a justice of the Supreme Court of the United States, comments on the excellence of juries in civil cases in his *Treatise on the Federal Constitution*: "The inestimable privilege of a trial by jury in civil cases, a privilege scarcely inferior to that in criminal cases, which is conceded by all persons to be essential to political and civil liberty." (Story, book 3, chap. 38.)

and under all forms of government, cannot be contrary to the spirit of justice.[4]

But let us leave this subject. To regard the jury simply as a judicial institution would be to take a notably narrow view, for if the jury has a great influence on the outcome of a trial, it has an even greater influence on the fate of society itself. Hence the jury is first and foremost a political institution and must always be judged as such.

By "jury" I mean a certain number of citizens chosen at random and temporarily invested with the right to judge.

To use juries in the repression of crime is in my view to introduce a distinctly republican institution into government, for the following reasons:

The jury system can be aristocratic or democratic, depending on the class from which jurors are selected, but it always retains a republican character in that it places actual control of society in the hands of the governed — or some of the governed — rather than of the government.

Force is never more than a fleeting element of success. The idea of right follows hard on its heels. A government unable to inflict damage on its enemies except on the battlefield would soon be destroyed. The true sanction of political laws

[4]If one wished to establish the usefulness of the jury as a judicial institution, many other arguments could be advanced, including the following:

The greater the use made of jurors, the more you can reduce the number of judges without ill effect, which is a great advantage. When judges are numerous, death creates voids in the judicial hierarchy and opens up new places for the survivors every day. Ambition therefore causes judges to pant constantly after higher office and of course makes them dependent on the majority or person who fills vacant judgeships. Judges advance in the courts as soldiers advance through the ranks in the military. Such a state of affairs is utterly at odds with the fair administration of justice as well as with the intent of the legislature. One makes it impossible to remove judges from office in order to keep them free, but what good is it that no one can take their independence from them if they sacrifice it voluntarily?

When the number of judges is large, many will turn out to be incompetent, for a great magistrate is not an ordinary human being. But I am not sure that a semi-enlightened tribunal is not the worst of all the possible ways of achieving the ends for which courts of justice were established to begin with.

As for myself, I would sooner leave the decision in a trial to ignorant jurors led by a skillful magistrate than surrender it to judges of whom a majority have only an incomplete knowledge of jurisprudence and law.

is therefore found in the penal code, and if that sanction is lacking, the law sooner or later loses its force. The man who judges in *criminal* cases is therefore the true master of society. Now, the jury system places the people, or at any rate one class of citizens, on the judge's bench. Thus the jury system really places control of society in the hands of the people, or of that class.[5]

In England, jurors are recruited from the aristocratic portion of the nation. The aristocracy makes the laws, enforces the laws, and judges infractions of the laws.* Everything is of a piece: thus England is in fact an aristocratic republic. In the United States, the same system is applied to the entire people. Every American citizen can vote, hold office, and serve on a jury.[†] The jury system as it is understood in America seems to me a consequence of the dogma of popular sovereignty just as direct and just as extreme as universal suffrage. Both are equally powerful means of ensuring that the majority reigns.

Sovereigns determined to draw their power from sources within themselves and to guide society rather than allow themselves to be guided by it have always destroyed or weakened the jury system. The Tudors imprisoned jurors unwilling to convict, and Napoleon had them selected by his agents.

However obvious most of the foregoing truths may be, some minds have yet to be struck by them: it seems that many of us still have only a confused idea of the jury system. When the question of the composition of jury lists arises, discussion is limited to the enlightenment and capabilities of the people summoned to serve, as if the jury were merely a judicial institution. But this, in my view, is the least important aspect

---

[5]An important remark has to be made, however:

The jury system, to be sure, gives the people a general right of control over the actions of citizens, but it does not give them the means to exercise that control in all cases, nor always in a tyrannical manner.

When an absolute prince can delegate the authority to judge crimes, the fate of the accused is fixed, as it were, in advance. But even if the people as a whole are determined to convict, an innocent person still stands a chance owing to the composition of the jury and that fact that it is accountable to no one.

*See Note XVI, page 501.

[†]See Note XVII, page 501.

of the subject. The jury is above all a political institution. It should be regarded as a form of popular sovereignty. If popular sovereignty is repudiated, the jury should be discarded entirely; otherwise it should be seen in relation to other laws establishing popular sovereignty. The jury constitutes the part of the nation charged with ensuring the execution of the laws, just as the houses of the legislature are the part of the nation charged with making the laws. And if society is to be governed in a stable and uniform way, jury lists must expand and contract with voter lists. In my opinion, this should always be the lawmaker's primary focus. The rest is nothing, so to speak, but frills.

So convinced am I that the jury is above all a political institution that I see its use in criminal cases in the same light.

Laws are always shaky unless they are supported by mores. Mores are the only robust and durable power in any nation.

When juries are reserved for criminal cases, people see them in action only at long intervals, and then only in particular cases. They become accustomed to doing without juries in the ordinary course of life and consider them to be one means of obtaining justice rather than the only means.[6]

By contrast, when juries are used in civil cases, their work is constantly in the public eye. It affects interests of every kind. Everyone serves on them. Thus they become a part of daily usage. The human mind becomes habituated to the jury's forms, and the jury itself comes to be identified, as it were, with the very idea of justice.

Thus, if the jury system is limited to criminal cases, it is always in danger, but once introduced into civil cases it defies time and human effort. If the jury could have been plucked from the mores of the English as easily as from their laws, it would have succumbed entirely under the Tudors. What really saved English liberties was therefore the civil jury.

No matter how juries are used, they cannot fail to exert an important influence on national character. But that influence increases immeasurably as their use in civil cases is extended.

The jury, especially the civil jury, imparts to the minds of all citizens some of the habits of mind of the judge. And those

---

[6]This is true *a fortiori* when juries are used only in certain criminal cases.

habits are precisely the ones that best prepare a people to be free.

The jury instills in all classes a respect for judicial decisions and the idea of law. Remove those two things and love of independence becomes a destructive passion.

The jury teaches men the practice of equity. Each man, in judging his neighbor, thinks that he may in turn be judged. This is especially true of juries in civil cases. Almost no one is afraid of one day being prosecuted as a criminal, but anyone can be sued.

From the jury every man learns not to shirk responsibility for his own actions — a virile disposition without which political virtue does not exist.

The jury vests each citizen with a kind of magistracy. It teaches everyone that they have duties toward society and a role in its government. By forcing men to be concerned with affairs other than their own, it combats individual egoism, which is to societies what rust is to metal.

The jury is incredibly useful in shaping the people's judgment and augmenting their natural enlightenment. This, in my view, is its greatest advantage. It should be seen as a free school, and one that is always open, to which each juror comes to learn about his rights, and where he enters into daily contact with the best educated, most enlightened members of the upper classes and receives practical instruction in the law in a form accessible to his intelligence, thanks to the efforts of the lawyers, the counsel of the judge, and the very passions of the litigants. I think that the primary reason for the practical intelligence and political good sense of Americans is their long experience with juries in civil matters.

I do not know if juries are useful to civil litigants, but I do know that they are very useful to the people who judge them. I see the jury as one of the most effective means available to society for educating the people.

The foregoing applies to all nations, but what I shall say next is specific to Americans and, more generally, to all democratic peoples.

I said earlier that, in a democracy, lawyers, and in particular magistrates, constitute the only aristocratic body capable of moderating the people's impulses. This aristocracy is not invested with any physical power; its conservative influence acts only on minds. And the principal source of its power lies in one institution: the civil jury.

In criminal trials, in which society is pitted against an individual, the jury is inclined to see the judge as the passive instrument of social power and is wary of his advice. Furthermore, criminal trials turn entirely on simple questions of fact easily resolved by common sense. On this terrain, judge and juror are equals.

Things are different in civil trials. There, the judge is seen as a disinterested arbiter between impassioned litigants. The jurors have confidence in him and listen with respect to what he says, for in this realm his intelligence entirely dominates theirs. It is he who unfolds for them the various arguments that have been set forth at such length as to try their memories, and he who takes them by the hand to guide them through the ins and outs of legal procedure. It is he who limits them to findings of fact and teaches them how they must answer questions of law. His influence on them is virtually unlimited.

Do I still need to explain why arguments based on the notion that jurors are ill-equipped to try civil cases carry little weight with me?

In civil trials — at least in all matters other than findings of fact — the jury is a judicial body in appearance only.

The jurors pronounce the judgment that the judge has rendered. To that judgment they impart the authority of the society they represent, and the judge imparts the authority of reason and law.[*]

In England and America, judges have an influence on the outcome of criminal trials that French judges have never known. It is easy to understand the reason for this difference: having established his power in civil matters, the English or American magistrate is merely exercising that power in another theater; he does not acquire it there.

There are cases — often the most important cases — in which American judges have the right to render judgment by

---

[*]See Note XVIII, page 503.

themselves.[7] They then find themselves for once in the usual position of the French judge. But their moral power is much greater: memories of the jury accompany them, and the voice of the judge is almost as powerful as that of society, of which jurors were the organ.

The judge's influence extends well beyond the walls of the courtroom. In the relaxations of private life as well as in the labors of political life, in public places and legislative chambers, the American judge is constantly surrounded by men accustomed to placing his intelligence above their own. His power, having been exercised in the courtroom, continues to shape the habits of mind and even the souls of those who helped him judge.

Thus the jury, though it seems to diminish the rights of the magistracy, actually establishes its empire, and nowhere are judges more powerful than in countries where the people share their privileges.

The civil jury has served the American magistracy as the primary means of imbuing even the lowermost ranks of society with what I have called the legal spirit.

Thus the jury, which is the most energetic form of popular rule, is also the most effective means of teaching the people how to rule.

---

[7]Federal judges almost always decide alone on questions that affect the government of the country most directly.

Chapter 9

ON THE PRINCIPAL CAUSES THAT
TEND TO MAINTAIN THE
DEMOCRATIC REPUBLIC IN
THE UNITED STATES

THE democratic republic in the United States continues to exist. The principal purpose of this book has been to explain the causes of this phenomenon.

Several of those causes have only been touched on from afar, as the main line of my argument took me in spite of myself in a different direction. Others I have been unable to take up at all. And those I have been able to discuss at some length have been left almost buried in detail.

Hence it occurs to me that before going on to speak of the future, I should collect within a brief compass all the things that explain the present.

This résumé will be brief, for I shall take care only to summarize what the reader already knows; and of the facts not yet in evidence, I shall mention only the most important.

Reflection suggests that the causes that tend to maintain the democratic republic in the United States can be reduced to three:

The peculiar, and accidental, situation in which Providence has placed the Americans is the first of these.

The second stems from the laws.

The third derives from habits and mores.

ON THE ACCIDENTAL OR PROVIDENTIAL
CAUSES THAT HELP TO MAINTAIN
THE DEMOCRATIC REPUBLIC
IN THE UNITED STATES

The Union has no neighbors. — No great capital. — The hazard of birth worked in favor of the Americans. — America is an empty country. — How this circumstance contributes powerfully to maintaining the democratic republic. — How the American wilderness is

being settled. — Eagerness of the Anglo-Americans to take possession
of the solitudes of the New World. — Influence of material well-
being on American political opinion.

There are a thousand circumstances independent of man's
will that ease the way for the democratic republic in the
United States. Some of these are well known; others are easy
to point out. I shall mention only the most important.

The Americans have no neighbors, hence no need to fear
major wars, financial crises, invasions, or conquests. They have
no need of heavy taxes, large armies, or great generals. They
have almost nothing to fear from a scourge even more terrible for republics than all these put together, namely, military
glory.

There is no denying that military glory exerts an incredible
influence on a nation's spirit. General Jackson, whom Americans have twice chosen to be their leader, is a man of violent
character and middling ability. Nothing in his career demon-
strates that he possesses the qualities required to govern a free
people. Accordingly, a majority of the enlightened classes of
the Union has always voted against him. What, then, put him
in the presidency and keeps him there even now? The memory
of the victory he won twenty years ago outside the walls of
New Orleans. Yet that victory in New Orleans was an unremarkable feat of arms that could attract such prolonged attention only in a country that seldom has occasion to resort
to battle. And the nation that has allowed itself to be so carried away by the prestige of glory is surely the coldest, most
calculating, least military, and, if I may say so, most prosaic
of all the nations of the world.

America has no great capital[1] whose direct or indirect influence is felt throughout the country. I consider this to be

[1]Although America does not yet have a great capital, it already has some
very large cities. In 1830 the population of Philadelphia was 161,000 and that
of New York 202,000. The lower classes in these vast cities constitute a rabble
even more dangerous than that of Europe. It consists primarily of freed Negroes condemned by law and opinion to a state of hereditary degradation and
misery. In its midst one also finds hordes of Europeans driven to the shores
of the New World every day by misfortune and mischief. These people bring
our worst vices with them to the United States, and they have none of the
interests that could combat the influence of those vices. As residents of

one of the primary reasons for the persistence of republican institutions in the United States. In cities it is almost impossible to prevent people from plotting together, finding common grounds for anger, and making sudden resolutions in the heat of passion. Cities are like great assemblies of which every resident is a member. There, the people have tremendous influence over officials and often impose their will directly, without intermediaries.

Therefore, to subject the province to the capital is to place the fate of the entire empire in the hands not simply of a portion of the people, which is unjust, but even worse, of the people acting on their own, which is extremely dangerous. The preponderance of capitals consequently poses a serious threat to the representative system. It causes modern republics to suffer from the same defect as the republics of Antiquity, which invariably perished because that system was unknown to them.

It would be easy for me to list many other, less important factors that facilitated the establishment and ensured the persistence of the democratic republic in the United States. Among this multitude of happy circumstances, however, I see two that stand out above the rest, and I want to point these out right away.

Earlier I said that I saw in the origin of the Americans, in what I called their point of departure, the first and most effective of all the causes to which one can attribute the present prosperity of the United States. The hazard of birth worked in the Americans' favor: their forefathers long ago imported equality of conditions and of intelligence into the land they

---

the country but not citizens, they are quick to take advantage of all the passions simmering within it. There have recently been serious riots in Philadelphia and New York, for example. Such disorders are unknown in the rest of the country, which is not alarmed by them because to date the urban population has no power or influence over the rural population.

I, however, look upon the size of certain American cities, and even more the composition of their population, as a veritable danger that threatens the future of the democratic republics of the New World, and I do not hesitate to predict that this is how they will perish, unless their governments succeed in creating an armed force obedient to the will of the national majority yet independent of the urban populace and capable of putting down its excesses.

settled, and from these the democratic republic would one day spring as from a natural source. And that is not all: along with a republican social state, they bequeathed to their descendants the habits, ideas, and mores most apt to give rise to a flourishing republic. When I reflect on what this original fact has produced, I see the entire destiny of America embodied in the first Puritan to land on its shores, just as the entire human race was embodied in the first man.

Among the other fortunate circumstances that facilitated the establishment and ensured the persistence of the democratic republic in the United States, the most important was the Americans' choice of a country to settle in. Their fathers instilled in them a love of equality and liberty, but it was God himself who, by giving them a boundless continent, granted them the means to remain equal and free for a long time to come.

General prosperity contributes to the stability of any government, but particularly to that of a democratic government, which depends on the attitudes of the majority, and especially of the neediest, of its people. When the people govern, it is essential that they be happy lest they overthrow the state. Misery does to the people what ambition does to kings. In America, the material causes of prosperity — independent of the law — are more numerous than they have ever been in any other country at any time in the history of the world.

In the United States, not only is legislation democratic, but nature herself works for the people.

Where in the memory of man can one find anything comparable to what is taking place before our eyes in North America?

The celebrated societies of Antiquity were all founded amid hostile peoples that had to be conquered before they could be supplanted. The moderns found in parts of South America vast regions inhabited by peoples who, though less enlightened than themselves, had already appropriated the land through cultivation. In order to found their new states, the moderns had to destroy or enslave vast populations, so that civilization was obliged to blush for its triumphs.

But North America was inhabited only by itinerant tribes that had never thought to avail themselves of the natural riches of the soil. North America was still literally an empty continent, a wilderness awaiting settlers.

Everything about the Americans is extraordinary, their social state no less than their laws. But what is still more extraordinary is the land on which they live.

When the Creator delivered the earth into the hands of men, it was young and inexhaustible, but they were weak and ignorant. And by the time they had learned to avail themselves of its treasures, they already covered its face and soon found themselves compelled to fight for the right to an asylum where they could repose in liberty.

It was then that North America was discovered, as if God had held it in reserve and it had only just emerged from the waters of the flood.

There one sees, as in the first days of creation, rivers that never run dry, verdant, well-watered solitudes, and boundless fields yet to be tilled by any plow. In this state the land lays itself out to man, who is no longer isolated, ignorant, and barbarous as in primitive times but already in possession of nature's most important secrets, united with his fellow man, and instructed by the experience of fifty centuries.

As I speak, thirteen million civilized Europeans are quietly spreading out across this fertile wilderness whose extent and resources they themselves still do not know for certain. Three or four thousand soldiers drive the wandering race of natives before them. Behind these armed men come woodsmen who penetrate the forests, scatter the wild animals, explore the rivers, and lay the groundwork for civilization's triumphant march across the wilderness.

In the course of this work I have frequently had occasion to allude to the material prosperity of the Americans. I have pointed to this as an important reason for the success of their laws. A thousand others had already made the same point before me: of all the reasons that have come to the attention of Europeans in one way or another, this is the only one that has become popular among us. Hence I will not go on at length about a subject that has been dealt with so often and is understood so well. I shall limit myself to adding a few new facts.

It is widely believed that the American wilderness is being populated by the European immigrants who arrive each year

on the shores of the New World, while the American population grows and multiplies on land settled by previous generations: this is a great error. The European who comes to the
United States arrives without friends and often without resources. In order to live, he is obliged to hire out his services,
and he seldom ventures beyond the great industrial zone along
the coast. One cannot clear land in the wilderness without capital or credit, and before a man can set off into the forest, his
body must adjust to the rigors of a new climate. The people
who daily depart the place of their birth to create vast estates
for themselves in far-off places are therefore Americans. So the
European quits his cottage to settle on transatlantic shores,
and the American born on those shores plunges deeper into
the wilds of the American heartland. This dual migratory flow
is never-ending: it begins in the heart of Europe, continues
across the great ocean, and pursues its course through the solitudes of the New World. Millions of men march together
toward the same point on the horizon: their languages, religions, and mores differ, but their goal is the same. Having
been told that fortune is to be found somewhere out west,
they hasten after it.

This constant displacement of human beings is unlike anything else in history, except perhaps what happened after the
fall of the Roman Empire. Then as now, hordes of people converged on the same destinations and there mingled in tumultuous confusion. But the designs of Providence were different.
Then, each newcomer trailed death and destruction in his
train. Now, each brings a seed of prosperity and life.

The ultimate consequences of this migration of Americans
toward the west still lie hidden in the future, but the immediate results are easy to recognize: every year, some people
depart from the states in which they were born, hence the
population of those states grows very slowly, though it also
ages. For example, the population of Connecticut, whose density is still only fifty-nine per square mile, grew by only a quarter over the past forty years, while that of England increased
by a third over the same period. Thus European immigrants
still arrive in a country that is only half full, where industry is
hungry for labor. The newcomer becomes a prosperous worker.

His son goes off to seek his fortune in an empty land and becomes a wealthy landowner. The former amasses capital that the latter uses to good advantage, and neither the foreigner nor the native lives in misery.

The laws of the United States do all they can to encourage the division of property, but a force even more powerful than legislation keeps that division within bounds.[2] One sees this clearly in states that are at last beginning to be full. Massachusetts is the most densely populated state of the Union with 80 residents per square mile, far less than the 162 inhabitants of the same space in France.

In Massachusetts, however, it is already rare for small holdings to be subdivided. Generally, the eldest son takes the land, and younger sons go off to seek their fortune in the wilderness.

The law abolished primogeniture, but Providence, one might say, reinstated it without giving anyone cause for complaint and, in these circumstances at any rate, without offending any principles of justice.

One fact will suffice to give an idea of the prodigious number of individuals who have left New England to make new homes for themselves in the wilderness. I have it on good authority that in 1830 thirty-six members of Congress could trace their birth to the small state of Connecticut. Thus Connecticut, with only one forty-third of the population of the United States, supplied one-eighth of the representatives.

Yet the state of Connecticut itself sends only five representatives to Congress. The other thirty-one represent the new states of the West. If those thirty-one people had stayed in Connecticut, they would very likely have remained small farmers instead of becoming wealthy landowners, would have lived in obscurity without any possibility of a political career, and would have become not useful legislators but dangerous citizens.

The Americans are as aware of these things as we are.

Chancellor Kent, in his *Commentaries on American Law*, says that "there can be no doubt that the division of estates must

---

[2] In New England, land is divided into very small plots, but it is no longer being subdivided.

produce great evils if carried to an extreme, such that each portion of land can no longer provide for the maintenance of a family; but these disadvantages have never been felt in the United States, and many generations will pass before they are felt. The extent of our uninhabited territory, the abundance of land available to us, and the constant stream of emigration from the Atlantic coast to the interior of the country suffice to prevent the parceling out of estates, and will suffice for a long time to come."

It would be difficult to describe the avidity with which the American hurls himself upon the immense prey that fortune offers him. In pursuit of it he fearlessly braves the Indian's arrows and the maladies of the wilderness. He is undaunted by the silence of the woods and unmoved by the approach of wild animals. A passion stronger than the love of life constantly spurs him on. Ahead of him lies a continent virtually without limit, yet he seems already afraid that room may run out, and makes haste lest he arrive too late. I have talked about emigration from the older states, but what shall I say about emigration from the newer ones? It is not fifty years since Ohio was founded. Most of the people who live in the state were not born there. Its capital is not thirty years old, and its territory still incorporates vast stretches of unclaimed wilderness. Yet already the population of Ohio has resumed its westward march: most of the settlers of Illinois's fertile prairies come from Ohio. These people left their original homeland in search of the good life. They left their second homeland in search of a still better one. Almost everywhere they go, they encounter good fortune but not happiness. For them, the desire for well-being has become an anxious, burning passion that grows even as it is satisfied. They long ago broke the bonds that attached them to their native soil and have formed no other bonds since. For them, emigration began as a need; today it has become a game of chance, which they love as much for the emotions it stirs as for the profit it brings.

Sometimes man advances so quickly that wilderness closes in again behind him. He tramples the forest underfoot, but as soon as he is gone, the forest springs back. It is not rare, when exploring the new western states, to come upon abandoned dwellings in the woods. One often finds the remains of cabins in the depths of solitude or stumbles on partially cleared land that attests not only to man's power but also to his inconstancy. The ancient forest loses no time in covering these abandoned fields and recent ruins with new shoots. Animals reclaim possession of their empire. Mocking nature buries the vestiges of man beneath verdant branches and colorful blossoms and hastens to erase his ephemeral trace.

I remember a trip through the wilds of New York State during which I came upon a lake completely surrounded by woodland, as if the world were still new. In the middle of the lake stood a small island covered with trees, whose foliage hid its shores entirely from view. Around the lake there was nothing to indicate the presence of man other than a column of smoke on the horizon that stretched perpendicularly from the treetops to the clouds and thus seemed to hang from the sky rather than rise toward it.

An Indian canoe was drawn up on the sand. I used it to visit the island that had initially attracted my attention, and soon I was standing on its shore. The island was one of those delightfully isolated places that one finds in the New World and that are almost enough to make a civilized man long for the savage life. The marvelous abundance of vegetation proclaimed the incomparable richness of the soil. The silence was profound, as it is everywhere in the North American wilderness, and it was broken only by the monotonous cooing of wood pigeons and the tapping of green woodpeckers. Nature here seemed to have been left so completely to herself that it never occurred to me that the place had ever been inhabited, but when I reached the center of the island I suddenly came upon what seemed to be vestiges of man. I then carefully examined all the objects in the vicinity and before long had dispelled any doubt that a European had once sought refuge on this very spot. But how utterly his work had been transformed! Wood that he had hastily cut to build himself a shelter had since sprouted anew. His fences had become living hedges, and his cabin had been transformed into a thicket. Among the shrubs one could still see a few fire-blackened stones scattered about a small pile of ashes. This had no doubt been his hearth. The fireplace had collapsed, leaving it covered with debris. For some time I silently admired the resourcefulness of nature and the weakness of man, and when at last I was obliged to leave that enchanted place, I muttered to myself sadly, "How astonishing! Ruins already!"

In Europe, we are in the habit of looking upon restlessness of spirit, immoderate desire for wealth, and extreme love of independence as great social dangers, but these are precisely the things that guarantee the American republics a long and tranquil future. Without these restless passions, the population would tend to concentrate in certain places, and before long people would begin to feel, as we do, needs that are hard to satisfy. Happy is the New World, where man's vices are almost as useful to society as his virtues.

This has an important influence on the way in which human actions are judged in the two hemispheres. What we call love of gain Americans see as praiseworthy industriousness, and they see a certain faintness of heart in what we regard as moderation of desire.

In France we regard simplicity of taste, tranquillity of mores, family spirit, and love of one's birthplace as important guarantees of tranquillity and happiness for the state, but in America nothing seems more prejudicial to society than virtues such as these. The French of Canada, who have faithfully preserved the traditions of their ancient mores, are already finding it difficult to live on the land they now occupy, and this tiny newborn nation will soon find itself prey to the miseries that afflict older nations. The most enlightened, patriotic, and humane Canadians have gone to extraordinary lengths to inculcate distaste for simple happiness in the people, who still deem it sufficient. They celebrate the advantages of wealth, just as their counterparts in France might extol the charms of respectable mediocrity, and devote more effort to stirring human passions than is lavished elsewhere on calming them. To exchange the pure and quiet pleasures that even the poor savor in their native land for the sterile enjoyments of prosperity under foreign skies; to flee one's ancestral home and the fields in which one's forebears lie buried; to abandon the dead and the living alike in order to court fortune — nothing, in their eyes, is more worthy of praise.

America today offers man resources so vast that industry cannot exploit them fast enough.

Hence in America no amount of enlightenment can ever be sufficient, for enlightenment is not only useful to those who have it but also profitable to those who do not. There is no reason to fear new needs, because all needs are easily satisfied. There is no reason to dread unleashing a surfeit of passions, because all passions find easy and salutary nourishment. Americans cannot have too much freedom, because they are almost never tempted to use their freedom improperly.

The American republics today are like trading companies organized to exploit the unclaimed territory of the New World, and business is booming.

The passions that move Americans most deeply are commercial rather than political, or perhaps it would be better to say that Americans take habits formed in trade and carry them over into the world of politics. They are fond of order, which business needs if it is to prosper, and in their mores they particularly prize regularity, the foundation of any sound enterprise. They prefer the common sense that creates great fortunes to the genius that often dissipates them. General ideas terrify minds accustomed to concrete calculations, and Americans honor practice above theory.

One must go to America to understand the power that material well-being exerts over political actions and even opinions, which ought to be subject to reason alone. The truth of this assertion is most apparent among foreigners. Most European immigrants bring with them to the New World that unbridled love of independence and change that is so often the fruit of our miseries. In the United States I occasionally met Europeans who had been forced to flee their native lands because of their political opinions. What they said always surprised me, but one in particular made a greater impression on me than all the rest. As I was traveling in one of the remotest corners of Pennsylvania, night fell earlier than I expected, and I went to seek shelter at the home of a wealthy farmer. He turned out to be French. He bade me sit next to his fire, and we conversed freely, as is only natural when two men meet in the backwoods two thousand leagues from where they were born. I was not unaware of the fact that, forty years earlier, my host had been a great leveler and ardent demagogue. History has not forgotten his name.

Hence it was strange and surprising to hear him talk about property rights as an economist — I almost said a landowner — might have done. He talked about the necessary hierarchy that fortune establishes among men, about obedience to established law, about the influence of good mores in republics, and about the support that religious ideas lend to order and liberty. At one point he even chanced to cite the authority of Jesus Christ in support of his political opinions.

As I listened to him, I marveled at the imbecility of human reason. A thing is either true or false: how do I find out which, given the uncertainties of knowledge and the diverse teachings of experience? A new fact emerges to dispel all my doubts. Once I was poor, now I am rich. If only prosperity, while influencing my conduct, had left my judgment free! But no, my opinions have in fact followed the change in my fortune, and in the happy event that made me wealthy I actually discovered the decisive argument I had previously missed.

The influence of well-being acts even more freely on Americans than on foreigners. In the eyes of the American, order and public prosperity have always been linked, have always marched in step. He cannot imagine that they can exist separately. Hence he has nothing to forget and, unlike so many Europeans, need not shed the lessons of his early education.

ON THE INFLUENCE OF LAWS ON THE PERSISTENCE OF THE DEMOCRATIC REPUBLIC IN THE UNITED STATES

Three principal reasons for the persistence of the democratic republic. — Federal form. — Local institutions. — Judicial power.

The principal purpose of this book was to familiarize the reader with the laws of the United States. If that goal has been achieved, the reader will already have been able to judge for himself which of those laws really tend to maintain the republic and which endanger it. If I have not succeeded in doing this in the book thus far, I shall be even less successful in this chapter.

Accordingly, I do not want to cover the same ground as before, and a few lines of summary will have to suffice.

Three things seem to contribute more than all others to the persistence of the democratic republic in the New World:

The first is the federal form that the Americans have adopted, which allows the Union to enjoy the power of a great republic and the security of a small one.

The second I see in local institutions, which not only moderate the despotism of the majority but also foster a taste for liberty among the people and teach them the art of being free.

The third is to be found in the constitution of judicial power. I have shown how much the courts serve to correct the aberrations of democracy and how, without ever thwarting the impulses of the majority, the courts are able to slow them down and guide them.

ON THE INFLUENCE OF MORES ON THE PERSISTENCE OF THE DEMOCRATIC REPUBLIC IN THE UNITED STATES

I said earlier that I regarded mores as one of the great general causes to which the persistence of the democratic republic in the United States can be attributed.

By *mores* I mean here what the Ancients meant by the term: I apply it not only to mores in the strict sense, what one might call habits of the heart, but also to the various notions that men possess, to the diverse opinions that are current among them, and to the whole range of ideas that shape habits of mind.

Thus I use this word to refer to the whole moral and intellectual state of a people. My purpose is not to paint a portrait of American mores. For now I shall simply be trying to find out which mores are favorable to the persistence of political institutions.

ON RELIGION CONSIDERED AS
A POLITICAL INSTITUTION:
HOW MIGHTILY IT CONTRIBUTES
TO THE PERSISTENCE OF THE
DEMOCRATIC REPUBLIC AMONG
THE AMERICANS

*North America populated by people professing a democratic and re-
publican form of Christianity. — Arrival of Catholics. — Why
Catholics today constitute the most democratic and republican class.*

Every religion has an affinity with some political opinion.

Allow the human spirit to follow its bent and it will impose
a uniform rule on both political society and the divine city. It
will seek, if I may put it this way, to *harmonize* earth with
Heaven.

The greater part of English America was populated by men
who, having broken away from the authority of the pope,
never submitted to any supreme religious authority again.
They therefore brought to the New World a Christianity that
can best be described as democratic and republican: this singularly favored the establishment of a republic and democracy
in temporal affairs. From the beginning, politics and religion
were in harmony, and they have remained so ever since.

Around fifty years ago Catholics began pouring into the
United States from Ireland. Meanwhile, American Catholicism made converts. In the Union today one finds more than
a million Christians professing the verities of the Roman
Church.

These Catholics demonstrate a great fidelity in their religious practices and are full of ardor and zeal for their beliefs.
Nevertheless, they constitute the most republican and democratic class in the United States. At first sight this fact may
seem surprising, but reflection easily uncovers its hidden
causes.

It is a mistake, in my view, to regard the Catholic religion
as a natural enemy of democracy. Of the various Christian
doctrines, Catholicism seems to me, on the contrary, among
those most favorable to equality of conditions. For Catholics,
religious society consists of just two elements: the priest and

the people. Only the priest stands above the faithful: below him, everyone is equal.

As for dogma, Catholicism sets one standard for every level of intelligence: scholar or ignoramus, genius or man of the people, the same faith is prescribed in detail for all. The same practices are imposed on rich and poor, the same austerities inflicted on the powerful and the weak. Catholicism makes no compromise with any mortal, and by applying the same standard to all human beings, it likes to blend all classes of society into one worshiping at the same altar, just as they are one in the eyes of God.

Thus Catholicism may dispose the faithful to obedience, but it does not prepare them for inequality. About Protestantism I would say the opposite: it generally encourages not so much equality as independence.

Catholicism is like an absolute monarchy. Remove the prince and you are left with conditions more equal than in any republic.

Often the Catholic priest has left the sanctuary to become a power in society, taking his place in the social hierarchy. At times he has used his religious influence to ensure the permanence of a political order of which he was a part. It was possible then to find Catholics assuming the role of champions of aristocracy in a religious spirit.

But once priests are excluded from government, or exclude themselves as they have done in the United States, no faith does more than the Catholic faith to encourage adepts to take the idea of equality of conditions and carry it over into the world of politics.

So, while the nature of Catholic beliefs in the United States is not such as to dragoon Catholics into embracing democratic and republican opinions, at least the faith is not naturally inimical to such views, and the social position of Catholics, as well as their small number, leads them to embrace those opinions as if compelled by law.

Most Catholics are poor, and if they are to take part in government at all, it is imperative that all citizens govern. Catholics are in the minority, and if they are to enjoy free exercise of their rights, it is imperative that all rights be respected. These

VOLUME ONE, PART II, CHAPTER 9

two causes lead them, unwittingly to be sure, to adopt political doctrines that they might be less ardent to embrace if they were wealthy and numerically predominant.

The Catholic clergy in the United States has not tried to counter this political tendency; it seeks rather to justify it. The Catholic priests of America have divided the intellectual world into two parts: in one they have left revealed dogmas, to which they submit without discussion; in the other they have placed political truth, and this they believe God has left for man to investigate freely. Thus American Catholics are at once the most docile believers and the most independent citizens.

Hence it is fair to say that in the United States there is not a single religious doctrine that is openly hostile to democratic and republican institutions. Clergymen of all persuasions speak the same language. Opinions accord with laws, and, in a manner of speaking, but a single current commands the human spirit.

While staying in one of America's large cities, I was invited to attend a political meeting, the purpose of which was to help the Poles by sending them arms and money.

I found two or three thousand people gathered in a large hall that had been prepared to receive them. Soon, a priest, wearing his ecclesiastical robes, moved toward the podium. The men in the audience removed their hats and stood in silence while he delivered the following speech:

Almighty God! Lord of hosts! Thou who didst strengthen our fathers' hearts and guide their arms when they fought for the sacred rights of independent nationhood. Thou who didst grant them victory over odious oppression and bestow upon our people the fruits of peace and liberty, look with favor, O Lord, upon the other hemisphere! Have pity on a heroic people who today are fighting for the very rights for which we, too, once fought! Lord, who hast created all men in thine own image, let not despotism spoil thy work, let it not perpetuate inequality on earth. Almighty God! Watch over the Poles and make them worthy of freedom. Let thy wisdom reign in their councils and thy strength fortify their arms. Sow terror among their enemies, divide the powers that plot their destruction, and let not the injustice that the world witnessed fifty years ago be consummated today. Lord, whose mighty hand encloseth the hearts of nations as of men, let allies be enlisted in the sacred cause of justice.

Let the French nation rise up at last, let it shake off the torpor in which it is kept by its leaders and once more venture forth to do battle for freedom on earth.

O, Lord! Turn not thy face from us, and grant that we may forever be the most religious as well as the freest of peoples.

Almighty God, hear our prayer this day and save the Poles. We beseech Thee in the name of thy beloved Son, our Lord Jesus Christ, who died on the cross that all men might live. Amen.

Everyone in attendance reverently repeated *Amen*.

INDIRECT INFLUENCE OF RELIGIOUS BELIEFS ON POLITICAL SOCIETY IN THE UNITED STATES

Christian morality found in all sects. — Influence of religion on the mores of the Americans. — Respect for the marriage bond. — How religion limits the imagination of Americans in certain ways and moderates their passion for innovation. — Opinion of the Americans regarding the political usefulness of religion. — Their efforts to extend and secure its empire.

I have just shown how religion directly influences politics in the United States. Its indirect influence seems to me more powerful still: it is when religion does not speak of freedom that it best instructs Americans in the art of being free.

There are countless sects in the United States. Each reveres the Creator in a different fashion, but all agree about man's duties to his fellow man. Each worships God in its own way, but all preach the same morality in God's name. Though it matters a great deal to each individual that his religion be true, this is not the case for society. Society has nothing to fear from the other life, and nothing to hope for, and what matters most to it is not so much that all citizens profess the true religion as that each citizen profess some religion. In any case, all sects in the United States are encompassed within the overarching unity of Christianity, and Christian morality is the same everywhere.

It is reasonable to assume that habit rather than conviction dictates the religious practices of at least some Americans. In the United States, moreover, the sovereign is religious, hence hypocrisy must be common. Nevertheless, Christianity maintains more actual power over souls in America than anywhere else. There is no better illustration of the usefulness and naturalness of religion, since the country where its influence is greatest today is also the country that is freest and most enlightened.

I stated earlier that American priests, including those who do not advocate religious liberty, generally favor civil liberty. They do not, however, support any particular political system. They are careful to remain aloof from public affairs and do not involve themselves in the machinations of the parties. Therefore one cannot say that religion in the United States influences the laws or the specifics of political opinion, but it does shape mores, and it is by regulating the family that religion endeavors to regulate the state.

I do not doubt for a moment that the great severity of American mores is due primarily to religious beliefs. Fortune tempts man in so many ways there that religion is often powerless to restrain him. Although religion cannot moderate his ardor for riches, which everything conspires to arouse, it nevertheless reigns supreme over the soul of woman, and it is woman who shapes mores. Of all the countries in the world, America is surely the one in which the marriage bond is most respected, and in which people subscribe to the loftiest and most just ideal of conjugal happiness.

In Europe, virtually all social disorders are born at home, close to the hearth and not far from the marriage bed. It is at home that men become scornful of natural ties and permissible pleasures and acquire a taste for disorder; their hearts grow anxious and their desires fickle. The European, agitated by the same tumultuous passions that have so often proved troublesome at home, finds it hard to submit to the legislative powers of the state. When an American leaves the discord of the political world behind and returns to the bosom of his family, he is greeted at once by an image of order and peace. There, all his pleasures are simple and natural, all his joys tranquil and innocent. And since it is regularity in life that brings him happiness, he readily becomes accustomed to regulating his opinions as well as his tastes.

While the European seeks to escape his domestic woes by stirring up trouble in society, the American's home is the well from which he draws his love of order, which he then carries over into affairs of state.

In the United States religion not only regulates mores but extends its empire over intelligence as well.

Some Anglo-Americans profess Christian dogmas because they believe them, others because they are afraid lest they seem not to believe them. Christianity therefore reigns without impediment, by universal consent. As I said earlier, the consequence of this is that everything in the moral world is certain and settled, though the political world seems given over to controversy and experiment. Thus boundless opportunity is never what the human spirit sees before it: for all its audacity, it sometimes runs up against seemingly insurmountable barriers. Before it can innovate, it is forced to accept certain basic assumptions and to mold its boldest conceptions to certain forms, and in the process it is slowed down or even brought to a halt.

The American imagination is therefore circumspect and hesitant, even in its wildest flights. Its wings are clipped, and its works remain incomplete. These habits of restraint are also found in political society and singularly favor the tranquillity of the American people and the duration of the institutions they have founded. Nature and circumstances have conspired to make the American audacious, as is clear from the way he seeks his fortune. If the spirit of the Americans were completely unfettered, one would soon find among them the boldest innovators and most implacable logicians in the world. But revolutionaries in America are obliged to profess a certain public respect for Christian morality and equity, so that it is not easy for them to violate the laws when those laws stand in the way of their designs. And even if they could overcome their own scruples, they would still be held in check by the scruples of their supporters. No one in the United States has yet dared to propose the maxim that everything is permitted in the interest of society — a wicked maxim that seems to have been invented in an age of liberty to legitimize all the tyrants of the future.

Thus even as the law allows the American people to do anything and everything, there are some things that religion prevents them from imagining or forbids them to attempt.

Although religion in the United States never intervenes directly in government, it must be considered as the first of
America's political institutions, for even if religion does not
give Americans their taste for liberty, it does notably facilitate
their use of that liberty.

This is how Americans themselves see their religious beliefs.
I do not know whether all of them have faith in their religion
— for who can read the bottom of men's hearts? — but I am
certain that they believe it to be necessary for the preservation
of republican institutions. This is not the opinion of one class
of citizens or one party but of the nation as a whole. One encounters it among people of every rank.

If a politician in the United States attacks a sect, that is no
reason for even proponents of that sect not to support him,
but if he attacks all sects at once, everyone will shun him, and
he will find himself alone.

While I was in America, a witness in a court in Chester
County (New York) stated that he did not believe in the existence of God or the immortality of the soul. The presiding
judge refused to swear him in on the grounds that the witness
had destroyed in advance any credibility that his testimony
might possess.[3] The newspapers reported the incident without commentary.

Americans so completely confound Christianity with liberty
that it is almost impossible to induce them to think of one
without the other. For them, moreover, this is by no means
a sterile belief, a legacy of the past that lies moldering in the
depths of the soul, but a vital article of faith.

I saw Americans form organizations to send ministers to

[3]The New York Spectator of August 23, 1831, reported the incident as follows: "The court of common pleas of Chester County (New York) a few days
since rejected a witness who declared his disbelief in the existence of God.
The presiding judge remarked that he had not before been aware that there
was a man living who did not believe in the existence of God, that this belief
constituted the sanction of all testimony in a court of justice, and that he knew
of no case in a Christian country where a witness had been permitted to tes-
tify without such a belief."

the new states of the West to found schools and churches there. They were afraid that religion might be forgotten in the backwoods and that the people who settled there might not be as free as their forebears. I met wealthy New Englanders who left the places where they were born to lay the groundwork for Christianity and liberty on the banks of the Missouri or in the prairies of Illinois. In the United States, religious zeal never ceases to warm itself at patriotism's hearth. You might imagine that these people act as they do solely out of concern for the other life, but you would be wrong: eternity is only one of their concerns. If you were to question these missionaries of Christian civilization, you would be quite surprised to hear how frequently they speak of the goods of this world, and you would find politicians where you had thought there were only men of religion. "All the American republics are intimately associated," they would tell you. "If the republics of the West lapse into anarchy or succumb to despotism, the republican institutions now flourishing along the Atlantic seaboard would be in great danger. It is therefore in our interest that the new states should be religious, so that we may remain free."

That is how the Americans see it, but obviously they are wrong, for every day men of very considerable learning offer me proof that all is well in America except for precisely the religious spirit that I admire, and I learn that the human race would have everything it needs to enjoy liberty and happiness on the Atlantic's other shore if only it could accept Spinoza's belief in the eternity of the world or Cabanis's assertion that the brain secretes thought. To that I truly have no response other than to say that the people who make such statements have never been to America and have never seen either a religious people or a people that is free. I await their return.

There are people in France who look upon republican institutions as a temporary instrument of their grandeur. With their eyes they measure the vast abyss separating their vice and their misery from power and wealth, and they think of bridging that abyss with ruins. Such people are to liberty what the freebooters of the Middle Ages were to kings: though they wear his colors, they make war to serve themselves. The republic, they wager, will surely endure long enough to rescue them from their current plight. These are not the people to whom I speak. There are others, however, who see the republic as a permanent and tranquil state, a necessary goal toward which ideas and mores are steadily sweeping modern societies, and who would sincerely like to prepare men to be free. When people such as these attack religious beliefs, they obey their passions rather than their interests. Despotism can do without faith, but liberty cannot. Religion is much more necessary in the republic they advocate than in the monarchy they attack, and most necessary of all in a democratic republic. How can society fail to perish if, as political bonds are loosened, moral bonds are not tightened? And what is to be done with a people that is its own master, if it is not obedient to God?

ON THE PRINCIPAL CAUSES OF RELIGION'S POWER IN AMERICA

Care taken by the Americans to separate church from state. — Laws, public opinion, and efforts of priests themselves contribute to this result. — Religion's power over souls in the United States must be attributed to this cause. — Why. — What is the natural state of man with respect to religion today? — What particular and accidental cause tends to prevent men from conforming to this state in certain countries?

The philosophers of the eighteenth century had a very simple explanation for the gradual attenuation of religious belief. Religious zeal, they said, was bound to dwindle as liberty and enlightenment increased. Unfortunately, the facts do not bear this theory out.

In Europe the unbelief of certain segments of the population is rivaled only by their brutishness and ignorance, whereas in America we find one of the freest and most enlightened peoples in the world zealously observing all of religion's outward requirements.

When I arrived in the United States, it was the country's religious aspect that first captured my attention. The longer I stayed, the more I became aware that this novel situation had important political consequences.

In France, I knew, the spirit of religion and the spirit of liberty almost always pulled in opposite directions. In the United States I found them intimately intertwined: together they ruled the same territory.

My desire to understand the cause of this phenomenon increased with each passing day.

In order to learn more about it, I questioned the faithful of all communions. I especially sought out the company of clergymen, who are not only the repositories of various beliefs but also have a personal interest in their duration. The religion that I profess brought me into contact with the Catholic clergy, and I soon developed close relationships with several of its members. To each of them I expressed my astonishment and revealed my doubts, and I discovered that they differed among themselves only on matters of detail: to a man, they assigned primary credit for the peaceful ascendancy of religion in their country to the complete separation of church and state. I state without hesitation that during my stay in America I met no one — not a single clergyman or layman — who did not agree with this statement.

This led me to examine more attentively than I had previously done the position that American clergymen occupy in political society. I was surprised to discover that they held no public employments.[4] I did not find a single one in the administration and discovered that they were not even represented in assemblies.

In several states political careers were closed to them by law,[5] and in the rest by opinion.

---

[4]Unless the role that many of them play in the schools is counted as a public employment. Much of education is entrusted to the clergy.

[5]See the constitutions of New York, art. 7, sec. 4; North Carolina, art. 31; Virginia; South Carolina, art. 1, sec. 23; Kentucky, art. 2, sec. 26; Tennessee, art. 8, sec. 1; Louisiana, art. 2, sec. 22. The article of the New York constitution reads as follows: "And whereas the ministers of the Gospel are, by their profession, dedicated to the service of God and the cure of souls and should not be diverted from the great duties of their functions, therefore, no minister of the gospel or priest of any denomination whatsoever shall . . . be eligible to or capable of holding any civil or military office or place within this state."

As for the spirit of the clergy itself, I found that most of its members seemed to steer clear of power voluntarily and to take a sort of professional pride in having nothing to do with it.

I listened to them blast ambition and bad faith in men of all political stripes. But as I listened, I also learned that in God's eyes no one is damnable for his political views so long as those views are sincere, and that there is no more sin in erring about matters of government than in being mistaken about how to build a house or plow a furrow.

I saw them carefully mark their distance from, and avoid contact with, all parties as zealously as if it were a matter of personal interest.

These facts convinced me that I had been told the truth. I then sought the causes behind the facts. I asked how it could be that diminishing a religion's apparent strength could actually make it more powerful, and it seemed to me that the answer should not be impossible to find out.

Sixty years is too brief a compass for man's imagination. The incomplete joys of this world can never satisfy his heart. Man is the only creature to exhibit both a natural disgust for existence and an overwhelming desire to exist: he despises life and fears nothingness. These divergent instincts constantly compel his soul to contemplate the other world, and religion leads him to it. Religion is therefore nothing other than a particular form of hope, as natural to the human heart as hope itself. Men stray from religious belief through a kind of aberration of the intelligence, and with the aid of a type of moral violence against their own nature: an invincible inclination brings them back. Unbelief is an accident; faith alone is the permanent condition of humankind.

Thus, looking at religions from a purely human point of view, one can say that all of them draw an element of strength from within man himself. This can never fail them, because it derives from a constitutive principle of human nature.

At times, of course, religion can add to this influence, which is inherent in its nature, the artificial might of the law and the material support of the powers that govern society. One knows of religions intimately associated with temporal governments that have ruled souls by terror as well as faith. But — I say without fear of contradiction — when a religion enters into such an alliance, it makes the same mistake that a man might make: it sacrifices the future for the sake of the present, and in obtaining a power to which it is not entitled, it risks forfeiting its legitimate power.

When a religion seeks to found its empire solely on the desire for immortality that torments the hearts of all men equally, it can aim for universality. But when it joins forces with a government, it must adopt maxims applicable only to certain peoples. Thus when religion allies itself with a political power, it increases its power over some but gives up hope of reigning over all.

As long as a religion rests solely on sentiments that console man in his misery, it can win the affection of the human race. But when it embraces the bitter passions of this world, it may be forced to defend allies acquired through interest rather than love, and it must reject as adversaries men who love it still even as they do battle with its allies. Religion cannot share the material might of those who govern without incurring some of the hatred they inspire.

The political powers that seem most securely established have no guarantee of longevity other than the opinions of a generation, the interests of a century, or, in many cases, the life of one man. A law can modify a social state that seems quite definitive and solid, and with that everything changes.

Like our time on this earth, the powers of society are mostly fleeting. They come and go quickly, like life's multifarious concerns. The government sustained by an invariable disposition of the human heart or founded on an immortal interest has yet to be seen.

As long as a religion draws its strength from sentiments, instincts, and passions that recur in much the same form in one historical period after another, it can resist the work of time, or at any rate it can be destroyed only by another religion. But when religion seeks the support of worldly interests, it becomes almost as fragile as any temporal power. Alone, it can hope for immortality; linked to ephemeral powers, it shares their fortune and often falls with the fleeting passions that sustain them.

Thus whenever a religion joins forces with political powers of any kind, the alliance is bound to be onerous for religion.

It has no need of their help to live, and in serving them it may die.

This danger exists in all ages, but it is not always visible to the same degree.

There are centuries in which governments seem immortal, and others in which the existence of society seems more fragile than that of a man.

Certain constitutions maintain citizens in a sort of lethargic slumber, while others bring feverish agitation in their wake.

When governments seem quite strong and laws quite stable, men fail to perceive the danger that religion courts when it joins forces with power.

When governments appear quite weak and laws quite variable, the peril is glaringly apparent, but by then it is often too late to do anything about it. One must therefore learn to recognize it from afar.

As a nation's social state becomes increasingly democratic, and as societies lean toward republican forms, it becomes increasingly dangerous for religion to join forces with authority, for power will soon pass from hand to hand, one political theory will replace another, and men, laws, and constitutions themselves will vanish or change from one day to the next — not just for a while but constantly. Agitation and instability are inherent in the nature of democratic republics, just as stasis and slumber are the rule in absolute monarchies.

If the Americans — who change their head of state every four years, choose new legislators every two years, and replace local administrators annually, and who have handed over the world of politics to the experiments of innovators — if the Americans had not created a place apart for religion, to what could it hold fast amid the surrounding swirl of human opinion? What respect could it command in the midst of partisan conflict? What would become of its immortality when everything around it perished?

The American clergy were the first to perceive this truth and to shape their behavior accordingly. They saw that they would have to renounce religious influence if they wished to acquire political power, and they chose to forfeit the support of power rather than share its vicissitudes.

Religion in America is perhaps less powerful than it has been at certain times in certain other countries, but its influence is more durable. It has been reduced to its own forces, which no one can take away. Its influence is limited to a particular sphere, but there it is pervasive and dominates effortlessly.

In Europe voices are raised in every quarter to deplore the absence of religious beliefs and to ask how some of the former power of religion might be restored.

The first thing that must be done, in my view, is to investigate carefully what man's *natural state* with respect to religion should be today. Then, knowing what we may hope for and what we must fear, we would clearly perceive the goal toward which our efforts should be directed.

Two great dangers threaten the existence of religions: schism and indifference.

In centuries of religious fervor, men may on occasion give up their religion, but they throw off one yoke only to bow to another. The object of faith changes, but faith itself does not die. In every heart the old religion then inspires either ardent love or implacable hatred. Some reject it angrily, while others embrace it with renewed ardor. Beliefs differ, but irreligion is unknown.

This is not the case, however, when a religious belief is silently undermined by what I shall call negative doctrines, because these assert the falsity of one religion without establishing the truth of any other.

The human spirit is then subject to prodigious revolutions, seemingly without the help of man's passions and almost without his knowledge. Men relinquish their fondest hopes as if inadvertently. Swept along by an imperceptible current which they lack the courage to fight yet to which they surrender with regret, they abandon the faith they love in order to follow doubt that leads to despair.

In times such as these, beliefs are abandoned coldly rather than out of hatred. People do not reject their beliefs; rather, their beliefs forsake them. The unbeliever ceases to believe in true religion but continues to deem it useful. Looking at religious beliefs from a human angle, he recognizes their power over mores, their influence on laws. He understands how beliefs can make men live in peace and prepare them gently for death. Having lost the faith, he nevertheless longs for it, and, fully aware of the value of his vanished possession, he is afraid to take it from anyone who possesses it still.

Meanwhile, the man who continues to believe does not hesitate to expose his faith to the view of all. Those who do not share his hopes he sees as unfortunates rather than adversaries. He knows that he can win their esteem without following their example. Hence he is not at war with anyone. And since he does not look upon the society in which he lives as an arena in which religion must constantly do battle with a thousand relentless enemies, he loves his contemporaries even as he condemns their weaknesses and grieves for the errors of their ways.

With those who do not believe hiding their incredulity and those who do believe showing their faith, public opinion develops in favor of religion. People love it, support it, and honor it, and one must look into the depths of their souls to see the wounds it has suffered.

So the mass of men, whom religious feeling never forsakes, see nothing to dissuade them from established beliefs. Their instinct for another life leads them straight to the foot of the altar and opens their hearts to the precepts and consolations of faith.

Why does this picture not apply to us?

Among us I see men who have ceased to believe in Christianity without embracing any other religion.

I see others who are stuck in doubt and already pretend they no longer believe.

Still others are Christians who continue to believe but dare not admit it.

Finally, alongside these lukewarm allies and ardent adversaries, I find a small number of believers prepared to brave every obstacle and scorn every danger for the sake of their beliefs. By struggling against human weakness they have succeeded in raising themselves above the common opinion. In the enthusiasm generated by their own exertions, they no longer know precisely where they ought to stop. Having seen that the first use their own countrymen made of independence was to attack religion, they fear their contemporaries and recoil in terror from the liberty those contemporaries seek. To them, disbelief seems to be a new thing, and consequently their hatred extends to everything else that is new. Hence they are at war with their century and their country, and in every opinion professed there they see a necessary enemy of the faith.

This, presumably, should not be man's natural state with respect to religion today.

Hence some accidental and particular cause must be at work among us that prevents the human spirit from following its bent and drives it beyond its natural limits.

I am deeply convinced that this particular and accidental cause is the close alliance between politics and religion.

Unbelievers in Europe pursue Christians as though they were political enemies rather than religious adversaries. They hate faith as though it were a party opinion rather than an erroneous belief, and what they reject in the priest is not so much the representative of God as the friend of power.

In Europe, Christianity allowed itself to become the close ally of temporal powers. Today those powers are collapsing, and Christianity finds itself buried, as it were, beneath their debris. A living thing, it has been lashed to cadavers: cut the ties that bind it to the dead and it will rise again.

I do not know what needs to be done to restore the energy of youth to Christianity in Europe. God alone can do it, but it is up to man to allow faith to use whatever strength it still possesses.

HOW THE ENLIGHTENMENT, HABITS, AND PRACTICAL EXPERIENCE OF THE AMERICANS CONTRIBUTE TO THE SUCCESS OF DEMOCRATIC INSTITUTIONS

What I mean by the enlightenment of the American people. — The human mind in the United States is less deeply cultivated than in Europe. — But no one has remained ignorant. — Why. — Rapid circulation of ideas in the semi-wilderness states of the West. — How practical experience is even more useful to Americans than literary learning.

Countless times throughout this work I have called the reader's attention to ways in which the habits and enlightenment of the Americans influenced the continuation of their political institutions. Hence there is little new for me to say.

America has thus far produced very few remarkable writers, no great historians, and not a single poet. The country's inhabitants harbor a kind of prejudice against literature proper, and there are third-rate cities in Europe that publish more literary works annually than all twenty-four states of the Union combined.

The American mind avoids general ideas. It does not seek out theoretical discoveries. Neither politics nor industry encourages it do so. In the United States new laws are constantly being made, but no great writer has yet emerged to investigate the general principles of the law.

The Americans have lawyers and commentators on the law but lack great legal scholars, and in politics they give the world examples rather than lessons.

The same is true for the mechanical arts.

Americans make shrewd application of European inventions, improving them and cleverly adapting them to the country's needs. They are industrious but do not cultivate the science of industry. Among them one finds good workers but few inventors. Fulton long hawked his genius abroad before he was able to dedicate it to his own country.

Anyone who wants to judge the state of enlightenment among the Anglo-Americans must therefore look at the same object from two different angles. If he pays attention only to the learned, he will be astonished by their small number. And if he counts the ignorant, the American people will seem the most enlightened on earth.

The population as a whole falls between these two extremes, as I said earlier.

In New England, every citizen receives instruction in the elementary notions of human knowledge. He also learns the doctrines and proofs of his religion. He is made familiar with the history of his country and the principal features of the Constitution that governs it. In Connecticut and Massachusetts, one seldom encounters any man whose knowledge of these things is merely superficial, and anyone absolutely ignorant of them would be something of a phenomenon.

When I compare the Greek and Roman republics with their libraries full of manuscripts and crude populace to the republics of America with their thousands of newspapers and enlightened citizenry and then think of all the effort that is still being expended on judging the latter in terms of the former and trying to predict what will happen today on the basis of what happened two thousand years ago, I am tempted to burn my books to make sure that I apply only new ideas to such a new social state.

What I say about New England should not be extended indiscriminately to the Union as a whole. The farther west or south one goes, the less educated the people are. In the states along the Gulf of Mexico there are people, as there are in France, who are strangers to the most basic elements of human knowledge. Still, one would search the United States in vain for a single county mired in ignorance. The reason for this is simple: the peoples of Europe began in darkness and barbarism and moved toward civilization and light. Their progress has been uneven: some have raced toward the destination, while others have done no more than walk. Several ceased to make progress altogether and slumber still along the way.

The situation in the United States was different.

When the Anglo-Americans first came to the land their descendants now occupy, they were already completely civilized. For them there was no need to learn; it was enough not to forget. Now, each year, the sons of these same Americans take not only their households but their acquired knowledge and respect for learning with them into the wilderness. Education has made them aware of the usefulness of enlightenment and placed them in a position to pass it on to their descendants. In the United States, therefore, society had no infancy; it was born into manhood.

Americans do not use the word *peasant*. They do not use the word because they do not possess the idea. The ignorance of primitive ages, the simplicity of the countryside, the rusticity of the village — they have preserved none of these things and have no conception of the virtues or vices, the coarse habits, or the naïve graces of a nascent civilization.

At the outer reaches of the confederated states, where society and wilderness meet, there subsists a population of bold adventurers who, fleeing the poverty that lay ready to afflict them had they remained beneath their fathers' roofs, fearlessly braved America's solitudes in search of a new homeland. No sooner does the pioneer reach his chosen place of refuge than he chops down a few trees and builds a cabin in the woods. Nothing is more wretched to look at than one of these forlorn shacks. A traveler who draws near as dusk descends can see the flicker of the hearth through chinks in the walls, and at night, if the wind picks up, he can hear the rustle of the leafy roof mingle with the other sounds of the forest. It is only natural to suppose that a cottage as poor as this must be home to coarse and ignorant people. Yet one must not assume that the pioneer in any way reflects the place he has chosen for an asylum. Everything around him is primitive and wild, but he is the product, so to speak, of eighteen centuries of effort and experience. He wears the clothes and speaks the language of the city. He knows the past, is curious about the future, and argues about the present. He is a highly civilized man who, having plunged into the wilds of the New World with his Bible, ax, and newspapers, has chosen to live for a time in the forest.

It is difficult to imagine how rapidly thought propagates through this wilderness.[6]

[6] I traveled through some of the American frontier in a kind of open wagon that people referred to as a mail coach. We traveled at a good clip day and night over barely cleared paths through vast forests. When the darkness became impenetrable, my driver set fire to some branches of larch to light the way, and we continued on. Every now and then we would come upon a cot-

I do not think that there is as much intellectual activity in the most enlightened and populous cantons of France.[7] There can be no doubt that the education of the people in the United States contributes powerfully to the perpetuation of the democratic republic. This will be so, I think, wherever the education that enlightens the mind is not divorced from the upbringing that regulates mores.

I would not make too much of this advantage, however, and I am even farther from agreeing with the many people in Europe who believe that it is enough to teach people to read and write to make citizens of them straightaway.

True enlightenment is primarily the fruit of experience, and if Americans had not gradually become used to governing themselves, their book-learning would not be of much use to them today.

I spent a good deal of time living with the people of the United States and cannot find words adequate to express how much I admired their experience and common sense.

Do not invite an American to talk about Europe, for he is likely to display a good deal of presumption and some rather foolish pride. He will content himself with vague general ideas of the sort that are of such great help to ignorant people everywhere. But ask him about his own country and the clouds obscuring his intelligence will suddenly dissipate. His language will become clear, sharp, and precise, as will his thoughts. He will tell you what his rights are and how they may be ex-

tage in the woods: the post office. The courier would drop an enormous bundle of letters at the door of this forlorn dwelling, and then we would gallop on, leaving it to each resident of the vicinity to come in search of his portion of the treasure.

[7]In 1832 each inhabitant of Michigan paid 1 franc 22 centimes in postal fees, and each inhabitant of Florida, 1 franc 5 centimes. (See *National Calendar*, 1833, p. 244.) In the same year, each inhabitant of the département du Nord paid the state 1 franc 4 centimes for the same purpose. (See *Compte général de l'administration de finances*, 1833, p. 623.) Now, in this period Michigan still had only seven inhabitants per square league and Florida had only five: education was less widespread and activity less great in these two districts than in most other states of the Union, whereas the département du Nord, with 3,400 inhabitants per square league, is one of the most enlightened and industrialized parts of France.

ercised. He understands the customs of the political world. You will find that he is aware of administrative rules and familiar with the workings of the law. Americans do not take their practical knowledge and concrete notions from books. Their literary education may prepare them for such learning, but it does not supply them with it.

The American learns about the law by participating in the making of it. He teaches himself about the forms of government by governing. He watches the great work of society being done every day before his eyes and, in a sense, by his hand.

In the United States, all of education is directed toward politics. In Europe, its principal purpose is to prepare people for private life. Citizens take part in public affairs too seldom to prepare them for it in advance.

A glance at the two societies reveals that these differences are apparent even in their outward aspect.

In Europe, we often take ideas and habits from private life with us into public life, and since we sometimes pass directly from the family circle to the councils of state, we often discuss the great interests of society in the same way as we converse with our friends.

By contrast, Americans almost always carry the habits of public life over into private life. With them, the idea of the jury turns up in games played in school, and parliamentary forms influence even banquet arrangements.

LAWS DO MORE TO MAINTAIN A DEMOCRATIC REPUBLIC IN THE UNITED STATES THAN PHYSICAL CAUSES DO, AND MORES DO MORE THAN LAWS

All the peoples of America have a democratic social state. — Nevertheless, democratic institutions have survived only among the Anglo-Americans. — The Spaniards of South America, though as favored by physical nature as the Anglo-Americans, cannot support a democratic republic. — Nor can Mexico, which has adopted the Constitution of the United States. — The Anglo-Americans of the West have more difficulty doing so than the Anglo-Americans of the East. — Reasons for these differences.

I have said that the perpetuation of democratic institutions in the United States must be attributed to circumstances, laws, and mores.[8]

Most Europeans are familiar with only the first of these three causes, to which they ascribe a preponderant importance that it does not possess.

It is true that the Anglo-Americans brought equality of conditions to the New World. Among them one finds neither commoners nor nobles: prejudices of birth have always been as alien to them as prejudices of profession. Since the social state was democratic in this sense, democracy had no difficulty establishing its empire.

But this fact is not peculiar to the United States. Nearly all the colonies in America were founded by men who either started out as equals or became equals by living in them. Nowhere in the New World were Europeans able to create an aristocracy.

Yet democratic institutions prospered only in the United States.

The American Union has no enemies to contend with. It stands alone, surrounded by wilderness as an island is surrounded by ocean.

But nature isolated the Spaniards of South America in the same way, and that isolation did not prevent them from maintaining armies. They made war on one another when no foreigners were at hand. To date, only the Anglo-American democracy has been able to maintain itself in peace.

The territory of the Union presents a boundless field to human activity. It offers inexhaustible nourishment to industry and labor. Hence love of riches there takes the place of ambition, and well-being quenches partisan ardor.

But where in the world can one find land more fertile, rivers mightier, or riches more untouched and inexhaustible than in South America? Yet South America cannot support democracy. If, in order for a people to be happy, it were enough to set it down in a corner of the world where it could multiply

[8]Here I would remind the reader of the general sense in which I use the word *mores*, by which I mean the whole range of intellectual and moral dispositions that men bring to the state of society.

at will in uninhabited territory, the Spaniards of southern America would have nothing to complain about. Even if they did not achieve the same degree of happiness as the settlers of the United States, they still should have been the envy of the peoples of Europe. Yet no nation on earth is more miserable than the nations of South America.

Thus, not only do physical causes fail to produce analogous results among South and North Americans; they cannot even bring South America up to the level of Europe, where the same causes work in the opposite direction.

Physical causes therefore do not influence the destiny of nations as much as people assume.

I met New Englanders prepared to abandon a homeland in which they might have lived comfortably in order to go and seek their fortune in the wilderness. Not far away, in Canada, I saw French settlers squeeze into a space too small to hold them even though the same wilderness was near to hand. And while immigrants in the United States could earn enough in a few days to pay for a large estate, Canadians paid as much for land as they would have done had they still been living in France.

Thus nature, in delivering the solitudes of the New World to Europeans, gives them goods they do not always know how to use.

The other peoples of America enjoy the same opportunities for prosperity as the Anglo-Americans, except for their laws and mores, and those peoples are miserable. The laws and mores of the Anglo-Americans therefore constitute the special reason for their greatness and the predominant cause I seek.

Far be it from me to claim that there is some kind of absolute goodness in American laws. I do not believe that they are applicable to all democratic peoples, and several of them seem to me to pose a danger to the United States itself.

Still, no one can deny that American legislation, taken as a whole, is well adapted to the genius of the people it must govern and to the nature of the country.

American laws are therefore good, and much of the credit for the success of democratic government in America must be attributed to them, but I do not think that they are the main reason for that success. And although laws seem to me to have a greater influence on the social happiness of the Americans than does the nature of the country itself, I also see reasons to believe that laws are less influential than mores.

Federal laws certainly constitute the most important part of the legislation of the United States.

Mexico, which is as happily situated as the Anglo-American Union, has appropriated those same laws yet has not been able to accustom itself to democratic government.

Hence there is a reason independent of physical causes and laws that enables democracy to govern the United States.

Indeed, the evidence proves still more than this. Nearly all the people living within the borders of the Union spring from the same blood. They all speak the same language, pray to God in the same way, are subject to the same physical causes, and obey the same laws.

Where, then, do the unmistakable differences among them originate?

Why, in the East of the Union, is republican government strong and orderly, and why does it proceed in a mature and deliberate fashion? Why are wisdom and duration the hallmark of all its actions?

By contrast, why do the powers of society in the West seem to proceed haphazardly?

Why does the conduct of public affairs there seem so disorderly, passionate, and one might almost say feverish — signs that do not presage a long future?

I am no longer comparing the Anglo-Americans to foreign peoples; now I am contrasting them with one another and trying to understand why they are not all alike. Arguments derived from the nature of the country and differences of law here carry no weight. Some other cause must be adduced, and where would I find such a cause if not in the mores of the people?

It was in the East that the Anglo-Americans experienced democratic government the longest and formed the habits and conceived the ideas most conducive to its maintenance. There, democracy gradually permeated customs, opinions, and forms — a fact that is apparent in every detail of social life and law. It was in the East that the literary instruction and practical education of the people were most perfected, and that religion and liberty became most fully intertwined. But all these habits, opinions, usages, and beliefs — what are they, if not what I have been calling mores?

In the West, by contrast, some of these same advantages are still lacking. Many of the Americans who live in the states of the West were born in the woods, and in them the civilization of their fathers is conjoined with ideas and customs drawn from the savage life. Their passions are more violent, their religious morality less powerful, their ideas less clearly defined. Men exert less control over one another, because they barely know their neighbors. To a certain extent the western states therefore exhibit the inexperience and unbridled ways of nascent peoples. Although the societies of the West are constructed of old elements, these are assembled in a new way.

What makes the Americans of the United States the only Americans capable of supporting the empire of democracy is therefore their mores. And what explains why some Anglo-American democracies are more orderly and prosperous than others is, once again, mores.

Thus Europeans exaggerate the influence of the country's geographical location on the longevity of democratic institutions. Too much importance is ascribed to laws and too little to mores. Physical causes, laws, mores: these are without a doubt the three major factors that have governed and shaped American democracy, but if I were asked to rank them, I would say that physical causes matter less than laws and laws less than mores.

I am convinced that even the most favorable geographical location and the best laws cannot maintain a constitution in spite of mores, whereas mores can turn even the most unfavorable locations and the worst laws to advantage. The importance of mores is a common truth, which study and experience have repeatedly confirmed. It is a truth central to all my thinking, and in the end all my ideas come back to it.

I have only one thing to add on this subject.

If, in the course of this work, I have failed to make the reader aware of the importance that I attach to the practical experience, habits, and opinions — in a word, to the mores — of the Americans in maintaining their laws, then I have failed to achieve the principal goal I set myself in writing it.

WOULD LAWS AND MORES SUFFICE TO MAINTAIN DEMOCRATIC INSTITUTIONS ELSEWHERE THAN IN AMERICA?

If the Anglo-Americans were transported to Europe, they would be obliged to modify their laws. — One must distinguish between democratic institutions and American institutions. — One can conceive of democratic laws better than, or at any rate different from, those adopted by American democracy. — The American example proves only that one need not despair of regulating democracy with the aid of laws and mores.

I have said that the success of democratic institutions in the United States was due more to laws and mores than to the nature of the country.

But does it follow that the same causes, if transported elsewhere, would by themselves have the same power? And that if the country cannot take the place of laws and mores, laws and mores can take the place of the country?

Clearly, evidence on this point is lacking. The Anglo-Americans are not the only people in the New World, and since other peoples were subject to the same physical conditions as the Anglo-Americans, I was able to make comparisons.

Outside of America, however, there is no nation which, lacking the physical advantages of the Anglo-Americans, has nevertheless adopted their laws and mores.

Lacking a useful point of comparison in this regard, we can only venture opinions.

To begin with, it seems to me that one must distinguish carefully between the institutions of the United States and democratic institutions in general.

When I think of the state of Europe, with its great nations, populous cities, formidable armies, and political complexities, I find it impossible to believe that if the Anglo-Americans themselves were transported to our soil with their ideas, their religion, and their mores, they would be able to survive there without considerable modification to their laws.

But one can imagine a democratic people organized in a different way from the American people.

Is it, then, impossible to conceive of a government based on the genuine will of the majority, but in which the majority, suppressing its natural egalitarian instincts for the sake of order and stability in the state, would consent to vest all the attributes of executive power in one family or one man? Is it impossible to imagine a democratic society in which the forces of the nation would be more centralized than in the United States and the people would exert a less direct and less irresistible influence over general affairs and yet in which each citizen, invested with certain rights, would, within his own sphere, participate in the operations of government?

What I saw among the Anglo-Americans leads me to believe that democratic institutions of this nature, if prudently introduced into society in such a way that people could become accustomed to them little by little and gradually absorb them into their opinions, could survive in places other than America.

If the laws of the United States were the only democratic laws imaginable, or the most perfect that could be found, I could understand how it would be possible to conclude that the success of those laws proved nothing about the success of democratic laws in general in a country less favored by nature.

But if American laws seem to me defective in many respects, and if I can easily imagine others, the special nature of the country does not prove to me that democratic institutions cannot succeed in a nation where, even though physical circumstances are less favorable, the laws may be better.

If men in America were different from men elsewhere, and if their social state gave rise to habits and opinions contrary to those produced by the same social state in Europe, then what happens in the American democracies would teach me nothing about what might happen in other democracies.

If Americans exhibited the same penchants as all other democratic peoples and if lawmakers had counted on the nature of the country and on circumstances to contain those penchants within just limits, the prosperity of the United States, being attributable to purely physical causes, would offer no encouragement to peoples wishing to follow the example of the Americans without possessing their natural advantages.

But neither of these assumptions is supported by the facts.

In America I found passions similar to those we see in

Europe. Some stemmed from the very nature of the human heart, others from the democratic state of society.

For example, I found in the United States that restlessness of the heart which is natural to men when, all conditions being almost equal, each person sees the same chance of rising. I found the democratic sentiment of envy expressed in a thousand different ways. I observed that in the conduct of affairs people often displayed a great mixture of presumption and ignorance, and from this I concluded that in America as in Europe, men were subject to the same imperfections and exposed to the same miseries.

But when I examined the state of society more closely, it was easy to see that the Americans had made great and successful efforts to combat these weaknesses of the human heart and to correct these natural defects of democracy.

Their diverse municipal laws struck me as so many barriers designed to confine the restless ambitions of citizens within a narrow sphere and to turn the very democratic passions that might overthrow the state to the benefit of the towns. It seemed to me that American lawmakers had contrived, not without success, to counter envious sentiments with the idea of rights; to counter the constant flux of the political world with the stability of religious morality; to counter the people's theoretical ignorance with their experience; and to counter the heat of popular desires with the people's habitual involvement in public affairs.

The Americans did not rely on the nature of the country to counter the dangers arising from their constitution and political laws. To ills that they share with all democratic peoples they applied remedies that had previously occurred to no one else; and, though they were the first to try those remedies, they succeeded.

American mores and laws are not the only ones appropriate to democratic peoples, but the Americans have shown that one need not despair of regulating democracy with the aid of laws and mores.

If other nations, borrowing this general and fruitful idea from America but without intending to imitate the particular application that the Americans have made of it, were to attempt to adapt themselves to the social state that Providence has imposed on men today, and if they were to seek in this way to avoid the threat of despotism and anarchy, what reasons do we have to believe that their efforts are doomed to failure?

The organization and establishment of democracy among Christians is the great political problem of our time. To be sure, the Americans have not solved this problem, but they offer useful instruction to those who wish to do so.

IMPORTANCE OF THE FOREGOING IN RELATION TO EUROPE

It is easy to see why I undertook to do the research set forth above. The question I raised concerns not just the United States but the entire world; not just one nation, but all mankind.

If peoples whose social state is democratic could remain free only as long as they lived in wilderness, one would have to despair of the future of the human race, for men are moving rapidly toward democracy, and the wilderness is filling up.

If it were true that laws and mores were inadequate to maintain democratic institutions, what refuge would nations have other than the despotism of a single individual?

I am well aware that many worthy people nowadays see nothing very terrifying in such a future; tired of liberty, they hope to find repose far from its tempests.

But these people are woefully ignorant of the port toward which they are headed. Preoccupied with their memories, they judge absolute power by what it once was and not by what it could be today.

If absolute power were once again to establish itself among the democratic peoples of Europe, I have no doubt that it would take a new form and exhibit features unknown to our fathers.

There was a time in Europe when the law, as well as the consent of the people, invested kings with almost limitless power. But they almost never had occasion to use it.

I shall say nothing about the prerogatives of the nobility, the authority of the sovereign courts, the rights of corporations, or provincial privileges, which not only softened the blows of authority but kept the spirit of resistance alive in the nation.

Apart from these political institutions, which, though often inimical to the freedom of individuals, nevertheless served to maintain the love of liberty in men's souls — in which respect their usefulness is obvious — opinions and mores erected barriers around royal power that are less well known yet no less powerful.

Religion, love of the prince by his subjects, the prince's goodness, honor, family spirit, provincial prejudices, custom, and public opinion — all these things circumscribed the power of kings and traced imperceptible limits around their authority.

In those days the constitutions of peoples were despotic and their mores free. Princes had the right to do whatever they pleased but not the capacity or the desire.

What remains today of the barriers that used to hold tyranny in check?

Religion having lost its empire over souls, the most visible of the boundaries that divided good from evil has been overturned. Everything in the moral world seems doubtful and uncertain. Kings and peoples have lost their bearings, and no one can say where the natural limits of despotism or the bounds of license lie.

Long years of revolution have forever destroyed the respect that once surrounded heads of state. Relieved of the burden of public esteem, princes can henceforth surrender without fear to the intoxication of power.

When kings sense that the people's hearts are with them, they are clement, because they feel strong. They are careful with their subjects' love, because that love is the mainstay of their thrones. The feelings that develop between prince and people exhibit a mildness reminiscent of the feelings in a family, but transposed to the bosom of society. Though subjects may murmur of their discontent with the king, they are nevertheless loath to displease him, and when the sovereign strikes his subjects, it is with a light hand, as a father would chastise his children.

But once the prestige of royalty has been swallowed up by the tumult of revolution and a succession of kings has revealed to the people both the weakness of *right* and the harshness of *fact*, no one sees the king any longer as the father of the state, and everyone sees him as a master. If he is weak, he is despised; if strong, he is hated. He himself is filled with anger and fear. He sees himself as a foreigner in his own land and treats his subjects as a conquered people.

When provinces and cities were so many nations within a common fatherland, each had a spirit of its own that stood in opposition to the general spirit of servitude. But now that all the parts of the same empire — having forfeited their franchises, usages, and prejudices, to say nothing of their memories and even their names — have become accustomed to obeying the same laws, it is no more difficult to oppress them all at once than to oppress any one of them separately.

While the nobility enjoyed power, and for a long time even after it had lost it, aristocratic honor lent extraordinary power to individual acts of resistance.

In those days men could be found who, though powerless, nevertheless entertained an exalted idea of their individual worth and dared to resist the pressure of the public authorities single-handed.

But now that all classes of society are on the point of being thoroughly mixed, and individuals are increasingly lost in the crowd and easily swallowed up in the common obscurity; now that the monarchical notion of honor has virtually lost its sway without being replaced by the notion of virtue, and nothing remains to lift man to a higher plane; who can say where the exigencies of power and the accommodations of weakness will end?

As long as family spirit endured, the man who fought against tyranny was never alone: he had clients, hereditary friends, and close relatives on his side. And if this support failed him, he still felt sustained by his ancestors and animated by his descendants. But when patrimonies are divided and within a few years races mix, what place is left for family spirit?

How powerful do customs remain when a people has changed its face entirely and continues to change it constantly; when every act of tyranny has its precedent and every crime its example; when one can find nothing so old that one hesitates to destroy it or think of anything so new that one dares not attempt it?

What resistance can mores offer when they have already yielded so many times?

What can public opinion itself accomplish when there are

not *twenty* people united by a common bond? When there is no person, family, body, class, or free association capable of representing that opinion and enabling it to act?

When each citizen, being equally powerless, equally poor, and equally isolated, has only his individual weakness to set against the organized force of the government?

To find something analogous to what would happen here under such circumstances, one should look not to our annals but perhaps to the monuments of Antiquity, to the terrible centuries of Roman tyranny, when, because mores were corrupt, memories effaced, habits destroyed, and opinions wavering, the liberty that had been banished from the law could find no refuge; when, because nothing protected citizens and citizens failed to protect themselves, men made sport of human nature and princes tried not so much the patience of their subjects as the clemency of the heavens.

People who think of reviving the monarchy of Henri IV or Louis XIV seem to me quite blind. When I think of the state in which several European nations already find themselves and toward which all the others are tending, I am inclined to believe that soon there will no longer be room in Europe for anything but democratic liberty or the tyranny of the Caesars.

Is this not worth thinking about? If there will inevitably come a time when all men must either be made free or become slaves; when all men must either be granted equal rights or be deprived of all rights; and if those who govern society were thereby reduced to either gradually raising the masses to their own level or allowing all citizens to sink below the threshold of humanity; would that not be enough to overcome any number of doubts, to reassure any number of consciences, and to prepare everyone to make great sacrifices?

Would it not then become necessary to consider the gradual development of democratic institutions and mores not as the best way to be free but as the only way left to us? And in that case, would not people, even without loving democratic government, be prepared to adopt it as the most useful and honorable remedy for society's present ills?

It is difficult to make the people participate in government. It is still more difficult to provide them with the experience and inspire in them the feelings they would need to govern well.

The will of a democracy is changeable; its agents are crude; its laws are imperfect — all this I grant. But if it were true that soon there is to be no intermediate between the empire of democracy and the yoke of one man, should we not strive toward the former rather than submit voluntarily to the latter? And if complete equality were ultimately inevitable, would it not be better to choose to be leveled by liberty rather than by a despot?

Anyone who, after reading this book, concludes that my goal in writing it was to suggest that every people whose social state is democratic ought to mimic the mores of the Americans is guilty of a serious error. Such a reader will have fastened on the form of my thought to the exclusion of the substance. My purpose was to show, by using America as an example, that laws and above all mores could allow a democratic people to remain free. I am, moreover, a very long way from believing that we ought to follow the example set by American democracy or imitate the means it has used to achieve its goal, for I am by no means unaware of the influence exerted by a country's nature and antecedent facts on its political constitution, and I should regard it as a great misfortune for the human race if liberty were obliged to exhibit identical features wherever it manifests itself.

But I do believe that if we do not manage gradually to introduce democratic institutions among us and ultimately to establish those institutions on a firm footing; and if we forsake the idea of instilling in all our citizens ideas and feelings that will first prepare them for liberty and then enable them to make use of it; then there will be no independence for anyone — not for the bourgeois or the noble, nor for the poor man or the rich man — but only equal tyranny for all. And I predict that if, in time, we do not succeed in founding the peaceful rule of the majority, we will sooner or later find ourselves subject to the *unlimited* power of a single individual.

Chapter 10

SOME CONSIDERATIONS CONCERNING THE PRESENT STATE AND PROBABLE FUTURE OF THE THREE RACES THAT INHABIT THE TERRITORY OF THE UNITED STATES

THE principal task that I set myself has now been fulfilled: I have shown, to the best of my ability at any rate, what the laws of American democracy are. I have described its mores. I could end here, but the reader might feel that his expectations had not been met.

America exemplifies something more than an immense and consummate democracy. There is more than one way to look at the peoples that inhabit the New World.

Although Indians and Negroes have come up frequently in the course of this work, I have yet to pause to show how these two races stand in relation to the democratic people I have been describing. I have discussed the spirit that shaped the Anglo-American confederation, and the laws that aided in that process. Only in passing was I able to touch on the dangers that threaten the confederation, and then only in the most incomplete way. It was impossible to explore in detail, and apart from laws and mores, the prospects for the confederation's survival. In discussing the united republics, I ventured no guess as to the permanence of republican forms in the New World, and though I often alluded to the commercial activity that dominates the Union, I was not able to treat the future of the Americans as a commercial people.

All of these topics were tangential to my subject: they are American but not democratic and it was above all democracy that I wished to portray. I therefore avoided them initially, but now, by way of conclusion, I must come back to them.

The territory nowadays occupied or claimed by the American Union extends from the Atlantic Ocean to the shores of the South Sea. To both the east and the west, therefore, its limits coincide with those of the continent itself. And it stretches from the edge of the tropics in the south to the frozen reaches of the north.

The people who have spread across this territory are not, as in Europe, all offspring of a single family. It is immediately apparent that they comprise three naturally distinct, and I might almost say hostile, races. Education, law, origins, and even outward features had raised an almost insurmountable barrier between them. Fortune brought them to the same soil, but it has mixed them together without being able to blend them, and each seeks its destiny separately.

Among these diverse men, the first to attract the eye, the first in enlightenment, power, and happiness, is the white man, the European, man par excellence. Below him appear the Negro and the Indian.

These two unfortunate races have in common neither birth, appearance, language, nor mores; they are alike only in their misfortunes, equal in their inferiority in the land they inhabit. Both suffer the effects of tyranny, and while their miseries are different, both can blame those miseries on the same tyrant.

Seeing what is taking place in the world, might one not say that the European is to men of other races what man himself is to animals? He makes them serve his needs, and when he cannot bend them to his will, he destroys them.

With one blow oppression has deprived the descendants of Africans of nearly all the privileges of humanity. The Negro in the United States has lost even the memory of his homeland. He no longer understands the language spoken by his ancestors. He has forsworn their religion and forgotten their mores. Thus he has ceased to belong to Africa, but he has not thereby acquired any right to Europe's goods. He is caught between two societies. He remains isolated between two peoples, sold by one and repudiated by the other, and in all the world the only semblance of an ancestral home that he has left is his master's household.

The Negro has no family. He cannot see in woman anything other than the fleeting partner of his pleasures, and his sons are his equals from birth.

Shall I call it God's blessing or a final curse of his wrath, this disposition of the soul that renders man insensible to extreme misery and, indeed, often inspires in him a sort of depraved taste for the cause of his misfortunes?

Plunged into this abyss of woe, the Negro scarcely feels his affliction. Violence made him a slave, but habituation to servitude has given him the thoughts and ambitions of one. He admires his tyrants even more than he hates them and finds his joy and his pride in servile imitation of his oppressors.

His intelligence has sunk to the level of his soul.

The Negro enters servitude when he enters life — nay, he is often bought while still in his mother's womb, so that he begins to be a slave even before he is born.

As devoid of needs as he is of pleasures, he is of no use to himself, and life teaches him from the beginning that he is the property of another man whose interest is to look after him. He recognizes that power over his fate has not been granted to him. Even the use of his mind seems to him a pointless gift of Providence, and he enjoys all the privileges of his baseness in tranquillity.

Should he become free, independence will often strike him as a chain heavier to bear than slavery itself, for life has taught him to submit to everything save reason; and when reason becomes his only guide, he cannot recognize its voice. He finds himself besieged by a thousand new needs, and he lacks the knowledge and energy necessary to resist them. Needs are masters that must be combated, and he has learned only how to submit and obey. Thus he sinks to the uttermost depths of misery: servitude stuns him, and freedom strikes the final blow.

Oppression has had no less of an impact on the Indian races, but to different effect.

Before Whites arrived in the New World, the people of North America lived tranquilly in the woods. Subject to the ordinary vicissitudes of the savage life, they exhibited the vices and virtues of all uncivilized peoples. The Europeans forced the Indian tribes to flee into the remote wilderness, thereby condemning them to a wandering, vagabond existence filled with unspeakable miseries.

Savage nations are governed by opinions and mores alone.

European tyranny attenuated the North American Indians' feeling for their native land, dispersed their families, obscured their traditions, severed the chain of memory, changed their habits, and increased their needs immeasurably, making them less disciplined and civilized than they were before. Meanwhile, the tribes' moral and physical condition grew steadily worse, and their barbarity kept pace with their wretchedness. Yet Europeans were not able to change the character of the Indians entirely, and though they had the power to destroy them, they were never able to reduce them to order and obedience.

The Negro exists at the ultimate extreme of servitude, the Indian at the outer limits of freedom. The effects of slavery on the former are scarcely more disastrous than those of independence on the latter.

The Negro, being the proprietor of nothing, not even his own person, cannot make decisions about his own life without committing a form of larceny.

The savage is his own master from the moment he can act. He is scarcely conscious of the authority of the family. He has never bowed to the will of another man. No one has taught him to distinguish between voluntary obedience and shameful subjection, and he knows nothing of law, not even the name. For him, to be free is to escape from nearly every social bond. He revels in this barbarous independence and would rather perish than sacrifice any part of it. Civilization has little purchase on such a man.

The Negro tries repeatedly to enter a society that wants no part of him. He bows to the tastes of his oppressors, adopts their opinions, and aspires, by imitating them, to become indistinguishable from them. He has been told since birth that his race is naturally inferior to that of the white man, and he is not far from believing it; hence he is ashamed of himself. In every one of his features he sees a trace of slavery, and if he could repudiate himself altogether, he would gladly consent to do so.

By contrast, the Indian's imagination is filled with the supposed nobility of his origins. He lives and dies amid dreams inspired by his pride. Far from wishing to bend his mores to ours, he clings to barbarity as a distinctive sign of his race, and he rejects civilization not so much because he hates it, perhaps, as because he is afraid of resembling the Europeans.[1]

He would oppose the perfection of our arts with nothing but the resources of the wilderness; our tactics with nothing but his undisciplined courage; the profundities of our designs with nothing but the spontaneous instincts of his savage nature. In this unequal contest he succumbs.

The Negro would like to blend in with the European, and he cannot. The Indian might to some degree succeed in such an enterprise, but he disdains to attempt it. The servility of the Negro dooms him to slavery, and the pride of the Indian condemns him to death.

I recall that once, while traveling through the forests that still cover the state of Alabama, I chanced upon a pioneer cabin. Not wishing to enter the American's home, I went to a spring in the nearby woods to rest for a while. As I sat there, an Indian woman arrived (we were not far from the territory

---

[1] The native of North America clings to his opinions and to the least modicum of his habits with a lack of flexibility unparalleled in history. In the more than two hundred years that the roving tribes of North America have been in daily contact with the white race, they have never borrowed a single one of its ideas or customs. Europeans have nevertheless exerted a profound influence on the savages. They have made the character of the Indian more reckless, but they have not made it more European.

In the summer of 1831 I found myself on the far side of Lake Michigan, in a place called Green Bay, the last outpost on the border between the United States and the territory occupied by the Indians of the Northwest. There I made the acquaintance of an American officer, Major H., who spoke to me at length about the inflexibility of the Indian character and then told me the following story: "I once knew a young Indian who had been educated at a school in New England. He did very well there and took on all the outward aspect of a civilized man. When war broke out between us and the English in 1810, I ran into this young man again. He was then serving in our army as the commander of a group of warriors from his tribe. The Americans had allowed Indians into their ranks only on condition that they refrain from the horrible practice of scalping their victims. When night fell after the battle of ———, C. came and sat at our campfire. I asked him what had happened during the day. Gradually warming to the recital of his exploits, he came eventually to a point where he unbuttoned his shirt and said, 'Don't give me away!' And I saw between his body and his shirt the hair of an Englishman still dripping with blood."

occupied by the Creek nation). She was holding the hand of a little girl of five or six, of the white race, whom I assumed to be the pioneer's daughter. A Negro woman followed along behind. Barbarous luxury of a kind was reflected in the Indian's dress: metal rings hung from her nostrils and ears; her hair, decorated with beads of glass, fell freely onto her shoulders, and I saw that she was not married, because she still wore the necklace of shells that virgins customarily leave on the nuptial bed. The Negress wore European clothing that was almost in tatters.

All three came and sat down by the spring, and the young savage, taking the child in her arms, lavished upon her caresses that one could easily believe dictated by a mother's heart. Meanwhile, the Negress tried to attract the little Creole's attention with a variety of innocent tricks. The child, with her every movement, displayed a sense of superiority that contrasted oddly with her weakness and her age. She seemed somehow to condescend to her companions even as she received their care.

Crouching before her mistress, alert for any indication of her desires, the Negress seemed equally divided between an almost maternal attachment and a servile fear, while even in the effusion of her tenderness the savage woman looked free, proud, and almost fierce.

I moved closer to them to contemplate this spectacle in silence. My curiosity no doubt displeased the Indian, for she abruptly stood, rather roughly pushed the child away, and with an irritated glance in my direction set off into the forest.

There were many occasions when I was able to observe individuals of the three races that populate North America together in the same place. I had already witnessed a thousand different ways in which the preponderance of the Whites manifested itself. But there was something particularly touching in the scene just described: here a bond of affection united the oppressed to the oppressors, and nature, in striving to bring them together, made the vast distance that prejudices and laws had placed between them even more striking.

CURRENT STATE AND PROBABLE FUTURE OF THE INDIAN TRIBES INHABITING THE TERRITORY POSSESSED BY THE UNION

Gradual disappearance of the native races. — How this comes about. — Miseries that accompany the forced migrations of the Indians. — The savages of North America had only two ways of escaping destruction: war or civilization. — They can no longer make war. — Why they did not want to become civilized when they could have done so and are no longer able to do so when they reach the point of wanting to. — Example of the Creeks and Cherokees. — Policy of particular states toward the Indians. — Policy of the federal government.

All the Indian tribes that once lived in New England — the Narragansetts, the Mohicans, and the Pequots — live now only in memory. The Lenapes, who welcomed Penn to the banks of the Delaware a hundred and fifty years ago, are now gone. I have met the last of the Iroquois: they begged for alms. All these nations used to live along the coast. Now one has to travel more than a hundred leagues inland to find an Indian. These savages did not simply retreat; they were destroyed.[2] As the Indians withdrew and died, a vast and steadily growing people came to take their place. Never has such a prodigious development been seen among the nations of the world, nor such a rapid destruction.

It is easy to show how this destruction came about.

When the Indians alone lived in the wilderness from which they have lately been exiled, their needs were few. They fabricated their weapons themselves, drank nothing but river water, and dressed in the hides of the animals whose flesh they ate.

Europeans introduced the natives of North America to firearms, iron, and whiskey. They taught the Indians to adopt our fabrics instead of the barbarous dress that these natives, in their simplicity, had previously been content to wear. The Indians acquired new tastes but not the means of satisfying them, for which they were obliged to turn to the industry of Whites. The savage, in exchange for these goods, which he

---

[2] Only 6,273 Indians remain in the thirteen original states. (See *Legislative Documents*, 20th Congress, no. 117, p. 90.)

lacked the skills to create, had nothing to offer but the rich furs with which his forests still abounded. Henceforth his hunting would not only supply his own needs but also flatter the frivolous passions of Europe. He would hunt the animals of the forest not just to feed himself but also to obtain the only commodities that we would accept in barter.[3]

While the needs of the natives were increasing in this fashion, their resources diminished steadily.

Whenever Europeans settle near Indian territory, any wild game in the vicinity immediately takes fright.[4] Thousands of nomadic savages roving the forests leave these animals unafraid, but let the unremitting din of European industry begin to be heard in a place and they will flee at once to the west, where they know instinctively that boundless wilderness still awaits them. "The herds of buffalo are constantly retreating," Messrs. Cass and Clark said in their report to Congress on February 4, 1829. "A few years ago, they still roamed at the foot of the Alleghenies; some years hence, it may be difficult

[3]Messrs. Clark and Cass, in their report to Congress on February 4, 1829, p. 23, said: "The time is long since past when the Indians could obtain necessary items of food and clothing without recourse to the industry of civilized men. Beyond the Mississippi, in a region where immense herds of buffalo are still to be found, live Indian tribes that follow the migrations of these wild animals. These Indians still find ways to live in conformity with the customs of their forebears, yet the buffalo are constantly receding. Without rifles and traps it is no longer possible to hunt the smaller species of wild animals such as bear, deer, beaver, and muskrat on which the Indians depend for the necessities of life.

"In the northwest primarily, Indians are forced to work excessively hard to feed their families. The hunter often spends several days pursuing his quarry without success. During that time, his family must feed itself on bark or roots, or perish. Many die of hunger every winter."

The Indians do not want to live like Europeans, yet they can neither do without Europeans nor live entirely as their fathers lived. As evidence of this I offer just one anecdote, which I also take from an official source: when some Indians from a tribe inhabiting the shores of Lake Superior killed a European, the American government banned further trade with the tribe until it surrendered the guilty individuals; they were surrendered.

[4]"Five years ago," says Volney in his *Tableau des États-Unis*, p. 370, when traveling from Vincennes to Kaskaskias, through territory now included in the state of Illinois but at that time (1797) entirely wild, "you could not cross the prairies without seeing herds of four to five hundred head of buffalo. Today, none remain. They swam the Mississippi, fleeing not only hunters but above all the bells of American cattle."

to see any on the vast plains that stretch along the Rocky Mountains." I have been assured that this effect of the white man's approach can be felt in many cases two hundred leagues beyond his border. Thus the white man's influence affects tribes whose names he barely knows, tribes that suffer the evils of usurpation long before they become aware of who is responsible for them.[5]

Hardy adventurers soon penetrate into Indian territory. They make forays up to fifteen or twenty leagues beyond the last White outposts, and there they build homes for civilized men in barbarous surroundings. This is easily accomplished: the territorial boundaries of a people of nomadic hunters are ill defined. In any case, the territory belongs to the nation as a whole and is not the property of any specific individual, hence no one has a personal interest in defending any part of it.

A few European families living in widely separated places then succeed in permanently driving all the wild animals out of the intervening region. The Indians, who had previously enjoyed abundance of a kind, find it difficult to survive, and more difficult still to procure the goods they need for barter. Causing their game to flee has the same effect as making fields barren would have on our farmers. These unfortunate people soon find themselves almost entirely deprived of the means of existence, and they take to prowling their depleted forests like famished wolves. Instinctive love of country attaches them to their native soil,[6] where nothing but misery and death awaits. At last they make up their minds to leave, and, trailing far behind the fleeing elk, buffalo, and beaver, they allow these

---

[5]The truth of this assertion can be seen by consulting the comprehensive data on Indians tribes living within the boundaries claimed by the United States. (*Legislative Documents*, 20th Congress, no. 117, pp. 90–105.) This document makes it clear that the tribes in the center of America are dwindling rapidly, even though Europeans are still a long way away.

[6]The Indians, say Messrs. Clark and Cass on p. 15 of their report to Congress, are tied to their country by the same feeling of affection that binds us to ours. What is more, they associate the idea of giving up the land vouchsafed to their ancestors by the Great Spirit with certain superstitious ideas that have great power over tribes that have as yet ceded little or nothing of their territory to the Europeans. "We will not sell the spot which contains the bones of our fathers," is almost always their first answer to anyone who proposes to buy their land.

wild animals to choose their new homeland. Strictly speaking, then, it is not Europeans who are driving out the native Americans; it is famine: this felicitous distinction, unknown to the casuists of old, is a discovery of modern scholars.

It is impossible to imagine the terrible afflictions that accompanied these forced emigrations. By the time the Indians left their paternal lands, they were already exhausted and diminished. The country they hoped to settle in was already occupied by tribes that felt only jealousy toward the new arrivals. Behind them lay hunger, ahead war, and everywhere misery. In the hope of escaping their many enemies, they split up. Each new arrival went off by himself to search stealthily for the means to stay alive, living in the immensity of the wilderness as an outlaw lives in civilized society. The social bond, long since weakened, now broke. Already these migrants had no homeland, and soon they ceased to constitute a people. At most a few families remained. Their common name was lost, their language was forgotten, and every trace of their origin disappeared. The nation ceased to exist. It survives, if at all, in the memory of a few American antiquarians and a handful of European scholars.

Let me assure the reader that the portrait I am painting is by no means exaggerated. I have seen with my own eyes many of the miseries just described. I have contemplated evils beyond my powers to retrace.

Toward the end of 1831, I found myself on the east bank of the Mississippi, at the place the Europeans call Memphis. During the time I was there, a large band of Choctaws arrived (the French of Louisiana call them Choctas). These savages had left their native land and were trying to make their way across to the west bank of the Mississippi, where they hoped to find the refuge promised them by the American government. It was then the heart of winter, and the cold that year was unusually bitter. The snow on the ground had frozen, and enormous chunks of ice floated on the river. The Indians traveled in families. Among them were the wounded and the sick, newborn infants, and dying elders. They had neither tents nor wagons, only scant provisions and some weapons. I watched them embark for the voyage across the great river, and the memory of that solemn spectacle will stay with me forever.

Not a sob or a cry was to be heard despite the large number of people; all were silent. Their misfortunes were old, and they sensed that there was nothing to be done about them. All the Indians had already boarded the vessel that was to carry them across the river. Their dogs had been left behind on the bank. When the animals finally realized that they were to be abandoned for good, they began to emit the most terrifying howls, then leaped into the icy waters of the Mississippi and swam after their masters.

Nowadays the dispossession of the Indians is often accomplished in a routine and — one might say — perfectly legal manner.

When the European population approaches a part of the wilderness occupied by some savage nation, the United States government ordinarily sends a solemn embassy to the tribe. The Whites assemble the Indians in a great plain, and after eating and drinking with them, they say, "What keeps you in the land of your fathers? Soon you will be obliged to dig up their bones to live here. What makes this part of the country better than any other? Are woods, marshes, and prairies to be found only where you live now? Is there no other sun under which you can thrive? Beyond those mountains you see on the horizon, beyond that lake on the western edge of your territory, lie vast regions where wild animals still abound. Sell us your land and find happiness out there." Having made this declaration, they lay before the Indians firearms, wool clothing, kegs of whiskey, glass necklaces, pewter bracelets, earrings, and mirrors.[7] If, after glimpsing all these riches, the

---

[7] See in the *Legislative Documents of Congress*, doc. 117, the account of what happens in these circumstances. This curious passage occurs in the previously cited report by Messrs. Clark and Lewis Cass to Congress on February 4, 1829. Mr. Cass is today Secretary of War.

"When the Indians reach the place where the treaty is to have effect," say Messrs. Clark and Cass, "they are poor and almost naked. There they find a very large number of objects which they consider precious, brought there by American merchants. The women and children, who want their needs met, then begin to importune the men with a thousand demands and use all their influence to see to it that the land is sold. The improvidence of the Indians is habitual and invincible. To gratify immediate needs and present desires is the irresistible passion of the savage: the expectation of future advantages has but a feeble effect on him. He easily forgets the past and does not concern

Indians still hesitate, it is insinuated that the offer that has been made to them is one they cannot refuse and that soon the government itself will be powerless to guarantee the enjoyment of their rights. What can they do? Half-persuaded, half-coerced, the Indians depart for the new wilderness, where they will be lucky if the Whites leave them in peace for ten years. This is how the Americans acquire for next to nothing entire provinces that the wealthiest sovereigns in Europe could not afford to buy.[8]

The evils enumerated above are great, and to me they seem irreparable. I believe that the Indian race in North America is doomed, and I cannot help thinking that by the time Europeans have settled the Pacific coast, it will have ceased to exist.[9]

---

himself with the future. It would be pointless to ask the Indians to cede part of their territory if one were not in a position to satisfy their needs at once. If one considers impartially the situation in which these unfortunate people find themselves, their eagerness to find relief for their woes is not surprising."

[8]On May 19, 1830, Mr. Edward Everett told the House of Representatives that Americans had already acquired by *treaty* some 230,000,000 acres east and west of the Mississippi.

In 1808, the Osages ceded 48,000,000 acres for a rent of $1,000.

In 1818, the Qapaws ceded 20,000,000 acres for $4,000. They reserved a territory of 1,000,000 acres for hunting. A solemn promise was given to respect this reservation, but soon it, too, was invaded.

On February 24, 1830, Mr. Bell, in his report to the Congressional Committee on Indian Affairs, said that "in appropriating wilderness land that the Indians claim to own, we have adopted the custom of paying the Indian tribes what their hunting grounds are worth after the game has fled or been destroyed. It is more advantageous, and certainly more in keeping with the forms of justice and more humane, to act in this way than to lay hold of the savages' territory by means of the sword.

"The practice of buying title to the Indians' land is thus nothing but a new mode of acquisition which humanity and expediency have substituted in place of violence, and which should serve just as well to make us masters of the lands that we claim by virtue of discovery and that is assured us, moreover, by the right of civilized nations to settle territory occupied by savage tribes.

"To date, various causes have steadily diminished the price of the ground that the Indians occupy in their eyes. Hence the practice of purchasing the right of occupancy from the savages has never retarded the prosperity of the United States to any perceptible degree."

[9]I believe that this opinion is shared, moreover, by almost all American statesmen.

"If we judge of the future by the past," Mr. Cass told Congress, "we must

Only two avenues of salvation were open to the Indians of North America: war or civilization. In other words, they had either to destroy the Europeans or to become their equals.

Had all the Indians joined forces at the inception of the colonies, they could have saved themselves from the small number of foreigners recently landed on the shores of the continent.[10] They tried to do so more than once and nearly succeeded. Today the disproportion in resources is too great for them to contemplate such an undertaking. Among the Indians, however, men of genius still arise from time to time, men who foresee the ultimate fate in store for the savage populations and hope to unite all tribes in common hatred of the Europeans; but their efforts come to naught. The tribes that live in proximity to Whites are already too weak to put up effective resistance; the others, giving in to that childish unconcern with the future that is characteristic of the savage, wait for danger to present itself before doing anything about it. The former cannot act; the latter will not.

It is easy to foresee that the Indians will never want to become civilized, or else that, by the time they do want to do so, it will be too late.

Civilization is the result of prolonged social endeavor in a particular place by a succession of generations that bequeath the fruits of their labor from one to the next. It is more difficult for civilization to establish its dominion over hunting peoples than over others. Pastoral tribes move from place to place, but their migrations follow a regular sequence, and they repeatedly travel the same routes. The home of the hunter varies with that of the animals he pursues.

There have been several attempts to bring enlightenment to the Indians without altering their vagabond mores. The

---

anticipate a progressive diminution in the number of Indians, and the eventual extinction of their race. For this not to occur, our borders would have to cease to expand, and the savages would have to settle beyond them, or else there would have to be a complete change in our relations with them, which would be rather unreasonable to expect."

[10]See, for example, the war launched against the settlers of New England in 1675 by the Wampanoags and other confederated tribes under the leadership of Metacom, as well as the attacks that the English in Virginia were obliged to endure in 1622.

Jesuits tried it in Canada, the Puritans in New England.[11] Neither achieved any lasting result. Civilization was born in the hut and went to die in the woods. The great mistake of those who made laws for the Indians was their failure to understand that in order to civilize a people, one must first persuade them to settle in one place, and this cannot happen unless they cultivate the soil. Hence the first challenge was to turn the Indians into farmers.

Not only do the Indians fail to possess this indispensable prerequisite of civilization, but it is very difficult for them to acquire it.

Men who have tasted the idle and adventurous life of the hunter feel an almost insurmountable distaste for the constant, disciplined labor required by agriculture. One sees this even in our own societies, but it is far more visible in places where the habits of the hunt have become national customs.

Independent of this general cause is another cause no less powerful that one finds at work only among the Indians. I mentioned it earlier but feel that I must come back to it now.

The Indians of North America view labor as not only an evil but also a disgrace, and their pride combats civilization almost as obstinately as their indolence.[12]

There is no Indian so miserable in his hut of bark that he does not entertain an overweening idea of his individual worth. He regards the chores of industry as degrading occupations. He likens the farmer to the ox hitched to its plow and in our arts sees nothing but the labor of slaves. Not that he lacks a high opinion of the power and intelligence of Whites, but while he admires the results of our efforts, he is contemptuous of the means by which we obtained them, and even as he submits to our ascendancy, he still thinks of himself as

[11]See the various historians of New England. See also *Histoire de la Nouvelle-France* by Charlevoix and *Lettres édifiantes*.

[12]"In all the tribes," says Volney in his *Tableau des Etats-Unis*, p. 423, "there is still a generation of old warriors, who, if they see anyone using a hoe, cannot refrain from denouncing the degradation of ancient mores and who insist that the decadence of the savages is due solely to these innovations and that in order to regain their glory and power they have only to return to their primitive mores."

superior. Hunting and warfare seem to him the only pursuits worthy of a man.[13] The Indian, in the depths of his sylvan misery, thus nurses the same ideas and the same opinions as the medieval nobleman in his fortified castle, and all he needs to end up resembling him is to become a conqueror. Indeed, it is remarkable that the old prejudices of Europe are found today in the forests of the New World rather than among the Europeans who inhabit its shores.

More than once in the course of this book I have sought to explain the prodigious influence that the social state seems to me to exert on the laws and mores of men. Let me add one additional comment on this subject.

When I note the resemblance between the political institutions of our ancestors, the Germanic tribes, and those of the roving tribes of North America, between the customs described by Tacitus and those that I was able to witness from time to time, I cannot help thinking that the same cause produced the same effects in both hemispheres and that in the midst of the apparent diversity of human things it is not impossible to find a small number of basic facts from which all others derive. In what we call Germanic institutions, therefore, I am tempted to see nothing other than barbarian habits, just as I am tempted to see the opinions of savages in what we call feudal ideas.

Whatever vices and prejudices may be preventing the Indians of North America from becoming civilized farmers, necessity sometimes drives them to it.

---

[13]An official document contains the following portrait:

"Until a young man has been in contact with the enemy and can boast of his prowess, he is held in no esteem and is regarded almost as a woman.

"In their great war dances, the warriors come one after another to strike the 'post,' as they call it, and recount their exploits. The audience for this occasion consists of relatives, friends, and companions of the narrator. The deep impression that his words make on them is obvious from the silence with which they listen and the loud applause that greets the end of his stories. A young man who has no story to tell on such occasions regards himself as unfortunate indeed, and it is not unknown for young warriors whose passions have been aroused to depart suddenly from these dances and to go alone in search of trophies to exhibit and adventures of which they may boast."

Several substantial nations of the South, including the Cherokees and the Creeks,[14] found themselves surrounded by Europeans who arrived in their vicinity simultaneously after landing on the Atlantic coast, descending the Ohio, or making their way up the Mississippi. Unlike the northern tribes, these Indians were not driven from pillar to post but gradually confined to a space that was too small for them, as hunters will first surround a part of the forest before plunging into it all at once. The Indians, caught at that point between civilization and death, were thus reduced to the shameful condition of living, like the white man, by their labor. They therefore became farmers and, without giving up their habits or mores entirely, sacrificed what was absolutely necessary in order to exist.

The Cherokees went further. They created a written language and established a fairly stable form of government. And since everything moves quickly in the New World, they had a newspaper[15] before all of them had clothes.

The development of European habits among the Indians was greatly encouraged by the presence of persons of mixed race.[16] The half-caste, by sharing his father's enlightenment without entirely forsaking the savage customs of his maternal ancestors, becomes a natural link between civilization and bar-

[14]These nations are today confined to the states of Georgia, Tennessee, Alabama, and Mississippi.

There were once four great nations in the South (remnants of which can still be seen): the Choctaws, the Chickasaws, the Creeks, and the Cherokees.

In 1830 the remnants of these nations still numbered about 75,000. It is estimated that roughly 300,000 Indians still live in territory occupied or claimed by the Anglo-American Union (see *Proceedings of the Indian Board of the City of New York*). Official documents provided to Congress put the number at 313,130. Readers curious to know the names and sizes of all the tribes living in Anglo-American territory should consult the documents I cited above. (*Legislative Documents*, 20th Congress, no. 117, pp. 90–105.)

[15]I brought one or two copies of this peculiar publication back to France with me.

[16]See the report of the Committee on Indian Affairs, 21st Congress, no. 227, p. 23, for a discussion of why individuals of mixed race multiplied among the Cherokees. The principal cause goes back to the Revolutionary War. Because many of the Anglo-Americans in Georgia took England's side in the war, they were obliged to hide out among the Indians, with whom they intermarried.

barity. Wherever individuals of mixed race have multiplied, one finds savages gradually modifying their social state and changing their mores.[17]

The success of the Cherokees proves that the Indians have the ability to become civilized, but it does not prove that they can succeed in that condition.

The difficulty Indians have in submitting to civilization stems from a general cause almost impossible for them to overcome.

Careful study of history shows that, in general, barbarian peoples have gradually raised themselves to civilization by their own efforts.

In cases where they drew enlightenment from a foreign nation, they occupied the rank of conquerors and were not in the position of a vanquished people.

When the conquered people is enlightened and the conquering people half-savage, as in the invasion of the Roman Empire by the nations of the north or of China by the Mongols, the power that victory secured for the barbarian was enough to place him on a par with the civilized man and enable

---

[17]Unfortunately, the number of half-castes in North America was smaller than anywhere else, and their influence was less extensive.

Two great European nations populated this part of the American continent: the French and the English.

The former were not slow to form unions with the daughters of natives, but unfortunately there was a secret affinity between the Indian character and the French. Instead of imparting the tastes and habits of civilized life to the barbarians, the French often developed a passionate attachment to the savage life: they became the most dangerous denizens of the wild and gained the Indian's friendship by exaggerating his vices and virtues. M. de Sénonville, governor of Canada, wrote to Louis XIV in 1685: "It was long believed that we should draw the savages to us in order to make them French. There is every reason to believe that this was a mistake. Those who have come to us have not become French, and the Frenchmen who frequented them have become savages. They affect to dress like them and to live like them." (*Histoire de la Nouvelle-France* by Charlevoix, vol. 2, p. 345.)

By contrast, the Englishman, by stubbornly clinging to the opinions, customs, and most insignificant habits of his forefathers, remained in the solitudes of America what he had been in the cities of Europe. Hence he had no desire to make contact with savages whom he held in contempt and carefully avoided mixing his blood with the blood of barbarians.

Thus, while the Frenchman had no salutary influence on the Indians, the Englishman was always a stranger to them.

the former to march as the latter's equal and, later, his emu-
lator. One has force, the other intelligence; the former admires the sciences and arts of the conquered; the latter envies
the power of the conquerors. Eventually the barbarians bring
the civilized man into their palaces, and the civilized man
opens his schools to the barbarians. But when those who possess physical force also enjoy intellectual superiority, the vanquished rarely become civilized. They either retreat or are
destroyed.

So one can say in a general way that savages go, arms in
hand, in search of enlightenment but will not accept it as
a gift.

If the Indian tribes now living in the center of the continent could summon up enough energy to attempt to civilize
themselves, they might succeed. Superior to the barbarian nations around them, they could then gradually acquire both
strength and experience, and if and when Europeans finally
appeared on their borders, they would be in a position, if not
to maintain their independence, then at least to insist on their
land rights and to be assimilated by their conquerors. It has
been the misfortune of the Indians, however, to come into
contact with the most civilized — and, I would add, the
greediest — people on earth at a time when they themselves
are still half-barbarous; to have masters for their teachers; and
to receive oppression together with enlightenment.

Living in sylvan freedom, the North American Indian is miserable but feels inferior to no one. Once he makes up his mind
to join the social hierarchy of the Whites, however, he cannot
aspire to anything above the lowest rank, for he arrives ignorant and poor in a society where knowledge and wealth reign
supreme. Having led an active life marked by suffering and
danger but at the same time rich in feeling and grandeur,[18] he

[18]In the adventurous life of hunting peoples there is something that the
heart finds irresistible, something that outweighs reason and experience and
carries man away in spite of himself. Anyone who has read Tanner's memoirs
will be convinced of this.

Tanner is a European who was kidnapped by Indians at the age of six and
who lived with them in the woods for thirty years. Nothing could be more
terrible than the miseries he describes. He shows us tribes without chiefs,
families without nations, isolated men, battered remnants of once-powerful

is obliged to submit to a monotonous, obscure, and degraded existence. To earn his daily bread by hard, ignoble labor — that, in his eyes, is the only result of this vaunted civilization. And even that result he is not always sure of obtaining.

When the Indians set out to imitate their European neighbors and farm the land as Whites do, they immediately become vulnerable to calamitous competition. The white man has mastered the secrets of agriculture. The Indian is a clumsy novice practicing an art he has never been taught. The one easily reaps huge harvests, while the other wrests fruits from the earth only with the greatest of difficulty.

The European lives among people whose needs he knows and shares.

The savage is isolated amidst a hostile people with whose mores, language, and laws he is not completely familiar, but whom he cannot do without. He can prosper only by trading his products for those of the white man, because his compatriots are no longer of much help to him.

---

tribes wandering aimlessly through the frozen wastes of Canada, pursued by hunger and cold. Every day seemed likely to be their last. Their mores and traditions lost all power over them, and they became increasingly barbarous. Tanner shared all these afflictions. Aware of his European origins, he was not kept away from Whites by force. On the contrary, he engaged in trade with them year after year, visited their homes, and saw their comfort. He knew that if he wished to return to civilized life, he could do so easily, yet he remained in the wilderness for thirty years. When he did at last return to civilized society, he confessed that the life whose miseries he described still held an indefinable charm for him. He returned to it repeatedly and could not tear himself away from its many afflictions without countless regrets. And when he finally settled among the Whites, several of his children refused to share his tranquillity and comfort.

I myself met Tanner at the eastern end of Lake Superior. He looked to me far more like a savage than like a civilized man.

Although Tanner's work exhibits neither system nor taste, the author does offer a vivid if unwitting portrait of the prejudices, passions, vices, and above all miseries of the people among whom he lived.

Vicomte Ernest de Blosseville, the author of an excellent work on England's penal colonies, has translated Tanner's memoirs. Along with his translation he has provided some very interesting notes, which allow the reader to compare the facts related by Tanner with the reports of a great many ancient and modern observers.

Anyone who wishes to learn about the present state of the Indians of North America and to predict their fate should consult M. de Blosseville's book.

Thus when the Indian wants to sell the fruits of his labors, he cannot always find a buyer, though the European farmer finds one easily, and what the European can deliver at a low price the native can produce only at high cost.

The Indian has therefore escaped the afflictions to which barbarous nations are exposed only to subject himself to the worst miseries of civilized peoples, and he finds it almost as difficult to live amid our abundance as surrounded by his forests.

Nevertheless, the habits of the wandering life have not been destroyed in him. Traditions have not lost their hold over him. His taste for hunting has not been extinguished. In his troubled imagination the savage joys he used to feel in the depths of the forest are painted in ever more vivid colors. By contrast, the privations he endured there seem less terrifying; the perils he faced seem less great. The independence that he enjoyed among his equals contrasts with the servile position he occupies in civilized society.

Meanwhile, the solitude in which he lived free for so long is still at hand: a few hours' march will suffice to take him there. For the half-cleared field that yields barely enough to feed him, his neighbor the white man is prepared to offer what seems to him a high price. Perhaps the money that Europeans are willing to pay him will enable him to live a happy, quiet life far from their presence. He abandons his plow, takes up his arms once more, and returns to the wilderness for good.[19]

[19]The destructive influence that very civilized peoples exert on those who are less civilized can be observed among the Europeans themselves.

Nearly a century ago, some Frenchmen founded the city of Vincennes on the Wabash in the middle of the wilderness. There they lived in great abundance until American immigrants arrived. The newcomers immediately began to ruin the earlier inhabitants through competition; then they bought their lands at low prices. At the time that M. de Volney, from whom I have borrowed this detail, visited Vincennes, the number of French residences had been reduced to about a hundred, most of whom were preparing to move to Louisiana or Canada. These Frenchmen were respectable but unenlightened and unindustrious people. They had acquired some of the habits of savages. The Americans, who may have been inferior to them from a moral standpoint, enjoyed an immense intellectual superiority over them: they were industrious, educated, wealthy, and accustomed to governing themselves.

In Canada, where the intellectual difference between the two races is much less pronounced, I myself have seen the English, who control commerce and

The accuracy of this depressing portrait can be judged by what is happening to the Creeks and Cherokees, whom I mentioned earlier.

In what little these Indians have accomplished, they have surely demonstrated as much natural genius as the peoples of Europe in their more ambitious enterprises. But nations, like men, need time to learn, however intelligent and industrious they may be.

While these savages worked to civilize themselves, the Europeans continued to envelop them and confine them within ever narrower limits. Today the two races have finally met; they have made contact. The Indian has already become superior to his father the savage, but he is still greatly inferior to his neighbor the white man. The Europeans, with the aid of their resources and their enlightenment, were not slow to appropriate most of the advantages that possession of the land might have provided the natives. They settled among the Indians, seized the land or bought it very cheaply, and ruined the natives through competition that the latter were utterly unable to withstand. Isolated in their own country, the Indians were reduced to a small colony of unwanted aliens in the midst of a numerous and dominating people.[20]

Washington, in one of his messages to Congress, said: "We are more enlightened and more powerful than the Indian

---

industry in Canadian territory, extend their dominion in every direction, restricting the French to very narrow limits.

Similarly, in Louisiana, nearly all commercial and industrial activity is concentrated in the hands of Anglo-Americans.

Something even more striking is going on in the province of Texas. The state of Texas is of course part of Mexico and is situated on that country's border with the United States. For some years now, Anglo-Americans have been individually entering this still sparsely populated province, buying land, taking control of industry, and rapidly supplanting the original population. It is clear that if Mexico does not soon put a halt to this process, it will lose control of Texas in short order.

If relatively minor differences in European civilization can lead to such results, it is easy to understand what inevitably takes place when the most highly perfected civilization in Europe comes into contact with Indian barbarity.

[20]See Legislative Documents, 21st Congress, no. 89, for excesses of all kinds committed by the white population in Indian territory. In some cases Anglo-Americans settled on Indian territory, as if land were in short supply elsewhere, and Congress had to send troops to expel them. In other cases they

nations. It is for us a matter of honor to treat them with kindness and even generosity."

This noble and virtuous policy has not been adhered to.

The greed of the colonists is regularly compounded by the
tyranny of the government. Although the Cherokees and
Creeks settled on land they inhabited before the arrival of
Europeans, and Americans often treated with them as with
foreign nations, the states in which they were living did not
want to recognize them as independent peoples and attempted
instead to make men who had only just emerged from the
forest subject to their magistrates, customs, and laws.[21] Misery
had driven these unfortunate Indians toward civilization; oppression is today driving them back to barbarity. Many are
abandoning their half-cleared fields and returning to their
savage ways.

If one carefully examines the tyrannical measures adopted
by the legislatures of the southern states, the behavior of their
governors, and the decisions of their courts, it is easy to see
that the ultimate goal of all their efforts is the complete ex-

---

stole the natives' livestock, burned down their houses, harvested their fruit,
or committed acts of violence against their persons.

All this evidence proves that natives are every day victims of the abuse of
force. The Union ordinarily maintains an agent among the Indians charged
with representing them. The report of the Cherokees' agent is included
among the documents I cited: this official's statements are almost always favorable to the savages. "The intrusion of Whites into the territory of the
Cherokees," he says on p. 12, "will lead to the ruin of the people who live
there and lead poor and inoffensive lives." Later we learn that the state of
Georgia, in order to shrink the Cherokees' territory still further, has begun
to put up boundary markers. The federal agent points out that because these
markers are set by Whites without any opportunity for the natives to challenge their location, they are worthless.

[21] In 1829, the state of Alabama divided the territory of the Creeks into
counties and subjected the Indian population to European magistrates.

In 1830, the state of Mississippi assimilated the Choctaws and Chickasaws
to Whites and declared that any of them who took the title "chief" would be
punished by a fine of $1,000 and a year in prison.

When the state of Mississippi thus extended its laws to the Choctaw Indians living within its borders, the Indians gathered. Their chief informed them
of what the Whites had done and read some of the laws to which they were
now supposed to submit. The savages unanimously decided that it would be
better to withdraw deeper into the wilderness. (*Mississippi papers.*)

pulsion of the Indians. The Americans who live in this part of the Union covet the natives' lands.[22] They sense that the Indians have not yet fully abandoned the traditions of savage life, and before civilization attaches them firmly to the land, they seek to reduce them to despair and force them to withdraw.

Oppressed by particular states, the Creeks and Cherokees turned to the central government. That government was not insensitive to their suffering and sincerely wished to save the remnants of the native tribes and ensure their free title to the territory that it had itself guaranteed.[23] But when it sought to carry out this plan, the particular states put up formidable resistance, whereupon the central government, rather than endanger the American Union, resolved without difficulty to allow these already half-destroyed savage tribes to perish.

Though powerless to protect the Indians, the federal government nevertheless wished to mitigate their fate. To that end, it undertook to pay the cost of transporting them to other locations.

Between 33 and 37 degrees north latitude extends a vast territory that has taken the name Arkansas from the principal river that runs through it. It stretches from the border with Mexico to the banks of the Mississippi. A host of streams and rivers flow through it in many directions; the climate is mild and the land fertile. A few bands of roving savages are the only inhabitants. The government of the Union proposed to transport the remnants of the indigenous populations of the South to the portion of this territory closest to Mexico, far from any American settlements.

At the end of 1831 we were assured that 10,000 Indians had already been settled on the banks of the Arkansas; others were

[22]Georgians, who find the proximity of the Indians such an inconvenience, occupy a territory that still counts fewer than seven inhabitants per square mile. In France, 162 individuals inhabit the same space.

[23]In 1818, Congress ordered that the Arkansas territory should be visited by American commissioners accompanied by a deputation of Creeks, Choctaws, and Chickasaws. This expedition was commanded by Messrs. Kennerly, McCoy, Wash Hood, and John Bell. See the various reports of the commissioners and their journal in the papers of Congress, no. 87, *House of Representatives*.

arriving daily. But Congress has yet to create consensus among those whose future it seeks to decide: some gladly consent to move far from the focus of tyranny; the most enlightened refuse to abandon their incipient harvests and new homes; they believe that if the work of civilization is interrupted, it will not be resumed; they fear that sedentary ways, recently adopted, may be irretrievably lost in still savage regions where nothing has been made ready for the subsistence of a farming people; they know that they will find enemy hordes in this new wilderness and that, to resist them, they no longer have the energy of barbarity but have yet to acquire the strengths of civilization. The Indians, moreover, are quick to divine all that is provisional about the settlement that has been proposed to them. Who will assure them that they may at last rest in peace in their new asylum? The United States pledges to keep them there, but the territory they now occupy had previously been guaranteed by the most solemn of oaths.[24] To be sure, the American government is not taking their land from them today, but it is allowing that land to be invaded. Within a few years, the same white population that has lately pressed in on them will likely hound their steps once more into the solitudes of Arkansas. Then they will face the same woes but without the same remedies. Sooner or later they will want for land, and they will again have to resign themselves to death.

There is less cupidity and violence in the Union's actions with respect to the Indians than in the policies adopted by the states, but in both cases there is the same absence of good faith.

The states, in extending what they call the benefits of their laws to the Indians, reckon that the Indians would rather depart than submit. And the central government, in prom-

---

[24]The 1790 treaty with the Creeks contains the following clause: "The United States solemnly guarantees to the Creek nation all lands that it possesses within the territory of the Union."

The treaty concluded with the Cherokees in July 1791 contains the following: "The United States solemnly guarantees to the Cherokee nation all land not previously ceded. If any citizen of the United States or anyone other than an Indian should settle in any of the Cherokee territories, the United States declares that it will withdraw its protection from that citizen and deliver him to the Cherokee nation, which may punish him as it sees fit." Art. 8

ising these unfortunates a permanent asylum in the West, is well aware that it cannot guarantee any such thing.[25]

Thus the states, with their tyranny, force the savages to flee; the Union, with its promises and the aid of its resources, facilitates their flight. The measures are different, but they tend toward the same goal.[26]

"By the will of our heavenly Father who rules the Universe," said the Cherokees in their petition to Congress,[27] "the race of red men in America has become small; the white race has become great and renowned."

"When your ancestors arrived on our shores, the red man was strong, and although he was ignorant and savage, he received them with kindness and allowed them to rest their weary feet on dry land. Our fathers and yours shook hands as a sign of friendship and lived in peace.

"Whatever the white man required to satisfy his needs, the Indian made haste to give him. The Indian was then the master, and the white man the supplicant. Today the scene has changed: the red man's strength has become weakness. As his neighbors grew in number, his power diminished more and more. And now, of the many powerful tribes that once covered the surface of what you call the United States, only a few remain, spared from the universal

---

[25]This does not prevent the government from making its promises in the most formal terms. See the letter from the president to the Creeks dated March 23, 1829 (*Proceedings of the Indian Board in the City of New York*, p. 5): "Beyond the great river (the Mississippi), your Father," he said, "has prepared a vast country to receive you. There your brothers the Whites will not trouble you. They will have no right to your lands. You and your children will be able to live there in peace and prosperity as long as the grass shall grow and the rivers flow. They will *belong to you forever*."

The Secretary of War, in a letter to the Cherokees dated April 18, 1829, states that they must abandon hope of retaining the territory they presently occupy, but he offers them the same positive assurance once they have crossed the Mississippi (*ibid.*, p. 6), as if he will then have the power he now lacks!

[26]To form an accurate idea of the policies of the individual states and the Union toward the Indians, one must consult: 1) the laws of the individual states pertaining to the Indians (contained in Legislative Documents, 21st Congress, no. 319); 2) the laws of the Union concerning the same, and in particular that of March 30, 1802 (these laws can be found in the work of Mr. Story entitled *Laws of the United States*), and finally, 3) to learn about the current state of relations between the Union and the various Indian tribes, see the report by Mr. Cass, Secretary of War, dated November 29, 1823.

[27]November 19, 1829. This passage is translated literally.

disaster. The tribes of the North, once renowned for their power, have already almost disappeared. Such has been the destiny of the red man in America.

"Here we are, the last of our race. Must we too die?

"Long ago, before anyone remembers, our common Father, who art in heaven, gave our ancestors the land that we occupy. Our ancestors passed it on to us as their legacy. We have preserved it with respect, for it contains their ashes. Did we ever surrender or lose that legacy? Allow us humbly to ask you what better right a people can have to a country than the right of inheritance and immemorial possession? We know that the State of Georgia and the president of the United States are today claiming that we have lost that right. But this allegation seems to us unwarranted. When are we supposed to have lost it? What crime did we commit to deprive us of our fatherland? Are we reproached for having fought under the flag of the king of Great Britain during the War for Independence? If that is the crime being invoked, why, in the first treaty following that war, did you not declare that we had lost ownership of our lands? Why did you not insert into that treaty an article such as the following: 'The United States wishes to grant peace to the Cherokee nation, but to punish it for having taken part in the war, it is hereby declared that the Cherokees shall henceforth be considered as mere tenants on the land and shall be subject to eviction as neighboring states may require.' That was the moment to speak in such terms. To no one did it occur to speak thus, however, and our ancestors would never have consented to a treaty whose effect would have been to deprive them of their most sacred rights and of their country."

Such is the language of the Indians. What they say is true; what they foresee seems to me inevitable.

From whatever angle one views the destiny of the natives of North America, one sees only irremediable afflictions. If they remain savages, they will be driven out as others advance. If they wish to become civilized, contact with more civilized people subjects them to oppression and misery. If they continue to wander from wilderness to wilderness, they will perish. If they try to settle in one place, they will also perish. They can gain enlightenment only with the help of Europeans, and the approach of Europeans corrupts them and drives them back into barbarism. So long as they are left alone in their solitudes, they refuse to change their mores; when they are finally obliged to do so, it is too late.

The Spaniards loosed their dogs on the Indians as though the natives were ferocious beasts. They pillaged the New World as if storming a city, indiscriminately and mercilessly. But to destroy everything is impossible, and frenzy has a limit: the remnants of the Indian population, having escaped the massacres, eventually mixed with the conquerors and adopted their religion and mores.[28]

By contrast, the conduct of the Americans of the United States toward the Indians exhibits the purest love of formalities and legalities. Provided that the Indians remain in the savage state, the Americans do not interfere in their affairs and treat them as independent peoples. They will not occupy Indian land until it has been duly acquired by contract. And if by chance an Indian nation can no longer live within its territory, the Americans offer a fraternal hand and lead the natives off to die somewhere other than in the land of their fathers.

The Spaniards, despite acts of unparalleled monstrousness that left them indelibly covered with shame, were unable to exterminate the Indian race or even prevent the Indians from sharing their rights. The Americans of the United States achieved both results with marvelous ease, quietly, legally, philanthropically, without bloodshed, without violating a single one of the great principles of morality[29] in the eyes of the world. To destroy human beings with greater respect for the laws of humanity would be impossible.

[28]The Spaniards, moreover, deserve no credit for this result. If the Indian tribes had not already been attached to the soil by agriculture when the Europeans arrived, they would no doubt have been destroyed in South America as they were in North America.

[29]See, for example, the report by Mr. Bell on behalf of the Committee on Indian Affairs, February 24, 1830, p. 5, where it is established by very logical argument and learned proof that "the fundamental principle that the Indians had no right by virtue of their ancient possession either of soil or sovereignty has never been abandoned expressly or by implication."

Reading this report, which, incidentally, is written by a clever man, one is astonished by the facility and ease with which the author, from his very first words, disposes of arguments based on natural right and reason, which he calls abstract and theoretical principles. The more I reflect on this, the more I think that the only difference between the civilized man and the uncivilized man with respect to justice is that the former contests the justice of rights, while the latter is content simply to violate them.

SITUATION OF THE BLACK RACE
IN THE UNITED STATES;[30]
DANGERS TO WHITES CREATED
BY ITS PRESENCE

Why it is more difficult for the Moderns to abolish slavery and eliminate its traces than it was for the Ancients. — In the United States, the prejudice of Whites against Blacks seems to grow stronger as slavery is destroyed. — Situation of the Negroes in the states of the North and South. — Why the Americans are abolishing slavery. — Servitude, which brutalizes the slave, impoverishes the master. — Differences between the north and south banks of the Ohio River. — To what these differences must be attributed. — The black race is concentrated in the South, as is slavery. — What explains this. — Difficulties faced by the southern states in abolishing slavery. — Dangers that lie ahead. — People's concerns. — Founding of a black colony in Africa. — Why the Americans of the South, though disgusted by slavery, are intensifying its hardships.

The Indians will die as they lived, in isolation, but the fate of the Negro is in a way bound up with that of the European. The two races are linked but have not therefore combined. It is as difficult for them to separate completely as to unite.

The most redoubtable of all the ills that threaten the future of the United States stems from the presence of Blacks on its soil. In seeking the cause of the Union's present difficulties and future dangers, one almost invariably arrives at this primary fact no matter where one starts.

[30]Before dealing with this subject, I want to call the reader's attention to a book I mentioned in the introduction to this work, which is soon to appear. In it, my traveling companion, M. Gustave de Beaumont, seeks primarily to make French readers aware of the situation of Negroes vis-à-vis the white population in the United States. M. de Beaumont goes into depth about an issue that my subject allows me only to touch on.

His book, the notes to which contain a substantial number of quite valuable and previously unknown legislative and historical documents, paints a picture so vivid that it can only be rivaled by the truth. M. Beaumont's work should be read by anyone interested in knowing the tyrannical excesses to which men may gradually be impelled once they begin to forsake nature and humanity.

In general, man can create lasting ills only through strenuous and unrelenting effort. But there is one evil that makes its way into the world surreptitiously: at first it is barely noticed among the ordinary abuses of power. It begins with an individual whose name history does not bother to record. Like an accursed seed it is planted somewhere in the soil. Thereafter it feeds on itself, spreads easily, and grows naturally with the society that accepted it: that evil is slavery.

Christianity had destroyed servitude; the Christians of the sixteenth century reinstated it. They never accepted it, however, as anything other than an exception to their social system, and they were careful to restrict it to only one of the races of man. Hence the wound they inflicted on humanity was not as large as it might have been, but infinitely more difficult to heal.

It is important to distinguish carefully between slavery in itself and the consequences of slavery.

The immediate ills resulting from slavery were almost the same among the Ancients as among the Moderns, but the consequences were different. Among the Ancients, the slave belonged to the same race as his master and was often superior to him in education and enlightenment.[31] Only freedom separated one from the other; freedom granted, they easily combined.

The Ancients therefore had a very simple way of delivering themselves from slavery and its consequences, namely, emancipation. When they made general application of this method, success was immediate.

That is not to say that the traces of servitude did not persist in Antiquity for some time after servitude was destroyed.

There is a natural prejudice that leads a man to scorn a person who has been his inferior long after that person has become his equal. The real inequality resulting from fortune or law is always replaced by an imaginary inequality rooted in mores. Among the Ancients, however, this secondary effect of

---

[31]As is well known, several of Antiquity's most celebrated authors were or had been slaves: Aesop and Terence were among them. Not all slaves were captives from barbarian nations: war subjected very civilized men to servitude.

slavery was of limited duration. The freedman so nearly resembled the freeborn that it soon became impossible to tell
the former apart from the latter.

What was most difficult for the Ancients was to change the
law. For the Moderns, it is to change mores, and for us the
real difficulty begins where Antiquity's ended.

This stems from the fact that for the Moderns, the immaterial and transitory fact of slavery combines in the most disastrous way with the material and permanent fact of racial
difference. The memory of slavery dishonors the race, and race
perpetuates the memory of slavery.

No African came in freedom to the shores of the New World.
From this it follows that all who now reside there are either
slaves or freedmen. Thus the Negro passes on the outward sign
of his ignominy to all his descendants at birth. The law may destroy servitude, but only God can obliterate its trace.

The modern slave differs from his master not only with respect to freedom but also with respect to origins. You can
make the Negro free, but you cannot make him anything
other than an alien vis-à-vis the European.

That is not all: this man, who was born in degradation, this
alien placed in our midst by servitude — we scarcely recognize him as possessing the common features of humanity. To
us his visage seems hideous, his intelligence limited, his tastes
base; we come close to regarding him as something intermediate between brute and man.[32]

After the Moderns abolish slavery, they must still destroy
three prejudices that are far more intangible and tenacious:
the prejudice of the master, the prejudice of race, and the prejudice of the white man.

To those of us fortunate enough to have been born among
men made similar to us by nature and equal to us by law, it is
very difficult to understand the unbreachable abyss that separates the American Negro from the European, but we can
form a remote idea of it if we reason by analogy.

In the past there existed among us great inequalities whose

---

[32] If Whites are to give up their belief in the intellectual and moral inferiority of their former slaves, the Negroes must change, but they cannot change
so long as this belief persists.

origins lay solely in legislation. What could be more facti-
tious than a purely legal inferiority! What more contrary to
man's instincts than permanent differences established between obviously similar people! Yet these differences per-
sisted for centuries. In many places they persist to this day.
Everywhere they have left traces which, though they exist
only in the mind, time is hardly able to efface. If inequality
created solely by the law is so difficult to eradicate, how can
one destroy an inequality that seems to possess an immutable
basis in nature itself?

As for me, when I consider how difficult it is for an aristocratic body of any kind to merge with the mass of the people,
and the extreme care that such bodies take to preserve for centuries the artificial barriers that separate them from that mass,
I despair of seeing the disappearance of an aristocracy
founded on visible and imperishable signs.

Hence, to my mind, those who hope that the Negroes will
one day blend in with the Europeans are nursing a chimera.
Reason does not persuade me that this will ever come to pass,
and I see no evidence for it in the facts.

Wherever Whites have been more powerful to date, they
have kept Negroes in degradation or slavery. Wherever Negroes have been stronger, they have destroyed Whites. Such
is the only reckoning that exists between the two races.

When I look at the United States today, it is clear that in one
part of the country the legal barrier between the two races is
tending to decrease, but not the barrier of mores. Slavery is receding; the prejudice to which it gave rise remains unaltered.

Have Negroes drawn closer to Whites in the portion of the
Union where they are no longer slaves? Anyone who has lived
in the United States will have noticed that the opposite has
occurred.

Racial prejudice seems to me stronger in the states that have
abolished slavery than in those where slavery still exists, and
nowhere is intolerance greater than in states where servitude
was unknown.

To be sure, marriage between Negroes and Whites is lawful
in the North, but public opinion would brand the white man
who married a Negress with a mark of infamy, and it would
be very difficult to cite a single instance of such a union.

In nearly all the states that have abolished slavery, voting rights have been granted to the Negro, but if he goes to the polls, he puts his life at risk. He can complain that he is oppressed, but all his judges will be white. The law grants him access to the jury box, but prejudice keeps him out. His son is excluded from the school where the child of European ancestry goes to study. No amount of money can buy him the right to sit next to his former master in a theater. In the hospital he lies apart. The Black is permitted to implore the same God as the Whites but not to pray at the same altar. He has his own priests and his own temples. The gates of Heaven are not closed to him, but it is scarcely as if inequality ends where the other world begins. When the Negro is no more, his bones are tossed aside, and the difference in his condition manifests itself even in the equality of death.

Thus the Negro is free, but he cannot share the rights, pleasures, labors, or sorrows — not even the tomb — of the person whose equal he has been declared to be. There is no place where the two can come together, whether in life or death.

In the South, where slavery still exists, less care is taken to keep the Negro apart. Negroes sometimes work alongside Whites and share their pleasures. Up to a point Whites are willing to mix with them. Legislation is harsher toward them; habits are milder and more tolerant.

In the South, the master is not afraid to raise the slave to his own level, because he knows that whenever he wishes he can cast him back down into the dust. In the North, the White no longer clearly perceives the barrier that is supposed to separate him from this debased race, and he shuns the Negro all the more assiduously for fear that he might one day become indistinguishable from him.

In Americans of the South, nature, reasserting its rights from time to time, does momentarily restore equality between Whites and Blacks. In the North, pride silences even the most imperious of man's passions. The American of the North might perhaps consent to make the Negress the fleeting companion of his pleasures if lawmakers had barred her from aspiring to share his bed; but she can become his wife, and he shuns her with a kind of horror.

Thus in the United States, the prejudice against Negroes seems to increase in proportion to their emancipation, and inequality is enshrined in mores as it disappears from laws.

But if the relative position of the two races that live in the United States is as I have just described it, why did the Americans abolish slavery in the North and why have they kept it and increased its hardships in the South?

The answer is easy. Slavery is being abolished in the United States not in the interest of the Negro but in that of the white man.

The first Negroes were imported into Virginia around 1621.[33] In America as in the rest of the world, servitude was therefore born in the South. From there it spread gradually, but as slavery moved northward, the number of slaves tended to diminish.[34] There have always been very few Negroes in New England.

The colonies were founded; a century had already elapsed when everyone began to be struck by an extraordinary fact. In provinces where people owned virtually no slaves, population, wealth, and prosperity were increasing more rapidly than in provinces where people did own slaves.

In the former, however, residents were obliged to cultivate the soil themselves or else to hire the services of others. In the latter, they could avail themselves of the services of workers who were not compensated for their efforts. Thus, labor and

[33]See Beverley's *History of Virginia*. See also Jefferson's memoirs for interesting details about the introduction of Negroes into Virginia and the first act prohibiting importation in 1778.

[34]The number of slaves in the North was smaller, but the advantages of slavery were not disputed there any more than in the South. In 1740, the New York state legislature declared that direct importation of slaves ought to be encouraged as much as possible and that smuggling ought to be punished severely as it tended to discourage honest traders. (*Kent's Commentaries*, vol. 2, p. 206.)

The Historical Collection of Massachusetts, vol. 4, p. 193, contains Belknap's interesting investigations of slavery in New England. From this it emerges that Negroes were introduced as early as 1630, but legislation and mores have manifested opposition to slavery from that time forward.

The same source also shows how public opinion and, later, law succeeded in putting an end to servitude.

expense on the one hand, leisure and economy on the other: yet the advantage lay with the former.

This result was difficult to explain, all the more so in that the immigrants, all belonging to the same European race, shared the same habits, civilization, and laws and differed only in rather subtle ways.

More time passed: leaving the shores of the Atlantic Ocean behind, Anglo-Americans daily plunged deeper into the solitudes of the West. There they encountered new terrain and new climates. They had to overcome obstacles of various kinds. Their races mingled: men from the South went north, and men from the North went south. With all these various causes at work, the same phenomenon recurred at every stage, and, in general, colonies where there were no slaves became more populous and prosperous than colonies where slavery was in force.

The farther they went, the more they began to see that servitude, so cruel to the slave, was also fatal to the master.

The ultimate demonstration of this truth came when they reached the banks of the Ohio.

The river that the Indians called the Ohio, or Beautiful River par excellence, waters one of the most magnificent valleys ever settled by man. The rolling land that stretches into the distance on both sides of the river is for the farmer a constant source of inexhaustible riches. On both banks the air is healthy and the climate temperate. The river forms the boundary between two vast states. The one that lies to the left as one travels downstream through the thousand twists and turns described by the Ohio River is called Kentucky; the one that lies to the right takes its name from the river itself. The two states differ in only one respect: Kentucky allows slaves, whereas Ohio has expelled them from its midst.[35]

Thus the traveler who lets the current of the Ohio carry him to the point where it joins the Mississippi navigates, as it were, between freedom and servitude, and he has only to look around to judge at a glance which is more propitious for humanity.

[35]Not only does Ohio not allow slavery, it also prohibits free Negroes from entering its territory and bars them from acquiring any property there. See the statutes of Ohio.

On the left bank of the river, the population is sparse. From time to time, a group of slaves can be seen ambling in their carefree way through half-cleared fields. The virgin forest never disappears for long. Society seems to slumber. Man appears idle, whereas nature is the very image of activity and life.

By contrast, the confused hum emanating from the right bank proclaims from afar the presence of industry. Rich harvests fill the fields. Elegant homes hint at the taste and fastidiousness of the farmers. Prosperity is apparent everywhere. Man seems rich and content: he is at work.[36]

The state of Kentucky was founded in 1775, the state of Ohio not until twelve years later: twelve years in America is more than half a century in Europe. Today the population of Ohio already exceeds that of Kentucky by 250,000.[37]

The contrasting effects of freedom and slavery are easy to understand. They suffice to explain many of the differences that one finds between ancient civilization and civilization today.

Labor is identified south of the Ohio with the idea of slavery, north of the Ohio with the idea of well-being and progress. To the south it is degraded, to the north honored. On the left bank of the river it is impossible to find workers of the white race; they would be afraid of looking like slaves. For labor, people must rely on the Negro. On the right bank one would search in vain for an idle person. The White applies his industriousness and intelligence to labor of every kind.

Hence those whose task it is to exploit the natural riches of the soil in Kentucky are neither eager nor enlightened, while those who could be both either do nothing or else cross over into Ohio so as to put their industriousness to good use in conditions where they need not be ashamed of it.

To be sure, masters in Kentucky make their slaves work without being obliged to pay them, but they derive little fruit

---

[36] It is not only man qua individual who is active in Ohio. The state itself is involved in immense undertakings. The state of Ohio has built a canal between Lake Erie and the Ohio River that connects the Mississippi valley to the rivers of the North. Thanks to this canal, European goods arriving in New York can be shipped by water all the way to New Orleans across more than five hundred leagues of the continent.

[37] According to the 1830 census, the exact figures are: Kentucky, 688,844; Ohio, 937,679.

from the slaves' efforts, whereas money paid to free workers would be returned with interest in the price of their products.

The free worker is paid, but he works more quickly than the slave, and speed of execution is an important factor in the economy. The White sells his services, but he finds buyers only when those services are useful. The Black has no claim on a price for his services, but he must be fed regularly. He must be supported in old age as well as in maturity, in barren childhood as well as in the fertile years of youth, in sickness and in health. Thus the work of both the White and the Black must be paid for: the free worker receives wages; the slave receives an upbringing, food, care, and clothing. The money that the master spends on the upkeep of the slave is meted out for specific purposes a little at a time; it is barely noticed. The wage paid to the worker is distributed in a lump sum and seems to enrich only the person to whom it is paid. In reality, however, the slave costs more than the free man, and his labor is less productive.[38]

The influence of slavery extends still further. It penetrates the master's very soul and imparts a particular direction to his ideas and tastes.

Nature has given man an enterprising and energetic character on both banks of the Ohio, but the uses to which these common qualities are put differ from one side to the other.

The White on the right bank, who must support himself through his own efforts, has made material well-being the principal goal of his existence. Because he lives in a region that

[38]Apart from the factors that make the labor of free workers more productive and economical than that of slaves wherever free workers are plentiful, I must point out one factor that is peculiar to the United States: it has not yet proved possible to cultivate sugar cane anywhere in the Union except on the banks of the Mississippi, near the mouth of that river, where it flows into the Gulf of Mexico. In Louisiana, the growing of cane is extremely profitable; nowhere does the farmer earn a higher price for his labors, and since there is always a certain ratio between the costs of production and the products, the price of slaves in Louisiana is very high. Now, since Louisiana is one of the confederate states, slaves can be shipped there from any part of the Union. The price paid for a slave in New Orleans therefore raises the price of slaves in all other markets. As a result, in regions where the land yields little, the costs of farming with slaves remains high, thereby giving a competitive advantage to free labor.

offers inexhaustible resources to his industry and endless incentives to his activity, his ardor to acquire has surpassed the ordinary limits of human cupidity: tormented by the desire for wealth, he boldly explores every path that fortune uncovers. He is equally ready to become a sailor, pioneer, manufacturer, or farmer, and equally willing to persevere in the face of the rigors and dangers with which these various occupations confront him. There is something wonderful about his ingenious resourcefulness and a kind of heroism in his avidity for profit.

The American of the left bank is contemptuous not only of labor but of all enterprises that succeed by virtue of labor. Living in idle comfort, he has the tastes of idle men. Money has lost part of its value in his eyes. What he seeks is not so much fortune as excitement and pleasure, and to that end he invests energy that his neighbor employs elsewhere. He has a passionate love of hunting and war. He enjoys the most violent forms of physical exercise. He is familiar with the use of arms, and as a child he learned to risk his life in single combat. Thus slavery not only prevents the White from making a fortune but diverts his will to other ends.

For two centuries, these factors, tending in opposite directions, have been constantly at work in the English colonies of North America, and they have led to a prodigious difference in the commercial abilities of southerners and northerners. Today, only the North has ships, factories, railroads, and canals.

This difference is apparent not only when the North is compared to the South but also when southerners are compared to one another. Almost all the men who engage in commercial enterprises and seek to use slavery in the southernmost states of the Union come from the North. Every day, northerners spread throughout this part of the country, where they have less to fear from competition. They discover resources that the residents had failed to notice and, adapting to a system of which they disapprove, capitalize on it more effectively than the people who founded it and still support it.

Were I inclined to press this parallel further, I could easily demonstrate that nearly all the evident differences between the southern and northern characters stem from slavery, but to do so would take me away from my subject: right now I am looking not at the effects of servitude in general but at the effects of servitude on the material prosperity of those who permit it.

Antiquity could have had only an imperfect understanding of this influence of slavery on the production of wealth. Servitude then existed throughout the civilized world; only among barbarian peoples was it unknown.

Accordingly, Christianity destroyed slavery solely by insisting on the rights of the slave. Today, one can attack it in the name of the master: on this point interest and morality are in accord.

As these truths became clear in the United States, slavery began slowly to recede in the face of enlightenment born of experience.

Servitude began in the South and expanded northward. Today it is receding. Freedom, emanating from the North, has been moving steadily southward. Among the large states, Pennsylvania today constitutes the extreme northern limit of slavery, but within its borders the institution is shaky. Maryland, which is just south of Pennsylvania, is on the point of abolishing it, and in Virginia, the next state to the south after Maryland, there is debate about its usefulness and dangers.[39]

Whenever a great change in human institutions occurs, the law of inheritance always figures among the causes.

When unequal division of estates was the law in the South, every family had as its representative a wealthy man, who felt neither the desire nor the need to work. Surrounding him like so many parasitic plants were the members of his family, who were legally barred from a share of the common inheritance

---

[39]There is a specific factor at work that is tending to detach the two last-named states from the cause of slavery.

The wealth of this part of the Union was formerly based primarily on the growing of tobacco. Slaves are particularly appropriate to this crop. Now, so happens that the market value of tobacco has been declining for some years now, but the value of slaves has remained steady. Thus the ratio between the costs of production and the products has changed. The residents of Maryland and Virginia therefore feel more disposed than they did thirty years ago either to grow tobacco without slaves or to give up both tobacco farming and slavery.

and lived as he did. In those days all southern families resembled the noble families that one still sees today in certain countries of Europe, where younger sons, though not as wealthy as the eldest, nevertheless lead lives just as idle. Similar effects sprang from entirely analogous causes in America and Europe. In the southern United States, the entire white race constituted an aristocratic body headed by a number of privileged individuals whose wealth was permanent and leisure hereditary. The leaders of the American nobility perpetuated the traditional prejudices of the white race in the body they represented and continued to set a high value on idleness. Within this aristocracy there were poor men but not workers; misery seemed preferable to industry. Negro workers and slaves therefore had no competitors, and no matter what opinion one might have held as to the utility of their efforts, one had to employ them, because there was no one else.

From the moment the law of inheritance was abolished, all fortunes began to shrink simultaneously, and all families moved closer to the condition in which it becomes necessary to work in order to exist. Many disappeared entirely. All sensed that a moment would eventually come when each individual would have to provide for his own needs. Today, wealthy individuals still exist, but they have ceased to constitute a distinct and hereditary body capable of fostering and maintaining an *esprit de corps* and instilling it in people of all ranks. By common accord they therefore abandoned the prejudice against labor, the stigma that once attached to the working man. The poor increased in number, and it became possible for them, without blushing, to concern themselves with ways of earning a living. Thus one of the most immediate effects of dividing estates into equal shares was to create a class of free workers. Once the free worker began to compete with the slave, the slave's inferiority became apparent, and slavery was attacked at its very root, namely, the self-interest of the master.

As slavery recedes, the black race has followed its retrograde march, returning to the tropics from which it came originally.

At first sight this may seem extraordinary, but we shall soon see the reason for it.

In abolishing the principle of servitude, the Americans did not set the slaves free.

What follows might be difficult to understand without an example, so let us take the state of New York. In 1788, the state of New York prohibited the sale of slaves within its borders. This was a roundabout way of prohibiting importation. Thereafter the number of Negroes increased only as fast as the natural rate of increase of the black population. Eight years later, a more decisive measure was taken, and it was announced that as of July 4, 1799, all children born to slave parents would be free. Every avenue of increase was then closed. Slaves remained, but, in a manner of speaking, servitude had ceased to exist.

Once a northern state had prohibited the importation of slaves, Blacks ceased to be taken from the South to be shipped north.

Once a northern state had banned the sale of Negroes, slave owners no longer had any way to get slaves off their hands, so that the slave became an inconvenient form of property, and the owner had an interest in shipping him south.

When a northern state declared the slave's son to be free at birth, the slave lost much of his monetary value, because his offspring could no longer be put up for sale; again, therefore, the slave's owner had a substantial interest in shipping him south.

Thus the same law both prevented southern slaves from coming north and drove northern slaves southward.

But another cause more powerful than those described thus far was also at work.

As the number of slaves in a state decreases, the need for free workers becomes increasingly apparent. To the extent that free workers take control of industry, the slave, whose labor is less productive, becomes inferior or useless property, so that its owner once again has a great interest in shipping him south, where there is no competition to fear.

Hence the abolition of slavery does not result in freedom for the slave. It simply results in a change of master from northerner to southerner.

Freed Negroes, as well as those born after slavery has been abolished, do not move from north to south but rather find themselves in a position vis-à-vis Europeans analogous to that of native Americans. They remain half-civilized and deprived of rights amid a population infinitely superior to them in wealth and enlightenment. They are exposed to the tyranny of laws[40] and the intolerance of mores. Less fortunate in some ways than the Indians, they have memories of slavery working against them, and they cannot claim ownership of any part of the land. Many succumb to their misery.[41] Others congregate in the cities, where they take on the grossest chores and lead a precarious and miserable existence.

In any case, even if the number of Negroes continued to grow as it did before they gained their freedom, the Blacks would soon be virtually engulfed by the influx of foreigners, because the number of Whites has been increasing since the abolition of slavery at twice the previous rate.

A region cultivated by slaves is generally less densely populated than a region cultivated by free men. America, moreover, is a new country. Hence when a state abolishes slavery, it is still only half settled. No sooner is servitude destroyed than the need for free workers begins to be felt, and countless bold adventurers rush in from all parts of the country. They come to take advantage of the new resources that are about to be opened up to industry. They divide up the land. A family of Whites settles on and takes possession of each parcel. Moreover, the European emigration is channeled into the free states. What would the poor European do if, having come to the New World in search of prosperity and happiness, he went to live in a region where labor was tainted with ignominy?

Thus the white population grows not only by natural increase but also by substantial immigration, while the black population receives no immigrants and dwindles. Before long

[40]The states that have abolished slavery usually try to make it uncomfortable for free Negroes to live within their borders, and since the various states come to emulate one another in this regard, the unfortunate Negroes can only choose among evils.

[41]There is a great difference in mortality between Whites and Blacks in states that have abolished slavery. From 1820 to 1831 only one of forty-two individuals belonging to the white race died, compared to one of twenty-one individuals belonging to the black race. Mortality is not nearly so high among Negro slaves. (See Emerson's *Medical Statistics*, p. 28.)

the proportions of the two races are reversed. The Negroes are reduced to nothing more than an unfortunate remnant, a small, poor, nomadic tribe lost in the midst of a numerous people that controls the land, and from that day on their presence is no longer noticed but for the injustices and hardships to which they are subject.

The Negro race never appeared at all in many of the western states, and it is now disappearing from all the northern states. The great question of the future is therefore confined within a relatively limited area. This makes it less redoubtable though no easier to resolve.

The farther south one goes, the more difficult it becomes to abolish slavery in an advantageous way. This is a consequence of a number of material causes, which need to be further elucidated.

The first of these is climate: there can be no doubt that the closer Europeans are to the tropics, the more difficult work becomes for them. Indeed, many Americans claim that below a certain latitude, work is fatal to them, whereas the Negro submits to it without danger.[42] But I do not believe that this idea, which the southerner uses to justify his laziness, is based on experience. It is no hotter in the south of the Union than in the south of Spain and Italy.[43] Why can the European not perform the same tasks in the American South? And if slavery could be abolished in Italy and Spain without the masters' perishing, why should it not be possible to do the same in the Union? Hence I do not believe that nature has barred the Europeans of Georgia and Florida from drawing their own subsistence from the soil on pain of death; but such work would surely be more arduous and less productive[44] than the labor

[42]This is true in places where rice is grown. Rice paddies, which are hazardous to health everywhere, are particularly dangerous in countries that swelter under the burning sun of the tropics. Europeans would find it very difficult indeed to cultivate the land in this part of the world if they insisted on growing rice. But are rice paddies indispensable?

[43]These states are closer to the equator than Italy and Spain, but the American continent is infinitely cooler than the European.

[44]Spain used to ship peasants from the Azores into a district of Louisiana known as Attakapas. As an experiment, they were not subjected to slavery. These people are still farming the land without slaves to this day, but they are so shiftless that they barely meet their own needs.

of New Englanders. Since the free worker thereby loses some of his superiority over the slave in the South, there is less advantage in abolishing slavery.

All European plants grow in the North of the Union; the South has special products of its own.

Slavery, as has been pointed out, is an expensive way to grow grain. Farmers who grow grain in countries where servitude is unknown generally employ relatively few farmhands. To be sure, they hire many additional workers at harvest and planting time, but these workers reside on the farmer's land for only a brief period.

To fill his storehouses or seed his fields, the farmer who lives in a slave state is obliged to maintain a large number of workers throughout the year even though he needs their services for only a few days. Unlike free workers, slaves cannot work for themselves while waiting for someone to hire their labor. They have to be bought before they can be used.

Slavery, apart from its general drawbacks, is therefore by nature less well adapted to regions that grow grain than to those that produce other things.

By contrast, tobacco, cotton, and especially sugar cane require constant attention. Women and children, who are of no use in growing grain, can be employed in these chores. Thus slavery is by nature more appropriate to regions that produce these crops.

Tobacco, cotton, and cane grow only in the South. They are the principal sources of that region's wealth. If southerners were to abolish slavery, they would find themselves in one of the two following situations: either they would be obliged to change their system of agriculture, in which case they would have to compete with more energetic and experienced northerners, or they would continue to grow the same crops without slaves, in which case they would have to face the competition of other southern states that had preserved slavery.

Thus the South has special reasons for retaining slavery that do not apply to the North.

There is, however, yet another reason more powerful than any that have been mentioned thus far. The South, if forced to do so, might well abolish slavery, but how would it dispose of the Blacks? In the North, slaves are being driven out along with slavery. In the South it is unreasonable to expect that the two things could be achieved at the same time.

When I showed that servitude was more natural and more advantageous in the South than in the North, I said enough to indicate that the number of slaves there was probably much larger. It was to the South that the first Africans were brought, and the majority of them continued to be sent there. The farther south one goes, the more powerful the prejudice in favor of idleness. In the states closest to the tropics, no white man works. Hence Negroes are naturally more numerous in the South than in the North. Every day they become still more so, as I noted earlier, for as slavery is destroyed at one end of the Union, Negroes accumulate at the other end. Thus the number of Blacks is increasing in the South, not only as a result of natural growth of the population but also owing to forced emigration of Negroes from the North. The reasons why the African race is growing in this part of the Union are analogous to the reasons why the European race is growing so rapidly in the North.

In the state of Maine there is one Negro for every three hundred inhabitants; in Massachusetts, one for every hundred; in New York, two for every hundred; in Pennsylvania, three; in Maryland, thirty-four; forty-two in Virginia, and, finally, fifty-five in South Carolina.[45] This was the proportion of Blacks relative to Whites in the year 1830. But this proportion is constantly changing: it becomes smaller every day in the North and larger in the South.

---

[45] In the American book *Letters on the Colonization Society* by Carey, 1833, one reads the following: "In South Carolina over the past forty years, the black race has been growing more rapidly than the white. Taking together the population of the first five states to have slaves — Maryland, Virginia, North Carolina, South Carolina, and Georgia," Mr. Carey goes on to say, "we find that from 1790 to 1830 the white population increased by 80 percent and the black population by 112 percent."

In the United States in 1830, the two races were distributed as follows: states in which slavery has been abolished, 6,565,434 Whites and 120,520 Negroes; states in which slavery still exists, 3,960,814 Whites and 2,208,102 Negroes.

It is obvious that slavery cannot be abolished in the south-ernmost states of the Union as was done in the North with-out running very substantial risks that the northern states did not have to face.

We have seen how the states of the North managed the transition from slavery to freedom. They keep the present gen-eration in irons and emancipate future generations. Such a course introduces Negroes into society only gradually. While the man who might make poor use of his independence is kept in servitude, the one who can still learn the art of being free before becoming his own master is emancipated.

It would be difficult to apply this method in the South. When it is declared that as of a certain date the Negro's chil-dren will be free, the principle and idea of liberty are intro-duced into the very heart of servitude: Blacks who are kept in slavery by lawmakers and who see their children freed are stunned by such unequal treatment at the hands of fate; this troubles and irritates them. From that moment on, slavery loses whatever moral power time and custom had given it in their eyes. It is reduced to nothing but a flagrant abuse of force. The North had nothing to fear from this contrast, be-cause in the North Blacks were few in number and Whites quite numerous. But if the first glimmers of freedom were to shine upon two million men at once, their oppressors would be obliged to tremble.

If the Europeans of the South were to emancipate the chil-dren of their slaves, they would soon be compelled to extend the same benefit to the black race as a whole.

In the North, as we have seen, once slavery was abolished — indeed, as soon as abolition began to seem likely — two things occurred: slaves left the region and were shipped south, and Whites from the northern states together with immigrants from Europe poured in to take their place.

These things cannot happen in the southernmost states. For one thing, there are too many slaves in the South for there to be any hope of persuading them to leave. For another, the Europeans and Anglo-Americans of the North are afraid of going to live in a region where work has yet to be rehabil-itated. Furthermore, they rightly regard states in which the

Negro population equals or exceeds the white population as likely to face serious woes in the future and refrain from investing their efforts there.

Hence if southerners were to abolish slavery, they would not be able to move the Negro gradually toward freedom, as their brothers to the north have done. They would not noticeably reduce the number of Blacks, and they would be left alone to hold the Negro in check. Within a few years, one would therefore find a large number of free Negroes living alongside an almost equal number of Whites.

The same abuses of power that maintain slavery in the South today would then become the greatest source of danger for Whites. Today, descendants of Europeans own all the land; they are absolute masters of the work force; they alone are rich, enlightened, and armed. Blacks have none of these advantages but can do without them because they are slaves. As free men, responsible for their own fate, could they remain so deprived and yet not perish? What made the white man strong when slavery existed would therefore expose him to innumerable perils if slavery were abolished.

So long as the Negro is left in servitude, he can be kept in a state bordering on brutishness, but once he becomes free, there is no way to prevent him from learning enough to appreciate the extent of his afflictions and conceive a vague idea of the remedy. More than that, a singular principle of relative justice lies deep within the human heart. Men are far more struck by inequalities within the same class than by inequalities between different classes. People understand slavery, but what are they to make of the lives of several million citizens eternally bowed down by the weight of infamy and abandoned to hereditary miseries? In the North, a population of freed Negroes feels those woes and suffers those injustices, but it is weak and submissive; in the South, it would be numerous and strong.

If we assume that Whites and emancipated Negroes are to occupy the same land and face each other as foreign peoples, it is easy to see that the future holds only two prospects: either Negroes and Whites must blend altogether or they must separate.

I have already stated my opinion as to the first of these possibilities.[46] I do not think that the white race and the black race will ever live anywhere on a footing of equality.

But I also believe that the difficulty will be far greater in the United States than anywhere else. It is possible for one man to set aside prejudices of religion, country, and race, and if that man is king, surprising revolutions may occur in society as a consequence; but an entire people cannot rise, as it were, above itself.

A despot who managed to reduce both the Americans and their former slaves to the same state of subservience might succeed in mixing them; so long as American democracy remains in charge of affairs, no one will dare attempt such a thing, and it is possible to predict that the freer the Whites of the United States become, the more they will seek to isolate themselves.[47]

I said earlier that the true bond between the European and the Indian was the half-breed. Similarly, the true bridge between the White and the Negro is the mulatto. Wherever mulattos are found in large numbers, fusion of the races is not impossible.

There are parts of America in which Europeans and Negroes have interbred to such a degree that it is difficult to find a person who is entirely white or entirely black. At that stage one can truly say that the two races have mixed. Or, rather, that a third race has emerged in their stead, a new race that takes after both without being precisely one or the other.

Of all the Europeans, the English have been least inclined to mix their blood with that of the Negro. One sees more mulattos in the South of the Union than in the North but far fewer than in any other European colony. Mulattos are not

[46]Furthermore, this opinion is supported by authorities far weightier than myself. In Jefferson's memoirs, for example, one can read the following: "Nothing is more certainly written in the book of fate than that these people are to be free. Nor is it less certain that the two races, equally free, cannot live in the same government. Nature, habit, opinion has drawn indelible lines of distinction between them." (See M. Conseil's excerpts from Jefferson's memoirs.)

[47]If the English of the West Indies had governed themselves, they surely would not have passed the act of emancipation that the mother country has just imposed.

very numerous in the United States. They do not constitute an independent force and in interracial disputes generally make common cause with Whites, just as in Europe the lackeys of great nobles will often lord it over the common people.

This pride of origin, natural to the Englishman, is markedly increased in the American by the individual pride born of democratic liberty. The white man in the United States is proud of his race and proud of himself.

Furthermore, since Whites and Negroes do not mix in the North of the Union, how could they possibly do so in the South? How can one possibly assume, even for a moment, that the American of the South, standing as he must between the white man in all his physical and moral superiority and the Negro, would ever think of combining with the Negro? Two powerful passions will always keep the American of the South apart from the Black: fear that he might come to resemble his former slave, the Negro, and fear that he might sink below the level of his neighbor, the White.

If forced to make a prediction about the future, I would say that it is highly likely that abolition of slavery in the South will increase the hostility of the southern white population toward Blacks. I base this opinion on what I have already seen of this kind of thing in the North. I said earlier that white men in the North shun Negroes all the more assiduously as the legal separation between them diminishes. Why should it be any different in the South? In the North, when Whites fear the possibility of being equated with Blacks, they fear an imaginary danger. In the South, where the danger would be real, I cannot believe that the fear would be less.

If one grants — and the fact is not in doubt — that Blacks are steadily accumulating in the far South, where their number is increasing much faster than that of Whites; and if, moreover, one concedes that it is impossible to foresee a time when Blacks and Whites might mix in such a way as to derive the same benefits from the state of society; then does it not follow that Blacks and Whites in the southern states will sooner or later end up in conflict?

What will the end result of that conflict be?

On this point, obviously, one must limit oneself to vague conjecture. It is difficult though not impossible for the human mind to circumscribe the future within certain broad limits, but beyond those limits chance plays havoc with all prediction. In our picture of the future, chance always leaves a zone of darkness, which the eye of intelligence cannot penetrate. What we can say is this: in the West Indies, it is the white race that seems destined to succumb; on the continent, it is the black race.

In the West Indies, Whites are isolated in the midst of an immense population of Blacks. On the continent, Blacks find themselves caught between the sea and an innumerable people that already fills the contiguous region stretching from the frozen wastes of Canada to the borders of Virginia and from the banks of the Missouri to the shores of the Atlantic Ocean. If the Whites of North America remain united, it is hard to see how the Negroes can escape the threat of destruction. They will end up either in irons or in misery. But the black population massed along the Gulf of Mexico might have a chance of surviving if the conflict between the two races came after the American confederation had been dissolved. Were the federal link to be broken, southerners would be wrong to count on the continuing support of their brothers to the north. Northerners know that the danger can never affect them. If no positive duty obliges them to march to the rescue of the South, one can anticipate that racial sympathies will not suffice to make them do it.

In any case, whenever the struggle comes, white southerners, even if abandoned to fight on their own, would join the fray with vast superiority in enlightenment and resources. Blacks would have numbers on their side, however, as well as the energy of despair. These are great advantages when a man has arms in hand. The white race in the South might then suffer the same fate as the Moors in Spain. After occupying the region for centuries, the Whites would be forced little by little to withdraw to the country from which their forebears came long ago, leaving the Negroes in possession of a land apparently destined by Providence to be theirs, since they live in it without difficulty and find it easier to work there than Whites.

The danger — more or less remote, but inevitable — of a struggle between Blacks and Whites living in the South is the distressing nightmare that haunts the American imagination. Northerners talk about these perils every day, even though they have nothing to fear from them directly. They search in vain for a way to ward off the misfortunes they anticipate. In the southern states, people are silent. No one talks with strangers about the future. People avoid delving into the question with their friends. In a sense, they hide it from themselves. The South's silence is in a way more frightening than the North's outspoken fear.

This general preoccupation has given rise to an undertaking which, though it has virtually been ignored, may alter the fate of a portion of the human race.

Fearing the dangers that I have just described, a group of American citizens have joined together for the purpose of paying the passage to the coast of Guinea of free Negroes who wish to escape the tyranny that oppresses them.[48]

In 1820, the society I speak of succeeded in founding a settlement in Africa, at seven degrees north latitude, and gave it the name *Liberia*. At last report, 2,500 Negroes had already been sent there. These Blacks have introduced American institutions into their former homeland. Liberia has a representative system, Negro jurors, Negro magistrates, and Negro priests. There are temples and newspapers, and in a notable reversal in the vicissitudes of this world, Whites are forbidden to settle within its walls.[49]

What a strange caprice of fortune! Two centuries have elapsed since Europeans first undertook to remove Negroes from their families and their homelands and carry them off to the shores of North America. Today we find Europeans involved in transporting the descendants of those same Negroes across the Atlantic Ocean once again, bringing them back to

[48]This organization is known as the Society for the Colonization of Blacks. See its annual reports, especially the fifteenth. See also the brochure mentioned earlier, entitled *Letters on the Colonization Society and On Its Probable Results*, by Mr. Carey (Philadelphia, April 1833).

[49]This last rule was laid down by the founders of the settlement themselves. They were afraid that something might happen in Africa similar to what is happening on the frontiers of the United States, and that if the Negroes, like the Indians, came into contact with a more enlightened race, they might be destroyed before they could become civilized.

the soil from which their fathers were so long ago uprooted. Barbarians imbibed civilization's enlightenment in the depths of servitude and learned in slavery the art of being free.

Until recently, Africa was closed to the arts and sciences of Whites. European enlightenment, imported by Africans, will perhaps penetrate that continent now. Hence in the founding of Liberia there is a great and beautiful idea, but that idea, which may prove quite fruitful for the Old World, is sterile for the New.

In twelve years, the Society for the Colonization of Blacks has transported 2,500 Negroes to Africa. During that time, roughly 700,000 Blacks were born in the United States.

Even if the colony of Liberia were in a position to receive thousands of new inhabitants every year, and there were Negroes in a condition to be sent there advantageously; and even if the Union were to take the place of the Society and draw annually from its own coffers[50] and upon its own vessels to export Negroes to Africa; it still would not be able to offset even the natural growth of the black population. And since it would not remove as many individuals as come into the world every year, it would not be able even to slow the development of a malady that grows worse with each passing day.[51]

The Negro race will never quit the shores of the American continent, to which it was brought by the passions and vices of Europe. It will disappear from the New World only if it ceases to exist. The inhabitants of the United States can put off the misfortunes they dread, but they cannot today destroy their cause.

---

[50]Such an enterprise would meet with many other difficulties as well. If the Union undertook to purchase black slaves from their owners for the purpose of transporting them to Africa, the price of Negroes, growing in proportion to their scarcity, would soon reach exorbitant heights, and it is scarcely believable that the northern states would consent to such an expenditure, the fruits of which they would never see. If the Union were to seize southern slaves by force or set a low price for their acquisition, it would foment insurmountable resistance in that part of the Union. Either choice would lead to an impossible situation.

[51]In 1830 there were 2,010,327 slaves in the United States, and 319,439 freedmen, for a total of 2,329,766 Negroes, or a little more than one-fifth of the total population of the United States at that time.

I am obliged to admit that I do not regard the abolition of servitude as a way to delay the struggle between the two races in the southern states.

The Negroes may long remain slaves without complaint, but once they join the ranks of free men, they will soon feel outrage at being deprived of nearly all the rights of citizens. And if they cannot become the white man's equal, they will not wait long before revealing themselves to be his enemy.

In the North it was profitable in every way to free the slaves. The white man thereby delivered himself from slavery yet had no need to fear free Negroes. There were too few of them ever to claim their rights. Things are different in the South.

For masters in the North, the question of slavery was a commercial and manufacturing question. In the South, it is a question of life and death. Hence slavery in the North should not be confused with slavery in the South.

God forbid that I should try to justify the principle of Negro servitude, as some American authors do. I say only that the people who embraced this dreadful principle in the past are not all equally free to let go of it today.

I confess that when I consider the state of the South, I see only two ways for Whites who live in the region to act: either free the Negroes and fuse with them; or remain isolated from them and keep them in slavery as long as possible. In my view, any intermediate measure will lead imminently to the most horrible of all civil wars and perhaps to the destruction of one of the two races.

Americans of the South look at the question from this angle and act in consequence. Since they are unwilling to fuse with the Negroes, they do not wish to set them free.

The point is not that all inhabitants of the South regard slavery as necessary to the master's wealth. On this point, many of them agree with northerners and readily admit that servitude is an evil; but they believe that they must preserve that evil in order to live.

As the South has become more enlightened, the inhabitants of that region have come to see that slavery is harmful to the master, and by the same lights they have also come to see, more clearly than ever before, that it is almost impossible to destroy. This has led to a striking contrast: slavery has become more and more firmly established in law as its utility has been more and more contested. And while its principle has gradually been abolished in the North, from that same principle increasingly harsh consequences have been drawn in the South.

Legislation pertaining to slaves in the southern states stands today as evidence of unprecedented atrocity, which by itself reveals some profound perturbation in the laws of humanity. It is enough to read the legislation of the southern states to judge the desperate position of the two races that inhabit them.

The point is not exactly that Americans in this part of the Union have increased the harshness of servitude; on the contrary, they have alleviated the material condition of the slave. The Ancients had only two ways of maintaining slavery: chains and death. Southerners have discovered more intellectual means of guaranteeing the duration of their power. They have, if I may put it this way, spiritualized despotism and violence. In Antiquity, people sought to prevent the slave from breaking his chains; nowadays, they seek to sap his desire to do so.

The Ancients chained the slave's body, but they left his mind free and allowed him to enlighten himself. In this they acted consistently. There was then a natural way out of servitude: from one day to the next, the slave could become free and equal to his master.

Southerners, who do not believe that Negroes will ever be capable of combining with them, have imposed harsh penalties for teaching them to read and write. Since they do not wish to raise the Negro to their level, they keep him as close as possible to the level of a brute.

The prospect of freedom has always been held out to slaves as a way of alleviating the rigors of slavery.

The Americans of the South understood that emancipation is always dangerous if the freed slave cannot some day assimilate with the master. To give a man freedom yet leave him in ignominious misery — what does this accomplish other than to provide some slave rebellion with a future leader? It was noticed long ago, moreover, that the presence of the freed Negro was vaguely disquieting to the souls of the unfree, in whom it aroused the first glimmerings of an idea of their rights. In

most cases, therefore, Americans in the South stripped masters of the prerogative to free their slaves.[52]

In the south of the Union I met an elderly man who had at
one time lived in illegitimate intercourse with one of his Ne-
gresses. He had had several children by her who became his
slaves at birth. On several occasions he had thought of granting them their freedom in his will, but his efforts to overcome
the legal impediments to emancipation dragged on for years.
In the meantime he had grown old and was about to die. He
pictured his sons being dragged from market to market and
passing from their father's authority to that of a stranger with
a whip. These horrible images haunted the dying man in his
delirium. Seeing him racked by despair, I understood how
nature avenges herself for the wounds inflicted by laws.

These evils are dreadful, to be sure, but are they not the pre-
dictable and necessary consequence of the very principle of
servitude in the modern world?

From the moment that Europeans began to take slaves from
another race of men, a race that many of them saw as inferior
to the other human races and with which they could never
contemplate assimilating without horror, they assumed that
slavery was eternal. For between the extreme inequality created by slavery and the complete equality to which independence naturally leads, there is no durable intermediate state.
Europeans were vaguely aware of this truth but never admitted it to themselves. Whenever the question of the Negro
arose, they followed the dictates either of interest and pride
or else of pity. With respect to the black man they violated all
the rights of humanity and then schooled him in the value and
inviolability of those rights. They opened their ranks to their
slaves, and when the slaves responded to this gesture, Whites
drove them out in shame. Desiring servitude, they nevertheless allowed themselves to be drawn unwillingly or unwittingly toward freedom, without the courage to be either
completely wicked or entirely just.

If it is impossible to foresee a time when Americans of
the South will mix their blood with that of the Negro, can

[52]Emancipation is not prohibited but rather subject to formalities that
make it difficult.

they, without mortal risk to themselves, allow the Negro to achieve freedom? And if, in order to save their own race, they are obliged to insist that the Negro be kept in irons, should they not be excused for adopting the most efficient means to that end?

What is happening in the South strikes me as both the most horrible and the most natural consequence of slavery. When I see the order of nature overturned and hear mankind cry out and struggle in vain against the law, I confess that my indignation is not directed at my contemporaries, the authors of these outrages; all my hatred is reserved for those who, after more than a thousand years of equality, introduced servitude into the world once more.

Furthermore, no matter how hard southerners try to preserve slavery, they will not succeed indefinitely. Restricted to one part of the globe and attacked by Christianity as unjust and by political economy as disastrous, slavery is not an institution that can endure in an age of democratic liberty and enlightenment. Either the slave or the master will put an end to it. In either case, great woes certainly lie ahead.

If freedom is denied to the Negroes of the South, they will some day seize it violently for themselves. If it is granted to them, they will not be slow to abuse it.

HOW LIKELY IS IT THAT THE AMERICAN UNION WILL LAST? WHAT DANGERS THREATEN IT?

Why the preponderance of force lies with the states rather than with the Union. — The confederation will last only as long as all the member states continue to want to belong. — Causes that should incline them to remain united. — Value of unity for resisting foreigners and keeping them out of America. — Providence has placed no physical barriers between the various states. — No material interests divide them. — Interest of the North in the prosperity and union of the South and West; of the South in that of the North and West; of the West in that of the two other regions. — Immaterial interests that unite the Americans. — Uniformity of opinions. — Dangers to the confederation stemming from differences in the characters and passions of its people. — Characters of southerners and northerners. — The rapid growth of the Union is one of the greatest perils it faces. — Movement of the population toward the northwest. — Gravitation of power in this direction. — Passions to which these rapid shifts of fortune give rise. — If the Union survives, will its government tend to gain strength or grow weaker? — Various signs of weakening. — Internal improvements. — Wilderness lands. — Indians. — Bank Affair. — Tariff Affair. — General Jackson.

The maintenance of whatever exists in the various states of the Union depends in part on the existence of the Union itself. Hence we must first examine the probable fate of the Union. Before that, however, I want to be clear about one point: if the present confederation were to collapse, I am certain that the member states would not return to their original separateness. Instead of one Union, they would form several. I do not intend to look into the possible bases of such new unions. What I want to show is what causes might lead to the disintegration of the confederation that now exists.

To that end, I shall be obliged to go over ground that I have covered previously. I am bound to delve into a number of subjects that will already be familiar to the reader. I am aware that this manner of proceeding is open to reproach, but the importance of the remaining material must serve as my excuse. I would on occasion rather repeat myself than be misunderstood and would sooner do harm to the author than to the subject.

The framers of the Constitution of 1789 strove to create a federal government that would exist in its own right and whose strength would be preponderant.

They were constrained, however, by the very nature of the problem they faced. Their charge was not to constitute the government of a single people but to lay down rules for the association of several peoples. Whatever their desires may have been, they were obliged in every instance to arrive at a solution in which the exercise of sovereignty would be shared.

To fully understand the consequences of that sharing, one has to make a rough distinction among different acts of sovereignty.

Some issues are national by their very nature: in other words, they pertain exclusively to the nation as a whole and can be dealt with only by the person or assembly that most fully represents the entire nation. I would include war and diplomacy in this category.

Other issues are provincial in nature: that is, they pertain only to certain localities and can be dealt with appropriately only in the locality itself. An example would be the budget of a town.

Finally, there are also issues whose nature is mixed: they are national, in that they interest all the individuals who make up the nation, and they are provincial, in that there is no need for the nation itself to take charge of them. An example would be the laws governing the civil and political status of citizens. No social state can exist without civil and political rights. Hence these rights interest all citizens equally. But the existence and prosperity of the nation do not always require that these rights be uniform and, consequently, that they be regulated by the central government.

Hence there are two necessary categories of issues with which sovereignty is concerned. These exist in all properly constituted societies, regardless of the basis of the social pact.

Between these two extremes, like a floating mass, lie any number of issues that are of general but not national interest, which I am calling mixed. Since these issues are neither exclusively national nor entirely provincial, responsibility for them may be assigned to either the national government or the provincial government by agreement of the partners, without prejudice to the purposes of their association.

The most common case is for ordinary individuals to join together to constitute the sovereign; their union creates a people. Below the level of the general government they establish for themselves, one therefore finds only such forces as an individual can muster, or else collective powers, each of which represents only a very tiny fraction of the sovereign. Hence it is most natural to call upon the general government to deal not only with issues that are national in their very essence but also with the vast majority of issues that I am calling mixed. Localities are thereby limited to that portion of sovereignty that is indispensable to their well-being.

Sometimes, a prior act of association results in a situation in which the sovereign consists of previously organized political bodies. In such a case, provincial government may assume responsibility not only for issues that are by nature strictly provincial but also for some or all of the mixed issues we have been discussing. This is because each of the confederated nations, having been sovereign prior to forming the union and continuing thereafter to represent a very significant fraction of the sovereign power, chose to relinquish to the general government only the exercise of those rights indispensable to the union.

When the national government, in addition to the prerogatives inherent in its nature, also has the power to deal with mixed issues of sovereignty, it becomes the predominant power. Its rights are many, and, more than that, whatever rights it does not possess are at its mercy, and there is reason to fear that it may go so far as to deprive local governments of their natural and necessary prerogatives.

By contrast, when the power to deal with mixed issues is vested in provincial government, the opposite tendency prevails in society, and there is reason to fear that the national government will eventually be stripped of privileges without which it cannot exist.

Unified peoples are therefore naturally inclined toward centralization, and confederations toward dismemberment.

All that remains is to apply these general ideas to the American Union.

The right to deal with purely provincial issues naturally fell to the individual states.

Furthermore, the states also retained the right to decide the civil and political status of their citizens, to regulate social relations, and to dispense justice. Though general in nature, these rights do not necessarily belong to the national government.

We saw earlier that the power to issue orders in the name of the entire nation was delegated to the government of the Union in cases where the nation is required to act as a single individual. The national government represents the Union with respect to foreigners, and it directs the nation's joint forces against the enemy. In a word, it is concerned with those issues that I am calling exclusively national.

In this division of the rights of sovereignty, the Union's share at first seems greater than that of the states. A more thorough examination reveals that it is in fact smaller.

The government of the Union is more ambitious in its undertakings, but its actions are rarely apparent. The state government's actions are smaller, but it never rests, and its existence is evident at every moment.

The government of the Union looks after the country's general interests, but the general interests of a people have at best a debatable influence on individual happiness.

By contrast, the affairs of the states visibly influence the well-being of everyone who lives in them.

The Union ensures the nation's independence and grandeur — things that do not affect individuals directly. The state preserves the liberty, regulates the rights, guarantees the fortune, and secures the life and entire future of each citizen.

The federal government stands at a great distance from its subjects. The state government is within the reach of all. To be heard by it, it suffices to raise one's voice. The central government is aided by the passions of a small number of superior men, who aspire to lead it. State governments are supported by the interests of men of a secondary order who do not hope for power beyond their own states, and because these men are close to the people, they exert the greatest power over them.

Americans therefore have far more to expect, and to fear, from the states than from the Union and, given the natural penchants of the human heart, are bound to feel more warmly attached to the former than to the latter.

In this, habits and sentiments accord with interests.

When a consolidated nation divides its sovereignty and transforms itself into a confederation, memories, customs, and habits continue for a long time to vie with laws, bestowing upon the central government a force that the law denies. When confederate peoples unite under a single sovereignty, the same causes work in the opposite direction. I have no doubt that if France became a confederated republic like the United States, its government would at first show itself to be more energetic than the government of the Union. And if the Union were to constitute itself as a monarchy like France, I think that the American government would for some time remain weaker than ours. When national life was first created among the Anglo-Americans, provincial existence already had a long past; necessary relationships had been established between towns and individuals of the same states; and people had become accustomed to looking at certain issues from a common standpoint and concerning themselves exclusively with certain undertakings as representing a special interest.

The Union is an immense body — a vague object for patriotism to embrace. A state has a definite shape and well-defined boundaries. It represents a certain number of things that its inhabitants know and cherish. It is indistinguishable from the image of the land itself and identified with property, with family, with memories of the past, labors of the present, and dreams of the future. Patriotism, which is usually only an extension of individual selfishness, has therefore remained attached to the state rather than going over, as it were, to the Union.

Thus interests, habits, and feelings conspire to concentrate authentic political life in the state, and not in the Union.

The difference in strength of the two levels of government is easily gauged by looking at how each acts within its own sphere of power.

Whenever a state government speaks to an individual or association of individuals, its language is clear and imperative. The same is true of the federal government when it speaks to individuals, but when confronted by a state, it begins to parley: it explains its motives and justifies its conduct; it argues, it offers advice, but seldom does it issue orders. If doubts arise as to the limits of the constitutional powers of each level of government, the state government boldly proclaims its rights and takes prompt and energetic measures to uphold them. In the meantime, the government of the Union reasons; it appeals to the good sense, the interests, the glory of the nation; it temporizes; it negotiates. Only when reduced to the ultimate extremity does it make up its mind to act. At first sight one might think that it was the state government that marshaled the armed might of the entire nation and that Congress represented but a single state.

The federal government, despite the efforts of the men who constituted it, is therefore, as I have already stated elsewhere, by its very nature a weak government, which, more than any other, needs the free cooperation of the governed in order to subsist.

It is easy to see that its purpose is to help the states fulfill their desire to remain united. When this primary condition is satisfied, it is wise, strong, and agile. It was organized in such a way that it normally finds only individuals standing in its way and can easily overcome any resistance to the common will. But the federal government was not established with an eye to the possibility that the states, or some number of them, would no longer wish to be united.

If conflict were to erupt today between the sovereignty of the Union and the sovereignty of the states, it is easy to foresee that the former would succumb. Indeed, I doubt that battle would even be joined in a serious way. The federal government will always give in to stubborn resistance. Experience has thus far shown that whenever a state has doggedly insisted on something and resolutely demanded it, it has always gotten what it wanted; and whenever a state has flatly refused to take action,[53] it was left to do as it pleased.

Even if the government of the Union had a force of its own, the material situation of the country would make it difficult to use.[54]

The United States covers an immense territory; long distances separate the states; the population is scattered through regions still half wilderness. If the Union undertook to maintain the confederation by force of arms, its position would be analogous to that of England during the War for Independence.

Furthermore, it is difficult for any government, even a strong one, to escape the consequences of a principle once it has accepted that principle as the basis of the public law that is supposed to govern its actions. The states formed the confederation of their own free will. In uniting, they did not

[53]See the conduct of the northern states in the War of 1812. In a letter to General La Fayette dated March 17, 1817, Jefferson wrote that "with four eastern states tied to us, as dead to living bodies, all doubt was removed as to the achievements of the war, had it continued." (*Correspondance de Jefferson*, published by M. Conseil.)

[54]The state of peace in which the Union finds itself offers no pretext for maintaining a standing army. Without a standing army, a government cannot be prepared in advance to seize a favorable opportunity, overcome resistance, and lay hold of sovereign power by surprise.

forfeit their nationality and did not merge into a single people. If one of those states today decided to remove its name from the contract, it would be rather difficult to prove that it could not. If the federal government chose to contest this decision, it is not obvious that it could back up its choice with either might or right.

If the federal government is to triumph easily over the resistance of some of its subjects, the particular interest of one or more of them must be intimately associated with the existence of the union, as the history of confederations has repeatedly demonstrated.

Suppose that, among the states joined by the federal bond, there are some to which the principal advantages of union exclusively accrue, or whose prosperity depends entirely on the union's existence; clearly the central government will receive very strong support from those states in its efforts to enforce obedience upon the others. In that case, however, its strength will be drawn not from itself but from a principle contrary to its nature. Peoples confederate only in order to derive equal advantages from the union, and in the case discussed above, the federal government is powerful because inequality prevails among the united nations.

Again, suppose that one of the confederated states becomes sufficiently preponderant to seize the central government by itself. It will then look upon the other states as its subjects and enforce its own sovereignty in the guise of the Union's sovereignty. Great things may then be done in the name of the federal government, but in reality that government will no longer exist.[55]

In both cases, the power that acts in the name of the confederation becomes stronger to the extent that it deviates from confederation's natural state and acknowledged principle.

In America, the present union is useful to all the states but not essential to any of them. Several states could break the federal bond without compromising the fate of the others, though the sum total of their happiness would be diminished.

---

[55] For example, the province of Holland in the Republic of the Netherlands and the emperor in the German Confederation have at times taken the place of the union and exploited federal power in their own interest.

Since there is no state whose existence or prosperity is wholly dependent on the present confederation, there is also no state prepared to make major sacrifices to save it.

Nor does there appear to be any state thus far with a great interest in maintaining, for the sake of its own ambition, the confederation as it exists today. To be sure, not all the states have the same influence in federal councils, but none seems to be in a position to dominate those councils or to treat its confederates as inferiors or subjects.

To me, therefore, it appears certain that if one portion of the Union seriously wished to separate from the other, it could not be prevented from doing so; indeed, no one would even try to prevent it. Hence the present Union will survive only as long as all of its member states continue to want to be part of it.

With that much established, our task becomes easier: the question is no longer whether the presently confederated states might be able to separate but whether they will wish to remain united.

Among the various reasons why Americans find the present union useful, two stand out sufficiently to be obvious to all observers.

Even though the Americans are, as it were, alone on their continent, commerce makes neighbors of all the peoples with whom they trade. Despite their apparent isolation, Americans therefore need to be strong, and they can be strong only if they remain united.

If the states became disunited, they would not only diminish their power with respect to foreigners but also create foreigners on their own soil. They would adopt a system of internal customs. They would divide valleys with imaginary lines. They would establish barriers to river traffic and in countless ways impede the exploitation of the vast continent that God has given them as their domain.

Today they have no invasion to fear, hence no armies to maintain and no taxes to levy; if the Union were to break down, it might not be long before the need for such things was felt.

Americans therefore have an immense interest in remaining united.

By contrast, it is almost impossible to see what sort of material interest any portion of the Union would have at present in separating from the others.

When one glances at a map of the United States and sees the Allegheny mountain range running from northeast to southwest over a distance of some 400 leagues, it is tempting to believe that Providence intentionally divided the Mississippi basin from the Atlantic coast by erecting one of those natural barriers which, by interfering with inveterate human relations, establish something like necessary boundaries between peoples.

But the average height of the Alleghenies does not exceed 800 meters.[56] Rounded peaks and valleys tucked into mountain folds offer easy access in a thousand places. More than that, the principal rivers that empty into the Atlantic — the Hudson, Susquehanna, and Potomac — have their sources beyond the Alleghenies, on an open plateau bordering on the Mississippi basin. Departing from that region,[57] they wend their way through a rampart seemingly destined to divert them westward, cutting natural passes that are open year-round.

Hence no barrier separates the various parts of the territory today occupied by the Anglo-Americans. The Alleghenies, far from serving as national boundaries, are not even state boundaries. New York, Pennsylvania, and Virginia all include portions of this range and extend as far west of the mountains as they do east.[58]

The territory occupied today by the twenty-four states and three large districts not yet counted as states though already inhabited covers an area of 131,144 square leagues,[59] or almost five times the size of France. Within its borders one finds varied soils, different temperatures, and a wide range of products.

---

[56]According to Volney (*Tableau des Etats-Unis*, p. 33), the average height of the Alleghenies is 700 to 800 meters; according to Darby it is 5,000 to 6,000 feet. The highest peak in the Vosges stands some 1,400 meters above sea-level.

[57]See Darby, *View of the United States*, pp. 64 and 79.

[58]The Allegheny range is not higher than the Vosges and presents fewer impediments to the efforts of human industry. The regions lying to the east of the Alleghenies are therefore as naturally linked to the Mississippi valley as Franche-Comté, upper Burgundy, and Alsace are to France.

[59]1,002,600 square miles. See Darby, *View of the United States*, p. 435.

The great extent of the territory occupied by the Anglo-American republics has given rise to doubts about their ability to maintain the Union intact. At this point, a distinction has to be made. Contrary interests sometimes arise in the various provinces of a vast empire, and these may eventually come into conflict; in such cases, the size of the state poses the greatest threat to its continuation. But if the people who inhabit this vast territory do not have contrary interests, the very extent of the state will inevitably contribute to their prosperity, for unity of government significantly encourages the possibility of exchange among various products of the soil and increases their value by easing the flow of trade.

It is clear to me that the different parts of the Union have different interests, but I do not see that those interests are in conflict.

The southern states are almost exclusively agricultural; the northern states specialize in manufacturing and commerce; and the western states engage in both manufacturing and farming. The South grows tobacco, rice, cotton, and sugar; the North and West harvest corn and wheat. Thus the sources of wealth are diverse, but the best means of tapping those sources is the same for all, namely, union.

The North, which ships the wealth of the Anglo-Americans to all parts of the world and brings the riches of the world to the Union, has an obvious interest in continuing the confederation as it exists today, in order to ensure that the number of American producers and consumers it is called upon to serve remains as large as possible. The North is the most natural intermediary between the South and West on the one hand and the rest of the world on the other. Hence the North must desire the continued unity and prosperity of the South and West, so that those regions may continue to supply its factories with raw materials and its vessels with cargo.

The South and West, for their part, have an even more direct interest in the preservation of the Union and the prosperity of the North. The South exports much of what it produces overseas. Hence the South and West need the commercial resources of the North. They are bound to want the Union to be a great maritime power in order to protect those resources effectively. The South and West are bound to contribute willingly to the cost of maintaining a navy even though they have no ships; for if the fleets of Europe were to blockade the ports of the South and of the Mississippi Delta, what would become of the rice of the Carolinas, the tobacco of Virginia, and the sugar and cotton that grow in the Mississippi valley? Thus there is no part of the federal budget that is not applied to the preservation of a material interest common to all the confederates.

Apart from considerations of commercial utility, the South and West derive great political advantage from remaining united with each other and with the North.

The South has a large slave population, which is a threat now and will be an even greater threat in the future.

The western states all lie in a single valley. The rivers that water their territory, whether they originate in the Rocky Mountains or the Alleghenies, all flow into the Mississippi and empty into the Gulf of Mexico. For geographical reasons, the western states are completely cut off from the traditions of Europe and the civilization of the Old World.

Southerners are therefore bound to want the Union preserved so as not to be left to face the Blacks alone, and westerners so as not to find themselves confined to the center of the continent and deprived of free communication with the rest of the world.

The North, for its part, is bound to want the Union to continue undivided so as to remain the link connecting that great body to the rest of the world.

Thus the material interests of all parts of the Union are closely intertwined.

I would say the same thing about those opinions and sentiments that one might call man's immaterial interests.

The inhabitants of the United States talk a great deal about their love of country. I confess that I do not trust this calculated patriotism, which is based on interest and which interest, by attaching to another object, may destroy.

Nor do I attach much importance to what Americans say when they daily proclaim their intention to preserve the federal system adopted by their forefathers.

What keeps large numbers of citizens subject to the same government is much less the rational determination to remain united than the instinctive and in some sense involuntary accord that results from similarity of feeling and likeness of opinion.

I cannot accept the proposition that men constitute a society simply because they recognize the same leader and obey the same laws. Society exists only when men see many things in the same way and have the same opinions about many subjects and, finally, when the same facts give rise to the same impressions and the same thoughts.

Once the question is framed in this way, anyone who studies what is happening in the United States can easily see that even though its inhabitants are divided among twenty-four distinct sovereignties, they nevertheless constitute a single people. Indeed, he may even reach the conclusion that there is more reality to the state of society that exists in the Anglo-American Union than in certain European nations, even though the latter are governed by a single set of laws and subject to a single ruler.

Although the Anglo-Americans have several religions, they all look at religion in the same way.

They do not always agree about the best means of governing or the most suitable forms of government, but they do agree about the general principles that ought to rule human societies. From Maine to Florida, from Missouri to the Atlantic Ocean, everyone believes that all legitimate power originates with the people. Everyone shares the same ideas about liberty and equality. Everyone professes the same opinions about the press, the right of association, juries, and the responsibilities of government agents.

If we turn our attention from political and religious ideas to the philosophical and moral opinions that regulate everyday actions and guide conduct in general, we find the same agreement.

The Anglo-Americans[60] believe that the source of moral authority lies in universal reason, just as the source of political power lies in the universality of citizens, and they hold that

[60]Needless to say, when I use the term "Anglo-Americans," I am speaking only of the vast majority of them. Outside the majority there are always a few isolated individuals.

consensus is the only guide to what is permitted or prohibited, true or false. Most of them believe that the man who properly understands his own self-interest has all the guidance he needs to act justly and honestly. They believe that every person is born with the faculty to govern himself and that no one has the right to force happiness on his fellow man. All share a strong belief in human perfectibility. They judge that the spread of enlightenment necessarily brings useful results and that ignorance leads to disaster. All consider society a body in progress and mankind a changing tableau in which nothing is or should be fixed forever, and they admit that what seems good to them today may be replaced tomorrow by something better but as yet hidden from view.

I do not say that all these opinions are correct, but they are American.

Not only are the Anglo-Americans thus united by shared ideas, they are also set apart from all other peoples by a feeling of pride.

For fifty years the inhabitants of the United States have been told repeatedly that they constitute the only people that is religious, enlightened, and free. They see that democratic institutions in their country have prospered, while in the rest of the world they have thus far foundered. They therefore have a very high opinion of themselves, and they are not far from believing that they constitute a distinct species within the human race.

Clearly, then, the dangers that threaten the American Union stem no more from diversity of opinion than from diversity of interest. They must be sought in the variety of American characters and passions.

The men who inhabit the vast territory of the United States nearly all spring from a common stock. But over a long period of time, climate and above all slavery have introduced marked differences in character between the English of the southern United States and the English of the North.

In Europe, it is generally believed that different parts of the Union have contradictory interests because of slavery. This is not what I found. Slavery did not create interests in the South contrary to those of the North, but it did modify the character of southerners and cause them to develop different habits.

I earlier pointed out how servitude influenced the commercial capacity of southerners. It also affected their mores.

The slave is a servant who does not argue and who submits without a murmur. Though he may murder his master on occasion, he never resists. No family in the South is so poor that it has no slaves. The southerner is born into a sort of domestic dictatorship. From the beginning, life teaches him that he is born to command, and the first habit he acquires is that of effortless domination. The southerner's upbringing all but ensures that he will be arrogant, quick-tempered, irascible, violent, ardent in his desires, and impatient of obstacles, but easily discouraged if triumph is not immediate.

The northerner has no slaves to wait on him in his cradle. Indeed, he has no free servants, either, for he is usually obliged to provide for his own needs. From the moment he comes into the world, the idea of necessity is borne in on him; hence he learns early on to gauge precisely, on his own, the natural limit of his power; he does not expect to subdue by force those who would thwart his will, and he knows that, in order to gain the support of his fellow men, he must first win their favor. He is therefore patient, reflective, tolerant, slow to act, and persevering in his designs.

In the southern states, man's most pressing needs are always satisfied. Thus the southerner is not preoccupied with life's material concerns. Someone else bears the burden of looking after these on his behalf. Free in this respect, his imagination turns to other objects, grander and less precisely defined. The southerner loves grandeur, luxury, glory, excitement, pleasure, and above all idleness. Nothing obliges him to exert himself in order to live, and since for him no labor is necessary, he sleeps and abstains from doing even that labor which might be useful.

With equality of fortune prevailing in the North and slavery no longer existing there, the northerner is absorbed, as it were, by the very material concerns that the white southerner disdains. From childhood on he must struggle against misery, and he learns to place comfort above all the pleasures of the mind and heart. His imagination, concentrated on life's petty details, suffocates; his ideas are fewer in number and less general, but they become more practical, clearer, and more precise. Since all his intellectual effort is bent solely to the study of well-being, he soon excels at it. He is admirably clever when it comes to availing himself of nature and men to produce wealth, and has a marvelous understanding of how society can be made to contribute to the prosperity of each of its members and how individual selfishness can be made to serve the happiness of all.

The northerner has knowledge as well as experience. Nevertheless, he does not prize knowledge as a pleasure but esteems it as a means, and only its useful applications whet his appetite.

The southerner is more spontaneous, wittier, more open, generous, intellectual, and brilliant.

The northerner is more active, reasonable, enlightened, and skillful.

One has the tastes, prejudices, weaknesses, and grandeur of every aristocracy.

The other has the qualities and flaws characteristic of the middle class.

Take two men from the same society. If both share the same interests and some of the same opinions but differ as to character, enlightenment, and civilization, then it is highly likely that they will not agree. The same can be said of a society of nations.

Slavery therefore attacks the American confederation not directly, by way of interests, but indirectly, by way of mores.

Thirteen states subscribed to the federal pact of 1790; today the confederation numbers twenty-four. The population, which stood at nearly four million in 1790, has quadrupled in forty years; in 1830 it stood at nearly thirteen million.[61]

Such changes cannot take place without danger.

For a society of nations as for a society of individuals, three things exert the greatest influence on the chance of survival: the wisdom of the society's members, their weakness taken individually, and the smallness of their number.

The Americans who flee the Atlantic coast and rush headlong westward are adventurers impatient of discipline of any kind, avid for wealth, and often outcasts from the states in

---

[61]Census of 1790, 3,929,328. Census of 1830, 12,856,265.

which they were born. They arrive in the wilderness as strangers to one another and find there nothing to restrain them — not traditions or family spirit or examples. The law has little power over them, and mores even less. The men who daily settle the valleys of the Mississippi are therefore inferior in every way to the Americans who live within the Union's former borders. They nevertheless exert considerable influence within its councils and find themselves in a position to govern the public's business before they have learned to control themselves.[62]

The weaker a society's members are individually, the greater the likelihood that that society will continue to exist, for in that case their only security lies in remaining united. In 1790, when the most populous of the American republics had fewer than 500,000 inhabitants,[63] each republic was aware of its insignificance as an independent people, and that thought made it easier to comply with federal authority. But when one of the confederated states has a population of 2,000,000, as New York does, and covers an area a quarter the size of France,[64] it feels strong in its own right, and while it continues to desire union as something useful to its well-being, it no longer sees it as necessary to its existence. Union is something it can do without, and if it agrees to remain, before long it will want to dominate.

Any increase in the number of states in the Union tends to put considerable strain on the federal bond. Even people who share the same point of view do not always see things in the same way. This is even more true when points of view differ. Hence as the number of American republics increases, the likelihood of getting all of them to assent to the same laws decreases.

The interests of the various parts of the Union do not conflict with one another today, but who can predict what changes the near future will bring to a country where new cities are born every day and new states every few years?

[62]This, to be sure, is only a passing peril. I have no doubt that society will in time learn to establish and regulate itself in the West as it has already done along the Atlantic seaboard.

[63]In 1790, the population of Pennsylvania was 431,373.

[64]New York covers some 6,213 square leagues (50,000 square miles). See Darby, *View of the United States*, p. 435.

Since the English colonies were founded, the population has doubled every twenty-two years, more or less. I do not see anything that is likely to halt this steady growth of the Anglo-American population over the next century. Within the next hundred years, I believe that the territory occupied or claimed by the United States will be filled with more than a hundred million people and divided into forty states.[65]

Let us assume that these hundred million people do not have different interests, indeed, that all perceive an equal advantage in remaining united. Even so, the very fact that there are a hundred million of them, divided into forty distinct nations of unequal strength, would make the survival of the federal government no more than a lucky accident.

I should like to believe in the perfectibility of man, but until human nature changes and men are 435completely transformed, I shall refuse to believe in the durability of a government whose task is to hold together forty diverse peoples spread over an area half the size of Europe,[66] to avoid rivalries, dampen ambitions, and eliminate conflict among them, and to direct their independent wills toward joint action aimed at achieving common designs.

The greatest peril the Union will face as it grows comes, however, from the continual shift of the forces at work within it.

As the crow flies, it is roughly four hundred French leagues from the shores of Lake Superior to the Gulf of Mexico. The frontier of the United States wends its way along this immense line. In places it does not reach quite that far westward,

---

[65]If the population continues to double every twenty-two years over the next century as it has done for the past two hundred years, the population of the United States in 1852 will be twenty-four million; in 1874, forty-eight million; and in 1896, ninety-six million. This will occur even if some of the land east of the Rockies proves to be unsuitable for cultivation. The land already occupied could easily support that number of people. A hundred million people spread over the area now occupied by the twenty-four states and three territories that constitute the Union would give a density of only 762 inhabitants per square league, still far less than the average density in France, which is 1,006; England, which is 1,417; and even Switzerland, which, despite its lakes and mountains, has a density of only 783 inhabitants per square league. See Malte-Brun, vol. 6, p. 92.

[66]The area of the United States is 295,000 square leagues; that of Europe, according to Malte-Brun, vol. 6, p. 4, is 500,000.

but more often than not it extends well on into the wilderness. It has been calculated that along this vast front Whites have been advancing an average of seven leagues every year.[67] Occasionally an obstacle is encountered: an unproductive district, a lake, an Indian nation unexpectedly turns up on the path. The column then halts for a moment; its two ends curve inward, and when they meet, the column begins to advance once more. There is something providential about this gradual and steady progress of the European race toward the Rocky Mountains: it is like a human flood, rising steadily and daily driven on by the hand of God.

Behind this conquering army's front line, cities are built and vast states are founded. In 1790 there were only a few thousand pioneers scattered among the valleys of the Mississippi. Today those same valleys are home to as many people as inhabited the entire Union in 1790. Their population has risen to almost four million.[68] The city of Washington was founded in 1800 in the very center of the American confederation; now it finds itself at one of the extremities. When representatives of the western states[69] go to take up their seats in Congress, they are already obliged to travel a distance as great as that from Vienna to Paris.

All the states of the Union are carried by the same tides of fortune, but it is impossible for all to grow and prosper at the same rate.

In the North, branches of the Alleghenies stretch right down to the Atlantic, forming spacious anchorages and ports that are open all year round to the largest vessels. But following the American coastline southward from the Potomac all the way to the Mississippi delta, one finds only flat and sandy terrain. In this part of the Union, the mouths of nearly all rivers are obstructed, and the ports that exist in the resulting widely separated lagoons are not as deep as the northern ports and far less well equipped for commercial operations.

Beyond this first inferiority, which is born of nature, there is another, which stems from laws.

[67]See *Legislative Documents*, 20th Congress, no. 117, p. 105.
[68]3,672,327, census of 1830.
[69]The distance from Jefferson, capital of the state of Missouri, to Washington is 1,019 miles, or 420 postal leagues. (*American Almanac*, 1831, p. 48.)

We have seen that slavery, which has been abolished in the North, still exists in the South, and I have shown the disastrous influence that it exerts on the well-being of the master himself.

The North is therefore bound to be more commercial[70] and more industrious than the South. It is only natural that population and wealth should accumulate there more rapidly.

The states along the Atlantic seaboard are already half-populated. Most of the land is owned. Hence these states cannot welcome the same number of immigrants as the western states, which still offer a boundless horizon to industry. The Mississippi basin is infinitely more fertile than the Atlantic coast. This, together with all the other factors, acts as a powerful force driving Europeans to the west. Statistics offer rigorous proof of this.

If one looks at the United States as a whole, the number of inhabitants has almost tripled over the past forty years. But if one looks exclusively at the Mississippi basin, it turns out that the population[71] increased thirty-one-fold over the same period.[72]

[70]A glance at the following statistics is enough to reveal the difference that exists between the commercial activity of the South and that of the North:

In 1829, the total tonnage of large and small commercial vessels belonging to Virginia, the two Carolinas, and Georgia (the four great states of the South) was only 5,243 tons.

In that same year, the ships of the state of Massachusetts alone amounted to 17,322 tons. (*Legislative Documents*, 21st Congress, 2nd session, no. 140, p. 244.)

Yet Massachusetts is only 959 square leagues in area (7,335 square miles) and has a population of just 610,014, while the four states I mentioned cover an area of 27,204 square leagues (210,000 square miles) and have a population of 3,047,767. Thus the area of Massachusetts is only one-thirtieth that of the four southern states, and its population is only a fifth of theirs. (See Darby, *View of the United States*.) Slavery harms the commercial prosperity of the South in a number of ways: it makes Whites less enterprising and prevents them from finding sailors when they need them. Sailors are generally recruited only from the lowest class of the population. In the South, that class consists of slaves, and slaves are difficult to use at sea. They allegedly do not perform as effectively as Whites, and there would always be the danger that they would rebel in the middle of the ocean or flee after landing on some foreign shore.

[71]Darby, *View of the United States*, p. 444.

[72]Note that when I speak of the Mississippi basin, I do not include the portions of the states of New York, Pennsylvania, and Virginia that lie west of the Alleghenies, which should also be considered a part of it.

The center of federal power is shifting daily. Forty years ago, the majority of the Union's citizens lived on the seacoast in the vicinity of where the city of Washington stands today. Now the center of population has moved deeper inland and farther to the north. There can be no doubt that within twenty years it will be located beyond the Alleghenies. If the Union survives, the Mississippi basin, owing to its fertility and extent, is surely destined to become the permanent center of federal power. Within thirty or forty years, the Mississippi basin will have assumed its natural rank. It is easy to calculate that by then the ratio of its population to that of the states along the Atlantic seaboard will be roughly forty to eleven. Within a few years after that, leadership of the Union will therefore pass entirely out of the hands of the founding states, and the population of the Mississippi valleys will dominate federal councils.

This steady northwestward drift of power and federal influence becomes apparent every ten years, as each new census of the population leads to a readjustment of the number of representatives that each state is supposed to send to Congress.[73]

In 1790, Virginia had nineteen congressmen. This number continued to increase until 1813, when it reached twenty-three. It then began to decrease. By 1833 it had dropped to twenty-one.[74] During the same period, New York followed a different pattern: in 1790, it had ten representatives in Congress; in

[73]The census shows that over the previous ten years, the population of, say, Delaware has increased by five percent, while that of, for instance, the territory of Michigan has increased by two hundred fifty percent. Virginia discovers that, during the same period, its population has increased by thirteen percent, while the population of the adjacent state of Ohio has increased by sixty-one percent. Look at the table in the *National Calendar*, and you will be struck by the inequalities in the fortunes of the various states.

[74]As we shall see later, the population of Virginia increased by thirteen percent during the latter period. Explanation is required for the fact that the number of a state's representatives can decrease while the state's population is not decreasing at all but actually increasing.

For purposes of comparison, let us take Virginia, which I have already mentioned. The number of Virginia's representatives in 1823 was proportionate to the total number of representatives for the entire Union. In 1833, the number of Virginia's representatives was again proportionate to the total number of representatives, taking account of the fact that both the population of Virginia and that of the Union had increased in that time. In order for the number of representatives from Virginia to remain constant, the ratio

1813, twenty-seven; in 1823, thirty-four; in 1833, forty. Ohio had only one congressman in 1803; in 1833 it could boast of nineteen.

It is difficult to imagine a durable union between two peoples, one poor and weak, the other rich and strong, even if the strength and wealth of the one are known not to be the cause of the weakness and poverty of the other. The difficulty of maintaining union is even greater when one people is losing strength and the other gaining.

The rapid and disproportionate growth of certain states threatens the independence of the others. If New York, with its two million inhabitants and forty representatives, wanted to lay down the law to Congress, it might well succeed. But even if the most powerful states did not seek to oppress the lesser ones, the danger would still exist, for the danger lies as much in the possibility as in the actual fact.

The weak seldom have confidence in the justice and reason of the strong. The states where growth is less rapid therefore look on the states favored by fortune with suspicion and envy. This accounts for the profound malaise and vague anxiety that one sees in one part of the Union, in stark contrast to the well-being and confidence that dominate the other part. This, in my view, is the sole cause of the hostile attitude adopted by the South.

Of all Americans, southerners should feel most attached to the Union, for it is they who would suffer most if left to themselves. Yet only they are threatening to break up the confederation. Why is this so? The answer is easy: the South, which provided the confederation with four presidents;[75] which today knows that its power is slipping away; which sees the number of its representatives in Congress decreasing every year while those of the North and West are increasing — the South, populated by ardent and irascible men, is vexed and

of the state's proportionate increase to the nation's would have to be inversely proportional to the ratio between the new number of representatives and the old. But if the ratio of the proportionate increase of Virginia's population to that of the Union's population is less than that of the ratio of the new number of representatives to the old, the number of Virginia's deputies will be smaller.

[75] Washington, Jefferson, Madison, and Monroe.

anxious. With a melancholy gaze it looks inward and, interrogating the past, asks itself every day whether it is not oppressed. Should it discover that a federal law is not obviously beneficial to it, it will bewail the abuse of power to its detriment; it ardently presses its demands, and if its voice goes unheeded, it becomes indignant and threatens to withdraw from a society whose burdens it bears without reaping the concomitant rewards.

In 1832, the people of Carolina offered the following observation: "Can it excite any surprise, that under the operation of the Protecting System, the manufacturing states should be constantly increasing in riches and growing in strength, with an inhospitable climate and barren soil, while the southern states, the natural garden of America, should be rapidly falling into decay?"[76]

If the changes I mentioned took place gradually, so that there was time at least for each generation to pass away along with the order of things to which it had been witness, the danger would be less great; but there is something precipitous, I would almost say revolutionary, in the progress that society is making in America. The same citizen who saw his state march at the head of the Union may subsequently have seen it reduced to impotence in federal councils. An Anglo-American republic can grow as rapidly as a man, experiencing birth, increase, and maturity all within the space of thirty years.

It would be a mistake, however, to think that states that lose power also lose population or wither away. There is no halt to their prosperity. Indeed, they continue to grow more rapidly than any kingdom in Europe.[77] To them, however, it seems

---

[76]See the report of the committee to the convention that proclaimed nullification in South Carolina.

[77]A country's population is certainly the primary ingredient of its wealth. In the period 1820 to 1832, while Virginia was losing two Congressmen, its population increased by 13.7 percent; that of the Carolinas by 15 percent; and that of Georgia by 51.5 percent (see *American Almanac*, 1832, p. 162). Now, Russia, the European country whose population growth is most rapid, had only a 9.5 percent population increase over a period of ten years; in France the rate of increase was 7 percent, and in Europe as a whole it was 4.7 percent (see Malte-Brun, vol. 6, p. 95).

that they are growing poorer because they do not grow richer as rapidly as their neighbors, and they think they are losing power because they suddenly find themselves in contact with a power greater than their own.[78] Thus their feelings and passions suffer more than their interests. Is that not enough, however, to place the confederation in peril? Had nations and kings looked only to their own true advantage since the beginning of the world, man would hardly know what war is.

Thus, the greatest danger that threatens the United States is born of its very prosperity, which tends to foster in a number of the confederated states the intoxication that goes with any rapid increase in fortune while filling the others with the envy, suspicion, and regret that usually attend the loss thereof.

Americans rejoice at this extraordinary development, but I think they should look upon it with regret and fear. No matter what they do, the Americans of the United States are destined to become one of the greatest peoples in the world. Their offspring will blanket all of North America. The continent they inhabit is their preserve: it cannot slip from their grasp. Why must they race to take possession of it today? Wealth, power, and glory will inevitably be theirs some day, yet they hasten after this immense fortune as though they had but a moment left to lay hold of it.

I have demonstrated, I believe, that the existence of the present confederation depends entirely on the willingness of all the confederates to remain united, and, starting from that premise, I have investigated the causes that might lead the various states to wish to separate. But the Union can die in two ways: one of the confederated states may wish to renege on the contract and thus break the common bond in a violent way; most of the remarks I have made thus far apply to this case. Or the federal government may gradually lose its power if for some reason all the united republics simultaneously reclaim their independence. The central power, deprived of its prerogatives one by one and reduced to impotence by tacit accord, would become incapable of fulfilling its purpose, and

---

[78] One has to admit, however, that the fall in the price of tobacco over the past fifty years has notably diminished the affluence of southern planters, but this has as little to do with the wishes of northerners as with their own.

the second Union would perish like the first in a kind of senile imbecility.

Furthermore, the gradual weakening of the federal bond, which leads ultimately to nullification of the Union, is in itself a distinct influence, which may yield many less drastic results prior to that. Well before the confederation ceased to exist, the weakness of its government could reduce the nation to impotence, leading to anarchy at home and hindering the country's general prosperity.

Having investigated the things that tend to drive the Anglo-Americans apart, it is therefore important to inquire whether, if the Union survives, the government will expand or contract its sphere of action, become more energetic or grow weaker.

Americans are obviously preoccupied by one great fear. They recognize that in most of the nations of the world, the exercise of sovereign rights tends to become concentrated in a few hands, and they are frightened by the thought that, in the end, it will be the same with them as well. Statesmen themselves experience these terrors, or at any rate pretend to experience them, for in America centralization is not popular, and there is no cleverer way to court the majority than to rail against the alleged encroachments of the central government. Americans refuse to see that in countries where this frightening tendency toward centralization manifests itself, there is only one people, whereas the Union is a confederation of different peoples. This is enough to upset any forecast based on analogy.

I confess that I consider this fear, which a large number of Americans feel, to be entirely imaginary. Far from sharing their dread that sovereignty may be consolidated in the hands of the Union, I believe that the federal government is becoming visibly weaker.

To prove my point, I shall adduce not old facts but only things that I was able to see for myself or that have occurred in recent times.

When one looks closely at what is happening in the United States, two contradictory tendencies stand out. It is as if two rivers flowing in opposite directions shared the same bed.

In the forty-five years that the Union has been in existence, time has refuted a host of provincial prejudices that initially militated against it. The patriotic sentiment binding each American to his state has become less exclusive. As the various parts of the Union have come to know each other better, they have grown closer. The postal service — a force for creating powerful intellectual bonds — today reaches into the depths of the wilderness.[79] Steamboats offer daily connections between all points on the coast. Trade flows up and down the rivers of the interior with unprecedented speed.[80] Beyond these opportunities created by nature and art, one also finds instability of desires, restlessness of spirit, and love of riches — forces that constantly drive Americans from their homes and into contact with large numbers of their fellow citizens. Americans travel all over their country and visit its many populations. There is no province in France whose people know one another as well as the thirteen million men and women who cover the surface of the United States.

As Americans mingle, they assimilate. Differences created by climate, origin, and institutions diminish. Everyone comes closer and closer to a common type. Every year, thousands of people leave the North and spread throughout the Union, taking their beliefs, opinions, and mores with them. Being more enlightened than the people among whom they settle, they soon take charge of affairs and alter society for their own benefit. This constant emigration from North to South significantly favors the fusion of all provincial characters into one national character. The civilization of the North therefore seems destined to become the common measure to which everything else must some day adjust.

As American industry progresses, the commercial ties uniting all the confederated states grow tighter, and the Union,

[79]As of 1832, the district of Michigan, which has a population of only 31,639 and is still virtually untouched wilderness, had developed 940 miles of post roads. The almost completely wild territory of Arkansas was already traversed by 1,938 miles of post roads. See *The Report of the Postmaster General*, November 30, 1833. Throughout the Union, the delivery of newspapers alone brings in $254,796 annually.

[80]In the ten years between 1821 and 1831, 271 steamboats were launched on the rivers of the Mississippi valley alone.

In 1829, there were 256 steamboats in the United States. See *Legislative Documents*, no. 140, p. 274.

no longer a matter of opinion, becomes a habit. The passage of time dissipates the many fantastic terrors that had tormented the imagination in 1789. Federal power has not become oppressive. It has not destroyed the independence of the states. It is not leading the confederates into monarchy. Within the Union, the smaller states have not become dependent on the larger ones. The confederation has grown steadily in population, wealth, and power.

So far as natural difficulties are concerned, I am therefore convinced that it is easier for Americans to live united now than it was in 1789; the Union has fewer enemies than it had then.

Yet anyone willing to devote careful study to the history of the United States over the past forty-five years will readily convince himself that federal power is decreasing.

The causes of this phenomenon are not difficult to point out.

When the Constitution was promulgated in 1789, everything was dying, and anarchy was everywhere. The Union that supplanted the previous state of disorder aroused considerable fear and hatred, but it also had ardent friends, because it was the expression of a great need. Though under heavier attack then than now, federal power therefore quickly reached its apogee, as is often the case when a government triumphs after summoning all its forces for battle. Interpretation of the Constitution in that period seemed to expand federal sovereignty rather than contract it, and the Union could be seen in several respects as offering the spectacle of a single people led internally as well as externally by a single government.

In order to reach that point, however, the people had in a sense risen above themselves.

The Constitution had not destroyed the individuality of the states, and all bodies, regardless of their nature, harbor a secret instinct that impels them toward independence. That instinct is more pronounced in a country like America, where each village constitutes a sort of republic accustomed to governing itself.

Hence it took effort on the part of the states to submit to federal preponderance, and effort, even when crowned with success, is bound to slacken with the waning of the cause that originally called it forth.

As the federal government consolidated its power, America resumed its rank among nations, peace was reestablished on its borders, and public credit was restored. Confusion gave way to a stable order, which allowed individual industry to follow its natural course and develop in liberty.

Prosperity itself made people lose sight of what had produced it. Once the peril was past, Americans could no longer summon up the energy and patriotism that had helped them avoid it in the first place. Delivered from the fears that had preoccupied them, they reverted easily to old habits and readily gave in to their usual penchants. The moment a strong government no longer seemed necessary, they began once again to think of it as a hindrance. Things in general prospered as the Union prospered, and no one severed his ties to it, yet everyone wished to feel the action of the power representing the Union as little as possible. In general, people wished to remain united, yet each of their particular actions tended to restore their independence. With each passing day, the principle of confederation was more readily accepted in theory and less applied in practice. Thus the federal government, by creating order and peace, brought on its own decadence.

Once this cast of mind manifested itself in public, party politicians, who thrive on the passions of the people, set about exploiting it for their own advantage.

At that point the federal government found itself in a very critical situation. Its enemies enjoyed popular favor, and candidates won the right to lead it by promising to make it weaker.

Since then, whenever the government of the Union has had to contend with the government of the states, it has almost invariably been forced to retreat. As occasions arose to interpret the terms of the federal constitution, interpretation has more often than not gone against the Union and proved favorable to the states.

The Constitution placed national interests in the charge of the federal government. The idea was that it should undertake or encourage major "internal improvements" intended to enhance the prosperity of the Union as a whole, such as the building of canals.

The states were alarmed by the idea that some authority other than their own might thus control a portion of their territory. They were afraid that if the central government thereby acquired substantial patronage within their borders, it might come to exert an influence that they wished to reserve exclusively for their own agents.

The democratic party, which had always opposed the expansion of federal power, therefore spoke out. Congress was accused of usurpation; the head of state, of ambition. Intimidated by this outcry, the central government ultimately acknowledged its error and strictly limited its action to the sphere prescribed.

The Constitution gives the Union the privilege of treating with foreign peoples. The Union had generally viewed Indian tribes living along its borders in this light. So long as these savages were willing to flee before civilization's advance, the federal right went uncontested. But the moment an Indian tribe sought to settle in one place, the surrounding states claimed possession of that tribe's land and sovereign rights over the people living on it. The federal government was quick to recognize both claims, and though it had previously dealt with the Indians as independent peoples, it now surrendered them as subjects to the legislative tyranny of the states.[81]

A number of the Atlantic seaboard states had no definite western boundaries and extended into wilderness regions where Europeans had yet to set foot. The states whose boundaries had been fixed irrevocably cast a jealous eye on the boundless future beckoning to their neighbors. The latter, in a spirit of conciliation and in order to facilitate the act of Union, agreed to set boundaries for themselves and ceded all territory beyond those boundaries to the confederation.[82]

Since then, the federal government has become the owner of all uncultivated land lying outside the thirteen states of the original confederation. It has assumed responsibility for

[81]See, in the legislative documents that I previously cited in the chapter on the Indians, the letter from the president of the United States to the Cherokees, his correspondence on this subject with his agents, and his messages to Congress.
[82]The first act of cession was passed by the state of New York in 1780; Virginia, Massachusetts, Connecticut, South Carolina, and North Carolina followed suit at various times, and Georgia, the last of the states to do so, did not act until 1802.

dividing up that land and selling it, and the money stemming from these sales goes exclusively to the treasury of the Union. With this income, the federal government buys land from the Indians, opens up roads into the new districts, and uses all its power to facilitate the rapid development of society there.

In due course, new states were organized in the former wilderness regions that the Atlantic seaboard states had ceded years earlier. Congress continued to sell the uncultivated land contained within the boundaries of those states for the benefit of the nation as a whole. Recently, however, the new states began to advance the claim that, once constituted, they should have the exclusive right to use the proceeds of these sales for their own benefit. As these claims became more and more threatening, Congress decided that it had better deprive the Union of some of the privileges it had previously enjoyed, and at the end of 1832 it passed a law which, though it did not cede ownership of uncultivated lands to the new republics of the West, did allow them to use the bulk of the revenue derived from the sale of such land for their own benefit.[83]

It is enough to travel through the United States to appreciate the benefits that the country derives from the Bank. These benefits are of several kinds, but one is especially striking to the foreigner: notes from the Bank of the United States are accepted on the edge of the wilderness at the same value as in Philadelphia, which is the seat of the bank's operations.[84]

The Bank of the United States is nevertheless the object of intense hatred. Its directors have spoken out against the President, and they are accused, plausibly enough, of abusing their influence to thwart his election. The President has therefore attacked the institution they represent with all the ardor of personal animosity. He is encouraged in his vendetta, moreover, by his sense that the majority with its secret instincts supports him.

---

[83]To be sure, the President refused to sign this law, but he fully accepted its principle. See *Message of December 8, 1833*.

[84]The present Bank of the United States was founded in 1816 with a capital of 35 million dollars (185,500,000 francs). Its charter expires in 1836. Last year, Congress passed a law renewing it, but the President refused to sign it. The ensuing struggle has today reached extremes of violence on both sides, and it is easy to foresee the bank's imminent collapse.

The Bank constitutes the great monetary bond of the Union, just as Congress is the great legislative bond, and the same passions that tend to make the state independent of the central government tend toward the destruction of the Bank.

The Bank of the United States always holds a large number of notes issued by state banks. Whenever it chooses, it can oblige those banks to redeem their notes for cash. No similar danger threatens it, however; it has sufficient resources available to withstand any demand. Because the existence of state banks is thereby threatened, they are obliged to exercise restraint and must issue notes only in proportion to their capital. The state banks are impatient of this salutary control. Newspapers that have sold out to them — along with the President, whose own self-interest has made him their mouthpiece — therefore attack the Bank with a kind of furor. They arouse local passions and the country's blind democratic instinct against the central bank. According to them, the directors of the Bank form a permanent aristocratic body whose influence is bound to be felt by the government and will sooner or later corrupt the principles of equality on which American society is based.

The Bank's struggle with its enemies is merely one episode in the wider war between the states and the central government in America — and between the spirit of independence and democracy and the spirit of hierarchy and subordination. I am not arguing that the enemies of the Bank of the United States are precisely the same individuals who are attacking the federal government on other points, but I am saying that the attacks against the Bank are a product of the same instincts that militate against the federal government, and that the fact that the Bank has a large number of enemies is a troubling symptom of that government's weakness.

At no time, however, has the Union's weakness been more clearly on display than in the notorious tariff affair.[85]

The French revolutionary wars and the War of 1812, by preventing free communication between America and Europe, allowed manufacturing to gain a foothold in the North of the

---

[85]The main source for details of this affair is *Legislative Documents*, 22nd Congress, 2nd Session, no. 30.

Union. When peace opened the New World to European products once again, the Americans felt obliged to establish a customs system both to protect their nascent industry and to pay off debts that war had forced them to acquire.

The southern states, being purely agricultural, had no manufacturing to encourage, and they were not slow to complain about this measure.

It is not my intention here to consider the extent to which these complaints may have been imaginary or real. I shall simply recount the facts.

In 1820, South Carolina declared in a petition to Congress that the tariff law was *unconstitutional*, *oppressive*, and *unjust*. Georgia, Virginia, North Carolina, and the states of Alabama and Mississippi subsequently lodged more or less strenuous protests along similar lines.

Taking no heed of these rumblings of discontent, Congress in 1824 and again in 1828 raised the tariffs and reaffirmed the principle.

At that point the South developed, or rather revived, a celebrated doctrine, which came to be known as *nullification*.

I showed earlier, at an appropriate place in my exposition, that the purpose of the federal constitution was not to establish a league but to create a national government. In all the cases foreseen by the Constitution, the Americans of the United States constitute a single and unique people. In each such instance, the national will is expressed, as with all constitutional peoples, by way of a majority. Once the majority has spoken, the duty of the minority is to submit.

That is the legal doctrine, the only one in agreement with both the text of the Constitution and the known intent of its framers.

By contrast, the *nullifiers* of the South claim that when Americans united, it was not their intention to fuse into a single and unique people but only to form a league of independent peoples; from which it follows that each state, having preserved its full sovereignty, if not in action then at least in principle, has the right to interpret the laws of Congress and, within its borders, to suspend execution of any such laws that it deems contrary to the Constitution or to justice.

The whole nullification doctrine was summed up by Mr.

Calhoun, the avowed leader of the nullifiers, in a speech he delivered to the United States Senate in 1833:

"The Constitution," he said, "is a contract in which the states figure as sovereigns. Now, any time there is a contract between parties who do not recognize a common arbiter, each of them retains the right to judge the extent of its obligation for itself."

It is manifest that such a doctrine would destroy the federal bond in principle and in fact restore the anarchy from which the Constitution delivered the Americans in 1789.

When South Carolina saw that Congress turned a deaf ear to its complaints, it threatened to apply the nullifiers' doctrine to the federal tariff laws. Congress stayed with its system. Finally, the storm broke.

In 1832, the people of South Carolina[86] called a state convention to advise on extraordinary measures that might still be taken. On November 24 of that year, the convention published what it called an ordinance, to wit, a law nullifying the federal tariff law, prohibiting the collection of the duties it imposed, and banning acceptance of any appeals that might be made to the federal courts.[87] The ordinance was not to be put into effect until the following February, and it was stipulated that if Congress modified the tariff before then, South

---

[86]To be precise, a majority of the people; for the opposition, known as the Union Party, continued to enjoy the support of a very strong and very active minority. Carolina must have had around 47,000 voters; 30,000 favored nullification, and 17,000 were opposed.

[87]This ordinance was preceded by the report of the committee charged with drafting it, which explained the nature and purpose of the law. The following passage appears on p. 34:

"When the rights reserved to the several states by the Constitution are deliberately violated, it is the right and duty of those states to intervene so as to stop the progress of the evil, oppose the usurpation, and maintain within their respective limits the powers and privileges that belong to them as *independent sovereigns*. If the states did not possess this right, in vain would they pretend to be sovereign. South Carolina recognizes no tribunal on earth that stands above her. It is true that she, along with other sovereign states, has entered into a solemn contract of union, but she claims and will exercise the right to explain what that means in her eyes, and when that contract is violated by her partners and by the government they have created, she will use the unquestionable right to judge the extent of the infraction and what measures are to be taken to obtain justice."

Carolina might agree not to act further on its threats. Later, it was intimated in vague and indefinite terms that the state wished to submit the matter to a special assembly of all the confederated states.

Meanwhile, South Carolina armed its militia and prepared for war.

What did Congress do? Having failed to listen to its suppliant subjects, it began to heed their complaints when it saw them take up arms.[88] It passed a law[89] stipulating that duties collected under the tariff would be reduced gradually over a period of ten years until they no longer exceeded the needs of the government. Thus Congress completely abandoned the principle of the tariff. It replaced a duty intended to protect industry with a purely fiscal measure.[90] To hide its defeat, the government of the Union resorted to an expedient often employed by weak governments: while it yielded in reality, it made a show of remaining inflexible as to the principle. Congress not only amended the tariff law but also passed another law granting the President special power to use force if needed to overcome a resistance that there was no longer any reason to fear.

South Carolina was unwilling to leave the Union with even this flimsy appearance of victory. The same state convention that had nullified the tariff law reconvened and accepted the concession it was offered, but at the same time it reaffirmed more strongly than ever its commitment to the nullifiers' doctrine and, to prove it, nullified the law granting special powers to the President, even though it was quite certain they would never be used.

Nearly all the events I have just described took place during General Jackson's presidency. There is no denying that Jackson shrewdly and vigorously defended the rights of the Union

---

[88] What finally persuaded Congress to adopt this measure was a show of force by the powerful state of Virginia, whose legislature offered to serve as arbiter between the Union and South Carolina. Until then, the latter state had seemed altogether abandoned, even by the states that had joined in its protest.

[89] Law of March 2, 1833.

[90] This law was suggested by Mr. Clay and passed within four days by an immense majority of both houses of Congress.

in the tariff affair. Nevertheless, I believe that among the dangers that the federal government faces today, one must count the very conduct of the man who represents it.

Some people in Europe have formed an opinion about General Jackson's influence over his country's affairs that seems quite extravagant to those who have witnessed the situation at first hand.

General Jackson is said to be a man who has won battles, an energetic individual given by character and habit to the use of force, eager for power, and despotic by predilection. All that may be true, but the consequences drawn from these truths are seriously mistaken.

Some think that General Jackson wants to establish a dictatorship in the United States, that he intends to promote a militaristic spirit and expand the central government in such a way as to endanger provincial liberties. In America, the time for such ventures, the century for such men, has yet to arrive: had General Jackson wished to rule in this manner, he would surely have forfeited his political position and compromised his life; hence he was not so imprudent as to attempt it.

The current President, far from wanting to extend federal power, in fact represents the party that wants to confine that power as much as possible within the limits clearly and precisely spelled out by the Constitution and is unwilling to accept any interpretation that might be favorable to the government of the Union. Far from presenting himself as the champion of centralization, General Jackson is the agent of provincial jealousies; it was *decentralizing* passions (if I may put it that way) that brought him to sovereign power, and it is by flattering those passions every day that he manages to remain and prosper in that position. General Jackson is the slave of the majority: he obeys its wishes and desires and heeds its half-divulged instincts; or, rather, he divines what the majority wants, anticipating its desires before it knows what they are in order to place himself at its head.

Whenever conflict arises between the government of the states and that of the Union, the President is almost always the first to doubt his own powers. He nearly always anticipates the legislative power. When there is room for interpretation as to the extent of federal powers, he takes a stand against himself, as it were. He minimizes himself, hides himself from view, shuns the limelight. Not that he is weak by nature or an enemy of the Union. When the majority took a stand against the claims of the southern nullifiers, he placed himself at its head, clearly and vigorously enunciated its position, and was the first to call for the use of force. To use terms borrowed from the lexicon of American party politics, General Jackson strikes me as *federal* by predilection and *republican* by calculation.

Having bowed to the majority to win its favor, General Jackson could once again stand tall. At that point he set his course straight for the objectives the majority had set for itself, or those that it did not regard with a jealous eye, overcoming every obstacle that stood in his way. Enjoying support that his predecessors lacked, he was strong enough to sweep his personal enemies aside more easily than any previous president. On his own responsibility he took measures that no one before him would have dared. At times he has treated the nation's representatives with disdain bordering on insult. He has refused to sign laws passed by Congress and has frequently failed to respond to that august body. He is a favorite who has been known at times to turn on his master. Accordingly, General Jackson's power is increasing steadily, but that of the President is diminishing. In his hands, the federal government is strong. When he passes it on to his successor, it will be weak.

Either I am strangely mistaken, or the federal government of the United States is daily growing weaker. It is withdrawing from one affair after another and steadily narrowing its sphere of action. Naturally weak, it is relinquishing even the appearance of strength. Meanwhile, however, it seemed to me that the sentiment of independence was growing more vigorous in the states and love of provincial government more pronounced.

Americans want the Union, but reduced to a shadow: they want it strong in certain cases and weak in all others. They pretend that in time of war it can gather all the nation's forces and all the country's resources in its hands, yet in time of peace that it can cease, as it were, to exist — as if this alternation of debility and vigor existed in nature.

I see nothing at present that can arrest the general tendency to think in such terms. Its causes remain unchanged. It will therefore continue, and one can predict that, barring some extraordinary circumstance, the government of the Union will grow weaker every day.

Nevertheless, I believe that the day is still far off when federal power, incapable of protecting its own existence and bringing peace to the country, will die, as it were, of its own accord. The Union is part of the nation's mores; people want it; its results are evident, its benefits visible. When people recognize that the weakness of the federal government is compromising the existence of the Union, I have no doubt that a reaction will take place in favor of force.

Of all the federal governments that have been established to date, the government of the United States is by its very nature the most likely to act. As long as it is not attacked indirectly through interpretation of its laws, and as long as its substance is not profoundly corrupted, a change of opinion, internal crisis, or war could promptly restore the vigor it needs.

The point I want to make is simply this: many people in Europe think that there is a tendency in the United States in favor of centralizing power in the hands of the President and Congress. I claim that a contrary tendency is plainly apparent there. As the federal government grows older, far from gaining strength and threatening the sovereignty of the states, it is, in my view, becoming weaker every day, and the only sovereignty in danger is that of the Union. This is what the present reveals. What will the final result of this tendency be? What events may halt, slow, or hasten the movement I have described? These remain hidden in the future, whose veil I do not pretend to be able to lift.

ON REPUBLICAN INSTITUTIONS IN THE UNITED STATES: WHAT ARE THEIR CHANCES OF SURVIVAL?

The Union is only an accident. — Republican institutions have more of a future. — The republic is, for now, the natural state of the Anglo-Americans. — Why. — In order to destroy it, one would have to change all laws and modify all mores at the same time. Difficulties faced by the Americans in creating an aristocracy.

A breakup of the Union, leading to war among the now confederated states and, with it, standing armies, dictatorship, and taxes, could in the long run compromise the fate of republican institutions.

Nevertheless, the future of the republic should not be confused with the future of the Union.

The Union is an accident, which will survive only as long as circumstances allow, but the republic seems to me the natural state of the Americans. Only the constant action of contrary causes, invariably acting in the same direction, could lead to its replacement by a monarchy.

The Union exists primarily in the law that created it. A single revolution or a change in public opinion could shatter it forever. The republic has deeper roots.

What the word "republic" means in the United States is the slow and tranquil action of society on itself. It is an orderly state truly based on the enlightened will of the people. It is a conciliatory government, whose resolutions ripen slowly, are debated deliberately, and are carried out only when mature.

Republicans in the United States value mores, respect beliefs, and recognize rights. They profess the opinion that insofar as a people is free, it must be moral, religious, and moderate. The name "republic" is applied in the United States to the tranquil reign of the majority. Once the majority has had time to identify itself and confirm its existence, it becomes the common source of power. But the majority itself is not all-powerful. Standing above it in the moral realm are humanity, justice, and reason, and, in the political realm, established rights. The majority recognizes these two barriers, and if it should happen to transgress them, it is because it has passions, just as individuals do, and, like them, can do wrong even though it discerns what is good.

In Europe, however, we have made some strange discoveries.

The republic, according to some of us, is not the reign of the majority, as people have hitherto believed, but rather the reign of those who present themselves as strong champions of the majority. It is not the people who rule in governments of this sort but those who know what is best for the people: this felicitous distinction makes it possible to act on behalf of a nation without consulting it and to claim the nation's gratitude while trampling it underfoot. Furthermore, a republican government is the only government that must be granted the right of doing whatever it wants and that must be allowed to scorn all that men have hitherto respected, from the highest laws of morality to the vulgar rules of common sense.

Before us, people thought that despotism in any form was odious. Lately, however, they have discovered that there are legitimate tyrannies in the world, and holy injustices, provided that they are exercised in the name of the people.

The ideas that Americans have formed about the republic significantly ease the task of living under it and ensure its survival. Although their practice of republican government is often bad, the theory at least is good, and in the end the people always bring their actions into conformity with theory.

In the beginning it was impossible, and it would still be very difficult, to establish a centralized administration in America. The people are dispersed over too wide a territory and separated by too many natural obstacles for a single individual to attempt to manage the details of their existence. America is therefore par excellence the land of provincial and local government.

These effects of geography were felt equally by all Europeans in the New World, but several other factors affected the Anglo-Americans in particular.

When the colonies of North America were established, municipal liberty was already firmly entrenched in English laws and mores, and the English immigrants adopted it not only as a necessary thing but also as a good whose value they fully appreciated.

We saw earlier how the colonies were founded. Each province, each district for that matter, was settled separately by men who did not know one another or who had joined together for a variety of purposes.

From the beginning, therefore, the English of the United States found themselves divided into a large number of small, distinct societies not linked to any common center, and each of these small societies was obliged to deal with its own affairs since there was no central authority that naturally would or readily could take care of these matters for them.

Thus the nature of the country, the very way in which the English colonies were founded, and the habits of the earliest immigrants all conspired to develop local and provincial liberties to an extraordinary degree.

In the United States, the institutions of the country in general are therefore essentially republican. In order to destroy permanently the laws on which the republic is based, one would almost have to abolish all the laws at once.

If a party attempted to establish a monarchy in the United States today, it would find itself in a more difficult position than a party that attempted to proclaim a republic in France. The crown would find no legislation prepared for it in advance, and it would really be a case of a monarchy surrounded by republican institutions.

It would be equally difficult for monarchic principles to influence American mores.

In the United States, the dogma of popular sovereignty is not an isolated doctrine unrelated to either habits or the whole range of dominant ideas. On the contrary, one can think of it as the last link in a chain of opinions that rings the whole Anglo-American world. Providence equipped each individual, whoever he might be, with the degree of reason necessary to guide his conduct in matters of exclusive interest to himself alone. This is the great maxim on which civil and political society in the United States is based: fathers apply it to their children, masters to their servants, towns to the people they administer, provinces to towns, states to provinces, the Union to the states. Extended to the whole nation, it becomes the dogma of popular sovereignty.

Thus, in the United States, the generative principle of the republic is the same principle that governs most human actions. Hence the republic penetrates, if I may put it that way, into the ideas, opinions, and general habits of the Americans at the same time that it establishes itself in their laws. In order for them to change their laws, they would in a sense have to change themselves through and through. In the United States, the religion of the majority is itself republican. That religion subjects the truths of the other world to individual reason, just as politics leaves the interests of this world to the good sense of all, and it allows each man free choice of the path that is to lead him to heaven, just as the law grants each citizen the right to choose his government.

Obviously, only a long series of circumstances all tending in the same direction could replace this combination of laws, opinions, and mores with a contrary one.

If republican principles are to perish in America, they will succumb only after a long, frequently interrupted, repeatedly renewed period of social travail. They will more than once seem to be reborn, and will disappear forever only when an entirely new people has taken the place of the one that exists right now. Such a revolution can have no harbinger, no premonitory sign.

What strikes you most upon arriving in the United States is the tumultuousness of political society. The laws change constantly, and at first sight it seems impossible that a people so uncertain of its wishes would not soon decide to replace its present form of government with an entirely new one. Such fears are premature. When it comes to political institutions, there are two kinds of instability that must not be confused. One has to do with secondary laws, and a settled society can live with such instability for long periods. The other continually strikes at the very foundations of the constitution and the generative principles of law; it is always followed by unrest and revolution; the nation that suffers from it is in a violent and transitory state. Experience shows that there is no necessary connection between these two kinds of legislative instability, for they occur not only together but also separately, at different times and in different places. The first kind of instability is found in the United States, but not the second. Americans frequently change their laws, but the constitutional foundation is respected.

The republican principle reigns in America today as the monarchical principle dominated France under Louis XIV. In those days the French were not just friends of monarchy; they could not imagine the possibility of putting anything else in its place. They accepted it as one accepts the course of the sun and the succession of the seasons. They were neither advocates nor adversaries of royal power.

This is how the republic exists in America: without combat, without opposition, without proof, by a tacit accord, a sort of *consensus universalis*.

Nevertheless, I believe that the Americans, by changing their administrative procedures as often as they do, are compromising the future of republican government.

If the people's projects are repeatedly thwarted by constant changes in the law, there is reason to fear that they will ultimately come to regard the republic as an inconvenient way of living in society. The harm done by instability in the secondary laws would then call the existence of fundamental laws into question and lead indirectly to a revolution; but that time still lies far in the future.

What can be foreseen right now is that if the Americans did abandon the republic, they would move quickly to despotism without tarrying for long in monarchy. Montesquieu said that there is nothing more absolute than the authority of a prince who succeeds a republic, because the indefinite powers once fearlessly entrusted to elected officials would then be placed in the hands of a hereditary leader. This is true in general, but particularly true of a democratic republic. In the United States, officials are not elected by a particular class of citizens but by the majority of the nation; they directly represent the passions of the multitude and are entirely dependent on its will. They therefore inspire neither hatred nor fear. Thus, as I noted earlier, little care has been taken to limit their power by circumscribing their action, and the range of arbitrary discretion left to them is vast. The habits fostered by this way of ordering things could outlast it. American officials could keep their indefinite power yet cease to be answerable to anyone, and it is impossible to say where tyranny would then end.

There are some among us who expect to see an aristocracy arise in America and who are already predicting exactly when it will seize power.

I will reiterate now what I said earlier, that the present tendency of American society seems to me more and more democratic.

Nevertheless, I have no wish to deny that the Americans may

some day decide to narrow the range of their political rights or confiscate those rights for the benefit of a single individual. I cannot believe, however, that they would ever entrust those rights exclusively to a particular class of citizens, or, to put it another way, that they would establish an aristocracy.

An aristocratic body consists of a certain number of citizens who, though not far removed from the crowd, nevertheless stand permanently above it; citizens whom other people may touch but cannot strike; with whom they may mix daily yet never blend in.

It is impossible to imagine anything more contrary to nature and to the secret instincts of the human heart than a subjection of this kind. Left to themselves, men will always prefer the arbitrary power of a king to the regular administration of nobles.

If an aristocracy is to last, it needs to establish the principle of inequality, legalize it in advance, and introduce it into the family even as it extends it to all of society — all things so repugnant to natural equity that they can be obtained only by coercion.

I do not think that one can cite a single example, since human societies have been in existence, of a people that, left to its own devices and through its own efforts, created an aristocracy in its midst. All the aristocracies of the Middle Ages were born of conquest. The victor became the noble, the vanquished the serf. Force then imposed inequality, which, once it became a part of mores, maintained itself and passed naturally into law.

There have been societies which, owing to events prior to their existence, were born aristocracies, so to speak, and subsequently, over centuries, moved closer to democracy. This was the case with the Romans and with the barbarians who established themselves later on. But a people that began in civilization and democracy, moved by degrees toward greater inequality of conditions, and ultimately established inviolable privileges and exclusive categories in its midst would be something new in the world.

There is nothing to suggest that America is destined to be the first to offer such a spectacle.

SOME CONSIDERATIONS ON THE CAUSES OF THE COMMERCIAL IMPORTANCE OF THE UNITED STATES

The Americans are destined by nature to become a great maritime people. — Extent of their coastline. — Depth of their ports. — Magnitude of their rivers. — Nevertheless, it is not physical so much as intellectual and moral causes that are responsible for the commercial superiority of the Anglo-Americans. — Reason for this opinion. — Future of the Anglo-Americans as a commercial people. — The collapse of the Union would not halt the flourishing of maritime commerce among the people who compose it. — Why. — The Anglo-Americans are destined by nature to serve the needs of the inhabitants of South America. — Like the English, they will become commercial agents for much of the world.

From the Bay of Fundy to the Sabine River off the Gulf of Mexico, the coast of the United States extends over a distance of almost nine hundred leagues.

These shores form a single, unbroken coastline dominated by one power.

No other nation in the world has deeper, wider, more secure ports with which to tempt commerce than the Americans.

The inhabitants of the United States constitute a great, civilized nation that fortune has located in the midst of wilderness, twelve hundred leagues from civilization's heartland. America therefore has daily need of Europe. In time, Americans will no doubt be able to produce or manufacture most of what they need for themselves, but the two continents will never be able to live entirely independent of each other. Too many natural links exist among their needs, ideas, habits, and mores.

The Union produces things that we have come to find necessary yet that our soil either utterly refuses to provide or can yield only at great expense. The Americans consume only a very small portion of these products; they sell us the rest.

Europe is therefore America's market, just as America is Europe's market. The inhabitants of the United States need maritime commerce as much to convey their raw materials to our ports as to transport our manufactured products to them.

Hence the United States was bound either to provide other maritime nations with a great deal of business (had Americans decided to forgo the shipping business for themselves, as the Spaniards of Mexico have done thus far) or to become one of the great maritime powers of the globe: the alternative was inevitable.

The Anglo-Americans have always demonstrated a decided taste for the sea. Independence, by breaking the commercial bonds that tied them to England, gave a new and powerful impetus to their maritime genius. Since that time, the number of Union vessels has increased almost as rapidly as the population. Today, Americans themselves carry nine tenths of the goods they import from Europe.[91] Americans also bring three quarters of the New World's exports to European consumers.[92]

United States vessels fill the ports of Le Havre and Liverpool. One sees only a small number of English and French ships in the port of New York.[93]

Thus, the American merchant not only braves competition on his own soil but also contends successfully with foreigners on theirs.

This is easy to explain: United States ships sail the seas more economically than any of the world's other vessels. As long as the United States merchant marine retains this advantage, it will not only keep what it has already won but add daily to its conquests.

Why Americans can navigate more economically than others

[91]The total value of imports for the year ending September 30, 1832, was $101,129,266. Imports carried by foreign ships accounted for only $10,731,039, or approximately one-tenth.

[92]The total value of exports during the same year was $87,176,943. The value exported on foreign vessels was $21,036,183, or approximately one-quarter (*Williams' Register*, 1833, p. 398).

[93]During the years 1829, 1830, and 1831, ships totaling 3,307,719 tons entered the ports of the Union. Foreign ships accounted for only 544,571 of this total, or roughly 16 percent (*National Calendar*, 1833, p. 304).

During the years 1820, 1826, and 1831, English vessels entering the ports of London, Liverpool, and Hull totaled 443,800 tons. Foreign vessels entering the same ports in the same years amounted to 159,431 tons, or roughly 36 percent (*Companion to the Almanac*, 1834, p. 169).

In the year 1832, the ratio of foreign ships to English ships entering the ports of Great Britain was 29 to 100.

is a difficult question to answer. It is tempting at first sight to assume that their superiority derives from certain material advantages that nature bestowed on them alone, but this turns out not to be the case.

American vessels cost almost as much to build as our own.[94] They are not better constructed and generally do not last as long.

The wages of an American sailor are much higher than those of a European sailor, as is proven by the large number of Europeans who work in the United States merchant marine.

What, then, accounts for the fact that Americans navigate more economically than we do?

There is no point, I think, in looking for material advantages that could explain this superiority. It has to do with purely intellectual and moral qualities.

The following comparison will make my thinking clear:

During the wars of the Revolution, the French introduced a new tactic into the art of war that confused older generals and nearly destroyed the most venerable monarchies in Europe. For the first time in history, they undertook to do without a host of things that had previously been deemed indispensable to war. They demanded new efforts of their soldiers that no civilized nation had ever asked its soldiers to make. Whatever had to be done they did at the double, and to obtain the desired result they did not hesitate to risk men's lives.

The French were not as numerous or as wealthy as their enemies and had far fewer resources. Yet they were constantly victorious — until the enemy made up his mind to imitate them.

The Americans have achieved something similar in commerce. What the French did for victory, they do to cut costs.

The European navigator is cautious about venturing onto the high seas. He sets sail only when the weather is inviting. If an unforeseen event occurs, he returns to port. At night he partly furls his sails, and when the ocean turns white with the approach of land, he slows his course and checks the sun.

---

[94]Generally speaking, raw materials cost less in America than in Europe, but the price of labor is much higher.

The American neglects these precautions and braves these dangers. He sets sail while the storm still rages; by night as well as day he spreads his full canvas to the wind; he repairs his storm-damaged ship while still under way; and when at last he comes to the end of his voyage, he continues to make for the coast at full speed as if he already had his port in sight.

The American often ends in shipwreck, yet no one else plies the seas as rapidly as he does. By doing what others do in less time, he cuts his costs.

Before reaching the end of a lengthy voyage, the European navigator feels that he must put in at several ports along his route. He wastes precious time searching for ports of call or waiting for opportunities to leave them, and he pays every day for the privilege of staying.

The American navigator sets sail from Boston to buy tea in China. He lands in Canton, stays there a few days, and returns. In under two years he has traveled the circumference of the globe and seen land only once. During a crossing of eight to ten months, he has drunk brackish water and lived on salted meat. He has battled constantly with the sea, with disease, and with boredom. But upon his return, he can sell his tea for a penny a pound less than the English merchant: his goal has been achieved.

There is no better way to express my thought than to say that there is something heroic about the way Americans do business.

The European merchant will always find it quite difficult to follow the example set by his American competitor. The American, in acting as I described above, is not just responding to a calculation but obeying the dictates of his nature.

The inhabitant of the United States experiences all the needs and desires born of an advanced civilization, but, unlike the European, he does not live in a society cleverly arranged to satisfy them. Hence he is often obliged to procure for himself various items that his upbringing and habits have made indispensable to him. In America, it is not unheard of for the same man to plow his own field, build his own house, fabricate his own tools, make his own shoes, and weave with his own hands the coarse fabric with which he covers his body. This impedes industrial improvement but offers a powerful impetus to the development of the workman's intelligence. Nothing is more likely to materialize man and eliminate every last vestige of soul from his works than great division of labor. In a country like America, where specialization is so rare, it is impossible to require every person who embraces a profession to undergo a long period of apprenticeship. Americans therefore find it quite easy to change their situation, and they take advantage of this as the needs of the moment dictate. One meets people who have been in turn lawyers, farmers, merchants, ministers of the Gospel, and physicians. The American may be less skillful than the European in each craft, but there is virtually no line of work that is entirely unfamiliar to him. His capabilities are more general, and the range of his intelligence is wider. Hence the inhabitant of the United States is never hindered by any guild's rule-of-thumb; he avoids every kind of occupational bias; he is no more attached to one system of operation than to another; he feels no more bound to an old method than to a new one; he has not created any habit for himself, and he readily sheds any influence that foreign habits might exert over his thinking, for he knows that his country is unlike any other and that his situation is new in the world.

The American lives in a land of wonders, in which everything seems to be in constant flux, and every change seems to mark an advance. Hence the idea of the new is coupled in his mind with the idea of the better. Nowhere does he perceive the limits that nature may have imposed on man's efforts. In his eyes, that which does not exist is that which has not yet been attempted.

The universal movement that dominates everything else in the United States, the frequent reversals of fortune, the unforeseen shifts in public and private wealth — all of these things combine to keep the soul in a sort of febrile agitation, which admirably disposes it to effort of all kinds and keeps it above the common run of humankind. An American experiences all of life as a game of chance, a time of revolution, a day of battle.

The same causes operating on all individuals at the same time ultimately impart an irresistible impetus to the national character. Hence an American chosen at random is likely to be a man ardent in his desires, enterprising, adventurous, and above all innovative. Indeed, the same spirit is found in all his works. He imparts it to his political laws, his religious doctrines, his theories of social economy, and his private industry. He carries it with him everywhere, whether into the depths of the forest or the heart of the city. It is this same spirit, applied to maritime commerce, that drives the American to make speedier, more economical voyages than any of the world's other traders.

As long as the sailors of the United States retain these intellectual advantages and the practical superiority that derives from them, not only will they continue by themselves to meet the needs of their country's producers and consumers, but they will tend more and more to act, like the English,[95] as commercial agents for other nations.

This is beginning to take place before our very eyes. We already see American shippers acting as intermediary agents in the trade of several European nations.[96] America holds out the prospect of an even greater future for them.

The Spanish and Portuguese established important colonies in South America, and these have since grown into empires. Civil war and despotism are today devastating these vast regions. The influx of population has halted, and the inhabitants, few in number and busy with the need to defend themselves, hardly feel the need to better their lot.

This will not always be the case, however. Left to itself, Europe managed to pierce the darkness of the Middle Ages by its own efforts. South America is Christian, like us. It has our laws and customs. It bears within itself all the seeds of civilization that developed within the nations of Europe and their offspring. And South America also has something that we do not: our example. Why should it always remain barbarous?

---

[95] It is wrong to assume that English vessels are employed solely in carrying foreign goods to England and English goods to foreign countries. Today, the English merchant marine is like a vast corporation of public carriers, ready to serve all the producers of the world and to open up channels of communication among all nations. The maritime genius of the Americans is encouraging them to set up a corporation to rival that of the English.

[96] Some Mediterranean trade is already carried on with American ships.

Obviously it is only a matter of time. Sooner or later, no doubt, a day will come when the people of South America will constitute enlightened and prosperous nations.

When the Spaniards and Portuguese of southern America begin to feel the needs of civilized people, however, they will still be a long way from being able to meet those needs themselves. As civilization's last-born children, they will have to endure the superiority already acquired by their elders. They will be farmers for a long time before becoming manufacturers and merchants, and they will need the help of foreigners to sell their wares overseas and obtain in exchange items newly felt to be necessities.

There can be no doubt that North Americans will one day be called upon to supply the needs of South Americans. Nature has placed them close together and made it very easy for the North Americans to know and appreciate the needs of the peoples to the south, form durable relations with them, and gradually take control of their market. United States merchants could squander these natural advantages only if they were very inferior to European merchants, whereas in fact they are superior in several respects. The Americans of the United States already exert a great moral influence over all the peoples of the New World. Enlightenment begins with them. All the nations that share the continent with them are already accustomed to look upon them as the most enlightened, most powerful, and wealthiest branch of the great American family. Hence they all look to the Union constantly and, insofar as it is within their power to do so, assimilate themselves to the peoples who compose it. They daily draw upon the political doctrines of the United States and borrow from its laws.

The Americans of the United States find themselves in precisely the same situation relative to the peoples of South America as their fathers, the English, do relative to the Italians, Spanish, Portuguese, and all the other peoples of Europe who, being less advanced in civilization and industry, receive most of their consumer goods from the English.

England is today the natural focal point of commerce for nearly all the nations that trade with it. The American Union is destined to play the same role in the other hemisphere. Therefore every nation that is born and develops in the New World does so in a sense for the benefit of the Anglo-Americans.

If the Union were to dissolve, the expansion of trade by its constituent states would no doubt be delayed, but less so than is generally supposed. It is obvious that, come what may, the trading states will remain united. They are contiguous; they share a perfect identity of opinions, interests, and mores, and by themselves they would constitute a very important maritime power. Even if the South became independent of the states of the North, it would not be able to do without them. I said earlier that the South is not commercial. There is as yet nothing to indicate that it will become so. Hence the Americans of the southern United States will be obliged for many years to rely on foreigners to export what they produce and import what they need. Now, of all the intermediaries they might choose, their neighbors to the north are surely the ones who can serve them at the lowest cost. Hence they will serve them, for "buy low" is the supreme law of commerce. Neither sovereign will nor national prejudice can hold out for long against low costs. There is no hatred more venomous than that which exists between the Americans of the United States and the English. Yet despite these hostile feelings, the English supply the Americans with most of their manufactured goods, for the simple reason that they charge them less than other countries do. Thus, despite the desires of the Americans, the growing prosperity of America is proving profitable to the manufacturing industry of England.

Reason suggests, and experience proves, that no commercial greatness can last unless it can ally itself, if need be, with a military power.

This truth is understood as well in the United States as anywhere else. The Americans are already capable of enforcing respect for their flag. Soon they will be in a position to make it feared.

I am convinced that the breakup of the United States, far from diminishing the naval forces of the Americans, would very likely strengthen them. Today the commercial states are linked to non-commercial ones, which are often reluctant to enhance a maritime power from which they profit only indirectly.

By contrast, if all the commercial states of the Union formed a single nation, commerce would become for them a national interest of the first order. They would then be disposed to make great sacrifices to protect their vessels, and nothing would stand in the way of their desire to do so.

I believe that nations, like men, nearly always reveal the main features of their destiny at an early age. When I see the spirit and ease with which the Anglo-Americans engage in commerce and note their success at it, I cannot help thinking that they will some day become the world's leading maritime power. They are driven to rule the seas, just as the Romans were driven to conquer the world.

CONCLUSION

I am nearing the end of my inquiry. In discussing the destiny of the United States, I have tried thus far to divide my subject into parts so as to study each of them with greater care.

Now I would like to look at everything from a single point of view. What I am going to say will be less detailed but more certain. I shall have a less distinct perception of each object but embrace general facts with greater certainty. I shall be like the traveler who, after passing through the gates of a great city, climbs a nearby hill. As he moves away from the city, the people he has just left vanish from his sight. Their houses blur together. He can no longer see the city's public places. He can barely make out the streets. But his eye takes in the city's contours more easily, and for the first time he apprehends its shape. In just this same way, I have the impression now that the whole future of the English race in the New World is taking shape before me. The details of this vast tableau remain in shadow, but my gaze takes it all in, and I conceive a clear idea of the whole.

The territory today occupied or owned by the United States of America amounts to approximately one-twentieth of the world's inhabited area.

As wide as its limits are, it would be a mistake to think that the Anglo-American race will always remain within them. It already reaches well beyond.

There was a time when we, too, might have created a great French nation in the American wilderness and swayed the destiny of the New World along with the English. France once owned territory in North America almost as vast as all of Europe. Three of the continent's largest rivers flowed entirely under French dominion. The Indian nations living between the mouth of the Saint Lawrence and the Mississippi delta heard no language but ours. Throughout this immense region, every European settlement stood as a reminder of the homeland: Louisbourg and Montmorency, Duquesne and Saint-Louis, Vincennes and La Nouvelle-Orléans — all names cherished in France and familiar to our ears.

But a series of circumstances that would be tedious to enumerate[97] deprived us of this magnificent heritage. Wherever the French were few in number and not well established, they disappeared. The rest crowded into a constricted space and passed under other laws. The four hundred thousand Frenchmen of Lower Canada are today like the debris of an ancient people inundated by the flood of a new nation. The foreign population around them is growing steadily, expanding in every direction. It even infiltrates the ranks of the former masters of the soil, dominates their cities, and denatures their language. This population is identical to that of the United States. Thus I am right to say that the English race is not stopping at the Union's borders but continuing to advance well beyond them, toward the northeast.

To the northwest one finds only a few Russian settlements of no great importance, but to the southwest Mexico stands as a barrier in the Anglo-Americans' path.

Hence the New World is in fact shared today by only two rival races, the Spanish and the English.

The boundaries that are supposed to separate these two races have been fixed by treaty. Yet no matter how much that treaty may favor the Anglo-Americans, I have no doubt that they will soon violate it.

---

[97]Foremost among these was the fact that free peoples accustomed to the municipal regime find it far easier to create flourishing colonies than do other nations. The habit of thinking for oneself and governing oneself is indispensable in a new country, where success invariably depends largely on the colonists' individual efforts.

Beyond the Union's border with Mexico lie vast regions that are still sparsely populated. The people of the United States will invade these empty spaces even before the people who have the right to occupy them. They will appropriate the land, settle on it and establish a society, and when the legitimate owners finally arrive, they will find the wasteland made fertile and foreigners in tranquil possession of their heritage.

The land of the New World belongs to whoever occupies it first, and empire is the prize in that race.

Even regions that are already populated will find it difficult to protect themselves against invasion.

Earlier I discussed what is happening in the province of Texas. Residents of the United States are filtering into Texas daily and acquiring land there, and even as they abide by the region's existing laws, they are founding an empire there — the empire of their own language and mores. The province of Texas is still under Mexican rule, but before long Mexicans will have vanished, as it were, from the vicinity. The same thing is happening wherever Anglo-Americans come into contact with populations of other origins.

There is no hiding the fact that the English race has acquired an immense preponderance over all the other European races in the New World. It is vastly superior to them in civilization, industry, and power. So long as it confronts only deserted or sparsely inhabited regions and does not encounter massed populations blocking its passage, it will expand steadily. It will not stop at lines traced by treaty, imaginary barriers that cannot resist the onrushing tide.

Yet another prodigious stimulus to the rapid development of the English race in the New World is the geographical position it occupies there.

North of its northern boundaries one encounters polar ice, while a few degrees south of its southern borders lie the blazing tropics. Thus the English of America are situated in the most temperate zone, the most habitable portion of the continent.

People imagine that the prodigious growth of the population of the United States began with independence, but this is a mistake. The population grew as rapidly under the colonial system as it does today: it roughly doubled in twenty-two years. But then there were only a few thousand inhabitants; now there are millions. The same phenomenon that went unnoticed a century ago is today striking to every observer.

The English of Canada, who are obedient to a king, are increasing in number and extent almost as rapidly as the English of the United States, who live under a republican government.

During the eight years of the War of Independence, the population did not cease to grow at the rate previously indicated.

Although great Indian nations allied with the English existed in those days on the western frontiers, the westward flow of immigration never slowed. While the enemy ravaged the Atlantic coast, Kentucky, the western districts of Pennsylvania, and the states of Vermont and Maine filled with settlers. Nor did the postwar disorders prevent the population from increasing or halt its steady march into the wilderness. Thus neither differences in law nor differences of situation — war or peace, order or anarchy — had any perceptible effect on the successive phases of Anglo-American expansion.

This is easy to understand: there are no causes general enough to make their influence felt simultaneously throughout such a vast territory. Thus there is always some substantial part of the country where a person can be certain of finding shelter from the calamities affecting others, and however great the ills may be, a greater remedy is always at hand.

Hence it must not be imagined that the rapid expansion of the English race in the New World can be halted. A breakup of the Union leading to war on the continent or abolition of the republic leading to tyranny might slow its growth but not prevent the inevitable fulfillment of its destiny. No power on earth can keep immigrants out of this fertile wilderness, which offers so many inducements to industry and refuge from every manner of misery. Whatever the future may hold, no event can deprive the Americans of their climate or their inland seas or their great rivers or their fertile soil. Neither bad laws nor revolutions nor anarchy can destroy the love of well-being and spirit of enterprise that seem to be the distinctive characteristics of their race, or altogether extinguish the enlightenment that guides their steps.

Thus, for all the uncertainty of the future, one thing is sure. In a period that, reckoned in terms of the life of a people, we may call imminent, the Anglo-Americans alone will blanket the vast region comprised between the polar ice cap and the tropics and stretching from the Atlantic to the South Seas.

Eventually, I believe, the Anglo-American race will cover an area three-quarters the size of Europe.[98] The climate of the Union is, all things considered, preferable to that of Europe. Its natural advantages are just as great. It is obvious that its population cannot fail some day to be proportionate to ours.

Europe, though divided among many diverse nations and despite incessant wars and the barbarity of the Middle Ages, has managed to achieve a population density of 410 inhabitants per square league.[99] What cause might be powerful enough to prevent the United States from some day achieving this same density?

Many centuries will pass before the various descendants of the English race in America will cease to exhibit a common physiognomy. One cannot foresee a time when it might be possible to establish permanent inequality of condition in the New World.

War or peace, liberty or tyranny, prosperity or misery may eventually create differences among the various descendants of the great Anglo-American family, but whatever those differences may be, all such descendants will at least share a similar social state and have in common the usages and ideas deriving from it.

In the Middle Ages, the bond of religion alone was enough to unite the various races of Europe in a single civilization. The English of the New World are united by a thousand other bonds, and they live in a century that tends to create equality in all things pertaining to man.

The Middle Ages were a time of fragmentation. Each people, each province, each city, each family had a strong tendency to assert its individuality. Today, an opposite tendency is apparent: peoples seem to be moving toward unity. Intellectual bonds join the most remote parts of the earth, and people

[98]The United States alone already covers an area half the size of Europe. The area of Europe is 500,000 square leagues, and its population is 205,000,000. Malte-Brun, vol. 6, book 114, p. 4.

[99]See Malte-Brun, vol. 6, book 116, p. 92.

cannot remain strangers to one another for a single day or ignorant of what is taking place in any corner of the globe. Accordingly, one finds less difference between Europeans and their descendants in the New World today, despite the ocean that divides them, than between certain thirteenth-century towns separated by nothing more than a river.

If this tendency toward assimilation brings foreign peoples together, it must *a fortiori* oppose any tendency for different offspring of the same people to become alienated from one another.

Hence there will come a day when North America will be home to 150,000,000 people,[100] all equal to one another, all members of the same family, sharing the same point of departure, the same civilization, the same language, the same religion, the same habits, the same mores, and among whom thought will circulate in the same form and take on the same colors. Everything else is doubtful, but this much is certain. And this is something entirely new in the world, the implications of which imagination itself cannot grasp.

There are today two great peoples on earth, who, though they started from different points, seem to be advancing toward the same goal: the Russians and the Anglo-Americans.

Both grew in obscurity, and while humanity's gaze was focused elsewhere, they abruptly vaulted to the first rank among nations: the world learned almost simultaneously of their birth and of their grandeur.

All other peoples seem close to achieving the limits traced for them by nature and henceforth need only to preserve what they already have; but these two are still growing.[101] All the others have stopped, or move forward only with the greatest of effort. Only these two march with an easy and rapid stride down a road whose end no eye can yet perceive.

The American does battle with the obstacles that nature has placed before him; the Russian grapples with men. One combats wilderness and barbarity; the other, civilization with all

---

[100]Assuming a population proportionate to that of Europe, with an average density of 410 per square league.

[101]Of all the nations of the Old World, Russia is the one that is growing the fastest, proportionately speaking.

its arms. The American makes his conquests with the farmer's plowshare, the Russian with the soldier's sword.

To achieve his goal, the American relies on personal interest and allows individuals to exercise their strength and reason without guidance.

The Russian in a sense concentrates all the power of society in one man.

The American's principal means of action is liberty; the Russian's, servitude.

Their points of departure are different, their ways diverse. Yet each seems called by a secret design of Providence some day to sway the destinies of half the globe.

NOTES

I, PAGE 24

Concerning regions of the West not yet penetrated by Europeans, see the two journeys undertaken by Major Long at the expense of Congress.

In regard to the great American wilderness in particular, Mr. Long says that a line should be drawn roughly parallel to the 20th degree of longitude (as measured from the meridian of Washington, which is roughly equivalent to the 99th degree measured from the meridian of Paris), from the Red River to the Platte River. From this imaginary line to the Rocky Mountains, which border the Mississippi valley on the west, stretch vast plains, generally covered with sand that is unsuitable for cultivation or strewn with granite boulders. These plains are without water during the summer, and empty, except for vast herds of buffalo and wild horses. On occasion hordes of Indians can also be seen, but they are few in number.

Major Long was told that if he had continued in the same direction up beyond the Platte, he would have had the same desert constantly on his left, but he was unable to verify the accuracy of this report for himself. *Long's Expedition*, vol. 2, p. 361.

However reliable Major Long's account may be, bear in mind that he simply crossed the region he describes without making any major zigzags to either side of his route.

II, PAGE 25

The tropical regions of South America produce an incredible profusion of the climbing plants known generically as liana. More than forty different species are found just among the flora of the West Indies.

Among the most graceful of these vines is the passion flower. As Descourtilz tells us in his description of West

Indian vegetation, this pretty plant uses its tendrils to attach itself to trees and form undulating arcades, colonnades made rich and elegant by the beauty of their decorative purple flowers, sometimes tinged with blue, whose fragrance is so enchanting; see vol. 1, p. 265.

The great-podded acacia is a very thick, fast-growing liana that runs from tree to tree, in some cases over a distance of more than half a league; see vol. 3, p. 227.

III, PAGE 26

ON AMERICAN LANGUAGES. The languages spoken by the Indians of America, from the North Pole to Cape Horn, are said to be based on a common model and to obey the same grammatical rules, from which it follows that in all likelihood the Indian nations all stem from a common stock.

Each tribe on the American continent speaks a different dialect, but there are very few languages in the strict sense — further evidence that the nations of the New World may not be very old.

Finally, the languages of America are extremely regular. Hence it is probable that the peoples who use them have yet to be subjected to great revolutions and have not mixed, willingly or unwillingly, with foreign nations, because it is generally the union of several languages into one that produces grammatical irregularities.

It is only recently that American languages, and in particular the languages of North America, have attracted the serious attention of philologists. Only then was it discovered that the idiom of these barbarous peoples was the product of a very complex system of ideas combined in clever ways. It was noticed that these languages were very rich, and that great care had been taken to make them easy on the ear.

The grammatical system of these American languages is different from all others in several respects, most notably the following:

Some European peoples, including the Germans, among others, have the ability to combine different expressions when necessary to give a complex meaning to certain words. The Indians have extended this ability in the most surprising way and have thereby succeeded in compressing a very large number of ideas into a single expression. An example cited by Mr. Duponceau in the *Memoirs of the American Philosophical Society* will help to make this point clear.

Duponceau tells us that when a Delaware woman plays with a cat or a puppy, she will sometimes utter the word *kuli-gatschis*. This word is composed as follows: *k* is the sign of the second person and signifies "you" or "your"; *uli*, which is pronounced *ouli*, is a fragment of the word *wulit*, which means "beautiful" or "pretty"; *gat* is another fragment, of the word *wichgat*, which means "paw"; finally, *schis*, pronounced *chise*, is a diminutive ending associated with the idea of smallness. Thus, with a single word, the Indian woman has said, "Your pretty little paw."

Here is another example, which shows how felicitously the savages of America put words together.

"A young man" in Delaware is *pilape*. This word is formed from *pilsit*, "chaste," and *lenape*, "man": in other words, "man in his purity and innocence."

This ability to combine words is most surprising when it comes to the formation of verbs. The most complicated actions are often expressed by a single verb; almost all the nuances of the idea act on the verb and modify it.

Anyone who would like more detail about this subject, which I have only touched on superficially, should read:

1. Mr. Duponceau's correspondence with Rev. Hecwelder on Indian languages. This correspondence can be found in the first volume of the *Memoirs of the Philosophical Society of America*, published in Philadelphia in 1819 by Abraham Small, pp. 356–464.

2. The grammar of the Delaware, or Lenape, language by Geiberger, together with Mr. Duponceau's preface. All this is found in the same collection, vol. 3.

3. A very well done summary of these works at the end of volume 6 of the *American Encyclopedia*.

IV, PAGE 28

Charlevoix gives a history of the first war between the French of Canada and the Iroquois in 1610. The Iroquois, though armed with bows and arrows, mounted a desperate resistance against the French and their allies. Charlevoix, though not much of a descriptive writer, brings out the contrast between the mores of the Europeans and those of the savages quite clearly, as well as the different ways in which the two races conceived of honor.

"The French," he says, "upon seeing Iroquois bodies lying out in the open, made off with the beaver skins that had draped them. Their allies the Hurons were scandalized by this spectacle. They then began to perform their usual cruelties on their prisoners and, to the horror of the French, devoured one whom they had killed. And so," Charlevoix adds, "these barbarians gloried in their disinterestedness, which they were surprised not to find in our nation, and failed to understand that it was far less evil to plunder the dead than to feast on their flesh like wild beasts."

In another place (vol. 1, p. 230), the same Charlevoix describes the first torture witnessed by Champlain and the Hurons' return to their village:

After covering a distance of eight leagues, our allies stopped and, seizing one of their captives, berated him for all the cruelties that he had visited on warriors of their nation who had fallen into his hands. They told him that he should expect the same treatment from them and added that, if he had any heart, he could show it by singing. He immediately launched into his song of death, followed by his song of war and all the other songs he knew, but in a very sad manner, according to Champlain, who had not been there long enough to know that there is something lugubrious about all the music of the savages. The torture of this man, along with all the other horrors of which we shall speak in due course, terrified the French, who did everything they could to put an end to it, but in vain. The next night, after a Huron dreamed that he was being pursued, the retreat turned into a veritable flight, and the savages would not stop anywhere unless there was absolutely no danger.

As soon as they saw the huts of their village, they cut long poles to which they attached the scalps they had jointly taken and raised them in triumph. When the women saw this, they dove into the water and, upon reaching the canoes, took the still bloody scalps from their husbands' hands and tied them around their necks.

The warriors gave Champlain one of these gruesome trophies as a gift, along with a number of bows and arrows — the only booty they had cared to take from the Iroquois — and asked him to show these prizes to the king of France.

Champlain spent a whole winter alone with these barbarians, during which his safety and property were never compromised for a moment.

V, PAGE 44

Although the puritanical strictness that presided at the birth of the English colonies in America has already been greatly relaxed, extraordinary traces of it remain in habits and laws.

In 1792, the very year in which the anti-Christian republic began its ephemeral existence in France, the legislature of Massachusetts promulgated a law to enforce Sunday observance. Here are the preamble and main provisions of that law, which deserve the most careful attention:

Whereas the observance of the Lord's Day is highly promotive of the welfare of a community, by affording necessary seasons for relaxation from labor and the cares of business; for moral reflections and conversation on the duties of the Maker, Governor, and Judge of the world; and for those acts of charity which support and adorn a Christian society: And whereas some thoughtless and irreligious persons, inattentive to the duties and benefits of the Lord's Day, profane the same, by unnecessarily pursuing their worldly business and recreations on that day, to their own great damage, as members of a Christian society; to the great disturbance of well-disposed persons, and to the great damage of the community, by producing dissipation of manners and immoralities of life:

Be it therefore enacted by the Senate and House of Representatives . . .

That no person or persons . . . shall keep open his . . . shop, warehouse, or workhouse, nor shall . . . do any manner of labor, business, or work . . . nor be present at any concert of music, dancing, or any public diversion, show, or entertainment, nor use any sport, game, play, or recreation on the Lord's Day . . . upon penalty of a sum not exceeding twenty shillings, nor less than ten shillings, for every offense.

That no traveler, drover, wagoner, teamster . . . shall travel on the Lord's Day . . . (except from necessity or charity) upon the penalty of a sum not exceeding twenty shillings, nor less than ten shillings.

That no vintner, retailer of strong liquors, innholder . . . shall entertain or suffer any of the inhabitants of the respective towns where they dwell . . . to abide and remain . . . drinking or spending their time either idly or at play or doing any secular business on the Lord's Day. . . .

That any person, being able of body and not otherwise necessarily prevented, who shall, for the space of three months together, absent him or herself from the public worship of God on the Lord's Day . . . shall pay a fine of ten shillings.

That if any person shall, on the Lord's Day, within the walls of any house of public worship, behave rudely or indecently, he or she shall pay a fine not more than forty shillings, nor less than five shillings. . . .

That the tithingmen[1] . . . in the several towns and districts within this Commonwealth shall be held and obliged to inquire into and inform of all offenses against this Act. . . .

And every tithingman is hereby authorized and empowered to enter into any of the rooms and other parts of an inn or public house of entertainment on the Lord's Day . . . to examine all persons whom they shall have good cause . . . to suspect of unnecessarily traveling as aforesaid on the Lord's Day and to demand of all such persons the cause thereof . . . and if any person shall refuse to give answer . . . he shall pay a fine not exceeding five pounds; . . . and if the reason given for such traveling shall not be satisfactory to the tithingman, he shall enter a complaint against the person traveling, before a Justice of the Peace in the county where the offense is committed." *General Laws of Massachusetts*, vol. 1, p. 410.

On March 11, 1797, a new law increased the fines, half of which were to go to the person prosecuting the offender. Same collection, vol. 1, p. 525.

On February 16, 1816, yet another law confirmed these measures. Same collection, vol. 2, p. 405.

Similar provisions exist in the laws of the state of New York, revised in 1827 and 1828. (See *Revised Statutes*, part 1, chap. 20, p. 675.) There it is stated that on Sunday no one shall be allowed to hunt, fish, gamble, or frequent houses where drinks are served, and no one shall be allowed to travel except for reasons of necessity.

This is not the only trace left in the laws by the religious spirit and austere mores of the first immigrants.

---

[1]Annually elected officials whose functions are similar to those of both the *garde champêtre* and the *officier de police judiciaire* in France.

The *Revised Statutes of the State of New York* contain the following article (vol. I, p. 662):

> Every person who shall win or lose at play, or by betting at any time, the sum or value of twenty-five dollars or upwards within the space of twenty-four hours shall be deemed guilty of a misdemeanor and on conviction shall be fined not less than five times the value or sum so lost or won; which . . . shall be paid to the overseers of the poor of the town.
>
> Every person who shall . . . lose at any time or sitting the sum or value of twenty-five dollars or upwards . . . may . . . sue for and recover the money . . . so . . . lost. . . . The overseers of the poor of the town where the offense was committed may sue for and recover the sum or value so lost and paid, together with treble the said sum or value, from the winner thereof for the benefit of the poor.

The laws just quoted are very recent, but who could understand them without going all the way back to the origins of the colonies? I do not doubt that the penal part of this legislation is very seldom applied nowadays. The laws remain inflexible, while mores have already adapted to changing times. Yet Sunday observance is still one of things that the foreigner in America finds most striking.

Indeed, in one large American city, social life all but comes to a halt on Saturday night. You can walk through the streets at a time that would seem to beckon mature men to business and youth to pleasure and find yourself quite alone. Not only is no one working, but no one seems to be alive. One hears neither the bustle of industry nor the accents of pleasure nor even the incessant hubbub of all large cities. Chains bar the way to churches, and only grudgingly do half-closed shutters allow even a ray of light to penetrate the citizens' homes. From time to time one may just glimpse a solitary figure silently making his way across a deserted intersection or down an abandoned street.

The next day, at daybreak, the rumble of carriages, the pounding of hammers, and the shouts of people can again be heard. The city comes back to life. Restless crowds hasten to places of business and work. All around, things begin to move, excitement is everywhere, the pace quickens. Lethargic torpor gives way to feverish activity. People behave as though they had but one day to make their fortune and enjoy its fruits.

VI, PAGE 49

Needless to say, I do not pretend that the chapter you have just read is a history of America. In writing it, my only purpose was to allow the reader to appreciate how the opinions and mores of the first immigrants influenced the fate of the various colonies and of the Union in general. I was therefore obliged to limit myself to a few unrelated fragments.

I may be mistaken, but it seems to me that, by pursuing the course that I have merely sketched out here, one could paint a portrait of the early days of the American republics that would not be unworthy of the public's attention and would no doubt provide statesmen with food for thought. Unable to undertake this work myself, I have tried at least to facilitate the task for others. To that end, I feel I ought to provide here a brief bibliography and concise analysis of the works I found most useful.

Foremost among the documents of a general nature that one might fruitfully consult I would place the *Historical Collection of State Papers and Other Authentic Documents, Intended as Materials for a History of the United States of America*, by Ebenezer Hazard.

The first volume of this compilation, which was printed in Philadelphia in 1792, contains the verbatim text of all the charters granted to immigrants by the Crown of England, along with the principal acts of the colonial governments during the earliest period of their existence. Among other things, one finds here a large number of authentic documents on the affairs of New England and Virginia during this period.

The second volume is almost entirely devoted to the acts of the confederation of 1643. This federal pact, which united the colonies of New England for the purpose of resisting the Indians, was the first example of a union among Anglo-Americans. There were several more confederations of a similar nature leading up to the one of 1776, which brought independence to the colonies.

There is a copy of this historical collection from Philadelphia in the Bibliothèque Royale.

In addition, each colony has its own historical records, several of which are invaluable. I shall begin by examining that of Virginia, which was the first state to be settled.

Virginia's first historian was its founder, Capt. John Smith. Captain Smith has left us a quarto volume entitled *The General History of Virginia and New England, by Captain John Smith, Sometime Governor in those Countries and Admiral of New England*, printed in London in 1627. (This volume can be found in the Bibliothèque Royale.) Embellishing Smith's work are some very interesting maps and engravings dating from the time it was printed. The historian's narrative covers the period from 1584 to 1626. Smith's book is well-respected, and deservedly so. The author was one of the most celebrated adventurers of the adventurous century in whose latter part he lived. The book itself breathes the ardor for discovery and spirit of enterprise characteristic of the men of that time. In it, one discovers that mix of chivalrous mores with the knack for trade that proved so useful in the acquisition of wealth.

What is most remarkable about Captain Smith, however, is that he combines the virtues of his contemporaries with qualities that remained foreign to most of them. His style is simple and clear, his stories all bear the hallmark of truth, and his descriptions are not ornate.

The author sheds valuable light on the state of the Indians at the time of North America's discovery.

The second historian to consult is Beverley. His work, in duodecimo, was translated into French and printed in Amsterdam in 1707. The author begins his narrative in 1585 and ends it in 1700. The first part of his book contains actual historical documents pertaining to the early days of the colony. The second part includes an interesting portrait of the state of the Indians in that remote period. The third part offers some very clear ideas about the mores, social state, laws, and political habits of the Virginians of the author's day.

Beverley was from Virginia, so that he begins by saying that he begs readers not to be too rigid in their criticism of his work, because, having been born in India, he does not aspire to purity of language. Despite this colonial modesty, the author makes it clear throughout his book that he is impatient of the supremacy of the mother country. There is abundant evidence in Beverley's work of the spirit of civil liberty that animated the English colonies in America from that time on. There is also evidence of the divisions that separated them for so long and delayed their independence. Beverley detests his Catholic neighbors in Maryland even more than he does the English government. His style is simple; his narratives are often extremely interesting and inspire confidence. The French translation of Beverley's history can be found in the Bibliothèque Royale.

I saw in America, but have been unable to find in France, a work that might also be worth consulting, entitled *History of Virginia*, by William Stith. This book contains interesting details but seemed to me long and diffuse.

The oldest and best document on the history of the Carolinas is a small quarto volume entitled *The History of Carolina*, by John Lawson, printed in London in 1718.

Lawson's book begins with a journey of discovery in western Carolina, recounted in journal form. The author's narrative is confused, and his observations are quite superficial. The only items of importance are a rather striking portrait of the ravages done by small pox and whiskey to the Indians of the time and an interesting description of the corruption of their mores, which the presence of Europeans encouraged.

The second part of Lawson's work reports on Carolina's physical state and products.

In the third part, the author gives an interesting description of the mores, usages, and government of the Indians of the period.

This portion of the book shows frequent flashes of wit and originality.

Lawson's history ends with the charter granted to Carolina in the time of Charles II.

The overall tone of the work is light and often licentious and stands in stark contrast to the profoundly serious style of works published in New England in the same period.

Lawson's history is extremely rare in America and impossible to obtain in Europe. There is, however, one copy in the Bibliothèque Royale.

From the extreme south of the United States I now turn directly to the extreme north. The intervening space was not settled until later.

I should first call attention to a very interesting compilation entitled *Collection of the Massachusetts Historical Society*, which was first printed in Boston in 1792 and reprinted in 1806. This work cannot be found in the Bibliothèque Royale or, I believe, in any other library.

This collection (which is still being added to) contains a wealth of very valuable documents pertaining to the history of the various states of New England. In it the reader will find unpublished correspondence and copies of documents that lay buried in local archives. The entirety of Gookin's work on the Indians has been included.

In the chapter to which this note refers, I mentioned several times the work of Nathaniel Morton entitled *New England's Memorial*. What I said about it should suffice to show that it merits the attention of anyone who would like to know more about the history of New England. Morton's book was reprinted in an octavo volume in Boston in 1826. It cannot be found in the Bibliothèque Royale.

The most respected and important document we have on the history of New England is the work of Rev. Cotton Mather entitled *Magnalia Christi Americana, or the Ecclesiastical History of New England, 1620–1698*, 2 vols. in octavo, reprinted in Harford in 1820. I do not believe that it can be found in the Bibliothèque Royale.

The author divided his work into seven books.

The first recounts the history of the events that laid the groundwork for and led up to the founding of New England.

The second contains lives of the first governors and of the region's most important officials.

The third is devoted to the lives and works of the ministers of the Gospel who tended to souls in the same period.

In the fourth, the author recounts the founding and development of the university in Cambridge (Massachusetts).

In the fifth, he sets forth the principles and discipline of the Church of New England.

The sixth is devoted to retracing certain events that, according to Mather, indicate the beneficent action of Providence on the inhabitants of New England.

In the seventh, finally, the author tells us of the heresies and troubles to which the Church of New England was exposed.

Cotton Mather was a minister of the Gospel who was born in Boston and spent his life there.

All the ardor and all the religious passions that led to the founding of New England animate and vivify his writing. His manner of writing reveals frequent traces of bad taste, yet he draws one in because his abundant enthusiasm is ultimately communicated to the reader. He is often intolerant and still more often credulous, but one never detects signs of an intent to deceive. There are even some beautiful passages in his work and some true and profound thoughts, such as these:

"Before the arrival of the Puritans," he says, "there were more than a few attempts of the *English* to people and improve the parts of *New England* . . . but the designs of those attempts being aimed no higher than the advancement of some *worldly interests*, a constant series of disasters has confounded them, until there was a plantation erected upon the nobler designs of *Christianity*; and that plantation, though it has had more adversaries than perhaps any one upon earth; yet, *having obtained help from God, it continues to this day*."

Mather sometimes softens the austerity of his descriptions with images of kindness and tenderness: speaking of an English lady brought to America along with her husband by religious ardor only to succumb soon thereafter to the fatigue and misery of exile, he adds: "As for her virtuous spouse, Isaac Johnson, he tried to live without her, liked it not, and died" (vol. 1, p. 71).

Mather's book paints an admirable picture of the time and country he sought to describe.

When he wants to tell us about the reasons that drove the Puritans to seek asylum across the seas, he says:

The God of Heaven served as it were, a *summons* upon the *spirits* of his people in the English nation; stirring up the spirits of thousands which never saw the *faces* of each other, with a most unanimous inclination to leave all the pleasant accommodations of their native country; and go over a terrible *ocean*, into a more terrible *desert*, for the *pure enjoyment of all his ordinances*. It is now reasonable that before we pass any further, the *reasons* of this undertaking should be more exactly made known unto *posterity*, especially unto the *posterity* of those that were the undertakers, lest they come at length to forget and neglect *the true interest* of New England. Wherefore I shall now transcribe some of *them* from a manuscript, wherein they were then tendered unto consideration.

First, it will be a service unto the *Church* of great consequence, to carry the *Gospel* into *those* parts of the world (North America), and raise a bulwark against the kingdom of *antichrist*, which the Jesuits labor to rear up in all parts of the world.

Secondly, all other Churches of *Europe* have been brought under *desolations*; and it may be feared that the like judgments are coming upon *us*; and who knows but God hath provided this place (New England) to be a *refuge* for many, whom he means to save out of the *General Destruction*.

Thirdly, the land grows weary of her *inhabitants*, insomuch that *man*, which is the most precious of all creatures, is here more vile and base than the earth he treads upon: *children, neighbors,* and *friends*, especially the *poor*, are counted the greatest *burdens*, which if things were right would be the chiefest earthly *blessings*.

Fourthly, we are grown to that intemperance in all *excess of riot*, as no mean estate almost will suffice a man to keep sail with his *equals*, and he that fails in it must live in scorn and contempt: hence it comes to pass that all *arts* and *trades* are carried in that deceitful manner, and unrighteous course, as it is almost impossible for a good upright man to maintain his constant charge, and live comfortably in them.

Fifthly, the *schools* of learning and religion are so corrupted, as . . . most children, even the best, wittiest, and of the fairest hopes, are perverted, corrupted, and utterly overthrown by the multitude of evil examples and licentious behaviors in these *seminaries*.

Sixthly, the *whole earth* is the *Lord's garden*, and he hath given it to the sons of *Adam*, to be tilled and improved by them: why then should we stand starving here for places of habitation and in the mean time suffer whole countries, as profitable for the use of man, to lie waste without any improvement?

Seventhly, what can be a better or nobler work, and more worthy of a *Christian*, than to erect and support a *reformed particular Church* in its infancy, and unite our forces with such a company of faithful people, as by a timely assistance may grow stronger and prosper; but for want of it may be put to great hazard, if not be wholly ruined.

Eighthly, if any such as are known to be godly, and live in wealth and prosperity here (in England), shall forsake all this to join with this *reformed church*, and with it run the hazard of an hard and mean condition, it will be an example of great use, both for the removing of *scandal* and to give more *life* unto the *faith* of God's people in their prayers for the plantation, and also to encourage others to join the more willingly in it.

Later, in setting forth the principles of the Church of New England in regard to matters of morality, Mather vehemently denounces the custom of drinking toasts at the dinner table — a habit he calls pagan and abominable.

He is just as harsh in his condemnation of women who wear ornaments in their hair and mercilessly condemns those who he says have taken up the fashion of baring the neck and arms.

In another part of his work, he gives an extremely long account of several incidents of witchcraft that sowed terror in New England. To him, the visible action of the demon in the affairs of this world is clearly an incontrovertible and demonstrated truth.

The spirit of civil liberty and political independence that was characteristic of the author's contemporaries is apparent at any number of places in the book. Their principles in regard to government are constantly in evidence. Thus we discover, for example, that in 1630, ten years after the founding of Plymouth, the inhabitants of Massachusetts set aside 400 pounds sterling to establish the university in Cambridge.

Turning now from general documents concerning the history of New England to documents pertaining to the various states contained within that region's boundaries, I am bound to mention first the work entitled *History of the Colony of Massachusetts*, by Hutchinson, lieutenant-governor of the Massachusetts province, 2 vols. in octavo. A copy of this work can be found in the Bibliothèque Royale: it is a second edition, printed in London in 1765.

Hutchinson's history, from which I quoted several times in the chapter to which this note refers, begins in 1628 and ends in 1750. An air of great veracity prevails throughout; the style is simple and unadorned. This is a very detailed history.

The best document to consult on Connecticut is Benjamin Trumbull's history, entitled *A Complete History of Connecticut, Civil and Ecclesiastical, 1630–1764*, 2 vols. in octavo, printed in

1818 at New Haven. I do not believe that Trumbull's work can be found at the Bibliothèque Royale.

This history gives a clear, dispassionate account of all events occurring in Connecticut during the period indicated in the title. The author relied on the best sources, and his accounts bear the hallmark of truth. Everything that he has to say about the earliest period of Connecticut's history is extremely interesting. See, in particular, "The Constitution of 1639," vol. 1, chap. 6, p. 100, and "The Penal Laws of Connecticut," vol. 1, chap. 7, p. 123.

Jeremy Belknap's *History of New Hampshire*, 2 vols. in octavo, printed in Boston in 1792, is rightly held in high esteem. See, in particular, chapter 3 of the first volume of Belknap's work, in which the author gives extremely valuable details about the political and religious principles of the Puritans, the reasons for their emigration, and their laws. One also finds this interesting quote from a sermon delivered in 1663: "New England must constantly remember that it was founded for a religious purpose and not a commercial one. Its profession of purity in matters of doctrine and discipline can be read upon its forehead. Let merchants and others who are busy piling penny upon penny therefore recall that religion and not profit was the purpose for which these colonies were founded. If anyone among us ranks the world as thirteen and religion as only twelve, he is not animated by the sentiments of a true son of New England." Readers will find in Belknap more general ideas and more forceful thinking than in any other American historian to date.

I do not know if this book can be found in the Bibliothèque Royale.

Among the central states that have already been in existence for some time, New York and Pennsylvania have the greatest claim on our attention. The best history of the state of New York is William Smith's *History of New York*, printed in London in 1757. There is a French translation of this, also printed in London in 1767, in one duodecimo volume. Smith provides us with useful details on the wars between the French and the English in America. Of all American historians, he gives the best account of the famous Iroquois confederation.

As for Pennsylvania, I can do no better than to call the reader's attention to *The History of Pennsylvania, from the Original Institution and Settlement of that Province, under the First Proprietor and Governor William Penn, in 1681 till after the Year 1742*, by Robert Proud, 2 vols. in octavo, printed in Philadelphia in 1797.

This work is particularly worthy of the reader's attention. It contains a wealth of very interesting documents on Penn, the doctrine of the Quakers, and the character, mores, and usages of the first inhabitants of Pennsylvania. It cannot be found, so far as I am aware, in the Bibliothèque.

There is no need to add that the works of Penn himself and of Franklin are among the most important documents concerning Pennsylvania. These works are known to many readers.

I consulted most of the books cited here during my stay in America. The Bibliothèque Royale was kind enough to entrust me with a number of them. The rest were lent to me by Mr. Warden, the former consul general of the United States in Paris and the author of an excellent book on America. I do not want to end this note without expressing my gratitude to him.

VII, PAGE 57

The following passage can be found in Jefferson's memoirs: "In the earlier times of the colony, when lands were to be obtained for little or nothing, some provident individuals procured large grants; and, desirous of founding great families for themselves, settled them on their descendants in fee tail. The transmission of this property from generation to generation, in the same name, raised up a distinct set of families, who, being privileged by law in the perpetuation of their wealth, were thus formed into a Patrician order, distinguished by the splendor and luxury of their establishments. From this order, too, the king habitually selected his councilors of state." (*Jefferson's Memoirs*.)

In the United States, the principal provisions of the English law of inheritance have been universally rejected.

"The first rule that we follow in regard to inheritance," says Mr. Kent, "is this: when a man dies intestate, his property passes to his direct lineal heirs. If there is only one heir or heiress, he or she alone receives the entire estate. If there are several heirs of the same degree, they divide the estate equally among themselves, without distinction as to sex."

This rule was prescribed for the first time in the state of New York by a statute of February 23, 1786 (see *Revised Statutes*, vol. 3, Appendix, p. 48). It has since been adopted in the revised statutes of the same state. It is now in force throughout the United States, with the sole exception of Vermont, where the male heir claims a double share. Kent, *Commentaries*, vol. 4, p. 370.

In the same work (vol. 4, pp. 1–22), Mr. Kent traces the history of American legislation concerning entails. It turns out that before the American Revolution, the English law of entail was accepted as common law in the colonies. Entailed estates per se were abolished in Virginia in 1776 (on a motion by Jefferson; see his memoirs) and in New York in 1786. Subsequently, North Carolina, Kentucky, Tennessee, Georgia, and Missouri followed suit. Entails were never in common use in Vermont, Indiana, Illinois, South Carolina, or Louisiana. Those states that felt obliged to preserve the English law of entail modified it so as to remove its most salient aristocratic features. "Our general principles in matters of government tend," says Mr. Kent, "to favor free circulation of property."

What is particularly striking to the French student of American estate law is that our laws in this area are infinitely more democratic than theirs.

American laws divide a father's property equally, but only when his wishes are unknown, for the law of New York (*Revised Statutes*, vol. 3, Appendix, p. 51) states that "every person shall have full and free liberty, power, and authority to give, dispose, will, or devise to any person or persons" (except bodies politic or corporate) "by his last will and testament."

Under French law, the rule is that the testator must divide his estate into equal or almost equal shares.

Most of the American republics still permit entails and limit themselves to restricting their effects.

French law does not permit entails under any circumstances.

Thus, while the social state of the Americans is still more democratic than ours, our laws are more democratic than theirs. This is easier to explain than one might think: in France, democracy is still busy demolishing; in America, it reigns tranquilly over ruins.

VIII, PAGE 65

SUMMARY OF VOTING REQUIREMENTS IN THE UNITED STATES. All states grant the right to vote at the age of twenty-one. All require residence for a certain period of time in the district in which a person votes. This period ranges from three months to two years.

As for property qualifications, the state of Massachusetts requires the voter to have an income of 3 pounds sterling or a capital of 60.

In Rhode Island, the voter must own real estate worth $133 (704 francs).

In Connecticut, he must have property yielding an income of $17 (approximately 90 francs). One year of service in the militia also gives a person the right to vote.

In New Jersey, the voter must have a fortune of 50 pounds sterling.

In South Carolina and Maryland, the voter must own 50 acres of land.

In Tennessee, he must own property of some sort.

In the states of Mississippi, Ohio, Georgia, Virginia, Pennsylvania, Delaware, and New York, it suffices to pay taxes to become a voter. In most of these states, service in the militia counts as equivalent to the payment of taxes.

In Maine and New Hampshire, it is enough not to be on the poor rolls.

Finally, in the states of Missouri, Alabama, Illinois, Louisiana, Indiana, Kentucky, and Vermont, no conditions are imposed as to the wealth of the voter.

I believe that North Carolina is the only state to impose different conditions on those who vote for senators and those who vote for representatives. The former must own 50 acres of land. To vote for a representative, it is enough to pay a tax.

IX, PAGE 107

The United States has a system of protective tariffs. Because the number of customs inspectors is small and the coastline long, smuggling is very easy. Yet there is much less of it than there is elsewhere, because everyone strives to prevent it. Because preventive measures are not taken in the United States, fires are more common there than in Europe, but generally they are extinguished more quickly, because neighbors are always quick to respond in case of danger.

X, PAGE 109

It is not accurate to say that centralization originated with the French Revolution; the French Revolution perfected but did not create it. The French penchant for centralization and mania for regulation date from the period when legists first joined the government, which takes us back to the time of Philip the Fair. Since then, the importance of both has increased steadily. Here is what M. de Malesherbes, speaking for the Cour des Aides, said to King Louis XVI in 1775:[2]

. . . Each body, each community of citizens retained the right to administer its own affairs, a right that was not, in our view, part of the primitive constitution of the kingdom, for it stems from a source significantly prior to that: natural right, the right of reason. Yet it has been taken away from your subjects, Sire, and we are not afraid to say that in this respect the administration has fallen into excesses that can be termed puerile.

Ever since powerful ministers made it a political principle not to allow a national assembly to be convoked, one thing has led to another to the point where even the deliberations of villagers can be declared null and void if not authorized by an *intendant*, with the result that if the community has to make some expenditure, it must first obtain the approval of the *intendant*'s underling and consequently follow whatever plan he has adopted, employ whichever workers he favors, and pay them whatever he deems appropriate. And if the community wishes to bring suit, it also needs the *intendant*'s authorization for that. The case must be argued before this tribunal first, before being taken to court. And if the opinion of the

[2] See *Mémoires pour servir à l'histoire du droit public de la France en matière d'impôts* (Brussels, 1779), p. 654.

intendant is at odds with that of the villagers, or if their adversary has influence with his office, the community is deprived of the means to defend its rights. It is by means such as these, Sire, that every last vestige of municipal spirit has been snuffed out in France, including, when possible, the sentiments of the citizens. The entire nation has in a sense been declared *incompetent* and placed in receivership.

Could one give a better description of the way things are today, now that the French Revolution has made its so-called *conquests* in regard to centralization?

In 1789, Jefferson wrote from Paris to a friend of his: "Never was there a country where the practice of governing too much had taken deeper root and done more mischief." (*Letters to Madison*, August 28, 1789.)

The truth is that the central power in France had for centuries done all it could to extend administrative centralization, and nothing but the limits of its own strength had ever prevented it from pursuing that course.

The central power born of the French Revolution proceeded further in this direction than any of its predecessors because it was stronger and cleverer than all of them. Louis XIV left the details of village life to the discretion of his *intendants*. Napoleon left them to the discretion of his ministers. The principle remained the same, but it was extended to ever more minute matters.

XI, PAGE 113

This immutability of the French Constitution is a necessary consequence of our laws.

To speak first of the most important of all laws, that which regulates the order of succession to the throne, what is more immutable in principle than a political order based on the natural order of succession from father to son? In 1814, Louis XVIII claimed the right of political succession in perpetuity on behalf of his family and insisted that it be enshrined in law. The men who decided what was to become of this law in the aftermath of the Revolution of 1830 followed his example, only they claimed the right of succession in perpetuity on behalf of another family. In doing so, they imitated Chancellor Maupeou, who made sure that the ordinance establishing the new Parlement on the ruins of the old one stipulated that the new magistrates would enjoy life tenure, just as their predecessors had before them.

The laws of 1830, like those of 1814, did not provide for any means of changing the Constitution. Clearly, ordinary legislative procedures are not adequate for this.

What is the source of the king's powers? The Constitution. Of the peers' powers? The Constitution. Of the deputies' powers? The Constitution. How, then, can the king, the peers, and the deputies join together to change any aspect of the law that is the sole source of their right to govern? Outside the Constitution, they are nothing: on what ground can they stand, therefore, to change the Constitution? There are just two possibilities: either their efforts are powerless against a charter that continues to exist in spite of them, in which case they continue to reign in its name, or else they succeed in changing the charter, in which case the law that gave them their existence no longer exists, hence they themselves have been reduced to nothing. By destroying the charter, they destroy themselves.

This is even more apparent in the laws of 1830 than in those of 1814. In 1814, royal power stood in a sense outside and above the Constitution. In 1830 it is by its own admission created by the Constitution, and absolutely nothing without it.

Hence one part of our Constitution is immutable, because it has been tied to the destiny of one family. And the Constitution as a whole is also immutable, because there is apparently no legal means of changing it.

None of this applies to England. Since England has no written constitution, who is to say that the constitution is being changed?

XII, PAGE 113

The most respected commentators on the English constitution seemingly try to outdo one another in asserting this omnipotence of Parliament.

Delolme (chap. 10, p. 77) says: "It is a fundamental principle with the English lawyers that Parliament can do everything except making a woman a man or a man a woman."

Blackstone is even more categorical, if not more forceful, than Delolme. This is what he says:

The power and jurisdiction of Parliament, says Sir Edward Coke (4 Inst. 36), is so transcendent and absolute that it cannot be confined, either for causes or persons, within any bounds. And of this high court, he adds, it may be truly said, *Si antiquitatem spectes, est vetustissima; si dignitatem, est honoratissima; si jurisdictionem, est capacissima.* It hath sovereign and uncontrollable authority in the making, confirming, enlarging, restraining, abrogating, repealing, reviving, and expounding of laws concerning matters of all possible denominations, ecclesiastical or temporal, civil, military, maritime, or criminal: this being the place where that absolute despotic power, which must in all governments reside somewhere, is entrusted by the constitution of these kingdoms. All mischiefs and grievances, operations and remedies, that transcend the ordinary course of the laws are within the reach of this extraordinary tribunal. It can regulate or new-model the succession to the crown, as was done in the reign of Henry VIII and William III. It can alter the established religion of the land, as was done in a variety of instances in the reigns of King Henry VIII and his three children. It can *change and create afresh even the constitution of the kingdom* and of parliaments themselves, as was done by the act of union and the several statutes for triennial and septennial elections. It can, in short, do everything that is not naturally impossible; and therefore some have not scrupled to call its power, by a figure rather too bold, the *omnipotence* of Parliament.

XIII, PAGE 125

There is no matter on which American constitutions are more fully in harmony than that of political judgment.

All the constitutions that deal with this subject give the House of Representatives the exclusive right to indict, except for the constitution of North Carolina, which gives this right to grand juries (article 23).

Almost all the constitutions give the Senate, or the assembly that takes its place, the exclusive right to judge.

The sole penalties that political tribunals can impose are removal from office and barring from future office. Only the constitution of Virginia allows the full range of penalties to be imposed.

Crimes that can give rise to political judgment are as follows: in the Federal Constitution (Art. 1, Sec. 4) and the constitutions of Indiana (Art. 3, pp. 23 and 24), New York (Art. 5), and Delaware (Art. 5), high treason, corruption, and other high crimes and misdemeanors;

In the constitutions of Massachusetts (Chap. 1, Sec. 2), North Carolina (Art. 23), and Virginia (p. 252), misconduct and improper administration;

In the constitution of New Hampshire (p. 105), corruption, criminal misconduct, and improper administration;

In Vermont (Chap. 2, Art. 24), improper administration;

In South Carolina (Art. 5), Kentucky (Art. 5), Tennessee (Art. 4), Ohio (Art. 1, Secs. 23 and 24), Louisiana (Art. 5), Mississippi (Art. 5), Alabama (Art. 6), and Pennsylvania (Art. 4), offenses committed in office;

In the states of Illinois, Georgia, Maine, and Connecticut, no crime is specified.

XIV, PAGE 193

It is true that the European powers have the ability to wage great wars with the Union at sea, but it is always easier and less dangerous to wage war at sea than on land. War at sea demands only one kind of effort. A commercial people that is willing to give its government the necessary funds can always be sure of putting a fleet to sea. It is far easier to hide the sacrifice of money from people than to disguise the sacrifice of men and personal effort. Furthermore, defeats at sea seldom compromise the existence or independence of the nation that suffers them.

As for land wars, it is obvious that the nations of Europe cannot wage any that would endanger the American Union.

It is quite difficult to transport 25,000 soldiers to America and maintain them there. Such a force would represent a nation of roughly two million people. If the greatest European nation were to mount such a force to wage war with the Union, it would be in the same position as a nation of two million waging war with a nation of twelve million. What is more, the Americans would have all their resources at hand, while the Europeans would be 1,500 leagues from theirs, and the immensity of the United States would by itself constitute an insurmountable obstacle to conquest.

VOLUME ONE, PART II

XV, PAGE 212

The first American newspaper appeared in April 1704. It was published in Boston. See *Collection of the Historical Society of Massachusetts*, vol. 6, p. 66.

It would be a mistake to assume that the periodical press has always been completely free in America. There have been attempts to impose something like prior censorship and surety.

The legislative records of Massachusetts for January 14, 1722, relate the following:

The committee named by the General Assembly (the legislative body of the province) to look into the case of the newspaper known as the *New England Courant*

finds that the tendency of said newspaper is to ridicule and heap scorn upon religion; that sacred authors are treated in a profane and irreverent manner; that the conduct of ministers of the Gospel is subject to malicious interpretation; that His Majesty's government is insulted; and that the peace and tranquillity of the province are disturbed by said newspaper; in consequence whereof, the committee is of the opinion that James Franklin, printer and publisher, should in the future be prohibited from printing and publishing said newspaper or any other text until he has submitted them to the secretary of the province. The justices of the peace of Suffolk County shall be enjoined to obtain from Mr. Franklin a bond of surety guaranteeing his good behavior during the coming year.

The committee's proposal was accepted and became law, yet it remained without effect. The newspaper evaded the ban by placing the name *Benjamin* Franklin rather than *James* Franklin at the end of its columns, and public opinion refused to accept the measure.

XVI, PAGE 314

To be a county elector (that is, a representative of landed property) prior to the Reform Bill of 1832, one had to possess, either in freehold or under lease for life, land yielding a net annual income of forty shillings. This law was promulgated under Henry VI around 1450. It has been calculated that forty shillings from the time of Henry VI might today be the equivalent of thirty pounds sterling. Yet this qualification, adopted in the fifteenth century, was allowed to subsist until 1832, which proves how democratic the English constitution had become over time, though it appeared to remain unchanged. See Delolme; see also Blackstone, Book I, Chap. 4.

English jurors are chosen by the county sheriff (Delolme, Book I, Chap. 12). The sheriff is generally a man of considerable importance in the county. His functions are both judicial and administrative. He represents the king, who confirms his appointment annually (Blackstone, Book I, Chap. 9). His position renders him immune from suspicion of corruption by the parties. Furthermore, if his impartiality is questioned, the jury he has appointed can be recused in toto, whereupon another official is charged with selecting new jurors. See Blackstone, Book III, Chap. 23.

To be entitled to be a juror, one must be in possession of land yielding an annual income of at least ten shillings (Blackstone, Book III, Chap. 23). Note that this condition was imposed during the reign of William and Mary, that is, around 1700, when the price of silver was far higher than it is today. Clearly, the English based their jury system not on capacity but on landed property, like all their other political institutions.

Ultimately, farmers were allowed to serve as jurors, but they had to hold very long-term leases and earn a net income of twenty shillings, independent of rent. (Blackstone, idem.)

XVII, PAGE 314

The federal Constitution established the jury system in the Union's courts, just as the states had established it in their courts. Furthermore, the Union did not impose its own rules for jury selection. The federal courts drew jurors from the regular jury lists that each state prepared for its own use. Hence one must study state laws in order to understand the theory of jury composition in America. See Story's *Commentaries on the Constitution*, Book III, Chap. 38, pp. 654–659 and Sergeant's *Constitutional Law*, p. 165. See also the federal laws of 1789, 1800, and 1802 on this matter.

Seeking a clear picture of American principles in regard to the composition of juries, I examined the laws in widely separated states. Here are the general ideas that emerged from my study.

In America, any citizen who is entitled to vote is entitled to serve as a juror. The great state of New York has, however, established a slight difference between the two capacities, but it is in the opposite direction from our laws: there are fewer jurors in New York than there are voters. In general, it is fair to say that in the United States, the right to serve on a jury, like the right to elect representatives, is extended to each and every citizen, but the exercise of that right is not indiscriminately entrusted to everyone.

Every year, a body of municipal or county officials, called selectmen in New England, supervisors in New York, trustees in Ohio, and parish sheriffs in Louisiana, selects a certain number of citizens from each county who are entitled to serve as jurors and presumed capable of doing so. Because these officials are themselves elected, they do not inspire distrust. Their powers are quite extensive and highly arbitrary, like those of republican officials in general, and it is said that they often make use of them, especially in New England, to eliminate unworthy and incapable jurors.

The names of the selected jurors are sent to the county court, and from this list of names a jury is chosen by lot to hear each case.

In addition, the Americans did everything possible to put jury service within reach of the people and reduce the burden of such service to a minimum. Because the number of jurors is large, each person is not required to serve much more often than once every three years. Sessions are held in every county seat; the county is more or less equivalent to the French *arrondissement.* Thus the court comes to sit close to the jury, instead of forcing the jury to come to it, as in France. Finally, jurors are indemnified for their service, either by the state or by the parties. In general, they are paid a dollar a day (5.42 francs), apart from traveling expenses. In America, jury service is still considered a burden, but a burden that is easy to bear and readily accepted.

See Brevard's *Digest of the Public Statute Law of South Carolina*, vol. 2, p. 338; vol. 1, pp. 454 and 456; vol. 2, p. 218.

See *The General Laws of Massachusetts Revised and Published by Authority of the Legislature*, vol. 2, pp. 331 and 187.

See *The Revised Statutes of the State of New York*, vol. 2, pp. 720, 411, 717, and 643.

See *The Statute Law of the State of Tennessee*, vol. 1, p. 209.

See *Acts of the State of Ohio*, pp. 95 and 210.

See *A General Digest of the Acts of the Legislature of Louisiana*, vol. 2, p. 55.

XVIII, PAGE 317

If the constitution of the civil jury in England is examined closely, it is easy to see that the jurors are always under the control of the judge.

To be sure, the jury verdict in civil as well as criminal cases is generally issued in the form of a simple statement covering both matters of fact and matters of law. Suppose, for example, Peter claims to have bought a house: a matter of fact. His adversary objects on the grounds that the seller was incompetent: a matter of law. The jury simply states that possession of the house is to be awarded to Peter; it thereby decides both the question of fact and the question of law. When the English brought the jury into civil matters, they did not persist in the view that the opinion of the jurors is infallible, as they hold it to be in criminal matters when the verdict is favorable.

If the judge believes that the verdict involves a misapplication of the law, he can refuse to accept it and send the jurors back for further deliberation.

If the judge allows the verdict to pass without comment, the case is still not entirely closed; there are several avenues of recourse in case the judgment is unfavorable. The main one is to ask the courts to overturn the verdict and summon a new jury. To be sure, such a request is seldom granted, and never more than twice, but I myself have seen it happen. See Blackstone, Book III, Chaps. 24 and 25.

Translator's Note

MORE than most writers, Alexis de Tocqueville was an architect of language. In *Democracy in America* he sought to create a harmonious edifice, a structure in which each part was carefully proportioned and subordinated to a conception of the whole. In a letter to his friend and traveling companion Gustave de Beaumont, he said, "I am more and more convinced that the overall effect is chief among the merits of a book and that one must have the courage to make all the sacrifices necessary to achieve it."[1] Tocqueville was perfectly conscious of the overall effect he wished to achieve. He described it well in characterizing the literary qualities that an aristocratic nation would be likely to value: "Style will seem almost as important as ideas and form almost as important as substance. Tone will be polite, measured, and even. The mind will invariably move at a stately pace, seldom with haste, and writers will devote more effort to perfecting their works than to producing them."[2] At the same time, he recommended avoiding "aristocratic jargon," because jargon excludes: "Any aristocracy that sets itself entirely apart from the people becomes impotent. This is true in literature as well as in politics."

In preparing this translation, these lines of Tocqueville's have been my guide. Fidelity to his ideas is perhaps easier to achieve than fidelity to his style — a style of classical sobriety, "almost anachronistic for the Romantic era."[3] His first tutor, Abbé Lesueur, had also been his father's tutor. As a citizen of the Republic of Letters, Tocqueville was therefore more a man of the 18th century than of the 19th, and he seems to have taken from his tutor something of the 18th century's love of clarity, elegance, and balance in prose. His father's library, filled with translations of ancient authors as well as the French classics of the 17th century and the great *philosophes* of the 18th,

---

[1] Françoise Mélonio, *Tocqueville et les Français* (Paris: Aubier, 1993), p. 34.
[2] See page 64.31–35 in volume two.
[3] André Jardin, *Alexis de Tocqueville*, (Paris: Hachette, 1984), p. 357.

probably influenced his writing even more than his classes in rhetoric, a subject in which he excelled.[4]

What stands out above all in Tocqueville's style is a remarkable and almost paradoxical combination of solidity and grace. His affirmations buttress one another without ever becoming ponderous or ungainly. Although he is the most quotable of authors, his sentences do not go in for what he disparaged as "facile beauties," nor do they depend on "surprise and novelty" or "intense and rapid emotions" for their effects. The "polite, measured, even tone" and "stately pace" at which he aimed may be prosaic qualities, but heedless translation can undo them all too easily. A writer of Tocqueville's mastery can cast a spell over his translator. The rightness of his French seems so incontestable that one hesitates to tamper with his choices. If an English cognate is available for a word he used in French, there is always a temptation to use it rather than cast about for a more adequate English equivalent. If he ordered his words and clauses in a certain way in order to achieve a balanced period in the original, there is a temptation to acquiesce in his example rather than make the extra effort necessary to achieve a similar equilibrium in English. Yet to succumb to these temptations is at times to betray the author by excess of fidelity. A fine discrimination is required, a tactful judgment as to what sacrifices are necessary and warranted in order to achieve the desired "overall effect." Each such decision may in itself be small and almost negligible, but a translation is the concatenation of thousands of small choices. Like the writer, the translator needs the courage to make sacrifices. At times, that may mean eschewing a misguided literalism in order to preserve some quality of the original that would not otherwise survive. At other times, it may mean translating literally even at the risk of producing a formulation that sounds oddly foreign in English.

In one instance it was necessary to take issue with Tocqueville himself. In Volume One, Part I, Chapter 5, Tocqueville placed the English word "township" in parentheses after the French phrase *la commune de la Nouvelle-Angleterre*. Previous translators have taken this as an indication that Tocqueville

[4] *Ibid.*, pp. 60–63.

intended the French *commune* to be equivalent to the English "township." Hence they have him refer in subsequent passages to "township meetings," "township officers," and the like. But New England was famous for its "town meetings"; Tocqueville took his local nomenclature from a book called *The Town Officer*; and a letter that he wrote to Jared Sparks on December 2, 1831, refers to *communes* as "towns." Sparks, his principal informant on these matters, consistently refers to "towns," not "townships."[5] Hence it seems forced and artificial to perpetuate what I believe to be a slip of Tocqueville's pen by emulating the choice that previous translators have made. I have accordingly broken with tradition on this point.

There are in *Democracy in America* certain words that amount to terms of art, words that acquire a special meaning from the way Tocqueville deploys them in his argument. One such term of particular importance is *mœurs*, which I have rendered into English using the cognate term "mores." Tocqueville uses "mores" to mean something more than "the accepted traditional customs and usages of a particular social group." Although he is usually content to allow special meanings to emerge from his use of a word in a variety of contexts, in this key instance he supplies a definition, but not until the word has been used many times: "By *mores* I mean here what the Ancients meant by the term: I apply it not only to mores in the strict sense, what one might call habits of the heart, but also to the various notions that men possess, to the diverse opinions that are current among them, and to the whole range of ideas that shape habits of mind. Thus I use this word to refer to the whole moral and intellectual state of a people."[6] Here the translation of a French word by a cognate is not misleading, because in both languages the meaning of the term is inflected by Tocqueville's idiosyncratic usage.

Tocqueville often uses the terms "nation" and "people" interchangeably as a stylistic device to avoid repetition. I have therefore allowed myself on occasion to substitute one for the other when necessary to achieve a more euphonious English

[5] I am grateful to Olivier Zunz for directing my attention to the Sparks-Tocqueville correspondence on this point.
[6] See page 331.27–33 in this volume.

sentence. There are places, however, where Tocqueville speaks of a nation composed of more than one people, and there the distinction has been rigorously maintained. In addition, he sometimes refers to the states of the Union as "nations" when he wants to emphasize their sovereign rights. Where a literal translation would have obscured his meaning, I have translated as "state" (and indicated the alteration in the Notes). *La souveraineté du peuple* is often rendered as "popular sovereignty," a phrase common enough in English and frequently conducive to less cumbersome translation than the more literal "sovereignty of the people."

Tocqueville refers to the various branches of the American government as "powers": *le pouvoir judiciaire*, for example. While it might be more natural to translate as "the judicial branch," something would surely be lost, so I have repatriated the Gallicism.

Tocqueville makes frequent use of the verb *se confondre*, whose translation proved problematic. Previous translators have generally rendered this as "intermingled," but this translation implies that the components of a mixture retain their identities, whereas *se confondre* suggests a loss of identity, a condition of indistinguishability, so I have preferred to translate the term in most instances as "blend." The nuance may be of some significance, particularly in the chapter on the "three races that inhabit the United States" (pages 365–476 in this volume), where the frequent occurrence of this verb is worth noting.

In one respect this translation departs significantly from previous translations of *Democracy in America*. Tocqueville translated passages from a substantial number of English texts into French and included them in his book. Some of his translations are quite faithful, while others are so free as to amount to interpretations of the originals. It was therefore decided to provide the reader with translations of Tocqueville's more liberal renderings. These retranslated passages have been incorporated into the body of the text; the original English passages are included in the Notes so as to allow the reader to judge what Tocqueville did in each case.

It is a rare honor for a translator to work on a classic of the magnitude of *Democracy in America*. I hope that I have been able to do it justice. I would like to thank Daniel Gordon, Patrice Higonnet, and Cheryl Welch for comments on portions of the manuscript and above all Jon Elster and Olivier Zunz for their careful reading of the entire text. These vigilant readers have improved the translation substantially. Any flaws that remain are of course entirely my own.

This is not the first translation of *Democracy in America*, nor will it be the last. I hope that it has qualities that will give the reader without French an idea of the stately grace of Tocqueville's style as well as a rigorous and faithful rendering of his ideas. Tocqueville enjoys a unique position in the history of literature and thought: a philosopher also notable as a literary stylist, he is the only Frenchman who can claim to be part of the American canon as well as the French. It is my fervent hope that the pleasure I took in translating his work will prove contagious.

Arthur Goldhammer
Cambridge, Massachusetts, 2003

Chronology

1805   Alexis Charles-Henri Clérel de Tocqueville is born in Paris on July 29, the third son of Hervé and Louise-Madeleine de Tocqueville. (Hervé Louis François Bonaventure Clérel de Tocqueville was born in 1772. His family owned the château de Tocqueville in Normandy, about 12 miles east of Cherbourg, and was of the *noblesse d'épée*, aristocrats whose nobility derived originally from their military service; one of his Clérel ancestors fought at the battle of Hastings in 1066. Louise-Madeleine Le Peletier de Rosanbo, born in 1771, was from a family predominantly of the *noblesse de robe*, aristocrats who derived nobility from their positions in the judiciary and royal administration. Her father, Louis Le Peletier de Rosanbo, served as a president of the Parlement of Paris, the highest appellate court; her grandfather, Chrétien-Guillaume de Lamoignon de Malesherbes, who had protected the *philosophes* while director of the book trade during the reign of Louis XV, served as a reformist minister early in the reign of Louis XVI, and then came out of retirement in 1792 to help defend the king at his trial before the National Convention. Hervé de Tocqueville and Louise-Madeleine de Rosanbo were married on March 12, 1793. They were arrested by the revolutionary regime in December 1793 along with Malesherbes, Rosanbo, and several other members of the family. Malesherbes; Le Peletier de Rosanbo and his wife, Marguerite; Louise-Madeleine's sister, Aline-Thérèse, and her husband, Jean-Baptiste de Chateaubriand, the older brother of the Romantic writer François-René de Chateaubriand — the great-grandfather, grandfather, grandmother, aunt, and uncle of Alexis de Tocqueville — were all guillotined in Paris in April 1794. While waiting for his execution, Malesherbes had to watch the beheading of his own daughter and granddaughter. Tocqueville's parents remained imprisoned until after the execution of Robespierre on July 28, 1794, or 10 Thermidor. Hervé de Tocqueville's hair turned prematurely white, while Louise-Madeleine suffered from persistent depression and anxiety as a result of her experiences. Hervé regained some of the family's fortune and became guardian of the orphaned Louis and Christian de Chateaubriand. Tocqueville's brother Hippolyte was born in 1797 and his brother Édouard in 1800.)

1805–13   The family resides in the winter in the Faubourg St. Germain in Paris and in the summer in a château at Verneuil-sur-Seine inherited from the Malesherbes family. Despite having fragile health, Tocqueville will remember having a happy childhood at Verneuil, where the family plays parlor games, has literary evenings with play readings and poetry recitations, and annually celebrates Saint Louis on the occasion of Louise-Madeleine's birthday. Chateaubriand occasionally comes to visit his nephews, and once greets Hervé de Tocqueville while disguised as an old woman. Tocqueville is tutored by Abbé Christian Lesueur, a conservative priest with Jansenist leanings who had been Hervé de Tocqueville's tutor. He studies French composition and writings by Blaise Pascal that emphasize strict morality and inward faith. Although two distant older cousins, Louis Honoré Félix Le Peletier d'Aunay and Louis-Mathieu Molé, who would become Tocqueville's political mentors in the July monarchy, rally to the Napoleonic regime, most family members remain "Legitimists" loyal to the deposed Bourbon dynasty.

1814   Tocqueville and his family join in a demonstration in Paris on April 3 calling for the restoration to the throne of Louis XVIII, the brother of Louis XVI. Napoleon abdicates on April 6 and Louis XVIII enters Paris on May 3. Hervé de Tocqueville is appointed prefect (the administrative representative of the central government in a French department) of Maine-et-Loire and moves to Angers. Tocqueville remains with his mother in Paris and continues his education with Abbé Lesueur; he will sometimes visit his father at his various posts. Hippolyte becomes an officer in the army (he will serve until 1830).

1815   Hervé de Tocqueville leaves Angers in March when Napoleon returns from his exile on Elba. After the Second Restoration of the Bourbon monarchy in July, Hervé de Tocqueville is appointed prefect of the Oise and moves to Beauvais.

1816   Hervé de Tocqueville is appointed prefect of the Côte d'Or and moves to Dijon. Édouard enters the army (he will serve until 1822).

1817   Hervé de Tocqueville is appointed prefect of the Moselle and moves to Metz.

1820   Tocqueville joins his father in Metz.

1821   When he is 16, Tocqueville is overcome by religious doubt when reading the works of the 18th-century *philosophes* in his father's library. In 1857 he described the experience in a letter to his friend, the Russian mystic and Parisian society figure Madame Swetchine: "My life up to then had flowed in an interior full of faith which had not even allowed doubt to penetrate my soul. Then doubt entered, or rather rushed in with unheard-of-violence, not merely the doubt of this or that, but universal doubt. I suddenly felt the sensation those who have witnessed an earthquake speak of, when the ground moves under their feet, the walls around them, the ceilings over their head, the furniture in their hands, all nature before their eyes. I was seized with the blackest depression, taken by an extreme disgust for life without having experienced it, and I was as if overwhelmed by trouble and terror at the sight of the road which I had still to travel in the world." He enters the lycée in Metz in November.

1822–23   Tocqueville is a brilliant student at the lycée, where he studies rhetoric and philosophy. At 17 he fathers a child, Louise Charlotte Meyer, with a servant at the prefecture. (Nothing is known of the child's life.) He later falls in love with Rosalie Malye, the daughter of a local civil servant. Perhaps because of a rivalry for the young woman, Tocqueville fights a duel in May 1823 with a classmate in which no one is hurt. Although his distant cousin and childhood friend Louis de Kergorlay dissuades Tocqueville from pursuing a relationship with a woman unsuitable for someone of his aristocratic background, the affair lingers until Malye is married in 1828. At the lycée Tocqueville also begins a lifelong friendship with Charles and Eugène Stöffels, young men of lesser social standing. He graduates with his baccalaureate in the summer of 1823, just as his father becomes prefect of the Somme and

moves to Amiens. In the fall Tocqueville enters the law
school of the University of Paris.

1824–26   Tocqueville studies Roman law, the Napoleonic civil
code, civil and criminal procedure, and criminal law, but
is a less distinguished student than at the lycée. Louis
XVIII dies in 1824 and is succeeded by his brother,
Charles X. Tocqueville receives his degree in 1826 after
writing two short theses, one in French and one in Latin.
In December he travels to Italy and Sicily with his brother
Édouard. During the trip he writes a journal in which he
notes the consequences for aristocratic society of the fragmentation of property ownership.

1827   In January, Hervé de Tocqueville, who has become prefect of Seine-et-Oise and settled in Versailles, writes to the
minister of justice to find a job for his son. As a result, in
April Tocqueville is appointed a *juge auditeur* (apprentice
judge) at the tribunal in Versailles; the position is an
unpaid internship in which he assists the judges and public
prosecutors in hearing and presenting civil and criminal
cases. In November Hervé de Tocqueville is named to the
Chamber of Peers, an institution recreated under the
Bourbon Restoration.

1828   In January Tocqueville moves into an apartment in Versailles with Gustave de Beaumont (born 1802), a lawyer
at the tribunal of Versailles with the rank of *substitut*, one
step above *auditeur*. In a speech he makes to the court on
dueling, Tocqueville explores the conflict between honor
and law. During the year he meets and falls in love with
Mary ("Marie") Mottley, an English woman of middle-
class origin, who lives with her aunt on the same street as
Tocqueville.

1829   Beginning in April, Tocqueville attends, along with Beaumont, the course on the history of French civilization
taught at the Sorbonne by François Guizot, whose lectures he finds "extraordinary." (Guizot was a leader of the
liberal opposition to the Bourbons, as well as one of the
most influential historians of the 19th century. Along with
the political philosopher and famous orator Pierre-Paul
Royer-Collard, he was a major figure in the "Doctri-
naires," a group of political thinkers who had reconciled

the liberal principles of the Revolution of 1789 with the legitimacy of the monarchy.) Tocqueville and Beaumont attend a few sessions of *Aide-toi, le ciel t'aidera* ("Heaven helps those who help themselves"), a liberal political society founded by Guizot in 1827. While traveling with Kergorlay in Switzerland, Tocqueville learns in October that Beaumont is leaving Versailles for a new position in Paris, and that the position of *substitut*, which he had hoped to receive, has been given to his childhood acquaintance Ernest de Chabrol. Although he is initially despondent about both pieces of news, he overcomes his disappointment and becomes a roommate and friend of Chabrol.

1830   Tocqueville closely follows the French expedition against Algiers, in which Kergorlay serves as an artillery officer. Algiers capitulates on July 5, beginning the French conquest of Algeria. Charles X promulgates ordinances on July 25 abolishing freedom of the press, restoring censorship, restricting the electoral franchise, dissolving the Chamber of Deputies, and calling for new elections under new electoral rules. Protests against the July ordinances in Paris lead to three days of street fighting ("les trois glorieuses") from July 27 to 29. Tocqueville helps his parents hide at St. Germain-en-Laye on July 29, then returns to Versailles, where he volunteers to serve in the newly reconstituted National Guard to help prevent violence between royalists and insurgents. Charles X withdraws the ordinances on July 30, then flees from the palace at St. Cloud outside Paris on July 31. Tocqueville watches with contempt as the royal convoy moves through Versailles on its way to Rambouillet. "As for the Bourbons, they have behaved like cowards and do not deserve a thousandth part of the blood that has been spilled over their cause," he writes to Marie Mottley. On July 31 the Marquis de La Fayette presides over the acclamation of the Duc d'Orléans at the Hôtel de Ville in Paris, the first step toward a new constitutional monarchy led by the junior branch of the royal family. Charles X abdicates on August 2 and the Duc d'Orléans becomes King Louis-Philippe on August 9.

Hervé de Tocqueville loses his seat in the upper chamber when the new regime abolishes the peerages created by Charles X. He refuses to serve the constitutional monarchy and goes into retirement. Tocqueville takes the oath of loyalty required of public officials on August 16 and repeats it in October, chilling relations with some members of his pro-Bourbon family, though his father and brother Édouard may have urged him to take the oath. On August 26 he writes to Charles Stöffels: "For a long time now, I have wanted to visit North America. I will see there what a great republic is. All I fear is that, while I am over there, a republic will be established in France." In October he and Beaumont petition the minister of the interior to be sent to the United States to study the American penitentiary system, a subject of great interest in French reform circles. Le Peletier d'Aunay, Tocqueville's cousin and a deputy in the Orleanist chamber, intervenes on their behalf.

1831   Tocqueville and Beaumont receive authorization for their trip from the interior ministry and an 18-month leave of absence from the ministry of justice. On April 2 they sail from Le Havre on an American ship. During the voyage Tocqueville and Beaumont discuss writing a book on American society and government in addition to their official prison report.

On May 9 they land at Newport, Rhode Island, a town that looks to Tocqueville like "an array of houses no bigger than chicken coops," then travel by steamboat to New York City, where they arrive on May 11 and move into a boarding house on Broadway. Their arrival is reported in the New York newspapers (stories about their activities will appear in other newspapers during their trip). Accompanied by the mayor and aldermen, the two commissioners visit the House of Refuge, a reformatory for delinquent minors; Bloomingdale hospital for the insane; an asylum for the deaf and mute; the poor house; and Blackwell's Island prison. They also attend parties given in their honor by local dignitaries in the city and in summer country homes.

Tocqueville and Beaumont interrupt their stay in the city for a visit, May 29–June 7, to Sing Sing, the 900-inmate prison in Ossining on the Hudson River. They watch inmates work in quarries and stonecutting sheds in total silence, under the threat of the whip, and then return to solitary confinement at night. (Inmates in French prisons were thrown together in large rooms, a condition that Tocqueville believed hindered their reformation.) Though

Tocqueville and Beaumont abhor the use of flogging at Sing Sing, they are impressed by the obedience and silence of the prisoners.

After their return to New York City they meet with James Kent, the former chief justice and chancellor of New York State, who gives them a copy of his *Commentaries on American Law*, and with the Swiss-born Albert Gallatin, who had served as secretary of the treasury in the Jefferson and Madison administrations. They also attend the trial of an accused thief in criminal court.

Upstate New York, June 30–July 19:

On June 30 Tocqueville and Beaumont leave New York City and travel by sloop and the steamboat *North America* up the Hudson to Albany, where they march with state officials in the Independence Day parade and inquire about the workings of the state government. They then travel by way of Utica to Syracuse, where on July 7 they interview Elam Lynds, the former warden of Auburn prison who had also overseen the construction of Sing Sing. From Syracuse they go to Oneida Lake and explore Frenchman's Island, which they believe to have been settled some 40 years earlier by a refugee from the French Revolution and his wife. In describing his impressions of the island to his sister-in-law Émilie, Hippolyte's wife, Tocqueville predicts his letter will keep her "daydreaming" for eight days. (Tocqueville later writes a longer account of his visit, *Voyage au Lac Onéida*, which is published posthumously by Beaumont in 1861.)

After visiting the Auburn prison, Tocqueville and Beaumont travel by horseback on July 16 to Canandaigua, where they visit the home of lawyer, state legislator, and former congressman John Canfield Spencer. Tocqueville encourages Spencer to talk about the ways American institutions affect social practices. Spencer shares his detailed knowledge of the workings of the judiciary; he explains that the freedom of the press in America is balanced by the heavy fines to which newspapers are subjected if convicted of printing libelous statements; tells them that religion in America supports liberty and free institutions; and stresses the importance of legislative bicameralism. During their stay at Canandaigua Tocqueville and Beaumont enjoy the company of Spencer's daughters,

Mary and Catherine. "We were more inclined to look at the daughters than at the father's books," Tocqueville writes Émilie. "They have among other charms, four blue eyes (that is, two each)" such as "you have never seen on the other side of the water."

On July 18 Tocqueville and Beaumont ride to Buffalo, where they see Indians waiting to receive government payments owed them for their land rights. Tocqueville, "full of memories of M. de Chateaubriand and of Cooper," had imagined encountering Indians bearing the "marks" of "proud virtues" and "liberty," and is disillusioned by the dependency and widespread drunkenness he sees.

The Great Lakes and Canada, July 19–September 2:

The next day the two friends board the steamboat *Ohio* on Lake Erie and reach Detroit on July 22 after a stop in Cleveland. In Detroit they interview Gabriel Richard, a French-born priest and educator, and John Biddle, the register of the land office, who explains to them the land acquisition and settlement process. His conversation with Biddle prompts Tocqueville to write to Chabrol: "How to imagine a revolution in a country where such a sequence of events can meet the needs and passions of men, and how to compare the political institutions of such a people to that of any other?" Tocqueville and Beaumont go on horseback to Pontiac, then cross the Flint River and travel through dense forest to the village of Saginaw, which is inhabited by about 30 Americans, French Canadians, Indians, and "bois brûlés" (children of French-Canadian men and Indian women). During their return Tocqueville turns 26 on July 29, a day he spends in the forest remembering the revolution in Paris the previous year.

On August 1 Tocqueville and Beaumont leave Detroit along with 200 other passengers on a steamboat excursion to Sault Ste. Marie, Mackinac Island, and Green Bay, Wisconsin. Tocqueville notes that Episcopalian passengers seem content to listen to a sermon by a Presbyterian minister, and writes: "This may be tolerance but may I die if this is faith." At Sault Ste. Marie they travel by canoe to Lake Superior, then go to Mackinac Island, where Tocqueville witnesses sectarian division between Catholics and Presbyterians. During the voyage he writes *Quinze jours dans le désert* ("Two Weeks in the Wilderness"), an account of their trip to Saginaw (it is published posthumously by Beaumont in 1861).

The *Superior* returns to Detroit on August 14, and on August 17 Tocqueville and Beaumont arrive in Buffalo by steamboat. They rent a carriage and spend two days exploring Niagara Falls, then take a steamboat across Lake Ontario and down the Saint Lawrence River to Montreal and Quebec City. "The old France is in Canada, the new one at home," Tocqueville notes. Although Tocqueville and Beaumont appreciate the hospitality shown to them, they do not like the dated French they hear and feel people lack spark. Tocqueville blames the Catholic Church for discouraging individualism and education, which he believes reduces the political effects of a broad electoral base. He also uncovers anachronistic, if limited, remnants of French feudal taxation and landholding practices.

New England, September 2–October 12:

Tocqueville and Beaumont leave Montreal on September 2. Traveling by way of Lake Champlain and Albany, on September 9 they reach Boston, where Tocqueville is overcome by sadness at the news in the mail of the death of his old tutor Abbé Lesueur.

During their stay in Boston Tocqueville and Beaumont visit the state prison at Charlestown three times. They also have numerous political conversations with former Federalists who oppose President Andrew Jackson, many of whom will later become members of the Whig party. At a rally in support of Polish independence they meet Josiah Quincy, the president of Harvard and a former congressman and mayor of Boston, who becomes a helpful source of information and documents. They form a friendship with Francis (Franz) Lieber, a German political exile who had been wounded during the Waterloo campaign while fighting with the Prussian army.

Their most important Boston informant is Jared Sparks, a Unitarian minister and former editor of the *North American Review* and future professor of history at Harvard, who explains to them that the "political dogma of this country is that the majority is always right." (Sparks will later protest that Tocqueville made too much of the idea of "the tyranny of the majority.") They also meet Senator Daniel Webster, but are disappointed by his dismissive attitude toward prison reform. At a dinner at the home of diplomat Alexander Everett on October 1, Tocqueville is seated next to former president John Quincy Adams, who had been defeated by Jackson in 1828; they discuss slavery and the South in French. Adams characterizes white southerners as a "class" with "all the ideas, all the passions, all the prejudices of an aristocracy," finding work "dishonorable" even though there is nothing in the southern climate that should prevent them from working. Before leaving Boston on October 3, Tocqueville and Beaumont discuss religion and democracy with the Unitarian minister William Ellery Channing. (In a letter to his mother, Tocqueville describes him as a leader of those Unitarians who "take from the Bible only what reason can admit.")

On October 5 they visit the Connecticut state prison at Wethersfield, where prisoners are punished by complete isolation in their cells and are rarely whipped. As they travel through Hartford and New York City, Tocqueville reflects on his conversations in New England regarding the jury, and writes that the institution is the "most direct and most powerful application of the dogma of popular sovereignty."

Philadelphia and Baltimore, October 12–November 22:

The two commissioners arrive in Philadelphia on October 12. Tocqueville and Beaumont make eight visits to the Eastern State Penitentiary, where Tocqueville individually interviews each of the inmates. They are deeply impressed by the Quaker-inspired "Philadelphia system" in which prisoners are encouraged to repent by means of uninterrupted solitary confinement and Bible study in cells large enough to provide individual workspaces. While in Philadelphia Tocqueville discusses American institutions, mores, population movements, and race relations with several informants, including Charles J. Ingersoll, a lawyer and former congressman, and Peter S. Duponceau, a French-born lawyer and expert on American Indian languages. He also meets with Quaker philanthropists and attends the theater, where he is struck by the restlessness of the audience.

As news of the cholera epidemic spreading through Europe reaches Philadelphia, Tocqueville sends Chabrol a shipment of cajeput oil, not available in France, with instructions not only to divide it among family members but to set a vial aside for Marie Mottley, the woman he loves "with all my soul." He also writes his mother: "The most valuable documents I am returning with are two small notebooks where I have written down, word for word, the conversations I have had with the most remarkable men of this country. . . . Up to now I have expressed only a few general ideas on America, in the letters I have sent to the family and a few other people in France. I have written them in haste, on steamboats or in some corner where I had to use my knees as a table. Will I ever publish anything on this country? . . . I have a few good ideas but I am not sure about what form to put them in and I am afraid of going public."

On October 28 Tocqueville and Beaumont travel to Baltimore, the center of American Catholicism, where Tocqueville is impressed by his conversations with lawyer John H. B. Latrobe on political parties, universal suffrage, and the American legal profession. They visit with 94-year-old Charles Carroll, the last surviving signer of the Declaration of Independence, before returning to Philadelphia on November 6. During their second stay in Philadelphia they speak with Nicholas Biddle, president of the Bank of the United States, and Joel Poinsett, a former ambassador to Mexico and strong supporter of Andrew Jackson.

The Ohio and the Mississippi, November 22–December 31:

Tocqueville and Beaumont leave Philadelphia on November 22 and travel by stagecoach to Pittsburgh, arriving on November 24 after crossing the Allegheny Mountains during a snowstorm. In Pittsburgh they visit the Western State Penitentiary before taking the steamboat *Fourth of July* down the Ohio. The vessel runs aground near Wheeling, but another steamboat brings its passengers to Cincinnati on December 1. In Cincinnati, Tocqueville discusses universal suffrage at length with the 23-year-old antislavery lawyer Salmon Portland Chase, who will later serve as secretary of the treasury and as chief justice of the U.S. Supreme Court, and also meets with U.S. Supreme Court Justice John McLean. Observing the contrast between Ohio and Kentucky, Tocqueville writes in a notebook that on one side of the Ohio "work is honored and leads to all else, on the other it is despised as the mark of servitude." He attributes the difference to slavery, which "degrades the black population and enervates the white." Tocqueville and Beaumont leave Cincinnati on December 4, intending to go down the Ohio and the Mississippi, but the next day their steamboat is blocked when the river freezes over in exceptionally cold weather. They go ashore at Westport, Kentucky, and walk 25 miles through snow to Louisville, then travel overland to Nashville by coach. While riding from Nashville to Memphis in a one-horse open coach, Tocqueville falls ill and the two friends have to stop for three days in an isolated log cabin inn. On December 17 they finally reach Memphis and discover that the Mississippi is full of ice. As they wait for navigation to resume, Tocqueville hunts birds in the nearby forests with Chickasaw Indians and reflects on Tennessee politics in his notebook: "When voting rights are universal, it is a strange thing how low the people's choice can descend and how far it can be mistaken. Two years ago the inhabitants of the district of which Memphis is the capital sent to the House of Representatives of Congress an individual called David Crockett, who had received no education, could read only with difficulty, had no property, no fixed dwelling, but spent his time hunting, selling his game for a living, and spending his whole life in the woods. His competitor, who failed, was a fairly rich and able man."

On December 25 Tocqueville and Beaumont leave Memphis for New Orleans on the steamboat *Louisville*, which also carries a group of 50 to 60 Choctaw Indians who are being sent by the federal government to the Indian territory west of Arkansas. This instance of "Indian removal" deeply affects Tocqueville, who predicts in a letter to his mother that American policy will eventually result in the extinction of the Indians. After the Choctaws disembark in Arkansas, Tocqueville and Beaumont discuss at length the situation of the Indians with their fellow passenger, Sam Houston, who had been living among the Cherokees in the Indian territory since resigning as governor of Tennessee in 1829.

1832   Tocqueville and Beaumont arrive in New Orleans on January 1 and stay until January 3, when they begin their return to the northeast without having visited a plantation worked by slave labor. (At some point in their American trip they apparently had received instructions from the French government to return sooner than they had originally intended.) They travel by steamboat to Mobile, then take a series of stagecoaches across Alabama, Georgia, South Carolina, and North Carolina, to Norfolk, Virginia, which they reach on January 16. In South Carolina they are joined by Joel Poinsett, who talks with Tocqueville at length about slavery, tariffs, and the nullification movement. From Norfolk they travel by steamboat to Washington, D.C., where they arrive on January 17.

In Washington they have a brief interview with President Jackson and attend debates in the Senate and the House of Representatives. Secretary of State Edward Livingston, an expert on the Louisiana penal system, helps them collect numerous books and documents. Tocqueville and Beaumont leave Washington on February 3 and return to New York City by way of Philadelphia. They embark in New York for Le Havre on February 20, with their trunks full of documents, sketchbooks, diaries, and records of conversations with over 200 known informants; they had also instructed their friends and families at home to keep all of their letters.

The date of their landing is not known, but by April 4 Tocqueville is in Paris. His return coincides with the arrival of the cholera epidemic, which claims more than 12,000 lives in Paris by the end of April. In May and June, he travels to Toulon, Geneva, and Lausanne to inspect their prisons. While in Toulon he learns that Beaumont has been dismissed from his post as a magistrate for a minor act of insubordination, and immediately resigns in solidarity. During his trip he also visits his friend Kergorlay, who was imprisoned earlier in May for his participation in a Legitimist plot, led by the Duchesse de Berry, to overthrow the July monarchy. After his return to Paris Tocqueville resumes his collaboration with Beaumont on their report on American prisons. Beaumont writes most of the report, while Tocqueville, uncertain about his future, makes comments and writes responses to his friend's queries.

1833   *Du Système pénitentiaire aux États-Unis et de son application en France* appears in January. Tocqueville and Beaumont contrast the Auburn system of collective work during the day, discipline by whipping, and night isolation with the

Philadelphia system of total isolation, without expressing a preference for either system. (An American edition, translated and edited by Francis Lieber, is published in Philadelphia later in the year.) On March 9 Tocqueville appears as co-counsel for the defense at the trial of Kergorlay in Montbrison in the Loire department. In his speech to the jury he defends Kergorlay's character and convictions, not the Legitimist cause. Kergorlay is acquitted. (This will be Tocqueville's only appearance as a defense attorney.) In early August Tocqueville travels to England to witness what he describes as "the last performance of a beautiful play" as English society moves away from aristocratic dominance. He watches debates in the House of Lords, visits Oxford, imagines scenes from Walter Scott's novels in the ruins of Kenilworth and Warwick castles, and becomes friends with Lord Radnor, a social reformer, and Nassau Senior, a political economist who is preparing a report on the British poor laws with a view to making them more restrictive. In September, Tocqueville returns to Paris and moves into an attic room in his parents' house to work on his book on America (he and Beaumont had abandoned their plan to collaborate on another book after the publication of the prison report).

1834   Tocqueville secures the services of two young Americans living in Paris, Theodore Sedgwick III, whom he had met in Stockbridge, Massachusetts, and Francis J. Lippitt, a secretary at the American legation. They provide him with summaries of over 200 books and documents, including *Commentaries on the Constitution of the United States* by Justice Joseph Story, *Notes on the State of Virginia* by Thomas Jefferson, and *The Federalist*, as well as of the many official papers Edward Livingston had helped assemble. Tocqueville also begins carefully to study a lengthy essay on the political history of New England towns that Jared Sparks had written at his request. Occasionally Tocqueville reads drafts of his work to friends and family and submits manuscripts to them for suggestions, which he frequently accepts. In the late summer he submits a complete manuscript to his publisher, Charles Gosselin, and corrects proofs in October.

1835   Volume One of *De la démocratie en Amérique* is published in Paris on January 23 in a printing of 500 copies. Uncertain of its reception, Tocqueville writes to Camille d'Orglandes "the best thing for me would be if no one read my book." Beaumont publishes *Marie ou l'Esclavage aux États-Unis, tableau de mœurs américaines*, a novel about the doomed love affair of a French immigrant and a white American woman with a distant mulatto ancestor; the book contains lengthy documentary appendices on slavery and race relations, religion, and American Indians. Tocqueville writes *Mémoire sur le paupérisme*, an essay published later in the year by the Academic Society of Cherbourg, in which he denounces aid to unwed mothers as "a dowry of infamy" while advocating charity to those incapable of fending for themselves. In March, Tocqueville meets Henry Reeve, a young Englishman who agrees, after some hesitation, to translate *De la démocratie en Amérique*. (*Democracy in America* is published in England later in the year; an American edition of the Reeve translation, edited by John Canfield Spencer, is published in 1838.) Chateaubriand introduces Tocqueville to the literary salon of Madame Récamier, where he meets members of the Parisian literary elite who will help make *De la démocratie en Amérique* a success (seven editions of the book are printed by June 1839).

In late April, Tocqueville and Beaumont travel to London. Tocqueville meets again with Nassau Senior, Lord Radnor, and Henry Reeve; is introduced to the Whig politicians Lord Lansdowne and Lord Brougham; and begins a friendship with John Stuart Mill, who is one year his junior. In late June they leave London and visit Coventry, Birmingham, Manchester, and Liverpool, investigating the growth of industrialization and urban poverty, before traveling to Ireland in early July. Tocqueville remains in Ireland until the middle of August; before returning to France, he writes: "If you wish to know what the spirit of conquest, religious hatred, combined with all the abuses of aristocracy without any of its advantages, can produce, come to Ireland." On October 26 he marries Marie Mottley. His family and friends, including initially Kergorlay and Beaumont, disapprove of the marriage. (As a commoner and a foreigner, and a woman nine years older than her husband, Marie is never fully accepted by the Tocqueville family, although she has formally abjured Protestantism and fervently embraced Catholicism.) In November Tocqueville begins work on the second volume of *De la démocratie en Amérique*.

Minister to France Edward Livingston returns to the United States late in the year with a copy of *De la démocratie en Amérique*, where he is singled out as the person most helpful in assembling the necessary documentation, but without having resolved the indemnity crisis that brought France and America close to war. French-American diplomatic relations are temporarily suspended (until February 1836) as President Jackson demands, and finally obtains, reparations for French seizure of American ships and cargoes during the Napoleonic blockade of the continent.

1836   Louise-Madeleine de Tocqueville dies in January. After his mother's death, Tocqueville is given the château de Tocqueville, uninhabited since the Revolution, and also the title of *Comte*, which he will never use. With the château he also receives land that will provide most of his income. The political philosopher Pierre-Paul Royer-Collard introduces Tocqueville into the fashionable literary salon of the Duchesse de Dino, a niece of Talleyrand. At the request of John Stuart Mill, Tocqueville writes *L'État social et politique de la France avant et après 1789*, his first study of the French Old Regime, in which he presents the French Revolution as a local manifestation of a larger European movement toward equality; the essay is published in translation in the April *London and Westminster Review*. The Tocquevilles spend the summer in Switzerland. During a brief stay in Bern, Tocqueville observes the functioning of the federal diet. In July Beaumont marries Clémentine de La Fayette, a granddaughter of the Marquis de La Fayette. While Marie is resting and taking the waters in Baden, Tocqueville reads Machiavelli's *Florentine History*, which he describes as a "learned lecture on the art of crime in politics," as well as works by the 17th-century Catholic bishop and famous pulpit orator Bossuet, whom he admires; by Voltaire, whom he resents as illiberal and anti-democratic; by Plato; and by the Church fathers. (Later that year, Tocqueville writes to Kergorlay: "there are three men with whom I live a little daily, they are Pascal, Montesquieu and Rousseau.")

1837   Tocqueville works on a second essay on pauperism (left unfinished) in which he considers the ways French industrial workers could gain economic security through savings accounts and the forming of associations. In June he and Marie go to the château de Tocqueville and remain there until November; in future years they will spend winter and spring in Paris and summer and fall in Normandy. Tocqueville publishes two unsigned letters on Algeria in the newspaper *La Presse de Seine-et-Oise*, June 23 and August 22, expressing hope that French colonists will be able to coexist peacefully with the Arabs in Algeria. With support from Marie, Tocqueville prepares to run for office, rejecting Royer-Collard's suggestion that his lack of oratorical ability will prevent him from becoming a politician. ("Do not believe that I have a blind enthusiasm, or indeed any kind of enthusiasm," he writes to Kergorlay, "for the intellectual life.") After considering the 10th *arrondissement* of Paris, Versailles, and Cherbourg, Tocqueville chooses the Norman town of Valognes, about 10 miles southwest of his family estate, as his electoral base. He runs for election to the Chamber of Deputies, but on November 4 loses in the second round of voting, 247–220, to the incumbent, Comte Jules-Polydor Le Marois. (As a self-proclaimed "liberal of a new kind," he had rejected the support of his cousin, prime minister Louis-Mathieu Molé, causing Molé to remark: "Isolation is not independence.") After John Quincy Adams writes to him contesting its accuracy, Tocqueville agrees to delete from the sixth edition of *De la démocratie en Amérique* a sentence stating that, while president, Adams had dismissed many officials from the preceding Monroe administration.

1838   Tocqueville is elected to the Académie des sciences morales et politiques on January 6. Although at first reluctant to sit with some former participants in the Revolutionary Terror, he comes to appreciate the opportunity to meet such historians as Jules Michelet, François Mignet, François Guizot, and the philosopher Victor Cousin. Tocqueville reads and makes notes on a French translation of the Koran. Without consulting Beaumont, he writes a letter to the *Journal de Valognes* endorsing the Philadelphia system of complete solitary confinement of prison inmates.

1839   On March 2 Tocqueville defeats Le Marois, 318–240, in the first round of voting and becomes the deputy for Valognes after an expensive self-financed campaign of banquets for the electors. His good friend Francisque de Corcelle is elected in the Orne, but Beaumont is defeated for the second time in Saint Calais (he is elected in December in another district of the Sarthe). Tocqueville, who insists on sitting on the left of the Chamber to avoid being labeled a Legitimist, supports the pro-monarchial center-left party led by Odilon Barrot; one of his main political aims is to overturn the "September Laws" restricting freedom of speech and of the press that were adopted in 1835 following an assassination attempt on the king.

He gives his first major speech on foreign affairs on July 2, outlining the diverging interests of France, Russia, and Great Britain in the Middle East and advocating French support for Muhammad Ali Pasha, the ruler of Egypt who had conquered Syria and effectively established his independence from the Ottoman Empire. On July 23 he submits a report to the Chamber on slavery in the colonies of Martinique, Guadeloupe, French Guiana, and the Isle of Bourbon (Réunion), calling for the immediate emancipation of all slaves, the payment of an indemnity to the slaveowners, and a state-guaranteed wage for the freedmen during a transition period, but the report is never debated. His involvement in politics makes it difficult for Tocqueville to complete the second volume of *De la démocratie en Amérique*, and he writes to Beaumont: "I must at all costs finish this book. It and I have a duel to the death — I must kill it or it must kill me."

1840   The second volume of *De la démocratie en Amérique* is published by Gosselin on April 20. (A translation by Reeve appears in London simultaneously, and it is published in New York with a preface by Spencer later in the year.) More abstract than the first volume, it is not nearly as successful, and Tocqueville writes to Royer-Collard: "I cannot hide from myself the fact that the book is not much read and not well understood by the great public." In the Chamber Tocqueville advocates adoption of the Philadelphia system in a report on prison reform submitted on June 20, but no action is taken on the proposal.

On July 15 Great Britain, Russia, Austria, Prussia, and the Ottoman Empire sign a treaty in London intended to preserve Ottoman sovereignty over Egypt and to force Muhammad Ali to withdraw from most of Syria. The exclusion of France from the concert of the great powers causes angry talk of going to war against Britain, and the Chamber votes extraordinary credits for military preparations. In late October Louis-Philippe refuses to endorse further belligerent measures and dismisses the ministry led by Adolphe Thiers. He appoints Guizot as foreign minister and effective head of government (a position Guizot retains for the remainder of the July monarchy). Unhappy with what he considers to be the policy of appeasement adopted by Guizot, Tocqueville proclaims in a speech to the Chamber on November 30 that "a government that is unable to make war is a detestable government." His speech prompts John Stuart Mill to retort in a letter to Tocqueville: "You know how repugnant to the English character is anything like bluster, and that instead of intimidating them, its effect when they do not treat it with calm contempt is to raise a dogged determination in them not to be bullied."

1841   In February the Ottoman sultan makes Muhammad Ali the hereditary ruler of Egypt under Ottoman sovereignty. Tocqueville travels to Algeria with his brother Hippolyte and Beaumont, arriving in Algiers on May 7. They are joined there by Corcelle and tour the nearby countryside, which Tocqueville describes in his journal as a "promised land, if one did not have to farm with a gun." He visits Oran and Philippeville (Skikda), meets with General Thomas-Robert Bugeaud, the recently appointed governor-general and army commander in Algeria, and interviews other senior French officials before falling ill with dysentery. Tocqueville returns to France on June 11 and goes to Normandy to recover. During his convalescence he drafts a long essay on Algeria (*Travail sur l'Algérie*, not published until 1962) describing its colonization as essential to preserving France as a great power and justifying the destruction of villages, orchards, and crops in *razzias* (raids) as a necessary means of crushing Arab resistance. France joins the four other powers on July 13 in signing a treaty governing the Turkish straits, a diplomatic move that restores the *entente cordiale* between France and Britain. Tocqueville is elected to the Académie Française on December 23.

1842   In his inaugural speech at the Académie Française, Tocqueville denounces Napoleon's despotism before an audience prone to commemoration of the Napoleonic legend. Along with Beaumont, he serves on a royal commission on Algerian colonization but becomes doubtful of its usefulness and withdraws. On July 9 he is reelected to the Chamber, defeating Le Marois, 465–177. Following the accidental death of the Duc d'Orléans, the heir to the throne, Tocqueville addresses the Chamber on August 18 during a debate over provisions for a future regency; in a letter to Marie, he laments that his speech was "horrible" and that he has "no talent for improvisation." To help in a study of modern moral philosophy he is undertaking for the Académie des sciences morales et politiques, Tocqueville recruits late in the year the young writer Arthur de Gobineau as his assistant (the project is never finished). In December he is elected to the Conseil général of his department, the Manche.

1843   In January, Tocqueville publishes in *Le Siècle* six unsigned letters in which he accuses "unprincipled" politicians of killing liberty while speaking in its name. Tocqueville has increasingly come to see Guizot as the leader of a centralizing, manipulative, and corrupt ministry and believes former prime minister Thiers to be equally unscrupulous. ("I despise them," Tocqueville had confided to Royer-Collard in 1841.) In the Chamber he opposes ratification of a treaty on suppressing the slave trade, sponsored by Great Britain and supported by Guizot, that would allow the British navy to stop and search foreign vessels. Tocqueville argues that the treaty is ineffectual, weakens national sovereignty, and permits abuses "in the solitude of the ocean"; as an alternative he advocates an international campaign to close the slave markets in Brazil and Cuba. In March he criticizes Guizot for his failure to support Spanish liberals, who have turned to Britain for help; he also opposes Guizot's support of British efforts to prevent the American annexation of Texas, believing that U.S. territorial expansion will help check British commercial and naval power.

    Tocqueville's marriage is often tumultuous, with frequent arguments. He writes Kergorlay in September that he cannot stop his "blood boiling at the sight of a woman" while Marie never accepts "the least deviation on my part." From October to December, Tocqueville publishes another series of six unsigned articles in *Le*

Siècle calling for emancipation in the French colonies. Tocqueville sees the French Caribbean as "the Mediterranean of the New World" and foresees the building of a canal across the Isthmus of Panama. During the fall he works on a study of British rule in India begun in 1840 (it is never finished). Contrasting French agrarian colonization in Algeria with the more flexible rule of the East India Company, Tocqueville is impressed by the British ability to manipulate Indian princes, control the economy by indirect means, and implement a new administrative and legal structure while accommodating local customs.

1844   During a debate in the Chamber over state control of Catholic secondary education, Tocqueville defends the independence of Church schools. The Chamber of Deputies passes a law, introduced by Tocqueville in 1843, instituting the Philadelphia system in French prisons, but the Chamber of Peers acts on it only in 1847 and the law is never implemented. Tocqueville joins with a group of friends in buying *Le Commerce* and establishing it on July 24 as an independent opposition newspaper. As the intense debate between ultramontanists and anticlericals over liberty of teaching continues, he writes in *Le Commerce* warning of the consequences of overturning the intellectual and moral authority provided by religion: "We will need soldiers and prisons if we abolish beliefs." He criticizes *Le Siècle* for its anticlericalism, leading to a sharp polemical exchange between the newspapers and a short, painful dispute with Beaumont, who resigns from the board of *Le Siècle* while praising its editor. Tocqueville publishes articles in *Le Commerce* on the French challenge of combining a "vast" administrative centralization with a "serious representative system," and writes a report for the Conseil général of the Manche advocating the construction of a direct rail line from Paris to Cherbourg.

1845   In June Tocqueville, who had discovered he did not like journalism, ends his involvement with the failing *Le Commerce* and loses his investment — "what amounted to my affluence."

1846   During a debate in the Chamber in June, Tocqueville criticizes Bugeaud and the Guizot ministry for failing to effectively promote agrarian colonization in Algeria. He easily wins reelection to the Chamber on August 1. In October he makes a second trip to Algeria, this time accompanied by Marie. Tocqueville meets again with Bugeaud, travels overland from Algiers to Ténès, and visits Oran, Constantine, and several villages in the interior before returning to France in late December.

1847   In the winter session of the Chamber Tocqueville and a few parliamentary friends fail in their attempt to create a "young left" party of "the really honest men" with a program to end corruption and reduce the burden of taxation on the poor. Tocqueville submits two reports on Algeria to the Chamber in late May criticizing the failure to establish effective political, legal, and administrative institutions in the colony. The reports contribute to Bugeaud's resignation as governor-general that year. Barrot holds a large public banquet in Paris on July 9 in support of enlarging the electorate, but Tocqueville declines to attend and abstains from the subsequent "campaign" of political banquets held by the opposition in public halls and parks throughout the country. Ambivalent about the adoption of universal male suffrage in France, he is also concerned about the potential for disorder. During the fall he drafts proposals for providing assistance to the poor. "There is little doubt," he writes, "that, one day, the political struggle will be between the haves and the have nots. Property will be the great battlefield, and the great political questions will be about how to change property rights and to what extent." Louis-Philippe and Guizot continue to refuse all suggestions of electoral reform.

1848   In a speech to the Chamber on January 27, Tocqueville warns of growing popular discontent. Sensing "the air of revolution," he points to those "opinions and ideas" that "tend not simply to the overthrow of such and such laws, such and such a minister, or even such and such a government, but rather to the overthrow of society." After the government prohibits a political banquet, demonstrations begin in Paris on February 22 that quickly turn into a popular revolution. The king dismisses Guizot on February 23, then abdicates on February 24 in favor of his nine-year-old grandson, the Comte de Paris. Tocqueville hopes that the boy can reign with his mother, the liberal Duchesse d'Orléans, acting as regent, and urges the poet Alphonse de Lamartine, a leading orator in the Chamber, to support this solution. Instead Lamartine declares that he will "join only a Republic," and the Second Republic is proclaimed at the Hôtel de Ville on the evening of February 24.

On March 5 elections are called for a Constituent Assembly to be chosen by universal manhood suffrage, and Tocqueville becomes a candidate in his department of the Manche. (He later writes in his memoir *Souvenirs* that he plunged "headlong into the fray, risking wealth, peace of mind and life to defend, not any particular government, but the laws that hold society together.") At a public banquet held on March 19 in Cherbourg, he calls for an alliance between the French and American republics to free the sea from British domination and praises the American example for the new French regime: "In America, the Republic is not a dictatorship exercised in the name of freedom; the Republic is liberty itself, true and real liberty for all citizens; it is the sincere government of the people by the people; the uncontested domination of the majority, the order of law." While campaigning he writes daily to Marie, describing "the great Democratic revolution now unfolding" as "God's will" one day, while on another day cautiously advising: "we must quietly keep as much money as possible at home, and preferably in coin. For I suspect paper money will soon lose much of its value." On April 24 Tocqueville is elected with 110,704 votes out of the approximately 120,000 cast (voters chose several candidates from various lists).

The Constituent Assembly meets on May 4 with moderate republicans in the majority. Tocqueville, Beaumont, and 16 other members are elected from May 17 to 19 to serve on a commission charged with drafting a new constitution. In June Tocqueville meets George Sand at the home of a mutual friend. Although prejudiced against women writers ("I detest women who write, especially those who systematically disguise the weaknesses of their sex," he writes in *Souvenirs*, "instead of interesting us by displaying them in their true colors"), he listens intently as she provides him with "a detailed and very vivacious picture of the state of the Parisian workers: their organization, numbers, arms, preparations, thoughts, passions and terrible resolves. I thought the picture overloaded, but it was not so, as subsequent events clearly proved." On June

21 the provisional government shuts down the public work-shops (*ateliers nationaux*), initiated in March, that employ as many as 120,000 people in Paris. A popular insurrection ensues, June 23–26, in which several thousand people are killed before troops led by General Louis-Eugène Cavaignac finally suppress the uprising. Tocqueville supports the quelling of the "class war" by Cavaignac, who becomes the head of the provisional government. He notes with sorrow the death of Chateaubriand on July 4.

In the constitutional commission, Tocqueville cites American examples and proposes creating a bicameral legislature in order to strengthen the power of local elites, but the commission rejects bicameralism, as well as his repeated attempts to lessen plans for centralized rule. (Tocqueville notes that centralization attracts strong support because "both the government and the enemies of the government love it.") Beaumont advocates limiting the president to one four-year term, a proposal that is adopted. The Assembly begins considering the proposed constitution on September 4 and approves the final version on November 4. During the debate the socialists unsuccessfully attempt to insert the right to work into the constitution's preamble. Tocqueville dismisses their claim to be the heirs of the Revolution of 1789, arguing that its "true heritage" is rather "the incorporation into politics of the divine dogma of charity." In this period, he also serves on a commission that reestablishes work in prisons after it was dispensed with by the provisional government (his last involvement with the penal system). Tocqueville supports Cavaignac in the presidential campaign, while Thiers backs Louis-Napoleon Bonaparte, whom he describes as "this imbecile we will manipulate." On December 10 Louis-Napoleon Bonaparte is elected with 74 percent of the vote.

1849   Confident of winning a seat in the Legislative Assembly established by the new constitution, Tocqueville leaves the Manche before election day to avoid the vexing local quarrels he describes as a "war of chamber pots." On May 13, he is elected with 82,404 votes out of the 94,481 cast. He goes to Frankfurt to understand the failure of the parliament, elected in Germany in 1848 by universal manhood suffrage, to create a federal Germany. Before returning to France he writes to Beaumont, predicting the victory of the German princes in the revolutionary conflict and observing: " I believe that the king of Prussia has refused the supremacy the Assembly offered him in the name of the revolution only with the intention of obtaining it by repressing this revolution."

On June 2 Tocqueville is appointed minister of foreign affairs in a cabinet presided over by Odilon Barrot. Tocqueville hires Arthur de Gobineau as his private secretary. While serving as foreign minister, he has his portrait painted by Théodore Chassériau. (It is likely that because Tocqueville had limited time to sit, Chassériau used as his model an earlier pencil portrait he had drawn in 1844.) Tocqueville's major diplomatic challenge is the restoration to temporal power of Pope Pius IX, who had been forced to flee Rome in 1848 by the republican coalition led by Giuseppe Mazzini. On July 3 a French expeditionary force occupies Rome. Tocqueville chooses his friend Francisque de Corcelle, a devout Catholic, as his envoy to the Pope, with instructions to lead Pius IX toward democratic reforms in the Papal States, but Corcelle proves unreliable and the pontiff refuses to make significant changes. In Europe, Tocqueville seeks to support moderate republican regimes throughout the continent while maintaining friendly relations with the reactionary powers of Prussia, Austria, and Russia. He helps Piedmont negotiate a peace treaty with Austria, and supports the Ottoman sultan when he refuses to surrender Hungarian and Polish revolutionary exiles wanted by the Czar and the Austrian emperor.

Tocqueville is also involved with affairs in Uruguay (there is a large French community in Montevideo), where since 1842 France has supported President José Fructuoso Rivera against his rival Manuel Oribe, who is backed by the Argentinean dictator Juan Manuel Rosas. (Although the French involvement is in contravention to the Monroe Doctrine, the United States does not intervene.) In October Tocqueville receives a letter from Secretary of State John Clayton demanding the recall of Guillaume-Tell Poussin, the French minister to the United States, for allegedly having used offensive language in official communications. Although Tocqueville dislikes Poussin (who had been a severe critic of *De la démocratie en Amérique*) and disapproves of his conduct, he refuses to receive the new American minister, William Cabell Rives, and writes to

Clayton asking for an explanation. (Poussin is eventually replaced, and the dispute is resolved.)

Tocqueville is minister of foreign affairs for only five months. On October 31, Louis-Napoleon Bonaparte, frustrated by the inability of French diplomacy to get the Pope to secularize the government of the Papal States and to acknowledge the French military contribution to the pontifical restoration, and vexed by Barrot's disregard for presidential concerns in the Assembly, dismisses the entire cabinet and replaces them with subservient ministers.

1850   In March Tocqueville is seriously ill and spits blood for the first time, showing symptoms of tuberculosis. He is granted a six-month leave by the Assembly. During the summer in Normandy he begins writing *Souvenirs*, his memoir of the 1848 revolution (published posthumously in 1893). On September 6 Tocqueville, as president of the Conseil général of the Manche, receives Louis-Napoleon Bonaparte in Cherbourg and renews his call for a railroad connecting the port town to Paris. In December the Tocquevilles, seeking a warm climate, rent a house in Sorrento in southern Italy. He continues working on *Souvenirs* and begins conceptualizing a major book on the French Revolution, writing to Kergorlay: "I believe myself in a better condition than I was when I wrote *Democracy* to deal well with a great subject of political literature. . . . For a long time I have had the thought of choosing in this great expanse of time that goes from 1789 to our day, and which I continue to call the French Revolution, the ten years of the Empire, the birth, the development, the decline and the fall of that prodigious enterprise."

1851   In April the increasingly autocratic Louis-Napoleon Bonaparte indirectly approaches Tocqueville about a possible new term as foreign minister, but the overture is rejected. Later in the month the Tocquevilles return to France. Tocqueville serves on an Assembly committee on revising the constitution; its recommendations fail to win approval. In September, he writes the third part of *Souvenirs* in Versailles. Prohibited by the constitution from seeking a second term, Louis-Napoleon stages a military coup d'état on December 2. Tocqueville is arrested along with more than 200 protesting members of the Assembly and is held in jail until December 4. He considers the coup to be "one

of the greatest crimes history has known" and condemns
it in an anonymous article, translated by Henry Reeve, that
appears on December 11 in the *Times* of London.

1852   Hoping that the Comte de Chambord, the grandson of
         Charles X and the Bourbon heir, can offer a political alter-
         native to the dictatorship of Louis-Napoleon, Tocqueville
         writes to him on January 14 outlining precepts for a con-
         stitutional monarchy. He becomes estranged from his
         brother Édouard when Édouard runs for office on a plat-
         form defending the coup. Tocqueville resigns from the
         Conseil général of the Manche to avoid swearing alle-
         giance to the new regime and retires from political life. In
         an address to the Académie des sciences morales et poli-
         tiques on April 12, he underscores the incompatibility of
         political science and the art of government, yet points to
         the role abstract writers had played in the making of the
         French Revolution, a theme he will fully develop in *L'An-
         cien Régime et la Révolution*. Returning to his château in
         the summer, he writes (referring to the events that led to
         Napoleon Bonaparte's coup on November 9, 1799, or
         18 Brumaire) about how once before "the republic was
         ready to receive a master" and describes his country in a
         letter to Édouard as "this tired, nervous, half-rotten
         France, which asks only to obey whoever will insure its
         material well-being." On December 2 Louis-Napoleon
         Bonaparte becomes Napoleon III as the Second Empire
         is proclaimed.

1853   With his health failing, Tocqueville is advised by his
         doctor to avoid the damp climate of Normandy, and in
         the late spring he settles in Saint-Cyr-les-Tours in the
         Loire Valley. In nearby Tours, he reads the files of the
         royal administration of the province of Touraine. After
         Gobineau sends him the first two volumes of his *Essai sur
         l'inégalité des races humaines*, Tocqueville writes in re-
         sponse: "You speak unceasingly of races that are regener-
         ating or deteriorating, which take up or lay aside social
         capacities by an *infusion of different blood* (I believe that
         these are your own terms). Such a predestination seems
         to me, I will confess, a cousin of pure materialism and
         be sure that if the crowd, which always takes the great
         beaten tracks in matters of reasoning, were to accept your
         doctrine, that would lead it straight from the race to the

individual and from social capacities to all kinds of capacities.... I remain situated at the opposite extreme of those doctrines. I believe them to be very probably wrong and very certainly pernicious."

1854   Early in the year Tocqueville decides to devote a full volume to the causes of the Revolution. After learning German, he goes with Marie to Bonn in June to research feudalism in Germany. He finds that feudal dues had survived much longer in Germany than in France, where they were hated most in the very regions where they had already largely disappeared. "I see with a certain satisfaction," Tocqueville writes to Beaumont, "that the ideas I had of Germany without knowing the country, purely from abstract reasoning, attempting to discover why the Revolution had happened among us rather than in Germany, appear to me to be fully confirmed by the factual details." The Tocquevilles return to France in September and spend the winter in Compiègne.

1855   Tocqueville takes an active part in the effort at the Académie des sciences morales et politiques to defeat government-backed candidates for membership. The government retaliates through various administrative measures, but the Académie becomes a symbol of liberal resistance to Napoleonic despotism. Tocqueville returns to Normandy in the summer after a three-year absence. Although he had actively sought his father's advice in the writing of *De la démocratie en Amérique,* he conceals the preparation of his new book from Hervé de Tocqueville, having not thought well of the two volumes his father had written on the reigns of Louis XV and Louis XVI.

1856   In January Tocqueville writes to his friend Madame Swetchine, describing the "moral isolation" he experiences: "to be alone in the desert often strikes me as being less painful than being alone among men." Beaumont helps him proofread the first volume of his book on the Old Regime. Seeing a continuity with the American work, he suggests "Démocratie et liberté en France" to Tocqueville as a possible title. Hervé de Tocqueville dies on June 9. *L'Ancien Régime et la Révolution* is published in Paris on June 16 by Michel Lévy and is given an enthusiastic reception. (*The Old Regime and the Revolution,* translated by Henry Reeve, is published simultaneously in London.) Tocqueville argues that the French Revolution, despite its own rhetoric of breaking with the past, was the outcome of many deep transformations begun in the Old Regime. He sees bureaucratic centralization under royal authority, which killed local liberty, as a long-term agent of destabilization, and argues that the monarchy itself, by depriving the nobility, the Third Estate, and even the royal administration of any real experience with politics, opened the way for inexperienced intellectuals to shape public opinion. The book is understood as a work of liberal opposition to Napoleon III and gives Tocqueville renewed political prominence.

1857   In June Tocqueville travels to London, where he is given authorization to read the diplomatic archives covering the years from 1787 to 1793. He returns to Cherbourg in July on a British naval ship provided by the Admiralty as a special courtesy. The financial panic in the United States worries Tocqueville. Fearing the loss of railroad bonds he had purchased in 1848, he asks Senator Charles Sumner to inquire about the fate of the Central Michigan and the Galena–Chicago railroads. In a letter to Sumner in November, Tocqueville wonders whether the election of James Buchanan in 1856 signaled the triumph of pro-slavery forces, but notes with pleasure the victory of Free-Soil candidates in the recent election for the Kansas territorial legislature.

1858   Tocqueville goes to Paris in April planning to do extensive research in the libraries for a second volume on the unfolding of the Revolution and the creation of the Empire. By the middle of May he feels so ill that he returns to his château, and in June he spits blood. In August he watches from the roof of his brother Édouard's château at Tourlaville as Napoleon III presides over the official opening of the Cherbourg–Paris railroad line. Tocqueville and Marie move to Cannes in late October, hoping that the Riviera climate will do him good. By this time, Tocqueville has drafted substantial sections of his second volume.

1859   John Stuart Mill sends Tocqueville a copy of *On Liberty*, but he is not able to comment on it as he had promised.

After a brief remission in February, Tocqueville continues to decline as his tuberculosis worsens. Beaumont and Kergorlay visit him. Marie convinces her husband to confess and receive Holy Communion but it is not known whether he recovers his faith. Tocqueville dies on the evening of April 16. As he wished, his body is taken back to Normandy and is buried on May 10 in the village cemetery of Tocqueville.

Note on the Texts

Drawn from *Tocqueville: Democracy in America* (Olivier Zunz, editor), volume 147 in the Library of America series, this Library of America Paperback Classic prints the text of volume one of *Democracy in America* (*De la démocratie en Amérique*) by Alexis de Tocqueville in a new translation by Arthur Goldhammer.

From May 9, 1831, to February 20, 1832, Tocqueville and his friend and fellow magistrate Gustave de Beaumont traveled through the United States, inspecting American prisons (the official purpose of their visit), but also conducting interviews with more than 200 informants on American politics, law, mores, and social beliefs. Following the publication in January 1833 of their report *Du Système pénitentiaire aux États-Unis et de son application en France*, which was written primarily by Beaumont, Tocqueville began work in the autumn of 1833 on *De la démocratie en Amérique*. In preparing his book Tocqueville drew on the letters, notebooks, and journals he had written during his American trip, as well as hundreds of books and documents he had collected in the United States and France. The first volume of *De la démocratie en Amérique* was published in Paris on January 23, 1835, by Charles Gosselin in a two-volume edition. Gosselin published six further "editions" between 1835 and 1839 (the 7th "edition" was a reprinting of the 6th). For the sixth, published in 1838, Tocqueville made a number of corrections.

Tocqueville began work on the second volume of *De la démocratie en Amérique* in the fall of 1835 but did not finish it as soon as he had expected for a number of reasons, including the time he devoted to his political career. The second volume of *De la démocratie en Amérique* was published in Paris by Gosselin on April 20, 1840, again in a two-volume edition (this is commonly known as the "8th edition" of the work). In 1842, Gosselin published the 9th, 10th, and 11th "editions," in which the first volume (1835) and second volume (1840) appeared together (the 10th and 11th "editions" were partially, and probably wholly, reprintings of the 9th). For what was called the 12th edition, published by Pagnerre in 1848, Tocqueville added a preface written after the February 1848 revolution in France that overthrew the July monarchy and established the Second Republic, as well as an appendix containing a report he delivered on January 15, 1848, to the Académie des sciences morales et politiques on *De la Démocratie en Suisse* by Élysée Cherbuliez. The new preface and appendix appeared in what was called the 13th edition, published by Pagnerre in 1850, along with an additional appendix printing the text of a speech Tocqueville made in the Chamber of Deputies on January 27, 1848, warning of a possible revolution in France. This was the last printing to appear before Tocqueville's death in 1859.

The translation by Arthur Goldhammer of the first volume of *Democracy in America* printed here is based on the text of the French 1850 text ("13th edition"), and the Goldhammer translation of the second volume of *Democracy in America* is based on the French 1848 text ("12th edition"); these texts have been shown by modern scholarship to be the most accurate ones published during Tocqueville's lifetime. In identifying and correcting typesetting errors in them, the historical-critical edition of *De la démocratie en Amérique* by Eduardo Nolla (Paris: Vrin, 1990), and the Pléiade edition of *De la démocratie en Amérique*, edited by André Jardin, Jean-Claude Lamberti, and James T. Schleifer (Paris: Gallimard, 1992), have been consulted. In the present volume, a new translation of the preface to the 12th "edition" is printed in the notes. The appendices added in the 12th and 13th "editions" have not been included in this volume.

Tocqueville included in his text numerous translated quotations from English-language sources. In cases where his translations are faithful to the English originals, this volume prints the texts of the original English-language sources; but in cases where Tocqueville freely translated or paraphrased the original sources, the quotations are retranslated into English, and the original passages are printed in the notes in this volume.

The translation presented here reproduces the volume, part, and chapter organization, and the sub-chapter headings, of the French texts it is based on, but it does not attempt to reproduce other features of their design. In presenting Tocqueville's footnotes, the present volume uses Arabic superscript numerals, and it numbers the notes continuously within each chapter. Tocqueville's endnotes are printed following the text and are assigned Roman numerals that proceed continuously through both volumes of *Democracy in America*; references to these endnotes are indicated in the text by footnotes using asterisks.

Notes

In the notes below, the reference numbers denote page and line of this volume (the line count includes headings). No note is made for material included in standard desk-reference books. Footnotes in the text are Tocqueville's own. For further biographical background and references to other studies, see André Jardin, *Tocqueville* (New York: Farrar, Straus & Giroux, Inc., 1988); George Wilson Pierson, *Tocqueville and Beaumont in America* (New York: Oxford University Press, 1938); Alexis de Tocqueville, *Journey to America*, edited by J. P. Mayer (London: Faber and Faber, Ltd., 1959); and *The Tocqueville Reader: A Life in Letters and Politics*, edited by Olivier Zunz and Alan S. Kahan (Oxford: Blackwell Publishing, 2002).

3.1   INTRODUCTION]   Tocqueville added the following preface to the 12th edition (1848):

As great and sudden as were the events that have just unfolded in an instant before our eyes, the author of the present work is entitled to say that they did not surprise him. This book was written fifteen years ago with but a single thought as the author's constant preoccupation: the impending, irresistible, universal advent of democracy in the world. Reread this book: on every page you will find a solemn warning to all men that the form of society and the condition of humanity are changing and that new destinies are at hand.

At the beginning these words were inscribed:

The gradual development of equality is a providential fact. It has the essential characteristics of one: it is universal, durable, and daily proves itself to be beyond the reach of man's powers. Not a single event, not a single individual, fails to contribute to its development. Is it wise to believe that a social movement that originated so far in the past can be halted by the efforts of a single generation? Does anyone think that democracy, having destroyed feudalism and vanquished kings, will be daunted by the bourgeois and the rich? Will it stop now that it has become so strong and its adversaries so weak?

The man who, in the face of a monarchy strengthened rather than shaken by the Revolution of July, wrote these lines, which events have made prophetic, may today, without fear, once again draw the public's attention to his work.

He should also be permitted to add that current circumstances give his book a topical interest and practical utility that it did not have when it first appeared.

Monarchy existed then. Today, it is destroyed. The institutions of America, which were merely a subject of curiosity for monarchical France, should be a subject of study for republican France. It is not force alone that provides the seat of a new government; it is good laws. After the combatant, the lawmaker. One has destroyed, the other lays a foundation. To each his work. If the question in France is no longer whether we shall have a monarchy or a republic, it remains to be seen whether we shall have an agitated republic or a tranquil one, a regular republic or an irregular one, a peaceful republic or a belligerent one, a liberal republic or an oppressive one, a republic that threatens the sacred rights of property and family or one that recognizes and consecrates them. An awesome problem, the solution to which matters not just to France but to the entire civilized world. If we save ourselves, we also save all the peoples who surround us. If we go down, they all go down with us. Depending on whether we have democratic liberty or democratic tyranny, the destiny of the world will be different, and it can be said that today it is up to us whether in the end the republic is established everywhere or abolished everywhere.

Now, this problem, which we have only just begun to face, was resolved in America sixty years ago. There, for sixty years, the principle of popular sovereignty that we have just now enthroned among us has reigned unchallenged. There it has been put into practice in the most direct, the most unlimited, the most absolute manner. For sixty years, the people that has made this principle the common source of all its laws has grown steadily in population, territory, and wealth, and — note this well — throughout that period it has been not only the most prosperous but the most stable of all the peoples of the earth. While all the nations of Europe were ravaged by war or torn by civil discord, the American nation has remained, alone in the civilized world, at peace. Nearly all of Europe has been turned upside down by revolutions; America has not even had riots. There, the republic has not disrupted all rights but preserved them. There, individual property has enjoyed more guarantees than in any other country in the world, and anarchy has remained as unheard of as despotism.

Where else can we look for greater hopes or greater lessons? Let us look to America not to copy servilely the institutions it has adopted but to better understand those that suit us, not so much to extract examples as to draw lessons, to borrow the principles of its laws rather than the details. The laws of the French republic can and should be different in many cases from the laws that govern the United States, but the principles on which American constitutions rest — principles of order, balance of powers, true liberty, and sincere and profound respect for what is right — are indispensable in any republic and should be common to all. And one can say in advance that where such principles are not found, the republic will soon have ceased to exist.

22.9   the South Seas]   The Pacific Ocean.

22.36   *toises*]   A *toise* was a unit of length equal to approximately 6 feet,
5 inches.

28.29–31   the old men . . . time of the Gauls]   This passage is from the
commentary on *Notes on the State of Virginia* written by Jefferson's friend
Charles Thomson, the secretary of the Continental Congress.

28.31–34   "there never was . . . insult and provocation."]   This quotation is from Thomas Jefferson's *Notes on the State of Virginia,* not Thomson's
commentary.

37.25–38.3   I have always . . . him as instruments.]   Retranslated from
Tocqueville's free translation from English into French. In the original:
"Gentle Reader, I have for some length of time looked upon it as a duty incumbent, especially on the immediate successors of those that have had so
large experience of those many memorable and signal demonstrations of
God's goodness, viz. The first beginners of this plantation in New-England,
to commit to writing his gracious dispensations on that behalf; having so
many inducements thereunto, not only otherwise, but so plentifully in the
sacred Scriptures, that so, what we have seen, and what our fathers have told
us, we may not hide from our children, shewing to the generations to come
the praises of the Lord. Psal. 78. 3, 4. That especially the seed of Abraham his
servant, and the children of Jacob his chosen, may remember his marvelous
works (Psal. 105. 5, 6.) in the beginning and progress of the planting of New-
England, his wonders, and the judgments of his mouth; how that God
brought a vine into this wilderness; that he cast out the heathen and planted
it; and that he also made room for it, and he caused it to take deep root, and
it filled the land; [. . .] Psal. 80. 8, 9. And not only so, but also that He hath
guided his people by his strength to his holy habitation, and planted them in
the mountain of his inheritance, (Exod. 15.13.) in respect of precious gospel-
enjoyments. [. . .] that as especially God may have the glory of all, unto whom
it is most due; so also some rays of glory may reach the names of those blessed
saints that were the main instruments of the beginning of this happy enter-
prize." Nathaniel Morton, *New England's Memorial,* first published in 1669,
5th edition (Boston: Crocker and Brewster, 1826), pp. 13–14.

38.13–29   So they left . . . be the last.]   Retranslated. In the original: "so
they left that goodly and pleasant city, which had been their resting place
above eleven years; but they knew that they were pilgrims and strangers here
below, and looked not much on these things, but lifted up their eyes to
heaven, their dearest country, where God hath prepared for them a city,
Heb. xi, 16, and therein quieted their spirits.

   When they came to the place, they found the ship and all things ready; and
such of their friends as could not come with them, followed after them, and
sundry came from Amsterdam to see them shipt, and to take their leave of
them. One night was spent with little sleep with the most, but with friendly

entertainment, and Christian discourse, and other real expressions of true Christian love. The next day the wind being fair they went on board, and their friends with them, where truly doleful was the sight of that sad and mournful parting, to hear what sighs and sobs, and prayers did sound amongst them; what tears did gush from every eye, and pithy speeches pierced each others heart, that sundry of the Dutch strangers, that stood on the Key as spectators, could not refrain from tears: [. . .] But the tide (which stays for no man) calling them away, that were thus loth to depart, their reverend pastor falling down on his knees, and they all with him, with watery cheeks commended them with most fervent prayers unto the Lord and his blessing; and then with mutual embraces, and many tears, they took their leave one of another, which proved to be the last leave to many of them." Morton, *New England's Memorial*, pp. 23–24.

39.1–17   "But before continuing . . . their eyes upward.]   Retranslated. In the original: "But before we pass on, let the reader, with me, make a pause, and seriously consider this poor people's present condition, the more to be raised up to admiration of God's goodness towards them in their preservation: For being now passed the vast ocean, and a sea of troubles before in their preparation, they had now no friends to welcome them, no inns to entertain or refresh them, no houses, much less towns, to repair unto to seek for succour. [. . .] and, for the season it was winter, and they that know the winters of the country, know them to be sharp and violent, subject to cruel and fierce storms, dangerous to travel to known places, much more to search unknown coasts.—Besides, what could they see but a hideous and desolate wilderness, full of wild beasts and wild men? And what multitudes of them there were, they then knew not; neither could they, as it were, go up to the top of Pisgah, to view from this wilderness a more goodly country to feed their hopes, for which way soever they turned their eyes (save upward to heaven) they could have but little solace or content." Morton, *New England's Memorial*, p. 35.

39.25–40.3   "We, whose names follow . . . submission and obedience."] Retranslated. In the original: "We whose names are under-written, [. . .] Having undertaken for the glory of God, and advancement of the Christian faith, and the honour of our King and country, a voyage to plant the first colony in the northern parts of Virginia; do by these presents solemnly and mutually, in the presence of God and one another, covenant and combine ourselves together into a civil body politick, for our better ordering and preservation, and furtherance of the ends aforesaid: And by virtue hereof, do enact, constitute and frame such just and equal laws, ordinances, acts, constitutions and officers, from time to time, as shall be thought most meet and convenient for the general good of the colony; unto which we promise all due submission and obedience." Morton, *New England's Memorial*, pp. 37–38.

42.19–20   "Whosoever shall . . . put to death."]   Retranslated. In the original: "If any man after legall conviction, shall have or worship any other

God but the Lord God, hee shall bee put to death." *The Code of 1650* (Hartford: S. Andrus and Son, 1821), p. 28.

46.32–47.3   "Whereas," says the law . . . of the Lord."]   Retranslated. In the original: "It being one cheife project of that old deluder, Sathan, to keepe men from the knowledge of the scriptures, as in former times, keeping them in an unknowne tongue, so in these latter times, by perswading them from the use of tongues, so that at least, the true sence and meaning of the originall might bee clouded with false glosses of saint seeming deceivers; and that learning may not bee buried in the grave of our forefathers, in church and commonwealth, the Lord assisting our indeavors." *The Code of 1650* (Hartford: S. Andrus and Son, 1821), pp. 90–91.

48.1–10   Make no mistake . . . our life for it.]   Retranslated. In the original: "Nor would I have you to mistake in the Point of your own *liberty*. There is a *liberty* of corrupt nature, which is affected by *men* and *beasts*, to do what they list; and this *liberty* is inconsistent with *authority*, impatient of all restraint; by this *liberty, Sumus Omnes Deteriores*; 'tis the grand enemy of *truth* and *peace*, and all the *ordinances* of God are bent against it. But there is a civil, a moral, a federal *liberty*, which is the proper end and object of *authority*; it is a *liberty* for that only which is *just* and *good*; for this *liberty* you are to stand with the hazard of your very *lives*." Cotton Mather, *Magnalia Christi Americana* (Hartford, 1820), pp. 116–17.

67.14   The locality (*commune*)]   Tocqueville uses the word *commune* in a variety of ways that no single English word can capture. Other translations have substituted the English "township" because Tocqueville himself, at one point in his text, places this word in parentheses after *commune*, but to translate *commune* always as "township" seems inadequate to Tocqueville's meaning. He clearly has in mind the most local form of government, and in this chapter is most often concerned with the New England town meeting (not "township" meeting). Moreover, he speaks of the *commune* as being a "part of nature," whereas a "township" is a political construct, not a natural human grouping. In a letter to Jared Sparks dated December 2, 1831, Tocqueville wrote: "It seems to me that, theoretically speaking, you have not adopted for *communes ordinaires* (not incorporated towns) the system of representative government established everywhere else." Elsewhere in this letter he refers to *institutions communales* as "local government." Therefore *commune* has been translated as "local government" or "town" or "locality" or "township," depending on which of the several facets of *commune* Tocqueville is emphasizing in each particular context.

69.2   The New England town]   Here Tocqueville inserted the English word "township" in parentheses after *la commune de la Nouvelle-Angleterre*, but the word has been translated as "town"; see the previous note and pages 874.34–875.12 in the Translator's Note.

78.17–18   the state, the center of all national powers]   Although Tocqueville here equates *nation* with *state*, as is natural for a European writer, he is referring in this passage to the powers of the state government, not the federal government.

78.22   *the administration*]   The French word *administration* has no precise English equivalent. Its sense is conveyed by the phrase "the machinery of government," i.e., routine governmental activity involving the application of general regulations to specific cases.

80.21–22   general regulations regarding public order]   Tocqueville wrote *règlements généraux de police*, using *police* to cover a broad range of matters including public order, health, welfare, morals, and safety.

80.35   secretary of state]   Tocqueville wrote *secrétaire de la république*.

82.3   general regulations regarding public welfare]   Tocqueville wrote *règlements généraux de police*; see note 80.21–22.

82.38   secretary of state]   Tocqueville wrote *secrétaire de la république*.

91.5   state legislature]   Tocqueville wrote *législature nationale*.

96.22   the state]   Tocqueville wrote *pays*, but clearly the state is meant.

96.25   the state]   Again, Tocqueville wrote *nation*, but the state is intended.

99.28–29   state power]   In the original, *la puissance nationale*, but the discussion is clearly about the power concentrated in the state governments.

100.31   the Convention]   The Convention was the supreme legislative and constituent body in France from September 21, 1792, to October 26, 1795; it abolished the monarchy and created the First Republic.

104.22   A talented writer]   Sébastien Saulnier, in "Nouvelles observations sur les finances des États-Unis, en réponse à une brochure publiée par le Général La Fayette," published in *Revue Britannique*, October 8, 1831.

111.32   the Parlement of Paris]   A court under the Old Regime, not a legislative body.

114.28   the three powers]   The King, the Lords, and the Commons.

118.10–11   Year VIII . . . a constitution]   The constitution was promulgated on December 15, 1799, or 24 Frimaire, a month after the overthrow of the Directory by Napoleon Bonaparte

120.32–33   Chambre des Pairs]   The Chamber of Peers was the upper chamber of the bicameral legislature under the July monarchy (1830–48) and had sole power to try government ministers.

124.20   Article I, Section 4]   The definition appears in Article II, Section 4.

129.10   remained the rule]   Tocqueville wrote *resta le droit commun*, literally, "remained the common law," but the phrase has been translated as "the
rule," in contrast to "the exception" raised by the federal government.

130.8–9   Nations, when dealing . . . than individuals.]   In French, *Les
peuples entre eux ne sont que des individus*. Here *les peuples entre eux* is taken to
mean one people when dealing with another people (or nation; Tocqueville
often uses the two interchangeably).

131.11   framers of the federal Constitution]   In the original, *les législateurs
fédéraux*. Here and elsewhere *législateurs* is translated as "framers" rather than
"lawmakers" when it is important to make clear that Tocqueville is referring
to the framers of constitutions, not to legislators in the usual sense.

131.20–21   *pays d'États*]   Provinces of France that maintained traditional
provincial assemblies.

145.24–25   Jefferson wrote . . . before the election]   The quotation is
from a letter Jefferson wrote to James Monroe on January 28, 1809, five weeks
before the inauguration of his successor, James Madison, who had been
elected on December 7, 1808.

158.3   *harmonious*]   In French, *corrélatifs*.

161.13   state governments]   In French, *gouvernements provinciaux*, literally,
provincial governments.

168.34   *the seven federal judges*]   The justices of the Supreme Court. From
1807 to 1837 the size of the Court was set by law at seven justices.

176.36–37   the separate governments included in the confederation]   In
French, *gouvernements particuliers*; the phrase refers to the several governments that composed the confederation.

177.17   patriotic spirit]   Tocqueville wrote *esprit national*, but he is referring to the spirit that binds each citizen to his particular state, so the phrase
has been translated as "patriotic spirit."

183.9   legislation by the states]   Tocqueville wrote *législations provinciales*.

183.32   small state]   Tocqueville wrote *petite nation*.

187.35   the union.]   Although Tocqueville capitalized "Union" as he does
when referring to the United States, he clearly has in mind confederal unions
in general, so the lower case has been used.

207.21–32   Throughout this whole . . . knows nothing of.]   This passage
has been retranslated. The original, from the *Vincennes* (Indiana) *Gazette*, has
not been identified.

213.14–15   A great man . . . *ends of knowledge*]   Blaise Pascal, *Pensées*, Brun-
schvicg edition, number 327.

215.33   purely abstract enemies]   In French, *des ennemis tout intellectuels*.

216.30   electoral bodies]   In French, *collèges électoraux*; literally, electoral colleges, but Tocqueville does not appear to want to limit his statement to the Electoral College that votes in presidential elections in the United States.

231.31–32   *forms the greatest* . . . *our governments*]   The italics are Tocqueville's.

248.3–4   state governments]   Tocqueville wrote *les gouvernements provinciaux*.

258.7   people in government]   Tocqueville wrote *hommes d'État*.

260.1–2   admirable letter . . . political testament]   Washington's Farewell Address was written as a public letter and published on September 19, 1796.

260.39   Previously, Washington gave expression]   The quotation that follows is also taken from the Farewell Address.

261.9–11   "Americans should never . . . grant any themselves."]   This has been retranslated from the French. The source has not been identified.

261.29   eminently one of wait-and-see]   In French, *éminemment expectante*.

262.20   a nation, as indivisible entity]   In French, *un peuple, comme individu*. Tocqueville is again applying the term *individu* to a people or nation to emphasize that he is thinking of the collectivity as an indivisible unit.

274.36   *Homo puer robustus*]   "A man is a boy with strength."

279.7   political rallies]   In French, *les clubs*, a term that strongly connotes a political association.

303.8   bestowed on lawyers]   The word that Tocqueville uses is *légiste*, or legist, a specialist in the laws, a jurist, and no more common a word in the French of Tocqueville's time than "legist" is in English today.

304.15   private interest]   In French, *l'intérêt particulier*.

307.21   a French lawyer]   Here Tocqueville used *avocat* rather than *légiste*.

312.39–42   "The inestimable privilege . . . and civil liberty."]   Tocqueville quotes this passage in English.

317.1   the people's impulses]   In French, *les mouvements du peuple*. The word *mouvement* in French has a semantic range rather different from the English "movement." For instance, one can do something *de son propre mouvement*, of one's own accord, and one can have *un mouvement de colère*, a fit of anger.

325.36–326.9   "there can be no . . . time to come."]   Retranslated. In the original: "it would be very unfounded to suppose that the evils of the equal partition of estates have been seriously felt in these United States, or that they have borne any proportion to the great advantages of the policy, or that such evils are to be anticipated for generations to come. The extraordinary extent of our unsettled territories, the abundance of uncultivated land in the market, and the constant stream of emigration from the Atlantic to the interior states, operates sufficiently to keep paternal inheritances unbroken." James Kent, *Commentaries on American Law* (New York: O. Halstead, 1826–30), vol. 4, pp. 380–81.

338.34–40   "The court of common . . . such a belief."]   Tocqueville quotes this article in English.

339.28   Cabanis's]   Pierre Cabanis (1757–1808), French physician and materialist philosopher.

340.18   *priests*]   In French, *prêtres*, translated in this volume variously as "priests" or "clergymen." Tocqueville includes Protestants as well as Catholics under this term.

344.28   local administrators]   Tocqueville wrote *administrateurs provinciaux.*

348.26–27   The Americans have . . . great legal scholars,]   Tocqueville wrote: *Les Américains ont des jurisconsultes et des commentateurs, les publicistes leur manquent.* The *Dictionnaire de L'Académie française* (1835) defines *publiciste* as a person who writes on public law and who has made a profound study of the subject and gives as an example the sentence, *C'est un jurisconsulte, mais non un publiciste.* A *jurisconsulte* is one who has studied law and offers professional advice on the subject. Thus the intention of the sentence appears to be to establish a gradation, and it has been translated accordingly.

356.11   the western states]   Tocqueville wrote *les nations de l'Ouest.*

363.1   not *twenty* people united]   The French "law of associations" of April 1834 prohibited associations of more than twenty persons.

366.34   ancestral home]   Here, *patrie* has been translated as "ancestral home."

372.15–373.2   "The herds of buffalo . . . Rocky Mountains."]   Retranslated. In the original: "But the buffalo is constantly receding. A few years since, they approached the base of the Alleghany, and a few years hence they may even be rare upon the immense plains which extend to the base of the Rocky Mountains." William Clark and Lewis Cass, *Report to the House of Representatives on Indian Affairs,* February 9, 1829, 20th Congress, 2nd Session, House doc. no. 117, p. 24.

372.20–32   "The time is long . . . hunger every winter."]   Retranslated. In the original: "The time when the Indians generally could supply themselves with food and clothing, without any of the articles of civilized life, has long since passed away. The more remote tribes, beyond the Mississippi, who live where immense herds of buffalo are yet to be found, and who follow those animals in their periodical migrations, could, more easily than any others, recur to the habits of their ancestors, and live without the white man or any of his manufactures. But the buffalo is constantly receding. [. . .] The smaller animals, the bear, the deer, the beaver, the otter, the muskrat, &c. principally minister to the comfort and support of the Indians, and these cannot be taken without guns, ammunition, and traps. [. . .] Among the northwestern Indians particularly, the labor of supplying a family with food and clothing is excessive. Day after day is spent by the hunter without success, and during this interval his family must subsist upon bark or roots, or perish. [. . .] Many die every Winter from actual starvation." William Clark and Lewis Cass, *Report to the House of Representatives on Indian Affairs*, February 9, 1829, pp. 23–24.

375.33–376.17   "When the Indians . . . is not surprising."]   Retranslated. In the original: "The Indians, as has been stated, reach the treaty ground poor, and almost naked. Large quantities of goods are taken there by the traders, and are seen and examined by the Indians. The women and children become importunate to have their wants supplied, and their influence is soon exerted to induce a sale. Their improvidence is habitual and unconquerable. The gratification of his immediate wants and desires is the ruling passion of an Indian. The expectation of future advantages seldom produces much effect. The experience of the past is lost, and the prospects of the future disregarded. This is one of the most striking traits in their character, and is well known to all who have had much intercourse with them. It would be utterly hopeless to demand a cession of land, unless the means were at hand of gratifying their immediate wants; and when their condition and circumstances are fairly considered, it ought not to surprise us that they are so anxious to relieve themselves." William Clark and Lewis Cass, *Report to the House of Representatives on Indian Affairs*, February 9, 1829, pp. 15–16.

376.26–40   "in appropriating wilderness . . . any perceptible degree."] Retranslated. In the original: "To pay an Indian tribe what their ancient hunting grounds are worth to them, after the game is fled or destroyed, as a mode of appropriating wild lands, claimed by Indians, has been found more convenient, and certainly it is more agreeable to the forms of justice, as well as more merciful, than to assert the possession of them by the sword. Thus, the practice of buying Indian titles is but the substitute which humanity and expediency have imposed, in place of the sword, in arriving at the actual enjoyment of property claimed by the right of discovery, and sanctioned by the natural superiority allowed to the claims of civilized communities over those of savage tribes. Up to the present time, so invariable has been the operation of certain causes, first in diminishing the value of forest lands to the Indians; and, secondly, in disposing them to sell readily; that the plan of buying their right of occupancy has never threatened to retard, in any perceptible degree, the prosperity of any of the States." Representative John Bell,

Report of the Committee on Indian Affairs, *Legislative Documents*, 21st Congress, 1st Session, House doc. no. 227, pp. 6–7.

376.43–377.36   "If we judge . . . unreasonable to expect."] Retranslated. In the original: "Judging of the future by the past, we cannot err in anticipating a progressive diminution of their numbers, and their eventual extinction, unless our border should become stationary, and they be removed beyond it, or unless some radical change should take place in the principles of our intercourse with them, which it is easier to hope for than to expect." William Clark and Lewis Cass, *Report to the House of Representatives on Indian Affairs*, February 9, 1829, p. 107.

379.29–40   "Until a young man . . . they may boast."] Retranslated. In the original: "Until a young man has been engaged with an enemy, and can boast of his prowess, he is held in no estimation, and is considered little better than a woman. At their great war dances, all the warriors in succession strike the post, as it is called, and recount the feats they have done. The auditory, upon these occasions, is composed of the relations, the friends, and the companions of the narrator, and the intensity of their feelings is manifested by the deep silence with which they listen to his tale, and by the loud shouts with which he is hailed at the termination. Unfortunate is the young man who has no deeds of valor to recount at these assemblages; and instances are not wanting, where young warriors, in the excitement of their feelings, have departed alone from these dances, in search of trophies to exhibit, and of adventures to relate." William Clark and Lewis Cass, *Report to the House of Representatives on Indian Affairs*, February 9, 1829, pp. 39–40.

382.35   Tanner's memoirs] John Tanner, *A Narrative of the Captivity and Adventures of John Tanner, during Thirty Years Residence among the Indians in the Interior of North America* (1830).

385.30   Texas . . . Mexico] Texas became an independent republic in 1836, a year after Tocqueville published Volume One of *Democracy in America*, and was annexed to the United States in 1845.

386.26–28   "The intrusions . . . poor and inoffensive lives."] Retranslated. In the original: "it would encourage and occasion a great number of white families to rush into, and settle on, the lands embraced within those lines, to the great annoyance, distress, and ruin, of the poor, helpless, and inoffensive Cherokees who inhabit them." Colonel Hugh Montgomery to Samuel A. Wales, May 13, 1829, "Intrusions on Cherokee Lands," U.S. House of Representatives, 21st Congress, 1st Session, 1830, p. 12.

388.36–40   "The United States . . . it sees fit."] Retranslated. In the original: "The United States solemnly guaranty to the Cherokee nation, all their lands not hereby ceded." (Article 7.) "If any citizen of the United States, or other person, not being an Indian, shall settle on any of the Cherokees' lands, such person shall forfeit the protection of the United States, and the Cherokees may punish him or not, as they please." Article 8. *Indian Treaties*

and Laws and Regulations Relating to Indian Affairs, Washington, D.C., 1826,
p. 117.

389.7–390.27   "By the will of our . . . of their country."]   Retranslated.
In the original: "By the will of our Father in Heaven, the Governor of the
whole world, the red man of America has become small, and the white man
great and renowned. When the ancestors of the people of these United States
first came to the shores of America, they found the red man strong—though
he was ignorant and savage, yet he received them kindly, and gave them dry
land to rest their weary feet. They met in peace, and shook hands in token of
friendship. Whatever the white man wanted and asked of the Indian, the latter
willingly gave. At that time the Indian was the lord, and the white man the
suppliant. But now the scene has changed. The strength of the red man has
become weakness. As his neighbors increased in numbers, his power became
less and less, and now, of the many and powerful tribes who once covered
these United States, only a few are to be seen—a few whom a sweeping pesti-
lence has left. The Northern tribes, who were once so numerous and powerful, are now nearly extinct. Thus it has happened to the red man of America.
Shall we, who are remnants, share the same fate? [. . .]

The land on which we stand we have received as an inheritance from our
fathers, who possessed it from time immemorial, as a gift from our common
Father in Heaven. We have already said, that, when the white man came to
the shores of America, our ancestors were found in peaceable possession
of this very land. They bequeathed it to us as their children, and we have
sacredly kept it, as containing the remains of our beloved men. This right of
inheritance we have *never ceded*, nor ever *forfeited*. Permit us to ask, what better
right can the people have to a country, than the right of *inheritance* and *immemorial peaceable possession?* We know it is said of late by the State of Georgia, and by the Executive of the United States, that we have forfeited this
right—but we think this is said gratuitously. At what time have we made the
forfeit? What great crime have we committed, whereby we must forever be
divested of our country and rights? Was it when we were hostile to the United
States, and took part with the King of Great Britain, during the struggle for
Independence? If so, why was not this forfeiture declared in the first treaty
of peace between the United States and our beloved men? Why was not such
an article as the following inserted in the treaty: 'The United States give peace
to the Cherokees, but, for the part they took in the late war, declare them to
be but tenants at will, to be removed, when the convenience of the States
within whose chartered limits they live, shall require it.' That was the proper
time to assume such a possession. But it was not thought of, nor would our
forefathers have agreed to any treaty, whose tendency was to deprive them
of their rights and their country." *Memorial of the Cherokees*, December 18,
1829, 21st Congress, 1st Session, 1830, House doc. no. 311, pp. 7–9.

389.26–30   "Beyond the great river . . . *to you forever*."]   Retranslated. In
the original: "Beyond the great river Mississippi, where a part of your nation

has gone, your father has provided a country large enough for all of you, and he advises you to remove to it. There your white brothers will not trouble you; they will have no claim to the land, and you can live upon it, you and all your children, as long as the grass grows or the water runs, in peace and plenty. It will be yours for ever." *Documents and Proceedings Relating to the Formation and Progress of a Board in the City of New York, for the Emigration, Preservation, and Improvement, of the Aborigines of America* (New York: Vanderpool and Cole, 1829), p. 5.

404.31–32   To the extent . . . of industry,]   In French, *A mesure que les travailleurs libres s'emparent de l'industriel.*

406.12–13   more difficult it becomes . . . advantageous way]   In French, *plus difficile d'abolir utilement l'esclavage.*

426.1   forfeit their nationality]   Tocqueville sometimes refers to states as "nations." Here he means their distinctive identity and sovereign power as states.

430.33–34   calculated patriotism]   In French, *patriotisme réfléchi*; the sense here is a patriotism that is reflected upon, mulled over, calculated, deliberate as opposed to instinctive and passionate.

435.34   states]   Tocqueville wrote *nations*.

449.6   state banks]   Tocqueville wrote *banques provinciales*.

449.23   between the states]   Tocqueville wrote *provinces*.

451.3–7   "The Constitution . . . obligation for itself."]   Retranslated. The quotation is presumably of a paraphrase of similar statements by Calhoun.

451.15–16   state convention]   Tocqueville wrote *convention nationale*.

451.31–42   "When the rights . . . to obtain justice."]   Retranslated. In the original: "when the rights reserved to the several States are deliberately invaded, it is their right and their duty to 'interpose for the purpose of arresting the progress of the evil of usurpation, and to maintain, within their respective limits, the authorities and privileges belonging to them as independent sovereignties.'* If the several States do not possess this right, it is in vain that they claim to be sovereign. [. . .] South Carolina claims to be a sovereign State. She recognizes no tribunal upon earth as above her authority. It is true, she has entered into a solemn compact of Union with other sovereign States, but she claims, and will exercise the right to determine the extent of her obligations under that compact, nor will she consent that any other power shall exercise the right of judgment for her. And when that compact is violated by her co-States, or by the Government which they have created, she asserts her unquestionable right '*to judge of the infractions*, as well as of the MODE and MEASURE of REDRESS.'†" "Message from the President of the United States, transmitting Copies of the Proclamation and Proceedings in Relation to South Carolina," January 16, 1833, Senate Document 30, 22nd Congress, 2nd Session, 1833, pp. 34–35. The first footnote is "Virginia Resolutions of 1798," the second "Kentucky Resolutions of 1798."

457.20–21   provincial and local government] Tocqueville wrote *gouvernement provincial et communal*.

458.3–4   local and provincial liberties] Tocqueville wrote *libertés provinciales et communales*.

458.27–28   provinces to towns . . . to the states.] Tocqueville wrote *la province aux communes, l'État aux provinces, l'Union aux États*.

466.15   guild's rule-of-thumb] In French, *axiome d'état*; Tocqueville appears to be thinking of assumptions that go with a particular "estate," hence the translation "guild's rule-of-thumb."

478.6   The great-podded acacia] *Entada gigas*, the monkey ladder vine.

482.40   *garde champêtre . . . police judiciaire*] Constable; police investigator.

486.1   having been born in India] Robert Beverley wrote in his *History and Present State of Virginia*: "I am an *Indian*, and don't pretend to be exact in my Language."

491.18–26   "New England must . . . son of New England."] Retranslated. In the original: "It concerneth New-England always to remember that they are originally a plantation religious, not a plantation of trade. The profession of the purity of doctrine, worship and discipline is written upon her forehead. Let merchants, and such as are increasing cent per cent remember this, that worldly gain was not the end and design of the people of New-England but religion. And if any man among us make religion as twelve, and the world as thirteen, such an one hath not the spirit of a true New-Englandman." Jeremy Belknap, *The History of New-Hampshire*, vol. I (Philadelphia, 1784), p. 59.

493.1–6   "The first rule . . . as to sex."] Retranslated. In the original: "The first rule of inheritance is, that if a person owning real estate, dies seised, or as owner, without devising the same, the estate shall descend to his lawful descendants in the direct line of lineal descent; and if there be but one person, then to him or her alone, and if more than one person, and all of equal degree of consanguinity to the ancestor, then the inheritance shall descend to the several persons as tenants in common in equal parts [. . .] without distinction of sex." James Kent, *Commentaries on American Law*, vol. 4 (New York: O. Halsted, 1826–30), p. 371.

493.25–26   "Our general principles . . . circulation of property."] Retranslated. In the original: "The general policy of this country does not encourage restraints upon the power of alienation of land." James Kent, *Commentaries on American Law*, vol. 4 (New York: O. Halsted, 1826–30), p. 17.

495.17–18   M. de Malesherbes . . . Cour des Aides]   The Cour des Aides was a law court that heard tax cases. Malesherbes was Tocqueville's great-grandfather; see Chronology, 1805.

495.21–22   for it stems . . . right of reason]   Malesherbes said: *car il remonte bien plus haut: c'est le droit naturel, le droit de la raison.* In French *remonte plus haut* is a standard idiom for priority in time, but the metaphorical use of the adjective *haut*, "high," lends the statement a different interpretation: the source of the right in question is not just earlier but "higher." The translation by "prior" is intended to capture the ambiguity between temporal precedence and hierarchy.

496.37–38   Chancellor Maupeou]   René de Maupeou (1714–1792) was chancellor of France from 1768 to 1774, during the reign of Louis XV.

498.6–8   *Si . . . est capacissima*]   "If you contemplate antiquity, it is the oldest; if dignity, the most honorable; if jurisdiction, the broadest."

500.18–29   finds that the . . . the coming year.]   Retranslated. The original has not been identified.

Index

Abolition of slavery, 394–97, 402, 404–10, 412, 416
Absolute monarchies, 47, 98, 109, 118, 131–32, 145, 154, 234–36, 256, 292–94, 296–99, 302
Absolute power, 360
Adair, James, 26n
Adams, John Quincy, 151
Administration: centralized, 97–110, 131, 191, 193, 301–2, 457, 496; instability of, 237–38, 242, 286–88; state, 94–97; town/county, 78–94
Aesop, 393n
Africa, 366, 394, 408, 414–15
African Americans. *See* Negroes
Agriculture, 24, 29, 34, 201, 429, 441, 450; of Indians, 378–80, 383–84, 388, 391n; and slavery, 397, 399, 400n, 402n, 407
Alabama, 369–70, 380n, 386n, 450, 494, 499
Alcohol abuse, 235, 236n, 257, 278
Allegheny Mountains, 22, 24, 372, 428, 430, 437, 438n, 439
Amendments, constitutional, 114–15
American Colonization Society, 408n, 414–15
American Revolution, 53, 57, 63, 79, 126–28, 165n, 172, 192n, 199–200, 228, 254, 296, 380n, 390, 425, 473, 493
Amphictyonic League, 177n
Anabaptists, 43n
Anarchy, 148, 298–99, 443, 445, 451
Appointments, presidential, 135–36, 140–41, 146, 152, 154
Apportionment, congressional, 133n, 439–40
Arbitrary power, 234–37, 291–92
Architecture, 246
Aristocracy, 51, 214, 285, 353, 395, 412, 460–61; American disdain of, 34, 52, 58–59, 131; benefits of, 8–10, 108, 255–56; corruption in, 251–53; during

crises, 255–56; in England, 263, 268, 289, 303–4, 308, 314; and foreign affairs, 262–63; in France, 3–6, 11, 109, 303; general tendency of laws, 265, 267–68; and lawyers, 303–9, 316; and parties, 202; and public expenditures, 241–45; in the South, 53, 63–64, 403, 434; wealth in, 203–4, 252–53, 256
Arkansas, 387–88, 444n
Arkansas River, 23, 387
Army, 100, 123, 127, 130, 141, 191–92, 249n, 250, 255, 320, 425, 427, 499
Arnold, Benedict, 263n
Articles of Confederation, 126–28, 176, 178, 192n, 200
Arts, 4–5, 348
Asia, 26n, 302
Assembly, freedom of, 216
Associations, political, 10, 204, 215–23
Athens, 46, 64. *See also* Greece
Atlantic Ocean, 21–22, 24–26, 28, 33, 38–39, 127, 142, 326, 339, 365, 371, 380, 398, 413–14, 428, 434, 435n, 437–39, 447–48, 473, 475
Australia, 36
Austria, 177n

Bail, 50
Baltimore, Maryland, 290n
Bank of the United States, 203, 263n, 448–49
Bankruptcy, 257
Beaumont, Gustave de, 15n, 392n
Bedford, Margaret, 43n
Belknap, Jeremy, 397n, 491
Bell, John, 376n, 387n, 391n
Bering Strait, 26n
Beverley, Robert, 35n, 397n, 485–86
Bible, 37–38, 42, 350
Bison, 372–73, 477
Blackstone, William, 51n, 120n, 498, 501, 504
Blosseville, Ernest de, 383n

About the editor:
OLIVIER ZUNZ is Commonwealth Professor of History at the University of Virginia. He is the editor (with Alan S. Kahan) of *The Tocqueville Reader: A Life in Letters and Politics* and *Alexis de Tocqueville and Gustave de Beaumont in America: Their Friendship and Their Travels* and the author of *Why the American Century?* and *Philanthropy in America: A History*, among other works. He has served as the president of The Tocqueville Society / La Société Tocqueville.

About the translator:
ARTHUR GOLDHAMMER has translated more than 120 works from the French, including Tocqueville's *The Ancien Régime and the French Revolution* and *Alexis de Tocqueville and Gustave de Beaumont in America: Their Friendship and Their Travels*. He is an affiliate of the Center for European Studies at Harvard University and a member of the editorial board of *French Politics, Culture, and Society*.

The Library of America Paperback Classics Series

American Speeches: Political Oratory from Patrick Henry to Barack Obama (various authors)
Edited and with an introduction by Ted Widmer
ISBN: 978-1-59853-094-0

The Education of Henry Adams by Henry Adams
With an introduction by Leon Wieseltier
ISBN: 978-1-59853-060-5

The Pioneers by James Fenimore Cooper
With an introduction by Alan Taylor
ISBN: 978-1-59853-155-8

The Red Badge of Courage by Stephen Crane
With an introduction by Robert Stone
ISBN: 978-1-59853-061-2

The Souls of Black Folk by W.E.B. Du Bois
With an introduction by John Edgar Wideman
ISBN: 978-1-59853-054-4

Essays: First and Second Series by Ralph Waldo Emerson
With an introduction by Douglas Crase
ISBN: 978-1-59853-084-1

The Autobiography by Benjamin Franklin
With an introduction by Daniel Aaron
ISBN: 978-1-59853-095-7

The Scarlet Letter by Nathaniel Hawthorne
With an introduction by Harold Bloom
ISBN: 978-1-59853-112-1

Indian Summer by William Dean Howells
With an introduction by John Updike
ISBN: 978-1-59853-156-5

The Varieties of Religious Experience by William James
With an introduction by Jaroslav Pelikan
ISBN: 978-1-59853-062-9

Selected Writings by Thomas Jefferson
With an introduction by Tom Wicker
ISBN: 978-1-59853-096-4

The Autobiography of an Ex-Colored Man by James Weldon Johnson
With an introduction by Charles R. Johnson
ISBN: 978-1-59853-113-8

Selected Speeches and Writings by Abraham Lincoln
With an introduction by Gore Vidal
ISBN: 978-1-59853-053-7

The Call of the Wild by Jack London
With an introduction by E. L. Doctorow
ISBN: 978-1-59853-058-2

Moby-Dick by Herman Melville
With an introduction by Edward Said
ISBN: 978-1-59853-085-8

My First Summer in the Sierra and Selected Essays by John Muir
Edited and with an introduction by Bill McKibben
ISBN: 978-1-59853-111-4

Selected Tales, with The Narrative of Arthur Gordon Pym
by Edgar Allan Poe
With an introduction by Diane Johnson
ISBN: 978-1-59853-056-8

Uncle Tom's Cabin by Harriet Beecher Stowe
With an introduction by James M. McPherson
ISBN: 978-1-59853-086-5

Walden by Henry David Thoreau
With an introduction by Edward Hoagland
ISBN: 978-1-59853-063-6

Democracy in America by Alexis de Tocqueville
The Arthur Goldhammer Translation
Edited and with introductions by Olivier Zunz
Volume One ISBN: 978-1-59853-151-0
Volume Two ISBN: 978-1-59853-152-7

The Adventures of Tom Sawyer by Mark Twain
With an introduction by Russell Baker
ISBN: 978-1-59853-087-2

Life on the Mississippi by Mark Twain
With an introduction by Jonathan Raban
ISBN: 978-1-59853-057-5

Selected Writings by George Washington
With an introduction by Ron Chernow
ISBN: 978-1-59853-110-7

The House of Mirth by Edith Wharton
With an introduction by Mary Gordon
ISBN: 978-1-59853-055-1

Leaves of Grass, The Complete 1855 and 1891–92 Editions
by Walt Whitman
With an introduction by John Hollander
ISBN: 978-1-59853-097-1

For more information, please visit www.loa.org/paperbackclassics/

☆ The Library of America